A WORLD ELSEWHERE

Erik Ryding and Rebecca Pechefsky

With a new introduction by the authors

University of Nebraska Press
Lincoln and London

First Nebraska paperback printing: 2006

Frontispiece: Bruno Walter (ca. 1911). Courtesy of Österreichisches Theatermuseum.

Library of Congress Cataloging-in-Publication Data
Ryding, Erik, 1953–
Bruno Walter: a world elsewhere: with a new introduction by the authors / Erik Ryding and Rebecca Pechefsky.
p.   cm.
Originally published: New Haven, CT: Yale University Press, c2001.
Includes bibliographical references, discography (p.   ), filmography (p.   ), and index.
ISBN-13: 978-0-8032-9008-2 (pbk.: alk. paper)
ISBN-10: 0-8032-9008-X (pbk.: alk. paper)
1. Walter, Bruno, 1876–1962.   2. Conductors (Music)—Biography.   I. Pechefsky, Rebecca.   II. Title.
ML422.W27R93   2006
784.2'092—dc22      2006003015

# Introduction

Since this book's first appearance in February 2001, interest in the life and times of Bruno Walter has continued to build with gratifying intensity. In October 2001 the Universität für Musik und darstellende Kunst in Vienna and the Orpheus Trust celebrated the 125th anniversary of Walter's birth with an exhibition, a concert, and the publication of a handsome collection of essays.[1] The year 2001 also saw the completion of Michele Selvini's marvelous biography of Walter, a lavishly illustrated work in three volumes.[2] Complementing this magnum opus was a documentary on Walter released in 2002, narrated by Selvini and directed by János Darvas for the Munich-based film company Metropolitan. In September 2004 the inauguration of the annual Bruno Walter Musiktage—a music festival offering concerts, master classes, lectures, an exhibition, and a commemorative program booklet in Slovak and German[3]—took place in Bratislava.

In addition to these tributes to Walter the conductor, performers have been increasingly drawn to Walter the composer. Naturally, his music formed part of the festivities in both Vienna and Bratislava.[4] But the most spectacular event connected with Walter's music was the masterly rendition of his First Symphony in New York's Avery Fisher Hall on October 15, 2004, by the American Symphony Orchestra conducted by Leon Botstein. This was the United States premiere of the work and only the third performance of it anywhere.

The symphony, lasting nearly an hour and requiring an orchestra of Mahlerian dimensions, reveals a composer whose imagination is teeming with ideas, a creator utterly in control of his massive forces, at home in large-scale forms, at once in step with the music of his time and ready to move in new directions. Some passages suggest contemporary works by Mahler and Elgar while others anticipate Korngold and even Shostakovich, but the symphony is not a pastiche; it is held together by a unified compositional style.

A number of Walter's other compositions *have* appeared on compact disc in recent years. Several previously unrecorded lieder from Walter's early song books were included in collections by Emma Bell and Christian Hilz, and even Walter's arrangement for piano four-hands of Mahler's First Symphony is now available in a performance by Zdeňka Hršel and Martin Hršel.[5] In addition, the German firm Ries & Erler has announced its intention to publish Walter's music, a move that may encourage others to explore the riches of his symphonic, chamber, and vocal scores.

Of course, the recordings that Walter himself made of standard and non-standard repertoire remain his chief legacy, and his final stereo sessions with the West Coast Columbia Symphony Orchestra, more than any of his other recordings, continue to attract new listeners. Although the orchestra has generally been characterized as a hand-picked group of musicians from Paramount Studios, the Los Angeles Philharmonic, and elsewhere in the Los Angeles area, the players often achieved a cohesion unexpected from a pick-up band. And in fact, some of these musicians had a history as an ensemble before recording with Walter since the players in Walter's Columbia Symphony Orchestra were drawn in large part from the Los Angeles Festival Orchestra, founded and directed by Franz Waxman.[6] Established in 1947, the Los Angeles Festival Orchestra performed regularly in late spring or early summer until 1966, mostly in Royce Hall at UCLA. Many of its members carried over from one season to the next, and by the late 1950s, when Walter began making his recordings with the Columbia Symphony Orchestra, a good number of these players came to the recording sessions with an established musical rapport.

Reissues of those recordings, as well as of Walter's other classic interpretations, continue to multiply. Sony Classical released a thirteen-disc set of Walter's best-known recordings of Mahler, Bruckner, and Wagner, and the French branch of Sony Classical has reissued many of Walter's superb New York Philharmonic recordings. The Great Conductors series, overseen by IMG Artists, devoted a two-disc set to Walter, and Andante has presented admirable transfers of several of Walter's live performances in deluxe packaging. The Tahra label has rescued some important live recordings from oblivion, and large historic sets by the Concertgebouw Orchestra and the Boston Symphony have also included Walter rarities.[7] All this bodes well for continuing interest in Walter's recorded legacy and his extraordinary life.

And Walter's life *was* extraordinary. We are learning more and more about this complex genius and the times in which he lived, and some fresh assessments are in order. The first printing of this biography, for example, offered no commentary on a remarkable premiere given by Walter—that of Ernst Krenek's Second Piano Concerto, which Walter introduced to the world in Amsterdam on March 17, 1938, with the composer as soloist. We were unable at the time to find either a score or a recording of this work but have since obtained both.[8]

The concerto is a twelve-tone work from beginning to end—apparently the only twelve-tone work that Walter ever performed—with a clear tone row subjected to standard dodecaphonic manipulation: transpositions, inversions, canon, and so on. The work ends with the piano drifting away in a deliberate anticlimactic gesture. Any sense of a tonal center is fleeting at best, and dissonance is the rule.

The Krenek premiere is noteworthy first and foremost because Walter had publicly condemned atonality and twelve-tone composition as unnatural only three years earlier in his essay *Von den moralischen Kräften der Musik*.[9] His attitude, however, might have softened after the publication of the essay. In 1946 Walter confessed that he had come to regret his "condemnation of atonality" because it had "deeply hurt" Alban Berg, a "stubborn wanderer on labyrinthine paths."[10] While Walter's feeling of regret doesn't necessarily mean that he had fundamentally changed his position on atonality, it shows that he had come to have second thoughts about his open condemnation of it. Perhaps Walter had become more receptive to the idea of exploring twelve-tone music—or perhaps, by 1938, he felt that being open-minded on the subject was politically correct, especially given the Nazis' hostility to atonal music.

As it happened, Walter's performance of Krenek's concerto occurred only a few days after Nazi troops peacefully filed into Austria. Although Walter probably did not anticipate Germany's annexation of Austria when he programmed the piece, he was painfully aware of the looming Nazi menace and surely knew that performing Krenek's concerto carried with it political implications. Krenek was already controversial as the composer of *Johnny spielt auf*, an opera incorporating jazz elements and touching on race relations in a way that offended the radical Right. Although Walter was no champion of *Johnny*, his decision to conduct a twelve-tone work by Krenek in 1938 shows bravery at a time when daring aesthetic choices could have grim consequences. It is nevertheless worth noting that when World War II ended and the Nazi threat had passed, Walter reverted to his earlier criticism of atonal and twelve-tone music as unnatural.[11]

Along with our increased knowledge of Walter the musician, we have learned more about Walter the man. Two sources have thrown light on Walter's relationship with his brother, Leo, in the years following World War II, when Leo and their sister, Emma, were living in Gothenburg, Sweden. One source is a collection of uncatalogued letters from Walter to his brother, mainly from the years 1946 to 1950, in the possession of the Bruno Walter Memorial Foundation. The other source, at the National Library of Canada in Ottawa, is also a collection of letters, mostly from Walter to his brother, supplemented by several photos.[12] The relationship that emerges is one in which Walter frequently acts as Leo's protector, inquiring into his and Emma's health, regularly sending them money, and visiting them in Sweden whenever possible. The photographs show a happy Walter with his adoring brother and sister, whose house is graced with images of the conductor.

The most significant aspect of Walter's personal life that has come to our attention, however, is the clandestine affair between Walter and Erika Mann, Thomas Mann's daughter, which took place during the 1940s.[13] The very idea of a romantic liaison between Walter and Erika Mann seemed unlikely when we wrote this biography. Born on November 9, 1905, Erika was thirty-one years younger than Walter and roughly the same age as Walter's daughters—Lotte (born in 1903) and Gretel (born in 1906)—with whom Erika played as a child. Erika's two husbands, the German actor-director Gustaf Gründgens and the poet W. H. Auden, were well-known gay figures, and Erika herself was known to be attracted to women.[14] In unpublished letters to her brother Klaus she often refers to Walter, but her references don't prove that he was her lover, in part because she used code to conceal Walter's identity. It also complicates matters that the code word she used, *Unhold* ("monster" or "fiend"), was one that she and her brother generally used to signify a lover and not a term reserved for Walter alone.[15] Nevertheless, the context of several letters dating from the mid-1940s makes it clear that Erika is describing Walter when she uses "Unhold" (or any number of variants, such as "U." or "Le monstre lui-même"). Of course, Erika's comments about Walter, though they reveal her passion for him, don't in themselves show that he reciprocated those feelings. But other details, taken along with Erika's letters, leave no real room for doubt.

So far as we can tell, the affair was noted in print for the first time in the memoirs of Albrecht Joseph (1901–1991). Joseph had been a stage director in Germany and was later a secretary to Thomas Mann and Franz Werfel. He worked in television and film in the United States, was one of Anna Mahler's husbands, and for a time in the 1940s dated Lotte Walter. Recalling that period in his life, he relates the following story in his memoirs:

> [A]t the time of my more intimate relationship with Lotte, we would sometimes meet each other not at my house but at the bathhouse behind the pool on the grounds of the Walters' residence. One evening Lotte pointed from there to a lit window on the upper floor of the main house. You could see the shadows of two people embracing each other. Lotte explained to me that they were her father and Erika [Mann],

who were having a love affair. . . . Lotte found the situation distasteful. She was indignant: "My best friend and my father . . ." I found it not shocking but natural.[16]

The tale of two shadows embracing each other is hardly conclusive, especially in an autobiography packed with diverting anecdotes. But further evidence surfaces in Irmela von der Lühe's important biography of Erika Mann, first published in 1993.[17] Von der Lühe cites not only Joseph's memoirs but also several of Erika's unpublished letters,[18] which make a much more persuasive case for an affair, though a skeptic could argue that the references in Erika Mann's letters were simply wishful thinking on her part.

The relationship became particularly strained when Delia Reinhardt reentered Walter's life. Walter had fallen in love with Reinhardt during his years in Munich, and although the two of them separated in the early 1920s, his affection for her never died. When Walter arranged for Delia Reinhardt to come to America after World War II, he resolved to end his affair with Erika and reportedly told her late in 1948 that he wanted his relationship with her to be on a "natural—that is, fatherly—basis."[19] Erika reacted with indignation and outrage, and well into the 1950s her relations with Walter were profoundly uneasy. In fact, the letters that Walter himself wrote to Erika in the late 1940s and mid-1950s present the clearest evidence of a romantic affair between them. Walter pleads again and again with Erika to be calm; he longs for the friendship that they once enjoyed; he insists that Delia Reinhardt knows nothing of the matter.[20] Neither his continued pleas for moderation nor his affectionate tone nor his comments about Delia Reinhardt's ignorance of their relationship make sense if Walter and Erika were simply old friends who had a falling out. And Erika's deep jealousy and pain, lasting for years, are also incomprehensible if not viewed as aftereffects of a love that, from her perspective, ended on a sour note. It comes as a great relief to read a letter from Erika to Walter—written in 1956, just days before his eightieth birthday—in which she seems finally to have achieved some reconciliation with him and can express "how very, very happy" she is to have figured in his life and "how grateful" she is for the many things he has given her over the decades.[21]

We may never know exactly how and when the relationship began, but it's easy to speculate on what brought them together. It seems likely that Walter and Erika began their relationship after they settled in the United States, both having been exiled from their homeland and having fought against the Nazi plague then spreading through Europe. Half Jewish herself, Erika was as much a racial outcast as Walter, and her years of producing anti-Nazi theatricals and writings resulted in her losing her German citizenship as the National Socialist machine was gaining deadly momentum. (The poet W. H. Auden came to her rescue in 1935, marrying her and thus allowing her to acquire a British passport just as her country was disowning her.) Walter had been a frequent guest in the Mann household while Erika was growing up, and his genial personality made him a particularly attractive father figure to her. She said, perhaps with some envy, that Walter's daughters regarded him as "not only the most affectionate, but also the most beguiling of parents. He played with them, and for them; he entertained them, and told them stories of which he was a great inventor—stories, which he was wont to perform, rather than merely to tell."[22] By Erika's adulthood, Walter seemed the embodiment of the culture and civilization that she was trying to preserve and that the Nazis threatened to destroy.

And to Walter, Erika must have seemed equally admirable, not only as a sharp-witted member of the talented Mann family but also as a splendid warrior in the cause of freedom. Perhaps she also reminded him of his beloved daughter Gretel, Erika's childhood friend, who was murdered in 1939.[23] Though Erika considered herself unattractive, she had magnetism—which is evident, for example, in her cameo appearance as a teacher of German classics in the 1931 film *Maedchen in Uniform.* And certainly the adoration of a clever woman in her thirties would have had a certain appeal to a man in his sixties known to enjoy the company of charming women. Nevertheless, Walter and Erika surely realized that a liaison between a young woman and a man literally old enough to be her father—indeed, a married man who had known her since childhood and was a close friend of her father's—would be unacceptable to many. They kept their relationship quiet and carefully hid it from Thomas Mann, though his wife, Katia, was in on the secret, as was Walter's daughter Lotte.

The sexual encounters appear to have been sporadic, and it would be wrong to view the relationship as merely physical. Walter and Erika spent time together publicly and engaged in lively exchanges of ideas. In 1944 Erika recalled the Walter of her youth: "how easy to amuse he was, how quickly touched, how readily impressed; the ideal audience; the perfect listener and reader."[24] She added that the Walter of the present day was much the same:

> He has grown immeasurably since the days of Munich. But the thirty years which turned the god of my childhood into a great figure in the world of music have left unchanged his youthful enthusiasm, his vast receptivity, his sprightly interest in all that is interesting. Going to

the movies with him is like going to the movies with a brilliant child. And hearing him discuss a book he has read, a play he has seen, or a speech he has heard, is like hearing somebody very young, if keenly intelligent, and oddly experienced. He reads more and writes better than many a man of letters.[25]

Erika's passion for Walter constituted, as Irmela von der Lühe has shown, "the great love of her life."[26] That's not to say that she had no interest in or passionate involvement with anyone else. But the memory of Walter remained strong with her well after his death; in her later years she wore Walter's wristwatch, showing it off to others, and on her night table she kept a photo of Walter and her father embracing on the occasion of her father's eightieth birthday.[27]

One might reasonably feel that Walter exercised poor judgment in allowing himself to get involved with Erika, no matter how the affair had begun or who initiated it. Yet after they broke off relations, the tender letters that he sent over the course of some seven years—during which Erika was evidently heaping abuse on him (in letters now lost or destroyed)—reveal a familiar figure, a gentle man who persists in seeking what he wants while remaining keenly aware of the feelings of those with whom he has a personal or professional relationship.

In preparing this revised edition we have incurred several new debts. We are grateful to the University of Nebraska Press and Yale University Press for allowing us to emend the text in a few places and to add a new introduction. We have also benefited from readers of the biography who generously offered helpful new information. Many of those thanked in the original list of acknowledgments deserve another round of thanks, particularly James Altena, Rolland Parker, and Steve Reveyoso. Unfortunately omitted from that list were Drs. Nergesh Tejani and Amir Tejani. We are also indebted to the following, who helped with this edition in various ways: Martin Anderson, Leon Botstein, Andrew Byrne, Christopher Gibbs, Juliane Braun-Giesecke, William Carragan, Claudia Daniel (Ernst-Krenek-Institut-Privatstiftung), Benjamin Epstein, Susanne Eschwé (Universität für Musik und darstellende Kunst), Mark W. Kluge, Irmela von der Lühe, Heather Lundine (University of Nebraska Press), Maureen Nevins (archivist, Music Division, National Library of Canada in Ottawa), Alexa Nieschlag, Joseph Patrych, David A. Pickett, Tully Potter, Cornelia Praetorius, Michael Schwalb, Barry Sheridan, Bob Thompson (Universal Edition), John Waxman, and Gabriele Weber (Monacensia Literaturarchiv und Bibliothek). We also renew our thanks to the Bruno Walter Memorial Foundation, especially Todd M. Brinberg, Craig M. Shumate, and W. Barry Thomson.

## Notes

1. Susanne Eschwé and Michael Staudinger, eds., *Bruno Walter: Der Wiener Nachlass* (Vienna: Verlag Lafite, 2001), with contributions from Susanne Eschwé, Gerhard Scheit, and Michael Schwalb, along with a list of works that were in Walter's library and are now housed at the Universität für Musik und darstellende Kunst.

2. Michele Selvini, *Bruno Walter: La porta dell'eternità*, 3 vols. (Milan: Fondazione culturale della collina d'oro, 1999–2001).

3. *Bruno Walter Musiktage* (Bratislava: Pressburger Philharmoniker, 2004).

4. Walter's Violin Sonata was performed at the Vienna celebration on October 19, 2001, by violinist Patricia Kopatschinskaja and pianist Claus-Christian Schuster (a recording of the performance is available at the Universität für Musik und darstellende Kunst in Vienna). The Violin Sonata now exists in four commercial recordings; see appendix for details.

   Also performed at the Vienna celebration were three of Walter's settings of texts by Joseph von Eichendorff and Walter's Piano Quintet, a work of distinctly Brahmsian stamp, especially in its opening movement—though Walter's own ecstatic musical voice makes itself heard throughout the work. (The songs were performed by soprano Margit Fleischmann and pianist Claus-Christian Schuster, who also took the keyboard part in Walter's Piano Quintet, with the Aron Quartet.) In Bratislava Walter's arrangement for piano four-hands of Mahler's Second Symphony had a performance by Ladislav Fančovič and Stanislav Galin on September 13, 2004, and movements of the String Quartet were performed by the Israel String Quartet on September 14, 2004. The quartet's slow movement—a twenty-minute piece sounding sometimes like Schubert, sometimes like early Schoenberg or Delibes—was also heard at the Bard Music Festival in Annandale-on-Hudson, New York, on August 17, 2002, in a performance by the Colorado Quartet.

5. See appendix.

6. We thank John Waxman, Franz Waxman's son, for calling to our attention the connection between the Los Angeles Festival Orchestra and the Columbia Symphony Orchestra.

7. See appendix for details on these recordings.

8. Thanks to Universal Edition, which lent us a study score, and the Austrian Broadcasting Corporation (ORF), which supplied us with a recording of the work as performed by the Vienna Philharmonic and Alfred Brendel.

9. See p. 244 of this biography.

10. Bruno Walter, *Theme and Variations*, trans. James A. Galston (New York: Knopf, 1946), 316.

11. Walter is quite clear about his hostility to atonality and twelve-tone music in his

1958 interview with Albert Goldberg, included in *Bruno Walter: The Maestro, The Man*, recently issued on DVD (VAI DVD 4235).

12. In the Bruno Walter Collection of the music division, manuscript section.

13. We are grateful to Michael Schwalb for first calling our attention to the relationship between Walter and Erika Mann.

14. See, for example, Peter Parker, *Isherwood: A Life Revealed* (New York: Random House, 2004). Parker writes that "the playwright Frank Wedekind's daughter Pamela . . . had previously been Erika [Mann's] lover" (198). Also, Don Bachardy noted in 1985 that the Manns "could hardly object" to Erika's marriage to the homosexual Auden "since Erika was a lesbian." See *Conversations with Christopher Isherwood*, ed. James J. Berg and Chris Freeman (Jackson: University Press of Mississippi, 2001), 193. Moreover, during some of the years of her relationship with Walter, Erika was also in love with the American war correspondent Betty Knox. See Irmela von der Lühe, *Erika Mann: Eine Biographie* (1993; revised edition, Frankfurt am Main: Fischer Taschenbuch, 1996), 289.

15. Irmela von der Lühe, e-mail message to Erik Ryding, May 10, 2005.

16. Albrecht Joseph, *Ein Tisch bei Romanoff's: Vom expressionistischen Theater zur Westernserie*, with an afterword by Stefan Weidle (Steidl, Göttingen: Juni-Verlag, 1991), 216.

17. Von der Lühe, *Erika Mann*, 284–89.

18. Now in the Erika Mann Collection (henceforth EMC) of the Monacensia Literaturarchiv und Bibliothek in Munich.

19. Katia Mann to Klaus Mann, Nov. 22, 1948 (EMC). Cited in von der Lühe, *Erika Mann*, 287–88. (It is unclear from the letter whether the gloss "that is, fatherly" represents the voice of Walter as cited by Katia Mann or that of Katia herself.)

20. See, for example, Bruno Walter to Erika Mann, Aug. 3, 1950; Apr. 10, 1954 (EMC).

21. Erika Mann to Bruno Walter, Sept. 9, 1956 (EMC).

22. Erika Mann, "For Bruno Walter," *Tomorrow* (July 1944): 24.

23. Walter wrote that he was happy that Erika kept Gretel in her thoughts, and that Gretel "lived on" in her. See Bruno Walter to Erika Mann, July 18, 1949 (EMC).

24. Erika Mann, "For Bruno Walter."

25. Ibid.

26. Von der Lühe, *Erika Mann*, 284.

27. Ibid., 288.

*For Emily, Mary, and William*
In memoriam *Rachel Kemper and Howard Pechefsky*

# Contents

CONTENTS

xviii

# Preface

During his sixty-seven years at the podium, Bruno Walter touched a huge number of listeners. At their greatest, his interpretations were revelatory, as audiences and critics acknowledged throughout his career. He succeeded again and again in discovering the essence of a musical composition and affording his listeners a passage to its inward panorama. He could make the opening theme of Beethoven's Fifth sound as fresh as a newly composed work, and he could galvanize Wagner and Verdi with an unsurpassed dramatic electricity. In doing so, he not only revealed the soul of the music he interpreted but also brought his listeners, through art, nearer to the passions and ecstasies and tragedies of life—all of which he knew from firsthand experience.

Walter's story constantly skirts tragedy yet finds a comparatively happy ending. An impassioned devotee of German art, he found himself persecuted by German nationalists as the Nazi Party gained momentum. He held key musical positions in Austria and Germany during the first two decades of the twentieth century and was friendly with some of the leading composers and authors of his day. Then the troubles began. Expelled first from Munich, then from Germany, then from Austria, and finally from Europe, Walter settled in the United States, where he would successfully reestablish his career. In this regard (though in few others) he somewhat resembled the ancient Roman war hero Coriolanus, who fought for his country but, through the political maneuverings of others, found himself an exile and ultimately joined the enemy forces. In Shakespeare's version of the story, as Coriolanus leaves Rome, he utters the famous line "There is a world elsewhere," from which we have taken our subtitle. The words, however, also seem appropriate for Walter if taken in a different sense, for throughout his mature life he was committed to the spiritual world, which had greater importance to him than anything on this temporal globe. In his final years he became a devoted student of the teachings of Rudolf Steiner and thought continually about the "higher spheres" and the dangers of materialism.

Assessments of Walter have varied over the years. Many have praised him for his sincerity, warmth, and musical genius, though in recent times some have been quick to characterize him as a sentimental, ambitious hypocrite. The truth, as is often the case, lies somewhere between the extremes. He was not a saint and had no desire to be treated as such. One can cite instances of backbiting, narrow-mindedness, and prevarication—which point to a distinctly unattractive side of his personality—but these were the exception rather than the rule. We have followed almost every day of his long career from about 1900 to 1962, scouring thousands of letters to and from Walter, and have interviewed over sixty people who had known him personally or worked with him professionally. The picture that emerges is of a man who was for the most part generous, open-minded, forgiving, and loyal to his friends. He could be evasive, especially when the feelings of others might be hurt, but he could also be brutally honest if a situation called for bluntness.

In searching for news of Walter's activities, we have combed through well over 20,000 reviews—most of them in German and Austrian newspapers—and there is no question that positive accounts of Walter's contribution to music have far outweighed negative ones, though certainly a chorus hostile to Walter existed almost from the beginning of his career. Without overloading the reader with passages from contemporary journals and newspapers, we have tried to give a balanced picture of Walter's critical reception, offering a somewhat greater percentage of negative reviews than we actually encountered—partly in an attempt to be even-handed, partly because critical reviews are often more revealing (both of Walter's stylistic manner and of his critics' prejudices) than sterling reports.

The most frequently cited grievances against Walter as a conductor are that he was "too sentimental" and that his "beat was unclear." Here it's surely best to turn to Walter's recordings and draw one's own conclusions. What seems sentimental to some might strike others as deeply sensitive; an unclear beat to one listener might sound like subtle rhythmic flexibility to another. While the relaxed tempi in some of Walter's later recordings seem flabby, unadventurous, and too *gemütlich* to some ears, those very recordings offer a mature, unhurried beauty, wedded to an almost erotic caressing of the lines, that few Walterians would be without. Even the most committed enthusiasts, however, will allow that some of Walter's stylistic peculiarities could be unfortunate; his tendency, especially in the earlier recordings, to slow down for the lyrical themes in works by classical composers like Mozart, even when the execution is skillfully carried off, can be disruptive and disconcerting. (This was, of course, a characteristic not of Walter alone, but of several generations of post-Wagnerian conductors; it is almost absent in his last recordings.) And his aversion to repeating the exposition in sonata form sometimes resulted in lopsided structure. But many will gladly tolerate such idiosyncrasies in return for the sumptuous musical banquet that Walter served.

Complaints of another kind dogged Walter for decades—indeed, whenever he performed before anti-Semitic critics. In some cases, the racial motives for a critic's animosity are made abundantly clear throughout a review, but in many instances the tastes of the critics could not obviously be attributed to racial bias. There are, for example, devastating reviews of Walter's original compositions that trounce him for lacking a genuinely creative gift— a line of attack often leveled at Mahler by those who believed that Jews were incapable of originality and higher creativity. It's tempting to see such attacks on Walter as part of the general propaganda against Jewish composers; yet one of the loudest critics in this vein was the Jewish reviewer Julius Korngold (father of the wunderkind composer Erich Wolfgang Korngold), whose attacks were hardly likely to have been prompted by a political or racial aversion to music composed by Jews. On the other hand, the Munich critic Paul Ehlers, who supported the Nazi Party early on, rarely wrote a harsh word about Walter over the course of several years.

Walter's style has often been characterized as "lyrical," but perhaps "vocal" would be a more accurate term. To be sure, Walter continually urged his players to sing, but singing is not just lyricism. "Sing out," yes, but always with different inflections; sing *recitativo* as well as *arioso*. In Walter's interpretations, we are often aware of intense drama; it is most obvious in the realm of opera, but the purely symphonic works are also often charged with feral energy. Even when his readings reach a frenzied pitch, however, the instruments are allowed to breathe, to create resonant tones that fit into deftly shaped lines; in *prestissimo* passages, one almost never feels that the instruments are gasping for breath. And the vocal model no doubt provided the textural ideal that Walter strove to achieve: the polyphonic fabric of his orchestral timbres surely owes a debt to the harmonies of human voices, where a subordinate line rarely serves as mere accompaniment but almost always has its own identity.

In his relations with orchestral musicians, Walter was perhaps the first world-renowned conductor to achieve a reputation for treating his players with courtesy rather than roughness, putting himself forward as *primus inter pares*. His disapproval was often expressed with the genial formula: "My friends, I am not quite happy. Please, once again." But this is not to say that he was a pushover; in fact, for all his courtliness, he could be quite firm with his players, until they gave him what he felt they were capable of giving. "Gentlemen, please give me my *piano*," he would say again and again, almost possessively. As Isaac Stern has remarked: "He was just as much an autocrat in his gentle way as Toscanini was in an explosive way. . . . But in a sense a musician must be, because above all a performer has to impose his will, firstly upon the orchestra, if he's a conductor, and then upon the audience, and that imposition of will comes from an inner strength and conviction at all times."[1]

Throughout his career, Walter was regarded as one of the greatest interpretive masters of the orchestral repertoire. In 1935, when Hans Joachim Moser's *Musik Lexikon* appeared in Berlin (a city that had effectively ousted Walter for racial motives two years before), the entry for Walter—his inclusion was a surprise in itself—astonishingly referred to the Jewish-born musician as "one of the most outstanding conductors of the present time."[2] Although short books on Walter began to appear as early as 1913, there has been no serious study of Walter's life in English since the publication of his own autobiography in 1946.[3] This is extraordinary, given both his importance as a twentieth-century figure and the wealth of primary sources available, which could furnish material for a study many times the length of the current volume. Ours is the first account of Walter's life to make full use of the Bruno Walter Papers at the New York Public Library for the Performing Arts, which contains some seven thousand letters to and from the conductor. In addition, we have combed through the substantial collections of the New York Philharmonic and Concertgebouw archives (each containing several hundred letters connected to Walter), and numerous smaller repositories of Walteriana, such as the Daniel Gregory Mason Collection at Columbia University and the Alma Mahler Werfel Collection at the University of Pennsylvania. Despite the temptation to add passages from every letter and every review that excited our interest, we have tried to be selective with our sources and to construct a readable narrative, in the hope that this biography, which necessarily omits much, will serve as an introduction to a life rich in event and richer still in musical achievement.

# Acknowledgments

We are grateful first and foremost to those people—several of whom have since passed away—who shared their memories of Walter with us, even if some of the interview material sadly but inevitably ended up on the "cutting-room floor": Kurt Adler, Pierrette Alarie, Lucine Amara, Georges Andre, Julius Baker, Rose Bampton, Samuel Baron, Schuyler Chapin, Van Cliburn, James Decker, Ranier De Intinis, Norman Dello Joio, Thea Dispeker, Maureen Forrester, Thomas Frost, Felix Galimir, Irma Geering, Maxim Gershunoff, Loren Glickman, Albert Goltzer, Ernst Haefliger, Nikolaus Harnoncourt, Walter Hendl, Jerome Hines, Laurel Hurley, Eugene Istomin, David Kates, Igor Kipnis, Henry-Louis de La Grange, Siegmund Levarie, William and Mary Lincer, David Lloyd, Ruth Martin, Kurt Masur, John McClure, Homer Mensch, Yehudi Menuhin, Alfio Micci, Arnold Michaelis, Mildred Miller, George Neikrug, Morris Newman, Jarmila Novotná, David Oppenheim, Martin Ormandy, Roberta Peters, Regina Resnik, Elsy Ruschmann, Virginia Sease, Léopold Simoneau, Johannes Somary, Maria Stader, János Starker, Risë Stevens, Wolfgang Stresemann, Nathan Stutch, Koho Uno, Theodor and Jean Uppman, William Vacchiano, Sandra Warfield, William Warfield, Theodore White, Frances Yeend, Manuel Zegler, and Bruno Zirato Jr.

Three devout Walterians, who were extraordinarily generous with their time and knowledge, deserve special mention: James Altena and Rolland Parker, who read through the entire manuscript in an earlier form and offered countless helpful suggestions for improvement, and Jon Samuels, who shared with us a large body of information on Walter's recordings and later concert programs, which Jon had gathered over the years.

Special thanks must also go to the New York Philharmonic's archivist/ historian, Barbara Haws, and to her colleagues Richard Wandel and Michele Smith. Barbara has served as an invaluable guide through the well-stocked archives of the Philharmonic—which include letters, contracts, live recordings, and memorabilia of immense value—and has also helped to bring some of Walter's long-lost broadcast recordings into circulation again.

Many others who helped with this biography have earned our heartfelt thanks: Jean van Altena, Allan Altman, Lisa Amend (Bayerische Staatsbibliothek), Jean Ashton (director, Rare Book and Manuscript Library, Columbia University), Stefana Atlas, Paul Banks, Charles Barber, JoAnne E. Barry (archivist, the Philadelphia Orchestra), Gregor Benko, Claudius Böhm (archives, Leipzig Gewandhaus), Andrew Bolotowsky, Joseph Boonin, John Canarina, Edward Cardona, Bridget P. Carr (archivist, Boston Symphony Orchestra), Matt Cavaluzzo, Donald Chankin, Sedgwick Clark, George Dansker, James Dixon, Stephanie Dyson (archives, Boston Symphony Orchestra), Michelle Errante, Mary Ann Feldman (program annotator and music adviser, Minnesota Orchestra), Roland Folter, Anthony Fountain, Ernestine Franco, Anita and Erika Frey, Walter Frisch, Takashi Fujita, Ernest Gilbert, Stanley Gillman (Bruno Walter Memorial Foundation), Johan Giskes (historian, Royal Concertgebouw Orchestra), Marie-Luise Hahn (Deutsches Exilarchiv 1933–1945, Die Deutsche Bibliothek in Frankfurt am Main), Tom Halliday, Jane Halpern, Gerda Hanf (Internationale Gustav Mahler Gesellschaft), Harry Haskell (Yale University Press), Johanna Hegenscheidt, Clemens Hellsberg (president and archivist, Wiener Philharmoniker), Mary Hurlbut, Betty Izant (festival archivist, Ojai Festivals, Ltd.), Jane Jackson (archives, Royal Opera House, Covent Garden), William Josephson, Jack Kamerman, Lars Karlsson (Royal Stockholm Philharmonic Orchestra), Ann Kersting-Meuleman (Musik- und Theaterabteilung, Stadt- und Universitätsbibliothek, Frankfurt am Main), James Klain, Friedrich Kleinknecht (chairman, Musikalische Akademie), Lotte Klemperer, Loanne Rios Kong, Karen Kopp, Orly Krasner, Michael Lalla, Lars Larson (Munich), David Lennick, Victor Litwinski, Luca Logi (librarian, Maggio Musicale Fiorentino), David Lowenherz, Wes Madison (library assistant, Cincinnati Symphony Orchestra), Victor Marshall (artistic administrator, Dallas Symphony Orchestra), H. Ward Marston, James North, Miwako Nozawa-Burleigh, Margaret Otzel, Emily Pechefsky, John Pennino (archives, Metropolitan Opera), Lisa Philpott (University of Western Ontario), Debra Podjed (Publications Department, San Francisco Symphony), Herbert Poetzl (Max Reinhardt Archive, Binghamton University, State University of New York), Doug Pomeroy, Edward Reilly, Steve Reveyoso, Philippe Reynal, Richard Rodzinski, Dennis D. Rooney, Angela Rückschloss (Stadtarchiv Würzburg), Karin Ryding, William Ryding, Harvey Sachs, Luitgard Schader (Paul-Hindemith-Institut, Frankfurt am Main), Edith Schipper, Helga Scholz (librarian, Universität für Musik und darstellende Kunst, Vienna), Axel Schröder (Landesarchiv Berlin), Jarrett Seals, Michele Selvini,

Peter Serkin, William Shank, Nancy Shawcross (Special Collections division of the Van Pelt-Dietrich Library, University of Pennsylvania), Wade Smith, Steve Smolian, Henriette Straub (archives, Royal Concertgebouw Orchestra), Mary Jean Stresemann, Brigita Stroda (Latvian National Opera), Hajime Suga, Don Tait, Anthony Thomas, Teri Noel Towe, Robert Tuggle (director, archives, Metropolitan Opera), J. Rigbie Turner (Pierpont Morgan Library, New York), Sam Ugbo (Munich), Koho Uno, Frank Villella (archives, Chicago Symphony Orchestra), Vita and Ishmael Wallace (the Orfeo Duo), Johann Weissensteiner (Diözesanarchiv, Vienna), Nóra Wellmann (archives, Budapest Opera), Irene Wenkel (Deutsche Oper Berlin), Antje Werkmeister (Berliner Staatsoper), Warren Wernick, Fredric W. Wilson, Seth Winner, Elizabeth Witherell (Special Collections, University of California at Santa Barbara), and Claude Zachary (University Archives and Manuscripts, University of Southern California).

We are also grateful to the following institutions: Brooklyn Public Library; Bundesarchiv (Berlin); Columbia University (New York); Czech Philharmonic; Deutsches Theatermuseum (Munich); Goetheanum (Dornach); Library of Congress (Washington, D.C.); Österreichische Nationalbibliothek (Vienna); Österreichisches Theatermuseum (Vienna); Prinzregententheater (Munich); Sony Music Entertainment; Staatsbibliothek (Berlin); Staatsbibliothek (Munich); TASIS, The American School in Switzerland (Montagnola); Texas Christian University (Fort Worth); and Yale University (New Haven, Connecticut).

Finally, we owe an enormous debt to all the helpful librarians at the New York Public Library for the Performing Arts, with its invaluable resources, particularly Karl Baranoff, Frances Barulich, George Boziwick, Charles Eubanks, Tema Hecht, Robert Kosovsky, John Shepard, and Channan Willner.

# *Bruno Schlesinger*

## Berlin, Cologne, Hamburg, 1876–1896

*A beautiful song, a masterly song—*
*How shall I grasp the difference?*
Wagner, *Die Meistersinger von Nürnberg*

Wagner's *Ring* cycle received its first complete performance in August 1876. The work's dimensions are huge even by operatic standards, its entire duration sometimes exceeding fifteen hours. A special theater was constructed in the out-of-the-way German city of Bayreuth specifically to stage the tetralogy, and audience members dutifully set aside four days to take in this tour de force, one day for each installment of the cycle. In its richness and scope, the work extended the limits of opera far beyond anything previously imagined, somewhat as Tolstoy's *War and Peace*, written at roughly the same time, reset the boundaries for the novel.

If Wagner's *Ring* signified the quintessential romantic deliverance from classical musical constraints, an event that took place shortly afterward—the premiere of Johannes Brahms's Symphony no. 1, presented on November 4, 1876—marked a move in a very different direction. This too was a large-scale orchestral work, employing the melodic and harmonic language of the later nineteenth century, yet it was written with due reverence to classical ideals. Balance, compact motivic development, artfully restrained passion, and an adherence to familiar forms were all among the earmarks of Brahms's first completed effort in the symphonic genre.

Grand in scope, both works demanded a virtuoso leader to keep the large forces together, to mold the thick textures into coherent works of art, and to tease out melodic strands from the rich fabric of sound. Each required an interpreter with insight and imagination, not just a time-beater. Between the premieres of these two nineteenth-century masterpieces fell the birth of Bruno Schlesinger, who would become not only a major interpreter of Brahms and Wagner but also one of the foremost conductors of the twentieth century, capable of both classic refinement and ecstatic surrender.

The son of Joseph and Johanna Schlesinger (née Fernbach), he was born on September 15, 1876, "not far from Alexanderplatz, at Büschings-platz and Mehnerstrasse, on the corner, no. 1."[1] His was a middle-class, Jewish family residing in the northern section of Berlin. He had a brother, Leo, three years his senior, and in 1878 acquired a sister, Emma. While his father, a bookkeeper in the garment industry, had a deep appreciation of music, it was his mother who possessed the actual talent and training, having attended the Stern Conservatory, founded in 1850 by the choral conductor and pedagogue Julius Stern. With a mixture of affection and vexation, Johanna Schlesinger recorded in a small collection of memoirs some of her son's earliest accomplishments. These included such irksome habits as stuffing every keyhole he could reach with paper cuttings and yanking pages out of musical scores.

But Bruno also displayed prodigious musical talent at an early age, and Johanna was the first to recognize her son's unusual abilities. At the age of five he gave a hint of his future profession. His mother regularly took him to the National Theater Garden, in which a little band entertained visitors. One day, the band became "the center of interest" to Bruno, "who, to everyone's delight, set himself up before them and imitated every movement of the conductor, without growing weary, and could not be removed before the music had ended."[2] His immovability on this occasion was paralleled by stubbornness on others. It was difficult for Johanna to satisfy her son's curiosity and to control his shifting moods; she could calm the "wild little colt" only by playing for him at the piano. "Then the little man listened, his mouth agape, and sat fully enchanted by it, and one day he asked: 'Mama, does that simply come out of your fingers, or are you doing something as well?' Then his mother placed him on her lap and showed him how the playing was effected; Bruno listened attentively to her words, then attempted to play on the keys. He said: 'Please, mother, let me learn how to play like you.'" Thereafter he received daily lessons from his mother and made rapid progress.

In school he was an intelligent but not exemplary student, his imagination already rebelling against the shackles of routine as it would, in a different way, later in his career. "The dreamer in him made him forget his pencil today, his tablet or notebook the next day," his mother wrote; yet when he learned to read, he would devour books, relishing works like *Robinson Crusoe* and the *Leather-Stocking Tales*, as well as legends of the ancient Greeks, which he knew well enough to identify scenes from ancient mythology depicted in works of art at the museum.

Aware that her son had talent beyond the ordinary, Johanna told her husband one day that she thought Bruno would "develop into a great musician."

He laughed. "Your maternal vanity is too great. I certainly think very highly of my children and will be proud and satisfied if they become competent, good people, but I don't envision anything like that."

"Time will tell," she replied.

Joseph's attitude toward his son changed soon enough. The occasion was a family wedding. The professional piano player, when asked by Bruno's uncle to let the boy play, shrugged his shoulders and unenthusiastically made room for him. Though unable to reach the pedals, Bruno played Mendelssohn's Song Without Words in F Major from memory. It was a "ravishing" performance, according to his mother's partisan account, and the professional pianist, predicting that the boy would indeed "become great," recommended taking him to the pianist and pedagogue Robert Radecke, one of the artistic directors of the Stern Conservatory and a conductor at the Berlin Royal Opera (as well as the composer of numerous lieder). Radecke tested his ear, confirmed his mother's declaration that he had absolute pitch, and admitted him to the conservatory.[3] Radecke's assessment of Bruno Schlesinger would remain with him for the rest of his life: "Every inch of this boy is music."

The conservatory was now developing and expanding under the directorship of Jenny Meyer, his mother's former voice teacher, who took a special interest in Johanna's son. Entering the conservatory at the age of eight, Bruno became known there as "the little Mozart" and soon enjoyed the attention of the young ladies, who "pampered and spoiled him, popping candies into his open mouth"; he would in fact enjoy the attention of female admirers for much of his life.

At the age of nine, Bruno decided to try his hand at composition. His mother asked her children to think up a "surprise for their father's approaching birthday. Without reflecting long, Bruno shouted: 'I shall compose a sonata for violin and piano and perform it with Leo [who had recently begun violin studies].'

" 'But you have no idea how it's done,' his mother said.

" 'You'll see; I'll be able to do it.'

"And indeed, without having any idea of theory or training in composition, he wrote a charming little duo. Unfortunately," his mother added, "the little piece has been lost, probably destroyed as a worthless thing by Bruno himself." She knew her son well.

He made good progress at the conservatory, though at first he needed "a special elevating contrivance" to allow his feet to reach the pedals. After a brief preparatory period under Franz Manstädt, he was assigned to the advanced piano class taught by Heinrich Ehrlich, at that time the most eminent piano and music-history teacher at the conservatory and a critic for the *Berliner Tageblatt*, one of the city's most prestigious newspapers. Ehrlich's course of study, to judge by his published technique manual, *How to Practice at the Piano*, was both careful and rigorous, giving Walter a secure technique that would stand him in good stead throughout the years to come.[4]

Indeed, by 1889, the twelve-year-old Bruno appeared destined for a career as a concert pianist. Not long after the Stern Conservatory had moved to a more spacious building on Wilhelmstrasse, Ehrlich informed Herr Schlesinger that his son was ready to play in public and arranged for him to take part in a concert with the Berlin Philharmonic.[5] According to the reviews, the debut was a complete success; the *Vossische Zeitung* reported that he "made an especially impressive appearance, playing a movement from Beethoven's Concerto in B-flat Major with graceful polish and a robust, almost manlike tone." The *Berliner Tageblatt* was hardly less effusive, reporting that "the boy Bruno Schlesinger" played his first movement "with full assurance and a freedom of expression reaching far beyond his age."[6]

In the year that followed, the young pianist continued to develop, driven by his desire to interpret the great literature for the piano and inspired by a concert he heard in Berlin by his contemporary, the prodigiously talented Josef Hofmann. "His brilliant Berlin success, which I witnessed, and his exceptional performance encouraged me in my own plans and hopes and kindled my zeal," Walter related in his autobiography.[7] In February 1890 he performed again, this time in a concert that included both solo works (the first movement of Bach's Italian Concerto and Chopin's Variations in B Major) and ensemble (Moscheles' Concerto in E-flat Major, once more with the Berlin Philharmonic). The *National Zeitung* praised his passagework, the reliability of his memory, and—significantly for a musician who would achieve fame for his work with others—the assurance of his ensemble playing, while the *Vossische Zeitung* commented on his natural phrasing and rhythm; he gave no appearance of being "drilled."[8] He was passing beyond the stage of mere student diligence and was already displaying the originality of interpretation necessary to a true concert artist. Yet despite his serious desire to excel as a musician, he lost none of his "childlike nature" while preparing for his recital; "when he finished work and his diligent practice, he could jump and romp like a playful child."[9]

Bruno Schlesinger was displaying other talents as well, drawing acclaim as accompanist for Jenny Meyer's students. If that was not enough, he continued to compose, though he was later to dismiss his compositions from that time as "wholly lacking in originality."[10] Developing concert pianist, accomplished vocal accompanist, and budding composer, the young musician seemed set in his path. But a momentous experience soon changed his musical plans forever: he saw Hans von Bülow conduct.

Until that time, Walter admitted later, he had scarcely noticed the conductors of the Berlin Royal Opera and the Philharmonic. But now he was seated on the stage, behind the timpani, with a full view of Bülow's facial expressions, and as he listened to the orchestra's expressivity, it became clear to him "that it was that one man who was producing the music, that he had transformed those hundred performers into his instrument, and that he was playing it as a pianist played the piano. That evening decided my future. Now I knew what I was meant for. No musical activity but that of an orchestral conductor could any longer be considered by me, no music could ever make me truly happy but symphonic music."[11]

Walter, of course, was not the only one upon whom Bülow's conducting made a deep impression. If Richard Wagner is to be believed, conducting earlier in the nineteenth century left much to be desired; orchestra directors were merely time-beating hacks, and some orchestras were even led by the concertmaster (though, as various orchestras without conductors have demonstrated, this in itself does not necessarily imply a lack of precision or interpretive subtlety). Even competent conductors like Mendelssohn, Wagner maintained, were too concerned with hurrying the music along;

they lacked the rhythmic flexibility necessary for an expressive perfor-mance. Wagner's opinions of his predecessors must certainly be taken with a grain of salt. Since he credits himself with being the first truly creative con-ductor, he surely exaggerates the defects of those who came before him, and Wagner's prejudices (racial and musical) with regard to Mendelssohn are well known. Nevertheless, Wagner must have infused his orchestras with a remarkable intensity of expression, for those lucky enough to hear him con-duct came away at once dazed and enlightened. Amy Fay, a young pianist from Boston who saw Wagner conduct in Berlin in 1871, described how he "controlled the orchestra as if it were a single instrument and he were play-ing on it. He didn't beat the time simply, as most conductors do, but he had all sorts of little ways to indicate what he wished."[12] By all accounts, Wagner is at least justified in claiming to be one of the first orchestra leaders to take the burden of musical interpretation upon himself, and Hans von Bülow was his self-styled heir.

Both Walter's and Felix Weingartner's recollections of Bülow's con-ducting accord with descriptions of Wagner's method, in that the "orchestra seemed to be a single instrument, on which Bülow played as on a pi-anoforte."[13] Weingartner, whom Walter would later encounter as Mahler's successor in Vienna, went on to describe how valuable Bülow's concert tours with the Meiningen orchestra in the 1880s were for both players and public: how, as a result of hearing them, other conductors and orchestra members realized that "it would not do to go on simply beating time and playing away with the old reprehensible carelessness and thoughtlessness, for that would certainly lower them in the eyes of the public, which, after once having nibbled dainties at the table of the great, would no longer be content with canteen-fare."[14]

Weingartner's estimation of Bülow's musical choices, however, was far from adulatory. In his essay on conducting, he described at some length what he considered the harmful features of Bülow's conducting, first and foremost of which was what he called Bülow's "pedagogic element." In his desire to make his interpretations audible to the listeners, Weingartner be-lieved, Bülow deliberately exaggerated his tempo modifications, took overall tempi that were either too fast or too slow, and was prone to give excessive prominence to details.[15] Weingartner admitted that these exaggerations be-came more pronounced at the end of Bülow's life, but that was the time when Walter would have heard him, and Walter himself reported that "a sublime artistic purity shone from [Bülow's] interpretations. They were never marred by disturbing liberties."[16] On the other hand, Walter confessed in his own book on interpretation that in his youth he, too, was guilty of excessive tempo modifications and that it took him some time "to learn enough from my mistakes to be able to correct them and attain to a purer style of making music," so it is certainly possible that he remembered Bülow's interpretations as "sublime" because they satisfied his youthful tendencies toward over-expressivity.[17] While it is always dangerous to judge a conductor by performances from the last years of his life, the recordings of Weingartner that have come down to us, particularly those of the Brahms symphonies made with the London Symphony Orchestra (1938–40), reveal a conducting style given more to subtly expressive phrases, rhythmic tautness, and clear dynamics than to changes in tempo, though Weingartner was certainly capable of skillful rubato when the music demanded it.

We can never know just how exaggerated Bülow's tempo modifications and interpretations of musical details really were, but Bülow's so-called pedagogic element had the effect of inspiring Walter to embark on a career as a conductor. He continued his piano studies with as much effort as ever and continued to accompany singers, an activity that he later stressed, both publicly and privately, as being among the most necessary for aspiring conductors. But meanwhile he also gained admission to Robert Radecke's conducting class at the conservatory and found himself in the fertile lands of score reading, thoroughbass (still considered an essential skill in those days), instrumentation, and eventually choral and orchestral rehearsals.

Most people passionately involved in music have had, in their adolescence or later, a sudden encounter with a previously unfamiliar composer that brings about a radical change in their musical tastes. What was once considered the height of musical expression now seems dull and commonplace; what was foreign and strange, the reason for existence. The young Bruno Schlesinger's encounter was with Wagner's *Tristan und Isolde*. At that time, however, the Stern Conservatory's faculty, as well as Walter's parents, other relatives, and acquaintances, were mostly anti-Wagnerians, holding up Brahms as the true mainstay of the classical tradition and eschewing Wagner's recent operas, though *Der fliegende Holländer* and *Lohengrin* were considered acceptable. Hearing Wagner constantly denigrated had the natural effect of making Walter curious, especially since he knew that one aspect of Wagner that his mentors considered dangerous was sensuality, which he "found rather interesting and by no means wicked."[18] So he decided to attend a performance of *Tristan* and judge for himself.

All the anticipatory excitement and high expectations in the world could not have prepared him for the effect the music actually had on him. He recalled how he sat in the topmost gallery of the Berlin Royal Opera House, astonished and overwhelmed: "Never before had my soul been so deluged with floods of sound and passion, never had my heart been consumed by such yearning and sublime blissfulness, never had I been transported from reality by such heavenly glory. I was no longer in this world. After the performance, I roamed the streets aimlessly. When I got home I didn't say anything and begged not to be questioned. My ecstasy kept singing within me through half the night, and when I awoke on the following morning I knew that my life was changed. A new epoch had begun: Wagner was my god, and I wanted to become his prophet."[19] Today Walter might be considered more the prophet of Mahler than of Wagner; since we lack any complete recordings of Walter conducting a Wagner opera, his youthful dreams of interpreting Wagner might seem to have fallen victim to impermanence. And Walter was never to conduct at Bayreuth, mainly because he was Jewish, though an unfortunate meeting with Cosima Wagner in 1901 in which he unwisely praised Verdi probably did nothing to increase his chances of being invited.[20] Still, audiences in Vienna, Munich, and Berlin, to mention only a few, would for many years thrill to the privilege of hearing Walter conduct Wagner.

There were, to be sure, other objections to Wagner besides sensuality that no doubt inspired extreme distaste on the part of Walter's relatives and instructors. Walter's piano teacher, Heinrich Ehrlich, actually admired Wagner's music and poetry to a high degree but had serious doubts about Wagner's personality and beliefs. Wagner was not only an anti-Semite, Ehrlich wrote in 1893, but a hypocrite as well: "If Wagner was so much against Jews that he repeatedly denied them all loftier understanding, how is it that he nevertheless took money from Jews to fund Bayreuth and also negotiated with them . . . ? And there's more. How was it possible that Wagner, who declared Jews incapable of understanding Christianity, appointed a Jew, Hermann Levi, the court Kapellmeister from Munich, to conduct his *Parsifal*?"[21] But despite his perception of Wagner's reprehensible qualities and less-than-honorable actions, Ehrlich could not help being moved by Wagner's creations. "How many insoluble riddles lie within his works," Ehrlich exclaimed; "how much that is great, beautiful, and sublime has this man created as musician and as poet!"[22] Ehrlich had, of course, hit upon one of the dilemmas that continue to plague lovers of Wagner today: how could someone capable of such reprehensible beliefs and dishonorable actions create such works of genius? As for the young Bruno Schlesinger, he must have heard remarks and insinuations concerning Wagner's undesirable qualities as a man, but he was evidently too caught up in his admiration of Wagner as a creator to let them tarnish his enthusiasm for Wagner's operas. In fact, Walter later came to believe that true geniuses should be remembered for their great works of art, rather than for their shortcomings as human beings. "Only musical value shall determine our choice of programs," he wrote shortly after World War II, in response to the suggestion that Hans Pfitzner's music should be banned from concerts. "To make this choice dependent upon political considerations means introducing a Nazi doctrine into our cultural life," he insisted, though he agreed that, in the case of true Nazis (he maintained that Pfitzner was not one), a "certain restraint" must be applied in the application of such an idealistic principle.[23]

Ehrlich's memoirs were published when Walter's studies at the Stern Conservatory were nearly at an end, and Walter probably never read them, for he makes no mention of them in his autobiography. Though he valued Ehrlich's thoroughgoing teaching methods from the standpoint of technique, he remembered considering him "old, devitalized, and barren," and, upon hearing him give a moving performance of Beethoven's "Hammerklavier" Sonata, was surprised at the "mighty spiritual sluice-break that evening."[24] Walter might have been even more surprised to read the praise Ehrlich heaped on Wagner as composer and poet, and it seems a pity that Walter remained unaware of another admirer of Wagner, another potential ally, at least in purely musical terms, in the Wagner–Brahms conflict that divided so many musical circles in late-nineteenth-century Germany.

This conflict is no neat fiction of twentieth-century musicologists and critics; it had a strong effect on many young musicians. Ethel Smyth, for instance, described how her first serious teacher in England played through Wagner scores for her, causing her to be "bitten by the operatic form of Art" and dream of someday having an opera produced in Germany, only to have these dreams quashed for a time when she entered the bitterly anti-Wagner circles in Leipzig.[25] But Walter, though now living more for Wagner than for any other composer, refused to give up Brahms. Instead, he "just loved both of them without trying to reconcile what, according to the opinion of so many high-principled people, was plainly irreconcilable."[26] Nonetheless, a certain amount of frustration and loneliness accompanied his attempts to gain intimate familiarity with Wagner's operas, necessitating as they did the scraping together of funds from his jobs as an accompanist in order to purchase tickets to performances, since he could hardly expect his parents to support his new obsession. He made secret trips to the Berlin Royal Library to study Wagner's scores and read his writings, which influenced him almost as much as Wagner's music, especially the famed essay on conducting. When Jenny Meyer had one of her students sing an excerpt from *Die Meistersinger*, kindly remarking that she didn't care for it herself but "wanted to give pleasure to our Bruno,"[27] he was naturally relieved. Absolved and encouraged, he could now devote himself to his new hero openly and wholeheartedly.

The Royal Library also helped him prepare for a conducting career in ways not directly connected to Wagner. Walter went there "almost daily" to familiarize himself with all the instruments, and the librarians "placed at his disposal—despite his youth—all the pertinent works," much to the irritation of the critic Wilhelm Tappert, a former editor of the *Allgemeine deutsche Musikzeitung* and an early scholar of lute music, who would become furious whenever he had to wait for a book from which Bruno was dutifully "making drawings of the instruments."[28] He also made his own piano reductions of orchestral scores—inexpensive study scores did not yet exist—and in the standing-room section of the opera house he would follow his reductions, scribbling notes to himself in the dim light of the gallery.[29]

The aspiring conductor, often lacking an instrument upon which to practice, is in a unique situation among musicians. Walter himself discussed this problem at some length in *Of Music and Music-Making*, stressing that since an orchestra would not be available to prospective conductors until the latter part of their studies, or even after their studies were complete, they must ready themselves in other ways, by coaching singers, attending concerts and observing other conductors, studying scores, and, more generally, by reading works of great minds and living life with relish: "The studies of the conductor must not be restricted to music. The world of music encompasses so much of the spiritual and human . . . that the value of a conductor's artistic achievements is to a high degree dependent upon his human qualities and capacities; the seriousness of his moral convictions, the richness of his emotional life, the breadth of his mental horizon, in short, his personality, has a decisive effect on his achievements."[30] The young Bruno Walter fed his imagination with works of great literature—by Defoe and Shakespeare, Goethe and Schiller, Kant and (later) Schopenhauer—and broadened his musical awareness, immersing himself in lesser-known operas by Russian composers, traveling to Bayreuth to hear Felix Mottl conduct (and, while there, visiting Wagner's grave). But he was eager to turn his newfound knowledge into practical experience in the opera house, for until that time came, he would be unsure if he truly possessed the ability to command those large and unruly forces that make up an operatic production.

Walter hoped to begin testing himself by acquiring a coaching position with one of the Berlin theaters. He was often called on by Jenny Meyer to accompany her students for theatrical auditions, and at a charity concert in December 1892 he played the piano for a number of conservatory singers. But at this time there appeared to be few openings for coaches in Berlin and, even more disheartening, no one to recommend Walter for the positions that might exist.

The tide began to turn for him when Arno Kleffel replaced Robert Radecke at the Stern Conservatory. Almost nothing is known about Kleffel today, beyond Walter's description of him as the leading conductor at the Cologne Stadttheater, but at that time he was familiar enough in Cologne circles for Walter to be called "a student of Arno Kleffel" upon making his debut. Walter studied composition with Kleffel and on March 18, 1893, appeared publicly in the capacity of conductor and composer, presenting his own *Meeresstille und glückliche Fahrt* for chorus and orchestra (a setting of Goethe's text), dedicated to Jenny Meyer. Presented in the hall of the Singakademie, the concert marked Walter's unofficial conducting debut with the Berlin Philharmonic, the not-so-humble assisting orchestra. While under Kleffel's tutelage, Walter also composed a song, "Der Ritter über den Bodensee," and was secretly working on an opera, *Agnes Bernauer*, "based upon Hebbel's tragedy," which he later condemned (after composing about two acts) as "thoroughly immature and, strange to say, quite un-Wagnerian."[31] Kleffel seems to have thought highly of his young protégé; his recommendation to Julius Hofmann, the artistic director in Cologne, resulted in a year's contract for Walter as a coach, beginning in September 1893. Thus ended Walter's student days, and he set off for the former Roman colony with trepidation and high hopes.

Any nervousness accompanying the assumption of his first real job was soon dispelled by the sheer burden of work. The position of coach appears to have been the equivalent of a dogsbody, for Walter's duties ranged from coaching the lead singers to giving the director opinions on new operas, auditioning new singers, and rehearsing backstage trumpets. In a letter to his parents of January 11, 1894, he apologized for having worried them with his long silence but said that the last four months had gone by quickly—"one day is just like another, and owing to this sameness you don't notice at all how swiftly the time flies."[32] He developed friendly relations with most of the main singers, particularly the baritone Baptist Hoffmann (who would later sing at the Berlin Royal Opera and become known especially for his interpretations of Wagner, making some recordings in the first decade of the twentieth century). Sometimes Walter's ability to work well with individual singers was a source of frustration, for details honed in coaching sessions were often lost in the actual stage productions; the "intensity of expression I had developed disappeared at the stage rehearsals and performances because of the conductor's excessively fast tempi, crumbled because of his dragging the music, or were rendered ineffective by the stage director's instructions."[33] He was, in fact, being introduced to the pitfalls of opera, to the never-ending pushing and pulling that stemmed from the struggle between musical ideals and theatrical shortcomings.

This struggle was by no means new or particularly prevalent in Cologne. Weingartner, too, complained bitterly of the problems an opera conductor faces: lack of adequate rehearsal, too many performances, stagings that don't afford singers a full view of the conductor, stage managers and stage directors who are ignorant of music, to cite merely a handful of Weingartner's grievances. Weingartner went so far as to regard his years in the theater as a "time of uselessly squandered labour, forcible suppression of my capabilities, and—a few isolated bright spots excepted—vain struggles to get even one step nearer the ideal."[34] Bruno Schlesinger at the age of seventeen was too much of an optimist to allow himself to lapse into that kind of bitterness. But he hadn't been in Cologne very long before he, too, began to be oppressed by similar frustrations. "I began to suffer from the dramatic and musical indifference of the performances," he recalled, "and from my powerlessness against the prevailing spirit of routine."[35] Further, he was discovering that he had higher ideals, both musical and dramatic, than most of his older colleagues. A picture now begins to emerge of an extremely talented young man, socially shy but musically confident, depressed when physical performances do not live up to artistic goals, but enabled by his buoyant spirit to strive for ideals in the next performance.

Perhaps Walter's frustrations would have grown more burdensome had he been relegated to the role of coach for many years. Early on, however, he was entrusted with the musical direction of two nineteenth-century light works—Carl Reinecke's *Von der Wiege bis zum Grabe* ("a cross between pantomime and ballet") and Johann Nestroy's play *Lumpazivagabundus*, which included musical numbers. Though Walter acknowledged that the works were "below the dignity of a regular operatic conductor," he was delighted to have an opportunity to direct the orchestra.[36] Then came the turning point, the work that Walter himself subsequently used to mark his official conducting debut. A mere seven months after arriving in Cologne, in March 1894, he was given the opportunity to lead a revival of *Waffenschmied*, a light and charming singspiel by Albert Lortzing. Known more for his comic and theatrical gifts than for serious operatic productions, Lortzing was naturally a far cry from Wagner, but his works contain enough melodic inventiveness and ensemble difficulties for a young conductor to prove himself. When *Waffenschmied* was first given in Vienna on May 30, 1846, the Viennese press and public appeared unimpressed; but it must have had a greater success in Germany, since by the late nineteenth century it was firmly ensconced in the repertoire of German opera theaters, and Walter would again be called upon to conduct it when he went to Breslau in 1896. Though never an enthusiast for light opera—he would later refuse positions where it seemed likely that he would have to conduct a large amount of it—Walter naturally retained a certain affection for this one, his first opera.

Reviews of Walter's debut were almost unmixed in their approbation. The *Köln-Zeitung* on March 21, 1894, praised his "keen rhythmic sense" and "great feeling for the beauty of sound." The *Kölner-Tageblatt* gives a more detailed picture of Walter's first professional conducting appearance: "Frequent acceleration of tempo was characteristic of the new conductor. Herr Schlesinger, undoubtedly a very talented musician, conducted with assuredness and determination, and displayed remarkable discretion. It is understandable, in a debut of so young a director (Herr Schlesinger might not yet have passed his nineteenth year), that he indicated and accompanied many inessential introductions and entrances with arm and head movements and also at times left the instruments in the rear to their fates—never, of course, disastrous for an orchestra such as ours."[37] From this description, one gains an impression of a young conductor who, though not completely in control when it comes to deciding which instruments to focus his attention upon, nevertheless has a clear idea of the overall musical interpretation, and one cannot help wondering whether these arm and head movements at "inessential" places were in fact symptoms of Walter's desire to let nothing go, to show to himself and others that he, like his hero Bülow, was more than a mere time-beater.

His debut was on a Wednesday, and the following Saturday, at the last minute, *Waffenschmied* was performed again. "Now, however, came an important event for me," Walter wrote to his parents early in April, proceeding to relate how, because of a singer's indisposition, the management decided to cancel *La Fille du régiment* and put *Waffenschmied* in its place, with two singers who hadn't performed their roles in years. When Walter heard the news, he was not even at the theater; assuming that he had the evening off, he had gone to coach Baptist Hoffmann. Walter rushed back to the theater, only to find the various directors in close consultation, evidently having serious doubts about entrusting a last-minute performance to a newcomer:

> I went into the director's office, and there stood the director, Ockert [the stage director], Mühldorfer, and Grossmann [two conductors]. I came in just as Grossmann said, "No, that seems to be too dangerous, I don't want to risk it, a much older conductor belongs there in order to hold the people together who no longer have any idea of what's going on." I went up to the director.
>
> "What, do you want something?" he said.
>
> "To conduct, of course, Herr Direktor," I said.
>
> Then Grossmann clapped me encouragingly on the shoulder and said, "Well now, you're going to get your miracle." Thus I conducted and happily held the performance together through alertness, energy, and attentiveness.[38]

Despite Grossmann's half-skeptical comment, Walter again came through his trial by fire unscathed, even with unrehearsed singers. But his two successes had the unfortunate effect of releasing a serpent of envy into the Cologne Opera. Probably this serpent had been slumbering for some time; the letters suggest that Walter was not one to keep his musical opinions to himself, and the sight of a seventeen-year-old, jumping up to the director's podium at the last minute and managing to hold things together as he seems to have done, was the final straw for those of his colleagues who were less secure in their abilities.

Earlier in his letter, Walter complained to his parents that, even after the first performance, neither Hofmann nor Ockert had said anything to show that they appreciated his success. Ockert in particular appears to have been put off by Walter's show of confidence; perhaps he and Walter had clashed over staging matters. In any case, after the Saturday performance, Ockert and the director continued to remain silent. What was worse, as Walter told his parents, the tenor, Bruno Heydrich, conspired with one of the newspapers to get Walter a poor review: "And then an article appeared in the *Sonntags-Anzeiger* which was written with such nastiness against me that I was speechless over it. Then another paper took my side, so a fierce battle has developed around me."[39] By this time, Heydrich was well known as a Wagnerian and had sung in many German opera houses in addition to the one in Cologne; but he was also the composer of two operas, one of which he conducted himself in Cologne the following year, so it is possible Heydrich feared that Walter was edging into the position he himself wished to occupy.

Walter's parents were no doubt intimately acquainted with their son's high ideals and his tendency to state them to the point of appearing critical. They must have expressed some reservations, even hinting that Walter might have brought some of this on himself, for in a letter the following week, Walter assured them that he was careful the entire time, that these people really were as difficult as he had described: "You wrote me that the hatred or the hostility . . . puzzled you, or was brought about through indiscretion on my part. In this last you are mistaken, for from the beginning, I have been very careful with remarks here. Heydrich is one of these people in whom the smallest success of every other person provokes the greatest envy and hatred."[40] Accompanying the letter are amusing, if unflattering and rather crudely drawn, caricatures of Heydrich and the others.[41] Though the entire episode motivated Walter to send in his resignation, he evidently held on to his boyish sense of humor.

Walter's pleasure and pride that his debut and subsequent emergency performance went so well were spoiled by these outbreaks of jealousy and ill will, and he was overjoyed to be engaged as a coach by the Hamburg Stadttheater. "The former choral director has been dismissed," he wrote to his parents. "A colossal bit of luck."[42] But Walter had no idea just what a stroke of luck this would turn out to be, for the leading conductor in Hamburg was Gustav Mahler.

Walter's meeting with Mahler in Hamburg was the beginning of a close personal friendship and artistic collaboration that would last until Mahler's death in 1911. According to one report, Mahler, on first seeing Walter, was struck by the young man's resemblance to his own younger brother, Otto, who had recently committed suicide; still pained by the loss, the composer felt it was Providence that had brought Walter into his life.[43] Walter, even before this initial encounter, had read unfavorable reviews of Mahler's First

Symphony, and, as with the earlier aspersions cast on Wagner by his colleagues and his family, the negative comments about Mahler had excited his curiosity. The first meeting between the two men, as recounted by Walter, became a much-cited incident among Mahler's sisters and is well known among Mahlerians and Walterians. Walter ran into Mahler at the Hamburg Opera House.

> "So you are the new coach," Mahler said. "Do you play the piano well?" "Excellently," I replied, meaning simply to tell the truth, because a false modesty seemed inappropriate in front of a great man. "Can you read well at sight?" Mahler asked. "Oh, yes, everything," I said again truthfully. "And do you know the regular repertoire operas?" "I know them all quite well," I replied with a great deal of assurance. Mahler gave a loud laugh, tapped me on the shoulder pleasantly, and concluded the conversation with "Well, that sounds quite splendid."[44]

Mahler was soon to discover that his young assistant had not exaggerated, and Walter would soon learn that Mahler's reputation as a virtuoso conductor was not inflated.

Mahler's conducting would have an even greater effect on Walter than his discoveries of Wagner and Bülow. As with Hans von Bülow, Mahler's control over the orchestra awed many listeners. The American composer Arthur Foote recalled that "with him you felt that it was *he* that played, the orchestra being his instrument."[45] In the very first rehearsal of Mahler's that Walter witnessed, he was both amazed and a little intimidated. "Never had I encountered so intense a human being," he remembered; "never had I dreamed that a brief, cogent word, a single compelling gesture, backed by absolute clarity of mind and intention, could fill other people with anxious terror and compel them to blind obedience."[46] Seeing what Mahler could do and what he could get others to do had the effect of making Walter dissatisfied with his own accomplishments thus far. His apparent ease in conducting those performances of *Waffenschmied* seemed a small achievement compared with the dramatic expression and depth of interpretation that Mahler exacted from his performers, though the Cologne review makes it clear that the *Waffenschmied* performances had much to recommend them. But now, under Mahler's influence, Walter wished to strive for greater heights of expression coupled with greater precision. Achieving a balance between passion and precision as Mahler seemed to do became his goal, and, he owned somewhat wryly in his autobiography, "There was much to learn for a lad of my questionable tendency to neglect musical correctness for the sake of feeling."[47]

Despite Walter's occasional feelings of depression that he would never achieve anything so exalted as Mahler's performances, observing Mahler's rehearsals was liberating insofar as he now saw what could be done. "Although I was still young, I had an old enemy: workaday triviality. I was no longer afraid of it. Here was a man against whom it was powerless, who renewed himself every minute, and who did not know the meaning of slackening either in his work or in his vital principles."[48] There can be no doubt that Mahler's influence on Walter, in terms of both working habits and musical aims, was profound and long-lasting—so profound that Walter was later to experience the anxiety of influence, and "at the cost of grave soul-searching," he took pains to establish that he was not a copy of Mahler but had his own artistic personality.[49] Nevertheless, Walter's highly charged 1935 recording of the first act of *Die Walküre*, made more than twenty years after Mahler's death, probably owes a debt to Mahler. Alma Mahler Werfel, recalling a performance of *Walküre* under Mahler in Vienna, observed that "there was a tempo in the orchestra such as I never heard before or since," and then, with somewhat underhanded praise, admitted that "Bruno Walter, at first awkward and inexperienced, came very near to realizing Mahler's ideals." And when it came to conducting Mahler's own works, of course, Walter gladly undertook to interpret the symphonies in accordance with his memories of Mahler's performances of them on the piano and in concert, as a comparison of Walter's recording of Mahler's Fifth Symphony with the New York Philharmonic and Mahler's piano roll of the first movement strikingly shows. Here Alma was more unstinting in her appreciation of Walter, asserting that he "mastered . . . every subtlety [of Mahler's music] and gave his own original interpretation."[50]

But even in Hamburg, where Walter willingly gave himself up to Mahler's guidance, he was learning that he could not be like Mahler in one very important way—he could not be a tyrannical dictator. For, as the critic Ferdinand Pfohl observed, "Mahler was a tyrant with the orchestra; he sat at his podium looking dark and threatening."[51] Pfohl, reminiscing on his acquaintance with Mahler from his Hamburg days, related how Mahler cruelly humiliated a flute player during a rehearsal, calling him a "wretched dilettante" in front of the entire orchestra when the poor musician could not, after several tries, play a phrase exactly the way Mahler wanted it (the flutist eventually ran from the room with tears in his eyes). Walter did not mention the incident himself, but he doubtless witnessed many similar occurrences. The problem of authority in conducting—how to keep so many different personalities and interpretations under one rule—began to plague the young conductor's thoughts. In order to achieve the kind of consummate, unified performance he so admired in Mahler, he felt the conductor must have authority, must reign supreme over the orchestra, and he was finding that he was decidedly wanting in this quality. His youth at that time prevented him from being able to exercise the control that comes with the musicians' respect for experience, and, despite his strong musical opinions, his compassionate nature precluded his humiliating people, even for the sake of artistic aims. So he began to search for ways to coax musicians, rather than command them: "What was more natural . . . than the desire of both singers and musicians to escape from the intimidating rule of the feared man and find restful relaxation in the presence of a wholly unfearsome youth? I could readily understand that, and so I tried to influence the artists by psychological methods appropriate to and in conformity with my nature. While my efforts were not always successful, they at least afforded me a comforting insight into a side of my nature to which I had paid no attention before: I became aware that I had an educational instinct."[52] This essential distinction between himself and Mahler, which Walter was discovering, even at an early date, was not all due to youth and was remarked on by contemporaries, including the poet and critic Richard Specht, whom Walter first met during his sojourn with Mahler in Steinbach am Attersee in the summer of 1896. Walter's conducting, Specht maintained, was outwardly similar to Mahler's and, during his first years as assistant to Mahler in Vienna (beginning in 1901), Walter even took on some of Mahler's mannerisms, particularly his "intense, imploring movements" while conducting. But Walter's innate personality was completely different from Mahler's. "Walter's nature was gentler, responded less vehemently to matters of life and art, had the wonderfully beautiful innocence of one who is cocooned only in his own special dreams."[53] The unrelenting tension Specht heard in Mahler's performances was relaxed somewhat in Walter's hands; for "Walter was more romantic, more dreamy, more exuberant . . . was not so fierce in the execution of climaxes, and often had for all that something wavering, irregular, since he gave himself up extemporaneously to his sudden inspirations, and in that way, for all his supreme command in wielding the baton, he sometimes made the members of the orchestra uncomfortable, since they always had to be ready for new surprises every moment."[54]

While Walter might have made the musicians uneasy by demanding their full concentration in order to bring out the smaller nuances Specht describes, his intent was not to embarrass them personally. Recordings and videos of rehearsals from his last years show a cajoling, even seductive, conductor, as opposed to an autocratic one, expressing his disapproval with words such as, "My friends, I am still not happy." Yet he was still quite capable of surprising his players, keeping them alert; during the initial read-through of the first movement of Brahms's Second Symphony in Vancouver, he lingers over the flutes' high F in the first statement of the opening theme; the next time through, he passes over it as if it were of no importance whatsoever.[55] Here we are seeing Walter at the pinnacle of his rehearsing skills; his special, relaxed stance was in part the result of the assurance that comes with years of experience, but it must have been something he aimed for early on. From his first observations of Mahler in Hamburg, Walter not only found new greatness in music, but learned more about himself.

During the summer of 1896 Walter had the pleasure of hearing the beginnings of Mahler's new symphony, the Third, a work that Walter himself would later conduct on several occasions to great acclaim. Mahler knew that he was at work on a masterpiece; he also predicted with painful accuracy that the critics would hate it.[56] In this massive symphony, he aspired to encompass what is awe-inspiring in the natural, human, and divine realms. When Walter arrived at Steinbach am Attersee in July, Mahler met him on the jetty and carried his luggage. On the way to Mahler's house, Walter gazed at the craggy Höllengebirge (literally, "Hellish Mountains"). Mahler commented: "You don't need to look—I have composed all this already!"[57] During Walter's sojourn, Mahler played what there was of the score to Walter, who in turn became well enough acquainted with the music to play some of it for the violist Natalie Bauer-Lechner.[58]

Walter's admiration of Mahler was not one-sided; Mahler was deeply impressed with Walter's abilities and, according to Ferdinand Pfohl, convinced the theater's director, Pollini (whose actual name was Bernhard Pohl), to let Walter conduct a performance of *Aida*, which, as Pfohl observed, is always a difficult opera, even in the hands of an experienced conductor. But Mahler appeared confident that Walter would distinguish himself, praising Walter so highly that he "led [Pfohl] to expect wonderful things, expectations which the most gifted beginner could not have ful-filled." Naturally Pfohl needed no urging from Mahler to attend the perfor-mance, which took place on November 21, 1895, during Walter's second sea-son in Hamburg. "In front of the conductor's podium," Pfohl recalled, "I saw a pale young man of about twenty, who through the assurance of his conducting, his energy, and his feeling for the scenes, without a doubt de-served the trust Mahler had placed in him." The performance proceeded smoothly until the finale of the second act, where some ensemble difficulties occurred that Pfohl attributed to the young director's not being completely equal to the task of commanding such large forces: "It was a dreadful confu-sion of chorus and soloists, of orchestra and on-stage musicians, which most surely would have led to a fatal catastrophe if with the entrance of the majes-tic Triumphal March the dispersed musicians had not found unity and pro-ceeded together to a satisfactory conclusion."[59]

Though Pfohl's narrative makes it seem as though this were the very first time he'd heard Walter conduct, he had actually reviewed a perfor-mance of Marschner's *Hans Heiling* two months earlier (in September) and had been favorably impressed then as well. "It is astonishing," he wrote, "how flexibly and prudently this young man conducted the orchestra, with what assurance he controlled the giant instrument, how tastefully he made music."[60] Evidently the size of Marschner's ensembles presented less of a technical challenge than that of Verdi's. Like Specht, Pfohl commented on Walter's exuberance, which he seemed to find refreshing, for he hoped that "we never detect in him that *phlegma* which persists when the spirit goes to rack and ruin." Walter's so-called exuberance, however, proved too much at times. After the performance of *Aida*, Mahler himself criticized Walter in a letter to his protégée Anna von Mildenburg, who had sung the title role, say-ing that the end of one of her arias had not gone as planned because Walter took the preceding aria too fast, not allowing her enough time to breathe.[61] But despite these occasional hitches—the natural result of the learning process, but no doubt displeasing to the young director who had set such high standards for himself—Mahler continued to hold his assistant in high esteem.

Mahler's relationship with Pollini eventually began to sour, since Pollini apparently liked to engage big-name singers and pay them high salaries but didn't schedule the necessary rehearsal time for the kind of tight, dramatic productions that Mahler wanted (Pollini also paid the chorus and orchestral musicians only a fraction of what the star singers received), and Mahler soon began to consider leaving Hamburg, eventually going to Vienna in 1897.[62] He took steps to secure a new position for his assistant, fearing that, if Walter stayed in Hamburg, their close association would be detrimental to Walter's career. Though infinitely grateful for Mahler's influence, Walter was eager to strike out on his own, for he worried that daily association with a musical personality as strong as Mahler's might be a hindrance to his own development.[63] As a result of Mahler's efforts, Walter was offered a position as second conductor in Prague and was on the point of accepting when he and Mahler noticed that, according to the local newspaper, the second conductor directed light opera more than anything else. "That was naturally not what I had in mind," Walter wrote to his parents.[64] So Mahler wrote another letter, this time to Theodor Löwe, director of the Breslau Stadttheater, who, Walter told his parents, wanted to engage him immediately. This would be Walter's first real position as a conductor; Löwe had a reputation for high artistic standards (before taking over direction of the theater, he was known mainly as a poet and a philosopher), which gave Walter confidence that the proffered appointment would be a fulfilling one.[65] But it was offered with one disagreeable condition: since there were so many Schlesingers in Breslau (the capital of Silesia, now known as Wrocław, Poland), Bruno Schlesinger would have to change his name.

Throughout Walter's life, and even after his death, people would now and then let fall remarks about his giving up his Jewish name in order to further his career, although Walter was neither the first nor the last to do such a thing. Whether Löwe's stipulation really stemmed from a desire to conceal the ethnic stamp of his second conductor's name is unknown; in any case, it was not something Walter did happily. Having to change his name was "terrible," he wrote to his parents; a name wasn't "just a piece of clothing that you can simply slip off." But, he continued, it seemed clear that he had to take this position for the sake of his career; the Mahlers (that is, Mahler and his sisters Justine and Emma) were also pressing him to change his name. "Makes you shudder, doesn't it?" he lamented.[66]

In his autobiography, Walter attributed the choice of name to its associations with Walther von Stolzing in *Meistersinger*, the medieval poet Walther von der Vogelweide (who also appears in *Tannhäuser* and was Walther's chief literary inspiration in *Meistersinger*), and Siegmund in *Walküre*, who wished to call himself *Frohwalt* but had been compelled to call himself *Wehwalt*.[67] Having a name that would remind him of these illustrious personages, whether real or fictional, might have made the change of name more palatable. But, as he described in a letter to his brother, Leo, Walter had actually suggested several names, which Mahler wrote down and gave to Löwe, who returned the contract with the name Bruno Walter. Walter suspected that Mahler had submitted that name alone, perhaps because it gave him the "best feeling." (Ironically, as German names go, Walter is even more common than Schlesinger.) Meanwhile, Leo Schlesinger seems to have been chastising his brother, for Walter asked him: "do you think positions for me grow on trees?"—adding, with a touch of bitterness perhaps left over from his Cologne disappointments, that if a person is out of the ordinary, "the entire world regards him with scorn; things come easily only to the mediocre." But, he hastened to add, this position was "a colossal stroke of luck."[68] So, armed with a new name and new hopes, refreshed from his summer vacation with Mahler in Steinbach am Attersee, he arrived in Breslau to take up his baton with renewed energy and, he expected, greater authority.

# Kapellmeister Walter
## Breslau, Pressburg, Riga, Berlin, 1896–1901

*A singer doesn't earn the title of master in a single day.*
Wagner, *Die Meistersinger von Nürnberg*

Almost immediately upon his arrival in Breslau, Walter was unfavorably impressed by what appeared to be indolence, indifference, and general laziness on the part of the singers and directors of the Breslau Stadttheater. The musicians seemed fonder of making cynical jokes than of rehearsing or improving their craft, and Löwe proved more interested in the staging than in the musical aspects of opera, virtually ignoring the young conductor. Walter apparently complained of this to his parents, who wrote back that he should simply speak up for himself; but the prospect of acquiring greater responsibilities within such a depressing work environment was thoroughly repellent. "It would, I think, take only a few words from me to get more [conducting opportunities], but I don't want it; that would in any case place me in a state of greater moral obligation to him [Löwe]," he wrote to his parents in December 1896, just a few months after arriving, filled with great expectations. It was, he thought, far better to distance himself as much as possible, which would make it easier to leave if a more attractive position presented itself.[1]

Meanwhile, the bleakness of the town, despite its distinguished university, also depressed him. This, coupled with the puritanical character of his landlady (who objected to his singing through parts of Bach's Mass in B Minor on Sunday, because music, even profoundly religious music, was forbidden on the Sabbath) and his lack of real friends, allowed him little in the way of social compensation for his unfulfilling work life.[2] "Breslau is a very dull town," he wrote to his parents; "despite the university, intellectual life is zero; Silesian *phlegma* is very great."[3] He enjoyed some evenings, drinking and smoking long Dutch pipes with colleagues in a Silesian tavern, but did not much care for the ensuing hangovers.[4] He did make friends with the great Swedish bass Johannes Elmblad, whose repertoire ranged from Mozart to Wagner; but, as he lamented to his parents, they had little time for each other.

Walter undoubtedly could have put up with these deficiencies in his social life if he hadn't felt himself being dragged down artistically. Despite his desire to avoid greater responsibility, he had already managed to attract attention by substituting for another conductor at the last minute. "Because nothing is appreciated so much at the theater as versatility and quick-wittedness, I found myself in favor all at once," he confessed in his autobiography. "Operas came pouring in on me. They were repertoire performances, operas that needed no rehearsing."[5] He began to take an almost sporting pleasure from jumping in at the last moment and holding things together, but this pleasure in itself depressed him, since it was so far removed from satisfying the lofty ideals and high aspirations he had acquired under Mahler's influence.

To be sure, his entire time in Breslau was not spent substituting; he was in fact entrusted with a production of *Lucrezia Borgia*, for which he was given a sufficient amount of rehearsal time and which, to judge by a review in the *Breslauer Zeitung*, was a decided success. The reviewer, Emil Bohn (a professor at the university), praised Walter's careful preparation, especially in the ensemble numbers, noting with a touch of irony that "serious classical German works seldom receive such a well-prepared performance."[6] Around the same time, Walter also directed a revival of *Die Zauberflöte*, in which Elmblad doubled as Sarastro and the stage manager. Walter now had the chance to work with someone whom he respected and with whom he could strive for higher goals, not to mention the opportunity of overseeing the production of a work that would come to have special meaning for him. Walter later remembered little about the actual production— only the anticipation coupled with relief when it was decided that he and

Elmblad would work together on it—but this series of performances was also successful.[7] The critic for the *Breslauer Morgen-Zeitung* noted that Walter conducted not only with "distinction and assurance," but also with "the proper feeling for style," through which the orchestra and chorus "were inspired to truly beautiful achievements." Interestingly, it was the chorus that particularly impressed this reviewer, who wrote that the "subtly nuanced, noble singing of our choristers deserves to be stressed especially, since this part of the company so seldom can earn praise for themselves."[8]

Despite these two respectable productions, Walter seems to have felt that his time in Breslau was spent regressing rather than progressing. But he was in fact learning a great deal, and though his conducting appearances did not match the high standards he had set for himself, he did not lapse into the dreaded role of time-beater but continued to experiment with a subtle and daring rubato. How much tempo modification was too much, however, gave rise to conflicting critical opinions in Breslau; reviews of a performance of *Waffenschmied* early in October disagreed on precisely this point. The reviewer from the *Breslauer Morgen-Zeitung* praised Walter for his "energetic and flexible rhythm" and observed that the "instrumental niceties, in which Lortzing is in no way lacking, were brought out in a loving manner."[9] On the other hand, flexibility—or an excess of it—was the very aspect of Walter's conducting that Emil Bohn criticized in the same performance. While praising the tightness of the production, particularly in the ensemble numbers, he carped that it was "only to be regretted that owing to the elegant working-out of the details, the regulation of the music did not keep to an overall uniform pace; the music for *Waffenschmied* scarcely needs to be handled with such delicacy."[10] Bohn, a distinguished scholar and the director of a series of concerts at the university, was no doubt a discerning listener.[11] Yet Lortzing was perhaps not to his taste; Bohn's concert series featured a remarkable amount of complex earlier music, including works by Frescobaldi and Byrd. His reviews of *Waffenschmied* and, later, of Lortzing's *Die beiden Schützen* carry an underlying hint of scorn, and he seems not to have considered light opera worthy of more subtle touches. The amount of rubato used by the young conductor and its appropriateness, however, are not as important as Walter's employing it in the first place; he was still trying for subtler effects, still attempting to refine his craft, even in the face of opposition or indifference.

On the whole, the tone of these reviews was encouraging, even welcoming. Despite Walter's feelings of loneliness, one senses that he had allies in the reviewers, who seemed overjoyed that someone was at last subjecting the company to more rigorous standards. It is almost poignant to read the *Breslauer Morgen-Zeitung*'s critic's hopeful observation that one "had the impression—and this impression became stronger and stronger during the course of the evening—that this young Kapellmeister will yet serve our opera extremely well," when we know that Walter, desperately unhappy, was already making plans to leave.[12] But the effort needed to maintain a high standard of musical production proved too great even for a young man of Walter's optimism and energy, and he declined Löwe's offer of a contract for an extended period. Strangely enough, though Walter was convinced at the time that Löwe took little interest in his activities, he heard years later that Löwe had spoken very highly of his achievements in Breslau. And during a chance meeting on a train, Walter "saw the eyes of the then aged man sparkle with pleasure and heard him say words of praise of myself."[13] In his estimation of the old theater director, Walter himself was eventually guilty of some hindsight glossing, writing for Löwe's hundredth-birthday celebration that he remembered "the friendly interest that he [Löwe] showed in the young musician."[14]

But at the time, Walter was convinced that he had fallen into the depths artistically, and he allowed his spirits to sink still further; he began to be plagued by feelings of worthlessness. In March 1897 he wrote a wistful letter to his uncle, longing for home, the company of his parents and their friends, and even the food he imagined they would eat. "Heavy clouds from the skies of Breslau hang over me," he groaned, "and I feel ill at ease."[15] Even the anticipated homecoming was not enough to assuage his bruised musical soul, however, for he spent the summer brooding over his "moral defeat in Breslau," though coaching the Berlin Opera's heroic tenor Ernst Kraus, with whom he would work on many subsequent occasions, kept him from wallowing too much in self-pity.[16] He must also have felt some sense of artistic accomplishment, for one of his finest songs, "Vorbei" (later published in his collection of lieder, opus 11), was performed publicly in a recital given by Louis Bauer on March 23. Although Walter played a few solo works for the concert under his new name, he apparently wished to keep his activity as a composer secret, since the song is attributed simply to "Schlesinger."

Meanwhile, he visited Mahler and his sisters in Vienna—Walter's first trip to the ornate, sensual city that he would one day, after many struggles there, consider his home. As he wandered around the Ringstrasse, eating bread and goulash, listening to Viennese music played by a ladies' orchestra, he quickly began to feel that this was where he belonged. "The Vienna dialect sounded harmoniously and pleasantly in my ear. I felt that I belonged in Vienna; that I had not found it, but had re-found it. Spiritually, I was a Viennese."[17] Writing from a distance of almost fifty years, Walter might have romanticized his spiritual homecoming; yet even at the time, he confidently informed his parents that, as a city, Berlin couldn't compete with Vienna.[18]

Walter determined to remain jobless rather than continue with what he regarded as mediocre activities in Breslau. Sometime near the end of the summer, however, he was offered the position of chief conductor at the Riga Stadttheater, where Wagner himself had conducted from 1837 to 1839—an offer he gladly accepted. Since the job in Riga was not to begin until 1898, he was wondering how he would spend the intervening year when he received a telegram from the director of the Stadttheater in Pressburg (now known as Bratislava, in Slovakia), also offering the position of chief conductor. Despite the city's distinguished history (it was once the capital of Hungary and the coronation site of its kings), the opera company in Pressburg was small and, by Walter's own admission, unpretentious; it was therefore a perfect place for the foundering—or so he felt—young conductor to regain his artistic integrity. In addition, it was only about an hour and a half's train ride from Vienna, which would allow him more opportunities to hear Mahler conduct. And so, in the fall of 1897, he sailed down the Danube for Pressburg, determined to make his mark on the city.

Outwardly, at least, he appears to have done so, for his earliest reviews were glowing. A review of his performance of *Pagliacci*, which must have taken place shortly after his arrival, reported: "For this year's opera performances, it appears that we have a splendid, musically sensitive conductor. Thus far Kapellmeister Walther has offered us quite beautiful performances, well rounded in ensemble. One might indeed have a differing view over the degree of individual strengths, but for the entirety, an air of pleasing security always rests over the performance when Mr. Walther has the conductor's baton in his hand."[19]

Indeed, Walter found to his surprise that there was none of the apathetic resistance he had encountered at Breslau, that his assistant conductors, the lead singers, choristers, and orchestra members (none of whom are remembered today) were more than willing to respond to his vigorous attempts to raise the little company's standards of performance. To judge by the reviews and by his own memories of crowded performances and loud applause, his efforts met with success. But inwardly, Walter was still suffering. He took long meditative walks along the Danube, subjecting himself to mental whippings, and descended into the cave of despair, which offered him "a wonderful solution" for his "disquiet": "I felt powerfully attracted by death."[20]

Walter's suicidal impulse during this period of personal confusion and professional uncertainty was eventually allayed by an epiphany that music, however intangible, was "not a dream. Let all material things be unreal; music's immaterial essence was surely not a deception of the senses. Here I had an unquestionable reality to which I could cling confidently."[21] This reversal of the importance of the material and immaterial spheres would become a leitmotif throughout his life. Perhaps not coincidentally, it was at this time, he wrote, that the writings of Jean Paul, especially *Titan*, led him "back again to the faith, to Christendom, to which I had come close years before, from which I had strayed, and which I was never to lose again."[22] Precisely when Walter had initially come close to Christendom is something of a mystery, but he would soon enough be compelled to adopt Christianity as his official religion.

While gazing within and wrestling with the eternal questions of life and whatever succeeds life, he was continuing his work in the everyday world, refining his abilities and developing his style. His interactions with other musicians—both vocalists and instrumentalists—grew more subtle, sometimes even oversubtle. Singers have often remarked on Walter's ability to direct with a firm hand while at the same time allowing them room to breathe. This sensitivity to the needs of singers, no doubt aided by his learning to coach and accompany at such an early age, figured prominently in one of the Pressburg reviews:

> We have followed Bruno Walter's direction of the Opera with great interest, and we believe that in him we have before us a musical personality who stands completely on his own two feet. In spite of a certain nervousness with which he directs the orchestra, chorus, and soloists, he demonstrates great assurance and, what is far more significant, a decided originality, which raises him above many far older and more established opera directors. The nuanced playing of his orchestra is uncommonly refined and sensitive, and we noticed with great pleasure how he managed to keep down every [potentially] obtrusive statement of the individual instruments and, at the same time, to *indulge* the soloists in their intentions. In this last instance, Herr Walter—may he forgive us this slight reproach—

perhaps went too far, for he acted contrary to his own taste on account of singers who were inclined "to drag."[23]

As he gained experience, Walter naturally became more assured and less likely to compromise his own interpretation, if that was in fact what he did. Regina Resnik, who sang Leonore in Walter's 1945 *Fidelio* at the Metropolitan Opera, recalled that Walter "was very definitive in his musical ideas," but at the same time "extremely elastic about singing," because "he wanted the most beautiful performance you could give."[24] Since the singers for this Pressburg performance have fallen into obscurity and are not preserved on any recordings, we have no way of knowing what kinds of liberties they might have taken, but the reviewer's comment gives us an intriguing glimpse of Walter's early awareness of the voice's unique demands.

After this busy year of outward triumphs and inward soul-searching, Walter took a trip through the Balkans, tasted his first Turkish coffee, and returned to Berlin by way of Budapest and Vienna, where, he tells us, he "spent the summer dreaming of the glories awaiting the future chief conductor of the Riga Opera."[25] And glories there would be, along with some discomforts concomitant on living in Riga (then part of Russia); for while the theater in those days was almost entirely run by Germans playing to German audiences, a large part of the population was, of course, Russian, with customs foreign to the young man from Berlin. Meanwhile, the Lettish portion of the population was, according to Walter, almost entirely denied the opportunity to hold important positions in society. In his autobiography Walter described how he received the score to an opera from a native Lettish composer accompanied by a letter written in faulty German, revealing to him "a striving for higher goals as well as the bitterness of the oppressed."[26]

Much as Walter had been forced to change his name when he assumed his duties in Breslau, so he had to agree to another major change in his life in order to work in Riga. As his daughter Lotte recalled, "In Russia you could not travel if you were a Jew at the time. It was completely anti-Semitic, and you didn't get a passport, and you couldn't get in."[27] So Walter converted to Christianity—almost certainly to Catholicism, for his remains rest in the Catholic cemetery of Sant' Abbondio in Montagnola, near Lugano. While Lotte admitted the very practical reason behind her father's conversion, she was quick to add that he would not have converted had he not truly been a Christian. "He *was* a Christian, and a very good one. And the older he got, the more religious he really became." Walter's own comments about the uplifting effect that Christianity had on him during his desperate stretch in Pressburg suggest that his official conversion truly reflected his inner leanings. "He talked to me very much about Jesus when I was a child," Lotte remembered. "He was completely engrossed with Jesus; the Jesus figure played a very important role in his life." In April 1919 Lotte was confirmed in Munich, as Thomas Mann noted in his diary, which points again to Walter's continuing acceptance of Christian orthodoxy.[28] Yet Walter's later willingness to embrace the ideas of Rudolf Steiner suggests that his notions of Christ's place in the history of Western thought and religion were flexible.

Before Walter even set foot on Riga soil to encounter the social lessons awaiting him in the capital of Latvia, another turning point had taken place. As he related somewhat formally in his autobiography, "a vital personal question had been decided . . . before my arrival"[29]—namely, his meeting with Elsa Korneck, a lyric-dramatic soprano of the Riga Opera and his future wife.[30] According to Walter, he did little more than gaze at her, reclining in a seat and looking rather ill from the voyage, before knowing with full certainty that he wanted to marry her. They married a few years later and remained married until her death in 1945. Yet, despite her near-constant companionship throughout the many changes of locale that Walter's dramatic career brought, it is difficult to form a clear picture of her character, or even of her appearance. A photograph taken shortly before their marriage reveals a serious young lady with a pleasing, round face; deep-set, almost poetic, dark eyes; and a determined mouth. In later photographs of Elsa and Walter with various friends, her face is almost always turned to one side, giving the impression of reticence; nevertheless, Wolfgang Stresemann referred to her as "the exceedingly lively, domineering wife of Bruno Walter."[31] Her position in these later photos probably stems not from reticence at all, but from a desire to talk with anyone standing nearby, for a series of home movies taken in Salzburg and elsewhere, sometime near 1938, reveals a very animated Elsa, who, in fact, is having a difficult time standing or sitting still.[32]

In her earlier years Elsa's energy, which must have been immediately apparent to Walter despite her seasickness, stood her in good stead on the stage. Reviews of her performances under Walter's baton attest to her ability as an actress, perhaps even more than as a singer. Of her performance as Agathe in *Freischütz*, the reviewer for the *Rigasche Rundschau* commented: "The young singer of Agathe, Frl. Korneck, possessed a very beautiful, highly engaging soprano voice. She sang with exemplary pureness and gave noble expression to the yearning and soulful feelings of love."[33] Of her performance as Marguerite in *Faust*, Carl Waack, the reviewer for the *Düna Zeitung* (and also the editor of several Wagner scores), praised the lack of sentimentality and the natural quality she brought to the role, though in this and in other reviews he tended to emphasize the smallness and lightness of her voice.[34]

That Elsa had a "soulful" side is clear, not only from these early reviews, or from the expression in her eyes in one of the few youthful photos that have survived, but also from a story told by Klaus Mann, Thomas Mann's oldest son and a playmate of Walter's daughters. Mann gives us one of the most extended accounts of Elsa, describing how Walter sometimes "managed to spare an hour or two" to sit down at the piano and to explain to his daughters and Klaus and Erika Mann "the charm and structure of an opera." Klaus recalled with palpable nostalgia Walter's impersonation of Papageno: "He is very funny. Our hilarity resounds throughout the house. Frau Walter rushes downstairs—all fluster and disapproval in her spectacular dressing gown. She laments and scolds: Bruno ought to change his clothes, it is high time for the opera; Gretel hadn't yet learned her lessons; Lotte ought at last to write that letter; and as for us, the Mann children, why, we had nothing in mind but mischief, as was generally known. But she could not help laughing as Walter answered her with the comic pantomime of Papageno, whose mouth has been locked by the three cruel ladies." Then Mann goes on to relate how the children begged Elsa to let Walter finish the act, and "naturally she surrendered. 'Ten minutes,' she decided, and added with a surprisingly tender smile: 'Of course, I'd like to hear Tamino's aria myself.'"[35]

Sadly, Walter provided no details in his autobiography of his and Elsa's early romance, nor is there even a mention of her in the letters to his parents (the only letters of his to have surfaced from this period), though this is not all that surprising, given how sluggish the young tend to be when it comes to informing their parents of their amatory relationships. So we can only guess at what point during the fateful steamer journey they were introduced. Perhaps the first meeting took place later, during rehearsals for *Freischütz*? Walter was, throughout his long life, intensely private and not inclined to reveal personal history and in his autobiography merely tells us that their engagement was announced on Christmas Eve of 1898. It might in fact have been 1899, for by December 1898, Walter and Elsa would have known each other only four months, though such whirlwind courtships are certainly not unheard of. In any case, their announcement was made at the home of the Irschick family, whose youngest son, Oskar, wrote to Walter some fifty years later, and the two old men exchanged a brief reminiscence of those long-ago days.[36] As to the courtship, Walter left it to the imaginations of his readers.

It is possible, however, that the stirrings of love fueled his long and somewhat breathless letter to his parents of early September 1898, in which he waxed rhapsodic about his successes in Riga: how well the orchestra followed him, how receptive the press and public had been, how the musical committees there wanted him to hold chamber music recitals and conduct orchestral concerts, what a nice place he had to live in, and so on.[37] At the same time, he was clearly beginning to feel firmly established as a musical force to be reckoned with, which in itself would be enough to inspire the joyous tone of this letter.

What must have been especially gratifying to Walter was the respectful tone of his first Riga reviews (of *Freischütz*), which mention his youth only in passing before going on to describe his conducting talents in some detail, though Carl Waack took Walter to task for what he considered excessive movements on the podium: "A man still very young, but from all appearances of a considerable efficacy, a capable, energetic conductor. One could indeed be happy with the seriousness and fervor that carried over from the podium to the performers. . . . With the exception of small, insignificant disturbances, he held the stage and orchestra apparatus firmly together and also knew how to make his intentions clear. . . . Herr Kapellmeister Walter must endeavor to break only one habit: making a showy display to convey the beat. Inner temperament and fire should not be mirrored too much in one's movements, otherwise conducting . . . can easily become foppery."[38] Excessive motion among conductors clearly irritated Waack, for two months later he again chided Walter, remarking in a review of *Lohengrin*—the performance of which he seemed to regard highly overall—that, "We do not wish for Herr Walter suddenly to stand still like a wall at the podium, but somewhat fewer gymnastics, somewhat smaller outward illustrations would nevertheless be desirable."[39] Despite Waack's preference for less movement, his accounts of Walter's performances throughout his tenure in Riga remained highly complimentary, even when it came to works by composers—Meyerbeer in particular—that Waack did not especially care for. Though a few years later Viennese critics also pointed to what they considered excessive motion, it is possible that Walter eventually paid some heed to these admonitions, for the critics around 1912 began to comment on his controlled movements, and footage of him conducting much later in life reveals almost spare, if impassioned, movements. But it is also certainly possible that he felt, perhaps rightly, that opera conducting required more energetic movement, and it is to be deeply regretted that little footage of Walter conducting opera survives. An excerpt of him conducting *Orfeo ed Euridice* in Salzburg is too fleeting for us to see if there are any "excessive" motions.[40]

In contrast, the other reviewers in town seem not to have been bothered by Walter's youthful propensity for exaggerated motions and were overwhelmingly positive in their accounts. Friedrich Pilzer, reviewer for the *Rigasche Rundschau*, expressed his immediate enthusiasm for Walter's *Freischütz*, summing it up as follows:

> There was no evidence at all that the new, young director, Herr Walter, was allowed only a few days to acquaint himself with new singers and musical personnel. On the contrary: the striking confidence in the collaboration of all these forces would have made one suppose that this was an ensemble that had played together for a long time. Most especially gratifying was the highly stimulating, musical-poetic exactitude that poured forth full of life, along with which there emerged, from this orchestral and vocal ensemble, the mysterious shiver of romanticism in nature, the blossoming of folk and popular characteristics, and the most ingenious as well as most powerful lyrical-dramatic transformations of the opera. Through this conducting achievement, Herr Walter introduced himself in such a way that, with his further musical direction and inspiration, the best can be expected from our Opera.[41]

With reviews such as these, and the first flowerings of romance, this must have been an uplifting time for the young conductor, unlike anything he had yet experienced, and it is no wonder that, in his autobiography, he describes his time in Riga in glowing terms. During his two-year tenure there, crammed full of standard repertoire, his local premieres included Spinelli's *A basso porto*, Rubinstein's *Der Makkabäer*, Massenet's *Werther*, and Siegfried Wagner's *Der Bärenhäuter*, and he introduced new productions of Nessler's *Der Rattenfänger von Hameln*, Glinka's *A Life for the Czar*, Wagner's *Der fliegende Holländer*, Goldmark's *Die Königin von Saba*, Gounod's *Roméo et Juliette*, Humperdinck's *Hänsel und Gretel*, Verdi's *Rigoletto*, and other works.[42]

There were, of course, occasional notes of criticism in some of the reviews, but here again they seemed to stem from the reviewer's personal preferences, and not from any signs of youthful inexperience on Walter's part. Of

Walter's performance of *Der fliegende Holländer*, for example, the reviewer for the *Rigasche Rundschau* admired the many fine details of the score brought out by Walter's interpretation, and in particular his ability to call attention to individual strands of the polyphonic fabric, but he felt that Walter's "contrasts," however thrilling, were overdone.[43]

In this case, however, Walter's use of excessive contrasts—excessive by the reviewer's lights, in any case—would appear to reflect a musical decision he made early on and adhered to through much of his career. Walter's recording of the *Holländer* Overture, made with the Royal Philharmonic Orchestra in the mid-1920s, displays a sharp contrast between the opening Dutchman theme and the following Senta theme, a contrast which, to be sure, is somewhat dictated by Wagner's use of the tempo markings *Allegro con brio* and *Andante*, respectively. Walter's somewhat broad interpretation of *Andante*, however, was not necessarily common practice, for in Karl Muck's contemporaneous recording of the same overture (made with the Berlin Staatsoper Orchestra), the opening tempo is comparable to Walter's, the *Andante* a bit quicker, so Muck's return to the opening theme does not require quite as much of an accelerando as Walter's, and the snatches from Senta's theme that creep in later on in the overture are not underscored with as much tempo modification. Further, Walter takes more liberties within the *Andante* itself, beginning the ritardandi marked by Wagner earlier than Muck (and earlier than many conductors do today), making the Senta theme sound even more expansive than its base tempo would indicate. Interestingly, Walter's stereo recording with the Columbia Symphony Orchestra from 1960 preserves all these tempo modifications, deviating less from his earlier interpretations than do some of his other late recordings. And very possibly it was just these distinctive liberties that impressed the Riga reviewer, though not so favorably.

Walter's first season in Riga contained one major source of unhappiness, his temporary clash with Mahler. In October 1898, only a couple of months into the season, Mahler wrote to him confidentially that Richter and Johann Fuchs were leaving the Vienna Hofoper and that he would like to engage Walter; if Walter agreed, they would "see how to get you out of Riga as fast as possible"—with any luck by the following fall.[44] Much as Walter admired Mahler and even sought to emulate him in many ways, he was unwilling to tear himself away from a musical environment in which he was scoring such high successes and in which he was regarded not as someone's assistant, but as the guiding musical force. So he refused Mahler's offer, writing to his parents that, as he had explained to Mahler, "The beginning of next fall would be too soon; in the first place I could not get away from here, in the second place I need another year in order to develop fully; the longer he [Mahler] would postpone my engagement, the surer he could be of my success in Vienna; I would ask him only that, if he engaged me, to introduce me openly as Richter's replacement; great demands would certainly be made on me, but I don't fear them; I only feared a so-called gradual introduction, since in the beginning it would not be known at all what I should actually do there, and I would perhaps be regarded as a kind of examinee, which would make my position very difficult at first."[45]

In addition to his desire to be given more time to develop his artistic personality independently, away from Mahler's influence (no doubt overwhelming at times), Walter's letter to his parents reveals his fear that simply showing up in Vienna to be Mahler's assistant would not guarantee the kind of position he might have, or what sorts of duties would be assigned to him. Having been exposed at a young age to the treacherous—at times downright nasty—political behind-the-scenes maneuvering so common in operatic establishments, he was clearly worried that Mahler's good word might not be enough and that, unless it was openly declared that he was the successor of the highly esteemed Richter, he might find himself with only a tentative position in Vienna.

Mahler, on the other hand, simply brushed aside his friend's reservations, and his reply from around November of that year makes light of the matter. "What is all this beating about the bush?" he asked. "If I make you an offer, I do really know what I am doing." He sought to persuade Walter by informing him that, at present, he was conducting everything himself, and if he didn't have Walter with him by 1900, he would most certainly be dead. "Besides," he added, "you will not be a 'finished' conductor in two or even ten years. If we are anything at all, we are always *learners*. You yourself will not be able to say where at present you could learn more than with me."[46]

This last remark, instead of persuading Walter to come to Vienna, probably had the opposite effect, making him all the more determined to stay in Riga; for, once having chosen the road to independence, artistic or otherwise, few care to hear they have taken a wrong turn. Nevertheless, as the days passed, he began to fear that his refusal would result in a serious breach between him and his most important mentor. By December he was already relenting, relating to his parents how he had refused an offer from Mannheim because the pay was too little (a position for which Mahler had originally recommended him), and thought Mahler would still be a good enough friend to let him go if he was unhappy.[47] A month later he was on the verge of despair, telling his parents that Mahler had not answered a twelve-page letter in which he told him he would come how, when, and as he wished.[48]

Without Mahler's support, Walter worried over what would become of him when his contract with Riga expired. Above all, he wanted to return to Germany, but he wondered if there would be any positions open. "Berlin is perfectly satisfied with its Muckish mediocrity," he wrote peevishly to his uncle; "it is the same in Munich with Stavenhagen and in Dresden with Schuch; people like myself are really quite superfluous." Perhaps, he mentioned in passing, he might even go to America. At least, he consoled himself, it was "splendid" in Riga, where "I am indisputably the master of the whole situation, and . . . everyone bows before me."[49] To be in artistic control was one of Walter's great desires, and we can only hope that his worries for the future did not prevent him from enjoying the advantages of the present, and that his nagging doubts about his career expressed in these letters to his relatives were not always uppermost in his thoughts.

In the end Walter's fear that Mahler's silence was symptomatic of deep resentment, and that there might even be a permanent breach between them, proved to be unfounded, for Mahler eventually wrote that Walter had completely misinterpreted his silence: "You know how lazy I am when it comes to writing letters. . . . Well—I have long since forgiven you, if there was anything to forgive. I cannot even remember what it was all about."[50]

As it turned out, neither Richter nor Fuchs was ready to leave the Vienna Hofoper just yet, so Walter's misgivings were justified. In any case, his short-lived conflict with Mahler was resolved, and when, in November 1899, Walter was offered a five-year contract as Royal Prussian Conductor by the Berlin Opera, he was careful to consult Mahler before accepting.[51]

Admired as he was by the press and public in Riga, and gratifying as it must have been to be "the master of the whole situation," he simply could not refuse such an offer. The caliber of the artistic personnel in Riga—respectable enough for what was basically a provincial theater—could not possibly match the likes of Emmy Destinn and Ernst Kraus (Walter's old friend), with whom he would be working in Berlin. Even before the Berlin offer came, by the beginning of the next season, Walter was already complaining to his parents that his performances were not going to be up to standard, that he was right to be worried about the new personnel engaged for that season, and that he would like to have a visiting card printed up that would read: "Bruno Walter, Conductor of the disgraceful performances at the Riga City Theater."[52] Further, the Berlin position would mean more financial security, allowing Walter and Elsa Korneck to marry. Above all, there was the lure of conducting in the opera house of his youth, where he had first heard Wagner's *Tristan*, an experience that had been partially responsible for launching him on his present course. "Think of it!" he exclaimed with unusual vehemence in his autobiography. "The venerable house in whose top gallery I had received the decisive impressions of my boyhood years . . . was to be the scene of my own activity."[53] Still, it was with a touch of nostalgia for what he was leaving behind that he described to his parents the farewell festivities accorded him in Riga, how people presented him with gifts and flowers, how it would be impossible to describe the ovations he received, how people waited for him in the street after a performance and applauded. "Isn't that incredible?" he ended the letter in wonderment.[54] Perhaps the goodwill of the audiences in Riga emboldened Walter to include six songs of his own composition, sung by Elsa and other singers from his troupe, in a concert given near the end of his tenure there.[55] This time he credited the author as Walter, not Schlesinger. It was no doubt with aspirations of becoming a great composer-conductor like Mahler that Walter prepared himself mentally for his return to Berlin.

But Royal Prussian Conductor or no, Elsa's parents persuaded the young couple to put off their marriage until the end of Walter's first season in Berlin; so Elsa accepted a one-year contract with the Stadttheater in Basel, while Walter procured a bachelor apartment for himself on Derfflingerstrasse near his old school, the Falk Real-Gymnasium, which, as he commented ironically in *Theme and Variations*, "about nine years before, I had left with so much impatience."[56]

Walter's seemingly triumphant homecoming was naturally picked up by the press. A number of articles stressing his Berlin origins appeared in various local newspapers. Some even printed a handsome engraving of the young conductor in which he sported a small goatee (grown at the urging of the Mahler family to make him appear older for his Riga engagement). His appearance at the podium was anticipated to the point where, in a harsh review of an apparently less-than-satisfactory *Lohengrin*, the critic exclaimed, "Where are Messers Strauss and Muck, where is the newly engaged Mr. Walter?"[57] (As it turned out, this critic's prayers were answered, for the hapless conductor who had been responsible for one of the worst performances the critic had ever suffered through was promptly relieved of his duties and replaced by Walter at the last minute in a performance of *Carmen*.) Nor, on the whole, did Walter disappoint; the opening reviews (of *Freischütz*) were respectful and complimentary. Three of the major Berlin papers—the *Berlin Lokal-Anzeiger*, the *Vossische Zeitung*, and the *Welt-am-Montag*—identified him as belonging to the same school of "modern" conductors as Mahler, with whom his association was well known, and Nikisch, in both his approach and movements.

Walter's notices for the fall of 1900 remained complimentary in tone, despite a performance of *Siegfried* that was, according to the *Berlin Lokal-Anzeiger*, not well rehearsed, and he received especial praise for a concert in which he conducted the Berlin Tonkünstler Orchester, performing Berlioz's *Symphonie fantastique*, Wagner's *Der fliegende Holländer* Overture, a funeral march from Pfitzner's *Rose vom Liebesgarten*, and Beethoven's Violin Concerto with Willy Burmester. (One critic, however, complained about the length of the program, which didn't end until after 11:00.) In the Violin Concerto, Walter experienced one of his earliest artistic differences of opinion with a soloist, for the conductor felt the third movement should be taken at a pace more moderate than the "exaggeratedly fast tempo" preferred by the violinist. The resulting tempo war did not escape at least one critic's ears.[58] On the whole, Walter's orchestral concerts in Riga—despite scattered remarks in his letters to his parents that the performances seemed less than perfect—prepared him well for orchestral conducting in Berlin. The assessments of the Berlin critics of Walter's opera and orchestral conducting were not so laudatory as those in Riga, often pointing to details of the performances that they felt were unsuccessful, but this was to be expected from critics in a major cultural center.

For the first time in his life, Walter was conducting at one of the foremost opera houses in Europe, directing singers considered the stars of the day; in addition to Emmy Destinn and Ernst Kraus were the bass Paul Knüpfer and the tenor Julius Lieban. He was also entrusted with some local premieres (including Weber's singspiel *Abu Hassan*), the most important of which was the first Berlin performance of Hans Pfitzner's neo-Wagnerian *Der arme Heinrich*, given on December 19, 1900. As he recounts in his memoirs, he had come across this score several years before, while in Hamburg. When he studied the music, he felt he had "struck pure gold. . . . At first, I was inclined to see in the initial scenes' deeply moving atmosphere of illness a powerfully expressive but rather Tristanesque sequel to Wagner. But the farther I got, the more clearly I recognized the inspiration and original inventiveness of a creative dramatic musician."[59] Many Berliners apparently agreed. The opera was a popular success, with the composer receiving numerous curtain calls throughout the performance. "He owed the greatest debt," the *Berliner Tageblatt* noted, "to Kapellmeister Bruno Walter, the conductor for the evening, who prepared the exceedingly difficult work with evident devotion."[60] Over the years, Walter recalled his first encounter with Pfitzner as having occurred in 1897 or 1899, but their work on *Der arme Heinrich* in Berlin—the first of many collaborations—no doubt marked a turning point in their relationship. Walter had gained a friend, though the friendship that ensued would travel on a bumpy road.

As the season passed, Walter found himself increasingly dissatisfied once again, mainly because the Berlin Opera was run by Prussian officials in a manner too bureaucratic for his taste. Artistic decisions were apparently dispensed in the form of commands, rather than suggestions, and Walter found himself face to face with the problem of whether performers could be ordered to produce certain results. Having already decided early on that it was more beneficial for all concerned to inspire rather than command, Walter quickly concluded that autocracy and art do not mix well. "Artists could be made into subordinates and commanded by instructions, but not in connection with the exercise of art, which in the absence of freedom loses its essential character," he wrote with regard to his year in Berlin. "No oboist obedient to a master's command is able to play a solo beautifully: his soul must lend charm to his playing, and the conductor, respecting its freedom, must influence it by methods more subtle than a superior's paralyzing command."[61] In addition to his inherent objection to bureaucrats' involving themselves in artistic matters—or perhaps because of it—Walter did not succeed in endearing himself to His Excellency Count Hochberg, the general director of both theaters for opera and drama in Berlin. This, however, made it easier for him to have his contract annulled when Mahler once again sought to entice Walter to Vienna.

Meanwhile, the Opera's general management decided to begin a series of lighter operas at the Kroll Theater, presumably to generate more income. As the youngest conductor, one who had proved his ability to handle light works with successful performances of Lortzing and Auber, Walter was naturally elected to conduct Gilbert and Sullivan's *Mikado*. Though no great lover of light opera, he rather enjoyed this one, and, as he recalled, the production's excellent cast made it a big success, so much so that the management hastened to present another, less attractive work (to Walter at least),

Lecocq's *La Fille de Madame Angot*, another local premiere. Faced with this and certain managerial absurdities—such as the casting of singers in productions at both houses on the same evening, which made them rush back and forth, hardly able to breathe, much less sing—Walter eventually petitioned Hochberg for an annulment of his contract, which was granted. He was now free to join Mahler in Vienna.

# THREE

# Mahler's Second-in-Command
## Vienna, 1901–1907

*Nothing is less important than what the press here says:*
*it is a company of idiots; they bark like hounds at every new face,*
*they growl for a while, and after a few years, you'll be "our Walter."*
Mahler, quoted by Walter in 1901

In the landscape of history, turn-of-the-century Vienna juts up as a cultural peak. The new and the old thrived in all the arts—in music perhaps more than anywhere else. Shortly before Walter's arrival in the fall of 1901, Richard Strauss had given the Viennese premiere of *Ein Heldenleben*; Gustav Mahler, the belated world premiere of his cantata *Das klagende Lied*. In the same year, the young tenor Leo Slezak joined the opera company at the Hofoper, where he would soon assume many of the leading heroic roles, and before the end of the decade, he would be thrilling audiences at the Metropolitan Opera House in New York. Eduard Hanslick, the champion of absolute music and the model for Beckmesser in Wagner's *Meistersinger*, was the senior music critic of Vienna's principal newspaper, the *Neue Freie Presse*, while Ferdinand Löwe—now remembered, if at all, as a misguided editor of Bruckner's scores—loomed as a notable force in Vienna's music world. As a conductor, he regularly presented masterpieces of the symphonic and choral repertoire, among them Bach's Mass in B Minor (then rarely heard), in a performance that featured an oboe d'amore.[1] The use of an "authentic" instrument in this performance, incidentally, serves as a reminder that an interest in early music and period instruments grew steadily during the years that Walter spent in Vienna. Indeed, Saint-Saëns himself was president of the Société des Concerts d'Instruments Anciens, which often performed in the city, introducing rare baroque and pseudo-baroque compositions to turn-of-the-century audiences. And Wanda Landowska also visited Vienna on many occasions, playing recitals on the piano and, of course, the harpsichord, an instrument that (in one form or another) Mahler and, later, Walter himself would employ for accompaniment.

While the racy plays of Arthur Schnitzler predictably appealed to many Austrian theatergoers, the Viennese imagination was excited as well by the writings of Oscar Wilde, who died in 1900, not long after a harrowing two-year prison sentence. His plays were performed frequently in the Austrian capital, and his other writings, in German translation, ran in the newspapers. Some composers closely connected with Walter recognized the artistic and commercial appeal of Wilde's works. For the text of his scandalous but undeniably successful opera *Salome*, Richard Strauss turned to Wilde's equally scandalous play, while Franz Schreker wrote music for a ballet based on Wilde's story "The Birthday of the Infanta," which in turn lent some of the inspiration for Schreker's later opera *Die Gezeichneten*.

Like music and literature, the visual arts were receiving new impulses that moved painting, sculpture, and architecture out of the nineteenth century and into the twentieth. In Vienna the most striking new movement in the visual arts was that of the Secession School, led by Gustav Klimt—a school that would inspire a kindred movement in music that counted Arnold Schoenberg and Bruno Walter among its members. The Secession School's best-known by-product was *Jugendstil*, the Austro-German version of Art Nouveau, which has left a lasting mark both on Vienna's public buildings and in art galleries around the world. Klimt's paintings—alive with sensuality, sometimes disturbingly decadent—helped pave the way for Expressionism (somewhat as the musical Secessionist Schoenberg moved from an aesthetic of the overlush to one of experimental pantonality). Among the women who came into intimate contact with Klimt at the turn of the century was the irresistible Alma Schindler, a woman soon to attract the attention of Gustav Mahler.

On May 2, 1901, a few months before arriving in Austria's splendid capital, Walter and Elsa Korneck were married in Berlin. The event was cause for celebration, but also for concern, since the position in Vienna was not absolutely secure. Mahler wrote that Walter would have a yearly salary of 6000 florins and a two-year contract, to be renewed at a higher rate after the first two years were completed.[2] The emperor's permission, however, was required before Walter could work at the Vienna Hofoper, and the "imperial assent" was long in coming. Walter's salary began on July 1, though he was not yet living in Vienna, and Mahler—who needed a healthy assistant at the opera, "not a nervous wreck"—advised him to "get a really decent holiday."[3] In August, relaxing at the seaside resort of Sopot, near Elsa's native city of Danzig, Walter wrote to his parents about his situation; Mahler, though desperately in need of help, would wait even till September for Walter to come as his assistant. He would have Walter or no one. "Mahler again behaved in a touching and splendid manner, a friend of the utmost loyalty and nobility. Without these assurances from Mahler," Walter confessed to his parents, "my situation would have been unbearable, making any rest and relaxation impossible."[4]

The "imperial assent" eventually came through, and on September 27 Walter was conducting the first of the countless operas he would lead at the Vienna Hofoper. Mahler had originally hoped to launch Walter's career in Vienna with something unusual—perhaps *Les Contes d'Hoffmann* or Puccini's *La Bohème* (which hadn't yet been performed in Vienna).[5] In the event, Walter conducted the old war-horse *Aida*, with a cast that included Anna von Mildenburg as Aida, Edyth Walker as Amneris, and Leo Slezak as Radamès. Walter viewed the performance as a great success, telling his parents it had gone "most excellently." The orchestra followed him with zest and thronged about him after the ends of the acts to offer kind words. Mahler had told him afterwards that he had "become quite a fellow."[6] In fact, according to Natalie Bauer-Lechner, Mahler was "delighted" with the performance, declaring that "from now on he could let Walter conduct in his place with complete confidence, and turn everything important over to him. Listening to somebody else conduct," she added, "he usually experiences so many musical discomforts that he becomes practically 'seasick'. But in this case you could see from his expressions and gestures—as from his frequent enthusiastic exclamations—that he was completely in agreement with what was going on."[7]

Nevertheless, when the critics' comments appeared, Walter found them unencouraging, irrelevant, stupid, even laughable. The *Neue Freie Presse* meted out praise and caution in about equal measure:

The conductor was certainly once undervalued! Nobody made much fuss if one conductor or another had superbly conducted a symphony or an opera. With the increasing difficulty of the scores, with the ever growing complexity of the modern orchestral apparatus, the conductor's duty acquired greater responsibility; the reputation of the spiritual leaders grew visibly, and their position naturally moved more into the foreground! Nowadays, we perhaps esteem the baton somewhat above its genuine value. Music, which to be sure readily follows fashion, has found its Superconductor! Herr Walter, who today sat for the first time at the conductor's desk in the Court Opera and conducted Verdi's inspired opera *Aida*, carried us off into this excursus. Still very young, he has been engaged previously at Breslau, Hamburg, and then Berlin; he seems unusually assured and quick-witted, thoroughly acquainted with his score, and inclined to rush rather than to drag. No liability there! But the fidgety movements, which at present belong—or so the uninitiated believes—to the tools of an "energetic" conductor, are also made by Herr Walter. These nervous gestures seem dashing and precise to the public, but for the performers they signify an unnecessary and dangerous annoyance![8]

The *Neues Wiener Journal* also raked Walter over the coals for his exaggerated movements; a strongly individual conductor like Mahler could get away with such gesticulations, which came naturally to him. Yet in Walter, the critic observed, they seemed affected. Nevertheless, Walter's devotion and energy left a positive impression.[9] The reviewer for the anti-Semitic *Deutsches Volksblatt* made sure to mention that "Herr Walther" and "Herr Schlesinger" were one and the same person.[10]

Despite the less-than-glowing reviews, Walter felt inspired by his outing before the opera orchestra that, then as now, doubled as the Vienna Philharmonic, and he entertained thoughts of conducting the players for the Philharmonic concerts. Mahler was no longer in charge of their concerts, and the musicians "didn't care much for Schalk"; they now had Joseph Hellmesberger, "a master-cobbler of the first order."[11] As a result, Walter was setting his sights on conducting the Philharmonic concerts as early as the following year, an aspiration that would not be realized quite so easily, nor quite so soon.

But he kept busy in the opera house. By the end of 1901 he had conducted *Der fliegende Holländer*, *Tannhäuser*, *Aida*, *Un ballo in maschera*,

*Carmen, Der Freischütz, Die lustigen Weiber von Windsor, L'Africaine, Orfeo ed Euridice,* and *Les Contes d'Hoffmann.* The *Neue Freie Presse* passed over the new Kapellmeister's part in most of these performances—most readers, after all, were interested only in the singers—though he received special mention for his *Ballo*: "The performance, carefully prepared and most skillfully conducted by Herr Walter, was a complete victory."[12] Some critics for other newspapers, however, made a special point of attacking Walter. One was Richard Wallaschek, chief music critic of *Die Zeit*, a Left-leaning newspaper focusing on literature and the other arts—a man who had gained an international reputation as a musical scholar in the late nineteenth century for his early work in what is now known as ethnomusicology.[13]

Wallaschek seems first to have encountered Walter in a performance of *L'Africaine* in October, which elicited an unpromising comment: "One Herr Walter conducted the performance. He is already the third conductor this year who wishes to learn something at our opera. On the damage accruing to our ensemble through these and other experiments, we shall return shortly for a more thorough treatment."[14] As promised, a lengthy essay appeared on October 26, ominously entitled "Conductor Woes in Vienna." Grumbling and despairing, it is a jeremiad over the sorry state of conducting in the Austrian capital. As Wallaschek tells the story, Mahler, patently overburdened at the Hofoper, had hired second-raters as his assistants, and they were now wreaking havoc on Vienna's musical life:

> In the course of the year . . . no fewer than three young, inexperienced conductors have appeared, one of whom (Herr Mickorey) disappeared immediately, while the other (Herr B[r]echer) is indeed still engaged, but he doesn't appear [at the podium].[15] A pity that the third conductor (Herr Walter) didn't follow his example. He appears rather often at the conductor's desk, and it was quite odd to see how, in the recent performance of *Ballo*, every singer, at the beginning of his aria, took his own tempo, without consideration for the interpretation of his partner. Where the conductor *did* enforce his will, as in the finale of Act I, this occurred with such unnatural distortions and affected shadings that the original conception of the work was scarcely recognizable.[16]

Walter's youth was also a liability in Wallaschek's eyes, since the mature artists he had to direct would feel a "legitimate displeasure" working under someone considerably younger than themselves and would not give their best in performance.

Like any other critic, Wallaschek had his own agenda, and Walter's use of rubato was clearly an irritant to him, as he made plain in several scathing reviews. He expressed quite definite opinions about rhythm, arguing at great length in one of his books that music had its origin therein: "Rhythm, taken in a general sense to include 'keeping in time,' is the essence in music, in its simplest form as well as in the most skilfully elaborated fugues of modern composers."[17] No doubt some of Wallascheck's hostility toward Walter sprang from a fundamental difference of opinion regarding the application of rubato, and indeed that very issue had already become (and would remain) a recurring motive in other critical assessments of Walter's work.

Certainly *Die Zeit* was not the only journal to criticize Walter. Other newspapers also pounced on Mahler's young new protégé. After a performance of *Tannhäuser*, Walter was shocked to read a "furious attack" in the *Neues Wiener Tagblatt*, a prominent, widely read newspaper. "It was the first time in my life," he wrote, "that I had been so violently abused. The expressions used were so extravagantly uncomplimentary—one of them was that 'I would not do as the leader even of a riflemen's band'—that the obvious malice should have weakened the general effect. I was nevertheless deeply dismayed, and my bewilderment increased when a number of similar voices were raised against me in quick succession."[18]

Mahler tried to comfort Walter by explaining that the attacks were largely indirect attacks on himself. Walter had obviously expressed concern about imprecision in the ensemble, for Mahler, with the voice of long experience, wrote to allay his fears in the winter of 1901: "If that goose [the soprano Elise Elizza] makes a mess of things and [Leo Slezak] is slovenly, then it simply means the ensemble can't be got to work. Don't worry yourself to death about it."[19] Nevertheless, faced with an onslaught of negative criticism such as he had never experienced before, Walter found himself thoroughly unnerved.

Social hostility added to the tensions created by critical abuse. If Walter felt Viennese in his heart, there were some in Vienna who were hardly willing to welcome him as one of their own, and the city's widespread animosity toward Jews brought him no comfort. Karl Lueger, an open anti-Semite, was Vienna's highly popular mayor. (He had once objected that the "Jew" Mahler was going to conduct the Vienna Philharmonic for a benefit concert in 1899; to their credit, the members of the orchestra "refused to play under anyone but the conductor of their choice," Mahler.[20]) In November Walter wrote to his father about the "spiteful" anti-Semitic newspapers, thanking God, in an unintentionally ironic aside, that no one read such papers in Germany. "Anti-Semitism is, at least on paper, immensely widespread. There are papers in which you find nothing but 'Jewish swindlers,' 'Jew-nastiness,' 'once again a Jewish dirty trick,' and so on."[21] By May 1903 the newspapers would carry stories of a particularly savage pogrom in Kishinev, on the Russian border near Rumania—one of many reminders that anti-Semitism involved far more than ugly words "on paper."

Before long, with critics against him and bigots spreading their venom, Walter faced a crisis; he was losing his self-confidence and didn't know how to regain it. The Cologne Opera made him an attractive offer that he was sorely tempted to accept, despite having a position as regular conductor in one of the greatest musical centers of Europe, working closely with perhaps the world's foremost composer-conductor. Elsa, concerned about her husband's well-being, secretly visited Mahler to ask his advice, and he told her that Walter had "lost the game," that anyone "who had once lost in Vienna could never again be victorious," a verdict she communicated to her husband. Despite his shock at hearing the grim prognosis from his friend and mentor, or perhaps because of it, Walter decided to stay: "I suddenly felt strong, was conscious of my responsibilities to myself, and quite certain of my decision: I had been done a wrong, and it would be cowardly to take it lying down."[22]

But his confidence in his technique wavered; he became wary of the rhythmic liberties he was taking and began to fear that perhaps he simply didn't know how to conduct. For all that, he was still capable of directing the orchestra, performance after performance, with a constantly varying repertoire. And soon an opportunity arose that allowed him to show he was a thinking musician, not just another baton-waving Kapellmeister. The music historian Ludwig Schiedermair was writing a series of articles for the new periodical *Die Musik* on the four Mahler symphonies then in existence. For the most recent symphony, the Fourth, Schiedermair hoped that Mahler himself would offer some exegetical assistance. Critics were doubtful about how to approach the symphony. Was it absolute music? If so, why was the last movement a song-setting of "Das himmlische Leben" from *Des Knaben Wunderhorn*? If it was a programmatic work, what was the program for the opening three movements?

Mahler deputized Walter, as the person who best understood his intentions, to respond to Schiedermair's inquiry. In a long letter, Walter explained that the opening movements were to be taken primarily as absolute music. Was a program really needed, Walter asked (speaking for Mahler), "in order to understand a movement that has a first theme, a second theme, a development section, and a recapitulation? Or a Scherzo with Trio? Or an Andante with Variations?" After a detailed explanation, Walter ended his opening statement with the assertion that the symphony was "absolute music and nonliterary from beginning to end, a four-movement symphony, organic in every movement, thoroughly accessible to anyone with a taste for subtle humor."[23] Then, having made his point, Walter surprisingly allowed that the piece could indeed suggest many possible extramusical scenarios. The opening three movements, for example, could portray a heavenly existence, anticipating the text of the last movement. The first movement, full of joy, might suggest a man who is experiencing the heavenly life, while the second movement could be entitled "Friend Hain [Death] Plays His Dance," with Death fiddling us up to heaven. The third movement might call to mind Saint Ursula, that most serious of saints, smiling and laughing at the prospect of heaven. But, Walter cautioned, this was just one way among many of interpreting the movements.[24]

Schiedermair cited much of Walter's letter in the last installment of his three-part series on Mahler, not always agreeing with the Kapellmeister's views but obviously respecting them, and this was almost certainly the first substantial musical statement of Walter's to appear in a widely read, serious publication.[25] It revealed a cultivated, intelligent mind, capable of making fine distinctions and of expressing them with grace and eloquence.

Another boost to his ego came in the form of an invitation to play with Arnold Rosé, the concertmaster of the Vienna Philharmonic, in the fifth concert of Rosé's chamber music series, which took place on March 4. The Rosé Quartet, often supplemented by other musicians, offered admirable performances of the classics—Beethoven, Brahms, Schubert, Mozart—and also regularly explored new music. In fact, the sixth concert in the series brought Vienna the first performance of Schoenberg's early masterpiece *Verklärte Nacht*. The concert on March 4 presented Schubert's Quartet in E Major, Beethoven's Quartet in E-flat Major, and a premiere, Robert Fuchs's Violin Sonata in D Minor (opus 68), with Walter at the keyboard accompanying Rosé on the violin. Though barely remembered today, Fuchs had been one of Mahler's teachers (Zemlinsky, Sibelius, and Schreker were also among his students), and he had won the admiration of Brahms, whose music patently served as the inspiration for much of Fuchs's own. A brief review of the recital in the *Neue Freie Presse* noted that the "piano part was effectively played by Kapellmeister Walter," without further elaboration on the piece or the performance.[26] Nevertheless, premiering a work by a composer with close connections to Mahler and Brahms must have given Walter a sense of accomplishment.

One key event in Mahler's personal life at the end of 1901 had an immediate impact on all his friends: his engagement to Alma Schindler, "the most beautiful woman in Vienna," as the phrase went. Mahler's sudden, intense affection for Alma took his friends by surprise, as did their engagement. Many of those closest to Mahler found out about the engagement only when they opened the newspapers. She was twenty-two, he forty-one. She was a celebrated beauty, accustomed to splendid society life, as Walter observed, whereas Mahler was otherworldly and solitary. People naturally harbored doubts about the union. Clearly embarrassed about the concealed engagement, Mahler awkwardly asked Walter not to congratulate him, "or congratulate me quite quickly, like this; now let's not say anything more about it."[27] A comical bridegroom, Walter thought. But a more serious side to the engagement was that the precious hours in which Walter and Mahler had shared their thoughts were, at least for the time being, disrupted.

Walter, of course, had other close friends, one being Hans Pfitzner, whose opera *Der arme Heinrich* Walter had introduced to Berlin the year before. Pfitzner became the recipient of long, confessional letters from Walter about his disappointments and frustrations in Vienna. Walter used the personal form of address to Pfitzner, *Du*, which he used sparingly throughout his life—Mahler and Walter addressed each other as *Sie*—and the tone of the letters is one of utter candor and trust. In March 1902 Walter confided to Pfitzner that the critics were against him and laid some of the blame, perhaps unfairly, on the conductor Franz Schalk, who had been hired at the Hofoper in 1900 and whose conducting both Mahler and Walter found dull and unimaginative. Along with Ferdinand Löwe, Franz Schalk and his brother Josef (both of whom had studied with Bruckner) were among the earliest editors of Bruckner's symphonies. Walter's senior by more than a decade, Franz Schalk was Viennese (unlike Walter) and had many friends; he was widely viewed—on dubious grounds, so Walter felt—as a man admirable for his sharp mind, his strong character, his deep nature, and his modest demeanor. His peace offerings to Walter, however, provoked skepticism and resentment in the younger conductor, who regarded Schalk as a slippery hypocrite out to ruin him. Whether or not Walter painted an unjust portrait of Schalk at this time, there is no doubt that strong and sometimes vicious factions were an inescapable reality in the city Walter admired so deeply.[28]

Naturally Walter wrote to Pfitzner about contemporary compositions, including their own works. He urged Rosé to perform Pfitzner's music in his concert series and waged a campaign to convince Mahler to bring Pfitzner's *Die Rose vom Liebesgarten* to the Hofoper. Unfortunately, Walter confided to Pfitzner with brutal honesty, Mahler had "an astounding antipathy" against his "whole style."[29] Some of the libretto, Walter pointed out, was too obscure and would prove puzzling to the audience; nevertheless, he would continue to work on Mahler. True to his word, Walter sat at the piano in December and performed a reduction of Pfitzner's Quartet in D Major for Mahler, Alma, and Arnold Rosé. Mahler was delighted with the masterly craft of the piece, enjoying particularly the expressive Adagio, a movement that Walter had initially found hardest to penetrate. Pfitzner also gained an important partisan in Alma, to whom he would later dedicate the quartet.[30] Only Rosé seemed to have reservations, which prompted Walter to brand him, privately (and unfairly), as a Philistine.[31] But Rosé must have soon overcome his doubts, for on January 13, 1903, the piece had its premiere in Vienna, given by the Rosé Quartet. Walter found the performance well executed but impersonal, objective to a fault.[32] Nevertheless, Mahler was deeply impressed and as a result reconsidered giving a performance of *Die Rose vom Liebesgarten*, which Walter reported to Pfitzner with palpable excitement.

However unsettling in some respects, the year 1902 brought Walter some good notices. The *Neue Freie Presse* ran complimentary reviews of his performances of Nicolai's *Die lustigen Weiber von Windsor*, Donizetti's *Lucia*, and Wagner's *Tannhäuser*, for which Walter, according to the *Neues Wiener Tagblatt*, now received such thunderous applause after the overture that he was obliged to bow several times.[33] Moreover, Julius Korngold, a music critic at the *Neue Freie Presse*, was gaining an increasingly important position at the paper, as Eduard Hanslick, then in his mid-seventies, prepared for retirement. (He died in 1904.) Like Hanslick, Korngold was an eloquent prose stylist with conservative musical tastes, admired and feared for his acerbic wit. Unlike Wallaschek, he took a distinct liking to the new conductor, singling him out for praise in a review of *Tannhäuser* in mid-September. As his status increased, Korngold began contributing longer musical essays to the paper; early in October he wrote a seven-column review of *Ernani* under Walter. "Herr Kapellmeister Walther led the performance with great fire," Korngold wrote; "in the third act, the true Verdian rockets rose up crackling."[34] Immediately afterward, on October 4, Walter scored another success by giving the Viennese premiere of Mozart's *Zaide*, an early, unfinished singspiel that the critic Robert Hirschfeld completed for turn-of-the-century audiences. The delightful concept of having a "new" opera by Mozart inspired nine columns of commentary from Korngold.[35]

Walter's conducting outside the opera house was also picking up. On the first day of 1903, Kapellmeister Walter no doubt took pleasure in seeing his name in bold print in a notice for a charity concert on January 16 by the violin virtuoso Amélie Heller and the heldentenor Leo Slezak.[36] It was to take place in the sumptuous Great Hall of the Musikverein, with its incomparable acoustics, its painted coffered ceiling, and its many columns of gilded, breast-baring women. Already the home of numerous historic symphonic performances, the hall where Brahms's Second and Third Symphonies had their premieres, it would become the venue for many of Walter's greatest triumphs. For Heller, the Konzertverein Orchestra performed Wieniawski's Second Violin Concerto, the first movement of Bruch's Second Violin Concerto, Paganini's Fantasy on *Moïse*, and Vieuxtemps's *Fantasia appassionata*. Slezak sang lieder by Beethoven, Schubert, Wolf, Brahms, and Boieldieu. Although Walter was still acting in the capacity of an accompanist, his duties were slowly extending into the orchestral repertoire, a direction he very much wanted his career to move in.

But what happened to Elsa's career? She apparently stopped singing publicly when she married Walter, yet in February 1903 she and her husband took a trip to Danzig and made what seem to have been their last professional appearances together. Elsa's sister, the contralto Gertrud Wirthschaft, was giving her recital debut at the Apollosaal, and this was probably the stimulus that recalled Elsa to the stage, with Walter accompanying at the piano. Elsa's singing, both technically and interpretively, was praised by the critics, and she included in the program two of her husband's songs, "Waltraut's Lied" I and II. Walter and Elsa also lent their services to a production of Gounod's *Faust* at the Stadttheater, much to the delight of the reviewers, one of whom asserted that the performance had ranked among the best of the season. Walter's ability to transform the orchestra into a flexible yet precise instrument receptive to his subtle intentions was admired as an astonishing accomplishment.[37] It must have been gratifying to read such positive reviews after the drubbings he had sometimes suffered in Vienna. Elsa no doubt enjoyed being in the limelight again, though her guest engagement in *Faust* appears to have been her farewell to the stage. Motherhood, which Elsa would soon experience, left women little time to maintain their art, especially at the turn of the last century.

It's hard to say whether Walter felt any pangs of conscience about his wife's divorce from her art, yet at the end of his career he offered a potentially telling comment to Mildred Miller, who was then preparing for a recording of Mahler's *Lieder eines fahrenden Gesellen* with Walter. Several months pregnant, she arrived for her piano rehearsal and brought along her husband. After the rehearsal Walter approached Miller's husband and reportedly said: "You know, your wife is not just a singer; she is an artist. And therefore, she must sing. You must allow her to sing. She must not have any more babies!"[38]

In the early 1900s conductors who wrote music were by no means exceptional. Felix Weingartner and Leo Blech both had serious reputations as composers, and the wunderkind George Szell would perform his compositions in Vienna during Walter's tenure there. Sharing his thoughts with Mahler, Strauss, and Pfitzner (all three capable of superb conducting), Walter was naturally spurred on to attempt a conquest of both arts. While some know that Walter dabbled with composition, the following passage, from a book on Walter's conducting published around 1913, will still come as something of a surprise to the modern reader: "I hope it will not occur to anyone to suppose that I am writing these observations down out of a tacit fear that Bruno Walter—who is incidentally, as everyone knows, also a creative artist—could be forgotten."[39] By "creative artist," the author, Mary Komorn-Rebhan, of course meant "a composer." Ironically, things turned out just the reverse of what she'd anticipated. Unable to predict the electrical recording process (to say nothing of the compact disc and its offshoots), she assumed that Walter's interpretations would perish in time, while his compositions would live on. Today, however, no one remembers Walter's compositions. He is known *only* as an interpreter.

Walter had already been writing short orchestral works and lieder for years, and by 1899 he had published a two-piano arrangement of Mahler's First Symphony as well as a four-hand reduction of the Second.[40] In 1901 (or early 1902) he would see twelve of his songs—two sets of six, opus 11 and opus 12—issued by Dreililien, a publisher in Berlin that also issued music by the young Arnold Schoenberg.[41] Walter had composed two of the songs as early as 1890 and had already programmed some of them in Breslau and Riga. On their publication, he sent Pfitzner copies and asked his friend for his frank opinion of them, but Pfitzner's replies have not surfaced. Among the texts Walter set were poems by Theodor Storm, Gustav Renner, Julius Wolff, Hermann Sudermann, Heinrich Heine, and Henrik Ibsen, as well as anonymous lyrics—including "Sehnsucht," from *Des Knaben Wunderhorn*, the famous anthology to which Mahler so often turned for inspiration. Despite Walter's initial excitement over the publication of the lieder, they seem to have drawn little if any critical attention and to have inspired no significant performances, though his friend, the tenor Ernst Kraus, possessed copies of them.[42] In a letter to his parents written in February 1907, Walter calmly stated that when he achieved fame, his songs would be performed often enough, which implies that, five years after their publication, his lieder were still languishing, unsung.[43]

Walter's facility and versatility as a composer immediately strike anyone who hears his music, and the early songs are no exception. Most of the songs make ample use of late-nineteenth-century chromaticism in the harmonies and melodies (some are littered with accidentals), and most are lyrical rather than dramatic, though the lengthy "Liebeslust" is an almost operatic profession of love. At his weakest, Walter can seem stylistically lost—some harmonies in "Meine Mutter hat's gewollt" seem best suited to the cocktail lounge, at least to modern ears—but this is rare. Many of the songs reveal a distinctive voice, which reappears in the later compositions. Some of the pieces, like the haunting "Vorbei" and "Tragödie II," are admirably crafted and musically unassailable. If we hear traces of Schubert, Debussy, Wolf, Wagner, and others in his songs, these elements are deftly integrated into his own style. Curiously enough, one genius of the art song seems to have had little if any influence on the early lieder: Gustav Mahler. To judge from later criticism of Walter's music, however, that influence would make its presence felt soon enough.

Walter had written to his parents already in 1897 that if he were to present himself to the public as a composer, his entire personality would be exposed, and he feared his songs would be "too intimate"; he therefore hoped to write a more substantial work in the coming years before grappling with the question of his future as a composer.[44] Though the songs were his first works to see print, he had clearly not lost sight of his aspiration to write large-scale works, for by 1903 he had composed a serious chamber composition and was ready to present it to that notoriously exacting audience, the Viennese public and press. The work, a String Quartet in D Major, was given its premiere performance by the Rosé Quartet on November 17.[45] Flanked by two other quartets—Beethoven's in A major (opus 18) and Brahms's in A minor—Walter's piece made its debut in the best possible company. The *Allgemeine Musikzeitung* allowed the quartet a mere sentence, but a complimentary one, describing the piece as "a rich, well-formed work, which often, however, pushes its way out of the limitations imposed by chamber music toward the area of orchestral music."[46] Korngold gave it plenty of attention in the *Neue Freie Presse*—more, perhaps, than Walter would have liked. He first ran a brief notice saying that the Rosé Quartet had recently brought forth a novelty by Walter that had been "awaited not without interest." Walter, it seems, had proved himself no less a follower of Mahler the composer than he had of Mahler the conductor. "Mahler is the creator of symphonies about which the last word will not be spoken for a long time. But he is surely the most dangerous example to pick for someone who ultimately aspires to write chamber music." Since a sharp difference of opinion had arisen after the recital, Korngold wrote, he promised "a little obituary notice" for Walter's quartet, to be run in a later issue. The five days that intervened between Korngold's initial comment and his longer review must have seemed an eternity to Walter, who was unlikely to have found any comfort when the threatened review actually appeared in print. Korngold grouped the newcomer with other "ultramodern musicians" who, to outdo their predecessors, ventured to defy the limitations of their medium:

> When four instruments of the same sound family, on which normally a sole voice is available, are to live fully in an important musical composition, they must remain four individuals. They should not want to play like an orchestra, and they simply cannot. Ultimately, there is no greater contrast than that between a quartet movement and the essence of a modern symphony. . . . We find orchestral episodes in [Walter's] work; an excess of movement and of obfuscating voices; dramatic breaking-off, connecting, building-up; all manner of playing with sounds—muted and pizzicato effects, a forcing of all the voices into the highest range. The spirit of the Mahlerian symphony, especially the Fourth, haunts Walter's quartet a little, even if fully eleven thousand virgins cannot dance within it. . . . Walter's concluding movement, in which two separate motives are varied, utterly falls apart.[47]

Reading this and other unfavorable reviews was undoubtedly a source of increased tension for Walter, who seems to have suffered from stress-related complaints throughout his life. A cause for joy during this period—the birth of his first daughter, Lotte, on October 4, 1903 ("indescribably lovely, so much that her entire being, her *melos*, seems like the purest poetry")—was probably also a source of anxiety, as Walter's responsibilities grew and the critics seemed determined to demolish his career.[48] And perhaps it was an accumulation of stress that forced him, less than a week after Korngold's review appeared, to abandon a performance of *Tannhäuser* after conducting only the first act. He had been "suddenly taken ill," and his rival Franz Schalk was called on to substitute for him.[49] The atmosphere in Vienna had grown so oppressive that Walter was actively seeking employment elsewhere. In a letter to Richard Strauss dated December 5, Walter confided that he'd applied for a position as Kapellmeister in Karlsruhe—hardly equal to Vienna as a cultural center—and had taken the liberty of listing the composer as a reference.[50]

However frustrated he might have felt professionally, his confidence in his compositional ability had not been thoroughly quashed by the reviews. In the same letter to Strauss, Walter also asked the older master to consider including a symphonic work of his in the next Tonkünstler-Versammlung in Frankfurt. Though inspired largely by Ibsen's *Peer Gynt*, Walter wrote, the tone poem was autobiographical enough that it might more properly be called *Bruno Walter*. In the end, Walter called it merely a "Symphonic Fantasy."[51] Strauss must have found some merit in the work, for it was indeed programmed for the Tonkünstler-Versammlung at the end of May 1904, an event that also included Strauss's *Symphonia domestica*. The musicologist Arnold Schering, then editor of the *Neue Zeitschrift für Musik*, assessed the entire series, giving Walter's piece a mixed review. The work was clearly programmatic, but the composer, "following the model of his teacher, Mahler, disdained to provide a program"; unfortunately, Schering felt, it couldn't stand on its own as a piece of "absolute music," as the composer would have liked. (A recurring grievance in reviews of this period revolved around the omission of printed programs in performances of tone poems.) Schering discovered some admirable spots in the piece—such as "the elegiac horn duet"—and commented on the "occasionally effective instrumentation," but these did not compensate for the lack of organizational clarity.[52] According to Alma (not always a reliable source), Walter played the piece for Mahler, who was overwhelmed by its "bloodless sterility" from the first measure onward, though he nevertheless managed to offer words of encouragement to his protégé.[53]

Despite the ill critical reception accorded his compositions, Walter's musical life continued to grow in exciting directions. As a pianist, Walter found an important new partner in the violinist Marie Soldat-Röger, who had studied under Joachim. Admired as a soloist, Soldat-Röger led an all-female string quartet whose personnel included the violist Natalie Bauer-Lechner, who had once hoped to become Mahler's wife. With members of the Soldat-Röger Quartet, Walter performed the Brahms Piano Trio in C Minor on January 11, 1904, and his work with these string players would continue throughout most of his tenure in Vienna.

Walter also established connections with the avant-garde composers of Vienna, some of whom had banded together to form a new musical organization. Early in 1904 the music scholar Guido Adler wrote an article in the *Neue Freie Presse* about the new Society for Creative Musicians in Vienna (Vereinigung schaffender Tonkünstler in Wien), whose members included, among others, Gustav Mahler (its honorary president), Alexander von Zemlinsky (chairman), Josef von Woess, Karl Weigl, Arnold Schoenberg, Oskar Posa, Gustav Gutheil (husband of the soprano Marie Gutheil-Schoder), Gerhard von Keussler, and Bruno Walter. Mahler and Strauss were both to conduct some of the concerts arranged by the society, whose goals, as stated in a circulated printed statement, were to bring contemporary composers into closer contact with the public, to break away from the current musical societies and create a musical secession, akin to the Secession School in the visual arts.[54] As a parallel activity to this musical "secession," Zemlinsky, Schoenberg, and the critic Elsa Bienenfeld were holding classes in music theory.

Composing, no doubt, with an eye to future performances at the Society for Creative Musicians, Walter worked on a piano quintet during the summer of 1904, a work that—so he confided to Pfitzner—brought him a sense of deep satisfaction.[55] It was some months before the society arranged its first concert, on November 23, for which Walter was originally scheduled to conduct three orchestral songs by Hermann Bischoff and two by Edgar Istel.[56] Shortly after the initial announcement, however, the program was changed; Zemlinsky would conduct the songs by Bischoff, and the work by Istel ceded its place to a *Dionysische Phantasie* by Siegmund von Hausegger; the second half of the concert was devoted to Strauss's *Symphonia domestica*, conducted by Mahler.[57] Why the change in program? Perhaps Zemlinsky felt that, as chairman, he should be represented at the inaugural concert of the new series, along with Mahler, the director of the Hofoper. Or perhaps Walter, in the view of the society, lacked the authority that its members no doubt desired for their first concert. In any event, Walter would have to wait until the following month before taking a more active part in the society's performances.

For all his emotional turmoil in 1904, Walter enjoyed his share of successes, opening the opera season with *Lohengrin*, which played to a nearly sold-out house. At the same time, he was clearly gaining a reputation as a proselytizer for Pfitzner's music. On December 20, 1904, Walter, Arnold Rosé, and Friedrich Buxbaum (the cellist of the Rosé Quartet and longtime solo cellist of the Philharmonic) performed Pfitzner's Piano Trio in F Major at a recital for the Vereinigung schaffender Tonkünstler. Korngold's review of the trio pointed out weaknesses but conceded that it conveyed a powerful gusto in the act of making music. Rosé, Buxbaum, and Walter, "the latter utterly aglow with the fire of propaganda," gave the performance their wholehearted devotion.[58] One is often surprised today to discover how ardently Walter championed certain modern composers earlier in his career, though the composers he favored tended to stem from the romantic tradition and were almost militantly proud of that heritage. It is often equally surprising to learn about some of the composers he rejected: "So far," he admitted to Pfitzner in November, "I can't understand a single measure of [Max] Reger's music."[59]

Another contemporary composer whose music occasionally proved difficult for Walter to appreciate was Richard Strauss, and the relationship between the two men—for personal as well as musical reasons—was strained for most of their professional lives. (In 1907 Walter bemoaned the great success of *Salome*, and of Strauss generally, as a sign of "these wretched times."[60]) Nevertheless, Walter performed Strauss's works even when—during and after World War II—some chose not to do so, in protest against the composer's political alliances. Strauss's Sonata for Violin and Piano in E-flat Major (1887) belongs to an early phase of the composer's career, and much of it sounds like fairly standard late-nineteenth-century romanticism, quite distinct from the Strauss of the famous tone poems. Some passages in the Violin Sonata could momentarily be mistaken for Schumann or Brahms. It was, in short, a work ideally suited to Walter's temperament, and on January 10, 1905, Walter accompanied Marie Soldat-Röger in a performance of the sonata; in the same recital he sat at the keyboard for a performance of Brahms's Piano Quartet in A Major. Once again, Walter's facility and dramatic interpretation impressed Korngold, though in places he found

Walter's attention to detail somewhat fussy: "He gladly seizes expression from the rhythmic sections and, with impassioned sensitivity to the music, concentrates on clarifying the phrase in an emphatic, sometimes overemphatic, way."[61]

If Walter's relationship to Strauss the composer was often uncomfortable, relations with Arnold Schoenberg were even more strained. Walter never concealed his antipathy to atonality and serialism; nevertheless, the compositions that Schoenberg wrote early in his career were of great interest to Walter, as they were to many Viennese musicians and music-lovers. "Schoenberg unquestionably outranked us all as a composer," Walter recalled decades later, "and he was also able to create more of a stir in Vienna's musical life than anybody else." *Verklärte Nacht*, which impressed him deeply, would appear on Walter's programs long after the composer had moved far away from its harmonic language. "In spite of its Wagnerian atmosphere and its infection with sequences," Walter wrote, "I found it highly original, full of ecstasy and convincing force in its moods, and at the same time rich in musical substance."[62] On January 25, 1905, in the Great Hall of the Musikverein with the Konzertverein Orchestra, the Society for Creative Musicians sponsored the premiere of Schoenberg's *Pelleas und Melisande* (conducted by the composer), along with Zemlinsky's *Die Seejungfrau* and some orchestral songs by Oskar Posa. Walter recalled in his autobiography, with almost palpable nostalgia, that *Pelleas*, like Mahler's Fourth, had created a "furor" on that occasion—a testament to the "widespread and passionate interest" the Viennese then took in music.[63]

For the third chamber music recital given by the Society for Creative Musicians, on February 20, 1905, Walter had the opportunity to premiere the Piano Quintet in which he had taken such pride the previous summer.[64] The Rosé Quartet assisted Walter, who played the piano part. The program, consisting of two works, opened with a Violin Sonata in C Major by Max Reger, whose music Walter had recently criticized as utterly incomprehensible, performed by Rosé and the composer. Like Walter, the veteran critic Gustav Schönaich of the *Wiener Allgemeine Zeitung*, who also reviewed Viennese musical events for *Die Musik*, had little sympathy for Reger's music; he unjustly condemned the work as "a truly disagreeable violin sonata that deliberately warded off any enjoyment through harmonic and rhythmic barbed wire" and far preferred the "beautiful-sounding, quite thoroughly interesting, and melodically successful Piano Quintet by Bruno Walter."[65] For its own series, the Rosé Quartet gave a second airing of Walter's Piano

Quintet at the end of February. Despite the two performances, however, Korngold omitted to review the piece. Perhaps it was for the best, given his antipathy to Walter's music.

The hostility that certain critics showed to Walter's compositions and conducting was surely the catalyst underlying an article Walter published in the *Österreichische Rundschau* during the first half of 1905. Immodestly entitled "On Understanding Art," the essay ostensibly treats the issue of the proper way to approach a work of art, and the opening paragraphs focus mainly on questions of aesthetics.[66] Walter holds that those who want to understand art must be prepared to surrender themselves to something "higher, purer, unknown" (Goethe's words) and to show gratitude before it—plainly setting up an argument whereby he can trounce those critics whose response to original art is anything but gratitude.

From a discussion of aesthetics, he soon turns to the question of criticism, the main topic of the essay. A noticeable defensiveness permeates the essay from this point onward. For Walter, certain critics simply don't have the proper background or attitude to pass judgment on a work of art. An ideal listener would be a great artist, brimming with life; the next best listener, a musically talented person, also full of life, "seeking the eternal and the one in the manifold and the mutable." Sadly, however, the self-appointed "connoisseur" (Walter has the hostile critic in mind) often uses a rigid set of criteria for judging art and "regards his relationship to the artist as akin to that of the examiner to the examinee, not infrequently to that of the judge to the delinquent."[67] The "individual" qualities that inevitably mark a work of genius are precisely what alienate the "connoisseur," who prefers to cherish the familiar works of the past and to praise works that follow the recognizable patterns of established masterpieces, while the genuinely original work is usually condemned by the "connoisseur," who cannot understand what is new and original, finding it "eclectic" and "confused." In contrast, true critics, if moved but puzzled by a new piece of music, will withhold judgment and attribute their confusion to the limitations of their perception, perhaps eventually gaining a just appreciation for the work in question.

As is often the case when we read Walter's early writings, it comes as a surprise that Walter should so aggressively attack the conservative critics who were praising, for the most part, the very music that Walter himself cherished above all. The critical responses he condemns were precisely the kind that his own music provoked, which adds an unfortunate self-serving tint to the essay; yet often enough hostility also greeted the music of Mahler,

Schoenberg, Elgar, and other composers of the twentieth century whose works are now regularly played in the concert hall. Walter was right to take the critics to task, though it's hard to imagine that his essay gained him any new allies in the critical world.

Preparations for the Viennese premiere of Pfitzner's *Die Rose vom Liebesgarten* made large demands on Walter's attention during the earlier part of 1905. He wrote to his friend on a number of occasions, informing him about casting and instrumentation, sets and costumes, setbacks and delays. Walter was patently thrilled that the production was finally taking place. There is a boyish exuberance in some of his dispatches ("IN A RUSH—IN HASTE—BREATHLESS!!!!!!"[68]). Though postponed several times, the premiere took place on April 6, 1905, under Mahler's masterly guidance. The performance received mixed reviews, largely due to the difficulties of the libretto, but it continued to generate interest for several weeks. On April 15 Walter, with irrepressible enthusiasm, wrote to Pfitzner that the performance on the following day was totally sold out: "Could the *Rose* become a box-office hit? Now really, Pfitzner!!"[69] Pfitzner, who had been present at some of the rehearsals, came to conduct on May 17, partly, no doubt, as a stratagem to maintain interest in the opera. When Walter conducted *Die Rose* in June, Korngold observed afterward that one felt, in every measure, Walter's fine enthusiasm for Pfitzner's music.[70]

Despite Walter's devotion to Pfitzner, the two had a brief but painful falling out at the end of the year, foreshadowing later clefts that would develop between them. Pfitzner had visited Vienna, apparently in October, to supervise a performance of his music.[71] On this occasion he seemingly had little time to spare for Walter, who took his friend's brusqueness as a slight. Affronted, Walter sent two letters to Pfitzner, one of them quite long, expressing his pain and anger at Pfitzner's perceived rudeness. "It seems to me," Walter wrote, "that all the warmth within you is related to art, and that human relations don't count for much to you."[72] Walter had also urged Pfitzner to be cautious when conversing with Alma Mahler, who by this time had begun waging a campaign for Pfitzner's music (she claimed to have regularly left the score of *Die Rose* for her husband to see on the piano's music stand[73]). She, in turn, seems to have suggested to Pfitzner that Walter had "complained about" him to her husband, when in fact, Walter protested, he was merely telling Mahler about an intellectual disagreement they'd had. "Feminine malevolence," he quipped, "describes this kind of thing as 'complaining.'"[74] Walter probably felt somewhat threatened by Alma, who had already altered his relationship with Mahler and was now developing an unsettling interest in Pfitzner. Walter's fears may have been justified; after all, throughout her life, Alma pursued her interests with a passion, and artists of genius ranked high among her interests and passions. By the end of the letter, Walter was again accusing Pfitzner of not taking human relations seriously, and saying that Walter's own "lofty conception of friendship" must therefore seem "exaggerated and exalted."[75]

These letters, while presenting a sorry picture of Walter's interior life, also suggest his alarming physical condition at this time. Elsa, it turns out, had to act as amanuensis for both letters (what did she think about Walter's petulant utterance on Alma's "feminine malevolence"?), for by the end of 1905 Walter could neither conduct nor play the piano nor write letters.[76] He was obliged even to back out of scheduled performances.[77]

The cause of all this was a serious problem in his arm that had developed sometime after his daughter Lotte's birth—he remembered the difficulty as beginning the following year, but the problem seems to have become critical about two years afterward. "Medical science called it a professional cramp, but it looked deucedly like incipient paralysis," he wrote. "The rheumatic-neuralgic pain became so violent that I could no longer use my right arm for conducting or piano playing. I went from one prominent doctor to another. Each one confirmed the presence of psychogenic elements in my malady." Living in turn-of-the-century Vienna, Walter had the luxury of consulting the father of psychoanalysis himself, Sigmund Freud. "Instead of questioning me about sexual aberrations in infancy, as my layman's ignorance had led me to expect," Walter recalled, "Freud examined my arm briefly. . . . [H]e asked me if I had ever been to Sicily. When I replied that I had not, he said that it was very beautiful and interesting, and more Greek than Greece itself. In short, I was to leave that very evening, forget all about my arm and the Opera, and do nothing for a few weeks but use my eyes."[78]

Walter dutifully followed Freud's orders, fully savoring the southern clime; but, upon his return, he still felt incapacitated by his ailing arm. Freud advised him simply to conduct. When Walter voiced his doubts about his ability to perform, Freud offered to take responsibility himself. Even reading about the ensuing performances creates tension. "I did a little conducting with my right arm, then with my left, and occasionally with my head. There were times when I forgot my arm over the music. I noticed at my next session with Freud that he attached particular importance to my forgetting."[79] In the end, Walter provisionally managed to control his problem (which dogged him into the 1950s) after reading Ernst von Feuchtersleben's *Dietetics of the Soul*,[80] a book on spiritual well-being and psychosomatic illness. It is typical of Walter, who often sought for enlightenment in unorthodox places, that he should have treated Freud's commonsense advice with some skepticism and found a book on the heatlh of the soul—a work once highly regarded and much read—more useful in dealing with his malady. His interest in Feuchtersleben would in some ways anticipate his fascination, several decades later, with Rudolf Steiner's writings on the spirit.

In the symphonic world the most important musical event in 1906 was undoubtedly the premiere of Mahler's Sixth Symphony during the forty-second music festival of the Allgemeiner deutscher Musikverein in Essen, held in late May. Mahler's "Tragic" Symphony was given on May 27; on the day before, a number of chamber works had been performed, including Walter's Piano Quintet and Pfitzner's Piano Trio. Both Walter and Pfitzner played the piano parts in their works, assisted by the Munich Quartet. *Die Musik* published a lengthy article on the festival, including musical examples drawn from the works to be performed, illustrating their principal motives and other thematic or structural points of interest.[81] Walter contributed a thematic table for his own piece, but Mahler's symphony held the dominant place in the article, as in the festival. Curiously enough, the colossal symphony that served as the festival's centerpiece, that staggeringly powerful musical statement, is the only symphonic work of Mahler's that Walter seems never to have conducted. The reason for this is perhaps impossible to ascertain, though Wolfgang Stresemann, who knew Walter well later in life, discovered a possible motive. During a walk one night, Mahler asked Walter quite directly what he thought of the Sixth Symphony. Walter replied, with undiplomatic frankness, that the second theme of the first movement, the "Alma" theme, struck him as too sentimental.

> "And what did Mahler say?" Stresemann asked.
> "Mahler didn't say anything," Walter replied.
> "What happened?"
> "We just continued our walk."
> They did so in silence.[82]

Perhaps the most revealing clue as to Walter's opinion of the Sixth is offered in Walter's biography of Mahler, published in 1936 but drawing on ideas that he had developed over the course of many years. There his assessment of the Sixth reveals a nearly morose reading of the work's deeper message: "The Sixth is bleakly pessimistic: it reeks of the bitter taste of the cup of life. In contrast with the Fifth, it says 'No', above all in its last movement, where something resembling the inexorable strife of 'all against all' is translated into music. 'Existence is a burden; death is desirable and life hateful', might be its motto. . . . [T]he work ends in hopelessness and the night of the soul. '*Non placet*' ['It does not please me'] is his verdict on this world; the 'other world' is not glimpsed for a moment."[83] How much this says about Walter, as opposed to Mahler, is open to question. But clearly a work that seemed so contrary to the life impulse and so skeptical of a benign providence went very much against the grain for Walter. (Curiously enough, the opening movement of Walter's own First Symphony struck some reviewers as presenting a relentlessly pessimistic world view to its listeners.)

In any event, Gustav Altmann wrote a long review in *Die Musik* of the works presented at the Tonkünstlerfest, expressing his views so bluntly that the editors found it necessary to place a disclaimer on the first page of his article to the effect that Altmann's ideas did not reflect those of the editors but were nevertheless being printed in the interest of free speech. For Altmann, Mahler's gigantic work was merely a bloated example of "Kapellmeistermusik"—trite, garrulous, and far too long. As for Walter's Piano Quintet, praised by Schönaich in an earlier issue of the same journal, Altmann dispatched it with one unflinching motion: "a plainly wretched work in which the sonic capabilities of the instruments are not once exploited; with its dry, rattling motives, it gave the impression of a musical skeleton."[84]

By 1906 Walter's status at the Hofoper had risen to the point where he was the one chosen to present the premiere traditionally given on the emperor's name day, October 4. Camille Erlanger's *Der polnische Jude* (*Le Juif polonais*), long since forgotten, was the opera selected to celebrate the occasion, and the composer himself attended the first Viennese performance. It was received, however, with something less than enthusiasm. The public responded only with "occasional interest, but no warmth."[85] Maximilian Muntz, of the nationalist *Deutsche Zeitung*, took the opportunity to attack Mahler for choosing, on such an occasion, a work unworthy of the institution entrusted to him. Mahler himself, Muntz argued, must have recognized the opera's worthlessness; after all, he simply "turned over" the opera to his "favorite, Kapellmeister Walther-Schlesinger."[86] Although Muntz claims to have been affronted on artistic grounds, his reference to Walter's original surname, Schlesinger, suggests a motive for his hostility far removed from aesthetics.

Meantime, Walter continued to compose, taking particular pride in his new Piano Trio, which members of the Rosé Quartet, with Walter at the keyboard (despite residual soreness in his arm), performed on January 8. The work inspired several reviews, most of them focusing on the weaknesses in the piece.[87] Long after the performances, in a survey of recent chamber works, Wilhelm Altmann wrote a distinctly unflattering, if not quite devastating, critique of the piece for *Die Musik*. Altmann owned that the piece had some admirable moments but judged it a disappointment overall, springing "more from reflection than from inspiration." The first two movements made a negative impression on him. The Scherzo, however, was "truly fine," being the "most unified and most clearly constructed" movement of the entire trio. The first half of the finale began well enough, but the second half lacked substance—hardly encouraging words for an aspiring composer. But Altmann was not yet finished with his victim. "That the composer also lacks a sense for beautiful sound," he added, "is shown especially by the treatment of the cello. A stricter sense of self-criticism would surely have led him to the same objections I have raised above." One final word, on Walter's piano playing: it was "rather loud."[88] Mahler, who attended a rehearsal of the piece, privately and regretfully confided to Alma that he found it soporific and that it was painful to see such creative fervor end in such wasted effort.[89]

Though his artistic creations met with indifference and hostility among friends and foes alike, one act of creation was less fraught with controversy. On September 21, 1906, Walter was blessed with another child, his daughter Gretel. She would become a captivating beauty, and her many talents—as pianist, singer, and actress—would often make her beaming father boast about her to his friends. Her violent death would come as an especially cruel blow to Walter during the critical year of 1939.

A pivotal moment in Walter's conducting career occurred early in 1907: he was appointed to conduct the Vienna Philharmonic's Nicolai Concert, held on January 27. Named after Otto Nicolai, the composer of *Die lustigen Weiber von Windsor* and the founder of the Vienna Philharmonic concerts, the Nicolai Concerts had begun in 1860 and were already a venerable institution by 1907. Members of the orchestra elected the conductor under whom they wished to play, and it was a rare honor to be chosen. Now Walter would at last have the chance to conduct major symphonic works with one of the finest orchestras in the world. The opening piece was Schumann's "Spring" Symphony. Walter studied the score in minute detail, buying the parts and marking them all. As he stood at the conductor's desk and took up the baton, he said to himself (or so he wrote to his parents): " 'I now hold my destiny in my hand. If things go amiss today, my career is over, and I'll have to resign myself to a modest existence at the Vienna Hofoper. If things go successfully, the whole case is altered.' Well, they went successfully." He sent his parents positive reviews, but far more important for him was the demonstrative support of the public and the orchestra, "which couldn't offer praise enough in its enthusiastic ovations." Nevertheless, Walter still felt bitter about the abuse he'd suffered during the six preceding years. Before this triumph, his battered reputation would have made it difficult for him to find a good position elsewhere; now, however, he had real negotiating power. If the Boston Symphony Orchestra or some other desirable ensemble were to invite him to conduct, he would go "in glory," with many regretting his departure.[90] Korngold certainly admired the performance, suggesting that the orchestra need not look far to find its regular conductor and hinting strongly that Walter would be a suitable candidate for the position.[91]

Along with his conducting duties, Walter kept busy as a pianist and a composer. He assisted the Hofoper's wind ensemble and performed the Brahms Piano Quintet in F Minor with the Soldat-Röger Quartet in February. At a Brahms celebration given by the Vienna Tonkünstler-Verein in mid-April, Walter accompanied Rosé in a rendering of one of Brahms's violin sonatas and the Trio for Piano, Violin, and Horn. (The day before, a young pianist-conductor from Berlin, Otto Klemperer, accompanied the Dutch cellist Jacques van Lier in a recital of Beethoven, Bach, Popper, and others.[92]) By September he had written a work for chorus, soloists, and full orchestra, based on Schiller's poem *Das Siegesfest*. Also in September Walter played his First Symphony—an ambitious work lasting nearly an hour—for Mahler, who offered no encouraging words to his younger colleague.[93] Though Walter was manifestly despondent at Mahler's indifference, he continued with his creative work. By February 1908 Pfitzner had examined the score of the symphony and, much to Walter's delight, asked for permission to conduct the first performance in Germany.[94]

At the Hofoper Walter gave a performance of Auber's *La Muette de Portici* at the end of February, in a production that first brought the young ballerina Grete Wiesenthal to the attention of the Viennese public. (As a choreographer, she would collaborate with the conductor again in 1930 for a

Salzburg production of Gluck's *Iphigenia in Aulis*.) But a far more important operatic event in Walter's life was the Viennese premiere of Saint-Saëns's *Samson et Dalila*, given on May 11. First presented in 1877, Saint-Saëns's dramatic masterpiece, which retains some of the qualities of an oratorio, did not initially fare well, largely because its biblical theme was deemed inappropriate for a sensual depiction on the operatic stage. Catholic Vienna was certainly slow to accept it, offering it only thirty years after its world premiere. Walter's cast included Erik Schmedes as Samson and, as Dalila, the American contralto Sarah Jane Cahier (better known as Madame Charles Cahier), who would later sing with Walter on many important occasions, most notably in the world premiere of Mahler's *Das Lied von der Erde*. Korngold lauded the performance (it "glistened thanks to the artistic polish seen in all new performances at the opera theater") and offered unstinting praise to Walter, "this warm-feeling, deeply probing musician," for his work on the musical portion of the production.[95]

Another new opera came Walter's way about this time, though he approached it at first with grave misgivings. An Englishwoman had written to Mahler, asking him to consider producing her new opera at the Hofoper. Neither Mahler nor Walter had high hopes for the work, though Walter, "Mahler's Second-in-Command," reluctantly agreed to hear it. Before she "had played him two pages," she recalled, "all was well."[96] The composer was Ethel Smyth, the early crusader for women's rights, and her opera was *The Wreckers*. She and Walter became warm friends, and although circumstances at the Hofoper prevented her opera from being presented, Walter would later conduct performances of the work in London, shortly after its English premiere under Beecham.

Walter advised Smyth "not to press the matter" of her opera with Mahler just then. In fact, a struggle that had been building for years was reaching a crisis. Since becoming director of the Hofoper, Mahler had given his lifeblood to Vienna, and many Viennese music-lovers knew it. Nevertheless, his enemies had persistently criticized him for spending too much money at the Hofoper, for his choice of casting, for conducting too often outside the city, for writing music they couldn't understand, for being Jewish—in short, for being Mahler. In March Walter remarked on an energetic campaign against Mahler that had begun in the press, "resulting principally from his justly disdainful relations" toward the critics.[97] By the end of May the news had reached the papers: Mahler would be leaving Vienna to take up a position at the Metropolitan Opera in New York. The news was a blow to the musical community, and the officials at the Hofoper scrambled to find a successor. After some anxious months of negotiation, Felix Weingartner, a man whose aesthetic sensibilities differed fundamentally from Mahler's, was named the new director. For his official farewell to Vienna Mahler conducted a performance of his Second Symphony with the Vienna Philharmonic, on November 24.

Fearing the consequences of Mahler's departure early on, when rumors of his resignation began to circulate, Walter wrote to his parents that all Mahler's efforts to get him new productions and premieres might be undone. The "old calamities might return," and, even if only half as bad as before, they would be doubly painful because they would now be *recurring* calamities.[98] The departure also seems to have released some pent-up resentment toward his mentor. "Despite everything that I suffered through him," Walter wrote to his parents shortly after Mahler left, "and perhaps will suffer still (there is a terrible side to him), he is one of the dearest men in the world to me, and will remain so; and despite all the pain, I still owe him an immeasurable heartfelt debt."[99] What suffering was Walter referring to? The question will probably remain unanswered, though Mahler's documented ruthlessness toward other musicians might well have extended to his younger colleague from time to time. Moreover, Mahler's distinct lack of enthusiasm for Walter's music, which the younger composer must often have sensed, would surely have left a wound.

To his friend and protégé Bruno Walter, Mahler wrote a short but touching letter of farewell: "Neither of us need waste words on what we mean to each other.—I know of no one who understands me as well as I feel you do, and I believe that for my part I have entered deep into the mine of your soul. Enclosed is the picture your wife asked for. Best wishes to both of you. Hoping to see you again in May."[100] The promise of seeing his friend again in May no doubt cheered Walter, and the thought of performing without competition from the greatest conductor he had ever known probably held a certain appeal for the younger man. Yet the departure of Mahler—who for so long had been a good friend, a magician at the podium, an inspiration as a composer, and a powerful ally in a notoriously political environment—must also have left Walter feeling awkward, vulnerable, and desolate.

# *Composer and Conductor*

### Vienna, 1908–1910

*Yes, graceful singer, accept the laurel crown;*
*Your song has gained you the master-prize!*
Wagner, *Die Meistersinger von Nürnberg*

Although Walter worried that his premieres and new productions would vanish with the change in directorship at the Hofoper, in reality a number of new works that Mahler had slated for performance fell directly into Walter's lap. Already on January 2, 1908, he found himself conducting the world premiere of Karl Goldmark's new opera, *Ein Wintermärchen,* based on Shakespeare's *A Winter's Tale*. Goldmark's works are little known today, though a handful of his pieces—the aria "Magische Töne," the Violin Concerto, and the "Ländliche Hochzeit" Symphony—have not been entirely consigned to oblivion. When Walter introduced *Ein Wintermärchen* to the Viennese public, however, the seventy-seven-year-old Hungarian-born composer had long been a favorite at the Hofoper, largely through the enormous success of his early opera *Die Königin von Saba,* an opera Walter had already conducted in Riga. With Leo Slezak as Leontes, Anna von Mildenburg as Hermione, Selma Kurz as Perdita, Leopold Demuth as Polixenes, and Richard Mayr as Valentin, the production was anticipated with great eagerness and received wide coverage in newspapers and journals. The composer attended the rehearsals and, according to the *Neue Freie Presse*, found Walter "the best and most sensitive man to carry out his intentions."[1] The opera itself was, for the most part, warmly received. Theodor Helm commented on the care with which Walter had prepared the production and his "extremely spirited conducting," which brought out "all the beauties into the brightest light."[2]

Walter now had a successful premiere to his credit under the new director, and his situation no longer looked so dire. Weingartner and Walter would never be close friends, but they acknowledged each other's talents. Impressed with Walter's performance, Goldmark sang his praises to Weingartner, who had heard his younger colleague in a performance of *Die Walküre* already in November 1907 and "said it had been a great pleasure" to hear him conduct.[3] Meanwhile, Walter's symphony was tentatively scheduled for a performance with the Konzertverein in March (it would be postponed till the following year), and he had become president of the Tonkünstlerverein. Everything seemed to be going his way.

Yet Walter felt alone. Midway through January the papers reported that Mahler had conducted *Tristan* at the Met to great acclaim. Shortly afterward Walter wrote to Pfitzner that he longed for companionship: "since Mahler's departure, it's become quite desolate here, and I might run aground again in the chilly atmosphere surrounding me. You've got to have an elephant's hide not to freeze to death in this terrain."[4] Despite the "chilly atmosphere," Pfitzner had warmed Walter a little by offering to dedicate his Piano Quintet to his friend.

But it was another piano quintet that Walter performed with the Soldat-Röger Quartet in February. The composer was Josef Labor, a blind pianist and organist as well as, miraculously, the editor of Heinrich Biber's violin music, whose pupils included Arnold Schoenberg, Alma Schindler (before she married Mahler), and Julius Bittner. All three pupils would have extensive dealings with Walter over the coming decades, and Bittner's music was to have an immediate impact on Walter's career.

On April 10 Walter gave the premiere (at the Hofoper) of Bittner's *Die rote Gred*, the composer's first staged opera. The work had provoked more than a little curiosity—partly because its thirty-four-year-old author had written the libretto as well as the score (in true Wagnerian fashion); partly because he was a man of law by profession, not a full-time musician, and therefore the event possessed an element of novelty; and partly because he was a native of Vienna and his story took place in Austria, which added the touch of local appeal. Yet for all his manifest talent, Bittner, to judge from the reviews, had not quite mastered his art in this eagerly anticipated work. Karl Schreder, in the racist *Deutsches Volksblatt*, gleefully spread the rumor that Walter had made many cuts in the score and had inserted his own material, much to the detriment of the piece; moreover, he had outdone his model, Mahler, in unnecessarily making the musicians slave away at their task.[5] Some, however, appreciated Walter's efforts; Richard Specht, for example, found much to praise in the conductor and noted that he seemed to be "ascending to the final step in the absolute mastery of conducting"; an interpretive artist of genius, Walter led the performance "with incomparable fire."[6]

Walter soon showed off his "incomparable fire" beyond the borders of Austria, traveling to Prague in May—accompanied by some of his leading singers—to score a triumph with Verdi's *Ballo*, played to a sold-out house. After nearly seven years, Walter could finally feel established as a major light in the musical scene. At the same time, he continued to make new friends among the Viennese intelligentsia. Walter's new acquaintances included the author Arthur Schnitzler and his wife, Olga, who had begun studying voice with Walter as her coach and later gave professional recitals in Vienna. Schnitzler was famous (or infamous) for his plays and stories that delved into sexuality in a manner deemed scandalous by many of his contemporaries, though by our jaded modern standards the works seem tame enough, and Walter seems not to have had any reservations about them. Indeed, in his final year, he remembered an especially close relationship with Schnitzler during this period. "Through [the] years of the first decade of this century," he wrote, "our connection remained one of my strongest contacts with the Viennese intellectual life of that time."[7]

Walter had already admired Arthur Schnitzler's works before getting to know the playwright personally and had recently spent "pleasant hours and days" reading *Der Weg ins Frei*, the author's latest literary creation.[8] The novel follows the activities of the aristocratic composer Georg von Wergenthin—a character, according to Walter, loosely based on the real-life Clemens von Franckenstein, a man who was later to play an active role in Walter's career.[9] A theme continually developed in the novel is the reaction of Viennese Jews to their city's anti-Semitism, a subject that the Jewish author no doubt knew from firsthand experience. The topic must have struck a chord in Walter, though—tight-lipped as he was on such matters—he doesn't elaborate on it in a letter to Olga Schnitzler praising the novel. Yet one potentially telling comment slips through his defenses: he finds the character Heinrich Bermann "extraordinary." It is Bermann who argues for individual, interior solutions to individual problems of race and religion: "Every one's life simply depends on whether or not he finds his mental way out. To do that of course it is necessary to see as clearly as possible into oneself, to throw the searchlight into one's most hidden crannies, to have the courage to be what one naturally is—not to be led into a mistake."[10] The sentiment may well have resonated in the mind of the man who would soon be teaching his elder daughter both about Noah's ark and about the birth of Christ, the mind of the future anthroposophist.[11]

While Walter made new acquaintances, he kept in touch with old friends. The Viennese newspapers regularly reported on Mahler, who periodically returned to Europe to compose and perform. His Seventh Symphony was one of the most important new orchestral pieces presented in 1908, and he traveled to Prague to give the premiere of his latest work on September 19. Walter, who was of course present, remembered the reunion fondly: "the rehearsals and performance . . . provided us with many occasions for lively discussion. . . . We made an expedition by car into the pleasant countryside; we talked together or in groups of friends and family; perfect harmony prevailed."[12] It was also on this occasion that Walter made the acquaintance of the young Otto Klemperer, who would go on to become one of Walter's greatest conducting rivals, especially of the Germanic repertoire.[13]

At the Hofoper, the year 1909 began with a performance of the *Ring*. The production had sparked controversy in Vienna, revolving not around Wagner's ugly prejudices—as is usually the case today—but around the cuts that Weingartner made in the score. He tried to justify the shortened *Ring* in a lengthy article, but many Viennese operagoers resented his presumption in depriving them of several choice passages in the cycle.[14] So when Walter conducted *Die Walküre* in January—despite a partial restoration of material that Weingartner had omitted—audience members responded to the still-remaining cuts with shouts of "Long live the complete *Walküre!*" and "Down with Weingartner!"[15] While the outcry must have been unnerving, Walter probably sympathized with the sentiment. One of Mahler's early decrees as director of the Hofoper was to insist on performing the Wagner operas complete, and the public was not about to yield a measure of the master's score.[16] The *Neue Freie Presse*, listing the exact number of deleted measures, observed with some asperity that the abbreviated performance of *Götterdämmerung* under Schalk ended only ten minutes earlier than usual.[17]

Of necessity, opera continued to be the focus of Walter's energies; in mid-January he gave the Viennese premiere of Xavier Leroux's *Le Chemineau*, a work that the critics instantly demolished. Such reactions no doubt served to increase his desire to become more closely associated with the symphonic repertoire, and he must have felt an edgy excitement when his own contribution to the genre was at last to have its unveiling before the public. Delayed for nearly a year, the performance of his First Symphony in D Minor took place on February 6, 1909, in the Grosser Musiksaal. The Konzertverein Orchestra played Walter's work as the last item in a concert consisting exclusively of premieres. Ferdinand Löwe opened the evening with *Eine Singspiel-Ouvertüre* by the critic Edgar Istel, Jan Brandts-Buys conducted his own *Illyrische Ballade*, and Walter wielded the baton for his own symphony. The work, which survives in neatly copied parts, employs a massive orchestra, and its temporal dimensions are Mahlerian in amplitude.[18] Walter wrote to Pfitzner that the symphony lasted somewhere between fifty and fifty-five minutes, the latter being the proper length—the Adagio would have to be taken as an "Allegro con fuoco," Walter noted, to result in the shorter timing.[19]

The work received enthusiastic applause from the audience, and the following month Walter wrote to his parents of its "colossal success."[20] Yet despite the strong vote of confidence from the public, critical reception of the work was sharply divided. Korngold published his review in a roundup of recent concerts that appeared two weeks after the event. He might have delayed it deliberately, since writing the review seems to have caused him pain. After all, for Walter the conductor, Korngold had nothing but the highest praise. But Walter the composer was another matter: "His new symphony did not make an impression on us that was substantially more pleasing than that made previously by his chamber music. . . . Witness, right off, the main theme of the first movement in D minor, which, over 'bitter' harmonies, tries to extend itself temporally in Mahler's manner, but simply meanders laboriously, thereby having little significance. The theme of the Adagio offers a similar picture. But even the development, the structuring, indeed the use of materials—skilled as the composer is in this—are lacking in clarity and deeper inner logic." Korngold owned that Walter's piece was not devoid of the occasional "interesting detail" or "stimulating episode," and he especially admired the "demonic" last movement; nevertheless, the work seemed misguided in its determination to shun earlier models. It was the "music of the modern conductor," a genre written by those who seek originality above all, because they "know the literature too well."[21]

Korngold's review was no real surprise; he had never liked any of Walter's music. Still, the harsh verdict must have wounded Walter. Few are impervious to the sting of a negative review, least of all in a prominent local newspaper. Other reviewers, if less brutal than Korngold, also felt that Walter was incapable of realizing his compositional ideal (a criticism, incidentally, that would be leveled at Mahler's music for decades to come).[22] One important exception was Richard Specht, whose assessment of the symphony for *Die Musik* was overflowing in its praise. The D minor symphony had "achieved a thunderous victory, under the masterly and persuasive conducting of the composer." It was a "weighty" piece, "compelling through its musical abundance," but nevertheless a work "not easily accessible, thanks to its gigantic dimensions." No doubt aware of Korngold's objections, Specht noted that, despite the difficulties the work presented to the listeners, "there wasn't the least objection to such an ecstatic creation," which "swelled expansively" and didn't shy away from roughness or sonic excess. This was true not only of the two crowd-pleasers, the "life-loving Waltz-Scherzo" and the eerily demonic finale (both of which excited loud cheers), but also of the opening two movements, which demanded more attention from the listeners. The audience intently followed the relentlessly grim first movement, which "offered no solace" and suppressed "every liberating sense of happiness with an iron fist," as well as the second movement, which allowed the "sense of happiness" to break free at last. "Indeed, at every moment one was conscious of music—even where, on first hearing, the motivic and architectonic coherence became lost—and one sensed a music whose inner urgency communicated itself to everyone." Walter's piece was "the direct expression of a personality," and artistically, notwithstanding any objections, this was the crucial point.[23]

Walter was probably too busy to ruminate over the reviews—whether encouraging or dismissive—for very long. By March 3 he found himself in London, giving his London debut with the Philharmonic Society at Queen's Hall. The centerpiece of his program was Schumann's "Spring" Symphony, the work with which he'd had such success at his first Nicolai Concert. The response in London was no less enthusiastic. The London *Times* said his performance "showed that he knows exactly what he wants from the orchestra and is able to secure it. What he most wants is tremendous rhythmic vigour; and this he got in the leaping subject of the scherzo and throughout the *finale*. But it was not all, for he kept a perfect balance of tone throughout the slow beautiful movement, and succeeded in making Schumann's orchestration sound unusually lucid and expressive."[24] Also on the program was a work by the Englishwoman who had visited the Hofoper in the hope that Mahler would put on her opera. Genuinely impressed by Ethel Smyth's work, Walter included the overture to her opera *The Wreckers* on his program. Smyth, who was present at the concert, came out to enjoy an ovation at the end of the piece. Emil Sauer joined Walter for a traversal of Beethoven's "Emperor" Concerto, and the concert concluded with Beethoven's "Leonore" Overture no. 3. Walter wrote to his parents of his "sensational success" in London and of the offer he'd received to conduct there again in November and December.[25]

Almost immediately after his return to Vienna, he gave the premiere of his Sonata for Piano and Violin in A Major on March 9. He obviously thought highly of the work, for it became the only purely instrumental work of his to appear in print.[26] Arnold Rosé presented it on a program that included Schumann's String Quartet in F Major and, with help from assisting artists, Mendelssohn's Octet. Rosé, to whom the work was dedicated, played the violin part from manuscript.

To the modern listener, the sonata is extraordinary in several ways. First and foremost, it shows that Walter was fully capable of writing serious music. This is not the work of a dabbler. Almost nothing in any of the voices is written merely for the sake of serving as an accompaniment to "the melody," for the motives and countermotives are always in play, always developing. The effect is perhaps closest to what Brahms achieved, though Walter's texture is even denser—one is at times reminded of an Isaac or a Bach working through a particularly intricate stretch of counterpoint—and his emotional outpourings sound almost utterly unrestrained. The rhythmically incisive, wailing first theme and the expansive second theme weave continually in and out of the fabric of the opening movement, as do many of the transitional and subordinate motives. But the effect of this continual development is anything but pedantic; a very personal voice runs through the movement, and through the piece as a whole, expressing extremes of pain, fear, rapture, and glory—with *espressivo* the most frequent marking. At one point in the opening movement, the piano alone plays with a three-note descending chromatic phrase that, surprisingly for this early date, seems to anticipate a key passage in Mahler's Ninth.[27] The second movement, which Walter recalled fondly in his later years, begins with a quiet, eerie passage that gives way to a section reminiscent of the famous Habanera from *Carmen*. Here, however, the mood is fundamentally different from what Bizet conjures up, for while there may be a touch of erotic seduction in the little rhythmic dance performed by the piano and violin, the seducer is of the Mephistophelian variety, inviting the listener into a dark realm teeming with demons. The final movement, arguably the most challenging interpretively, is a Moderato (perhaps a compromise between the Mahlerian *adagio* and the standard sprightly finale), and again it is the highly personal statement of a man who had already suffered much and enjoyed much.

Specht, perhaps predictably, gave the piece a sterling review. It was a "work of sweet and mature inwardness; music of a man who listens within, thoughtful, dreamily blissful—though also, to be sure, a work that is sometimes startled by sudden visions, breathing heavily, fearful, until it is soothed again to a state of tranquillity." While acknowledging a certain "brittleness" in the piece, which might "frighten off superficial listeners," Specht found it inconceivable that musicians would be insensitive to "what has been lived through and felt in this torrent of sound."[28]

As a composer, Bruno Walter was now reaching his peak. His most ambitious works had their unveiling in 1909, and the critics were beginning to take him seriously as a creative artist. Richard Specht, who had already evinced a serious interest in Walter's music on more than one occasion, ran an article in *Die Musik* entitled "The Young Viennese Composers," calling attention to those new composers who deserved encouragement and, more important, who needed support from publishers. Assuming a place alongside Zemlinsky, Schoenberg, Schreker, Bittner, and others, Walter had the honor of being the first composer under discussion, and one of Specht's most valuable observations concerned Walter's relationship to Mahler.[29] Although Walter's years of working with Mahler were, Specht observed, a great boon for the young conductor, they also carried with them a peril, for Walter's own personality was in danger of being dominated by Mahler's. Walter had come to imitate not only Mahler the musician but also Mahler the man, copying the older man's tricks of speech and physical gestures. Walter must have realized that the stronger musician's personality threatened to overpower his own, and, Specht conjectured, it was perhaps only when Mahler left Vienna that Walter was free to break away from his mentor's influence. Despite the inevitable pain he would have felt at losing his friend, he might also have breathed a sigh of relief: "In his music, especially in his new Sonata for Piano and Violin, one feels in certain passages as if the sounds were coming from a man who has escaped from a terrible oppression and who now, trembling afterward in anxiety, nevertheless sings his quiet song with inspiration. . . . In this regard, Walter is the only one for whom Mahler's departure has been profitable."[30] Walter could now be recognized for his own conducting, which carried on the traditions of Mahler, and could develop more as a composer with his own voice. "There is a corner in his soul in which demons dwell," Specht wrote, adding that although the demonic side of his personality had not vanished completely, a new element of tranquillity had entered Walter's more recent music.

But Mahler still loomed large in his life, and Walter's reputation as a concert conductor reached new heights when, in late October, he directed two performances of Mahler's Third Symphony with the Konzertverein Orchestra. To help the audience approach this massive work, Walter wrote a short essay for the inaugural issue of *Der Merker*, a music journal edited by his most vocal supporter, Richard Specht. Its central concern was the extent to which Mahler's symphony follows a program. The pieces, of course, originally bore descriptive titles (such as "Pan Awakens; Summer Marches In" and "What the Flowers of the Field Tell Me"); but Mahler did away with them after the first performances, wanting the music to be heard and judged as music, not as a story translated into symphonic sounds. Nevertheless, Walter pointed out, the titles were not without value as a guide; they had to be understood simply as starting points for the imagination. The idea was not to worry over exactly what the flowers of the field told us but, rather, to think "of everything that graciously moves the soul with gentle loveliness, with modest charm." The listener was to think not so much of the particular god Pan awakening as of the Dionysian ecstasy at the beginning of spring, "the wild, compelling force of Nature," "the triumphal procession of all blossoming life."[31] The symphony worked as "absolute" music, but a strong programmatic current ran through it. As in his commentary on the Fourth Symphony, Walter had it both ways.[32]

The two performances of Mahler's Third marked another milestone in his conducting career. This was the first time that Mahler's Third had been heard in Vienna without the composer at the helm, and some members of the audience—the critics especially—obviously approached the concert with skepticism. It is an enormous work whose first movement alone lasts longer than some nineteenth-century symphonies in their entirety. Up to this point, the demanding piece had had the conducting "magician" Mahler to work wonders with his materials. Could another conductor create the same magic? Walter proved himself up to the challenge. He was Mahler's "most animated and animating agent," wrote the *Neue Freie Presse* after the first concert. "The symphony is indebted to him for an exemplary and masterly rendition, and he is indebted to it for his greatest conducting triumph."[33] Korngold reviewed the repeat performance and found the opening movement more accessible than when the piece had previously been performed under Mahler himself. Without attributing his newfound appreciation of the opening movement specifically to Walter (it was more likely due to a better acquaintance with the score), he did credit Walter with interpreting "the work of his friend and master 'as if it were his own piece.' His heart is always beating along with each musical beat as he wields the baton, most especially on this occasion. His talent as a conductor, more promising every day, seemed to have increased formidably."[34] Though Walter never recorded the Third or performed it in the United States, it remained in his repertoire for many years (he conducted it with the Concertgebouw Orchestra as late as 1937), and he was widely regarded as one of its great interpreters.

At the end of the year, Walter traveled to London for his return engagement with the Philharmonic Society, and his repertoire included—along with standard works by Beethoven, Strauss, and Brahms—the overture to Ethel Smyth's *The Wreckers*, Goldmark's Violin Concerto, Liszt's *Mazeppa*, and Tchaikovsky's "Pathétique." On this occasion he had more leisure to explore the city and mix with its inhabitants, finding both very much to his taste. He visited the theater, taking particular delight in performances of operetta: "the charm of the dancing, the men's comedy, the loveliness of the women, and the elegant polish of the entire performance is unsurpassed," he wrote to his parents. But his appreciation was not wholly uncritical. "In serious works, by contrast," he added, "the English artists seem weaker." All in all, the friendliness he encountered among the English touched him deeply, and he felt that London could someday be "a kind of second home" for him—a feeling he'd "never had in Vienna over the last nine years."[35]

But Vienna was his home for now, and on his return he continued to advance the cause of new music. Joining members of the Soldat-Röger Quartet, he took part in the premiere of Bruno Morpurgo's Trio in F Major for Piano, Violin, and Cello, on January 15, 1910. Then, filling in for an indisposed Oskar Nedbal, he presided over the first Viennese performance of Guido Peters's Symphony in E Minor, played by the Tonkünstler Orchestra on

February 3. More important, he made more of his own compositions known to the world, for Universal published his settings of six songs to poems by Eichendorff early in the year.[36] The publication coincided with a concert of modern music given on February 8 at the Society for Art and Culture, an organization whose musical events were overseen by Paul Stefan, future biographer of both Mahler and Walter. The other composers featured at the recital were Anton Webern—a musician rarely associated with Walter—and Karl Weigl, while the singers for the evening included Gertrude Förstel (from the Hofoper),[37] Martha Winternitz-Dorda, and the Hungarian baritone Franz Steiner, to whom three of Walter's new songs—"Musikantengruss," "Der junge Ehemann," and "Der Soldat"—were dedicated.

Though written about the same time as the Violin Sonata, the songs show a far more intimate side of Walter's musical personality. The three songs dedicated to Steiner are written for middle voice range, while the remaining three ("Die Lerche," "Des Kindes Schlaf," and "Elfe"), dedicated to Walter's wife, are for a high voice.[38] All six have been recorded in recent times, the first three by Dietrich Fischer-Dieskau (who, early in his career, sang under Walter, and whose artistry Walter much admired), the remainder by MariAnne Häggander, who also recorded "Musikantengruss."[39]

As one might expect, most of the songs are marked by sensuous lyricism, though Walter was capable of adapting his style to suit his subject matter—witness the rough, declamatory style of "Der Soldat" ("The Soldier"). A more typically Walterian piece, however, is "Musikantengruss" ("Musicians' Greeting"), a gentle song that opens with an almost Debussian piano introduction, then shifts into a folklike idiom, with a grace-noted, pseudo-naive melody. Even in an outwardly simple song like this, however, Walter is striving for the ecstatic; the word *seligen* ("blessed") is treated to a rapturous high F-sharp, held for more than two measures.[40] It is also worth mentioning that "Die Lerche" ("The Lark"), dedicated to Elsa, begins with words that might have struck a poignant chord in the mind of the former singer: a lark laments that it cannot sing in its enclosed space.

On his third trip across the Channel, Walter was destined for Covent Garden. Although only a few recordings of Walter's interpretations of the Prelude and "Liebestod" from *Tristan und Isolde* have survived, the opera had special importance for Walter for much of his professional life, and on several occasions he performed it when making a debut at an opera house. So it was at Covent Garden on February 21, 1910, two days after Beecham had opened the season with the English premiere of Strauss's new opera *Elektra*. The Belgian tenor Jacques Urlus sang Tristan, while Zdenka Fassbender, from Munich, assumed the role of Isolde. Joining Walter from the Vienna Hofoper was Friedrich Weidemann as Kurwenal.

Yet Walter's Covent Garden debut seems to have been less than a smash hit. Apparently there was only a single rehearsal for *Tristan*, so the performance no doubt suffered from underpreparation.[41] *The Times* reviewer was somewhat disappointed with Fassbender's "pedestrian" Isolde, and even Walter earned only qualified praise.[42] In March, however, he conducted another performance of *Tristan*, this time with Anna Bahr-Mildenburg as Isolde, and his contribution to the production now received a glowing report: "Herr Bruno Walter conducted with real insight and skill, and the beauty of the orchestral playing was among the most remarkable features of the performance."[43]

But *Tristan* was not the only opera Walter conducted at Covent Garden. Ethel Smyth finally had the pleasure of hearing her opera *The Wreckers* performed by Walter on March 1. The score has plainly derivative stretches (Avis's Carmen-like first aria and several Wagnerian and Straussian passages as the work proceeds), but much of the music reveals an original voice, and Walter remained a loyal champion of Smyth's music for decades; in fact, through Walter she became the first woman to conduct the Berlin Philharmonic. When asked for his opinion of Smyth's music in 1912, he wrote an enlightened reply to a sensitive question:

> I consider Ethel Smyth a composer of quite special significance, who is certain of a permanent place in musical history. Real musical productivity is so rare that we are entitled to ask whether the impression of originality created by these compositions is not attributable to their femininity. Our ears are trained immediately to detect national differences in music, but are too inexperienced to detect sex characteristics. If we had a hundred female composers we might be able to establish a distinction between male and female music. I am, however, convinced that Dr. Ethel Smyth's thematic charm proceeds in an essential degree from her womanliness, though her work is at the same time English through and through. Yet in her case the sex question is comparatively unimportant in the presence of a talent so strong, thematic invention so original, and a temperament so deep and warm.[44]

The subtle balance that Walter strikes between artistic characteristics as a result of gender or ethnicity and of individual genius reveals an imagination that, from our vantage point, seems remarkably prescient.

Upon Walter's return to Vienna, preparations for the new two-act opera by Julius Bittner, *Der Musikant*—which took place in mid-April—occupied much of the conductor's attention. After that, with barely enough time to catch his breath, Walter took part in the first concert sponsored by the journal *Der Merker*, on April 16. Among the works performed was Walter's Violin Sonata, which Korngold had not reviewed at its premiere. He attended the *Merker* concert, heard the Violin Sonata performed by Walter and Rosé, and, uncharacteristically, enjoyed both the performance and the piece, judging it "superior to everything else" he'd heard by Walter.[45] It must have given Walter some satisfaction to receive, at last, a predominantly positive review from a critic who, over the previous seven years, could scarcely find an encouraging word to say about any of his compositions.

Perhaps inspired by his recent successes, Walter directed his thoughts toward music for the stage. He entertained the possibility of collaborating with Hugo von Hofmannsthal, the author now best known for his librettos to the operas of Richard Strauss. (In fact, Strauss and Hofmannsthal were just then collaborating on their most successful opera, *Der Rosenkavalier*.) Though Walter had met Hofmannsthal, his senior by two years, as early as 1896, there was a certain distance between them. Now he wrote directly to the poet-playwright, suggesting themes for operatic treatment and hoping that Hofmannsthal might provide a libretto.[46]

Although nothing in the operatic vein seems to have followed this overture, by June 1910 Walter had become involved in a new adaptation of *King Oedipus* that Hofmannsthal was working on with the already famous director Max Reinhardt, whom Walter had met in Berlin around 1895, when the two men were dating two sisters.[47] After a hugely successful—if controversial—performance in Munich on September 25, the production of *Oedipus* traveled to a number of large European cities, including Berlin, Cologne, and Vienna. Although the reviewers mention the music ("a mysterious music bursting out of the palace," "fanfares blast from behind the stage, followed by strange musical noises"[48]), they omit the composer's name, which was probably not listed on the program. It seems an odd omission, though certainly no odder than the omission of Hofmannsthal as translator, which puzzled the reviewer of the *Allgemeine Zeitung*. It's likely, in any case, that Walter's music was used.

While the few references to the music are tantalizing, the pieces were probably insubstantial works. Walter himself made only the most modest claims for them. If "carried out by a conductor with dramatic talent," Walter wrote to Hofmannsthal, the music could be "very effective. . . . I think it proper to recommend, above all, discretion in the execution of the music, since the lesser evil would be if one were too little aware of it."[49] And in an interview given by Walter, together with Alfred Roller and Hofmannsthal, on the topic of Max Reinhardt, one gets the distinct impression that Reinhardt's treatment of background music rubbed Walter the wrong way. For example, Walter listened to a description of Reinhardt's treatment of Humperdinck's incidental music to *The Merchant of Venice*, a production that opened with the ringing noises of Venice, followed by more clearly articulated sounds of gondoliers and masqueraders and then, at a particular spot in the text, by an unexpected, rough march motive. "It is certainly very fine and artful directing," Walter commented, "although to me," he added, "perhaps precisely because I am a musician, not even this way of using music is very appealing." Yet he admired Reinhardt's "incredible talent for transporting himself into the author's workshop" and his being able to reproduce the mood of an author in keeping with the period in which a work was written. It was, he said, very much what he himself strove for when giving a performance of a piece of music.[50] All politeness aside, though, there was already a palpable friction between Walter and Reinhardt at this early date, a friction that would surface on subsequent occasions and reassert itself even after Reinhardt's death—for although Walter gave a memorial concert for Reinhardt in 1943, Reinhardt's son later declared that the family would much have preferred Toscanini to Walter, "with whom [Reinhardt] had been at odds more than once."[51]

For the performances of *Oedipus*, Reinhardt caused a critical stir by employing a huge chorus and by staging the play in enormous auditoriums to create a grand effect. Something of a musical counterpart took place later that year in Munich, an event of unprecedented scale in the history of the symphony. On September 12, 1910, Mahler was back from New York for the summer to give the premiere of his Eighth Symphony, the "Symphony of a Thousand," so named—though not with Mahler's blessing—by the promoter of the concert, Emil Gutmann, because of the vast forces, both instrumental and vocal, required to perform the work. Even by Mahlerian standards, this was *big*. The piece had been in preparation for some months, and Walter had helped with the selection and coaching of soloists.[52] According to the author Siegfried Lipiner, a friend of both Mahler and Walter, at least some of the rehearsals for the soloists took place at Walter's home on Theobaldgasse, with Walter listening critically as Mahler sat at the piano directing the rehearsals, often checking with his younger colleague on matters of tempo ("Is the tempo right like this, my dear Walter? Or would you find it better if it were taken more slowly?").[53] Leading musicians and cultural figures came from afar to be present at the premiere in Munich, among them Willem Mengelberg, Oskar Fried, Gerhart Hauptmann, Lilli Lehmann, Max Reinhardt, Guido Adler, Hermann Bahr and his wife, Anna von Mildenburg (now Bahr-Mildenburg), Leopold Stokowski, as well as Walter, who felt that the sublime, overwhelming performance "marked a culminating point in Mahler's life."[54]

The Eighth Symphony was not the only significant event in Mahler's life in 1910. Mahler turned fifty that year. To celebrate the composer in general, and his fiftieth birthday in particular (few could have guessed it was his last), Paul Stefan put together a collection of tributes to Mahler. Among the many prominent contributors was, of course, Walter, who, having been asked to write an essay on the premiere of the Eighth Symphony, instead submitted a long, open letter to his friend and mentor.[55] Though he admitted that he might lack a certain distance from the subject at hand—normally expected in a critical evaluation—he flatly refused even to attempt a dispassionate discussion of his friend's works, declaring rather his "impassioned, ardent love for them."[56] But why did Walter "love" them? "Is it because the works, in their way, seek solutions to insoluble problems? Because they sing these problems? Because the solution to these problems is perhaps to sing them—at least in this earthly existence? Do your trumpets blow down the walls and ramparts surrounding the eternal secrets? Or do I love your works because they are 'beautiful music'?"[57] An implicit "Yes" is the answer to all these rhetorical questions. For Walter, "all pure music signifies, in its way, a solution to metaphysical problems," and Mahler's music "seems to speak with particular intensity of the secrets of our existence." These were, in fact, matters that Mahler himself had discussed with Walter, and clearly the two had similar views on music's ability to answer life's most pressing questions. In a letter to Walter of 1909 Mahler wrote: "Strange! When I hear music— even while I am conducting—I hear quite specific answers to all my questions—and am completely clear and certain. Or rather, I feel quite distinctly that they are not questions at all."[58] Along with the metaphysical reasons for his great love of Mahler's music, Walter added another, revealing reason: he found it "unfashionable." There was "no pure horizontality in the polyphony," nor were there any "purely harmonic, a-melodic lapses into mysterious relations between tones."[59] Even the huge formal structures seemed admirably retrograde to Walter in their sensitivity to proportional beauty. In Walter's view, the innovations were not so much radical departures from the symphonic tradition as extensions of the traditional boundaries to their very limits: the development section might grow to twice its usual size, or the coda might take on a life of its own, but the basic structure remained intact.

Walter's open letter ends with his recounting a dream he'd had about Mahler some years before. The dream reveals, almost more clearly than anything else Walter ever wrote about Mahler, how he viewed his ability as an artist as compared with Mahler's: "I went walking and saw you high above me, climbing up a high mountain on a steep path; after a while, blinded by the light, I had to close my eyes. When I opened them again, after searching for some time, I found you in an entirely different area on the mountain, making your way up a still-higher path. Again I closed my eyes, and again opened them, didn't find you, then caught sight of you again striving to attain a wholly different side. This occurred time and time again. I really dreamed this dream and believe that anyone who understands you will recognize its symbolism and say it was a truthful dream."[60] It is somewhat sad to think of Walter, in the deepest recesses of his subconscious mind, always viewing Mahler as on a plane higher than his own, able to see paths for exploration that Walter couldn't discover by himself. And this might well have been a critical year for Walter as a composer. He was wrestling with another symphony in 1910, a work that he evidently had trouble finishing.[61] It was never performed, and not long after writing his letter to Mahler, he seems to have ceased composing altogether.

In the opera house Walter kept active as always, but while his work at the Hofoper was important to him, he found it frustrating that his activities as a conductor were in large measure confined to works for the stage. His parents, upset to learn that Oskar Fried and Franz Schalk had been named as conductors for the Berlin and Vienna premieres of Mahler's Eighth, apparently blamed Mahler for the choice. Walter must have been equally distressed, but he came to his friend's defense: "Both [Fried and Schalk] are conductors of organizations that give performances of that kind—I'm just a theater conductor. Of course, when one knows my talent and then considers that of all my colleagues (Mahler excepted), one is astounded at the rapid progress of their careers and the slow pace of mine."[62]

Walter may have been frustrated with what he perceived as the slow pace of his career, but no one could accuse him of slacking off as an artist. The 1910 fall season was particularly busy for Walter and his longstanding colleague Arnold Rosé. The first of their immensely popular traversals of the Beethoven sonatas for violin and piano took place in mid-October. The two musicians also played in the second concert sponsored by *Der Merker*, given on December 11. On this occasion they were joined by Rosé's regular cellist Friedrich Buxbaum for the premiere of a new piano trio by a thirteen-year-old genius whose career would be linked with Walter's on several occasions.

How, one wonders, did Walter feel about playing the music of Erich Wolfgang Korngold, the son of the critic who had savaged Walter's compositions for years? Perhaps surprisingly, Walter seems to have held no grudges; he championed Erich's compositions from the beginning of the young composer's career to the end. Nevertheless, when he first examined the score, he must have been somewhat taken aback to see music written with such astonishing facility and originality by a mere boy. The history of music affords perhaps only two comparable examples of such prodigious talent: Mozart and Mendelssohn. An anecdote related by the Viennese critic Julian Sternberg in 1916 reveals the unusual circumstances surrounding Walter's earliest appreciation of the boy's talents, around 1908. Having recently moved into the house on Theobaldgasse, Walter found himself the downstairs neighbor of Julius Korngold, which must have made for some awkward encounters on the staircase. Korngold's young boy, born in 1897, was already allowing his imagination free reign at the piano, and his improvisations proved distracting to the conductor, who was "involuntarily" forced to listen because the boy was "a genius."[63]

Richard Specht, who understandably filled in for Julius Korngold as the reviewer for the *Neue Freie Presse* when covering the Piano Trio, praised the young composer's rich invention, his compelling structures, and his individual harmonic world.[64] The familiar earmarks of Korngold's musical language were already in place, immediately setting him apart from his contemporaries. Walter's compositions, by contrast, though full of emotional depth and joy and angst, never seem to spring spontaneously from an ever facile mind as Korngold's do. Not that an impression of spontaneity is a prerequisite for great music: neither Brahms nor Mahler nor even Beethoven creates a feeling of easy creativity. Nevertheless, for a composer not in their league, the appearance of a wunderkind like Erich Wolfgang Korngold must have been disconcerting. Walter, like his contemporaries, recognized Korngold's genius. He probably felt not only admiration but also a certain sympathy for the boy, whose father, as Walter knew all too well, was nothing if not critical. Even decades later, Julius could mention casually to Walter that, although Erich had been one of the most talented composers of his generation, he was "of course no Mahler."[65]

By the end of 1910, after much fruitless negotiation with the Hofoper, Weingartner decided to step down from the directorship. His successor, Hans Gregor, was—contrary to custom—not a conductor at all, but a stage director from the Komische Oper in Berlin who'd had some experience as an actor. His appointment as Weingartner's successor baffled and offended many—Walter among them, since he felt he could have filled the position and was wounded that the court chamberlain, Count Montenuovo, had preferred Gregor to him. Hofmannsthal described the appointment as "frivolous," an opinion in which Walter, who viewed Gregor as a "laughable buffoon," wholeheartedly concurred. But frustrated as he was at the Hofoper, Walter found some comfort in his new contract there, which allowed him much-needed time to compose, to spend with his daughters, to walk, to read.[66] Nevertheless, he was surely on the lookout, as he was during most of his tenure in Vienna, for better employment elsewhere, and a poetic death in Munich would soon turn his thoughts toward leaving the city with which he'd carried on a love–hate relationship for nearly a decade.

# *Premiere Performances*
## Vienna and Munich, 1911–1912

*I stand here waiting for my friend,*
*Waiting for the last farewell.*
After Mong-Kao-Jen, from *Das Lied von der Erde*

The year 1911 played a crucial role in Walter's life in many ways.
His close friend Mahler would leave him forever, and he would be
left bearing the great composer's mantle. It was a burden he bore
gladly, though it might ultimately have proved an impediment to
his composing. A more certain impediment was his assumption of
the duties of director of the Vienna Singakademie, a position held
by Brahms himself nearly half a century before. One of the singers
in Walter's chorus, Mary Komorn-Rebhan, detailed his methods
of conveying ideas to singers and of extracting from them the interpretations he desired. Her account, entitled *Was wir von Bruno
Walter lernten* ("What We Learned from Bruno Walter"), is the
first book-length work on Walter, an invaluable source—though
written quite obviously by a passionate enthusiast.[1] Nevertheless,
as a firsthand document, the book throws light on several facets of
Walter's approach to choral music. Working largely with amateurs,
he managed to breathe new life into the performers: "something
compelling emanates from him," Komorn-Rebhan wrote, "that

raises each member above his abilities; he takes fear away from every individual and gives him courage and self-confidence, suggesting to him, as it were, that he can perfectly well do everything required of him. The result is that one *actually can* do it."[2]

Other nontheatrical events drew Walter away from the Hofoper in 1911. In February he headed south for his first engagement in Rome, where he conducted the Orchestra of the Society of Santa Cecilia at the Augusteum in a concert of Berlioz's *Symphonie fantastique*, Richard Strauss's *Don Quixote*, and Goldmark's "Sakuntala" Overture. The composer and critic Alberto Gasco wrote a lengthy, complimentary review of the concert for *La Tribuna*, and the management engaged Walter for two further concerts in the coming season.[3]

Although Walter did not include his own compositions in his Roman programs, they were steadily reaching a wider audience. Gertrude Förstel, still one of the regular sopranos at the Vienna Hofoper, traveled to Munich to give a recital on February 10 in which she offered two songs by Walter, characterized as "charming" by Rudolf Louis and "insignificant" by the anonymous critic of the *Allgemeine Zeitung*.[4] Two days later, also in Munich, a chamber music recital of the Münchener Tonkünstler-Verein included Walter's Piano Trio on its program. Louis, reviewing the trio, was patently less impressed with it than he'd been with the songs, tactfully observing that Walter, though a "thoroughbred musician," perhaps lacked "creative talent."[5] Later that month, on February 22, Walter had occasion to conduct his Symphony in D Minor again, this time in Strasbourg (then part of Germany), where Pfitzner, who had been instrumental in arranging the concert, was the regular conductor.[6] Pfitzner's assistant, whom Walter met, was the young Wilhelm Furtwängler, whose path and Walter's would cross on many subsequent occasions. Performing the symphony again was an important event for Walter. Despite Korngold's negative remarks about it, the symphony had been enthusiastically received by many, and it was certainly Walter's most ambitious composition to date. The chance to expose it to a wider public, perhaps with a better orchestra, must have filled him with new hopes for his career as a composer, though the critical reception was not encouraging.[7] Gustav Altmann, who had bludgeoned Walter's Piano Quintet in 1906, reported on the concert for *Die Musik*, where Specht had earlier lavished praise on the symphony. Altmann once more seized the opportunity to put the would-be composer in his place, writing that the symphony was "emphatically rejected" in Strasbourg.[8] This was apparently the last time the symphony was performed.

A work still presented regularly, however, surely occupied Walter's attention in March, for he was preparing a performance of Handel's *Messiah*— in German, with plenty of cuts—which the Singakademie performed on April 4. It was the first concert they were to give under Walter as their new director, and he had a great deal to teach them. Above all, he wanted to convince them that the common association of oratorio with boredom was a fiction, that boring *performances* were the problem, not boring *music*. Walter knew that, to avoid dullness, it was critical to bring out the meaning of the words, and he expected his singers to create ever varying nuances to reflect the ever changing text. His manner, polite but firm, was not devoid of the occasional barb ("You're singing 'Behold the Lamb of God' as if it were on a signpost that read: 'This way to the Lamb of God'! Such a dearth of expression will not do!"[9]). Walter was also aware that a literal reading of the notes on the page would result in a deadly performance, and, as if in anticipation of baroque performance practice later in the century, deliberately overdotted certain passages, giving them a needed extra spring.[10] While Walter went through almost every phrase in detail, finding the right way to extract the proper affect from his singers, he seems to have had an especially adventurous (if anachronistic) approach to the "Hallelujah" chorus. It began with "a fairly measured *allegro moderato*," not too loud, and gradually worked into a clamorous frenzy, with the tempo having nearly doubled by the end. Komorn-Rebhan was ecstatic: "the floor under my feet seemed to fall away, and the glistening gilded ceiling seemed to open, and it was as if we were singing 'Hallelujah!' to the Creator himself."[11]

Along with this eighteenth-century masterpiece, newly minted works were being offered to Viennese music-lovers. Among the current offerings, two operatic premieres stood out in the spring of 1911. One was Richard Strauss's new work, *Der Rosenkavalier*, which Schalk conducted; the other, Debussy's *Pelléas et Mélisande*, which Walter introduced to Vienna. Mahler had considered giving a performance of *Pelléas* at the Hofoper during his tenure there, and the more progressive listeners felt that the work, which had had its premiere in Paris in 1902, should be performed at the great Austrian institution.[12] In December 1910 Debussy himself had come to Vienna to conduct a concert of his music, leaving a strong impression on the city's musical community. The time was favorable for bringing the French master's opera to the Hofoper, though the work was radically different from the prevailing Germanic and Italian fare at the house.

Walter's preparations for *Pelléas*, however, were carried out under extremely trying conditions—"anxiety, care, and grief" were his "daily bread" —as reports of Mahler's decaying health began to arrive with alarming frequency.[13] Bedridden in Paris, Mahler languished. His fever went up; it went down. He lost his appetite; he regained it. Overall, the symptoms were unencouraging. "I took a leave of absence and went to Paris with Mahler's sister, Justine Rosé," Walter recalled. "I found Mahler in a hopeless condition in a sanatorium in Neuilly. I spoke to him of his works, but he replied with bitterness, and I thought it best just to entertain him, which I partly succeeded in doing."[14] Though seriously ill, Mahler managed to return to Vienna. Walter visited him every free minute and was present to witness, on May 18, his friend's final moments on his deathbed, to see "his horrible struggle with death and his deliverance."[15] When asked for details of Mahler's last days, however, Walter couldn't bring himself to discuss the matter. "Let me just be silent about this horribly tragic occurrence," he wrote to Pfitzner, adding, somewhat mysteriously, "Perhaps I'll tell you someday *how* tragic."[16]

The day after Mahler's death, Walter, along with Arnold Rosé, Karl Moll, and Wilhelm Legler, watched the lid close upon Mahler's coffin, then followed it to the chapel in Grinzing. The funeral was scheduled for Monday, May 22, at 4:30, to allow members of the Hofoper to pay their last respects after their rehearsal for *Pelléas*.[17] To Alma, whose own health suffered after the funeral, Walter wrote a heartening letter of condolence: "The hardest part of the burden that fate has laid on your shoulders is still before you: to continue to live—for the child, the works, and everything that you possess through the long years of spiritual commerce with [Mahler]. He would also have fully approved of your nurturing your own talent. Art, to be sure, is a surrogate; that's how he viewed it as well. Our lives, so cold and dissonant, allow us in only a limited way to pour our ardent feelings into the world as love and to extend ourselves fully into the human sphere. It must be through art that we satisfy the greater part of our need for love." As for Walter's own sense of loss and his commitment to Mahler's music, there could be no doubt: "I have become uprooted and alone because of his death, but I won't grieve over that to you. I'll only say what you probably know: that I shall remain his . . . and that my ardent love for him, which has warmed my very soul every day since I first met him, will be active on the path that Nature has chosen for me: as protector and prophet of his work."[18] Less than a month after Mahler's death, Walter had apparently been selected to give the premiere performance of *Das Lied von der Erde*.[19]

With Mahler's prolonged illness, the premiere of *Pelléas et Mélisande* (in German) had been postponed several times. It took place, at last, on May 23. A widely covered event, it marked Hans Gregor's directorial debut at the Vienna Hofoper, and he earned the critics' respect for tackling a difficult work that his predecessor Weingartner had selected. Maeterlinck's tenebrous story found its ideal counterpart in Debussy's dark score, but for the Viennese the music was far too strange, too gloomy and static. Karl Schreder, of the *Deutsches Volksblatt*, lauded the performance rather than the work ("much ado about nothing"), remarking that Walter had "spent great effort on the production of this new musical work, for which he will certainly receive thanks from Vienna's musical modernists"[20]—a needed reminder that Walter, even at this phase of his career, was still associated with avant-garde trends.

The European musical community, still in shock over the death of Mahler, soon lost another of its leading conductors—Felix Mottl, whose romantic dying days are the stuff of legend. A renowned interpreter of Mozart and Wagner, Mottl began conducting at Bayreuth already in Wagner's lifetime and eventually became a Bayreuth institution. (Walter himself, during his student days, heard Mottl there.) In 1903 he became Generalmusikdirektor in the capital of Bavaria. While conducting his favorite opera, *Tristan*, in Munich's Hoftheater on June 21, 1911, Mottl sensed his imminent collapse and discreetly passed his baton to an assistant conductor. Two more conductors were called in to finish the opera. Mottl, meantime, was taken to the hospital. The Isolde of the production, Zdenka Fassbender (also the Isolde at Walter's Covent Garden debut), was romantically involved with Mottl, who had recently settled an ugly divorce suit and announced his engagement to Fassbender.[21] During his final days, in his hospital room, he married her.[22] He died on July 2, leaving one of Germany's most prestigious positions vacant. In almost Wagnerian manner, the demise of one of the demigods of the podium would allow for the rise of a young hero. But, as in Wagnerian music drama, such transitions take time.

A tenor of non-Wagnerian stamp—unquestionably the most popular singer of his day, revered wherever he performed—collaborated with Walter in 1911. Even today, when most of the great singers of the earlier twentieth century have sunk into obscurity, his name is still immediately recognizable. Enrico Caruso had visited the Vienna Hofoper several times over the previous few years, each time causing a sensation. He returned in September for a number of guest engagements (for which ticket prices were raised), including an Italian-language *Rigoletto* under Walter on September 23. Caruso played the Duke, and, as before, his performance stunned the audience and the critics. Although Caruso was, as always, the focus of critical attention, Walter earned praise for the "brio" he'd brought to the performance.[23] Walter wrote that he had conducted Caruso on several occasions, though he seems to have done so only once more, on September 25, in a performance of *Carmen*.[24] "I loved Caruso's voice," Walter recalled, "his vocal talent, the sense of beauty expressed in his tone coloring, his *portamento* and his *rubato*, his noble musicianship, and his naturalness. I may say that there was a perfect understanding between us."[25]

The opera house was also the venue for another well-publicized event in Walter's career, one that inspired public speculation about his future in Vienna. Julius Bittner's new opera, *Der Bergsee*, had its premiere at the Hofoper on November 9 under Walter.[26] In reviewing this post-Wagnerian work, Elsa Bienenfeld noted: "Walter is said to be leaving us for Munich. That would be a hard, unbearable, and, just now, irreplaceable loss for the Vienna Hofoper. He is currently the only important and interesting conductor at our institution in whose hands a performance is absolutely secure. He himself would be doing the right thing if he left. An artist of such talent and such experience must be conscious of his duty and power to fulfill great tasks."[27] The possibility of his departure for Munich was more than just a rumor. In September Walter had spoken to the manager of the Munich Opera, Albert von Speidel, about the position left vacant by Mottl's death. He wanted full directorial power and planned to ask for a salary of 30,000 marks (he was currently receiving 24,000). But Munich didn't want another "director"; a "first conductor" would serve just as well, and for less money. The proposal, as it stood, did not appeal to Walter.[28] To Richard Strauss, who had kindly offered to discuss the position in Munich with Walter, he wrote that the title he wanted was "Generalmusikdirektor"—a high honor for a relatively young conductor.[29]

Well before sealing an agreement with the authorities in Munich, Walter left a memorable impression on that city. One of the most important events in his life took place there in November 1911, a celebration of Mahler consisting of two concerts. On November 19 Walter accompanied the alto Madame Charles Cahier at the piano in a recital of Mahler songs, some of them receiving their first performance in Munich.[30] The following evening he presented a mammoth program, beginning with the world premiere of *Das Lied von der Erde*, billed as a "Symphony for Alto and Tenor Solo with Full Orchestra" and featuring Cahier and the tenor William Miller—both Americans, oddly enough. After this lengthy prelude came Mahler's enormous Second Symphony, performed by an amplified Konzertverein Orchestra ("100 musicians") and the Oratorio Society of Augsburg, 250 strong. Ossip Gabrilowitsch, a splendid pianist and talented conductor, was then working in Munich. Walter and he had met as early as 1906, at the music festival where Mahler's Sixth was premiered. Understanding the Herculean task that Walter faced, Gabrilowitsch offered his colleague as many extra rehearsals from his own time as he needed. From that time forward they were to remain good friends, and the bond was to extend beyond Gabrilowitsch's lifetime, for his wife, Clara Clemens (a professional singer, also Mark Twain's daughter), remained close to Walter long after her husband's death in 1936.[31]

*Das Lied* and Mahler's Second in one evening—nearly three hours of Mahler. It must have been an overwhelming and, by the end, a taxing experience for the audience. For the musicologist Eugen Schmitz (later the director of Peters Edition), the conducting of the Second Symphony prompted an encomium on Walter:

> Walter is without a doubt an artist of the very highest caliber. One indeed notices the Mahler school in his manner of conducting an orchestra: there is the same precision, the same exact firmness in his movements that the late maestro of the Vienna Hofoper had. The multitudes in the orchestra and the chorus were visibly under the spell of his artistic will, to the smallest detail, and followed his every movement with unquestioning certainty. And the interpretation that this will dictated was carefully thought out: clear and convincing, genuinely warm, with equal care given to the outward architecture and the inward soul. The most powerful effects of the evening were therefore surely due in large measure to the conductor.[32]

As if to demonstrate the pitfalls and the unreliability of historical documents, Rudolf Louis offered a far more qualified assessment of the evening.

For Louis, *Das Lied*, though better than many other compositions by Mahler, was still the work of a man whose "very high-striving artistic desire" outstripped his "actual creative *ability*." Walter, for his part, conducted the orchestra "securely and energetically" in *Das Lied*, but in the Second Symphony, Louis had reservations: "One got the impression from Bruno Walter of a very talented conductor, skillful and spirited, who also accompanies with particular excellence. Steadiness and composure in establishing and maintaining the tempo were sometimes lacking. Also notable was a certain tendency to drag, particularly in the first movement of the Second Symphony. But that can't seriously detract from the overall good impression one had of Walter. . . . There is something, however, that one should not think of if one wishes to be just to Herr Walter: the incomparable, unforgettable way in which Gustav Mahler himself interpreted this work."[33] Otto Klemperer— at the time, at least, an admirer of Walter's conducting—came from Strasbourg to hear the new work in Munich. He was apparently less moved than he expected to be and wrote to Alma Mahler late in November: "If only we could have heard the work once under Mahler."[34] No doubt Walter would have welcomed that opportunity as well. For him, Mahler was the greatest conductor, as well as the greatest musician, he'd ever known. He recalled how the ailing Mahler had handed him the score of *Das Lied* to study. "It was the first time that he did not play a new work to me. He was probably afraid of the excitement it might cause him. I studied the work and lived through days of a most violent mental upheaval. I was profoundly moved by that uniquely passionate, bitter, resigned, and blessing sound of farewell and departure, that last confession of one upon whom rested the finger of death."[35] Walter viewed the performance itself as a turning point; he felt as though he were "taking the master's place," and posterity, for the most part, has borne him out.[36]

Walter returned to Vienna to lead another memorial concert for Mahler at the beginning of December, and, as in Munich, the evening culminated in the Second Symphony (performed by the Vienna Konzertverein Orchestra and the Singakademie), though it opened with Beethoven's "Coriolan" Overture and Mahler's *Kindertotenlieder*, sung by Friedrich Weidemann. A few days later Walter returned to Munich to conduct his first opera in that city, giving the local premiere of Bittner's *Der Bergsee* at the Hoftheater in December. His return for a single performance of the opera provoked some curiosity among the critics about his eventual role in the musical life of Munich. Alfred von Mensi, of the *Allgemeine Zeitung*, thought the most interesting thing about *Der Bergsee* was that it had been conducted by Bruno Walter, who was "half and half regarded as Mottl's successor. The ovations raised at the conclusion of the work, recalling him again and again to the stage, were almost meant more for him than for the composer."[37] Several other rumors that Walter might take over the position left vacant by Mottl were circulating in Munich and Vienna. But Walter's artistic obligations in Vienna, along with a legally binding contract there, would detain him in Austria for more than another year.

In his last year at the Hofoper Walter enjoyed a continually increasing fame both in and out of Vienna. His schedule, never light, became even busier as he added more orchestral and choral concerts to the demands at the opera house. With Mahler dead, Walter became recognized as the composer's greatest living interpreter, and in 1912 he performed Mahler's greatest symphony, the Ninth, for the first time anywhere. In the same year he gave the Viennese premieres of *Das Lied* and the Eighth Symphony. Meanwhile, his activities in Munich increased significantly, as he slowly broke from the stranglehold that Vienna had on him.

Much of January was devoted to rehearsals for a work very dear to Walter's heart, Beethoven's *Missa solemnis*, with the Singakademie. Before getting down to business with his singers, he felt the need to prepare them for a choral work "entirely different" from Handel's oratorio. "In *Messiah*, a religiosity that is general, comprehensive, and (as it were) established through tradition is being expressed, whereas with Beethoven we are dealing with an independent soul's purely personal view of religion, with a profoundly individual belief in God."[38] This view of Beethoven's *Missa solemnis* would be thoroughly worked out in one of Walter's most important essays, published about a decade later. His approach to the *Missa solemnis* proved controversial, precisely because he was determined to break with the tradition that sought for classical repose and beauty—at the expense of expression—in ecclesiastical music. As with *Messiah*, Walter was bent on making the performance exciting, not the kind that audiences slept through. The one broadcast recording of this work under Walter is anything but dull.[39]

The precise methods Walter used to attain his desired effects make fascinating reading. Unlike those conductors who use the stick as their chief means of communicating their ideas, he discussed fine points of style in great detail; cutoffs and rests were as important as crescendi and diminuendi, and nuance was crucial. In the opening three statements of the word

*Kyrie*, Walter wanted not only an increase in volume, as Beethoven had already marked in the score, but also an increase in emotional intensity. As for the tone in general, Walter suggested the following: "imagine quite vividly that you're calling out to God three times from the greatest depths, that in Beethoven's Kyrie a soul lies in the dust and pleads for mercy. Then you will immediately have the expression that belongs here." But the address to Christ had to be quite different: "You come to the Lord fully in reverence and contrition, but with Christ, his intermediary, you have a much closer, more confidential relationship. To him, the Son of Man, you turn with a far more pressing entreaty, with far more passionate fervor."[40] The members of the Singakademie evidently appreciated Walter's constant attempts to put into words musical ideas that usually defied verbal description. His explanations were invariably accompanied by his own singing of the passages in question, which for the partisan Komorn-Rebhan was at least as illuminating as his carefully chosen words.

The concert took place as January drew to a close, and the program had its desired effect. Korngold swooned over the performance: "The excellent conductor plunged into the ecstatic and penitential moods of the work with all the musical fire that glows within him. It seems quite right for him to interpret this quarrelsome prayer, this passionate conflict with heaven, by means of sharp dynamic and rhythmic contrasts, *sforzando* outbursts, mystical *pianissimi*; with an impetuous rushing-forth and a sudden freezing of the movement; with an interpretation of the text searing with emotion!" And while the performance was "not without the occasional exaggeration," it gave the impression of "something genuine, felt through and through. . . . Not mass music—Prometheus music."[41]

While his rehearsals with the Singakademie must have been time consuming, Walter surely spent a great deal of time at the Hofoper as well during this period, since a new opera by Eugen d'Albert, *Die verschenkte Frau*, was scheduled for its premiere on February 6. As a boy, Walter had been deeply impressed with d'Albert's piano playing ("In his intimate contact with his instrument," Walter recalled, "he appeared to me like a new centaur, half piano and half man"), and since then d'Albert, still active as a concert pianist, had won considerable renown as a composer.[42] His opera *Tiefland* (1903) was immensely popular early in the century, and it must have pleased Walter to offer the first performance of a work by a musician he'd admired in his youth and whose fame stretched far and wide. *Die verschenkte Frau*, however, was a comic opera apparently verging on the operetta style of Lehár—

hardly Walter's favorite genre. It seems not to have left much of an impression on Walter, who says nothing about it in his memoirs.

February brought another significant event in Walter's life, this in the sphere of chamber music. The celebrated Spanish cellist Pablo Casals had recently given recitals in Vienna to great acclaim, and midway through February he was joined by Walter and Marie Soldat-Röger for a performance of Brahms's Trio in B Minor. The performance seems to have been one in which the musicians gave their all but enjoyed only a partial success owing to lack of rehearsal.[43] Curiously, Walter and Casals rarely worked together in later years. Whether this was because of artistic differences or simply logistical problems is hard to say, though Walter on a few occasions praised Casals both publicly and privately. The cellist, for his part, deeply admired Walter's musicianship and during the Nazi era refused to play in a Germany from which men like "Einstein, Thomas Mann, Bruno Walter . . . had to expatriate themselves."[44]

Mahler's ghost continued to hover over Vienna. In one week Walter devoted himself to Mahler's cause three times. On March 12 he accompanied Madame Cahier for another evening of songs by his late friend, and shortly afterward he conducted the first two Viennese performances of Mahler's Eighth, with the combined forces of the Singakademie, the Philharmonic Chorus, the Men's Chorus of the Railway Office (the work required every able voice in Vienna), and the Konzertverein Orchestra. A forty-eight-page thematic analysis by Richard Specht was published specifically for the local premiere. The Great Hall of the Musikverein was filled to the bursting point, with the performers themselves occupying half of it.[45] Though they suffered somewhat from nerves on the first night, the second night was a "*triumphant* success," both for the piece and the performers, with the applause lasting twenty minutes, according to Korngold.[46] Elsa Bienenfeld, having enjoyed one of the most moving experiences in her life when she heard Mahler conduct the work in Munich, judged Walter's performance nearly as impressive as his mentor's; in fact, the timbre was "more beautiful and rounded" in Vienna's Musikvereinssaal than in the Munich Tonhalle. "The extraordinary precision with which Walter brought out the rhythm and dynamics," she observed, "is the legacy he received from the conductor Mahler."[47]

Despite the gratification he felt when conducting this great tribute to Mahler, Walter was uneasy about his future. The position in Munich looked doubtful because of his contract at the Hofoper, binding until 1917.[48] His situation had changed since his initial arrival in Vienna; now, after being reviled for years, he was "our Walter," as Mahler had once predicted, and obviously there were those who wanted to keep him "our Walter." He wrote to Strauss again to say that he would be allowed to conduct at the Mozart and Wagner festivals in Munich that summer but added that he'd already advised Baron Speidel not to count on him for a long-term position.[49] Though he'd won a leave of absence from the Hofoper from May to the beginning of October to spend in Munich, a number of obligations would bring him back to Vienna during those months. With heavy responsibilities in Munich and Vienna, Walter could expect an exhausting year.

But Vienna and Munich were not the only cities requiring his presence. At the end of March he returned to Rome for two concerts at the Augusteum. While he again favored Germanic fare, he also added a recent piece by the young Alfredo Casella, an orchestral suite consisting of an ouverture, sarabanda, and bourrée. One of Mahler's earliest proponents in Italy, Casella had studied with d'Indy, Fauré, and others, and would rank among the foremost Italian composers of his generation. Alberto Gasco, the critic for *La Tribuna* (who had also studied with d'Indy), praised the bourrée in particular for the brilliant, varying timbres of the orchestral instrumentation and again complimented Walter on his conducting.[50] Walter was no doubt aware of Gasco's laudatory words, and perhaps as a show of goodwill he performed two of the Italian critic's tone poems in Munich at a concert of the Musikalische Akademie in 1914—to less encouraging comments from the German press.[51] It was on this visit to Italy that an incident occurred involving an audience request for a repeat performance of "Siegfried's Rhine Journey." The horn player gave a signal to the conductor that he was not eager to play his demanding part again, and Walter pressed on with the program, "only to be interrupted by a renewed outburst," he recalled. "The hornist finally decided to save the situation and informed me by a sign that I might repeat. Quiet reigned again, and when I started the Rhine Journey, a man in the gallery rewarded me for my *docilità* by a rather melodious shout of '*Bravo, Bruno!*'"[52]

After his return to Vienna, followed by a much-needed vacation, Walter contemplated with utter dread the further travels that lay before him. Preferring to stay in one place, he complained to his parents about the constant to-and-fro of his life.[53] But he wouldn't be staying in one place any time soon. In fact, his schedule for the next two months involved a dizzying amount of travel as he shuttled between Vienna and Munich, conducting works by Mozart (including *Bastien et Bastienne*), Wagner (the *Ring* operas and *Tristan*), Puccini, Bittner, and Mahler. The traveling time between the two cities now runs to about five hours; in Walter's day, it was closer to eight. Being in transit so much of the time, Walter began to draw on the language of locomotion to explain what he wanted from his singers in the Singakademie. "One doesn't say Eisen*bahn* [railway] but *Eisen*bahn," he commented during a rehearsal for another performance of the *Missa solemnis*. "In the same way, you shouldn't say Glori*a*, but *Glo*ria."[54]

A young Englishman, traveling in Germany with his mother in the summer of 1912, had the good fortune to hear Walter's performances of *Figaro*, *Così*, and *Don Giovanni* in Munich. He would become one of the leading conductors of his generation, and his admiration for Walter would never waver. "I didn't suppose I should ever hear Mozart performances of such all-round perfection," Sir Adrian Boult recalled six decades after the event, "and certainly I never have again."[55]

For the Mozart operas, mostly performed in the Residenztheater, an intimate rococo theater from Mozart's time, Walter himself accompanied the recitatives on the spinet; Alfred von Mensi remarked on Walter's discreet continuo playing, which contrasted sharply with Richard Strauss's elaborate improvisations. He also admired Walter's ability to rein in his singers' propensity for exaggeration. Walter's earlier tendency to imitate Mahler in his gestures, so often remarked on in reviews from Vienna, was evidently waning, for Mensi observed that Walter didn't favor "very abrupt and strict movements in the manner of Mottl and Mahler; on the contrary, he gladly lays down the baton in order, as it were, to depict the musical images three dimensionally, with both hands."[56]

In presenting the *Ring* operas, Walter appears to have provoked some debate—though not for his conducting. The Prinzregentheater, modeled after the Bayreuth Festspielhaus, had a sunken orchestra pit with a movable lid, to cover the orchestra in Wagnerian works. Walter chose not to employ the lid, and Mensi seems to have taken this artistic choice almost as a deliberate affront. Despite the powerful voices of the leading singers, he argued, their words would have been more clearly audible if the ingeniously designed lid had been employed.[57] But Alexander Dillmann, the chief music critic of the *Münchner Neueste Nachrichten*, had a far more positive reaction to Walter's performances of Wagner. Here was a conductor with "impulse, power, and style." His "three-dimensional" shaping of the lines, his crescendi and sforzandi, his sensitivity to the requirements of the sunken orchestra—all were singled out for praise. His management of the music, in short, "revealed a master."[58]

But the major work was still to come. Walter returned to Vienna to give a performance of *Figaro* and, more important, to prepare for the world premiere of Mahler's Ninth Symphony. It was to be given at the Vienna Music Festival Week, which ran from June 21 to July 1 and included two other "Ninths"—Beethoven's and Bruckner's, conducted respectively by Weingartner and Nikisch. There were few rehearsals, no doubt owing to Walter's hectic schedule and the demands placed on the orchestra by the other major works to be given. This was arguably the most important symphonic premiere of Walter's life (though *Das Lied*, if viewed as a symphony, shares an equal claim to that distinction), and he surely knew how important the occasion would be, how it would forever link his name with one of the great Ninths of the symphonic repertoire. Contemporary reactions to the work, however, were mixed. A young string player, Joseph Braunstein, attended the performance and recalled the concert some eighty years after the event. What stood out for him was a feeling of "deep disappointment," because after the jubilant Eighth Symphony there now came "these violent expressions—so it was shattering."[59] Some of the professional reviewers were also undecided about the merits of Mahler's great symphony, though Max Kalbeck immediately judged it "the trump card" of the festival, and Elsa Bienenfeld called the first movement Mahler's "most beautiful and mature music."[60] Its unusual sequence of movements—with the slow pieces at the outer ends and the faster ones in the middle—surprised some listeners, though not necessarily in a negative way. On the whole the infinitely beautiful first movement won over most of the critics, while the enormous ländler-like second movement and the demonic Rondo-Burleske proved harder to assess after a single hearing. Korngold found them "far inferior" to the first, while Specht commented on the indelible impression made by the "raw and powerful" scherzo: "at the end of this Michelangelesque brawl," he remarked, "one thinks one sees Goliath's bones lying about on the battlefield." He also admired the "shrill irony," the "infernal humor," and the "merciless" contrapuntal satire in the Rondo-Burleske.[61] Korngold observed the similarity in mood between Mahler's Adagio and that at the "end" of Bruckner's unfinished Ninth (he also mentioned its kinship with the last movement of Mahler's Third), though he carped that Mahler had placed too much emphasis on the short "melisma"—the "turn"—that forms a key theme in the piece. Walter was universally praised for his complete devotion to the score and to the spirit of Mahler, and by all accounts both he and the work received a roar of applause.

For all his success in Vienna, Walter must have sensed that his professional future awaited him in Bavaria. In August and September he gave seventeen more opera performances in Munich, offering pretty much the same Mozartian and Wagnerian fare as earlier, with the exception of a single performance of Strauss's *Der Rosenkavalier*. On September 29, however, he gave his first concert with the court orchestra at the Konzertsaal. The concert consisted of Schumann's First Symphony, Mozart's Violin Concerto in D Major (K. 218), and Beethoven's Seventh Symphony. The audience broke into spontaneous applause after the Scherzo of the Seventh, and Walter, in a collegial gesture, asked the orchestra members to rise from their seats, acknowledging his debt to his players.[62]

He returned to Vienna to present another Mahler premiere on November 4. This time the work was *Das Lied*, and it was the first and only occasion on which Walter used two male singers for the work. The American tenor William Miller and Walter's colleague from the Hofoper, Friedrich Weidemann, were the soloists. Walter never quite forgot the event. As late as 1957, when Wolfgang Stresemann asked him about using two male voices for *Das Lied*, Walter gave an unequivocal response. Yes, he'd once used a baritone, the great artist Friedrich Weidemann, because Mahler's instructions allowed for two male voices. But it was a serious error in judgment. "*Never again*, I said to myself then, and from that time onward I've always chosen an alto (Cahier, Thorborg, Onegin, Ferrier, and so on)."[63] Also on the program were several pieces by Ethel Smyth: the Prelude to Act II of *The Wreckers* and two choral works, "Sleepless Dreams" and "Hey Nonny No," sung by the Vienna Singakademie. It is a sign of the rich and changing musical atmosphere in Vienna that shortly before these works were introduced to the city, a radically new work by Schoenberg, *Pierrot Lunaire*, was also given its premiere; Korngold in fact discussed the new pieces by Mahler, Smyth, and Schoenberg in the same review.[64]

The year had been difficult for Walter emotionally and professionally. The position in Munich looked increasingly desirable, but Walter's contract in Vienna seemed an insuperable barrier. The venerable Prince Luitpold of Bavaria tried to intervene, indirectly asking the Austrian emperor if Walter could come to Munich. At the beginning of July Walter had written to his parents of the dream job awaiting him in Munich. He would be immediately designated Generalmusikdirektor with a lifelong contract that, after some six years, he could dissolve if he chose, but that could not be dissolved without his consent. His salary would be 36,000 marks; he would have all of July free, plus eight days off during the festivals in August, three weeks off after the festivals, and another four weeks off during the winter. The offer was as enticing artistically as it was professionally. Walter would have the option of directing the operas that he produced; he would engage singers and orchestra members, accept new works, designate who would conduct what, and determine repertoire. No other musician could boast such an offer. The generous vacation eliminated his worries about his health (or so he thought), which all too often had suffered during his stressful years in Vienna.[65]

But Vienna didn't want to let Walter go without securing an acceptable substitute. Baron Speidel, who had pressed to have Walter hired in Munich, died in the summer. In time he was replaced, however, by Clemens von Franckenstein. After much pleading, Walter finally won an interview with the Lord Steward in Vienna, who spoke for the emperor. "You got an exceptionally favorable contract from us only last year. What more can you want?" the Lord Steward reportedly asked. Walter bluntly answered that "the Munich post was far superior to that in Vienna both in function and in distinction." In Munich, he explained, he would be a director, whereas in Vienna, he would always be "overshadowed" by the director. Walter got his way, though he had to agree to sign a secret contract that would bind him to the Vienna Hofoper again after the six years that he would be committed to Munich.[66] It was a compromise that he readily accepted.

# SIX

# Generalmusikdirektor
## Munich, 1913–1915

*Alas now, pray you,*
*Work not so hard...*
Shakespeare, *The Tempest*

"But please have some *patience*," an overworked Walter wrote to Richard Strauss after scarcely two months in his new position; "if you could see the way I live—or, more accurately, don't live— you'd be the first to stop me."[1] Though it was only the beginning of March, Walter was feeling frayed at the edges. He had become the music director of a leading musical center, and his fame stretched further almost monthly. Later in life he never had any doubts about the importance of his years in Munich: they quite simply represented the "most important epoch" in his career.[2] Almost every day the local newspapers reported on his activities, and his departure from the city in 1922 would inspire front-page articles and countless eulogies. But this was also a period of constant exertion at the podium, continual travel, and romance both kindled and frustrated. Despite Walter's great productivity as a re-creative artist, it was a time when his own attempts at composition had ceased. It was a period when he became one of the leading celebrities of the city, but also a period that saw the rise of

Adolf Hitler, whose move from Vienna to Munich nearly coincided with Walter's.

After Mottl's death in 1910, the Munich-born Franz Fischer—who had known and worked with Wagner in Bayreuth and, along with Hermann Levi, had conducted the first performances of *Parsifal*—filled in as Royal Bavarian Generalmusikdirektor, relinquishing his title to Walter on January 1, 1913. Walter's duties in the capital of Bavaria were, first and foremost, related to operatic activity. Munich had three theaters in which serious opera was performed, two of which had a rich history. The ornate Residenztheater (or "Cuvilliés-Theater," after its architect, François de Cuvilliés), built in the mid-eighteenth century and accommodating an audience of a few hundred, had been the venue where, in 1811, Weber's *Abu Hassan* was first performed. Later in the nineteenth century, Wagner rehearsed *Tristan* there.[3] The space was ideal for the more intimate operas of Mozart, who himself had conducted in the Residenztheater, and for the plays that were regularly performed there. The largest theater, holding nearly two thousand people, was the Hof- und Nationaltheater (known only as the Nationaltheater after 1918). Built in the first quarter of the nineteenth century, it too had an illustrious history, which included the world premieres of Wagner's *Tristan und Isolde*, *Die Meistersinger*, *Das Rheingold*, and *Die Walküre*. These two older houses stood in easy walking distance of each other and were also near the principal orchestra hall, the Odeon. The third house, however, was situated far from the city center, on the other side of the Isar River. Its relative isolation lent it some of the feeling of Bayreuth, which was no doubt the designer's intended effect, for the middle-sized Prinzregententheater, which opened in 1901, was closely patterned after the Festspielhaus in Bayreuth, both internally and externally, and Wagnerian works were regularly performed there during the summer festivals. Each theater had its artistic assets and liabilities, and Walter had to adjust his conducting and directing accordingly—no easy task.

But his conducting duties did not end with opera, even if opera called on his services several times a week. The Musikalische Akademie, consisting of members of the opera orchestra, gave subscription concerts of symphonic music every year, as it continues to do to this day. Its principal venue was the Odeon hall, at the core of a building that was to suffer severe battering in World War II. The auditorium wasn't completely wiped out, however, and its walls and columns now form the courtyard of the Ministry of the Interior—an eerie spectacle for anyone familiar with the building's history. Though it presented a stark visual contrast to the sybaritic Musikvereinssaal in Vienna, the comparatively chaste Odeon hall appealed strongly to Walter, who admired its design and acoustics.[4]

A venerable institution, the Musikalische Akademie had celebrated its centennial the year before Walter settled in Munich. From 1913 till 1920, Walter conducted nearly all the academy concerts (about eight a season), including performances of works that stood outside the subscription series, especially Bach's *Matthäus-Passion*. This was the first time in his life that he had a symphony orchestra regularly at his disposal. Though the core of the repertoire played by the Musikalische Akademie was standard Austro-German symphonic fare, Walter frequently introduced "novelties," most of which were rarely heard again. In a perversely ironic twist, a number of the composers whose new music he made a distinct effort to bring to the public —such as Carl Ehrenberg, Paul Graener, Paul von Klenau, Hans Pfitzner, and Max Trapp—later found patronage and encouragement among the Nazis.

But most of Walter's work revolved around the perennial favorites of the opera house, and the year 1913 had special significance on that score. Two of the giants of nineteenth-century opera, Wagner and Verdi, had been born in 1813, and to mark the centennial of their births, theaters performed their works with even greater frequency than usual. Not surprisingly, the first opera the new music director conducted, on January 4, was *Tristan und Isolde*, presented in the very theater in which the work was first given. As at his Covent Garden debut, Walter's Tristan was Jacques Urlus, imported from Leipzig for this occasion, and his Isolde was Zdenka Fassbender—now Mottl-Fassbender. A new alto, Luise Willer, formerly of the Hoftheater chorus, played Brangäne; after hearing her in an audition, Walter decided that she was too good for the chorus and gave her a place among the soloists.[5] Winning popular and critical approval, Willer became the leading alto of his Munich troupe and was, like the soprano Maria Ivogün, one of Walter's many "discoveries." In his review Alexander Dillmann noted that the new conductor had chosen the opera with which Felix Mottl had ended his career and suggested that the new music director might have done so to assert his intention of carrying on his predecessor's work.[6] It must have been an especially poignant performance for Mottl-Fassbender, who gained Mottl's hand in marriage even as she lost him for life on that earlier occasion, though she had performed Isolde since that tragic event. Walter triumphed. A roar of applause burst out at the conclusion of the opera, but, curiously, the audience's attempts to call Walter to the stage proved futile.[7] Perhaps he felt, given the recent history of the opera at the Hoftheater and the high seriousness accorded the work by its composer, that returning for a bow would be in poor taste; the *Musical Courier*, in any case, applauded his actions: "The public showed its friendly disposition toward the new director by very hearty applause and calls for him at the end of the opera, to which he very modestly and properly did not respond."[8]

Walter had little chance to enjoy the warm response that his *Tristan* had inspired. Three days later he was in Vienna for rehearsals with the Singakademie, which gave a performance of Beethoven's *Missa solemnis* on January 11, with Adolf Busch as solo violinist. Another eight hours on the train, and Walter was back in Munich, ready to give performances of *Der Rosenkavalier* and *Il trovatore* in the Hoftheater. *Der Rosenkavalier*, which Walter had already conducted in Munich the previous summer, would become one of the works he performed most often during his tenure at Munich, ranking in frequency with *Tristan*, the *Ring*, and the great Mozart operas. It was inevitably well received. The performance of *Il trovatore*, however, was a special event, falling on the sixtieth anniversary of the premiere of the work, and it was Walter's first contribution to the Verdi centennial celebrations. On assuming his place at the conductor's desk, he was greeted with applause for several minutes. "His nimble hand," Max Mahler reported, "followed the lines of the score with the utmost elasticity, reined in the ensembles, and, through a spirited use of rubato, filled every phrase with glowing life. It was a sublime pleasure to follow the movements of this musical, fiery soul, which communicates itself to the entire organization."[9]

Again Walter scarcely had time to savor his victory, since he was headed for Russia to conduct what appears to have been his first concert in Moscow. Leading the Imperial Russian Music Society, he offered a program of Beethoven's Eighth, the "Liebestod" from *Tristan*, and Strauss's *Till Eulenspiegel*.[10] In his memoirs Walter also mentions operatic works that he later conducted at the Imperial Opera and the Simin Opera—*Pique Dame*, *Don Giovanni*—though it is difficult to trace his activity in Russia with much accuracy. In any case the visits to Russia left a vivid impression on Walter. After one performance of *Don Giovanni*, he was treated to a celebration with "carousing" that was "possible only in pre-war Russia." Around 3:00 A.M. his host, Simin, assured Walter that "he had been made very happy and grateful by the performance" and asked if he might grant a wish to "prove the sincerity of his sentiments." A lover of Russian literature, Walter confessed a curiosity about the troika, a "vehicle of past days"; he had always wanted to see "one of those sleighs drawn by three horses driven abreast" and asked his host "if such things still existed. Half an hour later," he recounted, "three troikas were at the door. Simin, my wife, and myself got into the first one, and the other guests crowded into the two vehicles following ours. A moment later, the horses, bells tinkling, rushed over the hard-frozen snow, through the icy air and the deeply snow-covered forest. After an hour's drive, we got to Strelna, a place frequently used to give the finishing touch to a gaily spent night in Moscow. A chorus of Russian gypsies, summoned by Simin, soon appeared in our private room. They delighted us with their magnificent voices and their singing of beautiful Russian folksongs."[11] On a different occasion Walter made the acquaintance of Serge Koussevitzky, another Jewish conductor who, like Walter, would later establish a new life in America.

Walter returned to Munich in late January to face the most demanding project in a month that had already severely taxed his energies. On January 30 he conducted the Munich premiere of Strauss's new opera, *Ariadne auf Naxos*—his first failure in Munich, though most of the fault lay with Strauss and Hofmannsthal rather than with Walter. Even at its premiere in Stuttgart the opera did not fare well. To understand its initial failure, we have to bear in mind the circumstances of its early performances. The original *Ariadne auf Naxos* was radically different from what we are now familiar with. Hofmannsthal had the idea of opening the evening with his adaptation of Molière's *Le Bourgeois Gentilhomme*, graced with incidental music by Strauss, under Max Reinhardt's inventive direction. The combination of play and opera—though attractive in theory—proved vexing to the audience in practice, since those who came for the opera resented having to wait so long for the singers to make their entrance.[12] The venue was also problematic. Walter had tried to convince Strauss and Hofmannsthal that the work should be performed in the Hoftheater rather than the Residenztheater, the house they particularly desired. The "raw acoustics" of the Residenztheater and its limited space for the orchestral musicians, he said, made it a poor site for *Ariadne*.[13] But despite his reservations, by December the case seems to have been settled in favor of the small rococo theater, "admirably suited" for a work of this kind, Hofmannsthal wrote to Strauss. "Walter," he continued, "seems to realize that a letter he appears to have written to you is pretty absurd (this strange man seems to be constantly in a fever, pro or contra, and never able to weigh anything calmly)."[14] If Hofmannsthal had known Walter's schedule, he might have found the conductor's feverish temperament a little less peculiar.

Strauss was on a concert tour in Russia when *Ariadne* had its first performance in Munich, with the American Maude Fay as Ariadne, Otto Wolf as Bacchus, and Hermine Bosetti as Zerbinetta. The composer, a native son of Munich, had a close relationship with the city, which held him in high esteem, and Alexander Dillmann of the *Münchner Neueste Nachrichten* showed due sensitivity in covering the opera; instead of writing a standard review, he poured out a seven-column open letter to Strauss in an attempt to explain why the audience had hissed its displeasure after the first act. Quite frankly, he stated, the Molière play had *bored* them—"not only because the performance of the play lacked sparkle but because Molière's comedy is simply unbearable today." Nevertheless, Dillmann was sorry that Strauss had not been present: "You would have enjoyed the performance of the opera and the love with which Bruno Walter immersed himself in your work."[15] For succeeding performances, Walter introduced cuts (most of them already adopted in Dresden) and moved *Ariadne* to the Hoftheater, much to Strauss's displeasure; to pacify the composer, however, he pointed out that attendance had since steadily risen. A move back to the more intimate but less capacious Residenztheater would spell financial disaster.[16] Despite the opera's inauspicious beginnings, Walter continued to conduct *Ariadne* throughout his Munich years, and after its revision, it became a favorite of both Walter and the Munich public.

During the following month Walter continued his manic schedule, shuttling between Vienna and Munich. He gave his first concert as regular conductor of the Musikalische Akademie on February 14 (Beethoven's Fourth, Wagner's "Faust" Overture, and Berlioz's *Symphonie fantastique*), and later that month he conducted his last concert as director of the Vienna Singakademie, the Verdi Requiem—a work that would remain in his repertoire into his final years.[17] But he was back in Munich at the end of February for another concert with the Musikalische Akademie. The solidly Germanic program consisted of Wolf's symphonic poem *Penthesilea*, Brahms's Second Symphony, and Weber's overture to *Euryanthe*. Walter's hectic schedule apparently took its toll on this performance, in which the reading of Wolf's tone poem was praised for its "splendidly worked-out details" but criticized for not offering more than details, while Brahms's symphony, "driven by nervous haste," lacked depth.[18]

Meanwhile, another awkward situation had developed. Though at one time the Musikalische Akademie had performed Bach's *Matthäus-Passion* regularly during the Easter season, it hadn't done so for five years. Walter decided to restore the great oratorio to the academy's concert schedule and set a performance for Palm Sunday. Unfortunately, the Concert Society for Choral Music, under the leadership of Eberhard Schwickerath, a choral conductor devoted to the corpus of great choral music, especially the works of Bach, had already scheduled a performance of the *Matthäus-Passion* for Good Friday. The Concert Society was palpably irritated at the competition from Walter, placing a notice in the *Münchner Neueste Nachrichten* to the effect that the society had made known its intention to present the oratorio in the fall of 1912 and now the Musikalische Akademie would be giving an earlier performance of the work.[19] To judge from contemporary reports, two more different approaches to Bach's masterpiece would be hard to imagine. Critics who attended both performances judged Schwickerath's reading more faithful to Bach's intentions, while Walter's seemed operatic, at times even sentimental—both qualities the legacy, no doubt, of his long association with the opera house. Yet while they sympathized with Schwickerath, whose earnest reading of the score left a deep impression, the critics also conceded that Walter had a "far stronger individuality," was technically far more skilled than Schwickerath, and had brought out a wealth of subtleties.[20] Among Walter's soloists were two women imported from outside Munich, Gertrude Förstel and Madame Cahier, both of whom had worked with Walter before. Felix Senius, from Berlin, was his Evangelist, and Paul Bender, one of Munich's leading basses, his Jesus. (Senius died later that year after contracting food poisoning at a banquet held in his honor.[21]) Even with cuts, which later caused Walter an acute sense of artistic guilt, the performance lasted about two hours and forty-five minutes. While awkwardness surrounded this first performance of the *Matthäus-Passion*, for the next seven years Walter's annual performances of Bach's oratorio would be eagerly anticipated in Munich.[22]

The first complete *Ring* cycle that Walter gave as Generalmusikdirektor also took place in March. He had conducted the *Ring* in Munich on a few occasions during the previous year as a guest conductor, but now he was being judged as the successor to Mottl and Fischer and as the representative of the Wagner tradition in Munich. The careful preparation, the serious work, the organic fusion of music and drama—all made a deep impression on Alexander Dillmann, who tendered a lengthy panegyric on Walter's performance:

> First and foremost, we should thank Bruno Walter, Munich's Generalmusikdirektor, for this gratifying achievement. He has thrown himself into his new field of work with holy zeal, I might almost say with a Mahlerian fanaticism for art. It was again confirmed that

Walter, under the given conditions, was the right man—at least as principal conductor—to take over the leadership of the Munich Opera, orphaned since Mottl's death. . . . Walter is a detailed, precise worker of rare conscientiousness, of hard industriousness and extraordinary technical ability. There are few conductors with such a sharply stamped rhythmic delicacy, scarcely any that combine such an outward calm and deliberation with such a motoric temperament.[23]

Nevertheless, because Munich had a strong Wagner tradition—it was, after all, where many of the music dramas had received their first airings—the critics and citizens had fixed expectations about how their Wagner should be performed, and even Walter couldn't come through this rite of passage without provoking some quibbles. On the one hand, there were the "countless little details" of the true Wagner style that had been passed down over the years in Munich and with which Walter was not yet familiar. On the other, there was the problem of his becoming too engrossed in the details, not allowing himself simply to be swept away by the music and led fully by the heart. All in all, however, Walter turned in an "imposing" performance: "The whole musical structure sparkled brilliantly with a purity and clarity scarcely known before."

A steady diet consisting mainly of Wagner, Mozart, and Strauss dominated Walter's life in the opera houses. Two events that stand out were the first performance at the Hoftheater of Pfitzner's *Der arme Heinrich* on April 17, 1913 (it had played earlier at the Prinzregenten theater), and a new production of Wagner's *Rienzi* on May 1. *Rienzi*, of course, comes so early in the Wagnerian canon that for some it scarcely qualifies as Wagner; few today have heard more than the overture. Though it was warmly received, Walter seems to have conducted *Rienzi* only on this one occasion in Munich—and then, one assumes, mainly out of a sense of duty during the Wagner centennial year—but Pfitzner's Wagnerian spin-off, *Der arme Heinrich*, the work that first attracted Walter to Pfitzner, would enjoy numerous performances under Walter's baton in Munich.

Taking stock of his situation near the end of April, Walter on the whole felt content with his life, however exhausting. "I feel as satisfied with my position in Munich," he wrote to his parents, "as one can feel at all in the theater, which is a very odd and difficult and contradictory institution. I get along excellently with Baron Franckenstein and we have almost become friends. He lets me have my way and supports me to the best of his abilities. The orchestra is heartily devoted to me, and this good relationship is likely to last for some time. They are indebted to me for the great success of their concerts, and since they receive the proceeds from the concerts, they owe me a good relationship on account of their own financial interest. But in this case, I almost believe that the orchestra's attachment to me would prove lasting even without this important motivating factor." The members of his opera troupe were, with few exceptions, devoted to him, and the public had demonstrably shown its support—a storm of applause recently greeted him when he assumed his position at the podium to conduct the second act of *Siegfried*. His home life also brought him considerable comfort: "Above all, however, I feel good about the delightful home that we have established here. Of course it isn't fully paid for yet, but since I've inherited my father's insouciance, it doesn't bother me that much. I have a house of my own, a small garden in which the children can play, a large terrace along this garden and the many surrounding gardens, all in a charming area of Munich that quite resembles a park, utterly serene."[24]

Walter, however, had to deny himself the serenity of his delightful new home for a short while to return to his native city, where on June 21 he opened a series of seven concerts for the German Music Festival in Berlin. A "monster" orchestra, composed of instrumentalists from fifty-four German orchestras, greeted the conductors invited to the festival.[25] The effect must have been overwhelming, if a touch vulgar. According to contemporary reports, Walter's performance of Wagner's *Kaisermarsch* employed forty first violins, thirty-two second violins, twenty-seven violas, twenty-three cellos, twenty double basses, and a comparably lush panoply of wind, brass, and percussion instruments. It created an impression of "unprecedented pomp," but despite the massive organism that Walter had to govern, one reviewer felt that he'd turned in a "sensitive and subtle" performance of Beethoven's Seventh, the centerpiece of his concert.[26]

As his contract stipulated, Walter had most of July to himself. He certainly deserved a rest, and the coming months would afford no time for him to gather his strength. August and September were bursting with *Ring* cycles, *Tristans*, *Don Giovannis*, *Figaros*, *Zauberflötes*, and the odd *Ariadne*. At the end of October, in honor of the Verdi centennial, Walter presented a highly successful new production of *Falstaff*—"a novelty for Munich"— which, unlike *Rienzi*, became one of his regular operas for several months.[27] And he managed to work a world premiere into his tight schedule. On November 16 he gave the first performance of *Sulamith*, by the Danish composer Paul von Klenau, a short opera in six scenes (usually supplemented by

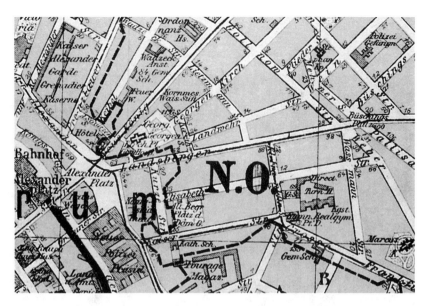

Kiessling's neuer kleiner Plan von Berlin, *details showing the exact location where Walter was born, near Alexanderplatz, at the intersection of Büschingsplatz and Mehnerstrasse, Corner no. 1 (Berlin, 1875).*
Courtesy of Map Division, The New York Public Library,
Astor, Lenox and Tilden Foundations.

*Emma, Joseph, Johanna, Leo, and Bruno Schlesinger (Berlin, 1880).*
Courtesy of Sony Music Photo Archives.

*Bruno Schlesinger and his father, Joseph, whose "pockets were always crammed with testimonials" of his son's success (Berlin, ca. 1885).*
Courtesy of Sony Music Photo Archives.

*Walter at the age of twenty, about the time he worked with Mahler in Hamburg*
*(ca. 1896).*
Courtesy of Sony Music Photo Archives.

*Walter, following advice from Mahler and his sisters, grew a beard to make himself look older (Berlin, 1900).*
Courtesy of Sony Music Photo Archives.

*Gustav Mahler and his future brother-in-law, Arnold Rosé, concertmaster of the Vienna Philharmonic and Walter's frequent chamber music partner (ca. 1899).*
Courtesy of Bruno Walter Papers, Music Division, The New York
Public Library for the Performing Arts, Astor, Lenox and Tilden Foundations.

SECHS LIEDER

FÜR EINE

SINGSTIMME

MIT

KLAVIERBEGLEITUNG

KOMPONIERT

VON

BRUNO WALTER

OP. 11

VERLAG

DREILILIEN

BERLIN

| | | | |
|---|---|---|---|
| No. 1. | Meine Mutter hat's gewollt . . . . . | Theodor Storm. | Pr. M. 1,20 |
| No. 2. | Vorbei . . . . . . . . . . . . . . . | Gustav Renner. | Pr. M. 1,20 |
| No. 3. | Waldtrauts Lied I . . . . . . . . . . | Julius Wolff. | Pr. M. 1,20 |
| No. 4. | Waldtrauts Lied II . . . . . . . . . . | Julius Wolff. | Pr. M. 1,20 |
| No. 5. | Weisst du, wie lieb ich dich hab'? . . | Hermann Sudermann. | Pr. M. 1,20 |
| No. 6. | Liebeslust . . . . . . . . . . . . . | Fliegende Blätter. | Pr. M. 1,80 |

*Walter's first collection of original printed music, his* Sechs Lieder, *op. 11, in print by the early part of 1902.*

Dienstag, 17. November, abends halb 8 Uhr,

im kleinen Musikvereinssaal:

## Zweites

# Rosé-Quartett.

### PROGRAMM:

1. **Beethoven:** Quartett A-dur op. 18 Nr. 5 (comp. 1801).
2. **Bruno Walter:** Quartett D-dur (Manuskript
I. Auff.) 8. **Brahms:** Quartett A-moll op. 51 Nr. 2
(comp. 1873).

Cerclo à fl. 3, Parterre à fl. 2 u. 1.50, Galerie à fl. 1.20
und fl. 1 bei

### Alexander Rosé, Concertbureau, I., Kärntnerring 11.

*Notice for the premiere of Walter's String Quartet on
November 17, 1903, performed by the illustrious
Rosé Quartet.*

### Konzert-Direktion Albert Gutmann.

**Mittwoch den 20. Februar, abends ½ 8 Uhr,**

im Bösendorfer-Saale:

## III. (letzter) Kammermusikabend

# Soldat-Roeger-

## Quartett

I. Violine: Marie Soldat-Roeger.      Viola: Natalie Lechner-Bauer,
II.   „   Else Edle v. Plank.      Violoncell: Leontine Gärtner,
Unter Mitwirkung des Hofopern-Kapellmeisters **Bruno Walter.**

### PROGRAMM:

1. **Mozart:** Streich-Quartett C-dur, Nr. 6.
2. **Mendelssohn:** Streich-Quartett E-moll, op. 44, Nr. 2.
8. **Brahms:** Klavier-Quintett F-moll, op. 34.
Klavier: Hofopern-Kapellmeister **Bruno Walter.**

Karten zu fl. 4, 3, 2 und 1 in

## GUTMANN's k. u. k. Hof-Musikalienhdlg. (Hofoper)

und Klavier-Etablissement, I., Himmelpfortgasse 27.

*Walter often worked with the Soldat-Röger Quartet, an all-
female ensemble; on February 20, 1907, he took the keyboard
part in Brahms's great Piano Quintet in F minor.*

**Wiener Konzert-Verein.**

Samstag den 6. Februar 1909, 1/28 Uhr abends:

Im grossen Musikvereinssaale:

# Ausserordentliches Konzert
## (Novitäten-Abend).

### PROGRAMM:

Edgar Istel: Eine Singspiel-Ouvertüre, Dirigent Ferd. Löwe.
Jan Brandts-Buys: Illyrische Ballade, } unter Leitung der
Bruno Walter: Symphonie, } Komponisten.

Karten von K. 1.50 bis 6.— bei Kehlendorfer, I., Krugerstr. 3.

*Walter's First Symphony had its premiere on February 6, 1909, in the Grosser Musikvereinssaal, where the Second and Third symphonies of Brahms had their first performances, and where Walter would introduce Mahler's Ninth Symphony.*

19.—20. November:

## Gedächtnisfeier
### für

# Gustav Mahler
### I.

Sonntag, 19. November, Abends 8 Uhr          K. Odeon

## Gustav Mahler Lieder-Abend

Mme. Charles Cahier ══════════ Am Klavier: Bruno Walter

Frühlingsmorgen, Erinnerung, Scheiden und Meiden, Ablösung im Sommer, Nicht wiedersehen, Ich ging mit Lust, Hans und Grete, Starke Einbildungskraft, Das irdische Leben, Die schönen Trompeten, Rheinlegendchen, Wer hat dies Liedchen erdacht, Ich bin der Welt abhanden gekommen, Urlicht, Ich atme einen Lindenduft, Um Mitternacht.
(NB. Die unterstrichenen Lieder zum erstenmal!)

### II.

Montag, 20. November, Abends 8 Uhr          Tonhalle

#### 1. Abteilung:

## Uraufführung: Das Lied von der Erde
Symphonie für Alt- und Tenorsolo und grosses Orchester

#### 2. Abteilung:

## Zweite Symphonie (C-moll) für Soli, gemischter Chor grosses Orchester u.Orgel (Auferstehungssymphonie)

### Dirigent: Hofkapellmeister BRUNO WALTER (Wien)

Soli: Mme. Charles Cahier (Alt), Marie Möhl-Knabl (Sopran), K. K. Hofopernsänger William Miller (Tenor), Chor: Der Oratorienverein Augsburg (250 Sänger), Orchester: Das verstärkte Konzertvereinsorchester (100 Musiker), Orgel: Hoforganist Prof. L. Maier.

Eintrittskarten pro Abend à M. 10.20, 8.20, 6.20, 5.10, 4.10, 3.10 und 2.— (einschl. Steuer)

*Perhaps Walter's most important performance, the world premiere of Mahler's* Das Lied von der Erde, *given in Munich on November 20, 1911, during a memorial celebration of the composer's works. On the same program as* Das Lied *was Mahler's "Resurrection" Symphony.*

*Bruno Walter as Bavarian Generalmusikdirektor (Munich, ca. 1913).*
Courtesy of Deutsches Theatermuseum, Munich.

*Walter and his wife, Elsa, with their two daughters, Lotte* (left) *and Gretel (Munich, ca. 1918).*
Courtesy of Deutsches Theatermuseum, Munich.

*Delia Reinhardt as Carlotta, the heroine of Franz Schreker's opera*
Die Gezeichneten *(Munich, 1920).*
Courtesy of Deutsches Theatermuseum, Munich.

*Walter in the covered pit of Munich's Prinzregententheater, patterned after the Festspielhaus at Bayreuth (Munich, ca. 1913).*
Courtesy of Sony Music Photo Archives.

*Walter, Hans Pfitzner, and Ludwig Kirschner (set designer), during preparations for the world premiere of Pfitzner's* Palestrina *(Munich, 1917).*
Courtesy of Sony Music Photo Archives.

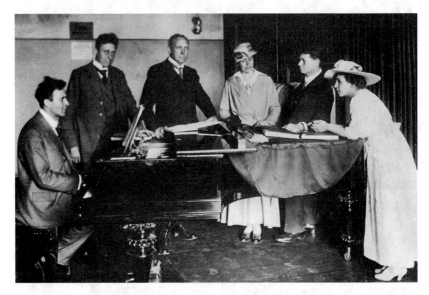

*Walter at a piano rehearsal for* Palestrina. From left to right, standing: *Karl Erb,*
*Fritz Feinhals, Emmy Krüger, Fritz Brodersen, and Maria Ivogün (Munich, 1917).*
Courtesy of Sony Music Photo Archives.

*Walter in his study, surrounded by the likenesses of Beethoven, Mahler, and Brahms (Berlin, ca. 1930).*
Courtesy of Sony Music Photo Archives.

*Walter and Paul Whiteman, who conducted the world premiere performance of* Gershwin's Rhapsody in Blue *(Hollywood, 1927).*
Courtesy of Sony Music Photo Archives.

another short work, like *Cavalleria rusticana*), based on that most sensual book of the Old Testament, the Song of Solomon.

Later in November Walter presented the most ambitious program of his first year as director of the Musikalische Akademie. It included two rarely heard works: W. F. Bach's Sinfonia for two violins, viola, bass, and two flutes (with harpsichord continuo, played by Hans Rohr)—given "for the first time," according to the notices—and Mahler's Third Symphony, with Luise Willer as alto soloist. Walter, of course, had enjoyed one of his great triumphs in Vienna when he had conducted Mahler's Third in 1909 and no doubt hoped for a similar victory in Munich. But while the reviewers praised Walter's "excellent" performance of the work, they criticized what they viewed as compositional weaknesses in Mahler's hour-and-a-half-long, six-movement symphony, which struck them as unconvincing, a work in which the composer strove for goals beyond his reach.[28]

Nevertheless, Walter's fame was spreading rapidly, and leading orchestras sought his services. After giving an ebullient charity performance of Suppé's *Die schöne Galathée*, Walter again traveled to his native city for his first engagement as guest conductor of the Berlin Philharmonic on December 29. For this important concert he chose an ambitious program: Schumann's First Symphony—by now almost obligatory for his debut with an orchestra—and Beethoven's Ninth, with a chorus of about 250 voices.[29] The significance of Walter's return to Berlin was not lost on Leopold Schmidt, the chief music reviewer for the *Berliner Tageblatt*, whose coverage of Walter's activities in Berlin spanned many years. He reminded his readers that Walter had studied at the Stern Conservatory and had returned briefly (at the turn of the century) as an opera conductor. "We were vexed with the management in those days for not having allowed a greater field of activity for this man, whose great talent was obvious, and for having let him move to Vienna after a short while. It was easy to note how seriously the young musician took his job and to see that he had no desire at all to fall into the role of a *routinier*."[30] As music director of Bavaria, Walter had now joined the ranks of the "finest conductors in Germany," Schmidt observed, and his appearance in Berlin was an event followed with interest. Small wonder that, after this impressive debut, Walter would return to conduct the Berlin Philharmonic almost every year until 1933.

However frenzied and overburdened Walter's first year in Munich might have been, the year 1914 would begin a period of stress and confusion such as he had never before experienced. World War I ushered in not only the usual calamities of war but, in its wake—devastating for Germany—provided the spark that would ignite a number of radical political movements affecting the entire course of Walter's life, though neither he nor anyone else could have foreseen the long-term consequences of those political upheavals.

While the year began with familiar works in the opera house, Walter's concert calendar in January included something new for him, a major work that would remain in his repertoire till the end of his career: Bruckner's Fourth Symphony. Although Walter was regarded in the 1940s and 1950s as one of the foremost exponents of Bruckner's symphonies—or at least of the four that he then conducted—his status as a Brucknerian was far from established in 1914, when he seems to have conducted Bruckner for the first time. On the program with Bruckner's "Romantic" Symphony were Pfitzner's ballade "Herr Olaf" and his occasional music to Kleist's *Kätchen von Heilbronn*. Reviewing the concert, Rudolf Louis admired Walter's handling of the works by Pfitzner but felt that Bruckner's compositional method was somewhat alien to the conductor, and that the first and last movements were wanting in "fluidity and liveliness."[31] Walter himself later confessed that he came to understand Bruckner only after he'd lived for half a century. "The emotional substance of his music," he wrote, "had stirred me by its soulful force and depth and delighted me by its occasional Austrian charm, but I had not been able to feel at home on his soil." But after a bout with double pneumonia, which forced him to rest and reflect for some weeks, he was visited by a sudden revelation. "The increased maturity and deeper tranquillity gained during my illness may have had something to do with it. . . . I recognized in the melodic substance, in the towering climaxes, and in the emotional world of his symphonies the great soul of their creator, pious and childlike. This stirring recognition, in turn, made me comprehend effortlessly the substance and form of his music."[32] Despite his claims not to have understood Bruckner before this revelation, and despite Louis's criticism of the outer movements, Walter seems to have turned in an impressive performance: the details were "worked out with extraordinary subtlety," Louis noted, and the "beautiful" orchestral sound "left nothing to be desired."[33]

While taking pains to include novelties on his concert programs—among them, Debussy's *Printemps* suite and Wilhelm Mauke's *Einsamkeit*, both offered in February 1914—Walter also pressed to have new operas produced. For some years, he had been interested in the music of an innovative young musician, another of Robert Fuchs's seemingly endless supply of talented students, Franz Schreker. His bold, lush harmonies, his compositional facility, his virtuoso orchestration, and his controversial libretti made him the object of praise, envy, and scorn, in about equal measure. His music, which initially created a sensation, fell into eclipse during the Third Reich but has enjoyed a steadily growing renaissance since the 1980s, thanks to the ever increasing exploration of the "degenerate music" condemned by the Nazis. He was a professor at the Academy of Music in Vienna as well as the conductor of its Philharmonic Chorus, an ensemble he founded. Like Wagner, he wrote his own texts, often laced with erotic and entertainingly subversive strains. Already in Vienna, during Weingartner's tenure as director, Walter had tried to have Schreker's first opera, *Der ferne Klang*, produced at the Hofoper, though the change in leadership at the opera house frustrated his plan. (The opera eventually received its premiere in Frankfurt in 1912.) Walter heartily recommended Schreker to others in a position to help the radical composer, Richard Strauss being among those to whom he made a direct appeal.[34]

On February 28, 1914, Walter gave the Munich premiere of *Der ferne Klang* at the Hoftheater, with Karl Erb and Luise Perard-Petzl as the protagonists Fritz and Grete. The piano–vocal score, arranged by Alban Berg, bore a dedication from Schreker "to Bruno Walter, in gratitude."[35] Schreker claimed to have worked on the libretto already in his early twenties, and in some ways the plot reveals the workings of a young mind.[36] (The young artist Fritz abandons Grete, the woman who loves him, to pursue "the distant sound" of a nebulous artistic ideal. Fifteen years pass during the course of the opera, Grete falls into a life of ill repute, and Fritz, in the end, learns too late that "the distant sound" he had sought for so many years was within his reach the whole time.) The opera ranks among the most daring and modern works that Walter ever brought to the stage, and he gave it his wholehearted devotion. The large number of rehearsals he demanded were already the stuff of local legend before opening night, and the performance showed that the work had been worth the effort. "We've heard about the fantastic number of rehearsals for weeks," Max Mahler wrote. "Bruno Walter, working tirelessly with utter devotion and love, has awakened this tremendously complicated score into resounding life. Under his superlatively beautiful direction, the court orchestra played with sparkling sonic splendor."[37] The work itself generated considerable debate. The critics acknowledged Schreker's prodigious musical talent and his revolutionary compositional style, and Max Mahler cautioned those who found the music too strange not to condemn it out of hand: the new, Mahler pointed out, is bound to be difficult to absorb at first. Some critics, however, were not willing to give Schreker the benefit of the doubt. Everything about the adventurous work seemed too radical for Alfred von Mensi, and the interest the public took in Schreker's work was an indication to him of an alarming move toward "a Schreker—or shall we say a *schrecklich* [terrible]—era."[38]

Although Walter had already acquired a reputation for having conservative taste, the fact remains that he often chose works that were new and innovative. Despite loud and demonstrative objections raised by some critics, Walter continued to schedule fresh and even more radical works by Schreker at the Munich Hoftheater for several years to come. He confessed to not always understanding the music he performed, yet (at least in the case of Schreker and some other composers) he seems to have followed his own advice to critics by attributing his lack of understanding to the limitations of his own perception.[39]

While Schreker's opera drew a mixed response from the press and the public, another premiere that Walter conducted in 1914 elicited far more encouraging words and considerably more attention from the critics, even though the piece in question was not new. The work was Wagner's final masterpiece, *Parsifal*, first performed in 1882 and written specifically for Bayreuth; the composer was utterly opposed to having it performed outside his custom-built theater, and especially to having it transported to an urban opera house where the solemnity of the music and the story would be compromised by commercial surroundings. After Wagner's death, the work was protected by copyright, at least in Europe, until 1913. Nevertheless, the Metropolitan Opera House in New York (the very home of Wall Street), unaffected by the copyright restrictions on the opera, became the first to ignore Wagner's wish, staging *Parsifal* as early as 1903, which prompted many a venomous article from the European press.[40] But surely a fair amount of envy was mixed with the venom. *Parsifal* was, after all, one of Wagner's crowning achievements, and limiting performances to Bayreuth meant that many music-lovers, even ardent Wagnerians, would have few chances to experience the work.[41]

When the performance restrictions on *Parsifal* were lifted in 1913, productions abounded. Several had already occurred in Germany before the Munich production, which took place on Wagner's birthday, but because of the long association of Munich with Wagner's works, and because of the Prinzregententheater's close structural kinship with the Festspielhaus, the performance that Walter conducted on May 22 had special significance. Max Mahler, declaring the aptness of the Prinzregententheater for *Parsifal*, commented that "among all Wagner's works, the music of *Parsifal* most requires the invisible sunken orchestra."[42] The difficult stage work necessary for the production forced some other plays and operas in the theater to be rescheduled. Anton Fuchs, who had worked with Wagner at Bayreuth and had played Klingsor there in the early productions, was in charge of the stage direction (he also worked with Walter on several other operas). Much to Mensi's relief, Walter chose to make use of the "covered lid" in the Prinzregententheater, "which we missed very much at last year's Festspielen," the critic added.[43] The great Karl Erb assumed the role of Parsifal, while Kundry was played by Zdenka Mottl-Fassbender. The first performance was deemed a huge success, with Walter receiving credit for the devotion and care he had brought to preparing the work. "Under his single-minded conducting, the orchestra proved its old reputation. The Prelude, Transformation Music, Good Friday Spell—these prominent parts of the score seemed filled with an atmosphere of utter nobility. And the contrasting moods (the restless haste of the Prelude to the Klingsor scene, for example) were also brought out with precision."[44]

Walter's success in Munich no doubt aroused the jealousy of some of his colleagues, one of whom, Otto Hess (who specialized in Wagner), was given a chance to grapple with *Parsifal* late in June, turning in a laudable performance. According to Walter, Hess profoundly resented Walter's presence in Munich; if so, it's easy to understand why. When Walter became Generalmusikdirektor, Hess fell into the shadows, though he still had many opportunities to conduct major works that Walter rarely (or never) touched. He was "a difficult and unfortunate man," Walter wrote. "At the slightest difference of opinion in a harmless conversation, two fiery spots would appear on his cheeks, and his heavy breathing would make it advisable to stop the talk. I did my best to give him a sphere of activity that ought to have satisfied any conductor. But so inordinate was his ambition that he would have considered my suicide but the first instalment payment on the immense debt fate owed to his justified demands."[45] To what extent this is an honest assessment of Hess, rather than a caricature, is hard to know. Walter might have sensed a resentment that stemmed from more than habitual biliousness on the part of Hess, for there were certainly critics who stressed Hess's truly "German" conducting in a way that suggested the possibility of racial tension at the opera house. As a native son of Munich, moreover, Hess had old allies in the city. Nevertheless, the press was capable of treating him with indifference, as when, in the early days of June, the two conductors collaborated in an evening honoring Richard Strauss on his fiftieth birthday. Walter opened with a performance of *Tod und Verklärung*, and Hess followed with *Salome*. Though Hess bore the greater part of the conducting duties, only Walter's conducting was mentioned in the *Allgemeine Zeitung*.[46]

With the sheer mass of work that burdened Walter during the first part of 1914, it is hard to imagine that he had much time for anything other than preparing and giving performances in Munich and elsewhere. But, as throughout his career, he took time out to help the careers of especially talented musicians whom he'd encountered. So it was that in June he wrote to Ernst von Possart—reputed to have a "decisive voice" in the proceedings of the Munich Konzertverein—recommending the young Wilhelm Furtwängler, who was to conduct one of the upcoming concerts given by that orchestra. "If I can convince you to hear this concert, I'll be able to forgo any further recommendation of the young artist. I have the highest opinion of his talent and ability, his deep and true musicality, and his effectiveness before an audience. As you probably already know, he comes from Munich, the son of the well-known scholar (the late university professor)."[47] Furtwängler secured a position in Mannheim the following year—with help from Walter, which the younger conductor never forgot—and went on to become the most celebrated conductor in Germany.[48] When Walter's impending departure from Munich became public knowledge in 1922, Furtwängler's mother, Adelheid, wrote the Generalmusikdirektor a letter expressing her regret that her name hadn't been included on a petition circulated in the city, adding: "You know how my son reveres you with his entire soul and is delighted that you have shown him your friendship. Every time he's here, he looks forward to seeing you and hearing you."[49] The subsequent deterioration of the promising relationship between Walter and Furtwängler would constitute one of the most painful chapters in Walter's life.

The end of Walter's second season in Munich coincided with an unexpected and devastating event. On June 29, 1914, the *Münchner Neueste Nachrichten* carried an ominous headline: "The Archduke, Successor to the Throne, and his Consort Killed." World War I broke out suddenly and lasted far longer than anyone could have predicted. For musicians in general, it would take a drastic, sometimes disastrous, toll on their livelihood. Theaters closed, orchestras disbanded. For Walter, who worked in theaters supported by the court and the state, the war would result in fewer performances of works requiring large forces, and programs would strongly favor the German repertoire. A considerable number of charity concerts, "Fatherland Concerts" (with huge choral ensembles), and "People's Concerts" found Walter at the helm, conducting German favorites and patriotic songs. By October, in fact, Walter was arguing that popular concerts, directed by major conductors and given either in beer halls (providing a pleasant, informal atmosphere) or in standard auditoriums, were an excellent way to boost morale and to aid needy musicians and unemployed music teachers. Walter, Strauss, and other conductors gave such concerts in Munich, waiving their fees, and the audience response was encouraging. Thomas Mann later recalled the "joy and verve" of Walter's conducting on these occasions.[50] "The orchestra divided up among its members eighty percent of the net proceeds," Walter wrote; "twenty percent was allotted to the musicians' relief fund."[51] It was a good method of keeping musicians employed and of doing one's social duty. (The idea of Walter's leading rousing renditions of "Die Wacht am Rhein" and "Deutschland über Alles," and his confidence in a glorious victory for Germany, may cause some discomfort to the modern reader, but the songs had not yet acquired the taint of National Socialism, and Walter was merely being a loyal patriot. Very much in favor of the German cause, he even flirted with the idea of joining the armed forces as a volunteer in 1915.[52]) In addition to these concerts, Walter was in charge of music for various celebrations of German culture focusing on such luminaries as Schiller, Beethoven, and Wagner.

In the opera house, light and comic works predominated. Walter revived Peter Cornelius's comic work *Der Barbier von Bagdad* and a short pastoral attributed to Gluck, *Les Amours champêtres* (*Maienkönigin*), both to great acclaim, and he conducted the usual works by Mozart and Strauss, adding performances of Verdi's *Ballo* and Rossini's *Barbiere di Siviglia* (the other "Barber" opera) to vary the almost exclusively Germanic fare being offered. His first performance of *Die Meistersinger* in Munich occurred on Christmas Day, 1914. It received a detailed review from Alexander Dillmann, who heaped praise on Walter's "decided feeling for sonic beauty, his acute dissection of the score's subtle and complex architecture, his intoxication with analytical niceties, and his overall care in the handling of the orchestra." Walter "pulled instruments that are otherwise scarcely heard out of their hiding places—here a graceful woodwind figure, there the contemplative voice of a bass tuba, whose *Wahn*-motive, making its way through the figuration, would usually be absorbed into the general pattern of sound."[53] Nevertheless, some aspects of the performance provoked criticism; the loud passages could have profited from brighter brass playing, and—at least "for the time being"— certain qualities were missing in this *Meistersinger*: "*inner, tranquil strength,* composure, simplicity, and unaffected music-making, so different from the brilliant dissection and the conjuring, ecstatic display of energy with which Walter has attempted to reach this work, which is German, straightforward, and indeed very great." The patriotic emphasis on the opera's "German" essence, though hardly remarkable in time of war, might have been cause for concern, since there lurked a potential implication that the Jewish-born Walter, though a native Berliner, couldn't fully understand the German mentality. If this sounds oversensitive, it is worth bearing in mind that a few years later, that exact charge would be leveled directly at Walter.

Despite the occasional criticisms, however, Walter was becoming recognized as one of the great European conductors. News of another conductor, one whose career would eventually eclipse that of all his contemporaries, reached Walter around the end of 1914. Arturo Toscanini, on whom Mahler had bestowed qualified praise to Walter in 1908 ("He conducts [*Tristan*] in a manner entirely different from ours . . . but magnificently in his way"), was now a major force at the Metropolitan Opera House.[54] One of his performances was heard by the Russian-born Ossip Gabrilowitsch, who, with his wife Clara, had left Europe at the outbreak of World War I. Gabrilowitsch soon found employment in the United States, where he remained until his death, and he maintained a correspondence with Walter for many years. Shortly after arriving in New York, Gabrilowitsch attended a performance of *Tristan* at the Met under Arturo Toscanini and was disappointed with what he heard. He reported to Walter that the Italian conductor's strong suit was drama and that he lacked poetry and lyricism. Technically he was great, but not to be compared with Mahler or Walter himself. Essentially an orchestral conductor, he didn't have as "spontaneous and compelling" an effect on the singers as Walter had.[55] But later in life both Gabrilowitsch and Walter would become allies of Toscanini, admiring his formidable gifts and his courage in the face of totalitarianism. Over a decade passed before Walter met his rival, yet their friendship endured, despite the occasional disagreement, until Toscanini's death in 1957.

Throughout the early months of the war, Walter's activities with the Musikalische Akademie seem to have continued unabated. Among the choral works he performed were Mozart's Requiem in November—a sober work for troubled times that made a deep enough impression on the audience to warrant a repeat performance—and, in December, Haydn's *Die Schöpfung*, which offered a much-needed vision of creation (and, by extension, regeneration) to a country at war. Walter also managed to find works that were new to the Munich audience. Some were, in fact, neglected older pieces, like Mozart's ballet suite *Les Petits Riens* and his concert aria "Popoli di Tessaglia" (sung by Maria Ivogün), both billed as "novelties." But he also offered at least one new work, Karl Bleyle's *Legende* for orchestra, giving its world premiere on December 28, 1914. The piece was politely reviewed but less enthusiastically received than another work on the same program, naturally from the standard repertoire: Schumann's Piano Concerto in A Minor, with Artur Schnabel as soloist.[56]

"Work, work, work," Walter wrote to his parents in April 1915, summing up his life in Munich. "The behavior of the press is as vile as ever; in fact, during the war it's stooping to new lows, but the public is full of love and enthusiasm."[57] Whatever Walter found offensive in the press was plainly matched by a goodly amount of praise in many of the leading papers, though his enemies would soon enough begin to voice their objections, vociferously and nastily, to his interpretive manner. At the beginning of 1915, however, the press seemed quite satisfied with Walter's accomplishments. It was a year that saw few surprises in Walter's repertoire at the opera house and on the concert stage, though his schedule remained as hectic as ever. Something new for Munich occurred on March 20, when Walter accompanied Arnold Rosé, with whom he still played the occasional recital during his visits to Vienna, in a program of Beethoven violin sonatas. This concert presented the music director "for the first time as a piano soloist in Munich" and naturally piqued the critics' interest.[58] Richard Würz of the *Münchner Neueste Nachrichten* focused almost exclusively on Walter, expressing admiration for his ability to impress his strong artistic personality even on chamber music. Walter's technical security at the keyboard, his fine nuances, his gentle pianos and full but never brittle fortes—all were singled out for praise. For the next few years, Walter would appear many times in chamber music recitals, much as he had done in Vienna, sometimes joined by the visiting Rosé. Along with the Beethoven violin sonatas (and several piano trios), Walter served as pianist in works by Brahms, Mozart, Pfitzner, Rachmaninoff, Schubert, and Tchaikovsky.

Though his attitude toward Richard Strauss could be lukewarm, Walter promoted the composer's music many times in his career, and on April 17,

1915, he gave what was his first Munich performance of Strauss's *Elektra*. His "painstaking rehearsals" resulted in a performance of "uncommonly rich shading, bathed in glowing colors," according to the *Münchner Neueste Nachrichten*, though Strauss himself, a mere four months later, complained bitterly that his works weren't being kept up in his "native city" and blamed Walter and Franckenstein for the putative neglect.[59] A composer whose works Walter could never be accused of neglecting, however, was Mahler, whose *Lied von der Erde* he conducted in Vienna on February 21 and again on April 27, with Luise Willer and Otto Wolf as his soloists and the Vienna Philharmonic as his orchestra. (The piece hadn't been heard in that city since Walter introduced it to the Viennese in 1912.) In Munich standard orchestral repertoire dominated his programs with the Musikalische Akademie: a cycle of the Beethoven symphonies, a performance of Mahler's Fourth (with Ivogün as soprano soloist), Bruckner's Seventh, Mozart's "Jupiter," and so on. At least one reviewer questioned the wisdom of performing Beethoven's Ninth during the war; odes to joy—so the reasoning ran—should wait for times of peace.[60]

With his usual desire to mix the new and the old, Walter injected some novelties into his subscription series, the first two of which, to judge by their titles, were unlikely to prompt charges of indecorous levity: Hans Pfitzner's *Klage* ("Lament"), for baritone, men's chorus, and orchestra; Paul von Klenau's *Gespräch mit dem Tod* ("Dialogue with Death"), for alto and orchestra; Heinrich Noren's Violin Concerto, with Alexander Petschnikoff as soloist; and Paul Graener's *Musik am Abend* ("Music in the Evening"), included on a program that also featured the first performance in Munich of Strauss's new *Alpensinfonie*. Walter entertained the idea of writing his own music again, but his soul wasn't "free enough" during those troubled times to attempt anything "so bold," and in any case he was "perhaps too exhausted" to compose.[61]

Worked nearly to the point of collapse, Walter would sometimes give the impression in his correspondence that he was in danger of fizzling out. His complaints of exhaustion became more frequent as the years passed, and his schedule remained as punishing as ever. It would have been natural for him to seek out something new to rekindle the hard, gemlike flame with which he strove to burn. And, in fact, a new source of invigoration was shortly to enter his life.

# SEVEN

# *Delia*

## Munich, 1915–1922

*People will no longer know what is German and pure.*
Wagner, *Die Meistersinger von Nürnberg*

The theater offers ample opportunity for both artists and their admirers to fall in love. A leading heroine or hero in the spotlight easily becomes the object of desire—and just as easily the conductor who wields the baton, magically holding the ensemble together. With his schedule crammed with rehearsals and performances, Walter could not have had much free time to develop a romantic attachment, yet, like many another overworked performer, he managed to find the time. The year 1915 introduced a key player into his life, the lyric soprano Delia Reinhardt. They were brought together when two staples of German opera—*Die Zauberflöte* and *Der Freischütz*—were given under Walter on August 29 and September 5, and Reinhardt, a guest from the Breslau Stadttheater (where she had begun her professional career in 1913), assumed the roles of Pamina and Agathe. She was being considered for a position with the Munich troupe and had some manifest strengths on her side; her early publicity photos, for example, display a wide spectrum of poses and facial expressions. As Sieglinde she looks feminine, slender, and frail; as

Octavian and Ighino, boyish and aristocratic; as Elsa, pious and untouchable; as Carlotta, sensuous and robust, with large, manly hands. Though the informal shots taken during her Munich years often show her as unattractive, overweight, and oppressed, snapshots taken after the war reveal a melancholy beauty in her features and a figure that had aged gracefully. With her controlled, coolly plaintive voice, she would attract several important musicians of the day, including the baritone Gustav Schützendorf and the conductor Georges Sébastian (both of whom were married to her for a time), as well as Bruno Walter.

The handful of recordings Reinhardt made in the early electrical period have often been reissued—testimony to her long-standing popularity in Germanic countries. Her recorded repertoire includes famous arias and set pieces of Agathe, Cherubino, Eva, Elisabeth, Elsa, and Sieglinde. Much in her voice is admirable: there is some of the steely strength of a Frida Leider, some of the impassioned drama of a Lotte Lehmann. In a way, it was the perfect voice for the standard German operatic repertoire. Unfortunately, for those who have heard her more successful peers, Delia Reinhardt may prove something of a disappointment, sounding like an undeveloped Leider or Lehmann, giving us too little of what the other singers gave in such abundance.

Even some of Reinhardt's own contemporaries initially felt that certain qualities were wanting in her delivery. Alexander Dillmann reviewed her guest performances and noted, after hearing her Pamina, an utter lack of "warmth" in her voice; hers was a "chaste, almost cool" voice, one that she used, however, with "a great deal of taste and even more skill."[1] He withheld judgment on her until he had heard her portrayal of Agathe, which convinced him that she did not belong with the Munich opera company. "When I heard her," he wrote, "I thought I was attending an interesting singing lesson rather than a performance of one of the liveliest works of German opera." Though proper enough from a technical standpoint—even "immaculately pure"—her singing lacked drama and personality.[2] Yet despite Dillmann's reservations, by the following year she had become an active member of the Munich company, and her singing and stage presence would win her many admirers. In January 1917 Thomas Mann praised her as a "happy acquisition" for the Hoftheater.[3]

It's hard to say just when Walter fell in love with Delia Reinhardt, but at some point after she joined the Munich troupe she seems to have become the woman closest to Walter's heart. Irma Geering, long a good friend of Reinhardt's and the person with whom Reinhardt spent her final years, said that a year after Reinhardt joined the troupe in Munich, Walter wanted to marry her.[4] This, of course, is the recollection of an event that had taken place about eight decades before, and the details might have become blurred over time. But there is little question that Walter developed a deep affection for Reinhardt during his years in Munich, and that the two were on intimate terms, though she had become the wife of the baritone Gustav Schützendorf sometime before November 1919, and Walter himself remained married until his wife's death in 1945.[5] Other affairs between Walter and his singers (or fans) have been rumored, and Walter certainly received large quantities of mail from adoring female admirers, some of whom must have presented a strong temptation. But if there was one great love in Walter's later life, it was Delia Reinhardt.

The complications of love—with both tragic and comic consequences—were at the thematic core of a double bill that Walter gave at the Hoftheater on March 28. Overshadowing almost everything else that Walter conducted in 1916, the two works, both being given for the first time, were one-act operas by Erich Wolfgang Korngold: *Violanta* and *Der Ring des Polykrates*. Though no longer a child, Korngold was presenting two compositions showing such mastery of the orchestra, such knowledge of dramatic structure, and such depth of expression and harmonic sophistication that it was hard to believe a teenager had written them. Walter never forgot the experience of listening to the young man singing through his two operas while playing his own accompaniment at the piano. "One could have compared his interpretation of works of his on the piano," Walter wrote many years later, "to the eruption of a musical-dramatic Volcano, if the lyric episodes or graceful moments had not also found their insinuating expression in his playing."[6]

The first item of the evening, *Violanta*, offers a plot that smacks of Jacobean tragedies of blood (and their Victorian derivatives). Set in fifteenth-century Italy, it is rife with those ingredients so comforting to the box office: lust, revenge, and violence. Korngold's suavely luxuriant score serves as a perfect complement to the decadent plot, in which the heroine, Violanta, sets out to arrange the murder of her sister's seducer but instead falls in love with him. After the story of Violanta's decline and fall, Korngold cleared the air with a comedy set in eighteenth-century Saxony, *Der Ring des Polykrates*. The action centers on a game that pries into the amorous past of the central female character, Laura, and her servant, Lieschen, while a recurring theme pits artistic originality against mere imitation. Fully in keeping with that theme, the score is marked by both imitation and originality; hints of *Rosenkavalier* are easily discernible, but Korngold's own voice speaks far more loudly than Strauss's, and the Straussian passages should surely be viewed as homage to an older master rather than pilferings.

The son of Julius Korngold clearly found a sympathetic spirit in the Bavarian music director. In fact, Willi Gloeckner seems to have felt that Walter bestowed rather too much attention on the boy: "One asks oneself how it comes about that this sensation was prepared with such a brilliant production, in which everything fit together in an almost unprecedented manner? I have never seen Bruno Walter apply himself with such enthusiasm."[7] Erich Korngold, of course, was overjoyed by the conductor's wholehearted commitment. "What can I say to an artist like you," he wrote to Walter afterwards, "one who is great, pure, understanding, and loving? You must have felt how delighted I was to hear my music resound in such a way—I believe I may safely say this—that it will doubtless never be heard again."[8] Yet for all Korngold's satisfaction with the performance and for all the fanfare surrounding the two operas by the wunderkind, neither work held the public's attention for very long. They enjoyed only a handful of performances in Munich immediately following the premiere, and a few more the following season.

While Korngold's works were unquestionably the most exciting offerings of the year, Walter presided over another operatic first in 1916, a work by his former chief at the Vienna Hofoper, Felix Weingartner. *Dame Kobold*, based on the seventeeth-century comedy by Pedro Calderón, had its Munich premiere on November 23, 1916, with Weingartner supervising the final rehearsals and attending on opening night. One wonders how Walter, who had recently expressed regret at not being able to compose, felt about performing a large-scale work by a major rival conductor. And what did Weingartner feel? Not disappointment in Walter, who offered a committed, sympathetic, and beautiful performance of the opera, according to the reviewers. Weingartner himself recalled the "polished performances of this opera, carried out with particular care by Bruno Walter in Munich."[9]

But while opera remained the dominant responsibility in his musical life, Walter continued to perform in orchestra and chamber concerts, and occasionally performers would include some of the music director's own compositions on their programs. On March 14, 1916 (as part of a chamber music recital given by Walter, Alexander Petschnikoff, and Johannes Heger), Maria Ivogün sang several songs by Pfitzner and Walter. For once, Walter's works seemed to be winning unqualified praise. One critic judged the songs "noble" and "spirited," and the audience, which demanded an encore for the Eichendorff song "Elfe," evidently shared his enthusiasm.[10]

Bach's *Matthäus-Passion*, which Walter usually performed at Easter time, was absent from his concerts in 1916, but he by no means neglected oratorios that year. In mid-March he revived Schumann's rarely heard *Das Paradies und die Peri*, a charming work that merited a reprise in December, and in November he presented Handel's *Samson*. For both oratorios the Musikalische Akademie provided the instrumental support, and Walter's subscription concerts with that orchestra continued in full force through 1916, mostly offering standard repertoire. One unusual item, presented on November 27, 1916, was the premiere of Clemens von Franckenstein's Four Songs for Baritone and Orchestra, opus 34, with Emil Schipper as the baritone soloist.

As a pianist, Walter continued to lend his services to singers and chamber musicians, including the renowned Wagnerian Anton van Rooy and the violinist Alexander Petschnikoff. Such recitals no doubt added to Walter's many professional burdens, but it was the unrelenting work at the opera house that took its toll on Walter in 1916. At the end of May, Hugo Röhr had to substitute for Walter, who had fallen ill and would need an extended vacation to recover. By late November, Walter was desperate to leave the theater, which for "eleven months of the year" drained him to his "last drop of blood," as he wrote to Gabrilowitsch. He hoped for a position in America, perhaps with the Boston Symphony Orchestra if Karl Muck left his post there.[11] Muck, of course, would leave his post soon enough—involuntarily, however, and only to be interned on the dubious charge of espionage. Germans were not welcome in Boston (or any number of other American cities) during the war.

Despite his time-devouring musical schedule, Walter's engagement with art was not limited to performing music. He remained an avid reader and an eloquent writer. Authors often figured among his close friends. In Vienna he had known Arthur Schnitzler, Siegfried Lipiner, and other professional writers; in Munich one of his neighbors was Thomas Mann, who became a lifelong friend. The acquaintance probably began shortly after Walter arrived in Munich, though the beginnings of their friendship are hard to pinpoint. As Mann's diaries show, the two men frequently spoke about literature, music, politics, and life. On one occasion, Mann was clearly touched by Walter's enthusiasm over the lengthy poem "Gesang vom Kindchen," which the author had just sent him; he recorded that Walter "repeated his warm praise of the poem, which he has now read three times, once aloud to his wife. His response to it is by far the most favorable I have had so far." On another occasion, during a performance of Pfitzner's *Der arme Heinrich*, "Walter threw glances" at Mann "from the podium to call [his] attention to the monks' chorus," much to Mann's delight.[12]

While hobnobbing with one of Germany's leading authors, Walter himself continued to write essays on music and aesthetics. In Vienna he had already shown himself capable of wielding a pen with great skill, and he turned to the written word once more in 1916 to express his thoughts on the state of opera in Munich during the war years and—the real purpose behind the essay—to voice his anger over what he viewed as hostility from the press.[13] Walter's most substantial literary work to date, the essay bore the Wagnerian title "Art and Public Opinion" and appeared in the *Süddeutsche Monatshefte*, a periodical edited by Paul Cossmann, a conservative nationalist, a close friend of Pfitzner's, and a Jew turned Catholic who would ultimately die in the concentration camp at Terezín.

The heart of the essay is an extended invective against the critics. Whether qualified to pass judgment or not, Walter argues, the critics write what they will, and artists are helpless if they receive bad reviews. Indeed, the artist, however strong, "cannot remain fully uninfluenced" by the reviews. With various reference works ready to hand, the critic can become the scourge of young artists striving for lofty goals, condemning a composer's supposed paucity of invention; if the public gives a new work an ovation, the critic can contend that "the loud applause was not for the composition but for the performers."[14] The examples Walter adduces might have been inspired by recent reviews of works by Schreker and Korngold, though he could just as easily have been ruminating on reviews of Mahler's works—or, even more to the point, reviews of his own compositions.

Whatever hostility some of the critics felt toward Walter would certainly have been aggravated by Walter's essay. His implication that many reviewers are inept and should be weeded out, and his suggestion that a court of appeals might be established to ensure critical justice, probably even made him a few new enemies.[15] Shortly after Walter's piece appeared, Thomas Mann published "Music in Munich," a follow-up essay to "Art and Public Opinion," asserting the author's solidarity with Walter, though Mann's decision to write such an essay in the first place smacks of damage control.[16] In any event, neither essay seems to have had its desired effect. The year 1917 saw the advent of an anonymous critic for the *Allgemeine Zeitung* who frankly styled himself "Severus," a professional taste-maker whose unflagging attacks on Walter's rubato could not have made the conductor any happier with the role of the press in recording public opinion.

If the two operas by Korngold stood out in Walter's career in 1916, the opera that had its premiere in the Prinzregententheater on June 12, 1917—Hans Pfitzner's *Palestrina*—was in Walter's view one of the highest artistic peaks in his entire life. The publicity accorded this work was phenomenal, far outstripping that given to the first Munich performance of, say, Wagner's *Parsifal* or Korngold's double bill. For many, certainly for Walter, this was the greatest German opera of the day, and its premiere in Munich drew forth comparisons with the premieres of *Tristan* and *Meistersinger*. It led off a "Pfitzner Week," which also included performances of *Der arme Heinrich* under Pfitzner and *Die Rose vom Liebesgarten* under Walter, as well as chamber-music and song recitals. Delia Reinhardt, who sang Minnelied in *Die Rose*, had a small part as one of the angels in *Palestrina*. The role of Palestrina was taken by Karl Erb, Borromeo by Fritz Feinhals, and Ighino by Maria Ivogün. The performance, prepared with exemplary attention to detail, was praised to the skies.

Before the premiere, Walter told Thomas Mann that the "musical part" of *Palestrina* was matched "only by the supreme composers of the past."[17] Deeply impressed by the opera, Mann himself attended several performances and wrote a warm appreciation of the work in his essay "On Virtue."[18] In November Walter and his troupe took the production to Basel, Bern, and Zurich as propaganda for German art and culture. Outside Germany, however, it has never even come close to reaching the popularity of *Lohengrin*, to say nothing of *Tristan* and *Meistersinger*. What, then, made Walter and others feel so passionately attached to this work?

The theories about art that permeate *Palestrina* intersected with Walter's own beliefs, which he held steadfastly throughout his life. Pfitzner had worked on the opera for years, writing the libretto himself; the ideas he wanted to express were too personal to entrust to another. The key theme is that of the artist's duty to art. The archetypal artist in the opera, the sixteenth-century composer Giovanni Pierluigi da Palestrina, has the task of saving the great tradition of polyphonic music at a time when it is threatened by two forces, the first being the new style promoted by neoclassical enthusiasts like Giovanni Bardi. These musicians, who condemned complex polyphony for its lack of classical precedent and its text-garbling counterpoint, experimented with monody—melody with a simple chordal accompaniment—and their experiments led to the birth of opera. The other force was the Catholic Church, then in the throes of the Counter-Reformation. Some church officials felt that the intricate settings that obscured the all-important texts of the Mass and sacred motets had no place in the house of God; praises sung to the Lord, they argued, should take the form of simple chant.

Palestrina plainly stood for Pfitzner himself, who was trying to save the great musical tradition from avant-garde composers like Schoenberg and Stravinsky. (There was a decided irony, surely not lost on Pfitzner, that the Italian monodists in effect invented the very art form that Pfitzner employed to criticize the twentieth-century avant-garde.) While creating something new, the artist must be keenly aware of the past, contributing to it rather than abandoning it. It was all doctrine that Walter subscribed to with absolute conviction. But another aspect of the opera must have haunted both Walter and Pfitzner as the political events of the next three decades unfolded. For the artist Palestrina is an individual working within an institution that seeks to use art as a political tool. Recognizing the divine nature of his art, he will not profane the muse. The institution here is the Catholic Church—portrayed in the opera as bureaucratic, hypocritical, and anti-German—but it clearly represents any organization that treats individuals in general (and artists in particular) as pawns, imprisoning them if they refuse to follow orders. It was perhaps this aspect of the opera that made Walter write, in a defense of his friend after the war, that "the noble emotions reigning in Pfitzner's poem . . . are astronomically far from Nazi standards."[19]

Though Pfitzner's opera was the premiere that loomed largest in Walter's schedule for 1917, it was not the only new work that he introduced to Munich operagoers that year. On March 3 he brought two novelties to the Hoftheater by composers whose music he had championed before: Julius Bittner's new singspiel *Das höllisch Gold* (with Luise Willer and Gustav Schützendorf in the leading roles), followed by a new ballet by Paul Klenau, *Klein Idas Blumen*. Later in the year, on November 3, Walter gave the world premiere of Walter Courvoisier's Arthurian *Lanzelot und Elaine*, a four-hour work apparently full of muted subtleties that demanded much from the audience but also rewarded those who followed attentively. Emil Schipper sang the role of Lanzelot, Delia Reinhardt that of Elaine. The performance was hailed as superb, and even "Severus," usually critical of Walter, gave the conductor credit on this occasion for bringing the work to life.[20]

Of the three choral works that Walter programmed in 1917, two were oratorios well known in Germany—Bach's *Matthäus-Passion* and Mendelssohn's *Elias (Elijah)*—and the other was the Mass in C Minor by Mozart, a piece familiar now, but not when Walter performed it in Munich. Both the Mass and the "Exsultate, jubilate" (given shortly afterward) were billed, astonishingly from our vantage point, as first-time performances.[21] After the explosion of Mozart celebrations in 1991 and the huge success, both on stage and on screen, of Peter Shaffer's *Amadeus*, it's easy to forget how much of the composer's music was virtually unknown earlier in the century.

Also in 1917 Walter's commitment to new music led to more premieres with the Musikalische Akademie. *The Chinese Flute*, a poetic anthology that had supplied the texts for *Das Lied von der Erde*, inspired Walter Braunfels to write three orchestral "Chinese" songs, and on March 12, 1917, Delia Reinhardt sang them for the first time in Munich, under Walter's direction. Both the settings and the performance drew critical acclaim. Yet a more important item on the program, as far as Walter's personal career is concerned, was the principal piece of the evening, Bruckner's Ninth Symphony (Ferdinand Löwe's edition), prepared by the conductor, as the critics noted, with "religious care."[22] Walter was probably introduced to the piece in February 1903, when Löwe himself gave its posthumous premiere in Vienna. But Walter's 1917 performance was almost certainly his first encounter, as a conductor, with Bruckner's last, unfinished masterpiece, a work that would gain both musical and spiritual importance for him during the course of his life and would appear on his programs with increasing frequency in his final years. The "religious care" with which he prepared his first performance seems to have stayed with him to the end. In the 1950s he helped the Bruckner scholar Max Auer successfully petition to have the piece recognized by the Catholic Church as a religious work, playable in church.[23]

Two of the novelties that Walter chose to perform with the Musikalische Akademie at the end of the year showed the direction in which Walter's taste was moving and also, in hindsight, suggest unsettling connections between musical and political reactionism. Carl Ehrenberg's Suite für Orchester, played from manuscript, had its world premiere on December 3. Ehrenberg, then a conductor in Augsburg, was a friend of Thomas Mann's—indeed, at the turn of the century Mann harbored a particular fondness for Paul Ehrenberg, Carl's brother—and as a composer he earned a reputation for writing "thoroughly tonal" music.[24] The tone poems that constituted his orchestral suite betrayed the influence of Richard Strauss, according to Richard Würz, who judged him more a "schooled" composer than a "born" one and attributed the success of the piece largely to Walter's sensitive conducting and the orchestra's "very beautiful" playing.[25] A week later, on December 10, Walter offered Max Trapp's *Sinfonia giocosa* "for the first time" in Munich. Like Ehrenberg's Suite für Orchester, Trapp's *Sinfonia giocosa* drew inspiration from Richard Strauss, so much so that Paul Ehlers felt that the composer hadn't found own his voice yet.[26] Both works bore a distinctly conservative stamp, and both composers joined the Nazi Party before 1933, enjoying official support and encouragement during the Third Reich.[27]

Throughout much of his career, Walter's interactions with family members were recorded only in the occasional letter, the memoirs of his friends, and chance references in the newspapers. Yet in spite of the dearth of material giving us glimpses into his nearest relations, it's clear that the demands of his job did not utterly blind him to the presence and needs of his family. While away on business, he wrote to his daughter Lotte, checking on her education and her friendships. Walter—or "Kuzi," as his daughters called him—was delighted that Lotte was making friends but, like a Victorian patriarch, became anxious when he learned that his thirteen-year-old daughter had developed an association with a young man called Pepi. "I'm happy that you have a girlfriend; that's very good for you," he wrote in the summer of 1917. "I'm less pleased about your friendship with Pepi. Young boys at this age in particular are at their worst, even if it doesn't in the least seem so, and can have a bad influence on your surroundings—even without your knowing it. As politely and unobtrusively as possible, please avoid frequent encounters with him; at all costs," he warned, "avoid being alone with him."[28] On her birthday Walter sent Lotte greetings and a suggestion for reading, apparently in response to some Dickens novels she'd acquired. *A Tale of Two Cities*, he thought, would be more fitting than *Little Dorrit* or *Martin Chuzzlewit*; those two novels were "unsuitable for such an eager learner," and he advised her to turn them over to her mother.[29] Walter's tone to his daughter, while gentle and affectionate, is also unmistakably protective, and it must have been hard for Lotte to develop on her own. Though she married twice, her father seems to have remained the central male figure in her life. She and her second husband lived with Walter in Beverly Hills until his death, and she died less than a decade afterward, not long after assembling a collection of his letters and seeing them through the press.

Artistically, the year 1918 saw few surprises from Walter. Three orchestral songs by Walter Braunfels—"An die Parzen," "Auf ein Soldatengrab," "Der

Tod fürs Vaterland"—had their very first performance on November 25 under Walter, sung by Emil Schipper. The concert also included Schoenberg's *Verklärte Nacht*, a piece that Walter championed despite the resistance he almost invariably encountered wherever he performed it.[30] To commemorate the hundredth anniversary of the opening of the Nationaltheater, Walter presented a new production of Joseph Weigl's early nineteenth-century singspiel *Die Schweizerfamilie*; and another singspiel, Pfitzner's *Christelflein* (a reworking of material formerly used as incidental music), enjoyed its Munich premiere under Walter on December 7, 1918, with the composer present to receive a hearty ovation from the audience.[31]

Pfitzner's former assistant, Wilhelm Furtwängler, maintained his ties with Walter. Like Walter, he aspired to become a professional composer, and throughout his life he returned to composition, writing in a late romantic style that became increasingly dated as his technique improved. From time to time he would turn to Walter for encouragement and inspiration. After the summer of 1918 Furtwängler apparently expressed his regret at missing a performance of *Tristan* under Walter, and Walter was sorry as well. "What I missed in your letter," he added in his letter to Furtwängler, "was any information about creative work you'd actually done during the summer, and I conclude from your silence that your work was interrupted by the end of the vacation, which grieves me deeply. It would be most desirable for you to succeed in obtaining a position as a concert conductor, which would allow you to be able to follow your true calling. The theater simply makes too many demands on a composer." Walter was speaking from painful, personal experience, and he sympathized with the plight of his colleague, whom he then regarded as a kindred spirit. In discussing Furtwängler's projected program in Vienna, Walter wished him a great success there—"since, because of the affinity of our natures (despite any differences), I always feel as if the things that touch you were my own affair."[32]

That year, both conductors—along with Siegfried Ochs, Arthur Nikisch, Felix Weingartner, and Max von Schillings—took part in a debate that revolved around a new system of notating orchestral scores. Schoenberg had devised a method to save space and to eliminate some of the confusion that arose from reading a full score, advocating a system whereby an entire orchestral score would be distilled into one or a few treble-and-bass-clef arrangements (akin to piano reductions), with running commentary on the changing instrumentation. When the leading conductors of Germany and Austria were canvassed for their opinions of the proposed system, they rejected it roundly. Nikisch complained that a conductor would have to reorient himself to the changing instrumentation in almost every measure: "The most complicated score by Richard Strauss is mere child's play by comparison." Weingartner sneeringly added that Schoenberg's notation was "fully in keeping" with his music. Walter, however, raised a musical objection that reflected some of his foremost concerns as an interpreter. He granted that the new system would ease a "vertical" reading of the score, but it would hinder a "horizontal" reading and thus prevent one from clearly following the voice leading. That in itself, in his view, invalidated the system.[33] Keenly sensitive to the underlying harmony in counterpoint and to the counterpoint inherent in harmony, Walter rebelled against a system that threatened to bury individual melodic strands in a chordal fabric. His brief but respectful grievance could not have strengthened his relationship with the composer, who admired Walter's conducting but would grumble against his personality for decades to come.

The year 1918 was, perhaps more than most other years, a time of transition. The arts lost two of their most innovative creators, Claude Debussy and Gustav Klimt. Radical transitions took place in the field of politics. World War I came to an end, with Germany emerging as the loser. The time was ripe for radical reformers to swoop in, and in November the Communists seized control of Munich. Gunfire rang through the streets "deep into the night," as Thomas Mann recorded, and looters took advantage of the chaos that temporarily reigned. "In the afternoon I stayed dressed and only rested on the chaise longue," Mann wrote on November 8, 1918, "since Walter, pale and beside himself, had warned Katia [Mann's wife] of the approach of a 'mob' that never, in fact, arrived. Katia and the children cleared out the pantry and hid three-quarters of our provisions in various rooms of the house.—Now, after tea, I hear shooting again."[34] Controlled by the new regime, the *Münchner Neueste Nachrichten* printed the *Communist Manifesto* in its pages. Old positions were dissolved; the Hoftheater became the Nationaltheater. In fact, according to Walter it was largely owing to his proests against the "revolutionary" contingent that the name wasn't changed to Volkstheater or Landestheater. Walter's aristocratic ally Clemens von Franckenstein would for a time be ousted from his position as manager, and Walter himself was on the verge of resigning, only being dissuaded by Franckenstein, who urged him to stay.[35] Though Walter did not get along with the new regime, he retained his post as Bavarian music director. The new regime was short-lived—its prime mover, Kurt Eisner, was assassinated on February 21, 1919, and shortly afterward the socialist government began to crumble—

but no one in 1918 could have predicted the consequences of the November revolution.

For months to come, the strain of living in a state of revolutionary overthrow would take its toll on Walter, who remained as overworked as ever. In April 1919 he wrote to his parents of the "terrifying nights" and "the constant fears" he and his family endured—despite which, they continued to be more or less well.[36] He feared a financial collapse at the opera house, though the worst-case scenario he was envisioning inspired some positive thoughts, or at least some gallows humor: "Maybe," he wrote to his parents in June, "after the collapse of the theater (it won't necessarily come, of course), I'll lead a life that is, to be sure, more modest, but also more healthy."[37]

Though Walter seems to have written no music during his years in Munich, those who knew and worked with him continued to perform his works. On January 18, 1919, an ensemble composed of the pianist August Schmid-Lindner, the violinist Jani Szántó, and the Belgian cellist Josef Disclez (Walter's frequent recital partner and principal cellist in the opera orchestra) performed the music director's Piano Trio. Premiered in 1906 in Vienna, it was a piece that Walter obviously thought highly of, and it had even been given a hearing once before in Munich, in 1911. In both cases, the critics had for the most part been unimpressed, and the same held true on this occasion. A curious review appeared in the *Münchner Neueste Nachrichten*, written by neither Paul Ehlers nor Richard Würz, the critics who normally covered such events, but by one H. Ru., who confessed that he couldn't attend the performance himself but was merely reporting what his unnamed deputy passed on to him. It's tempting (if not quite justifiable) to assume that the leading reviewers deliberately avoided the recital, not wanting to be in a position where they might have to criticize the compositions of Munich's most influential musician. As it turned out, the review was hardly offensive, but its reservations were such as to discourage further attempts at composition. The piece, written some time ago, inclined toward romanticism (the critic's polite way of saying that the music already sounded out of date), and for all its praiseworthy construction and its effective lively movements, it left "no deeply moving impression."[38] Walter had heard it all before, from Julius Korngold and others, usually expressed less delicately. Surely if the piece left no memorable impression, it had failed, however admirable its construction. Szántó and Schmid-Lindner made another attempt to place Walter's music before the public in February 1920, when they performed the Violin Sonata, but the critic Richard Würz, echoing words that were all too familiar to

Walter, wrote that the piece left "scarcely any doubt that the re-creative talent of this eminent artist is stronger than his creative talent."[39] One can almost hear that criticism still resounding in the opening paragraph of Walter's autobiography, which ends with a poignant lie: "I have made only the music of others sound forth, I have been but a 're-creator.'"[40]

An event that drew far more attention than any of Walter's compositions had ever attracted was the Munich premiere of Schreker's new opera, *Die Gezeichneten*, given on February 15, 1919. Delia Reinhardt starred as Carlotta, Karl Erb as Alviano Salvago, Gustav Schützendorf as Adorno, and Emil Schipper as Tamare. Even more luxuriant in sound and more lubricious in subject matter than *Der ferne Klang*, *Die Gezeichneten* elicited both excitement and outrage from the press and, presumably, the public. Set in Renaissance Italy, the story is plainly meant to shock—though not only to shock. It is a substantial work of art. On an island near Genoa, the ugly Alviano has built a paradise devoted to beauty and pleasure, where young gentlemen abscond with the fairest beauties of the city and indulge themselves in wild orgies. Throughout the score the harmonies are almost vertiginously lush. Carlotta, daughter of the Podestà, desires to paint Alviano's soul, to which he consents after some initial hesitation. Alviano soon falls in love with Carlotta, but despite her affection for him, she eventually succumbs to the lecherous advances of the rakish Tamare, whom Alviano murders in the final scene. Schreker himself wrote the libretto, which wades dangerously deep into the waters of erotic desire, both male and female, at a time when such matters were usually treated more obliquely, even on the operatic stage.

Did Walter approve of the opera? He himself would have been the first to admit that Schreker's work was in some ways alien to his own personality. At some point between 1913 and the end of 1916, Walter and Schreker had become good enough friends to use the familiar form of address, *Du*, in their correspondence. (Walter commonly used the more formal *Sie* with his colleagues.) There had been serious discussion about a Munich performance of *Die Gezeichneten* already in 1916. But the local press, Walter wrote to Schreker, had attacked the Munich Opera for favoring Viennese composers and was particularly wary of Schreker.[41] By November 1916 Walter was explaining to Schreker why the manager of the Munich Opera had decided to postpone the performance. He indignantly brushed aside Schreker's apparent suggestion that "foreign influences" had turned him against the composer. But the hostile reviewers (still very active) and the public's uneasy response to *Der ferne Klang* were, Walter explained, unpleasant realities that couldn't be ignored. About his own feelings on Schreker's work, Walter was quite candid: "For me personally, your creative work, both poetic and musical, remains in a certain sense foreign. The purity of your artistic will, the nearly fanatical traits that characterize your relation to your art, and finally your undoubted artistic, if not purely musical, productivity—all these things always genuinely (or, better yet, powerfully) attract me." The letter ended with an unusual rhetorical strategy: "To describe my relation to your work with words that will be fully understandable to you, I'd like to say the following, given from your point of view: 'Walter is conservative, indeed, even somewhat reactionary, and I am a representative of the most extreme modernism.' I, for my part, would of course not accept this characterization, but I've attempted to speak with your language and your thoughts to be as clear as possible for you."[42] It's evident that Walter had already grown accustomed to being branded a conservative, "even somewhat reactionary," musician, though just a few years before he'd been chided by the conservative press for writing ultramodern music. He seemed resigned to the fact that some would view him as an unadventurous churner-out of the established repertoire, even if he himself didn't share their verdict. Charges of conservatism, however, should be weighed against the bold programming that Walter continually fought for in Munich. And Schreker's opera, however controversial, regularly filled the house during the opening performances.[43]

The other major operatic performance that Walter offered in 1919 was the Munich premiere of Strauss's *Die Frau ohne Schatten*, given on November 9 in the Nationaltheater, less than a month after its world premiere in Vienna. It was also the first anniversary of the Communist revolution, as Paul Ehlers commented in his review, noting that the Strauss premiere had brought back many of the old regulars who had avoided the opera house since the revolution.[44] The cast included Otto Wolf as the Emperor, Delia Reinhardt as the Empress, Zdenka Mottl-Fassbender as the Nurse, Emil Schipper as Barak, and Margot Leander as Barak's wife. Next to *Die Gezeichneten*, Strauss's opera seems almost chaste in its harmonies and story line. Nevertheless, the new work was complex and sonically rich, employing the full palette of Straussian tone colors. Though now widely regarded as one of the greatest collaborative efforts of Strauss and Hofmannsthal, the opera initially drew some curmudgeonly grumbling from the press. Even in Munich, which prided itself on being Strauss's city, the reviews of this masterly offering were mixed at best. The opera, running to about four hours, was too long and its plot too convoluted to score an easy victory. With its strong symbolism and its Eastern setting, the opera inescapably invited comparison with *Die Zauberflöte*, though Pidoll of the *Allgemeine Zeitung*, who detested Strauss and Hofmannsthal's latest creation, wrote that to compare the two works was "blasphemy."[45] The performance, however, received high praise, with Walter's total devotion to the production and his firm control over the "gigantic apparatus" winning special mention.[46]

Delia Reinhardt, the Empress in *Die Frau ohne Schatten*, was receiving leading roles in more and more operas directed by Walter, and she sang in Walter's *Matthäus-Passion* for the first time in 1919, on which occasion she was introduced to Thomas Mann in the greenroom.[47] (Mann's son Klaus, future author of the novel *Mephisto*, was singing in the chorus.) And as Elsa Korneck had once done, Delia Reinhardt sang Eva in Walter's *Meistersinger*. Walter and Reinhardt also joined forces on November 13 in a lieder recital, with Walter accompanying on piano. During this time, her then husband, Gustav Schützendorf, had been absent from Munich for some months. He'd traveled to Milan to work on his vocal technique, and there he reportedly developed a case of typhoid fever. By November 21 Reinhardt had traveled to Milan to tend her ailing husband.[48] It is hard not to speculate that the constant close contact of Walter and Reinhardt, and the absence of Schützendorf, might have contributed to the intimacy that eventually grew between them.

Along with his growing relationship to Delia Reinhardt, another development in Munich must have touched Walter personally. More and more frequently the newspapers reported on "the Jewish question" and on unrest among certain malcontents. In April the Jewish League of Soldiers at the Front placed a large open letter to the Bavarian government in the *Münchner Neueste Nachrichten*, protesting the "unbelievable hatred of Jews" that certain groups in the city had been fostering for months. To us it seems inevitable that a Jewish music director would eventually come under fire from the fledgling Nazi Party, at the time still widely dismissed as a fringe group. The previous year, articles had appeared denying rumors that Walter was to leave Munich, but obviously word was spreading that he might find employment elsewhere, and perhaps he had indeed begun to look for another, more welcoming environment in which to work.

Like most other Germans, Walter was utterly dissatisfied with life in postwar Germany. The Treaty of Versailles demanded massive reparations from Germany for its part in World War I, and Walter was as concerned about its effect on his country as were the loudest demagogues of the Left and the

Right. The German people had collectively become ill, he wrote to Ossip Gabrilowitsch in March, and suicide attempts were on the increase. He worried about the future of his children "in a country that, through the Treaty of Versailles, is doomed for generations to the profoundest debasement and to the greatest misery."[49] Nevertheless, he pressed on with his life, deriving pleasure from his two daughters, both of whom were then studying music with him. "Lottchen," he continued in his letter to Gabrilowitsch, "is a grown-up young lady who is already taking singing lessons with her father; Gretchen is unusually musical and plays the piano splendidly—right now she's playing Chopin's Scherzo in B Minor. Both study piano with their father."

During his last two years in Munich, Walter's long-distance friendship with Gabrilowitsch continued to grow stronger. Gabrilowitsch sent the Walters a veritable cornucopia of American foodstuffs, much appreciated during the deprivations of postwar Germany.[50] While that relationship prospered, however, another was threatening to dissolve. Hans Pfitzner had moved to Munich after the end of the war, having lost his position in Strasbourg when the city was turned over to France as part of Germany's reparations for World War I. In Munich he hoped to land the position of Oberregisseur at the opera. When he did not get the job—the decision was by no means Walter's—he seems to have held Walter responsible, perhaps having been misinformed by his wife, Mimi.[51] Walter complained that Pfitzner had cut him off, and his mute hostility pierced Walter to the heart. "It's impossible for me," he wrote to Pfitzner in June, "to follow your method of keeping silent in a matter like ours. You should at least know that I'm deeply hurt and affronted. . . . How shall I have satisfaction for this horrible injury? It weighs heavily upon me and preys on my mind. Since you've been in Munich, I've had nothing but injustice from you. There hasn't been a single friendly word coming from your mouth or a single friendly look from your eyes."[52] By all accounts, Pfitzner was no easy person to get along with. (After his death, Walter commented that Pfitzner "was not tolerant—couldn't be—and thus when a fundamental difference of opinion arose, reaching an agreement was impossible. In other words, he was easier to love from afar than up close."[53]) It was typical of Walter, though, that on this occasion, as on others, he insisted on bringing these disagreeable matters into the open, maintaining human contact. The various psychological pressures bearing down on him were taking their toll on his constitution. At the end of the letter, he apologized for his bad handwriting: his arm was ailing again, and his nerves were frayed.

The punishing life of the opera house was also a regular source of stress for Walter, yet he continued to look for new and ambitious projects for his theaters. His most successful new productions were of Hugo Wolf's comic opera *Der Corregidor* and Weber's *Oberon*, the latter touched up by Mahler. There were also two premieres in 1920, *Das Spielwerk*, by the ever controversial Franz Schreker, and *Die Vögel* (based on Aristophanes' *The Birds*), by Walter Braunfels. Schreker's opera, a revision of his *Das Spielwerk und die Prinzessin* (first performed in 1913), had its world premiere in the Nationaltheater on October 30, 1920. Like his other works, *Das Spielwerk* reveled in the sensuous and the sensual, drawing praise and condemnation alike from contemporaries. *Die Vögel*, in which the central characters appeared in striking bird costumes, had its premiere on November 30, also at the Nationaltheater. A brilliant work, lacking the scandalous elements of Schreker's plots and showing off the strengths of the singers in the Munich troupe, it scored an unqualified success.

Beyond the walls of Munich in 1920, tributes to Gustav Mahler, marking the passage of sixty years since his birth, took the form of two extraordinary concert series—one in Amsterdam, under Willem Mengelberg's direction, the other in Vienna, led by Oskar Fried—as well as several smaller concerts, one of which involved Walter. Though he conducted nothing so grand as the cycles presented by Mengelberg and Fried, Walter did offer what was, for him, an unusual token of esteem to his late master. On March 6 and 7 he conducted Mahler's Seventh Symphony, apparently for the only time in his career. The ensemble was composed of the Konzertverein and Tonkünstler orchestras, organizations that would eventually merge to form the Vienna Symphony. Both concerts, along with the open rehearsal on March 5, were sold out, and in his enthusiastic review of the performances, R. Hoffmann succinctly commented: "Walter conducted; I'll say no more."[54] Despite the positive reaction to Walter's performance, Mahler's Seventh was a symphony that the conductor consciously avoided on later occasions, at least in part because he wanted to present to the public "only the strongest [works] that Mahler wrote," and he clearly did not consider the Seventh such a work.[55]

Another massive piece—one that Walter had dreamed of performing almost since his arrival in Munich—finally received its first performance in that city on April 12, 1920: Schoenberg's *Gurre-Lieder*.[56] The Musikalische Akademie and the Lehrgesangverein joined forces to perform this vocal and orchestral tour de force, which Walter and his contemporaries praised almost as passionately as they reviled the composer's later music. The soloists were Karl Erb as Waldemar, Delia Reinhardt as Tove, Luise Willer as the Voice of the Wood-Dove, Emil Grifft as the Peasant, and Alfred Jerger as Klauss-Narr. It was a work that Walter would perform later in Vienna and would gladly have conducted in New York, though the financial burden it carried made this impracticable.[57] As late as 1960 Walter was writing that Schoenberg's "powerful work" deserved a permanent place in the concert hall; nevertheless, he was aware of its logistical problems—the huge forces and many rehearsals needed.[58] In a panegyric on the performance and the piece itself, Paul Ehlers, remarking that the work made great demands on the conductor, pointed out that Walter put his "entire personality" into the work, infusing it "with rich sonic and spiritual life."[59] For all that, the notoriously ill-tempered composer apparently felt little gratitude toward Walter in later years. At the time of a performance of *Gurre-Lieder* in February 1951, led by Thor Johnson in Cincinnati, people were "astounded" to learn from Wolfgang Stresemann, who attended the concert, that Walter had performed the work in Vienna. "Schoenberg hadn't reported on these performances," Stresemann wrote to Walter, "or rather he gave the impression that he himself had conducted them in Vienna."[60]

The unending demands of work kept Walter's thoughts occupied, but his home life gave him much to think about as well. An epidemic of influenza, which killed millions of Europeans, was racing through Germany in 1919 and 1920. One person affected by it was Gretel, Walter's thirteen-year-old daughter, who had developed into a fetching young lady with enough talent to make her father gush over her accomplishments. "She's filled with music to her very fingertips," he wrote to Ossip Gabrilowitsch, "full of spirit, wit, and sparkling life; she's the warmest, most golden heart under the sun, a ray of happiness for anyone who comes in contact with her, and for us—well, I don't need to spell it out."[61] When she became feverish and showed no signs of improvement after several days, Walter consulted a doctor in Munich, who diagnosed her bronchial glands as having been infected with tuberculosis. Walter panicked. He was prepared to arrange for a costly treatment in Switzerland that would entail taking out a loan and paying it back over five years, but fortunately her malady was not so severe as he'd imagined. His elder daughter, Lotte, tersely noted half a century later that the "mild infection of the bronchial glands was cured in German sanatoriums," and one senses in her no-nonsense remark the tone of a daughter who still felt a twinge of jealousy that her father had agonized so deeply over her younger sister.[62]

His familial concerns, however, certainly didn't cause him to neglect the 150th anniversary of Beethoven's birth in 1920. On October 30 the *Münchner Neueste Nachrichten* printed a special Beethoven supplement in which prominent musicians and music historians expressed their thoughts on that colossus straddling the classical and romantic eras. Walter contributed a long essay on the *Missa solemnis*, a work he would perform three times in November. Though forgotten now, Walter's essay was an ambitious piece of *Kunstprosa*, replete with visions of nearly Blakean intensity. It reveals more strikingly than any of Walter's other essays the pictorial vividness of his imagination. The central point is that Beethoven, while working within the context of the Mass, was continually bursting out of the confines of ecclesiastical music, letting his humanity overtake his piety. Walter goes through the Mass, movement by movement, almost phrase by phrase, freely drawing on literature and painting to elucidate his conception of Beethoven's *Missa*. The presto in the Gloria, for example, conjures up a memorable fancy:

> It is a roaring, overwhelming shout of Gloria from millions of rejoicing voices; the arms are raised, the eyes enraptured: the jubilation of all humanity. Beethoven calls out his Hosanna almost like the unbelieving philosopher of Ivan Karamazov, from Dostoevsky's famous novel; after death, to atone for his disbelief, he had to wander through a quadrillion-kilometer darkness until he reached the gate of Paradise. But when he entered, after wandering for an eternity, he called out after two seconds that, for these two seconds in Paradise, one could wander through quadrillions of quadrillions of kilometers, and he sang his Hosanna with such rapture that, as Dostoevsky writes, "the more proper angels felt embarrassed straightaway."

Thomas Mann was familiar with this extraordinary essay, which he apparently heard Walter read as a lecture, though Mann wasn't wholly satisfied with the actual performance of the *Missa* at the open rehearsal. "The expectations aroused by Walter's talk," he wrote in his diary, were "fulfilled at best sporadically. In order to enjoy music I need to have heard it *often*, know it *thoroughly*." And in any case, Mann's thoughts weren't focused solely on the music. "My chief impression," he continued, "was of a remarkably handsome young man, Slavic in appearance and wearing a sort of Russian costume, with whom I established a kind of contact at a distance."[63]

Another work that Walter performed during the Beethoven celebrations was an opera that would come to have special significance for him, *Fidelio*. It was also, curiously, a work that Walter did not perform in Munich during his first few years there, leaving it to his colleagues, one of whom, Otto Hess (Walter's nemesis), died on November 8. As would often be the case in his later career, Walter's *Fidelio* was a thorough triumph.[64]

Adrian Boult, the Englishman who had been so impressed with Walter's Mozart performances in 1912, visited Munich again around 1920. This time he came to Walter with a letter of introduction from the editor of the *Daily Telegraph* and was invited to attend a rehearsal of *Figaro* in the Residenztheater. His description serves as a reminder that Walter, like his mentor Mahler, was not content merely to conduct the music; he strove to direct the action on stage as well: "The rehearsal took this form: three hours were called for the singers, joined by the orchestra for the last hour and a half. The singers assembled at 9:30 and Bruno had a pianist to do the recitatives. He stood at the footlights directing the proceedings and sometimes he would run up to a singer and say 'No, you should be there,' and pull him or her along. Then he would suddenly turn round to a shadowy figure who was sitting in the darkness of the rear stalls and ask: 'May I have your permission, Herr Professor?' That was the producer, who knew his job when Bruno Walter was conducting."[65] Walter had already entered the director's domain, and for the rest of his career he would make an impression on singers by extending his activities into the sphere of stage direction. Sometimes he was openly credited for the direction, as in Berlin, but more often not, as at the Metropolitan Opera, where he nevertheless frequently interjected his ideas about managing the action.

While his personal engagement with the musical and dramatic aspects of the standard operatic repertoire remained undiminished, the era for controversial operas in Walter's Munich career seems to have drawn to an end by 1921. Few critics could find anything to attack in Walter the musician. He continued to look for new works and to dust off old ones. A light opera by Paul Graener, *Schirin und Gertraude*, premiered on February 8, was one of the first new works performed by Walter in his next-to-last year as music director of Bavaria. An apparent success, the opera starred Delia Reinhardt, Luise Willer, and Alfred Jerger. A fresh production of Gluck's *Iphigenia in Aulis*, based on Richard Wagner's arrangement, enjoyed critical acclaim at the Nationaltheater. With leading members of his local troupe, Walter made a guest appearance in Berlin, performing *Don Pasquale* at the Metropoltheater at the beginning of January 1921, in a special concert to benefit the

Union of the Berlin Press.[66] In the spring he took several of his singers to Barcelona for more operatic performances. The circle of his fame continued to spread.

But despite these victories, all was not well. It is easy to forget how early the Nazi Party developed its characteristic identity. Adolf Hitler had already gained a reputation for incendiary oratory, and as a music-lover he had followed with outrage the rise of Bruno Walter from his years as Mahler's assistant in Vienna to his position as Royal Bavarian Generalmusikdirektor. It clearly rankled. As late as 1929 Hitler was claiming that Walter's increased fame and success in 1912 had been the result of Jewish maneuvering in the liberal press.[67] In 1921 the organ of the Nazi Party, the *Völkischer Beobachter*, was already a regularly published newspaper in Munich. Strewn with swastikas and packed with Jew-baiting articles, it included music reviews among its columns on the arts. The city's Jewish music director was a target waiting to be fired at, and the first shots came when the regular reviewer for the newspaper, who went by the initials H. B. (later, Dr. H. B.), gave place to the notorious Hermann Esser, one of Hitler's earliest supporters. Even in the company of thugs, Esser seems to have been regarded as a boor and an embarrassment, and his anti-Semitism knew no bounds. He eagerly capitalized on the economic discontent in the land. In April "the Allies had presented Germany the bill for reparations [for World War I], a whopping 132 billion gold marks—33 billion dollars—which the Germans howled they could not possibly pay."[68] Runaway inflation soon began its disastrous course in Germany. It is surely no coincidence that Esser's first attacks on Walter came at a time when the populace was painfully overtaxed and badly in need of a scapegoat.

In May, Esser wrote two essays that glanced at Walter, the first entitled "Scandal at the State Theater." Did the Bavarian Nationaltheater actually nurture German art any more, he asked, or had it become a playground for Jews? The hard-working people were taxed beyond reason to support a theater that charged prohibitively high admission fees. The taxpayers' money, meanwhile, was simply being tossed out the window. Walter, referred to scornfully as "the Jew conductor Isidor *Schlesinger*, alias Walter," is attacked for hiring a "Jewess singer" from Vienna and overpaying her for her allegedly inadequate services. "*We National Socialists*," the article concluded, "*at the beginning of this year publicly and collectively promised to take care that the artistic life of Munich—of which the Nationaltheater is a part—remains German in character.*"[69] Esser's second essay on the Nationaltheater, equally inflammatory, ended by mentioning that Walter was to conduct a performance of *Meistersinger* in honor of the German air force. "Naturally," Esser wrote, "Bruno (truly a beautiful name!) will conduct. Now I urge all German countrymen not to become vexed but to contemplate in all composure a veritable oddity: In a commemoration for our heroic German aviators, in the company of German aviators—a Hebrew who conducts Richard Wagner's *Meistersinger*.

*"Perhaps there's still enough time to find someone German?"*[70]

Walter claimed to have distanced himself from such attacks. "The National Socialist *Völkischer Beobachter* indulged, I was told, in orgies of insults, but I refused to read the paper and steadfastly ignored hostile sentiments, whose political weight I was unable to foretell at the time," he wrote in his autobiography.[71] There is no reason to doubt Walter on this point; the newspaper was clearly beneath contempt, its authors no-name barbarians. But Walter knew of their hostility and must have heard and read about the city's anti-Semitism with a sense of discomfort.

The far Right, however, could find no fault with the conductor Karl Muck, the great Wagnerian with whom the very young Walter had worked during his tenure at the Berlin Staatsoper in the 1900–1901 season. Muck had returned to Germany after bidding an unpleasant farewell to the United States, which had treated him like a spy rather than an artist, and presented himself to Walter in the hope that the music director might be able to make use of his services. "I had not seen him in almost twenty years," Walter recalled, "and was moved by the contrast between the energetic, firm, and caustically sarcastic man in his forties whom I remembered and the serious and obviously tired man of more than sixty now facing me."[72] Muck had been a guest before in Munich during Walter's reign, and during the summer of 1921 Walter allowed him to conduct many of the Wagner operas while Walter took the Mozart operas, *Palestrina*, and a few other favorites. With his close connections to Bayreuth, Muck was already something of a legend in his own time, and his conducting of the Wagnerian masterpieces drew strong praise from the critics. How did Walter feel about this? A couple of decades before, he had referred unflatteringly to Muck's "mediocrity," yet the recordings Muck made in 1917 and the later 1920s show him to have been an extremely sensitive and controlled interpreter, if far more conservative than Walter in the use of rubato and dynamics.[73] For the public record, at least, Walter seems to have changed his opinion of his colleague and rival: "His clear interpretative style revealed simplicity, greatness, and strength.

These Munich guest appearances led to extremely amicable personal relations between us."[74]

But Walter's own guest appearances in other cities (which included Barcelona and Rome, as well as Vienna, where he conducted Mahler's Eighth and Bach's *Matthäus-Passion*) led to less-than-amicable relations with some denizens of Munich. "Bruno Walter seems to me like our dear Lord: I *believe* in him, but I never *see* him" was a witticism said to have circulated in Munich during Walter's final years there.[75] In 1922 a large number of performances were being led by Walter's new assistants, among them Robert Heger and Karl Böhm. It was fairly clear that Walter was looking for a new position, hoping to land a job that wouldn't squeeze out the last drop of his lifeblood, and an opportunity to escape in fact materialized. On January 23, 1922, the conducting giant Arthur Nikisch died, leaving vacant two highly desirable conducting positions—one at the Berlin Philharmonic, the other at the Gewandhaus Orchestra in Leipzig. Walter, who had returned to conduct the Berlin Philharmonic on several occasions since his debut with the orchestra in 1913, was one of the chief contenders for that post. Already in 1916 Max Marschalk, of the *Vossische Zeitung* in Berlin, had grouped Walter with Richard Strauss and Nikisch as among the most important conductors of the day; a little over two years later, when Walter substituted for Nikisch, Marschalk lavished praise on the young conductor for his rare gifts, his mastery and persuasiveness at the podium.[76] But Walter was not the only contender.

Felix Weingartner, whose career had overlapped with Walter's in Vienna, was a serious candidate. Another was the prodigiously talented Wilhelm Furtwängler; a decade younger than Walter, he had already established an impressive reputation in Germany. Notwithstanding Weingartner's weighty credentials, Walter thought the decision would be between himself and Furtwängler. In March he wrote to Gabrilowitsch from Rome: "Since Nikisch's death, Furtwängler has been staying in Berlin, moving heaven, hell, and any number of other spheres to get the position; he's rapidly been conducting everything that could inspire only applause and is now probably awaiting the results of my concert like Isolde, anxiously waiting for Tristan in Act II—though with opposite feelings." Walter, by contrast, had not gone out of his way to win the approval of the influential in Berlin. He tried, as he told Gabrilowitsch, to let his actions determine his life's path. But, he confessed, he was planning to leave Munich in October, and "it would be of decisive importance for me to be Nikisch's successor."[77]

By the middle of March, the news had been made public that Walter would leave his position as Bavarian Generalmusikdirektor. Despite his frequent absences, which might have been a tip-off signaling a change of direction in Walter's career, the news struck like a lightning bolt. For days the announced departure was front-page news. A huge, horrified music-loving public banded together to sign a petition, which read as follows:

> The undersigned feel compelled to express their sincere reverence and their warmest thanks for the great artistic experiences that you have offered to Munich in nearly ten years of activity. Understanding classical and modern works, in the opera and in the concert hall, with sympathetic love and reverence for the work of art, you created impressions of lasting power with your interpretive art, governed by your entire personality. With the expression of our reverence and love for you, we add the wish that you might remain true to our city, which would suffer a heavy loss in its artistic and cultural life in the event of your departure.
>
> 2523 citizens of Munich, representatives of all professions and classes, have signed the address that stands before you and present it midway through March, 1922.[78]

A much-abbreviated listing of the signatories ran in both the *Münchner Neueste Nachrichten* and the *Münchener Zeitung*. Tributes by Walter Courvoisier, Clemens von Franckenstein, Thomas Mann, Hans Pfitzner, Emil Preetorius, and others appeared in the *Münchner Neueste Nachrichten* on March 21.

In marked contrast, the *Völkischer Beobachter*, delighted to rid the city of its Jewish music director, jeered at this outpouring of affection for Walter: "The Munich Generalmusikdirektor claims that he wishes to leave. He is tired of his job, makes more money abroad, and has sincere friends elsewhere. This last fact may have prompted his partisans and kindred companions in Munich to direct a written homage to that most controversial figure, sending a heartfelt plea for him not to throw in the sponge. The *Neueste Nachrichten* has published this cultural document: sadly, only in summary. It would have been interesting to determine statistically what percentage of those who took part, by signing the document, were Jews, Social Democrats, much-busied university professors, councilors of commerce, and artists with and without reputations."[79] But many in Munich, the author argued, were surely of the opposite feeling, and it would be interesting to assemble a list of their names. Bruno Walter, to be sure, had his "circle of friends," and he had his talents, but he "never conquered" Munich's musical world "because he simply was, is, and always will be of a different sensibility. He has no sense for the German way of life; he has always promoted artists from the East; he opposed those artists living in Munich who had German style and sensibility." The last point is a jingoistic swipe at the various singers in Walter's troupe—like Zdenka Mottl-Fassbender, Maria Ivogün, Hermine Bosetti, and Emil Schipper—who came from the Austro-Hungarian region; it conveniently ignores German-born leading artists like Paul Bender, Berta Morena, Delia Reinhardt, Gustav Schützendorf, and Otto Wolf.

The positions in Berlin and Leipzig, which Walter had set his sights on, both went to Furtwängler, and some contemporary reports sensed an anti-Semitic slant in the rejection of Walter. César Saerchinger, in the *Musical Courier*, noted that Walter "was, with Furtwängler and Weingartner, one of the three leading favorites," but "the premises on which things are decided in Germany are not wholly musical. Bruno Walter's original name was Schlesinger; and a Schlesinger on the highest musical throne of Germany is almost unthinkable in these 'democratic' days. These are the disabilities of birth."[80] Yet anti-Semitism may have had little to do with the decision. Wolfgang Stresemann heard directly from Louise Wolff, the famous artists' manager in charge of the Berlin Philharmonic concerts, that Furtwängler had presented himself to be considered as Nikisch's successor, and that although "she would have preferred Bruno Walter," Furtwängler was then simply the "more popular" conductor.[81] Wolff, who had many close ties to Jews, was not likely to have been anti-Semitic, though the real or supposed prejudices of her clientele might well have influenced her decision.

Why did Walter leave Munich? He himself strongly denied that anti-Semitism had anything to do with his departure. "It was generally assumed that Nazi persecutions were driving me out of Munich," Walter wrote in *Theme and Variations*. "I repeat that to the day of my departure I was actually not made to suffer from political hostility, and that my leaving was partly caused by a feeling that I had completed my task and partly by personal considerations."[82] Among the contemporary observers who blamed Nazi hostility for his departure was Paul Bekker, who mentioned both Fritz Reiner and Walter as musicians who'd been forced to seek employment elsewhere because of pressure imposed by the "anti-Semitic movement."[83] Walter's own daughter Lotte, in a radio interview given after her father's death, also accused the Nazis of having been a contributing factor in Walter's decision to leave Munich.[84] It seems unlikely that the gathering hostility played no part in Walter's departure. Two items among the huge number of letters sent to Walter on the occasion of his leaving Munich mention the critic Paul Ehlers as one of Walter's influential enemies.[85] Ehlers was, as his later writings show, a genuine anti-Semite, and he eventually came to hail Hitler as the savior of German music.[86] In all fairness to Ehlers, though, his reviews almost inevitably offered laudatory assessments of Walter's performances during the Munich years.

But another motive surely played a part in Walter's choosing to relocate. He touches on it in his autobiography: "Those were for me days of great and passionate involvement, bearing the seeds of tragic development. The thought of leaving Munich, generated by artistic considerations, offered a way out of a tormenting human situation."[87] The "tormenting human situation" would seem to have been his involvement with Delia Reinhardt, though it's by no means certain that this is what he is alluding to. Already in September 1921 negotiations were well under way for Reinhardt to sing at the Metropolitan Opera House in New York.[88] By November 1922 Gustav Schützendorf was singing at the Met, and his wife made her debut there in January 1923. Whether Walter's move out of Munich would have alleviated the "tormenting human situation" by allowing the two to meet in another city is unclear. As Irma Geering recalled the event, Walter wanted to marry Reinhardt, "and for this reason he went to America, left his family and went to America: officially to conduct for Gabrilowitsch, unofficially to wait for Delia. This must have been around 1923. And Delia Reinhardt—she didn't come. She told me . . . that Bruno Walter was too intense and passionate for her. She was in fact very delicate—outwardly strong, but inwardly very delicate and fine."[89] Some of the statements and implications of this account are questionable. (Was Walter planning simply to abandon his family and run off with Delia? Was she expected to leave her husband while they were both engaged at the Metropolitan Opera?) But the central idea that Walter wanted to establish a closer bond with Reinhardt seems likely, given his relationship with her after his wife's death in 1945. And the "tragic development" that Walter mentions in his autobiography, published in 1946, might well refer to his separation from Reinhardt—first during the 1920s, when Reinhardt and Walter's relationship seems to have been mainly professional (they frequently worked together at Covent Garden), then from 1933 to 1945, most of which time Reinhardt remained in Germany. The two were reunited only in the late 1940s.

Though Walter spent much of 1922 outside Munich, he offered a novelty of sorts on June 7, when he presented Handel's *Acis and Galatea* done in eighteenth-century dress, with Delia Reinhardt as Galatea. Then in August and September, he returned for a veritable Walter marathon. Among the works he performed in this limited period were *Die Meistersinger*, *Così*, *Die Entführung*, *Tristan*, *Palestrina*, *Der Rosenkavalier*, *Iphigenia in Aulis*, *Die Vögel*, *Die Zauberflöte*, the *Ring*, *Ariadne*, *Der Corregidor*, Beethoven's Ninth, as well as a triple bill of Handel's *Acis and Galatea*, Pergolesi's *Serva padrona*, and Schenk's *Dorfbarbier*; the Munich premiere of Pfitzner's new cantata, *Von deutscher Seele* (on August 29, repeated on October 2); and, as his farewell to Munich, *Fidelio* at the Nationaltheater, on October 3. The veteran manager Thea Dispeker—who, in school, had once played a four-hand version of a Haydn symphony with one of Walter's daughters, while Walter conducted—recalled his final operatic performance in Munich: "I will never forget his last opera, his farewell performance; it was *Fidelio*. . . . I was up in the gallery, a schoolgirl, and I cried my eyes out. He was such an integral part of the Munich opera, and the father of it all."[90] Her feelings were echoed by many in Munich; in a mawkish, elegiac poem by Maria von Hofmann Cortens, which circulated on a postcard, a desolate Nationaltheater grieves after Walter's last concert there:

> Oh, stay with us, master of heavenly music;
> The National Theater, where thou long hast led,
> With woeful glance bids thee a mute farewell.[91]

At the conclusion of that last *Fidelio*, members of the audience were unwilling to budge from the theater, and Walter was eventually led "in triumph through the city at night."[92] At an open rehearsal for his final concert with the Musikalische Akademie, the orchestra and the entire audience rose on his arrival to greet him with deafening applause; "the ladies waved their handkerchiefs, and people called out, 'Walter, stay here! Don't go! Stay here!'"[93]

On October 4 the racially unobjectionable Hans Knappertsbusch took over as Walter's successor. The *Völkischer Beobachter* noted with approval that the new director's plans for the concert hall and the opera house would include no "futuristic" music and would consist almost exclusively of German works.[94] Walter, of course, had also emphasized German music in his programs, and shortly after the article in the *Völkischer Beobachter* appeared, Alfred Einstein wrote an essay on Walter's activity in Munich in which he pointed out that Walter's programming had been the "most German" to be found on any stage.[95]

Adrian Boult was also present during Walter's farewell season. Boult himself was to conduct in Munich that November, and he'd found a loyal friend in Walter, who attended the first of his concerts. Boult, in turn, could scarcely find enough praise to bestow on Walter in later years. One memory of Walter's performances that Boult recalled involved the audience's reaction to Walter in the Prinzregententheater: "It is an absolute fact," he wrote to Walter, "that with all conductors but you there was always an appreciable movement in the audience UNTIL the first sound was heard. With you there was dead silence before the lights were fully lowered, and so we had silence for several seconds before we heard the music. . . . What a lot there is still to be learnt about telepathy and the influence of concentration!"[96]

Another visitor to Munich that season was Walter Damrosch, the impresario-conductor of the Symphony Society of New York, which had afforded Mahler his first opportunity to conduct symphonic concerts in New York. Damrosch had been alerted to Walter's excellent qualities by Ossip Gabrilowitsch earlier in 1922, and Walter's performance made a distinctly favorable impression.[97] Eight years later Damrosch recalled the incident in his memoirs:

> The town was in great excitement over the approaching performance of Handel's "Acis and Galatea" in dramatic form. Their conductor, Bruno Walter, said to me: "We are very proud of this stage performance, as it is the first since Handel's time." He was amazed and, as he told me, much chagrined when I informed him that I had given it in New York nearly thirty years ago. He gave it a beautiful performance. I had costumed my singers in classic Greek, but the Munich stage director had given the work an additional and rather piquant flavor by dressing the singers and dancers as in Handel's time, when all performers, in no matter what age their plays were supposed to take place, wore the costumes and huge periwigs of their own period.[98]

After this impressive introduction, it is little wonder that a few months later Walter himself would be conducting Damrosch's orchestra in New York.

Walter bade a formal farewell to the singers, instrumentalists, technicians, dancers, and actors who worked either with him or alongside him in Munich's principal theaters. It was a fine speech to end an era that in future years he would always regard as his "most important epoch"; it came from the heart and went to the heart:

> You see me before you at a grave moment in my life, bidding you farewell. For me, leaving the Munich opera means being cut off from my life's work. This is such a serious and weighty step for me that I simply don't feel myself equal to the farewell party that you good people have prepared for me here today. Yet to go my own way quietly (as one might do), when the separation affects one so heavily, and as if the separation had suited my entire way of life—that would hardly have been a satisfying conclusion to our ten years of close collaboration. . . . And thus we stand here to bid each other farewell eye to eye. But understand and excuse me if not even my words can come close to expressing the feelings and depths of that which moves me. The feeling of which I am most strongly conscious at this hour is gratitude. I have been allowed to revel in an artistic existence. I was able, over time, to perform all the works that I loved, those dearest to my heart, as they existed in my imagination, which never grew tired of molding the beloved objects. Thus I was able to build a repertoire out of the greatest treasures of German art. I could experience the fulfillment of this ideal. For this, my life's goal, you the artists of this house delivered your invaluable powers with a never ceasing joy in creation.
>
> Thus no one will doubt that I bear a debt of lasting and ardent gratitude to those who helped me realize my artistic dreams. But please don't misunderstand me, as though I meant that I'd *achieved* my ideals or that my dreams had been *fulfilled*. Ah, ladies and gentlemen, *achieving* and *fulfilling* are not words found in the dictionary of human existence. But to strive after achievement and fulfillment; to rouse all your forces fervently for this purpose; in short, to live intensely—that is the pattern by which happiness has been prolonged for the children of men.
>
> . . . Fare you well and think back kindly upon me.[99]

In Walter's typescript copy of this speech, the phrase "the greatest treasures of German art" originally read "the greatest treasures of art." The qualifier was an afterthought, a reminder, perhaps, that Walter was very much a German, wholeheartedly devoted to what Wagner called "holy German art." At the time of Walter's departure, Adolf Schiedt, editor of the *Münchener Zeitung*, wrote Walter a personal letter praising his contribution to German culture in Munich and in regions beyond, where his "musical accomplishments" would be "inseparably bound with [his] German soul."[100] The last comment, on Walter's "German soul," was no doubt in part an allusion to the final concert piece that Walter had performed in Munich, Pfitzner's *Von deutscher Seele* ("On the German Soul"), and there is a decided irony in Walter's bidding farewell to Munich—amid cries from the radical Right that he was no German at all but a "Hebrew," a "Jew conductor"—with a work that grappled directly with the German soul.

# *New and Old Worlds*
## USA and Berlin, 1923–1925

*Ha, proud ocean,*
*In a short time you will carry me again . . .*
Wagner, *Der fliegende Holländer*

"On the ocean, we had three stormy days altogether, the worst
yesterday. I actually suffered from queasiness and dizziness the
whole time, and except for a few moments I never had the emotional composure that would have allowed me to take pleasure in
the prodigious grandeur of the ocean in agitation and at rest, the
sun, the moon, tempest and calm." Thus Walter, on board the *S. S.
Manchuria*, wrote to his daughter Lotte, then studying voice in
Vienna, as he sailed to America for the first time. He had boarded
on January 20, and the journey was taking longer than expected.
Though the rough waters made him feel ill, he prided himself on
not having been technically "seasick." He needed his strength for
the ordeals ahead and thought he would be "in good bodily condition to encounter New York."[1]

He had entertained fantasies about traveling to Boston already
at the turn of the century, when the Viennese public and press initially turned against him, and the thought of escaping to America
would become a leitmotif in his correspondence. On this, his first

trip to America, Walter had engagements in New York, Detroit, Minneapolis, and Boston. The journey marked an important step for him, and he knew it, though he had no idea that he was visiting his future home.

Despite the huge distance that separated America from Europe, Walter was to find a number of links with the Old World when he landed in New York. Singers with whom he had worked closely in Munich—like Paul Bender, Gustav Schützendorf, and of course Delia Reinhardt—were now singing at the Metropolitan Opera House. Ossip Gabrilowitsch gave a piano recital in February, and Rachmaninoff played his Second Piano Concerto with the Symphony Orchestra under Damrosch at the beginning of March. Some works that had become familiar, if not necessarily accepted, in Europe were now being introduced to New York. On February 4 Schoenberg's atonal *Pierrot Lunaire* had its American premiere in that city, while Max von Schillings's *Mona Lisa* had its first American airing at the Metropolitan Opera House as March began. Between those two premieres, Walter's New York debut took place.

Little fanfare surrounded Walter's arrival in the United States. Carnegie Hall, a large auditorium for a large city and already a venue with an illustrious past—Tchaikovsky conducted at its opening, and Mahler performed there on many occasions—was the site of Walter's first concert in New York, on February 15, 1923. Opened in 1891, decorated with simple designs, it remains one of the most satisfying halls in the world for orchestral music: resonant and warm without being cavernous and turbid. The ensemble was Walter Damrosch's New York Symphony Orchestra, which still retained some musicians who had played under Mahler in 1908, and the program consisted of Beethoven's "Leonore" Overture no. 2, Mozart's "Haffner" Symphony, and Brahms's First Symphony—the first two items, as the critics pointed out, then rarely played.

The reviews were respectful but hardly ecstatic. Richard Aldrich of the *New York Times* expressed admiration for Walter's rhythmic subtlety, the simplicity of his conducting technique, and his seriousness of purpose, devoid of empty flamboyance. Of the Brahms, Aldrich noted that Walter "sought for the finest and subtlest exposition of the outline: delicate contrasts, significant phrasing, pulsing rhythms, subtle modifications of tempo—modifications that were not thrown at the listener's head, but were such as to be felt, rather than noticed."[2] Both the *Times* and the *Herald* commented that Walter had tried, somewhat unsuccessfully, to perform the symphonies without pauses for applause between movements. If Walter checked the *Daily News* for a review of his debut (there was none), he would have found a grim reminder of a nagging problem at home that showed no signs of disappearing. On the back page were three sizable pictures of National Socialists staging "a huge demonstration" in Munich, "marching behind the emblem they have made their own"—an emblem that would become sickeningly familiar.[3]

Not surprisingly, his presence as a guest from afar gave rise to speculation in the press about his intentions. One reviewer pointedly asked, "Why is he here?" Henry Finck, of the *New York Evening Post*, postulated that Walter's guest appearance might be not merely a means of offering variety to the audience but a possible sign of his being a permanent fixture in the city: "Will he or will Albert Coates conduct this orchestra if Walter Damrosch succeeds in the ambition attributed to him—with what truth I know not—of being added to the President's Cabinet as Minister of the Fine Arts?"[4]

The now defunct Aeolian Concert Hall on 43rd Street—a smaller, more sumptuously adorned space, whose stage was graced with a rich array of organ pipes—was the venue for Walter's next program with the Symphony Orchestra, on Sunday, February 18. He again offered "serious" music (by contemporary standards) rather than crowd-pleasers: Mozart's "Haffner" Serenade, Mendelssohn's overture to *A Midsummer Night's Dream*, Schumann's "Spring" Symphony (his old standby), and the Prelude to Wagner's *Meistersinger*. The seriousness of the program was often paralleled by reserve in the conductor's stage presence, and W. J. Henderson of the *New York Herald* observed that Walter's manner—in the Mozart at least—held nothing of interest for "that large number which has to see as well as to hear," noting with some relief the conductor's more animated demeanor in the romantic works. Nevertheless, he concluded, "Mr. Walter is not a conductor who relies on pictorial effects. He is a direct, magnetic and authoritative leader of musicians, and he conveys his commands to them in the shortest and simplest manner."[5]

While the critics admired Walter's high seriousness, their practical concern over his discreet bearing at the podium was well founded. Although Walter made several return visits to the Symphony Orchestra, he would be rejected, two years after his debut, as a possible musical director of the organization. In reporting to the Symphony Society's board of directors, Harry Harkness Flagler sadly noted the "lack of drawing power of our principal guest conductor, Bruno Walter, who while possessing the highest talent and musicianship did not loom large in the eye of a public seeking for sensational or striking methods."[6] So Walter, often criticized in his youth for his excessive movements and his musical exaggerations, would become an undesirable commodity because of his controlled and dignified manner at the conductor's desk.

Though the public relations work surrounding Walter's debut in the United States was generally weak, at least some effort was made to publicize his presence in the New World when *Musical America* interviewed him for a substantial piece that ran shortly after his engagements in New York. A point he stressed in the interview was the dire financial situation of orchestras in postwar Germany. Even the Berlin Philharmonic, he pointed out, was in trouble. "The players do not receive a living wage, and it has seemed at times as if the body would be disbanded. . . . There has been a rumor also of the difficulties faced by the Gewandhaus Orchestra of Leipzig, but I cannot verify this."[7] The cynic might be tempted to detect a trace of smugness in these comments—after all, Walter had recently been rejected in favor of Furtwängler as the conductor of both orchestras—but such public utterances had their desired effect: he eventually collected five hundred dollars for the financially strapped Berlin Philharmonic, an instance of generosity that later inclined him to "speak very favorably about America."[8]

The interview also touched on the present state of composition in his native country. For Walter, composition in Germany currently "served as a voice to bitterness and pain of the spirit. It is a far cry from the sunlit Mozartean melody to the latest productions of German genius." There were, of course, some exceptions, such as Richard Strauss, Pfitzner, and Braunfels. "Yet the crass and raucous are also prominent." About the Schoenberg of *Fünf Orchester-Stücke* Walter had particular misgivings. Here he set forth ideas that he would develop at greater length in his pamphlet *On the Moral Forces of Music*; the Schoenberg who promoted atonality "may be right," Walter allowed. "But I believe that in the nature of music there are certain innate laws. If these are violated, the essential nature of music is destroyed." Yet he was quick to add that he had "much admiration" for Schoenberg's earlier works.[9] Those who have found Walter's criticisms of atonal music exceedingly ill timed in 1935—and so they were—should remember that the conductor had uttered similar criticisms well before they were associated with the tastes of the Nazi Party.

After his New York concerts Walter took the train to Detroit, where Gabrilowitsch had arranged for him to give concerts later in February. Walter found the orchestra "simply fabulous," and the players seemed equally pleased with their guest conductor.[10] Immediately following his concerts in Detroit, Walter headed for Minneapolis, where several guest conductors demonstrated their abilities during the 1922–23 season. Walter and Henri Verbrugghen were at this time apparently both being seriously considered as permanent conductors for the orchestra, so Walter was engaged to lead six concerts in Minnesota—some in Minneapolis, some in St. Paul—during the month of March.[11] His friend and colleague Maria Ivogün joined him for his first concert. (Her old vocal instructor, Amalie Schlemmer-Ambros, was now giving Lotte Walter singing lessons, much to her father's pleasure.) The opening concert was a first for both Walter and the orchestra, in that it was broadcast live to a huge, nationwide audience. "Imagine playing to an audience all across the continent, with thousands listening!" Walter reportedly said.[12] As a performer who would become one of the most frequently broadcast musicians of his generation, he would eventually grow quite accustomed to performing before the microphone. For the remaining concerts he offered much the same fare as in New York and Detroit, supplemented by a substantial number of other works, some of them unusual for Walter— Franck's Symphonic Variations for Piano and Orchestra; Haydn's Symphony no. 12 (a Minneapolis premiere); Chopin's Andante spianato and Polonaise for Piano and Orchestra and Liszt's Piano Concerto no. 1, both with the Polish virtuoso Ignaz Friedman as soloist. In addition, Walter also assumed the role of piano accompanist for recitals of lieder and cello sonatas. At the Symphony Club he took the opportunity to reach potential philanthropists, giving a lecture on the desperate state of musicians in Germany. "I didn't exactly speak the best English," he wrote to his daughter Lotte, "but it still made a deep impression and will, I think, bring money to German musicians."[13]

Boston, a city that had appealed to Walter's imagination already for two decades, awaited him at the end of his first United States tour. On March 30 Walter gave his first concert in Symphony Hall, conducting the orchestra in a program that included Beethoven's Piano Concerto no. 4, with Artur Schnabel at the keyboard. At least one major European musical figure was present in the audience for Walter's Boston debut. Pierre Monteux, the French *chef d'orchestre* who had already given the world premieres of such modern masterpieces as Stravinsky's *Le Sacre du printemps* and Ravel's *Daphnis et Chloé*, was the orchestra's regular conductor; that night, he was seated in the balcony, no doubt with a smile under his bushy walrus-like mustache, listening "to the concert free from responsibility for it."[14]

One critic who would later review Walter on countless occasions for the *New York Times* was then already a veteran reviewer for the *Boston Post*; Olin Downes offered some of the most astute comments on Walter's method yet to appear in print: "Mr. Walter's rhythm [is] very striking, very much a living, breathing thing. 'Breathing' is the word. When a musical phrase is truly felt by the conductor, and when the orchestra feels it with him, the orchestra breathes, and this natural, deep rhythmical respiration of the instruments is one of the inalienable qualities of a good performance. Then the conductor has ceased to merely beat time. Then his baton is a pulse-beat which affects every part of the orchestral organism."[15] A long, complimentary, gossipy column appeared in the *Transcript*, speculating on whether the real purpose behind Walter's conducting the Boston Symphony Orchestra had anything to do with the impending expiration of Monteux's contract. "By common consent," the article noted, "Mr. Walter is a conductor of high ability and large prestige. By recorded fact, he is also a conductor 'out of a job' and not indisposed, presumably, to new employment. On many a score these United States are accounted conductors' paradise. May there not . . . be anticipations at the back of Mr. Walter's head as he goes 'a-guesting' up and down this broad land?"[16]

Before heading back to Europe, Walter returned to New York to discuss the following year's program with Walter Damrosch. All in all, a successful tour. One reviewer, according to Walter, wrote that the impression he had made on the New York audience was comparable only with that made by Toscanini when he first appeared in the city.[17] But Walter still hadn't secured any permanent position and would spend months continuing to search for employment in Europe. Engagements were not hard to come by. He received invitations from the Netherlands, Italy, Rumania, Hungary, and Denmark, and had plenty of work with which to occupy himself in Germany and Austria. The oppressive economy in Germany, however, made him feel strongly that America was the place to go in search of regular work, as he confided to Gabrilowitsch in August. Indeed, even working for the cause of Germany, which Walter planned to do for the rest of his life, could be "achieved better abroad than in Germany itself."[18] Walter asked his colleague to keep an eye out for possible opportunities in the United States.

All the while, the house in Munich, at Mauerkirchstrasse 43, continued to serve as his home base, though he planned to move to either Berlin or

Vienna, the cities where he would be most often engaged professionally. Neither option appealed much to him: "In Berlin, serious disturbances are sure to come, and Elsa is decidedly antipathetic toward Vienna. But to live in Munich, where we have this house, after all, makes no sense whatsoever, since I never conduct here and would therefore never see Elsa or Gretel."[19] By the winter the family may have moved to Vienna; Walter wrote as much in his memoirs, though several of his letters throughout 1924 continue to give Munich as his home address.[20]

As we now know, Walter was right to be concerned about future disturbances in Berlin; yet the city continued to draw him back for guest engagements, and indeed one of his first concerts upon returning to Europe was with the Berlin Philharmonic in late April. While the program was not particularly adventurous, it offered the rare combination of Walter and the great Irish tenor John McCormack, who sang arias by Mozart and Beethoven. Leopold Schmidt's glowing comments on Walter show that a substantial portion of the Berlin audience sympathized with him, both as a man who had left Munich under less than ideal conditions and as a potential leader of the Berlin Philharmonic who had recently been rejected in favor of Furtwängler: "The hall was filled with an audience whose excitement very quickly reached the boiling point. Mixed with the roaring applause for Walter's performance were undertones of unmistakable meaning: joy over a man who returns home in glory, support for a man unjustly wounded, desire to tie him more closely to our musical life. (Does he have any desire at all to be tied down?)"[21]

Walter's guest engagements—always hard to pinpoint—become especially difficult to follow in the 1920s. He visited Vienna in April and May 1923; no doubt he worked elsewhere, with nearly every moment devoted to traveling, rehearsing, or conducting. After some restful weeks in Switzerland during the summer, Walter returned to his punishing schedule, revisiting familiar cities and making new contacts, especially in Leipzig and Amsterdam.

His debut with the Leipzig Gewandhaus Orchestra, an organization that would later play a central role in his career, took place on August 28, 1923. Supplanting the hall in which Mendelssohn had conducted, the new Gewandhaus opened in 1891, elaborately decorated in splendid nineteenth-century neo-baroque style. (Like several other houses in which Walter worked, it was destroyed during World War II.) The orchestra was one of the most venerable in Europe, and Leipzig itself, while it couldn't compare with nearby Berlin as a cultural center, could boast strong ties to both Bach, the most celebrated cantor of the Thomaskirche, and Mendelssohn, a former Gewandhaus director.

When Walter visited Leipzig for his first concert there, the hall was sold out, though the core of his program held no surprises: Brahms's Second Symphony, Schubert's Ballet Music for *Rosamunde*, and Weber's *Euryanthe* Overture (to which were appended a scene from Bruch's *Achilleus* and four Brahms lieder sung by Margarete Krämer-Bergau). The Gewandhaus, of course, was another of the orchestras for which Walter had recently been considered as a potential regular conductor. He had his partisans in Leipzig, and Furtwängler had his critics. But Max Steinitzer, reviewing Walter's performance for the *Leipziger Neueste Nachrichten*, seems to have admired both conductors almost equally. While noting that the audiences had grown accustomed (through Furtwängler) to performances that couldn't be surpassed, he complimented Walter, who had had little rehearsal time, on his "extraordinary" achievement: "His conducting is outwardly and inwardly the strongest contrast of everything that is ponderous, hard, stiff, and violent—free and light, like the most natural expression of life. If there were—if there could be—a woman conductor of genius," Steinitzer added, "that conductor would undoubtedly conduct certain passages in a like manner." Apart from the condescending attitude toward aspiring female conductors, the aside jolts because of its utter unexpectedness. Others, however, have commented on Walter's gentleness, and perhaps this was uppermost in the critic's mind when he drew the conjectural comparison. But about one quality—Walter's slowing down for certain passages (a characteristic also prominent in Furtwängler's readings)— Steinitzer voiced reservations, arguing that the same effects could be achieved without such extreme measures.[22]

Another orchestra that Walter would conduct many times was the Concertgebouw in Amsterdam, with which he made his debut on October 11, 1923. Though not as elaborately decorated as the Gewandhaus of Walter's time, the Concertgebouw was and still is a majestic hall, its acoustics ranking among the wonders of the musical world, and its construction had attractions beyond its superb sonics. Instead of prosaically walking to center stage by way of a side wing, the conductor at the Concertgebouw of necessity makes a dramatic entrance by emerging from double doors atop a long staircase that leads to the stage below. Walter relished every minute of the show. "I liked to look down for a little while from the raised, darkened box on the right before swinging open the half-door in its front and setting foot on the top step of the platform, thereby exposing myself to the public gaze. There followed the long descent down the steps between the orchestra and the part of the audience seated along the side of the platform, until I finally reached the conductor's desk."[23]

It is fitting that Walter should have commenced his work with the Concertgebouw Orchestra with Mahler's First Symphony. Mahler himself had conducted and admired the orchestra, and Willem Mengelberg, its regular conductor, was one of the most ardent champions of Mahler's works. Walter's program also included Pfitzner's new Piano Concerto in E-flat Major, with the pianist Walter Gieseking, who in March had premiered the work under Fritz Busch. The newspapers found much to praise in the guest conductor—his spontaneity, his lively rhythm, his attention to detail, his affinity for Mahler's music—and the public response was equally enthusiastic.

Less well received was an item from the United States that Walter introduced in his next Concertgebouw concert, Cecil Burleigh's Concerto for Violin in E Minor, given its first Amsterdam performance on October 14. The solo violinist, also an American, was Amy Neill, one of Leopold Auer's pupils, then making a concert tour of Europe. This may well have been the first work (at least the first substantial work) by an American composer that Walter ever conducted, and its fate, sad to say, was similar to that of many other American compositions that Walter performed. Some reviewers might have turned against the piece after reading the program notes, which perhaps unwisely mentioned that Burleigh had received a thousand-dollar prize for his composition in America. It was a kingly sum, and the piece didn't convince the reviewers that it was worthy of such a regal reward. The composer Sem Dresden, a critic for *De Telegraaf*, dismissed the concerto as "utterly unimportant," a "mediocre work that could have been written just as well in the Old World as in the New."[24] More and more, Walter's attempts to include novelties would provoke such hostile critical responses, either because the works were too conservative or because they were too radical.

While programming freshly minted works, Walter continued to take an interest in neglected older pieces, and it was inevitable that he would become entangled in the controversy surrounding Mahler's unfinished last symphony. As one of the musicians who had been closest to Mahler, Walter felt responsible not only for performing his friend's music but also, to an extent, for protecting his legacy. Alma Mahler was in charge of overseeing her late husband's works, and she allowed the young composer Ernst Krenek—

who in the mid-1920s was briefly married to Anna Mahler, Gustav and Alma's daughter—to complete the two movements of Mahler's Tenth Symphony that the composer had almost finished. (The movements were eventually performed in October 1924.) Alma had apparently asked Walter for his assessment of Mahler's sketches, which she'd shown him a decade before, but Walter claimed not to have seen the two nearly complete movements. He recalled true "sketches" that were hard to read, sometimes supplemented by personal remarks. There could be no talk of a "score," he wrote, and the finished movements, "intentionally or unintentionally," had not been shown to him.[25] A distinct testiness runs through Walter's letter to Alma. He made his opposition to a public performance very clear: "No composer was less inclined than Mahler to make known an unfinished work; you know that as well as I. And I very much regret that you haven't taken into account this aversion, which was deeply rooted in his being and work, and that you are placing before the public a torso lacking the final improvements and polishings of Mahler's unique hand—moreover, for the world premiere you're using a venue that is thoroughly unsatisfactory, on acoustical grounds, for a symphonic work." The venue in question was the Vienna Staatsoper, designed for operatic, not symphonic, works. Much later he confided that Alma's decision to allow the piece to be performed almost led to a rift between them.[26] For the rest of his life Walter would remain adamant about leaving Mahler's last work in peace. He never performed any parts of the Tenth and as late as 1961 strongly opposed the performance of Deryck Cooke's now famous reconstruction of the entire symphony: "The unfinished work of a musical genius," he wrote to Alma, "should not be touched, not even by the most talented and devoted musician."[27] Nevertheless, given the greatness of the symphony, even in its unpolished state, we can only be grateful that Walter did not have his way in this matter.

Having become a lodestone for great European artists—especially those in need of cash—America drew Walter back early in 1924. Now a known quantity, he received somewhat more attention on his second visit to New York than on his first. The cover of the *Symphony Society Bulletin* bore a dramatic shot of Walter, underneath which was an announcement of his return to Aeolian and Carnegie halls. Before giving his Manhattan concerts, however, Walter conducted the Symphony Society at the Brooklyn Academy of Music on February 9. His program included the Beethoven Violin Concerto, with the composer and violin virtuoso Georges Enesco as soloist. A month later Walter and Enesco appeared together on a special program sponsored by the Beethoven Association; Walter accompanied Julia Culp in Schumann's *Liederkreis*, and other featured artists were Enesco and the pianist Elly Ney (then married to Willem van Hoogstraten, a new conductor with the New York Philharmonic; she would later become the musical darling of the Nazi regime). Walter came to know Enesco personally during this time and learned that the Rumanian composer, amid the political struggles of 1917, had lost a substantial number of his compositions, which had been sent to Moscow. When Walter wrote to his contact in Moscow later that year, he explained Enesco's plight in detail and offered to retrieve the music and return it to the composer on his next trip to the city. "If Mr. Enesco has had to live without his manuscripts for seven years, he can live without them longer, perhaps till I come to Moscow and can then bring them to him then and there," Walter wrote (more coolly than the composer might have liked). "But I'd very much like to be able to give him some concrete information; he longs so much for news, feeling no doubt like a father whose son is lost in the war."[28]

On this visit Walter conducted eight programs with the Symphony Society in Manhattan, offering somewhat more variety than on his previous American tour. It was a rich sampling of music, but at least one critic commented that Walter lacked adequate time for rehearsal and therefore had "no opportunity to show what he could do."[29] Among the less frequently played items were Schoenberg's *Verklärte Nacht*—which created a scandal when Walter conducted it in Rome, though it sounded "very tame indeed" to New Yorkers—and Volkmar Andreae's Little Suite, condemned by Olin Downes, now of the *New York Times*, as "obvious and witless in its attempts at what is fantastical or poetic or whimsical."[30] And Walter also chose to perform Mahler, a composer conspicuously absent from his American programs of the previous year. Although he picked the readily accessible First Symphony, many in New York were still not prepared for the composer whom Walter would champion vigorously throughout his life. Was their hostility simply a result of their being unacquainted with the music? The reviewer for the *Musical Courier* dismissed that idea out of hand: "When one stops to think of the other works written about the same time that have become favorites, the argument fails to convince. . . . Lack of ideas seems to explain it, and perhaps also excessive length, which will kill any work, however beautiful."[31] Such were the discouraging arguments that Walter often encountered, in Europe and even more so in America, when he performed the works of his departed friend. At the dawn of the twenty-first century, when Mahler's symphonies are among the most popular works in the orchestral repetoire, it's easy to forget how far into the twentieth century the resistance to Mahler reached.

A number of soloists—some now immortal, some long since forgotten—appeared with Walter in New York: Efrem Zimbalist played the Glazunov Violin Concerto in A Minor; Dusolina Giannini sang a Mozart aria and the Gypsy Songs of Dvořák, with Walter accompanying at the keyboard; Heifetz triumphed in the Goldmark Violin Concerto in A Minor (a rare collaboration between the violinist and the conductor, perhaps the first); Gustave Tinlot, the orchestra's concertmaster, performed Rimsky-Korsakov's Fantasy on Russian Themes; and Moriz Rosenthal "reeled off" Liszt's E-flat Piano Concerto "with perfect ease as a mere bagatelle."[32]

During the time that Walter was conducting in New York, singers from his old Munich troupe were still assuming leading roles at the Metropolitan Opera, including Gustav Schützendorf and Delia Reinhardt. How much contact Walter had with Reinhardt is hard to know, but by May she was singing under his direction in London, so presumably they were in touch with each other. It must have been a somewhat difficult situation for both of them, and one curious occurrence in the opera house makes one wonder whether Walter's presence in New York might not have added considerably to the stress a performer always feels on stage. The occasion was an afternoon performance of *Meistersinger* under Bodanzky, on February 23, with Delia Reinhardt as Eva and Gustav Schützendorf as Beckmesser. Reinhardt had sung Eva many times, often under Walter. The part should not have caused her any great trouble. Yet in this performance, as the papers duly reported, she "fainted on the Metropolitan stage midway in act three . . . just as the curtains were about to close on the famous quintet. Her companions for the moment gathered around her and she recovered in time to resume the heroine's slight remaining share in the final scene."[33] Did Walter attend the performance? (He was not conducting the Symphony Society that day.)

As on his first trip to the United States, Walter made excursions to Detroit and Minneapolis (where he played piano accompaniment to Henri Verbrugghen's violin in a charity concert to benefit "starving German children"[34]). Taking leave of the United States early in April, Walter boarded the *Albert Ballin* in New York to steam toward Europe. By late April he was in his native city, conducting Mozart's Requiem with the Berlin Philharmonic, and his thoughts turned with ever greater frequency toward Berlin as a possible home. The city itself was clearly giving plenty of thought to him as well, as evidenced by a variety of reviews and articles that mention Walter as a potential candidate for musical openings in the city. His new concert manager was Robert Sachs, who would ensure Walter's frequent presence in Berlin for the coming years.[35] In June, as he considered sending his daughter to the Hochschule für Musik in Berlin, Walter wrote to Franz Schreker, then director of the school, to ask about the entrance requirements and the curriculum. Gretel's education, Walter admitted, had been uneven—partly as a result of his peripatetic career. Further, she was talented at many things, not just music. "She's uncommonly gifted, plays splendid piano, has a charming voice, is theatrically very talented and full of wit and liveliness," he wrote with evident pride. "I myself am undecided whether I should send her to drama school or for piano lessons, vocal instruction, lessons in theory, or something else."[36] Walter, Elsa, and Gretel would live in Berlin, starting in October. His elder daughter, Lotte, was to continue her musical studies in Hanover with Rudolf Krasselt, a conductor and former solo cellist of the Berlin Philharmonic, whose association with the family reached back to the preceding century (Krasselt had performed a recital with Elsa in 1898). By the fall, Lotte had secured her first professional engagement as a soprano at the Stadttheater in Hanover.[37]

Walter's international career continued to grow in 1924. Covent Garden, which had received him warmly in 1910, had gone without a German opera season since the outbreak of World War I, and Walter had the honor of being the first conductor to restore the German season to the venerable institution. Looking like a brilliant commercial tie-in, a new movie by Fritz Lang, *The Niebelungs*, had its London premiere—with live Wagnerian music provided by the London Symphony Orchestra—shortly before Walter came to conduct the *Ring* cycle at Covent Garden. The restoration of German opera was a much anticipated event, and the "ablest players from the several orchestras in London" were called on for the occasion.[38] On three consecutive nights, beginning May 5, Walter conducted the first three parts of the tetralogy, which elicited mixed reviews. But the real excitement was sandwiched between *Siegfried* and *Götterdämmerung*. It was a performance of *Tristan* that featured, in the title roles, Jacques Urlus—less than sterling on this occasion, according to the reviews—and a seasoned soprano in her Covent Garden debut: the splendid, incomparable Frida Leider. (She recalled her partner on this occasion as Lauritz Melchior, who in fact did perform with her later that season.[39]) For those who know her singing, it will be no surprise to learn that she stole the show that night and won a devoted following among British Wagnerians. In the middle of May, Walter offered a second, more successful *Ring* cycle to London, with a stronger cast that included such stellar artists as Lauritz Melchior, Frida Leider, Maria Olszewska, Emil Schipper, Friedrich Schorr, and Gertrud Kappel.

Some of the German operas at Covent Garden that season were taken by Karl Alwin, the husband of Elisabeth Schumann, who was also present. Schumann had already performed in recital with Walter during his Munich years and was now singing with him in an opera that would become a favorite offering of Walter's in London, *Der Rosenkavalier*; his first Covent Garden performance of Strauss's rococo opera was presented to a grateful English public on May 21. The dream cast included Lotte Lehmann as the Marschallin, Delia Reinhardt as Octavian, Schumann as Sophie, and Richard Mayr (in his English debut) as Baron Ochs. "One knew from the very first bars of the orchestral music last night that we were in for a good thing, and the great joy of last night's performance, surely one of the best of any opera which has been seen and heard at Covent Garden within present memory, lay in the way Herr Bruno Walter and his players handled the good gifts of the composer. The range of tone was enormous, and yet the general impression of the score, at any rate through two-thirds of the opera, was one of extraordinary lightness."[40] These performances, of rare quality, became the stuff of legend. In a BBC tribute to Walter on his eightieth birthday, the musicologist and radio personality Julian Herbage recalled the early productions of *Rosenkavalier* and other German works given during Walter's first years at Covent Garden after World War I: "Those performances showed me the meaning of perfection in operatic singing, and convinced me that Walter can extract more out of singers than any other living conductor—I'd even be rash enough to say, than any other conductor that has ever lived."[41] Nevertheless, the stage machinery and technical coordination of the production sometimes left much to be desired. Walter recalled a particularly awkward moment in *Rosenkavalier*, "when the waiters . . . touched the wall candles at the left with their lighters, while those at the right flamed up"—which inspired both laughter and an ovation.[42]

One of Walter's closest friendships began on the occasion of that production of *Rosenkavalier*, though its beginnings were far from auspicious. Lotte Lehmann, who knew the roles of Sophie and Octavian, had never performed as the Marschallin before accepting the engagement at Covent Garden. "I can imagine that he was not very pleased with me," she wrote; "the Marschallin is not a part that one can master at the first go. And Walter, with his passion for throwing light on every detail of a part, must have missed in me the entire exhausting of all the possibilities of the part. I confessed that I had never sung the Marschallin before and had only accepted for fear the lovely Covent Garden engagement would come to nothing—and I begged him to help me." He did help, on this and many later occasions. "How many old operatic parts became new and living under his direction! Often a word from him would make pale shadows flash into new life!"[43]

Later that year, Walter took the Vienna Philharmonic on tour through Germany.[44] Though he was leading the life of a wanderer, in the fall Walter and his family moved into "a furnished apartment on Lützowplatz" in Berlin.[45] The Deutsches Opernhaus in Charlottenburg played host to him several times in the second half of 1924. In his guest appearances there, he conducted *Tristan*, *Die Walküre*, *Die Zauberflöte*, and *Aida*. For Paul Stefan, writing about a decade later, the impressive performances of *Tristan* and *Aida* seemed, in retrospect, to anticipate the conductor's future career in that house.[46]

Other work also kept Walter busy in Berlin. Midway through November he lent his services for a charity production of *Die Fledermaus* at the Metropol-Theater, with Fritzi Massary as Adele and Leo Slezak, his old heldentenor from Vienna, as Alfred. Massary was a hugely popular star in the world of German operetta, and Walter found himself utterly charmed by her from the moment they met. "I had expected to meet a *diva* type, spoiled by popularity . . . ," Walter wrote. "Instead, I found a great artist who disdained popular routine and centered all of her highly-tensed nature upon the essentialities of her task."[47] Walter's own dazzling contribution to the production drew words of wonder from Max Marschalk, who noted that the conductor, known for his seriousness, was able to adapt his style to that of Johann Strauss by increasing the light and happy touch he used with such success in Mozart.[48]

At the same time, he was keeping up his chamber music activities. Near the end of 1924 he provided piano accompaniment for the cellist Emanuel Feuermann (then in his early twenties) and his violinist brother Siegmund in recitals of music by Brahms, Schumann, Tchaikovsky, and others in Berlin's Beethoven-Saal. A student of Walter's old colleague Friedrich Buxbaum, Emanuel Feuermann became one of the most renowned cellists of his day— and, as if to extend the student–teacher connection to the end of Walter's career, Feuermann's own pupil George Neikrug would become a regular cellist in the California-based Columbia Symphony Orchestra, Walter's last recording ensemble.

Though in his chamber and operatic work Walter limited himself to established classics, several contemporary compositions appeared on the various orchestral programs that he offered with the Berlin Philharmonic in the final quarter of 1924, including Reznicek's *Chamisso Variationen*, Korngold's *Viel Lärm um Nichts* Suite, and, most important, Prokofiev's First Violin Concerto, given its first Berlin performance on December 1, with Joseph Szigeti as soloist. The Hungarian-born violinist, already a renowned artist, would perform with Walter on a number of occasions and, through his two recordings of the Beethoven Violin Concerto under Walter, became widely associated with the conductor. Walter's connection with Prokofiev, however, is less well known, though Walter championed the Russian composer's music several times and even had the distinction of conducting Prokofiev's Third and Fifth piano concertos with the composer at the keyboard. (Not always appreciative of these efforts on his behalf, Prokofiev complained to a friend in 1928 about Walter's perceived "swinishness" when he decided not to stage *The Fiery Angel* in Berlin because the composer had missed his "deadline for delivering the music."[49]) At the time of the Berlin premiere of the Violin Concerto, Prokofiev had not yet established his credentials worldwide, and the critics were fully prepared to pounce on the new composition. Leopold Schmidt condemned the piece for its putative lack of substance—the three movements seemed like "technical studies" to him—and attributed the audience's loud applause to the courageous violinist, who "performed his thankless task in truly marvelous fashion."[50]

While Prokofiev had yet to be recognized as one of the preeminent musical figures of the twentieth century, by the 1920s Sir Edward Elgar had already secured his status as the greatest living English composer. In London, on December 4, Walter conducted the Royal Philharmonic Orchestra in a performance of Elgar's First Symphony, with the composer present in Queen's Hall for the event. This seems to have been the first time that the two men met, though Walter—perhaps forgetting which of the two symphonies he had conducted—remembered the encounter as having occurred at a performance of Elgar's Second. One might expect the Germanic density and romantic brooding of Elgar's music to have held a special appeal for Walter, but he rarely programmed Elgar's compositions, confessing with painful honesty that he was "not very strongly attracted by his works," even though he admired Elgar's "mastery" in the Enigma Variations, the Violin Concerto, and at least one of the symphonies. "I was more deeply affected by his *Dream of Gerontius*," he wrote, "and no less so by his serious and sincere personality, revealed to me at a luncheon to which he had invited me."[51]

Walter's interpretation of Elgar's sweeping symphony generated great enthusiasm from the audience, who "let themselves go when the end was reached and called the composer from his place in the grand circle to receive a vociferous greeting"; yet at least the *Times* critic felt that Walter had missed that indefinable English inflection in the music.[52] Elgar himself, however, may not have harbored such doubts about Walter's interpretation; certainly in later years he came to hold Walter in the highest esteem. In the politically decisive month of March 1933 Elgar wrote to a friend: "I am in a maze regarding events in Germany—what are they doing? In this morning's paper it is said that the greatest conductor Bruno Walter &, stranger still, Einstein are ostracised: are we all mad?"[53]

Walter is best known today for his recordings of the standard (and occasionally nonstandard) repertoire. Curiously enough, exactly when his long recording career began is hard to say; he dated it from 1900 or 1901, and while that early date seems unlikely, his own word must be given some weight.[54] Certainly by the early 1920s he was in the studio, making recordings of shorter pieces mainly with the Berlin Philharmonic. The Polydor catalogue of 1924–25 (the company later known as Deutsche Grammophon) listed several items conducted by Walter: the preludes to the third and fourth acts of *Carmen*, Beethoven's "Coriolan" Overture, Wagner's "Faust" Overture, Berlioz's "Carnaval romain" Overture, and Mendelssohn's "Hebrides" Overture. These were acoustic recordings, recorded through a horn rather than an electronic microphone, and the sound is predictably disappointing. In order to make certain parts audible, various alterations to the instrumentation were often necessary. Little amplifying horns were sometimes attached to the violins, and brass instruments played along with the double basses. The result, especially in symphonic works, ranged from almost acceptable to risible or excruciating. Walter, however, was hardly reluctant to endorse the technological miracle of recorded sound: "Today I have spent over an hour listening to your records, which greatly pleased me," he wrote in a statement used to promote Polydor records in the mid-1920s. "What sonic beauty in the voices, what pure reproduction and instrumental subtleties, what clarity and fullness in the recording of the orchestra's performance."[55] To the modern listener accustomed to crystal-clear digital sound, the words are hard to take seriously. But Walter no doubt foresaw at this point in his career that his claim to lasting recognition depended on his interpretations. Only recordings could preserve those interpretations, and throughout his later career he followed every improvement in sonic reproduction with considerable interest and enthusiasm. It's possible that he was genuinely delighted to have some record—however inadequate—of his performances to bequeath to posterity. At the very end of his life, however, he described the earliest record-player as "a mechanical device emitting ugly imitative musical noises."[56] And in 1956, when looking back on his first recording, he recalled a less than satisfactory arrangement in which the musicians were seated as in "animal cages": "I was very highly posted, and the orchestra [was] around me; far below me, the tuba and the brass, and on my sides the strings. And there was no double bass allowed to play without being supported by the bass tuba—otherwise, the low tones could not be recorded. And the outcome was not so very enjoyable."[57]

Exact dates for the acoustic recordings with the Berlin Philharmonic are unavailable, though most were done in the years 1923 and 1924.[58] Walter also recorded several pieces with the Royal Philharmonic Orchestra in London. The recordings, again using the acoustic horn, were made between December 1924 and February 1925, and the works were generally more substantial than those recorded with the Berlin Philharmonic: Strauss's *Tod und Verklärung*; Berlioz's "Dance of the Sylphes" from *La Damnation de Faust*; Weber's *Freischütz* Overture; the Nocturne from Mendelssohn's *A Midsummer Night's Dream*; Wagner's *Siegfried Idyll*, "Siegfried's Rhine Journey," an abbreviated version of the Prelude to Act III of *Die Meistersinger*; and an instrumental arrangement of the "Liebestod" from *Tristan* (curiously, given its importance in Walter's musical development, his only studio recording of any part of the opera). Of these, the *Tod und Verklärung*, the Mendelssohn Nocturne, and the "Liebestod" are sonically the least successful, depending too often on murky timbres that defy satisfactory reproduction using the acoustic process. The other works, however, are surprisingly clear and effective.

In addition to the 78s that Walter made with the Berlin Philharmonic and the Royal Philharmonic Orchestra, several recordings by the Berlin Staatskapelle Orchestra, probably made in 1925, featured Walter at the conductor's desk. Three of these, all overtures from the classical era, were particularly successful: two belonged to operas by Mozart, *Così fan tutte* and *Idomeneo*, the other to an opera by Cherubini, *Les Deux Journées, ou Le Porteur d'eau* (*Der Wasserträger*). The Mozart overtures, taken at a very brisk clip (perhaps to fit each work on a single side), are rhythmically incisive yet flexible, muscular yet graceful. The Cherubini overture, though less brilliant, is still an impressive performance, showing Walter's sensitive shaping to good advantage. Schumann's *Manfred* and Berlioz's *Benvenuto Cellini* overtures were also among the Staatskapelle recordings. But the most significant set was of Tchaikovsky's "Pathétique," historically important because it was the first complete recording of the work, as well as the first recording of an entire symphony by Walter. A recent Deutsche Grammophon transfer of the hard-to-reproduce sides reveals far more subtlety in this problematic recording than one might expect, given that the score creates even more difficulties than most for reproduction through the acoustic horn.[59] The lower strings are wispy at best, and Tchaikovsky's wide range of dynamic markings—one passage is to be played *pppppp*—can scarcely be followed faithfully when everything must be played loud enough to leave an audible impression on the master disk. There are moments of rhythmic waywardness, especially in the first movement, and intonation problems (perhaps the result of awkward instrumental doublings) plague every movement. The recording is "not so very enjoyable," to use Walter's words, but there are exhilarating moments, such as the thirty-second-note runs in the Allegro molto vivace, even if the effect of the movement as a whole is slightly comical, conjuring up cartoon images of a flea-circus band. The last movement, perhaps the most satisfying, offers some aptly plangent passages.

By the end of 1925 Walter would at last land a steady position in Berlin, but the first half of the year kept him very much on the move. At the beginning of the year, he spent several weeks in Amsterdam with the Concertgebouw, conducting mainly standard Germanic repertoire, though he also programmed some rarer items like the Prokofiev Violin Concerto and Debussy's *Nocturnes*, and offered some light Viennese music by Johann Strauss Jr. and Joseph Lanner. He headed for London in February to give a concert of Wagner and Berlioz with the Broadcasting Symphony Orchestra at Covent Garden. Performing with him was the baritone Wilhelm Rode, who sang popular Wagnerian excerpts.[60] Rode had joined the Munich troupe not long before Walter announced his intention to leave, and at that time he wrote a touching letter to Walter in which he wondered who could possibly regret Walter's departure more than he himself did.[61] Whether he was being sincere or merely opportunistic, however, is open to question. He worked with Walter on several other occasions, but when he saw which way the political wind was blowing, he became one of the first to join the very party that had waged a campaign to expel Walter from Munich in 1922. By 1938 he could publish (apparently without shame) a fawning tribute to Hitler: "Whatever the Führer wishes and demands, him I will follow, ever and always enthusiastic, with an obedient, faithful and grateful 'Yes!'"[62]

Walter returned to New York for concerts from late February to the end of March. He continued to look for new works by American composers, especially works that fit into a classical mold, and in Daniel Gregory Mason—composer, teacher, and author—he found a kindred spirit, another musician hostile to jazz and dissonance yet searching for a way to keep serious music in step with changing times and tastes. The composer came from a distinguished musical family whose forebears included the organist-composer Lowell Mason (his grandfather) and the pianist-composer William Mason (his father). It was Walter's friend Ossip Gabrilowitsch who gave Mason's career its first important push forward by promoting his Elegy for Piano, opus 2, both in America and in Europe, and no doubt Gabrilowitsch first brought the composer to Walter's attention.[63] Mason would later become one of Walter's key advisers on American music, and the two musicians maintained a lively correspondence until Mason's death in 1953, discussing in detail matters both personal and musical. For the conservative Mason, Walter was a sign of hope for the future. Walter, in turn, programmed Mason's original but by no means modernist music on several occasions, the first being on March 15, 1925, when he performed Mason's Symphony in C Minor. Olin Downes gave the work a detailed review that was, despite the odd quibble, quite positive: "This is the work of a composer who turns his back upon sensationalism of any kind and who has more than a theoretical admiration for what is noble and heroic."[64] Downes never wrote anything so complimentary about Mahler.

One more Symphony Society concert, given on March 26, deserves mention. Two items make the program stand out from the rest: Elgar's First (which as a composition received indifferent reviews, though the performance was lauded) and a set of vocal numbers sung by the great tenor Roland Hayes. It was almost certainly the first time Walter had worked with an African-American musician. Hayes sang "Endure, My Soul" ("Geduld"), from Bach's *Matthäus-Passion*, and two spirituals accompanied by the orchestra, "Go Down, Moses" and "Bye and Bye." The last two items are not music that one associates with Walter, and it was probably Damrosch who suggested Hayes, famed for his spirituals, as soloist. (Hayes sang spirituals again the following year, when Klemperer was guest conductor of the Symphony Society.) But on this occasion, as on many others, Walter showed his willingness to explore repertoire that was foreign to him.

Shortly after his return to Berlin, he received some vexing news. When he left New York, he had been led to believe by George Engles, the orchestra's manager, that the Symphony Society would invite him back the following year. The last concert, Walter wrote to Gabrilowitsch, had been sold out. Yet he later read in the newspapers that Otto Klemperer, then a rising new star associated with a more modern, "objective" approach to scores, had been engaged instead. Walter was wounded, not only because of the slight but also because of the devious way in which the matter had been handled. Why hadn't Damrosch been open about his intentions? "I'm negotiating with the Vienna Opera and the Deutsches Opernhaus in Berlin," he closed his letter to Gabrilowitsch, "and am curious to know where I shall rest my weary (very weary) head."[65]

But there was no rest for him yet. By the spring, the German season at Covent Garden beckoned to Walter once more. At a dinner given early in June, Herman Klein asked him whether the tenors singing at Covent Garden—the Wagnerians included Fritz Soot, Laurenz Hofer, and Fritz Krauss—were an adequate sampling of what Germanic countries had to offer. Walter blurted out to Klein (perhaps not realizing that his confidences would be shared with Klein's reading public): "By no means. How it has come about is not for me to say; but the fact remains that there are at this moment at least three, and possibly half a dozen, splendid *Helden* (= heroic) tenors in Germany and Austria, any one of whom is superior to those whom London has lately been hearing."[66]

Still jobless more than two years after leaving his position in Munich, Walter pressed on with his peregrinations, hoping to find a resting place, and an island of repose finally came into view. Though in Munich he had found the life of an opera director utterly enervating, a tempting offer—a challenge, really—came from Charlottenburg (a district of Berlin), whose privately run Deutsches Opernhaus, which had enjoyed visits from Walter in 1924, had recently gone bankrupt. The theater was taken over by the city, which turned to Walter to build a high-quality ensemble without making unreasonable demands on the municipal coffers.[67] If anyone could accomplish the task, Walter could: already in Munich, Adolf Weissmann noted, he'd proved his ability to discover and cultivate budding talent.[68] This would give the city another important opera house, one that would vie with the venerable Staatsoper, and soon Otto Klemperer would be offering radical productions at the refurbished Kroll Opera—all of which made Berlin in the late 1920s a paradise for lovers of German opera, even if some Berliners feared a "Twilight of Opera."

The plan was to have Walter as the principal musical force behind the opera and Heinz Tietjen, himself a thoroughly competent conductor, as its general manager. But Walter had nearly burned himself out in Munich and wasn't about to embark on another life-draining enterprise without discussing terms in detail. He negotiated shrewdly with Tietjen over his conditions. It was eventually agreed that Walter would take over as Generalmusikdirektor on August 1, 1925, with his contract lasting till August 31, 1928.

That summer, Walter—no doubt acutely aware of the pressures awaiting him in the fall—found time to relax and read. Thoroughly taken with *Der Zauberberg* (*The Magic Mountain*), the new novel by his friend Thomas Mann, Walter deemed it the "most beautiful and profound work" Mann had thus far written. The time he'd spent with it was more like "timelessness— it's remarkable that this book not only reports about the metaphysical but also, like music, brings us into the sphere of the metaphysical."[69]

Late in August one more important engagement called on his services. Since the 1870s Salzburg had been the venue for summer festivals centering on the city's most famous native son, Wolfgang Amadeus Mozart. In 1920 the Salzburg Festival became an annual event, placing the works of Mozart at its core but also including the medieval drama *Jedermann* (*Everyman*), as produced by Max Reinhardt. Eventually the scope of the festival broadened to embrace composers other than Mozart and dramatic works other than *Jedermann*. In 1925 a new Festspielhaus opened, and on August 26 Bruno Walter appeared for the first time at the festival, leading a performance of Donizetti's *Don Pasquale*. The opera followed performances of *Don Giovanni* under Muck and *Figaro* under Schalk. Even in the company of these Mozartian masterpieces, however, Walter made Donizetti's opera stand out, prompting Julius Korngold to remark that, thanks to the "extraordinary performance" under Walter, it surpassed even *Figaro* in effectiveness.[70] In addition to *Don Pasquale*, Walter gave a concert with the Vienna Philharmonic, which included Mozart's Piano Concerto in E-flat Major (K. 482), featuring

Rudolf Serkin as soloist, and he accompanied Joseph Schwarz at the piano for an evening of song. From his debut at Salzburg till his banishment from Austria after the Anschluss, Walter was one of the most highly esteemed regular conductors at the festival.

Though gratifyingly feted in Salzburg, Amsterdam, New York, Vienna, and elsewhere, Walter must have felt relieved that a regular position now awaited him in his native city. The lack of a secure job and his nomadic life had weighed heavily on him for over two years. He could finally lay his weary head to rest—at least for the moment.

# NINE

# A New Opera Company
## Berlin, 1925–1929

*Hence shall we see,*
*If power change purpose, what our seemers be.*
Shakespeare, *Measure for Measure*

Already in his early career Walter had proved his talent for landing himself in artistically vibrant centers, and now he had done so again. Berlin in the Weimar period was the beating heart of German culture, especially for avant-garde artists. When Walter assumed his position at the Städtische Oper, Max Reinhardt's German Theater continued to thrive (even if Reinhardt himself was rarely in town), and the original genius of Bertolt Brecht was beginning to make itself known. At the same time, Mies van der Rohe, the future leader of the Bauhaus, was drafting designs for buildings that would be inextricably linked with modern architecture. And the city certainly did not suffer from a dearth of great conductors in the 1920s; among the master interpreters who regularly worked there were Wilhelm Furtwängler at the Berlin Philharmonic, Erich Kleiber at the Staatsoper, Otto Klemperer at the Kroll, and Bruno Walter at the Städtische Oper. (Of course, Kleiber, Klemperer, and Walter also gave regular concert series with the Philharmonic.) If ever there was a golden age of conducting, this was it. A famous photograph taken on the occasion of Arturo Toscanini's visit to

Berlin in 1929 shows the five conductors banded together—truly an embarrassment of riches—in apparent solidarity, though shifts in the political landscape would soon expel four of the five men in that gathering to lands far from their native countries.

The last phase of Walter's operatic career in Germany began on September 18, 1925, with a performance of Wagner's *Meistersinger*. Lotte Lehmann, as in a Covent Garden performance earlier that year, assumed the role of Eva, and the other principals included Emil Schipper, Fritz Krauss, Eduard Kandl, and Alexander Kipnis. Awaited with great anticipation, the inaugural performance by the company proved very much an "event," even if it was not satisfying in every particular. The old house had been refurbished to make it more appealing to the eye, but some complained that the end result smacked of cheapness and haste, and there was general agreement that the acoustics had suffered in the process. "The brass sounded raw as never before," Max Marschalk complained, "and during the entire overture—conducted somewhat uneasily and nervously—one couldn't be happy with the sound."[1] Furthermore, the orchestra continually threatened to overwhelm the singers. But, for all that, much in the performance itself pleased. "Already in the course of the first act," Marschalk wrote, "it became increasingly clear how much the performance owed to [Walter's] will and his ability to vivify and animate the details, to bring out the truth of the dramatic expression." In fact, the veteran critic went as far as to claim that he'd never experienced such a lively and intelligent interpretation of the first act.

There could have been no argument about who would conduct the first performance, since Walter was, in a way, the star of the show; but his long experience had taught him much about delegating responsibility and pacing himself. The day after the performance of *Meistersinger*, a new opera was put on, *Die heilige Ente* by Hans Gál. Perhaps surprisingly, Walter did not conduct; instead, his colleague Fritz Zweig gave the Berlin premiere. And indeed, Zweig would conduct many performances at the Städtische Oper until 1927, when he left to join Klemperer at the Kroll. While Walter's frequent absence from the podium was undoubtedly healthy for his constitution, the critics began to grumble early on that the operas were being led too often by conductors of middling talent. So Walter was now in the position that Mahler had been in at the turn of the century, and Walter's assistants were now being treated as he had been in those trying early days.

Although the second work performed at the new opera house was a local premiere, most of the repertoire would be quite familiar to contemporary audiences: *Der Freischütz, Tiefland, Carmen, Don Pasquale, Faust, Les Contes d'Hoffmann*, the favorites by Mozart, Verdi, and Wagner, and so on—largely the works offered at the three Munich theaters. In some cases Walter would act as producer. He programmed nothing so daring as, say, *Wozzeck* (which had its premiere in December at the Staatsoper), and the reviewers gave him nowhere near the attention he'd enjoyed in Munich. Nevertheless, now and again a new work or a strikingly novel approach to an old work would pique the critics' curiosity. In November, for example, Walter presented a successful new production of Gluck's *Iphigenia in Aulis*, with sets by Emil Preetorius. The title role was assumed by a familiar guest artist, Delia Reinhardt, now a member of the Berlin Staatsoper. It is notable that Emil Schipper, another principal in the production, had been a regular under Walter in Munich, for again and again leading singers from his Munich troupe would appear on the stage of the Städtische Oper, some of them as members of the new company.

Walter's work in the opera house kept him busy, but it represented only part of his activity in Berlin, since he also had a series of concerts with the Berlin Philharmonic. His first Philharmonic program of the season, given in October, consisted of a coupling he admired and recommended to others: Schubert's "Unfinished" Symphony followed by *Das Lied von der Erde*.[2] One of the singers in his latest traversal of *Das Lied* was Madame Cahier, who had sung at the premiere performance and whose professional relations with Walter had lasted many years.

Another artist with whom Walter would enjoy a long working relationship was the violinist Erica Morini, who performed as his soloist in November, playing the "rarely heard" Glazunov Violin Concerto in A Minor; the program also included Tchaikovsky's "Pathétique" (which Walter had recently recorded). The choice of pieces might not seem especially bold, but it is worth bearing in mind that Walter's continual interest in the works of Russian composers—he would later offer new productions of Tchaikovsky's *Pique Dame* and *Eugene Onegin* in the opera house—could be interpreted as a subversive political statement in a country with a rapidly growing number of ardent nationalists.

Though settled in Berlin, Walter continued his exhausting travels; by late November he was in England again, conducting the London Symphony Orchestra in a concert that featured the Schumann Cello Concerto with Pablo Casals as soloist. It was another of those precious collaborations between two musicians who admired each other deeply but rarely worked together. On this occasion the great Spanish cellist's compulsive practicing astounded Walter, who, after the concert, impishly chastised him for not instantly taking up his instrument and getting back to work.[3]

If collaborations between Walter and Casals were rare, those between Walter and Béla Bartók—a giant figure in twentieth-century music—were rarer still; but on January 18, 1926, the Hungarian pianist-composer joined Walter and the Berlin Philharmonic for a performance of his early and stylistically conservative Rhapsody for Piano and Orchestra, opus 1, seldom heard in Berlin. Yet most of Walter's orchestral repertoire, like his operatic repertoire, consisted not of rarities but of works that the conductor, the orchestra, and the audience pretty much knew by heart. Making them sound fresh was a constant challenge. How did one approach such pieces? For Walter, it was crucial to make a piece like the "Eroica," however familiar and even overplayed, sound new in performance. This was the central point of an essay he wrote for the *Deutsche Tonkünstler-Zeitung* in 1926: "The work must sound as though it were being played for the first time, and the conductor must feel that he bears the responsibility for making the piece rise fully into the spirit and temper of its creator. I use the day before an important performance to prepare myself for it in this way. Keeping the obtrusive noise of the everyday far from me, I wander about in open nature and try to awaken the mood that seized me when I heard the work for the first time."[4] His striving for that first-time experience, a constant goal in his performances throughout his career, left a lasting impression on Yehudi Menuhin, who as a boy first worked with Walter in 1929: "He was always trying to look for that first moment of rapture . . . when you listen or meet or find something that you've never seen before and which reveals some magic," Menuhin recalled. "And he was trying to look for that magic each time he made music."[5]

That spring, Walter returned to Covent Garden, where his appearances were becoming a much anticipated yearly event. In the early part of May 1926, however, England was in the throes of a general strike, just when Walter was scheduled to launch the German season. It was with considerable interest that he observed the strike and the English way of coping with it. "A feeling of solidarity manifested itself in a general and spontaneous readiness to be of help, while a vigorous sense of humor tended to mitigate annoying inconveniences," he recorded in his memoirs. "With but a few exceptions, a spirit of moderation and self-discipline prevented outbursts of violence."[6] How typical of Walter to admire "moderation and self-discipline" in a time of civil unrest; sadly, he would soon see immoderate behavior and iron discipline gaining the upper hand in his own country.

One important concert in London took place outside the operatic arena, when at the end of May, Walter accompanied Lotte Lehmann at the piano for an afternoon of Wagner and Richard Strauss. Lehmann sang not only songs written for voice and piano but also operatic selections, including the final scene from *Salome*, "which was really sung and not screamed out, so that one could enjoy the sound of it despite its unpleasantness," as the *Times* critic remarked.[7] It was a great success, and over the years Walter and Lehmann would join forces on many occasions, their lieder recitals being an eagerly anticipated annual event in Salzburg.

While preparing the various operas for their performances at Covent Garden, Walter found time to exchange letters with Tietjen, discussing guest conductors, casting, repertoire, and finance. Tietjen's letters to Walter are often long and detailed, and one has to feel some sympathy for a man who was so committed to his work and whom Walter so clearly disliked. Although Tietjen, who negotiated behind Walter's back and later flourished during the Third Reich, may today look like a crafty opportunist, he seems to have respected his music director immensely. (After hearing the first two acts of Walter's *Tristan* in April at the Städtische Oper, he wrote that he'd never in his life heard it performed as Walter had interpreted it, that there was no one who could match what he'd accomplished.[8]) One of the subjects that Tietjen brought up concerned Puccini's last opera, *Turandot*, given its world premiere in April 1926. The Städtische Oper was striving to be the first Berlin company to stage Puccini's posthumous work, and Tietjen had studied the score thoroughly. "It's magnificent indeed," he wrote Walter, "even if it becomes somewhat kitschy at the end. But who's to sing Turandot, with eighty-six high Cs?"[9] The Italian-born Mafalda Salvatini, who established her career outside Italy, would eventually sing the high Cs in Berlin, for Tietjen succeeded in securing *Turandot* for the new company.

But not all Tietjen's attempts at programming novelties at the Städtische Oper would prove so successful. Franz Schreker, whose operas Walter had championed in Munich, remained a powerful musical force in Berlin. His latest work, *Irrelohe*, was even more startling and subversive than his earlier operas (depraved aristocrats have raped the local women, and incendiary commoners raze the castle of Irrelohe in retribution); it seemed as good an example of a "modern German work" as you could get. Apparently Tietjen wanted to fend off criticisms that the Städtische Oper was programming works that were too conservative and neglecting contemporary operas, for he very much wanted Walter's permission to acquire *Irrelohe* for the company. It's unclear whether a rift had actually developed between Walter and Schreker; in any case, despite Tietjen's urgings, *Irrelohe* was not performed at the Städtische Oper during Walter's tenure there.

If having a regular position in Berlin was a comfort for Walter, he continued to lead the life of a wanderer for much of the year. Milan's great opera house, La Scala, was a major venue that had so far eluded him, but on June 23, 1926, he gave his debut concert there in a program consisting of Weber's *Euryanthe* Overture, Mozart's "Haffner" Symphony, Respighi's *Fontane di Roma*, and Strauss's *Don Quixote*. The reviewer for *Corriere della Sera* remarked on the audience's enthusiastic response but took a native's liberty of criticizing Walter's approach to Respighi's tone poem, especially "La fontana di Trevi al meriggio," which seemed somewhat rushed and did not emphasize the brass as much as listeners had come to expect.[10] Walter's refined sensibilities apparently did not lend themselves to Respighi's raucous ebullience.

While in Milan Walter at last met a conductor whom he had heard about for many years. The man he now encountered—well known for his penetrating eyes, hollow cheeks, and devilish mustache—immediately reminded him of Lucifer.[11] This demonic master of the baton was Arturo Toscanini, who would become a close friend of Walter's and whose career would parallel and intersect with Walter's on several occasions; both would be driven from their native lands to find new homes in America.

The Salzburg Festival invited Walter to return in August 1926, and the operas he conducted there were *Die Entführung* and *Die Fledermaus*, which featured (though only once in the same performance) Fritzi Massary as Adele and Richard Tauber as Eisenstein. It must have been a delightful evening. Walter was again working with Massary, whose artistry in *Die Fledermaus* he had already savored two years before in Berlin, and Tauber was no less satisfying. Though the tenor had plenty of experience in serious lyric-tenor roles, he gained a large and loyal following for his work in lighter opera, especially the operettas of Lehár, who highly prized Tauber. Walter was certainly among his fans; in 1948, when asked to write a tribute for the recently deceased Tauber, he recalled hearing the tenor for the first time in Dresden: "I had the feeling that there on the stage stood a born musician and one to whom was given the secret of beauty."[12]

Two noteworthy events took place midway through September 1926, as the new season began. One was a splendid new production of *Fidelio* at the

Städtische Oper on September 14, with sets by Alfred Roller (who had designed the sets for Mahler's famous production at the Vienna Hofoper in 1904). After the performance the Oberbürgermeister Gustav Böss threw a banquet in honor of Walter's fiftieth birthday, the other significant event. Several prominent musical figures were invited, including Tietjen. Delighted that Walter and Tietjen had so quickly raised performance standards at the new theater, Böss thanked them both heartily, though the festivities that night focused on Walter. As a token of his esteem, Böss presented Walter with a special baton, "a pretty and valuable product of the jeweler's art." Walter, for his part, gave a speech on one of his favorite themes, the difficult choice of focusing on the art of one's own time or on art for all time, and during the performance of *Fidelio* "he again had the feeling that only art that 'stresses the eternal' is the genuine article." That didn't mean, he hastened to add (perhaps sensing that his words would sound reactionary), that modern works shouldn't be performed on the stage, for they too could "stress the eternal." The obvious implication behind Walter's statement, of course, is that works that don't stress the eternal and that follow fads are not worth pursuing or producing.[13]

The birthday celebration touched Walter, yet on September 16 the *Berliner Tageblatt* brought an unpleasant surprise: news that Tietjen had been appointed general manager of the Berlin Staatsoper. Incensed, Walter called up his colleague and demanded an explanation. Tietjen explained that he had been sworn to secrecy on the matter but argued that this turn of events would allow both of them to realize their plan for a merger between the Städtische Oper and the Staatsoper. Walter remained unsatisfied: "I replied that he should not have included me in his obligation of secrecy, as I was more vitally affected than anybody else by his assumption of a new sphere of activity. . . . Suggestions made by me on behalf of the Municipal Opera would from now on have to be considered by him from the standpoint of whether or not they conflicted with the interests of the State Opera."[14] For all the praise that had recently been bestowed on Walter, this new turn of events seemed like a slap in the face, and indeed his days at the Städtische Oper were numbered from that time forward.

Nevertheless, he pressed on with his work there. His most important operatic production in 1926 was the Berlin premiere of Puccini's *Turandot*, which took place on November 6. Walter conducted, and Tietjen was the director. Mafalda Salvatini sang Turandot; Lotte Schöne, Liù; Anton Baumann, Timur; and Carl Martin Oehmann, Calaf. Puccini's posthumous work had already played in Milan, Rome, Dresden, Cologne, and Vienna; its historical significance was recognized immediately, and seizing it before the Staatsoper represented a coup for the young company. Leopold Schmidt wryly commented that the Staatsoper, preferring to dabble with fruitless experiments (like *Wozzeck*?), had allowed the Städtische Oper to celebrate a genuine triumph. Walter's attitude to Puccini's music at this time is hard to pin down. He had conducted *Madama Butterfly* on a number of occasions, often eliciting highly enthusiastic responses from the public and the press. In conducting *Turandot* he again gave his all, accomplishing wonders with his forces, and while the orchestra was not, as Schmidt observed, on a par with those in Milan or Dresden, Walter inspired the players to bring out "all the wondrous sound in the score; he uncovers buried subtleties and gives us not only what is terrifying and powerfully monumental but also a fairy-tale sweetness and gentleness. He was justly hailed as the hero of the evening."[15] Yet some had reservations about Walter's approach to the work. Adolf Weissmann found that Puccini's opera "became lyricized in Bruno Walter's hands"; the elements of grand opera and orientalism receded "into the background."[16]

So much for the reception of the opera. But what did Walter himself think of *Turandot*, and of Puccini generally? One would think that Puccini's extraordinary lyric gift, his virtuoso orchestration, his deft manipulation of well-wrought themes would have appealed strongly to the conductor. Yet Walter says nothing of this premiere in *Theme and Variations*. After the initial performances, he passed the work on to Fritz Zweig, though this in itself is no indication that Walter felt indifferent toward it, since he often turned operas over to colleagues after a few performances during this phase of his career. Nevertheless, he probably found Puccini's work less satisfying than, say, the *Ring* or *Fidelio*. In 1955 he wrote to a young music student in Japan who had expressed his admiration for *Madama Butterfly*, "Please discriminate in music. Do not put a certainly charming work of theatrical and musical talents like Butterfly on a level with our lofty classic music by Brahms or Mozart, Beethoven or Brahms, Schubert or Bruckner."[17] Admittedly, more is involved here than just Puccini versus the Teutonic masters; theatrical music is pitted against lofty symphonic works. Nevertheless, Walter seems never to have appreciated Puccini as deeply as one might have expected from a man with a penchant for lyrical beauty.

After the premiere of *Turandot* Walter returned for the most part to familiar repertoire at the opera house and in the concert hall. The more out-of-the-way operas performed at the Städtische Oper were taken by Walter's colleagues, mainly by Egon Pollack and Fritz Zweig. Walter led a highly successful new production of *Falstaff* early in March 1927 and later that month offered a sampling of Beethoven's works with the Philharmonic, giving a speech on Beethoven for the hundredth anniversary of the composer's death.[18] His friendship with Hans Pfitzner continued to manifest itself in tangible ways: at the end of March, a Pfitzner Week, less ambitious than the one arranged in Munich in 1917, took place in Berlin, with *Der arme Heinrich* and *Von deutscher Seele*, both under Walter, at its core. By this time, it should be noted, Pfitzner's conservative political stance had crept to the extreme Right. In 1923 Pfitzner met Adolf Hitler and soon developed a profound admiration for the aspiring leader of Germany.[19] Walter, however, surely knew nothing of his friend's Nazi leanings and, after the war, expressed utter disbelief when confronted with some of Pfitzner's more discreditable actions.

Success shone on Walter whenever he performed in Berlin, yet complaints grew ever louder and more frequent that the director of the Städtische Oper was too often absent from his post. In January 1927 Walter wrote to Gustav Böss, chairman of the opera's supervisory board, that he was deeply upset by the rebukes leveled at him for his supposed neglect of his duties during a recent trip to Russia. The grievances had been raised not only privately, by the supervisory board, but also publicly, by the press, which had apparently been informed by members of the board. With his patent devotion to the Städtische Oper, he wrote, he was surprised that he had to endure such abuse. Prepared to dissolve his relationship with the opera company after his current contract expired, he hoped that delicate decisions made by the board would not be leaked to the press. Böss wrote back that the decisions of the board were a matter of public record and recommended that Walter patch things up with his colleagues at the Städtische Oper.[20]

The grievances about Walter's absence, however annoying to the conductor, were not groundless. He had left Berlin on many occasions and would continue to do so throughout 1927; some of his ventures outside the city's boundaries, though, were perfectly unobjectionable, since his contract allowed for a fair amount of guest conducting. In May, for example, he returned to Covent Garden for his annual performances there. While Walter conducted in London, a young guest conductor, Georg Sebestyen (better known by the name he later adopted in France, Georges Sébastian), appeared at the Städtische Oper. The Hungarian-born Sébastian had admired

Walter on many occasions in Munich and had even written a eulogistic essay on him for *Die Musik*.[21] His connections with Walter would in fact reach beyond the limits of their musical collaborations, for he became Delia Reinhardt's second husband, after her divorce from Gustav Schützendorf. (Schützendorf, in turn, married the soprano Grete Stückgold, another singer who frequently worked with Walter.)

While Sébastian and Walter always remained on friendly terms, the same could not be said about Walter and another conductor, Wilhelm Furtwängler. During Walter's brief stay in England, in fact, a business transaction developed that was hardly likely to ease tensions between the two German conductors, though neither was at fault. Anton Weiss of the Vienna Philharmonic had invited Walter to conduct three or four of its subscription concerts, along with Schalk and Furtwängler. Walter wrote back on May 20 that he was perfectly happy to conduct the concerts offered by the orchestra; as for his payment, the "quickest and most painless" solution was to pay him whatever Furtwängler would receive.[22] (Walter didn't bother to inquire into Schalk's remuneration.) When Walter received his next letter from Weiss, the news it brought proved irritating and insulting. Dated May 24, it arrived in Walter's hands only on June 2, and Weiss claimed in it not have received Walter's letter of May 20. Furtwängler, it turned out, had agreed to conduct five or six concerts, so the Philharmonic now offered Walter only two subscription concerts and one nonsubscription—roughly half as many concerts as Furtwängler would be conducting.[23] This prompted a bitter reply from Walter, who found the postal delays in their correspondence "puzzling" and "incomprehensible." "But for me the *most incomprehensible* thing," he wrote, "is that you, *after* officially offering me three to four of your regular concerts, have accepted Herr Furtwängler's demand to conduct five to six concerts, which therefore forces you *retroactively* to reduce the offer made earlier to me. You will understand that I cannot accept this, since it is not compatible with my prestige."[24]

Though plans for his guest engagements in Vienna crumbled, Walter had offers in abundance to conduct outside Berlin, some of them from the other side of the Atlantic. Early in June 1927 he again set off for New York. This time, however, his destinations lay far from his initial landing place; he would cross the entire country to perform first in Cleveland and then in San Francisco and Los Angeles. On this occasion Elsa and Gretel joined him. Lotte remained in Europe, perhaps in Würzburg, where she was engaged as a singer at the Stadttheater during the 1926–27 and 1927–28 seasons. There she sang a number of lighter roles and met a young director, Arthur Maria Rabenalt, whom she married.[25] It was around 1929 that Rudolf Bing first met Rabenalt—who later scored a number of successes in major theaters— at the opera house in Darmstadt. Bing recalled him as "young and very talented," but "married, rather unsuitably, to Bruno Walter's daughter Lotte— they had been working on annual contracts at a little theater in Würzburg, she as a soprano, and in these little towns one has nothing else to do, so they were married. Soon they were divorced."[26] It was evidently not a happy union, but the correspondence that has surfaced so far has shed no light on Lotte's brief first marriage.

We do, however, know something about Walter's visit to the United States. He had never experienced an American summer before, and on his arrival in New York, where his cross-country journey began, the heat overwhelmed him. "Cleveland," he wrote, "was hardly more bearable."[27] The event that drew Walter to Cleveland was the triennial Sängerfest of the North American Sängerbund, a three-day festival beginning June 22. "A crowd of some 12,000 filled Public Hall and marveled at the chorus of 4,000 voices that filled the huge auditorium with song," the *Musical Courier* reported. "Artistically the engagement was a triumph, and financially the results were most gratifying."[28] The orchestra consisted of players from the Cleveland and Detroit orchestras, and Walter's first appearance in Cleveland was an unqualified success. He opened the ceremonies with the overture to *Tannhäuser* and returned throughout the festival to conduct other works by German and Austrian masters—mostly standard repertoire, with the exception of the "Transformation Music" from *Monika Vogelsang*, an opera by Rudolf Schueller, a local composer and one of the participating choral conductors.[29] Though by no means the only conductor, Walter was clearly the big star. At the conclusion of the festival, according to the *Musical Courier*, "the 12,000 people who attended the final concert united in giving Bruno Walter a rousing farewell that must have made a most pleasant memory for that talented conductor to carry back with him to Germany."

But before returning to Germany, the Walters had to travel farther west. In a sweltering train compartment they sweated their way to California, where Walter made "his Pacific debut" in Hillsborough on Sunday, July 3— a well-attended event, even though it fell in the middle of a holiday weekend. This was followed on July 5 by his San Francisco debut at the Exposition Auditorium, which drew a crowd of eight thousand. Again the popular and critical response was enthusiastic. Like others before him (and after), Alfred

Metzger was especially impressed at what Walter could achieve in such a short time. "Throughout the program the conductor was able, although he had but two rehearsals, to impress his individuality and personal touch upon the orchestra. . . . He belongs to that class of leaders who accomplish remarkable results with just the least hint of what he wants and he has his men so well in hand that they grasp his slightest meaning without fail. In short, he is a great conductor."[30]

Another immense auditorium awaited him in Los Angeles, the Hollywood Bowl (seating ten thousand), which Walter approached with due caution, though this enormous outdoor stadium would become one of his regular venues in the 1940s and 1950s. Hollywood hype surrounded his debut there: Elsa was identified as having been "one of the best-known singers in Germany," Gretel as "a stage celebrity in Berlin."[31] Despite his doubts about the amphitheater, Walter was surprised to find that conducting in a space whose acoustics were patently inadequate could nevertheless produce satisfactory results. "What had happened to me to make me undisturbed by the night wind threatening the sheets on the musicians' desks, to make me overlook the insufficient brilliance of the *fortissimo* and the unreliability of the *pianissimo*? There was the splendor of the California night, of the starry sky, and of the dark mountains surrounding us; there was the touching silence of the immense throng."[32]

The trip to America, however enjoyable, took its toll on Walter's health. Upon his return to Europe he learned that he had double pneumonia. Unable to participate in the Salzburg Festival, he rested in St. Moritz, Switzerland, during August and early September. Though this was a brief professional setback, his illness and convalescence had the advantage of bringing to him an "increased maturity and deeper tranquillity," which helped him acquire a deeper understanding and appreciation of Bruckner.[33] But his attention was not devoted solely to aesthetics. This was also a period for solemn reflection on the course his life had taken, with his difficulties in Berlin preying on his mind. In disgust he wrote to Hans Pfitzner in late August that, though still enervated, he hoped to arrive in Berlin midway through September, "ready for work—'ready for aggravation' would be more like it." A public break with the Städtische Oper had thus far been avoided, but Walter ruled out staying there beyond the coming season, and he doubted whether he could last even that long.[34]

One of the aggravations that Walter had to prepare himself for was a new opera (first presented in Leipzig earlier that year) by Ernst Krenek, the young composer who had completed two movements of Mahler's Tenth Symphony and had married Mahler's daughter Anna. Krenek's latest creation, *Jonny spielt auf*, had become a smash hit in Germany in a very short time. One disenchanted reviewer characterized the work's fast-spreading popularity as an epidemic, labeling it "Jonnytis vulgaris."[35] Injecting jazz elements into opera, *Jonny* was a daring and controversial work, different from anything the Städtische Oper had thus far presented. But the combination of jazz and classical elements would always rub Walter the wrong way. In 1929, when asked whether the present time could bring forth great composers, he responded, "Well, why not? . . . We have some great talents today; unfortunately, they have all let themselves be influenced so strongly by *jazz* that they can no longer develop their own personalities."[36] And later in his life, in a notorious interview, he went so far as to offer a flat condemnation of jazz as "an insult. . . . The monotony of the use of percussion, the uninterrupted shrieking of the muted brass is nearly unbearable to me."[37] Tietjen admitted that *Jonny* was no more to his taste than to Walter's, characterizing it as a "revue"; yet he also felt that Krenek became "magnificent" when he introduced the jazz rhythms—a telling difference between the two musicians' aesthetic sensibilities.[38] Not surprisingly, Walter gave no performances of the opera, which went to the new member of his conducting staff, Georges Sébastian.

Other modern works, probably recommended by the business-minded Tietjen, made their way onto the performance calendar of the Städtische Oper. Robert Denzler, another conductor then on the roster, led a double bill of two older works by Stravinsky, an opera and a ballet, *The Nightingale* and *The Firebird*. Both were billed as being presented "for the first time"—at the Städtische Oper, at least. While Sébastian and Denzler were offering Krenek and Stravinsky, Walter refreshed operas that had become part of his repertoire. In October he gave a new production of Gluck's *Orfeo ed Euridice*, using his own arrangement, which mixed elements of both the French and the Italian versions, and which concluded not with the standard ending but, curiously, with the finale from Gluck's *Echo et Narcisse*.[39] In December Walter revisited an opera he had introduced to Vienna, Debussy's *Pelléas et Mélisande*.

During the same period, the Berlin Philharmonic continued with its Bruno Walter Concerts, one of the more noteworthy taking place in early November, when Walter and Vladimir Horowitz collaborated in a performance of Tchaikovsky's Piano Concerto in B-flat Minor. The concert marked the first time that Walter and Horowitz performed together;

Horowitz, of course, would go on to become the most celebrated pianist of his generation and would marry Wanda Toscanini, daughter of the century's most celebrated conductor. The concert was covered by Alfred Einstein, the new chief music reviewer for the *Berliner Tageblatt*, who took over the position left vacant after Leopold Schmidt's death in April. A man of extraordinary cultural breadth, Einstein became one of the leading musicologists of the twentieth century, remembered above all for his monumental study of the Italian madrigal, though he published books on a wide variety of musical subjects. He had heard many of Walter's concerts in Munich, where he'd reviewed for the *Münchener Post*, and he had written a short tribute to Walter for the journal *Musikblätter des Anbruch*.[40] Though one of Walter's strongest supporters in Berlin, Einstein could also be one of his loudest critics. In reviewing the concert with Horowitz he made no attempt to conceal his disdain for the concerto that the musicians had chosen. Nevertheless, he was utterly won over by Horowitz's performance; the Russian pianist "played with such élan, with such a rich palette of colors, with such fine taste, and the playing was so far removed from the brutal and the saccharine, that one was absolutely delighted by his virtuosity and musicianship."[41]

Two months later Einstein reviewed the world premiere of a work by Richard Strauss, which should have been an event of great moment. As it happened, the piece that Walter introduced on January 16, 1928, is one of Strauss's least-heard works—*Panathenäenzug*, written for Paul Wittgenstein, the famous pianist who lost his right arm in World War I. A brother of the philosopher Ludwig Wittgenstein, Paul came from a Viennese family that had long supported the arts in general and music in particular; Walter recalled having played music at the Wittgensteins' during his earlier years in Vienna.[42] Strauss was by no means the only composer to write music specially for Paul Wittgenstein; indeed, the list of distinguished composers who wrote with his special requirements in mind includes Ravel, Prokofiev, Korngold, and Britten. The piece, running to about half an hour, took the form of a passacaglia and was strikingly different from the aggressively postromantic Straussian tone poems that Walter usually conducted, though it had an eighteenth-century neatness and restraint that would be in keeping with some of Strauss's later works, like *Capriccio* and the Oboe Concerto. Unimpressed, Einstein admired the pianist's artistry but found the composition itself banal and empty; Strauss, he commented, was lost without a program.[43] The piece seems to have been forgettable for Walter as well, for in his memoirs he made no attempt to note Strauss's *Panathenäenzug* as one of the works he'd introduced to the world.

If Einstein handled Strauss roughly in his review, his treatment of Walter shortly afterward was plainly a case of tough love. Walter's absences had become intolerable for the reviewer, and a mediocre production of Handel's *Ezio*, conducted by Robert Denzler at the Städtische Oper, seems to have pushed Einstein over the edge. The production was very poorly prepared, wholly unworthy of a major opera house in Berlin. Who was to be held accountable? Surely Walter himself. "It is *his* institute," Einstein wrote. "If I may be permitted to say so, he doesn't trouble himself enough over his institute. *His* performances are good, but his are almost the only good ones. And his are far too infrequent. We simply can't have enough of him. . . . Bruno Walter's successes in London, Amsterdam, New York, and Oklahoma [*sic*] bring us heartfelt joy, but the Städtische Oper is going to the dogs. And if he really wants to have thirteen vacations in twelve months, then he must allow a leader and conductor who is up to standard to take the reins during his absence."[44]

It was true that Walter's constant traveling outside Berlin had a deleterious effect on his opera company, but the city also profited from his wanderings, for he encountered new soloists and young composers abroad, and brought both foreign performers and fresh compositions to Berlin. One of the new talents he discovered during his travels would become the foremost symphonist of his generation. In 1926, while Walter was guest-conducting in what was then called Leningrad, the conductor Nicolai Malko asked him to listen to the first symphony of a man barely past twenty, Dmitri Shostakovich.[45] Walter immediately recognized the budding composer's originality and talent and later arranged to have the work played by the Berlin Philharmonic. So it was that on February 6, 1928, Shostakovich's First Symphony had its German premiere. The four-movement work, lasting somewhat over half an hour, bore the stamp of an individual composer who knew what he wanted and how to achieve it. In shunning extreme experiments, the symphony won over not only Walter but several of the critics, including Einstein and Max Marschalk. "He can do a great deal, this young Russian," Marschalk wrote, "and he can do more than some who, in recent years, have caused a great fuss. He has a sense for line and color, and his instrumentation is exceedingly skillful, one could almost say refined."[46] Walter's "total devotion" to the performance was duly noted, as was his beautiful accompanying of Artur Schnabel in Mozart's Piano Concerto in G Major (K. 453), also on the program—which ended with Beethoven's Fifth. Clearly a memorable night.

Although Walter and his parents lived in the same city, his schedule was so full that he rarely had time to see them. Late in February, he wrote to them from Budapest, "You ought to receive at least a greeting from me 'from a far-away country,' since when I'm in Berlin you hardly see me at all any more. Here, despite all my work (I had a concert yesterday, I'm conducting today and tomorrow), I'm still relatively free."[47] He would be coming back to Berlin for a few days to rehearse some operas and concerts, then off to Prague by March 4. His regret at not being able to spend more time with his parents must have increased exponentially over the next two years, for his mother died in 1929, his father in 1930, both in their mid-eighties. Later, however, from the vantage point of one who had seen the horrors of World War II, he could find comfort in the thought that they'd been spared the ordeal of witnessing the Nazis' rise to power.[48]

A new opera made its way onto the stage of the Städtische Oper in April 1928. The first major work by Erich Wolfgang Korngold that Walter had per-formed since the famous double bill of *Violanta* and *Der Ring des Polykrates* in 1916, *Das Wunder der Heliane* had had its world premiere the previous October in Hamburg. Korngold's fame, which had continued to grow since his early successes, was reaching its peak; in 1930 a poll conducted by the *Neues Wiener Tagblatt* listed him as one of the most highly esteemed men in Austria.[49] Nevertheless, much of his fame had revolved around his arrange-ments of operettas and his spirited conducting of lighter works, so *Heliane* represented, in some ways, Korngold's reminder to the world that he was still a serious composer.

The Berlin production of *Heliane*, on April 5, 1928, starred Grete Stückgold in the title role, Hans Fidesser as the Stranger, Emil Schipper as the Ruler, and Alexander Kipnis as the Jailer. The audience responded warmly, offering ovations to the composer—who attended the performance —after the second and third acts. Putting a subversive spin on the issues, the opera deals with such loaded themes as sexual repression and erotic libera-tion, political and spiritual tyranny, patriarchal authority, and that perennial favorite, adultery. To add another controversial touch, the plot has Heliane raising the Stranger (whom she loves) from the dead, with a Christ-like power that is not lost on the characters themselves. In the first act, Heliane is to bare herself on stage for the Stranger, and even if she is actually wearing a "chemise of airy thinness" underneath her cloak, the disrobing must have achieved a stunningly sensual effect. While some of these themes had made their way into opera long before, the thin edge of the wedge was slowly prying open the door of propriety; Einstein, who had reviewed the world premiere, reiterated his thorough distaste for the libretto, though he allowed that the music was "incomparably better than the book." All the same, the music (like the book) was too derivative for him—too Puccinian (though to modern ears Korngold's distinctive voice is far louder than Puccini's). Walter's interpretation stressed the drama above all, and Einstein noted the impressive dramatic intensity that Walter built in the final act.[50] Although the opera had been a box office success in several cities and, as a cultural artifact, was widely viewed as a foil to the enormously popular *Jonny spielt auf*, its run in Berlin was short-lived.[51] Walter's yearly commitments at Covent Garden took him away from the opera soon after its initial performances, and even those had hardly won over the critics. One of the reviewers, Adolf Weissmann, commenting on its ill reception in Berlin, conceded that the libretto contained matter potentially effective on the stage, and also that Korngold knew how to write opera as almost no one else did. "It's only a pity," he added, "that he has so little taste."[52]

While the earlier part of May found Walter again conducting Wagner in London—the *Ring* cycle, *Die Meistersinger*—the real excitement awaited him at the end of the month. On May 17 he arrived in Paris to lead a month-long Mozart marathon that would prove a revelation to the French while taxing Walter's stamina to the point of collapse. Already in 1927 plans had been made for a Wagner Festival to be held in March at the Grand Théâtre des Champs-Élysées, with Walter and Erich Kleiber sharing the conducting duties, but the festival never materialized.[53] Now Walter alone, beginning on May 25, 1928, was scheduled to conduct a series of five Mozart operas, each work receiving three performances, all in close succession: *Don Giovanni* (in Italian), *Così fan tutte* (in Italian), *Die Zauberflöte* (in German), *Die Entführung* (in French), and *Le nozze di Figaro* (in French). Before leading the operatic performances, he gave a concert with the Orchestre de la Société des Concerts, and at some point he found time to record several sides with the Festival Orchestra. Almost predictably, exhaustion overwhelmed him just as he reached *Figaro*, and doctors ordered him to rest. On very short notice, Reynaldo Hahn—critic, composer, singer, conductor, and erstwhile intimate of Marcel Proust—kindly agreed to take over the last leg of this journey through the major Mozart operas.[54]

For his concert performance, on May 20 in the Salle Pleyel, Walter offered Mahler's Fourth, with Renée Destanges as soprano soloist, and Stravinsky's Piano Concerto, with the composer himself at the keyboard. Furtwängler had just visited Paris on tour with the Berlin Philharmonic, leaving a stronger impression than Walter, who, as one critic noted, wasn't conducting his own ensemble and hadn't had adequate time to rehearse.[55] (Walter must have flinched to hear the unflattering comparison with his younger rival, which would doubtless have opened old wounds—the missed positions in Leipzig and Berlin, the frustrated concert series in Vienna.) Nevertheless, despite far from ideal conditions, Walter managed to deliver a memorable performance. Robert Brussel, reviewing the concert in *Le Figaro*, had previously known Walter only as an operatic conductor who captured "the spirit of the works" mainly through his "fidelity to the texts." He found many of the same qualities when Walter directed an orchestra in concert. "His gestures are precise without ever being automatic, firm but not at all hard, passionate without being bombastic."[56]

While Mahler's Fourth was a work that Walter conducted with great frequency throughout his career, the music of Igor Stravinsky—by some accounts, the greatest composer of the twentieth century—rarely appeared on Walter's programs. During the 1927-28 season, however, he had programmed Stravinsky's *Pulcinella* Suite in Berlin and Leipzig. That suite, of course, belongs to Stravinsky's neoclassical period, the movements being based on eighteenth-century works once attributed to Pergolesi. It is therefore not surprising that the Piano Concerto, the Stravinsky piece that Walter chose for his concert in Paris, was also markedly neoclassical in character—Brussel drew a comparison with Bach's Fifth Brandenburg—though the angular lines, dissonances, and sharp syncopations represented a tangible link with modernism. How did Walter approach the piece? One reliable eyewitness, Stravinsky himself, offered a surprising account: "The performance was a pleasure altogether unanticipated. I expected a 'Romantiker,' from such a different and *vergangenen* generation, to lack the technique for this kind of music, but my scrambled meters gave him no trouble at all and he conducted the Concerto as well as any conductor with whom I played it. (I, on the other hand, would never have the technique to do 'his' music; I sorely envied his rubato.)"[57] It was a gracious tribute indeed to a conductor who had never performed (and had probably never liked) *Le Sacre du printemps*.[58]

If the orchestral concert drew qualified praise from the critics, the Mozart operas were a colossal success. They took place at the Théâtre des

Champs-Élysées, and the ensemble was again the Orchestre de la Société des Concerts du Conservatoire. One of the purposes of the festival was to bring together musicians from different nations to collaborate artistically, and among Walter's cosmopolitan cast of singers were Mariano Stabile, Frida Leider, Alexander Kipnis, Lotte Schöne, Marie Gerhardt, Hans Fidesser, Paul Bender, Renée Destanges, Georges Meader, Gabrielle Ritter-Ciampi, and René Maison.[59] The event won popular and critical acclaim; according to one report, so many Parisians flocked to the theater to hear *Die Zauberflöte* that over five hundred had to be turned away from the last performance.[60] In his reviews, Pierre-Barthélemy Gheusi of *Le Figaro* attributed much of the success of the Mozart cycle to Walter's masterly conducting, which showed what could be accomplished with the musicians who performed regularly in Paris. "It would be saddening," he wrote, "if such lessons were lost on our conductors."[61]

The only sound documents of the festival itself are studio recordings of the overtures to *Die Zauberflöte* and *Le nozze di Figaro* (the latter very rare and never officially released), both with the Festival Orchestra.[62] Walter takes decidedly brisk tempi for both overtures, and the effect is exhilarating. He also conducted the same orchestra in a recording of Schumann's Fourth Symphony, with more uneven results. The intonation, especially between the strings and the woodwinds, leaves much to be desired, and a number of uneasy transitions from one tempo to another suggest very limited rehearsal time. Nevertheless, this is a vigorous performance, and some of the accelerandi and crescendi are particularly forceful. There is nothing cautious or routine in the playing.

After the Mozart cycle Walter felt thoroughly drained and, according to one report, irritated at how the business side of the festival had been managed.[63] During his enforced period of relaxation in Switzerland, he ruminated on the unsatisfactory state of affairs at the Städtische Oper. Tietjen had the misfortune of having to consult him on several vexing business matters. The tenor Hans Fidesser, who had worked with Walter in Berlin and Paris and whom Walter wanted to retain at the Städtische Oper, was apparently trying to negotiate an arrangement with the Kroll Opera allowing him to perform in both houses.[64] It was not the kind of news that Walter wanted to hear. In general, he was also suffering from a malaise over the current state of opera. He voiced some of his concerns in a 1932 essay with the ominously Wagnerian title "Operndämmerung" ("The Twilight of Opera").[65] His point of departure is the question whether opera as a medium, as an "idea," has become obsolete. He thinks not. "How should one accept that such riches would lose their charm or that the capability for inspired surrender, the love for the human voice and for music, the interest in dramatic development, and so forth, could wither? Then we would stand before a 'Twilight of the Soul,' and it would be not opera but rather the human heart and its role in culture that would be in danger." For Walter, the real enemy to the future of opera lurks in "the carefully prepared new production . . . that alters the spirit of the work, lifting it from its proper sphere in order . . . to force upon it the allure of novelty." He makes a plea for "authenticity" and, in doing so, apparently sides once again with the more conservative element. Walter, however, doesn't want to "conserve" what is dead but to maintain vitality in what is living, as his concluding analogy shows: "The institutions to whose care opera is entrusted almost have the duty of a zoological garden, whose directors must provide living conditions corresponding to the nature of each of the creatures in their care in order to keep it healthy and to allow the full development of its being." Such thoughts about the future of opera had no doubt troubled him during his tenure at the Städtische Oper, where another problem—his unsatisfactory relationship with Tietjen—eventually led to open conflict.

By August, Walter had regained his strength and was ready to face yet another Mozart Festival, this one in Salzburg, where he conducted *Così* as well as three concerts with the Vienna Philharmonic. But while he entered Mozart's world of well-governed harmonies, surrounded as he was by gorgeous landscapes and splendid architecture, he no doubt felt a need to resolve the ever growing dissonance in his operatic work at the Städtische Oper. After much frustrating correspondence with Tietjen and others about running the theater, Walter wrote a long letter in September to Gustav Böss, who had been one of his staunchest supporters. In 1925, Walter wrote, he had become musical director of an independent opera house. Tietjen had discussed the possibility of establishing a connection between the Städtische Oper and the Staatsoper, a collaboration that could work, in Walter's opinion, only if the two companies merged under the joint directorship of himself and Tietjen. This might well have led to the building of a single, very strong Berlin company. But Tietjen alone had assumed the directorship of the Staatsoper, while still acting as manager of the Städtische Oper, and Walter was limited to being music director at the new house. "I am now the captain of a ship," Walter moaned, "that has been coupled by a cable to the journey of another ship." As an example, he cited the difficulties with Fidesser, whose services were sought by the Kroll and the Staatsoper. Walter felt that, for aesthetic and practical reasons, Fidesser would have to confine his activities to the Städtische Oper, and Tietjen had shown solidarity with Walter. Yet several weeks after the matter had apparently been settled, Tietjen allowed Fidesser to sing at the Staatsoper—an utterly unacceptable turn of events for Walter. And there were bound to be other situations in which Tietjen, as manager of both houses, would make decisions regarding casting and repertoire that would be in his own interests, not in Walter's, and on which Tietjen would have the final word. The current state of affairs was galling for Walter, who had grown accustomed, in Munich, to having a clearly defined role regarding the organization and development of a unified, independent company, whereas now he had an unclear position in a company that had lost its independence. After voicing his grievances, Walter asked for Böss's confidential promise to accept his resignation. The affair would be kept quiet unless the situation grew so unbearable that Walter would feel compelled to make a public statement, and then the two of them could agree on the exact form that statement would take.[66] The negotiations recalled, in some particulars, those awkward months in 1912 before Walter's departure from Vienna, when he desperately wanted to quit the city.

As Walter's relationship to the Städtische Oper continued to deteriorate, his connection with the Gewandhaus Orchestra grew stronger. For the 1928–29 season, Walter was allotted the better part of the Gewandhaus concerts, and on October 11 he made a positive impression on the critic Adolf Aber in Leipzig with the first of his concerts for the new season. Aber's preference for Walter over Furtwängler—who had recently left his position at the Gewandhaus—is unmistakable. For Aber, Furtwängler had done much to eliminate the freedom that Arthur Nikisch had achieved with the orchestra, and Walter, "no despot," was liberating the players again:

> He doesn't have to force upon the orchestra his thoughts on every quarter note and every eighth; he even allows himself to be carried for a while by the waves until, when the climax approaches, he retakes the helm with greater firmness and pulls every last bit from his musicians. Such music making requires from the orchestra its own highly developed joy in playing music, its own ardor. All this Arthur Nikisch once cultivated in the orchestra to the highest degree. And it seems to me that quite some time must pass before the orchestra, which in recent years has been accustomed to uncondi-

tional subordination under Wilhelm Furtwängler's victorious will, finds its way again to this freer sort of music making.[67]

It may come as a surprise to see Furtwängler, now often viewed as an exponent of rhythmically "free" interpretation, portrayed as something of a musical dictator, while Walter, today remembered largely for the sensuously flexible yet controlled performances of his last years, is admired for the freedom he gives to the orchestra. Yet how sharp-sighted of Aber to recognize Walter's striving for a communal effort on the part of the orchestral players, who were expected to have their own "highly developed joy in playing music."

At the opera house in Berlin, standard repertoire prevailed, though Robert Denzler gave the local premieres of Kurt Weill's *Der Protagonist* and *Der Zar lässt sich photographieren* in October. Walter enjoyed a triumph with a new production of the Paris version of *Tannhäuser* and, on November 13, 1928, gave the world premiere of Julius Bittner's *Mondnacht*. The new work, strongly Viennese in plot and music (like Bittner's earlier operas), was well received—largely, as the reviewers noted, because Walter himself had brought so much to the production. Another triumph was Walter's new production of Verdi's *Otello*, given in December, with Carl Martin Oehmann as Otello, Maria Müller as Desdemona, and Wilhelm Rode (a guest from Munich) as Iago. To judge from the many clippings that Walter had amassed, it was a production that he was particularly proud of.

Highlights of Walter's concerts with the Berlin Philharmonic at the end of 1928 included a performance of Mahler's Third, a Schubert program in which Walter accompanied Dusolina Giannini at the piano, and a performance of Ernest Bloch's Concerto Grosso, also with Walter at the keyboard. The reviewer Karl Westermeyer noted that, several weeks before, Bloch's piece had been introduced to Berlin by Heinz Unger, at which time it had met a lukewarm reception; now, for the same piece under Walter, the "applause was great."[68]

An entire program of out-of-the-way music, coupled with an unprecedented choice for a conducting partner, distinguished a concert Walter gave at the end of the year. Always aware of women's contributions to musical culture, Walter made history at the Berlin Philharmonic on December 19, 1928, by helping to break down a long-held gender barrier. He devoted an entire program to the music of his old friend Ethel Smyth and, since they shared duties at the podium, Smyth became the first woman to conduct either the Berlin Philharmonic or the Bruno Kittel Choir, which participated in the concert. The program began with the overture to *The Boatswain's Mate*, conducted by Walter; then Smyth directed a performance of her Concerto for Violin, Horn, and Orchestra, with Marjorie Hayward playing the violin and Aubrey Brain the horn. Walter returned for the Prelude to Act II of *The Wreckers*, followed by love scenes from the same act, sung by Rose Pauly—one of the century's most celebrated Elektras, then known as Rose Pauly-Deesen—and Carl Martin Oehmann. The concert concluded with two choral numbers, "Nacht" ("Sleepless Dreams") and "He holla ho" ("Hey Nonny No"), under Smyth. The audience responded with tremendous fervor, though Westermeyer later wrote that the benevolent applause was not to deceive anyone into thinking the concert had been a success: "She is not a composer in the true sense of the word, not a creative nature," he carped, "for the derivative character of her music is unmistakable."[69]

While Walter enjoyed his share of triumphs and endured ever-growing frustrations in Berlin, his reputation outside his home city continued to reach new heights. It is a sign of Walter's increasing importance in the worldwide musical scene that, at the beginning of 1929, when Toscanini was unable to conduct the Philharmonic Symphony-Society of New York—an ensemble that had come into being when the New York Philharmonic and its rival the New York Symphony Orchestra merged in 1928—Arthur Judson asked Walter in confidence whether he could take Toscanini's place. It was obviously in the best interest of the newly assembled organization to have conductors who would draw the largest audiences and whose names enjoyed the highest prestige. Despite the tempting offer, Walter cabled back: "CURRENT SEASON FULLY OCCUPIED."[70]

The concerts with the Berlin Philharmonic held few surprises in the earlier part of 1929. One novelty for Berlin was Janáček's *Taras Bulba*, though the piece was then over a decade old. While Janáček's music rarely appeared on Walter's programs, this tone poem seems to have appealed to him, for he continued to perform it well into the 1930s. Other high points in the Philharmonic's programs included the Brahms Piano Concerto in D Minor, with Edwin Fischer as soloist; Beethoven's *Missa solemnis*, with the Bruno Kittel Choir; and Mozart's Concerto for Two Pianos in E-flat Major (K. 365), with Walter and Ossip Gabrilowitsch playing the keyboards.

The inevitable news was made public in the latter part of March 1929: Walter would be leaving the Städtische Oper at the end of the current season. His frustrations with the present state of affairs—in which Tietjen controlled both houses while Walter was music director of only one—had become intolerable. He had longed to transform the two opera companies into a unified ensemble, with a stable roster and plenty of first-rate singers. Instead, he was forced to accommodate two separate institutions and to put up with unstable personnel and casts that juxtaposed mediocre and superb talents. For years he had asked for greater cooperation and had found it wanting. Seeing no indication that the situation would improve, and having informed the management long before that he would leave if no steps were taken to rectify the situation, he chose to relinquish his duties at the Städtische Oper.[71]

Some were stunned by the news. In Vienna Lotte Lehmann heard reports so contradictory that she didn't know what to believe. "Should you not remain the leader of the Städtische Oper," she wrote, "I also wouldn't want to sing there any more. This opera company stands and falls with you, and it will turn into a second-rate institution the moment your hands have left the reins."[72] The Berlin critics were united in viewing this turn of events as an artistic blow to their city. The *Vossische Zeitung* carried a long front-page story explaining the events that had resulted in Walter's departure.[73] In the *Berliner Tageblatt* Einstein ran a tribute to Walter, sympathizing with his desire for a merger between the Staatsoper and the Städtische Oper under unified artistic direction.[74] Though it was common knowledge that Walter was next in line to conduct the Gewandhaus Orchestra, for a while there was hope that he might reconsider leaving the Städtische Oper; but by the early days of April, Einstein had reconciled himself to the inevitable. "From my own memories," he wrote, "I don't know what the institute was before his arrival, but I know what it became when he himself prepared and conducted a performance, to what heights of accomplishment it could rise." Though pained by the loss of such a great artist, Einstein knew that Walter's departure was based largely on his convictions: "Walter himself is inclined to see a symbolic act in his departure from the Städtische Oper. He is turning away from a moribund cultural form that now leads an artificial existence—a luxury item, for which there is no longer a vital need. Perhaps he is right, though our point of view must differ from his. It is saddening that one of the strongest props of the opera tradition is leaving the Berlin opera in the lurch at a critical moment, and it becomes all the more crucial for all those who are responsible to support this tradition or, better yet, to create it anew."[75]

As in Munich, Walter chose to perform Pergolesi's *La serva padrona* and Schenck's *Dorfbarbier* (but not *Acis and Galatea*) after announcing his departure. The comic operas, presented on March 23, were perhaps meant as a sugar coating to the bitter pill he was offering. The same double bill of comic operas was scheduled for April 12; Walter's services, however, were required elsewhere. A violin prodigy had been scheduled to perform three concertos with the Berlin Philharmonic under Fritz Busch, but Busch had to travel to Dresden at the last minute owing to the death of his father. The concert agent Louise Wolff quickly contacted Walter, who agreed to substitute on very short notice. The young violinist, Yehudi Menuhin, recorded in his memoirs his gratitude to Walter on the occasion of his Berlin debut: "I do not believe that anyone else of his eminence would have cancelled an engagement at the opera, as he did, to conduct for a twelve-year-old traveling fiddler known to him only by report." Not only was Walter canceling an engagement at the Städtische Oper; he was canceling one of his farewell appearances there. Menuhin recalled the tremendous musical support he felt playing under Walter: "It seemed that whatever I did, he was always there, perfectly with me, an accompanist such as I had never known, who left me with no sense of pushing, no sense of pulling."[76]

Walter's final opera during his tenure at the Städtische Oper, given on April 14, was *Fidelio*—another echo of his farewell to Munich. Then he was off to London for the German season from late April to late May, once again with his usual singers: Reinhardt, Lehmann, Leider, Olszewska, Melchior, Kipnis, and the rest. On his return to Berlin he enjoyed a special musical treat. His friend Arturo Toscanini and his Milan troupe toured Vienna and Berlin in May. "All the scenery, stage machinery, and costumes" were imported from Milan, and "even the stage directors, electricians, tailors, hairdressers, and shoemakers" of the "Scala family" were brought along.[77] Berlin audiences sat spellbound as they listened to Toscanini's intensely driven interpretations of *Aida*, *Falstaff*, *Lucia*, *Manon Lescaut*, *Rigoletto*, and *Il trovatore*. The Italian conductor ran a tight ship, and his unsentimental approach to Verdi, Donizetti, and Puccini proved revelatory. Walter attended some of these performances, admiring them for their "perfection and stylistic sureness."[78] For a Berlin Festival held the following month (during which Furtwängler led a performance of Beethoven's Ninth), Walter conducted one work, *Das Lied von der Erde*, with Sigrid Onegin and Jacques Urlus, on June 10. After that, aside from his occasional guest engagements, which included his popular concert series with the Philharmonic, Walter's work in Berlin was over.

In an interview given after his departure from the Städtische Oper, Walter lamented the financial crisis in Europe that made it difficult for music-lovers to attend concerts. In America, things were quite different. "The American has above all the desire to advance culturally, to learn something, to see something new," Walter observed. "The cost of going to a concert doesn't play a role in his budget. He is not burdened by it; on the contrary, he has the inner freedom to enjoy the evening, which is to bring him new sources of stimulation." In fact, the atmosphere at a concert in America was well-nigh ideal, and the American public could be "reckoned among the most artistically knowledgeable in the world."[79]

Perhaps with these idealized thoughts in mind, Walter spent the summer in the United States again, this time limiting himself to West Coast appearances, conducting in San Francisco and Los Angeles (again at the Hollywood Bowl) in late July and August. In both cities he included Bloch's Concerto Grosso for String Orchestra and Piano Obbligato, taking the keyboard part himself. While most of the other repertoire was predictable, a few items that were unusual for Walter made their way onto his programs: Prokofiev's "Classical" Symphony, Charpentier's *Impressions d'Italie*, Ravel's *Rapsodie espagnole*, and Tchaikovsky's *Nutcracker Suite*.

On his return to Europe Walter paid a visit to Sweden, where, on October 2, he gave his first concert with the Stockholm Philharmonic Orchestra. The heart of the program was Mahler's First, complemented by Strauss's *Don Juan* and Mozart's *Eine kleine Nachtmusik*. While the orchestra would enjoy his intermittent visits until 1950, Sweden itself would have special significance for Walter when the political climate in Germany grew hazardous, since Gothenburg not only served as a sanctuary for his brother and sister during the Nazi period but eventually became their new home. The situation in Germany, however, had not yet become critical, and Walter headed back to Berlin and Leipzig to commence the last phase of his career in his mother country.

# *Gewandhauskapellmeister*
## Leipzig, 1929–1933

*I did not understand a world*
*Where such a thing might happen . . .*
Pfitzner, *Palestrina*

The position of music director of the Gewandhaus Orchestra of Leipzig, one of Europe's most venerable musical establishments, with its roots in J. S. Bach's Leipzig collegium, appealed strongly to Walter's love of cultural continuity. The orchestra's twofold tradition of keeping alive the great musical works of the past while championing important new compositions was close to Walter's heart, and he was prepared to commit the rest of his active career to it. "To care for its continued mission and its enduring importance in the musical life of Europe seemed to me, a man of fifty-three, a worthy task for the rest of my life," he stated in his autobiography, adding a little sadly: "Like so many others, I expected to see Nazism decline . . . and, with the Gewandhaus as the center of my work, looked forward to a flourishing activity in a progressively musical and decreasingly political world."[1] As late as 1931 he would still maintain, at least publicly, that such an illustrious institution should not be affected by unsettling political events— that it must be allowed to carry out its artistic tasks in the higher sphere in which it belonged, "just as earthquakes cannot disturb the bird in flight."[2]

Walter's esteem for Leipzig as a musical center was reciprocated by the players, many of whom wrote to Walter after the war, and especially by the music devotees who had experienced Walter's conducting as early as 1924 and must have had "vivid memories" of his concerts during the 1924–25 and 1926–27 seasons, in addition to his ten concerts of the 1928–29 season.[3] "Walter's manner of conducting reminded some of Nikisch," a history of the Gewandhaus reported, "and that was felt at once by the Gewandhaus. The people of Leipzig could 'relate to' Walter more than to Furtwängler."[4] One of the leading Leipzig critics, Adolf Aber of the *Leipziger Neueste Nachrichten* (also the Leipzig correspondent for *Die Musik*), emphasized how lucky the Gewandhaus was to have secured someone of Walter's stature and international reputation so soon after Furtwängler's abrupt departure. Aber, whose high opinion of Walter hardly ever wavered, patently regarded Walter as Nikisch's true successor, writing that with Walter's appointment, "an unsettling chapter in the history of the Gewandhaus, an interregnum of several years, has been brought to an end." Enthusiastic about Walter's programming, he noted how the conductor "supported the promotion of contemporary creations with especial warmth."[5]

There was, however, one aspect of the Leipzig job that was less attractive to Walter—the prospect of residing in the city itself, a place "singularly devoid of charm," in Walter's words.[6] To his disappointment he could find no trace of the young student Goethe, and, on the whole, the city seemed socially and architecturally (perhaps even gastronomically) uninspiring, despite its thriving university life. So he decided to keep his Berlin home, especially since he was still conducting a regular series of Bruno Walter Concerts with the Berlin Philharmonic. The Gewandhaus season was sufficiently light to allow him to travel back and forth between the two cities; the distance at that time could be covered in about two and a half hours by car.

Though it is doubtful that Walter voiced his disenchantment with Leipzig to any of its public officials, his harsh judgment of the city as a place to live and his decision to remain in Berlin—the acknowledged center of German culture during the Weimar period—may not have sat so well with the denizens of Leipzig. For instance, Alfred Heuss, the critic for the *Zeitschrift für Musik* (and formerly its editor), initially doubted Walter's dedication to the orchestra, wondering in January 1930 if Walter would really be a true Gewandhauskapellmeister or merely a semi-regular guest conductor.[7] At some point Heuss apparently decided on the latter, for in a review of a concert devoted to Haydn, the performance of which he did not care for one bit, he remarked that Walter's programming was incoherent—because "for Bruno Walter, Leipzig is nothing more than a side occupation."[8] Even Aber, Walter's champion, fretted that Walter's many international activities might prevent him from wholeheartedly dedicating himself to the Gewandhaus's well-being, though he was soon reassured on that score.[9]

Walter's first concert in his new role as Gewandhauskapellmeister took place on October 10, just a week after the death of chancellor Gustav Stresemann and just eighteen days before the fateful New York Stock Exchange crash, which plunged the German economy into the worldwide Great Depression, undoing the small amount of economic recovery that had taken place during the previous six years under Stresemann. Loans from America had been a large part of that recovery; when the crash instantly dried them up and the older loans suddenly became due, Germany's still fragile economy began to collapse. Many historians agree that it was this combination of economic events that enabled Hitler and his Nazi Party to begin their final successful campaign for political power; once again Walter had rounded a bend in what he hoped would be a purely artistic, nonpolitical career, only to be thwarted by political events after all.

Nevertheless, his first season with the Gewandhaus, in which he conducted ten of the regularly scheduled nineteen concerts (and two additional concerts), seems to have gone fairly smoothly. Both Aber and Max Steinitzer, the other critic for the *Leipziger Neueste Nachrichten*, wrote accounts of Walter's performances that glowed off the page. For them, a new era in Gewandhaus history had begun. But Walter got only mixed, if respectful, reviews from Alfred Heuss, a founding member of Alfred Rosenberg's Kampfbund für deutsche Kultur, formed in 1929 to fight modernism. A Mozart scholar of some repute, Heuss seems to have had very definite expectations concerning the proper performance of Mozart's (and other earlier composers') music—expectations that Walter failed to meet. "Walter's music-making was exceptionally rich," he reported in his review of Walter's first Gewandhaus concert; "that is to say, too rich in the classical first movement of the Concerto Grosso in G Minor by Handel and the Eighth Symphony of Beethoven, so that the overpotent luxuriousness of sound—wonderfully lovely at first—with time dulls somewhat." But with Strauss's *Tod und Verklärung*, Heuss declared, Walter (here politely referred to as "the great conductor") was "completely in his musical element."[10]

Clearly grouping Walter in the "romantic" school of conducting, Heuss described, in an article on the performance practice of Mozart and other classical composers, how Walter made undue use of crescendi. He decried Walter's "relapse" into a Wagnerian style of conducting, which, with all the new understanding of the proper way of executing dynamics in the works of classical composers (that is, with sudden shifts from piano to forte, rather than gradual crescendi), Heuss found "not really justifiable today."[11] Ironically, Walter's performance of Tchaikovsky's Fifth Symphony the following season, in December 1930, seemed too classical in style: "It was played with such sharp articulation, as if it were by Haydn."[12] So for Heuss, Walter's classicism was too romantic, his romanticism too classical. Unfortunately, Walter's performances with the Gewandhaus from this period have not, so far as we know, been preserved on private recordings, but his studio recordings of Mozart's Symphony no. 40 in G Minor with the Berlin Staatskapelle (January 1929) and the overture to *Le nozze di Figaro* with the British Symphony Orchestra (April 1932), as well as recordings of classical symphonies with the Vienna Philharmonic from a few years later, reveal clean (almost "period") articulation, tapered phrases, and generally quick tempi.[13] Of course, Heuss might have taken exception to the occasional Wagnerian relaxation of tempi for lyrical second themes.

Heuss was, not surprisingly, vastly more conservative in his tastes than Aber or Steinitzer, both of whom were fairly favorable toward the new compositions Walter chose, with a few reservations from time to time. But Heuss, a few years earlier, had published a long, three-part article entitled "Discussions of the Style of New Music," in which he lamented the decline of Germanic music.[14] While citing French Impressionist influences, among other causes, as being to blame, he also offered some not very positive comments concerning Schoenberg's music, to which an entire section was devoted. Heuss was unhappy with many of the new works that Walter chose to perform, though not because they were too modern. Rather, they seemed too lightweight by comparison with the great German masters. Of the works performed during October and November of Walter's first season, Kurt Thomas's Serenade "was no joy," "lacking in style and emotionally somewhat limited," while Ravel's gorgeous song sequence *Shéhérazade* had "little musical to say" to Heuss, and Krenek's *Kleine Sinfonie* provoked the critic's open contempt.[15] On Shostakovich's First Symphony, he at least bestowed cautious praise, concluding that more should be heard from this "composer discovered by Walter."[16] But in Walter's almost four seasons as Gewandhauskapellmeister, the only modern work to earn Heuss's outright praise was a piece by Hermann Wetzler, the German-born son of American parents: a symphonic poem entitled *Assisi*, given on March 12, 1931, which Heuss described as a "beautiful, noble work."[17]

Though Heuss's estimation of Walter's conducting was by no means entirely negative, the overall tone of his reviews was generally much less complimentary than that of the other Leipzig reviewers and that of Heuss's Berlin colleague Fritz Stege, who reviewed Walter's Berlin activities for the *Zeitschrift für Musik.* Oddly enough, Stege's views were more straightforwardly racist than Heuss's—he was the musical adviser to the Deutschvölkische Freiheitsbewegung, an organization that later merged with the Nazi Party. Yet his estimation of Walter's conducting during these last, decisive years was generally quite approving. His reviews and those of others, like Alfred Einstein, are sufficiently complimentary to reassure us that Walter's batteries were not running down, as Heuss would often have his readers believe.

In fact, early in 1930 Walter conducted a program with the Berlin Philharmonic that must have required especial liveliness on his part: "Tänze aus zwei Jahrhunderten," with orchestral dances by Beethoven, Mozart, Rossini, Dvořák, Glinka, Mussorgsky, Borodin, Schubert, and, of course, Johann Strauss. There was also a striking work by Richard Strauss, an arrangement of keyboard dances from François Couperin's harpsichord suites. Einstein gave this unusual program an encomiastic review, admiring Walter's ability to breathe life into so many different styles (though he admitted that the Strauss work had little to do with Couperin): "One can hardly say which piece from this abundance Walter brought off with more fulfillment, more freedom, more life: the clarity and resilience of the classical or the sensuous rubato of the Slavic pieces. It was a feast."[18]

Walter was especially fond of Viennese waltzes; Thomas Mann recorded an occasion on which the Manns and the Walters met in a Viennese café, where Walter eventually sat down at the Bösendorfer piano and played.[19] We can actually get some idea of how this might have sounded from a recording he made in his Beverly Hills home in 1952 that included Strauss's "Wiener Blut" and "Wienerwald."[20] Though Walter's piano is out of tune and his technique rusty, hardly the match for his great flexibility of rhythm and liveliness of articulation, his obvious enjoyment at rendering these Viennese standards resonates in every bar. Alex Nifosi of the BBC Symphony Orchestra described the dedication and sense of style Walter displayed when conducting a Strauss waltz: "It was almost as if he were showing off his beloved Vienna . . . There was certainly no hint in it that he was playing music of a quality any different from his normal symphonic repertoire."[21] And the same could easily be said for the Strauss selections that he recorded with the Columbia Symphony Orchestra in 1956, though the liveliest and most sweeping of all his extant Strauss performances were captured in 1947, when in Edinburgh he led the Vienna Philharmonic for the first time after the end of World War II.[22]

Given his enthusiasm for Strauss waltzes, it is no surprise that Walter had a high regard for *Die Fledermaus*, considering it "a work of art unique in its kind," possessing "beauty without heaviness, levity without vulgarity, gaiety without frivolity, and a strange mixture of exuberant musical richness (somewhat resembling Schubert), and popular simplicity." That, at least, was how he described the charm of the work, adding the qualifier "that all magical attraction—and happily so—remains inexplicable, simply because it is magic."[23] Early 1930 would find him conducting it once again, this time in Amsterdam on February 24 at the Wagner-Vereeniging in a highly successful production directed by Franz L. Hörth. Indeed, it was so successful that it piqued the interests of both Covent Garden and the banker Baron Henri de Rothschild, who invited Walter and the Amsterdam organization to bring the production to Paris at the Théâtre Pigalle (which Rothschild had built) in March. When the impending Paris *Fledermaus* performance was announced, a controversy broke out, for Max Reinhardt was making plans to bring *his* Berlin production to the Théâtre des Champs-Élysées in June of that same year. Walter apparently did not consider this a great drawback since, as he wrote to a friend in Paris, the two *Fledermaus* productions would be very different, his being a traditional *Fledermaus*, Reinhardt's a "fantasy of a modern director-genius on the theme of *Fledermaus*."[24] He also felt that, despite the German dialogue, Parisian audiences would enjoy the work immensely, for "what Parisian could resist the Danube waltzes?"[25] The idea, however, of having the two *Fledermaus* productions within just three months, each involving one of Germany's most prominent artists, predictably led to a series of articles in Viennese and German newspapers. Though one critic did maintain that it would be interesting for Parisian audiences to compare the two, this view was not shared by everyone. An article in a Berlin newspaper even hinted that Rothschild's bringing Walter's *Fledermaus* to the Théâtre Pigalle, the superlatively beautiful modern theater, would spell financial disaster for Reinhardt and would not bode well for future German productions in Paris. The reasoning was apparently that Walter's *Fledermaus*, though it featured German singers, could not be considered German because it was produced in Amsterdam.[26]

And Walter was sensitive to the potential insult to his old colleague (with whom relations never seemed quite cordial), writing him a carefully worded letter in which he assured Reinhardt that he would do everything in his power to "relieve" the situation, though he is sketchy about the kind of relief he would be able to provide. Reinhardt sent back an equally diplomatic telegram in which he proposed canceling his Paris engagement, not believing that a typically German work would do well financially in Paris and concluding, with palpable irritation, that he didn't want to hear any more words on the subject. Walter would not let Reinhardt off so easily, however, and responded with a two-and-a-half-page letter, urging him to go ahead with his production, stressing the differences between the two, and insisting that, since Reinhardt's production was uniquely his, he should not be afraid of any duplication.[27] In the end, Walter lost the argument; Reinhardt sent a telegram to Rothschild, allowing the Pigalle performance to take place, and Reinhardt presented his *Fledermaus* at the Pigalle a couple of years later.

No such controversy, fortunately, accompanied the plans to bring the production to Covent Garden. Walter had evidently wanted to conduct *Die Fledermaus* in London for some time but had encountered difficulty persuading the board to mount a production.[28] Again—though it is hard to imagine today (with *Fledermaus* a popular New Year's Eve offering in many parts of the world)—there appears to have been some feeling among theater managers and critics that such an innately Viennese work would not appeal to audiences outside Austria or Germany. In any case, the success of the Amsterdam production was such that Colonel Blois, the new managing director of the Grand Opera Syndicate Limited, was finally persuaded and, as in the Théâtre Pigalle production, the sets were lent by the Amsterdam Wagner-Vereeniging.

The opera's enthusiastic reception was sufficient to quash any nagging, skeptical voices, and Walter, mainly known to Covent Garden audiences for his conducting of Wagner and Richard Strauss, once again demonstrated his special love for the Viennese waltz. "Last night, the *finale* of the second act showed the younger generation what dancing really is," the London *Times* reported, "and before the third act, Herr Bruno Walter and the orchestra played the famous 'Blue Danube' with all its supple insinuating measures charged with that blend of languorousness and excitement which makes the Viennese waltz unique in music."[29] The opera was such a success that a special performance took place on May 21 at the request of the King and Queen and was revived the following year.

While *Die Fledermaus* was remembered fondly by many who were fortunate enough to attend the performances, Walter himself, oddly enough, had some reservations about the production. Years later Harold Rosenthal (Covent Garden's archivist from 1950 to 1956, the editor of *Opera*, and the author of two books on Covent Garden) wrote to Walter asking him to record a few words for a planned centenary celebration of Covent Garden. He hoped Walter would talk about German opera in the 1920s, especially about how Walter's *Fledermaus* "transformed" Covent Garden. Surfeited, however, with the glitter and gaiety of the "Waltz King" at this stage in his career, Walter—while happy to contribute to the celebration—retained a very different set of memories: "I don't think I was able to 'transform the atmosphere of Covent Garden by introducing "Die Fledermaus." ' On the contrary, I never felt happy with this experiment."[30] With his usual epistolary reserve, Walter does not specify what made him unhappy about his "experiment," and we can only hope that he enjoyed it more at the time than in retrospect, since it was so obviously enjoyed by his London audience.

Meanwhile, during the course of his 1929–30 season, Walter continued to conduct all over Germany—a Hamburg *Otello*, concerts in Mannheim, Chemnitz, Munich, and Nuremberg, to name only a few—but was conspicuously absent from Vienna, even while he was championing Viennese music in Amsterdam, Paris, and London. In fact, though Walter still felt deep ties with Viennese culture and music, a behind-the-scenes intrigue had taken place the previous year, temporarily cooling his relations with the Vienna Staatsoper. At the end of 1928 Schalk had resigned as director, and many Viennese operagoers and critics, especially Julius Korngold, wondered why the Generalintendant, Franz Schneiderhan, did not appear to be making any attempts to secure Walter as Schalk's successor and instead courted Furtwängler, who seemed unenthusiastic about the job.[31] (Furtwängler was, in fact, negotiating with the Berlin Philharmonic.) The not-so-soft whispers in Walter's favor finally culminated in an open letter, printed on the front page of the *Neue Freie Presse*. "Can anyone dare to claim," the editors asked, "that this firebrand, this great student of Mahler, this sympathetic, spirited musician who radiates love of life and the force of creativity, that he is not suited to our environment, that he is not the right person to improve the ensemble, to reorganize the concert programming, to exert authority and to recover those great heights that today can still be found as a living presence on good evenings?"[32] In the face of so much public pressure, Schneiderhan eventually wrote to Walter, proposing that they meet in private to discuss the matter; Walter suggested the Westbahnhof railway station and went there at the appointed time, but neither Schneiderhan nor anyone else from the opera management came to meet him. Though Walter eventually received a letter of apology from Schneiderhan, he was not pleased when a notice appeared in the *Neue Freie Presse* stating, in short, that he had asked for too much money. Addressing the concern expressed by Korngold and in the open letter—namely, that the opera company would sink into mediocrity—Schneiderhan published a response praising Clemens Krauss, who in the meantime had gotten the appointment, stressing his Austrian origins (and Walter's lack of Austrian birth). The intrigues and the jingoism must have brought back unpleasant memories of Walter's early days in Vienna as Mahler's assistant.

Recounting the whole sequence of events in *Theme and Variations*, Walter was convinced that the Ministry of Education, then ruled by the Christian Socialist Party, opposed his appointment and that the Ministry's "confidential man," a former music critic who had been hostile to Walter when he was Mahler's assistant, had deliberately misrepresented his demands in order to dodge the issue. When Walter encountered Schneiderhan years later in Salzburg, however, the director assured him that it had all been a grave misunderstanding.[33] The whole incident was doubtless part of a larger tangled web that Walter couldn't fully unravel, so he was content to stay away from the Vienna Opera for a few years. But his uneasy relationship with the Staatsoper during the early 1930s did not prevent him from conducting the Vienna Philharmonic at the Salzburg Festival over the next few summers, while the dearth of his performances in Vienna during the Leipzig years was keenly felt by the Viennese public. Describing Walter's appearance with the Vienna Tonkünstler-Orchester in the spring of 1931, Victor Junk remarked that hardly any other artist received such a warm reception. "A thousand hands are stretched toward him, and the roaring applause, translated into the language of words, wants to say: Why are *you* not with us?"[34] As it happened, Walter would be "with" Vienna in less than two years, for reasons that, in 1931, were probably far from the minds of those Viennese stretching out their hands.

The rise of the Nazi Party, however, was already casting long shadows in the autumn of 1930. With the elections on September 14—just a day before Walter's birthday—the National Socialists secured 107 seats in the Reichstag, making it Germany's second largest party, whereas previously it had been the smallest. Walter was hardly unaware of the ominous turn politics had taken: "I vividly remember the night preceding September 15. We spent it at our Berlin apartment, listening to the radio. Emanuel Feuermann was with us. Every few minutes, the triumphant voice of the announcer would tell of the progress of the election. We knew at about three in the morning that Hitler had polled about 6,500,000 votes. . . . Feuermann, usually so gay, left us with the words: 'It's all over with Germany; all over with Europe.'"[35] But for many German intellectuals and artists it was still difficult not to hope that their country would weather what might be just a political tempest in a teapot, that the Nazis' apparent gain in power would prove no more lasting than the attempted Communist takeover of Munich in 1918. The historian Golo Mann has described in his autobiography how, even as late as 1932, life in academia continued sedately: "Everyone pursued, as best he could, his obligations, his interests, his pleasures. The professors faithfully went on giving their lectures and seminars, which had absolutely no bearing on the misery in the country."[36] Even Golo Mann himself, cannier than most by virtue of being Thomas Mann's son and a keen observer in his own right, admitted that he was not unhappy to vote for Hindenburg in the presidential elections of 1932, unaware of how dangerous Hindenburg's conciliatory attempts to contain Hitler would be. "Who could foresee that we had made a bad choice—but then," he wondered, "what alternative did we have?"[37]

Walter, too, carried on as best he could, conducting, in addition to his regular season in Leipzig and his series of six Bruno Walter Concerts in Berlin (which included the local premiere of Lopatnikoff's First Symphony on February 18), a *Meistersinger* in Hamburg, *Das Lied von der Erde* in Munich, a Brahms Requiem in Vienna, *Don Giovanni* at La Scala (his only appearance conducting opera there), a radio performance of *Die Zauberflöte* in Berlin, a Mahler Second with the Queen's Hall Orchestra in London, as well as concerts in Amsterdam, Budapest, Prague, Frankfurt, and so on. But unlike Golo Mann's acquaintances, Walter, unable to lose himself completely in his work, began to experience a growing sense of dread. "From that moment, even my stubborn optimism began to wane," he recalled. "Although I could not dimly foresee what was to come, I felt oppressed by the increased darkening of life."[38] It is poignant to imagine Walter repeating his performance of *Die Fledermaus* at Covent Garden that spring, a work that, he felt, "causes human errors to assume the appearance of delightful misunder-standings, and life in its entirety that of a fugitive paradise," while his daily life must have been pervaded by a growing dread.[39]

Given the unsavory political situation in his native land, Walter was ea-ger to continue his activities abroad, so the termination of his engagements at Covent Garden hit him especially hard. In April and May of 1931 he con-ducted his German season as usual and was once again warmly received, though perhaps not quite so favorably reviewed. Of this year's *Fledermaus*, the *Times* reported that "Bruno Walter gave us all the impetuosities and lan-guors of the music, but not quite all its lightness. There was just a touch of deliberation in the hanging-up of the rhythm."[40] The critics also found some of his Wagner performances too frenetic: of his *Rheingold*, for instance, the *Times* reviewer complained: "We could wish that he would not insist on vividness so incessantly, particularly that he would not make the drums cari-cature Wagner's majestic writing for them, and not urge the wind players to such energy that they splutter and miss their notes. A simpler reading might secure better playing."[41] This spring's series of London *Times* reviews, of course, also contained many appreciative comments, and audiences, though smaller than in previous years, were larger than those for the Italian season. Yet it may have been partly these reviews that inspired some to think that Walter and Heger's German seasons were becoming tired and even sloppy, that fresh blood was needed to inject life into an opera company that was foundering, both artistically and financially—in other words, the return of Sir Thomas Beecham.

Beecham had meanwhile raised a great deal of money for something he called the Imperial League of Opera, and securing him as music director would mean consolidating his proposed opera company with the Royal Opera Company. The popular conductor's presence would not only gener-ate more ticket sales but also guarantee some ready money. With Europe's shaky economic situation and England's Gold Standard crisis of 1931, the National government had recently cut the opera's subsidies. Desperate times called for desperate measures.[42] To begin with, the German singers were re-engaged for lower fees. Further, as Walter learned only by reading the newspapers, Beecham was to take his place as chief conductor. Unin-formed of these plans by the company itself, Walter was understandably quite upset; moreover, since he had not been consulted on how to make pub-lic the circumstances surrounding his replacement by Beecham, he feared that people might view his dismissal in a bad light. "I do think," he wrote indignantly to Colonel Blois, "that after all my work in Covent Garden I deserved a more considerate action from your side."[43]

His ties with two of Europe's leading opera companies having been severed in less than three years, Walter appeared to be drawing away from opera and becoming more and more a purely symphonic conductor. Such a career progression was (and remains today) common enough—it is widely acknowledged that conducting opera requires great stamina and emotional resilience. And, though the art of electric recording was being refined throughout the 1930s, Walter's records during these years still consisted mainly of short orchestral selections, including a solemnly potent rendition of the "Funeral Music" from *Götterdämmerung* with an unnamed London orchestra (1931). At the relatively young age of fifty-four, however, Walter was not yet finished with opera, and during the summer of 1931 he once again returned to the Salzburg Festival, conducting his share of Mozart operas (*Don Giovanni* and *Die Zauberflöte*), as well as a new production of Gluck's *Orfeo ed Euridice*, directed by Karlheinz Martin with choreography by Margarete Wallmann, who would serve as ballet director for the Vienna Staatsoper from 1934 to 1937. By all accounts the production was a great success. The reviewer for *Die Musik* described it as "sensational," and the reviewer for the *Neues Wiener Journal* wrote three lengthy paragraphs, praising Walter's conducting; Martin's ingenuity in working with a difficult stage; Wallmann's choreography, especially the "unforgettable moments" in the "Dance of the Furies"; Sigrid Onegin's performance as Orpheus; and everything else about the production.[44] Walter had always held the opera in extraordinarily high esteem, writing years later to Stresemann that it was, "in its way, the most sublime work of musical drama," and that "neither in Gluck nor in some of our other great masters would such heights of musical and dramatic inspiration [again] be reached."[45] So it must have been especially gratifying to work on what was clearly one of his favorite operas with such talented colleagues.

Both Walter and Wallmann looked back on their collaborations with pleasure, though Walter could not resist teasing Wallmann about her working methods, somewhat at odds with his own. "I think back gladly on the time we spent together," he wrote to her in 1954, "and the renewed acknowledgment of the artistic understanding between us. This understanding does not, however, include our working methods, as four-hour, midnight rehearsals in the dew were not 'my cup of tea' and should really not be yours. I can only hope that you will refrain from such extravagances in the future."[46]

Meanwhile, there was another, more materially obvious reason why Walter was unable to ignore the growing economic difficulties (and ensuing political instabilities) in his country: the venerable Gewandhaus Orchestra, like so many of Germany's cultural institutions, was again suffering from lack of funds. The 1931–32 season would be the 150th anniversary of the Gewandhaus Hall, but at the end of the 1930–31 season, despite a successful tour with its "famous Director" Walter, its grave financial outlook cast a pall over the planned celebration, and many wondered if there would be much festivity at all, or even a normal concert season.[47] Nevertheless, plans went ahead; the number of subscription concerts was reduced from twenty to sixteen to lessen subscription prices, and programming became more conservative, focusing on standard repertoire to ensure good audience attendance. Walter agreed to commit to a significant number of concerts (thirteen out of sixteen, including the "Festkonzert" planned for November 25) at the expense of offers from other cities, even though it was not certain that the Gewandhaus season would remain intact. This earned him a long round of applause at the end of a performance of Beethoven's Ninth Symphony and ecstatic praise from Adolf Aber: "It is really an inestimable bit of luck for the Gewandhaus that an artist with such a great sense of responsibility for the institution remains at its disposal during this critical time."[48] That July an appeal was made to the music-loving population of Leipzig for support, but the funds received were insufficient, and the Gewandhaus, traditionally a financially independent institution, now had to rely on municipal funds to continue its operations. The willingness of the Leipzig town officials to save the institution from possible extinction was seen by some as highly commendable, but, as with the Berlin Philharmonic, the intertwining of music and public money would give rise to unpleasant complications.[49]

From an artistic standpoint, however, the institution's festival week (November 19–26) contained special events for the Leipzig public, including a "historic" concert, the programs of which were printed on cream-colored paper to look like 1781 programs. From the first violinist's desk, Charles Munch, then the Gewandhaus's concertmaster, led the orchestra in pieces by Dittersdorf, J. C. Bach, Reichardt, Hiller, and Haydn. Walter's two concerts on November 25 and 26 were the crowning events of the festival. For the first concert Beethoven's Fifth Symphony, Mozart's Symphony no. 39 in E-flat Major, and Weber's overture to *Euryanthe* were supplemented by readings from Goethe and Schiller, and Hans Hermann Nissen sang Hans Sachs's final monologue from Wagner's *Meistersinger*, in which Sachs speaks of the endurance of German art. The selection from *Meistersinger* must have seemed especially meaningful to both audience and performers; for wasn't this celebration of one of Germany's oldest musical institutions in the face of economic hardship a clear demonstration of Wagner's sentiments? The irony in programming what later came to be regarded as a harbinger of anti-Semitism—Sachs, as Wagner's mouthpiece, speaks of German art's withstanding "pernicious" or "evil" influences—was perhaps only seen in retrospect.

The following evening's concert, consisting of Mendelssohn's Overture to *A Midsummer Night's Dream*, Schumann's Piano Concerto with Edwin Fischer, and Brahms's First Symphony, was admired even by Alfred Heuss, who called it "one of the most marvelous evenings that we owe to Bruno Walter, the house conductor." Heuss also went on to praise Walter's dedication, saying that he had proved his true loyalty to the institution during this important time.[50] All in all, despite the orchestra's uneasiness over its shaky financial status, there seems to have been a general feeling that the festival concerts established Walter as Gewandhauskapellmeister once and for all, a difficult time had been survived, and a new era had well and truly begun.

But Walter, like others, heard the distant rumblings of trouble ahead. Earlier in 1931 he had received an invitation from Harry Harkness Flagler to conduct the New York Philharmonic during the 1931–32 season. Since the New York Symphony Orchestra had merged with the Philharmonic in 1928, Flagler had become the orchestra's new president. As early as January 1929, in fact, Arthur Judson had tried to secure Walter as a guest conductor, but Walter's busy schedule in Europe had always prevented him from accepting. Now, however, there were more urgent reasons for doing so, and although Walter had already committed himself to all the Gewandhaus concerts not conducted by either Thomaskantor Karl Straube or the chamber orchestra director, Edwin Fischer (the celebrated pianist), the Gewandhaus management generously agreed to free him for January 1932, realizing, according to Walter, "that in view of the threatening internal situation in Germany everything should be done to facilitate the resumption of my relations with American musical life."[51] As a result, Walter was engaged for a seven-week period, beginning mid-January and extending to the end of February. Coincidentally, Hermann Abendroth, who would soon replace Walter as Gewandhauskapellmeister, was engaged for Walter's January Gewandhaus concert.

As with his Gewandhaus and Berlin concerts, Walter was determined that his programs should contain a significant number of works by living composers; but Arthur Judson cautioned him against having too many, saying that, while the board had a policy of presenting new works of value, the public had become skeptical about their worth, since so many pieces were performed once and never repeated. He suggested that Walter pick two or three "novelties" that he considered especially important. In the end it was decided to include four of the various new compositions that Walter proposed: Ernst Krenek's *Der Triumph der Empfindsamkeit* ("it belongs to the best novelties possible"); Franz Schmidt's *Variationen über ein Husarenlied* ("very excellent, effective . . . the orchestra can excel"); Prokofiev's *Prodigal Son* Suite ("very important, interesting, serious and grateful [i.e., gratifying]"); and Daniel Gregory Mason's Second Symphony ("an excellent, important work").[52] Two of Walter's suggestions—Bruckner's Fifth and a Mozart piano concerto with himself as soloist—did not come to fruition, possibly because, as Judson hinted in one of his letters, the board felt that both Mahler's Fifth (which Walter did conduct) and Bruckner's Fifth in the same season would be heavy going for New York audiences, so the Bruckner symphony was saved for the following year. As for the Mozart concerto, its omission remains a mystery, especially since Walter tried to impress on Judson how much he would like to perform something in that vein. "I would of course charge nothing for that and consider it included in my obligations," he wrote. "It is a kind of a specialty of mine." He proceeded to name an impressive array of cities in which he had performed as soloist and conductor, but it was not until December 1934 that Walter actually played and conducted the Mozart D Minor Piano Concerto in New York.

Though Walter had been cordially and enthusiastically received by the New York public and critics in his performances with the New York Symphony Orchestra, his debut with the Philharmonic seems to have taken the megalopolis by storm. "Walter in Triumph" read the headline of Olin Downes's first review. The already eminent New York critic nearly gushed over the evening: "The instant the string choir sounded the opening harmonies of a Handel 'Concerto Grosso,' with a tone superb in its depth, fullness and virility, the audience realized the presence of an authoritative and inspired interpreter. Interest and excitement grew as the concert went on. At the end the audience did not hurry from the hall, but remained to applaud and cheer the conductor."[53] While Downes admired Walter's Handel and Haydn, he waxed rhapsodic when it came to describing Walter's rendition of Brahms's Second Symphony: "Theme merged into theme," he wrote, "thought into thought with a perfect enchainment." The second movement he characterized as "noble and impassioned," the Allegretto as "bewitching," and the finale as "irresistible."

The remainder of Walter's long stretch of concerts received many reviews abounding in praise, especially his rendition of Berlioz's *Symphonie fantastique*. Walter's collaborations with soloists such as Ossip Gabrilowitsch in Brahms's Second Piano Concerto and Yehudi Menuhin in Brahms's Violin Concerto also enjoyed enthusiastic words from the press. In some respects, however, Olin Downes proved the counterpart to Alfred Heuss back in Leipzig, in that he simply did not find much to like in the new works Walter had chosen. True, Downes was more charitable to Krenek than the German critic had been, finding "ingenuity" in *Der Triumph der Empfindsamkeit* but also a "facetiousness and grimacing" that grew a little tiring. Schmidt's *Variationen über ein Husarenlied*, performed on the same program, seemed "hard on the innocent bystander," while Prokofiev's *Prodigal Son* Overture was deemed "not very impressive. It is strained, and it echoes other pages of Prokofieff."[54] In this verdict, Downes could have found some sympathy from the composer himself, who considered the suite less important than his other compositions; indeed, he described to his friend Vernon Duke how he put it together "so that the remaining material of the ballet would not go to waste," not having foreseen that "Walter would get so fixated on the suite."[55]

Daniel Gregory Mason's Second Symphony was a work Walter particularly liked; he wrote to the composer that his musical language had "developed the capacity of personal confession without sacrificing musical purity."[56] Nevertheless, Downes—who had praised Mason's First Symphony in 1925—deemed the new piece "unoriginal" and its orchestration "none too successful."[57] Mason and Walter had become friends by now, and Downes's words no doubt wounded on personal as well as aesthetic grounds. How much more painful it must have been to hear Downes's harsh judgment on Mahler, which had not softened since Walter first conducted his mentor's music in New York in 1924. While Downes admired Walter's conducting of Mahler's Fifth Symphony, particularly since Walter conducted from memory, he couldn't hear that Mahler's symphony contained anything subtle or complex. "Everything is a big pose or a big noise," he wrote, adding with just a touch of defensiveness that "German musicians . . . are disposed to believe that Americans do not understand Mahler as yet . . . but with every performance of Mahler the conviction grows that he is understood here entirely too well. . . . Mahler is not a profound composer."[58] Downes did note that, while a few audience members left during the symphony, there was also a contingent that applauded furiously and called Walter back to the stage many times. If Walter could not change Downes's low opinion of Mahler, it is doubtful that anyone could.

Not every critic was fully swayed by Walter. Herbert Peyser, who would also write for the *New York Times* and had often heard Walter conduct, wrote a short sketch of him for the periodical *Disques* that appeared directly after Walter's concerts in New York. It was the most critical assessment of Walter to appear in America, raising objections to the conductor's style that would often be echoed by others (such as that he was "feminine" and "sentimental"), as well as grievances that few have since voiced (that his *fortissimo* was "harsh, raucous, crass," that he was "not a conductor of what the Germans call large *Format*"). But even Peyser compared Walter only to the towering conductors of the early twentieth century—Furtwängler, Mahler, Muck, Nikisch, Toscanini—and confessed that there was "no question of [Walter's] rank among the most popular and deeply esteemed conductors of the present age."[59]

So, with a successful return trip to New York to his credit, Walter headed back to Leipzig and Berlin for another round of concerts. In that spring, also, Walter conducted his first concert with his friend Adrian Boult's BBC Symphony Orchestra on April 20. Then it was on to Salzburg for repeat performances of *Orfeo ed Euridice*, followed by an array of fall concerts. By December he was back in New York for a new series of Philharmonic concerts. In an article entitled "Concerts and Their Function," he had recently defended the preponderance of "classical" works in the few concerts he was giving that season in Berlin—"All our relationships need to be nurtured and renewed if they are to remain a part of our life and our being"—but he was quick to add that he was not in principle averse to programming unfamiliar compositions.[60] Indeed, undeterred by Downes's negative comments concerning the previous year's novelties, Walter programmed several more in New York, including Prokofiev's *The Gambler* Suite, the Bloch Concerto Grosso with Walter as piano soloist (a work he had already performed in San Francisco, Los Angeles, Stockholm, and several cities in Germany), and Arthur Shepherd's *Horizons: Four Western Pieces for Orchestra*. Another rarity on Walter's programs was Charles Martin Loeffler's *The Death of Tintagiles*, which featured as a prominent solo instrument the antique viola d'amore, with its unearthly resonance. The works by Shepherd and Loeffler attracted special attention, having been composed by living Americans—one native-born, the other a naturalized citizen. Daniel Gregory Mason had brought Shepherd's work to Walter's attention two years earlier, and it evidently piqued the conductor's interest, for he kept the score longer than originally planned—though one wonders what Walter thought of Shepherd's use of "cowboy tunes," which, according to one reviewer, represented "a not unsuccessful effort to express in music something of the spirit of one of the most characteristically American parts of this country."[61] The work by Loeffler, on the other hand, "might have been written in his native Alsace as well as in Boston" and is based on a hair-raising drama by Maeterlinck, though its themes struck one critic as too lyrical for the story they were supposed to convey, and the viola d'amore, played by Zoltan Kurthy, "was like a hopelessly sweet crying rather than the expression of terror."[62]

One of Walter's last concerts in this series included Mahler's Second Symphony, and while reviews of Mahler's composition were naturally mixed, most critics had something positive to say about Walter's performance, as if to imply that the performance was more impressive than the piece itself. The reviews make one regret that RCA Victor's carefully worked-out plans to issue a live recording of the performance fell through, possibly because of the high expenses involved.[63] It would have been Walter's first record with the Philharmonic, and its players would have included several musicians who had performed under Mahler.

In Germany, meanwhile, the Nazi Party was swiftly spreading its poison through the German government. On January 29 Walter was conducting a Sunday afternoon concert at the Brooklyn Academy of Music, while across the ocean, where it was already evening, Hitler, Göring, and the rest were celebrating what would certainly be Hitler's appointment the following day as chancellor of Germany. Coincidentally, Walter was joined in the Brooklyn concert by another soon-to-be expatriate, Lotte Lehmann. At noon the following day, the Nazis' expectations were fulfilled, and Hindenburg made Adolf Hitler chancellor. Walter's last concert in New York that year was on February 26, the day before Berlin storm troopers burned the Reichstag. Nevertheless, Walter and Elsa sailed back to Germany, with Walter planning to conduct his March concerts as usual. Later, he would remember vividly the strained atmosphere on board the ship as all the passengers avoided speaking of politics, taking pains to hide their anxieties or their high hopes, depending on their attitude toward the Nazis. When the Walters disembarked in Cuxhaven, they were met by Lotte and Gretel, who had both driven up from Berlin, and the sight of them was Walter's "last joyful experience on German soil." Or rather, he added, "symbolically—prior to my landing. For no sooner had I set foot on firm ground than I felt a chilling wave of strangeness flow toward me from the outwardly familiar surroundings."[64] The sight of swastikas flying everywhere was a source of revulsion; Walter at first refused to eat in any restaurant where they were displayed, only to be informed by his daughters that they would go hungry as a result.

Max Brockhaus, the Gewandhaus Committee president, had been frantically telephoning Walter's Berlin apartment. Over the telephone he would only hint at the emerging unpleasantness, and it was not until Walter arrived in Leipzig the next day that he was apprised of what was happening: Manfred von Killinger, Leipzig's Chief of Police, had threatened to forbid Walter's upcoming concert if the management itself refused to cancel it. This the management was unwilling to do; nor would it accept Walter's proffered resignation, for the Gewandhaus had always prided itself on its cultural integrity and independence, though with its recent dependence on city money, such autonomy would prove harder to maintain. Thereupon Brockhaus, with Walter assisting, spent the next few days telephoning influential people in the hope that someone would exert influence upon the new government on behalf of one of Germany's oldest musical institutions. "In those early days of Nazi rule, such dreams were still entertained," Walter commented ruefully.[65] In Leipzig such dreams were entertained only for a few days, for despite Brockhaus's best efforts, on the morning of the concert the management received word from the police that, in the name of the Saxon Ministry of the Interior, they were forbidding both the concert and the general rehearsal. Brockhaus, the other members of the management, and the musicians themselves were so devastated that they could hardly speak. After a series of muted good-byes, Walter left, pausing only to gaze for a moment at the noble Gewandhaus hall—which a few years later would be deprived of its statue of the Jewish-born Mendelssohn.

"So ended a chapter in the history of the Gewandhaus, before it had even rightfully begun!"[66] And in fact, Walter's brief spark of accomplishment in Leipzig was swiftly extinguished and buried, like the transitory flame that the Nazis hoped it would be. "Arthur Nikisch's direct descendant stands on the conductor's podium of the Gewandhaus once again," began a review of the next Gewandhaus concert, which Furtwängler conducted.[67] Adolf Aber was gone, and the *Leipziger Neueste Nachrichten*'s new critic,

Julius Goetz, expressed opinions clearly more in keeping with the party line of the new regime. A history of the Gewandhaus written in 1943 mentioned Walter only in passing, lumping his nearly four seasons with the previous, directorless one of 1928–29 (and, predictably, making mention of Walter's original name, Schlesinger). In short, the whole of Walter's activities amounted to little more than a transition between Furtwängler and Abendroth, the "true" conductors.[68] A festschrift written some years after the war in 1956 (for the orchestra's 175th anniversary) did little to change this view of history, though now Abendroth's tenure was viewed as the first stable period after the Nikisch years.[69] It was not until 1962 that Fritz Hennenberg wrote of Walter's three-year directorship as an actual era in the orchestra's history, if a sadly shortened one.[70] But Walter attached no blame to the institution itself for its historians' revisionism, writing a congratulatory letter for that very 1956 festschrift in which he is treated as little better than a guest conductor: "The time in which I served as Gewandhauskapellmeister lives on in my heart in its wealth of uplifting artistic experiences."[71] Soon after the war he also showed his appreciation of the orchestra in a more practical way by donating money to several elderly players or their widows.

Walter's abrupt departure from Leipzig was only the beginning of his misfortunes at the hands of the Nazis. When he arrived in Berlin, he found Louise Wolff and her colleagues Sachs and Simon in distress, for they had just received a warning from Goebbels that Walter's Berlin concert should be canceled because there might be unpleasant demonstrations. No one could decide exactly what this meant, so, at Walter's suggestion, Erich Sachs telephoned the Propaganda Ministry directly. Louise Wolff's daughter, Edith Stargardt-Wolff, related how they all listened to his end of the conversation, increasingly aware of how complicated the situation was becoming. "Then the concert cannot take place and must be canceled," they heard him say. "But it is a 'Bruno Walter Concert,' in a series which carries his name, and so can't be conducted by anyone else." Nevertheless, Walter Funk, who later became the Nazis' minister of economics, insisted that they were not going to forbid the concert, but that if it took place, they could expect violence in the concert hall. Therefore the concert must take place under another conductor. Stargardt-Wolff described how shocked they all were, how they had been naive enough to believe that Walter could still conduct in Berlin, even after he had been forbidden to do so in Leipzig. At this point, she related, Walter stood up, looking pale but controlled, and said, "Then I have no further business here," and departed with "great dignity, leaving them deeply depressed."[72]

According to Walter, Funk had closed his thinly disguised ultimatum with the following mysterious statement: "Besides, Herr Walter is politically suspicious."[73] When Elsa Walter, who had been waiting outside the office, heard this menacing remark, she told her husband that he should leave Berlin at once. They decided he should not even go back to their apartment. So Walter and Lotte went almost immediately to the train station and boarded a train for Semmering, leaving Elsa and Gretel behind to close up their cherished Berlin home and prepare for a permanent move to Austria.

As is well known, it was Richard Strauss who eventually conducted Walter's Berlin Philharmonic concert on March 20. How Strauss came to agree to this, and who exactly suggested that he take over, are the questions that mark where the accounts of Walter and Stargardt-Wolff diverge. In Walter's version, when Sachs told Funk that they had decided to cancel the concert, Funk informed them that the concert would take place with Strauss conducting, and, Funk assured them, Strauss would certainly agree. Walter, it seems, had no reason to doubt the truth of this, writing acerbically in his autobiography that "the composer of *Ein Heldenleben* actually declared himself ready to conduct in place of a forcibly removed colleague."[74] But, according to Stargardt-Wolff, no definite candidate to replace Walter had been suggested until the following day, when Elsa arrived at Louise Wolff's office and, after allaying their anxiety over Walter by informing them that he was already in Austria, stated that it was Walter's wish to have Richard Strauss take over the concert. This seemed like a good idea to all concerned, especially since Strauss was already in Berlin. But Strauss at first refused, even when told that Walter had suggested him. Then Louise Wolff was visited by two Nazi journalists, one of whom was Hugo Rasch of the Nazi news organ, the *Völkischer Beobachter*. Stargardt-Wolff leaves the other journalist unnamed, but he was probably Julius Kopsch (who in 1954 was president of the Internationale Richard-Strauss-Gesellschaft). Wolff had meanwhile engaged the Bremen conductor Ernst Wendel to take Walter's place, but these two party men informed her that the government wanted Strauss to conduct the concert.

Julius Kopsch himself wrote to Walter in 1950 with the intention of clarifying some of the circumstances of Strauss's agreeing to take over the concert (in other words, to defend Strauss's actions). According to Kopsch, Louise Wolff had asked *him*, as a friend of Strauss's, to convince Strauss to take over, which Strauss agreed to do only when he learned that the orchestra would suffer a serious financial blow if another conductor took over.[75] Walter replied that he could accept Kopsch's version, yet the fact remained that Strauss had directed a concert that Walter himself, as a result of political circumstances, was unable to conduct. But, he assured Kopsch, his admiration for Strauss as a musician remained unaffected by these events, though the two conductors kept their distance for the remainder of their lives.[76]

Four years after Kopsch wrote to Walter, Stargardt-Wolff published her account, and almost immediately Kopsch telephoned her, questioning whether her version was accurate. Since Kopsch was very likely the second "Nazi" journalist, we can only speculate as to his reasons for wanting to draw attention to events that, on further examination, might reveal his own activities as a Nazi Party member. Meanwhile the Strauss family was also not happy that the Stargardt-Wolff version linked Strauss's name more closely with the Nazi Party than even Walter's had. Eventually, Stargardt-Wolff published an "explanation" in a publication of the Richard-Strauss-Gesellschaft, in which she denied any intention to darken Strauss's name and insisted that it was Walter's own wish that he take over.[77]

Ironically enough, Walter had written an introduction to Stargardt-Wolff's book, but he clearly had not had an opportunity to read her manuscript in its entirety. Instead, he caught sight of her "explanation" in the society publication and, deeply disturbed, wrote to her, insisting that he had had no say in who would take over his concert and asking her to publish a correction.[78] Stargardt-Wolff's reply was adamant; she was, she said, the sole surviving witness, and she had to convince Walter that her version of the story was absolutely accurate, that Elsa really did say it was Walter's own idea for Strauss to conduct.[79] Together, they came up with a compromise, rewording the passage to state that, after speaking with Elsa, Louise Wolff had received only an "impression" that Walter had suggested Strauss, and this was subsequently published in the Richard-Strauss-Gesellschaft's next bulletin (December 1955).[80] Despite Walter's astonishment at reading a version of the story so at odds with what he remembered, the ensuing exchange between him and Stargardt-Wolff was not really hostile. One gets the impression that each felt the other was simply remembering events incorrectly and not that there was any deliberate attempt on either side to falsify the record. In the end, we must consider the possibility that Elsa, who was not averse to taking matters into her own hands, put forth Strauss's name herself.

As might be expected, Nazi newspapers such as the infamous *Völkischer Beobachter* hailed Strauss as a hero. Hugo Rasch wrote that Strauss's substituting for Walter, as well as Erich Orthmann's taking Fritz Stiedry's place in a performance of *Der fliegende Holländer*, proved that Germans were "absolutely not dependent on foreign-blooded conductors."[81] In an interview (also infamous) in the *Berliner Lokal-Anzeiger*, Hans Hinkel denied that Walter's concert had been either banned or made impossible in any way; as far as he knew, the concert management had wanted to cancel it, but Strauss had stepped in, earning the German people's thanks.[82] For the *New York Times*, however, Hinkel modified his story, claiming that it was simply not possible to provide police guards for Walter's protection, since "our storm troops have more important functions than providing protection for concerts." As for the threatening letters from America, Hinkel maintained that the German people resented "that the American public made itself the spokesman for Herr Walter in a conspicuous manner."[83] A draft of a chilling statement that the new regime planned to make concerning Walter's concert has survived, drawn up by the office of the Kampfbund für deutsche Kultur (KfdK). A model of obfuscation, it not only states that Walter freely chose to give up his concert when protection could not be provided but also implies that the reason protection might have been necessary was that Walter had chosen for his soloist the Czech soprano Jarmila Novotná, who had supposedly spoken out against Germany and German culture in the "most unacceptable manner."[84] This sort of rhetoric coming from the Prussian State Commissioner for Science, Art, and Culture, who may have been one of the prime movers behind Walter's persecution, is hardly surprising. But Fritz Stege, who, despite his politics, had thus far treated Walter favorably in his Berlin reviews for the *Zeitschrift für Musik*, quickly jumped ship. It is painful to read his description of the audience's enthusiastic reception of Strauss, who had not let threatening letters from "Jewish-incited America" deter him from taking over the concert—this from a paper that had in years past referred to Walter as a great "German" conductor.[85]

These were still early days, however, and not every journalist in Germany immediately clambered onto the Jew-banning bandwagon. Fritz Klein, editor of the liberal Berlin newspaper the *Deutsche Allgemeine Zeitung*, a man whom Walter had met at the Berlin Rotary Club, published a long and courageous article on a front page loaded with headlines concerning the activities of Germany's new chancellor. Though he chose his words carefully, Klein wondered how the loss of such important artists—Walter in particular—could possibly be good for Germany. He was "so great an artist and so musical a person," Klein argued, that it was impossible to banish thoughts of Walter in connection with the German musical scene, and whatever people believed about there being too many Jews in Germany, there was "no reason to retaliate with an extreme anti-Semitism that then throws out the baby with the bath water."[86] As events unfolded, Klein published other criticisms, which may have cost him his job. A similar article appeared in the *Frankfurter Zeitung* after Walter canceled a concert he was scheduled to conduct in Frankfurt, in which the author recalled that nobody had done more since World War I to bring back recognition for Germany's cultural values than Walter.[87]

In fact, though Daniel Goldhagen in a controversial book has recently gone to great lengths to show that, by the nineteenth and early twentieth centuries, anti-Semitism in Germany had evolved into a deeply ingrained fear and hatred amounting almost to a collective memory, many Germans of Walter's acquaintance, if they were indeed possessed of such hatred, never felt it toward Walter.[88] As soon as they learned that Walter had been driven out of Berlin, outraged German music-lovers, helplessly watching the new extremist government running roughshod over their culture, poured out their feelings privately in letters to Walter and his wife. Over and over they thanked Walter for the hours of enjoyment he had given them, expressed their dismay, and wondered how this could possibly be happening. Anyone who could conduct Mozart as Walter did must be a true German in his heart, one particularly impassioned letter cried; its author heard the morning bells marking some celebration of the German state but stayed in his room and was ashamed of his Germany.[89]

This outpouring of supportive letters, both from his former country and from abroad, enabled Walter to cling to his underlying faith in humanity. Though Germany appeared to be slipping into the abyss, people in other parts of the world were still displaying the sort of admirable sentiments that, Walter had always maintained, people were capable of. And his ability to make music would carry him through this darkest hour of his life (and that of so many others). "I have loved Germany as well as one can love and have always felt myself to be German," he wrote to a friend of Elsa's, but since he was considered foreign where he believed himself at home, music must now be his home.[90] At this time especially, he felt that musicians had an obligation—even a moral duty—to attempt to counterbalance the spreading darkness, and his belief in music's ability to bring out the best in humankind was, in some ways, his greatest comfort. Indeed, the importance of all the arts was as great as it had ever been. In a stalwart speech given at a dinner of the London Music Club on April 26, at which he was the guest of honor, he declared, "What we have to do is to stand our ground, to keep faith and loyalty to our arts, to the great thoughts, which the noblest minds of humanity created, to keep faith and loyalty to the ideals of freedom of thought and of understanding and peace between the single persons and between the nations."[91]

But privately, with his closest friends, Walter found it difficult to speak of recent events without lapsing into great sorrow. "The loss of my home country was a real sadness for me, but let me tell you that even this great personal loss is not the most tragic part of those last experiences and of my present feelings," he wrote to Harry Harkness Flagler, who as the years passed would become one of Walter's closest American friends. "Imagine, that it is not only I and the very many other artists and scientists and so on, who have lost Germany by being compelled to leave her, no, we must think that the whole world lost Germany, because this Germany which was such a Royaume [i.e., realm] of Spirit and Humanity, a center of artistic and scientific life, does not exist anymore." Despite his belief that musical performances might alleviate people's suffering in some way, Walter, like the German intellectuals he'd had to leave behind, felt powerless, unable to help. "I feel my helplessness to quench a huge fire with a glassful of water," he wrote in the same letter. "This mourning has not a great style, it is a daily torture and I am not the coward to make my escape and be satisfied that I personally and my family are not damaged, at least not materially." Nevertheless, Walter shied away from giving in to hatred or revenge, which some of his contemporaries who had also suffered persecution simply could not understand and even considered a bit suspect. But he was adamant—he did not want to be regarded as a political martyr. "I loved Germany dearly, I suffered terribly by her suffering, but I never felt the least inclination to judge a person after his or her Nationality, race or religion," he told Flagler.[92] And he refused to grant the North American Newspaper Alliance an interview, asking them to "understand that my language is music which lacks possibility of telling political tales."[93]

But now things had gone too far for Walter to remain completely detached from politics, so shortly after leaving Berlin he asked Count Kanitz— the former Minister of Agriculture and a devotee of Walter's conducting, a man with some influence among the older government officials—to inquire into the meaning of "politically suspicious." Kanitz's inquiries revealed that, according to the Propaganda Ministry, some Communist documents containing Walter's name had been uncovered. It surely did not help that Walter's programs in Leipzig and Berlin had included what some viewed as a disproportionately large number of Russian compositions, with premieres by Prokofiev, Shostakovich, and Lopatnikoff. The Lopatnikoff symphony was doubtless especially repugnant to the Nazis, since its program notes claimed that its style was a kind of Russian pastiche, "working against all the 'German' symphonic leather."[94] Despite his disinclination for things political, Walter felt he must take some steps to deny any Communist involvement, especially since the accusations made against him might put him and his family in some danger, even outside Germany. As he wrote to Kanitz, he sent proof of his noninvolvement with Communism to a lawyer in Berlin, not only to right himself, but to protest the treatment of one who had led such a "blameless life."[95] To this lawyer, Dr. Korn, Walter described in great detail his opposition to the Communist uprising in Munich in 1918. He had stood, he said, very badly with Kurt Eisner, the leader of the short-lived Bavarian socialist government, doing his best to hinder his influence at the Munich Nationaltheater. He refused to direct a concert organized by Eisner, though, at the advice of friends, he agreed to conduct a short overture in a long concert and did so without a red ribbon in his buttonhole—he believed he was the only participant to eschew the Communist emblem.[96] Though Walter felt strongly that art and politics did not mix, he clearly was capable of taking a political stance when the occasion demanded it.

Meanwhile, the *Deutsche Wochenschau* published the news of the supposed finding of Bolshevist Walter material, a news item soon picked up by the *Zeitschrift für Musik*, which had been moving further and further to the Right ever since Gustav Bosse (not to be confused with Walter's friend, Gustav Böss) became its publisher in 1929 and Fritz Stege had joined Heuss as editor-in-chief.[97] Here again Walter felt the need to set the record straight, writing terse statements to both Bosse and the publisher of the *Deutsche Wochenschau* to the effect that there was no such material, that Walter had never taken an active role in politics, that he had never belonged to a political party, and that his life was devoted solely to art.[98] To his credit, Bosse wrote back, agreeing to include Walter's statement and, true to his word, printed it in its entirety in the June issue of the *Zeitschrift für Musik* without any disclaimers or sarcastic asides.[99] By this time the newspaper was laced with articles in support of the steps that the new government was taking to counteract "evil influences," and some were written by Bosse himself; so his willingness to help Walter defend himself, albeit it in a very small way, reveals a complexity of attitude beyond simple racism. Oddly enough, another German music journal, the *Allgemeine Musikzeitung*, blithely reported on Walter's activities at least as late as May 1934, devoting an entire column in that issue to both Walter's and Furtwängler's concerts in Vienna as if they were simply two distinguished guest conductors taking Vienna by storm—though there is perhaps an underlying irony in the article's opening statement that "Bruno Walter, who for many years could only come to his musical home for a couple of days, has this time been in Vienna for several weeks and has imprinted the entire musical season that is even now coming to a close with the stamp of his personality."[100]

Very shortly after Walter's expulsion from his native land, Wilhelm Furtwängler boldly defended Walter against his detractors. Despite their rivalry, Furtwängler had continued to regard the older conductor as an exemplary figure. In his private notebooks, for example, Furtwängler had jotted down in 1929 that "true conductors"—he listed only two, Toscanini and Walter—did not follow academic precepts on how to conduct. And though he respected both his chief rivals, there were times when he clearly preferred Walter's approach. In 1930, while ruminating on Toscanini's recent performance of Haydn's "Clock" Symphony in Berlin, he condemned the "stiff and soulless effect" of Toscanini's approach to a passage in the Andante, adding, "I should like to hear a passage like this done by Bruno Walter, for example."[101]

Not all of Furtwängler's thoughts on Walter, however, were hidden from the public. In an open letter to Joseph Goebbels that ran in the *Vossische Zeitung* on April 11, he expressed how shocked he was to witness Walter and other proponents of German culture suddenly fleeing for their lives, and he urged "that men like Walter, Klemperer, Reinhardt, and so on, must be allowed to be heard in Germany in the future as well." But he also added an unfortunate comment on good and bad art, revealing his own prejudices and exposing a chink in his rhetorical armor: "If the battle against Jewishness is directed principally against those who, rootless and destructive, attempt to operate through kitsch, dry virtuosity, and the like, then it is only proper. . . . If this battle, however, is directed against true artists, then it is not in the best interest of our cultural life." So retention of the "good" Jews who had risen above the limitations of their race, the argument seems to run, might be a politic move for the greater good of Germany.

Public utterance of sentiments so critical of Nazi ideology did nothing to endear Furtwängler to Joseph Goebbels, who immediately shot back an outwardly civil response in the *Berliner Lokal-Anzeiger*. Instead of lamenting that men like Walter, Reinhardt, and Klemperer would no longer be heard in Germany, Goebbels wrote, it would be better to view the current turn of events as a liberation of the true German artists whose voices had been smothered throughout the previous fourteen years of the Weimar Republic. (Presumably he was writing of such men as Paul Graener and Carl Ehrenberg, recent Nazi converts, whose music Walter had promoted.) And while it was true that some non-Jewish German composers were guilty of writing bad music—"rootless and destructive," full of empty virtuosity, and so on—this was only a sign, Goebbels maintained, of how deeply the roots of Jewishness extended into German culture. [102]

While the plight of exiled Germans was being debated in the papers, Walter and his family prepared themselves to settle permanently in Austria, with no immediate hope of returning to their homeland. Some might wonder at Walter's decision, expedient though it was, to take up residence in a country that in some ways had long had a more openly anti-Semitic strain than Germany itself and where, in 1933, the Nazi Party already had strong support. Many expatriates, such as the Manns, stayed away from Austria on the advice of friends who felt that it was "sinister and to be avoided," opting instead for Switzerland. [103] Gino Baldini, who had served as Walter's personal representative during his New York appearances, asked him why he did not return to America, where he was loved, and wondered whether Germany or Austria merited Walter's loyalty. [104] Walter told him not to worry, that he would be perfectly fine in Austria, where he had been a naturalized citizen for the last twenty-three years. He described how the president of Austria (Wilhelm Miklas) had asked Walter to come to his box at a concert and had allowed them to be photographed together as a "kind of paying political homage to an artist to whom has been done a political wrong from his own country." [105] Writing to Harry Harkness Flagler, however, he was less optimistic, commenting doubtfully that "if Austria would keep clean of the poison of the germs who made Germany so sick, we would perhaps settle in Vienna." [106] Those germs remained dormant for only the next five years.

# ELEVEN

# Nomad Again
## 1933–1936

*I have already wandered far and wide . . .*
Wagner, *Siegfried*

"Germany, in expelling Walter, has made a present of its greatest conductor to the rest of the world."[1] This was how one London newspaper put it, and it was certainly the opinion of music directors in many countries who, surmising that Walter suddenly had more free time, hastened to invite him to conduct. In fact, Walter was allowed only one day of relaxation in the mountain air of Semmering, outside Vienna. The following day he received a telephone call from Rudolf Mengelberg, who asked him to replace the indisposed Willem Mengelberg (Rudolf's uncle) for several concerts with the Concertgebouw Orchestra in Amsterdam. A mere ten days earlier Walter had written to Rudolf that he hoped to be able to conduct the Concertgebouw at some point and that he would let him know when his schedule was clear.[2] With his schedule now open, he was happy to accept, for conducting the Concertgebouw, with which he had such a friendly relationship and had enjoyed many special performances of Mahler in particular, was a welcome musical solace for his battered heart. So he took the *Edelweiss* train through Switzerland, France, and

Belgium, traveling to Amsterdam from Vienna without crossing into Germany—no easy proposition. In fact, the number of lengthy trips he would take in the next five years in order to continue conducting throughout Europe while avoiding Germany is staggering.

If Walter had hoped that the Amsterdam presses would simply report on his concerts and leave politics out of it, he was to be disappointed. No sooner had he crossed the Dutch border than several journalists boarded the train and sought to interview him, doubtless hoping he would let out some scathing remarks about the new German regime. But Walter's replies were necessarily cautious; Elsa and Gretel, as well as his brother Leo and sister Emma, were still in Germany, and he feared that they might suffer reprisals for any strong words on his part published in foreign papers. Instead, he talked mainly of his future plans and his happiness at returning to the Netherlands, "the land that was also so close to Gustav Mahler's heart."[3]

Upon his arrival at the Amsterdam train station, where Rudolf Mengelberg and Eduard van Beinum greeted him, Walter encountered a peaceful demonstration staged by the Amsterdam Social Democrats. They cheered him as he stepped onto the square, and a spontaneous chorus began to sing "De Stem des Volks," an old Netherlands freedom hymn. For Walter, it was "a surprise, hardly bearable because of the deep emotion it caused" him.[4] Another surprise lay in waiting for him; during one of the rehearsals Gretel, still residing in Germany with her husband, came up from the audience to greet him as he left the podium. Though not given to public displays of emotion, Walter could not contain himself and, before the orchestra and the press, stroked her hair and exclaimed, "Gretel, it gives me infinite happiness that you're here." Then the father and daughter gazed at each other for a long time without speaking, one of the papers reported, and their eyes filled with tears.[5]

In this charged atmosphere, Walter conducted concerts with the Concertgebouw in Amsterdam, The Hague, Rotterdam, and Haarlem (the programs included Mahler's Fourth and Fifth symphonies, music now banned in Germany), then returned to Vienna, where his wife arrived soon afterward with tales of the horror she had left behind in Berlin. "She, who had hardly ever shed tears, fell on my neck crying bitterly when she alighted from the train," Walter recalled later.[6] The sight of Nazi mobs wrecking Jewish shops and beating people in the streets was bad enough, but—even worse for Elsa—some of her relatives had defended them, and she'd had to sever relations with her own family members.

In Vienna, meanwhile, Walter was a hero. In addition to the planned performance of Mahler's Eighth by the Vienna Singverein, the Vienna Philharmonic invited Walter to conduct an extra concert on April 9. The program was tailor-made for him, consisting of the Mozart Piano Concerto in D Minor with himself as soloist, three of Wagner's *Wesendonk-Lieder* sung by Rosette Anday, and Mahler's First. Vienna was naturally not free of Nazi sympathizers, but none seem to have attended this concert, and Walter received an ovation the intensity of which was "rare, even in Vienna."[7] The Viennese Nazis could not leave Walter completely alone, though, and on April 12, the day of the Singverein performance, the *Deutschoesterreichische Tageszeitung* published an "offensive" article about the concert.[8]

If this article had any effect, however, it was to make even more people attend the Singverein concert. "The house was completely sold out," reported the *Neue Freie Presse*, and the audience was full of prominent Viennese citizens, including President Wilhelm Miklas. The performance won accolades, while a separate article was devoted to the ovations that followed, which lasted over half an hour. Much as Walter disliked addressing audiences after performances, the feeling here was too great for him simply to walk off silently. He motioned with his hand, waited for the audience to calm down, then declared that "the best thing we have in the world is music—here in Vienna, music has its home. I am fortunate!"[9] According to Paul Stefan, half an hour passed before the lights in the Musikverein were finally dark.[10]

Walter might have felt that Vienna was music's home, but many other cities were waiting to welcome him. After conducting in Budapest, it was on to London, where more plaudits awaited him. First he conducted the newly reconstituted London Philharmonic in a concert of Mozart, Wagner, and Beethoven at Queen's Hall. The *Times* review must have pleased him, for it was a model of restraint, describing only the concert itself, with absolutely no mention of his recent political experiences. An account of this event a couple of weeks later in New York's *Musical Courier* was not nearly so understated: "No conductor, not even Toscanini at the head of the New York Philharmonic, has received the ovation that greeted [Walter] when he emerged on the platform of Queen's Hall."[11] Following the two repeat performances of this highly acclaimed concert was a dinner in Walter's honor given by the London Music Club at the May Fair Hotel, with Sir Thomas Beecham presiding in place of Sir Edward Elgar, who was seriously ill. Adrian Boult (not yet "Sir Adrian") was unfortunately also unable to attend, but among the guests was one of Walter's other great English friends, Dame

Ethel Smyth. At the dinner Beecham related how, twenty-three years before, he had asked Smyth if she knew of anyone who could conduct her opera *The Wreckers* better than he could. "Certainly: I have a young friend in Vienna whom you ought to invite to London—Mr. Bruno Walter," she replied.[12]

Walter's trip to London was not entirely taken up with conducting and banquets; it was on this visit that Smyth introduced him to Virginia Woolf. On the whole, the two were favorably impressed with each other, though Woolf wrote somewhat disparagingly in her diary that Walter was "swarthy" and "fattish." Yet she was deeply moved, both by his intense personality (or even "genius") and by his visceral reaction to the recent events in Germany. "He is very nearly mad; that is, he cant get 'the poison' as he called it of Hitler out of him," she wrote, describing how Walter spoke to them for some time about Germany's "disgrace" and the terrible state of the world. Perhaps because of his long friendship with Ethel Smyth, Walter spoke more frankly to her friends the Woolfs than he did to most people, telling them: "We must refuse to meet any German. We must say that they are uncivilised. We will not trade with them or play with them—we must make them feel themselves outcasts—not by fighting them; by ignoring them."[13]

Despite these strong words to friends, Walter was still not inclined to make public declarations of his private anguish. After being feted in London, he could perhaps have gone to Paris; but, as he explained to Flagler, he had postponed any Paris engagements "because I was afraid that the demonstration there would have changed so far to a political character that, at once, I may have been considered more an object of political interest than an artist."[14] Instead he retreated to Switzerland for a rest, to ready himself for the upcoming Salzburg Festival. He had, of course, been conducting in Salzburg regularly for the last several years. But now his appearance had added significance for Austrians—he was no longer a visiting conductor from Germany but one of their own. Both Walter and Max Reinhardt, also barred from his native land, had become heroes of the festival and were followed by adoring crowds wherever they went. "An artist such as this must certainly remain at the forefront of the festival, which would be hard to imagine without him," wrote Hermann Ullrich, reviewing Walter's first concert with the Vienna Philharmonic, a subtle dig perhaps at those who had lost him.[15] The audience, however, didn't waste time with subtleties, showering Walter with roses at the end of the concert.[16] Meanwhile Nazi sympathizers, hard at work, did everything in their power to turn people against the festival, sending airplanes overhead to drop leaflets denouncing the anti-Nazi government under Chancellor Engelbert Dollfuss and attaching fake bombs (which turned out to be little more than firecrackers) to telephone poles—much to the derision of the music-lovers who had come to hear the concerts. There were naturally some German singers who had canceled—or been forced to cancel—their Salzburg engagement, but their places were swiftly filled.

From a purely musical standpoint, this summer's festival was also special because it included Walter's first Salzburg *Tristan*—in fact, his first *Tristan* in Austria. Ironically, it was the first Wagner opera conducted at the festival, which up to this point had consisted mainly of operas by Mozart, Strauss, Gluck, and other non-Wagnerians. Though Walter's *Tristan* was clearly one of the high points of the festival, repeats of *Die Zauberflöte* and *Orfeo ed Euridice*, three concerts with the Vienna Philharmonic, and his annual song recital with Lotte Lehmann also gave audiences many chances to show their appreciation, both publicly and privately. One of the greatest novelists from America's Gilded Age attended the festival that year, and her discriminating palate was not disappointed with the proffered fare. "Mozart Symphony Concert *supremely* conducted by Bruno Walter," Edith Wharton wrote to a friend.[17]

Walter appreciated both his audience and the singers who stepped in at the last minute, for now, more than ever, he regarded Salzburg as a special sanctuary dedicated to art and beauty, divorced from worldly upheavals. "In America you have a great beauty spot called Yellowstone Park," he told a *New York Times* reporter. "Within its borders all the last disappearing beautiful things—birds, animals and everything else it is good to keep on earth—are preserved and safe. Why cannot Salzburg, why cannot, in fact, all Austria, which is small and weak politically, be made such a refuge for art and for music, under the protection of the League of Nations, for instance?"[18] In hindsight, it's hard to believe that Walter and some other Austrians could actually have entertained such hopes; but at the time, with Dollfuss's strongly anti-Nazi regime, the idea did seem plausible. Thus it was with some renewed optimism that Walter set sail for America in September for a conducting stint lasting from early October to mid-December.

At the same time, Walter was still trying his best to avoid undue publicity and to concentrate on conducting. "I do not at all like the idea of being interviewed and photographed on the liner, when I arrive and getting political headlines and attributes in the papers," he wrote to Bruno Zirato (his liaison at the New York Philharmonic) before leaving Europe. "If you see a way for me and Mrs. Walter to get off the boat unobserved I would appreciate it highly."[19] Naturally Zirato was unable to keep the press at bay entirely, but at least the article in the *New York Times* announcing Walter's arrival began with a musical headline, "WALTER SELECTS AMERICAN MUSIC," before moving on, in smaller type, to "CONDUCTOR NOW 'NOMAD.'"[20] And in Walter's opening concert, at which he was received with "a welcoming demonstration of unusual length and ardor," Olin Downes commented in his review that "no doubt the demonstration received added impetus from the fact that Mr. Walter is one of the great artists who have been driven from Germany by Hitlerism."[21] For the rest of his conducting run in New York, however, the critics confined themselves to discussing details of the performances—no doubt a great source of satisfaction for Walter.

Driven from Germany or no, in America as in Austria, Walter was still considered one of the foremost interpreters of German music, and his programs in the fall of 1933 contained perhaps even more Germanic works than usual. Wagner, Beethoven, Brahms, and Strauss, along with the Austrians Haydn, Mahler, Mozart, and Bruckner, dominated his repertoire, which led Downes to grouse that "all music was not made in Germany."[22] But his grievance stemmed from purely musical considerations—it was too early for the recent political developments in Germany to become inextricably linked to German culture. In any case, as the above headline trumpeted, Walter did not neglect American music, giving the New York premieres of Randall Thompson's Second Symphony and David Stanley Smith's *1929, a Satire*. Walter, retaining fond memories of Thompson's work, wrote to the composer over a decade later: "I always remember with great pleasure your Second Symphony which belongs to the best compositions I had the good luck to perform."[23]

In truth, as this series of concerts with the Philharmonic wore on, Downes's griping notwithstanding, it could certainly be said that there was something for everyone—English works by Bax and Elgar; Gallic compositions by Chausson, Franck, Ravel, and Berlioz; Slavic contributions from Janáček and Tchaikovsky; the Polish Chopin and the German Schumann; a Viennese program complete with waltzes and sleigh bells; and even a tone poem by Respighi, *Vetrate di chiesa*. Elgar's Violin Concerto with Jascha Heifetz, the first performance of the work by the Philharmonic, attracted particular attention, as did Berlioz's *Symphonie fantastique*, by now one of Walter's specialties.

One program that also intrigued the critics included excerpts from Wolf's *Der Corregidor*. This was another much-maligned work that Walter seems to have taken pains to resurrect and reinstate. In America as in Germany, it appears to have worked; Lawrence Gilman, for one, was completely convinced of its worth. "What makes one disinclined to take too seriously the charge of theatrical ineffectiveness that is sometimes brought against 'Der Corregidor' is the plain fact—evident, I should suppose, to anyone who knows the score—that the music is charged with an almost unflagging dramatic vitality," he wrote; and in answer to the objection that the score is "chiefly a series of beautiful vocal numbers" (which, he is quick to point out, is a criticism that could be leveled at many works in the standard repertoire), the "comment is grotesquely inapplicable to 'Der Corregidor.' This music fits the delectable comedy like a glove—is perfectly shaped to its wit, its gayety, its gusto, its recurrent tenderness." As for the performance, "Mr. Walter conducted with complete authority."[24] The conductor maintained his affection for the work until the end of his career, writing to a friend in 1960 that, in spite of its weaknesses, he could not understand why *Der Corregidor* had not found a permanent place in the German operatic repertoire.[25]

The year 1933 was now drawing to a close, an indescribably tumultuous year for Walter personally, and yet as a musician he seemed to be more in command than ever before. But all these artistic triumphs could not completely wash away the sorrow in his heart. "It is no cheerful world, no happy time within which this day falls," he wrote in a letter congratulating his brother Leo on his sixtieth birthday. "But it will only be to your credit to hold your head high and to be cheerful when the circumstances call for the opposite."[26] Walter's advice to his brother no doubt echoed the advice he had been giving himself all along, and one can imagine that Walter, as he sailed back to Europe for a vacation in St. Moritz, was wondering what further upheavals the new year would bring.

For the moment, however, life seemed to be settling into a pattern: living in Austria, vacationing in Switzerland, and conducting just about everywhere in Europe outside Germany. In mid-January he conducted the Orchestra Stabile Fiorentina; on January 31 he gave a concert with the BBC Symphony in which Prokofiev played the British premiere of his Fifth Piano Concerto. He went back to Amsterdam in February for a series of concerts rich in Mozart and Mahler. In March and April he returned to Vienna to conduct concerts with the Vienna Philharmonic and, even more exciting for the Viennese public, to appear at the Staatsoper, where he had not conducted opera since leaving in 1912.

"This year Vienna will not have to visit Bruno Walter in Salzburg," began Walter's old supporter Julius Korngold, reviewing the first of his three

Vienna Philharmonic concerts and describing the jubilant reception Walter received. The audience, Korngold declared, "stripped Walter of his internationality so to speak, and reclaimed him as a Viennese conductor."[27] Both Korngold and Josef Reitler, the *Neue Freie Presse*'s other music critic, emphasized Walter's connection to Mahler, and both implied that such a Mahler disciple belonged only in Vienna; so it was fitting that the last of Walter's three concerts contained *Das Lied von der Erde*. But the truly wondrous thing was to have Walter back at the Staatsoper, where he directed new productions of Verdi's *Ballo*, Tchaikovsky's *Eugene Onegin*, and a special performance of *Tristan*. One has to give credit to Clemens Krauss—a rival conductor—for recognizing how meaningful Walter's opera conducting would be to the Viennese public and for allowing the success of the season as a whole momentarily to outweigh his personal ambitions. Marcel Prawy recalls that "his idea was to make the Vienna Opera a one-man band, and the one man was Clemens Krauss," and Krauss was especially determined to reserve all the new productions for himself.[28] But, his personal ambitions notwithstanding, Krauss held Walter in high esteem, once declaring in an interview that Walter's concerts at Salzburg had made a great impression on him, that he admired Walter's personality, and that working with him was "a great, unalloyed pleasure."[29] His giving Walter the opportunity to take over not one but *two* new productions for his return to the Staatsoper reveals not only his respect for Walter but also a more generous spirit than most people are willing to grant him.

Krauss's artistic integrity did not go unnoticed by Josef Reitler; in his review of *Ballo*, he commented, "Certainly every production conducted by Walter will have its cachet and attract the interest of the opera-going public. We value the high artistic and insightful principles of Director Clemens Krauss, who does not easily let productions rehearsed by him out of his hands."[30] Reitler himself, to be sure, belonged to the group of operagoers for whom Walter's conducting had a "cachet," for he described all three operas in the warmest terms, stressing especially Walter's great sense of theater. "It is a sign of a born theater director," he wrote, reviewing *Onegin*, "that he always makes music in the closest contact with the stage; catching inspiration from the moment, he gives his all to the work, bestowing upon it his nerves and spirit, drawing from his own spirit."[31] We do not know if Krauss read the review and regretted giving up these productions, or if, like the rest of Vienna, he too felt that Walter was back in Vienna where he belonged and rejoiced in it, for the moment at least.

Walter had reestablished his home base in Vienna, but during these years of wandering, London and Paris became his frequent late spring haunts. At the beginning of May he conducted *Don Giovanni* in Paris, then sailed across the Channel to London to take part in Boult's London Music Festival, a series of six concerts at Queen's Hall. The programming was sufficiently standard—largely Brahms and Beethoven (with Walter conducting some Richard Strauss and Bruckner)—to cause the press to carp about the festival's somewhat grandiose title. After Walter's two London concerts, he set sail for another Paris *Don Giovanni* in mid-May, then returned to London to record Brahms's Fourth Symphony and Mozart's Symphony no. 39 with the BBC Symphony Orchestra. No doubt he would have appreciated the Chunnel.

For the London Music Festival it was originally intended that the conducting duties be split evenly between Boult and Walter, but Weingartner was eventually engaged to conduct the last concert because Walter felt uncomfortable at the idea of having Wilhelm Backhaus as his piano soloist, writing to the management with surprising vehemence that Backhaus was an "official favourite of Hitler." When the management demurred, Walter wrote again that "there is remaining in myself a very strong resistance against a collaboration with a fellow-being in sympathy with the most anti-spiritual (and in consequence anti-artistic) system of our times."[32] Clearly Walter's recent wounds had not yet healed; it was rare for him to denounce a colleague so strongly, and his unwillingness to do so after the war often earned him harsh criticisms. Ironically, Backhaus and Walter appeared to have had some sort of reconciliation shortly afterward, when they were both living in Switzerland, for Backhaus wrote to Walter in 1945, after Elsa's death, to offer his condolences. Writing from Lugano, he recalled passing Walter's old house and the memories it evoked of the prewar years they had experienced together.[33] A few years after the war, moreover, Walter suggested to Bruno Zirato that Backhaus might be used as a soloist with the New York Philharmonic, noting that he "behaved very well politically—as a matter of fact, he left Germany for good and spent all these years in Switzerland," so there could be no political objection to his appearing with the orchestra.[34]

Despite these continued brushes with politics, the year was proceeding smoothly—summer was on its way, and Walter was preparing for another Salzburg Festival. Then near the end of July, Chancellor Engelbert Dollfuss was assassinated when a group of armed Austrian rebels incited by German Nazis stormed a cabinet meeting. Walter describes how his drive from

Hallein to Salzburg, normally forty-five minutes long, took twice the time that evening, as his car was stopped repeatedly by the Austrian militia, demanding to see his papers.[35] There had been a Nazi plot to take over the Austrian government by force or even assassination if necessary. Though Dollfuss had received a last-minute warning from one of the plotters who had changed his mind, he dismissed his cabinet and remained to confront the rebels, bleeding for two and a half hours before finally dying. So the cabinet members escaped, and the plot failed, but Dollfuss, who has been called the "heartbeat" of Austria, was dead, and once again political earthquakes were threatening to leave gaping fissures in Walter's world.[36]

Dollfuss's successor, Kurt von Schuschnigg—though history has portrayed him as a weaker, more contemplative man, lacking Dollfuss's strength of leadership—nevertheless impressed Walter with his idealism and belief in Austria. Walter was introduced to him by Alma Mahler Werfel, and Schuschnigg apparently was equally impressed by the conductor of Beethoven's *Missa solemnis*, a piece that he especially enjoyed. "He may have been lacking in the political instinct that would have scented the terrible dangers of the international situation and possibly averted them," Walter admitted, but "he was given strength and inspiration by his firm belief in Austria's political and cultural mission."[37] Walter clearly identified with Schuschnigg's idealism and felt that as long as such a man remained chancellor, Austria would be safe for him. But although Walter greatly underrated the danger from the Nazi menace, he and his family were hardly unaware of it. Two reels of home movies, possibly filmed by Lotte, show a man and two women in Salzburg enjoying a pleasant luncheon on a terrace overlooking the mountains. The camera focuses on them, then pans to one side, sweeping over the graceful Austrian countryside. Then the camera pans in the other direction until it comes upon a banner with a large swastika hanging from a nearby chalet, where it lingers for a moment, making the contrast between the peaceful countryside and the foreboding emblem eminently clear.[38]

For the most part, however, Walter kept his thoughts focused on music and his first *Don Giovanni* in Salzburg. He'd never been quite satisfied with his previous attempts at solving what he saw as problems in the work. "At any rate, my repeated experiences and disappointments had made me thoroughly acquainted with them," he recalled.[39] In Salzburg he was confident that the designer Oskar Strnad and the director Karlheinz Martin would help him overcome some of the difficulties, but one major obstacle remained—finding the perfect singer for the title role. Then Walter heard that

Ezio Pinza had successfully sung the Don in New York. Walter remembered how he had invited Pinza to meet him in New York and how Pinza, famous for his effect on the female sex, had particularly enchanted the Walters' Bohemian cook. Upon opening the door, she went rushing back and whispered to Elsa, "Ma'am, there's such a beautiful man outside," leading Walter to hope that Pinza would be able to "produce that immediate personal effect" he thought was crucial for the role.[40] Pinza, as it turned out, was to have a personal effect on Walter's daughter Gretel, but for now his importance to the conductor was as a singer whose voice and charisma were ideal for Don Giovanni.

Pinza, for his part, was deeply impressed by Walter. "Once more I found myself working with a person of Toscanini's caliber," he recalled, "but one who was neither distant nor harsh. . . . Walter welcomed challenge, meeting it in the spirit of intellectual and artistic give-and-take, making of it an enriching experience."[41] Under Walter's guidance Pinza changed his portrayal of the Don as "a conquering male, hopping from bedroom to bedroom," to that of a "magnetic rogue . . . doomed by his quest for the perfect woman."[42] Gretel may indeed have seen Pinza himself as a kind of magnetic rogue, for, as Pinza recalls, she kept her distance when they first met in the summer of 1934. Meanwhile, both Pinza and Gretel were in the process of separating from their spouses; Pinza's present wife, Augusta, was of a volatile, highly jealous nature, and Pinza shied away from "involving the deeply respected Bruno Walter family in one of Augusta's terrible scenes."[43] So although Gretel made an immediate impression on Pinza, their relationship would not develop until the following summer.

In the meantime Walter's and Pinza's attempt to make something more subtle out of the opera's title role caught the attention of the critics, one of whom described Pinza as a "fascinating Don Giovanni, full of a passionate, effervescent love of life."[44] The Austrian audiences and critics also appreciated Walter's using a version of the opera closer to that of the Viennese premiere in 1788, restoring certain numbers that were usually cut in Vienna in the earlier part of the twentieth century. The rest of the cast, which included Dusolina Giannini as Donna Anna, was also highly praised, and the entire production was a great hit. This summer's season also boasted a return performance of *Tristan*, Weber's *Oberon*, Vienna Philharmonic concerts, and Walter's customary lieder recital with Lotte Lehmann.

The young conductor Erich Leinsdorf, who had been hired as Walter's assistant, contributed to the success of *Don Giovanni*, though not quite in the way he had envisioned. He recalled how his first day was a "big letdown. Walter, holding piano rehearsals with the cast, showed me in no uncertain way that he needed my assistance like the proverbial hole in the head." Leinsdorf spent most of the day turning pages for Walter. During the staging rehearsals Leinsdorf's big chance came when "the rehearsal pianist had to go to the men's room" and he had the opportunity to accompany at the piano for a full ten minutes, during which time he translated "one or two messages from the Italian singers to the Viennese singers." As the rehearsal continued, Leinsdorf noticed that the Viennese prompter (who could pronounce Italian but otherwise did not know the language) was confusing the Italian singers. Leinsdorf, who had studied Italian, could prompt both the Italian- and the German-speaking singers with far greater success than the official prompter, and Pinza begged him to prompt at the performance. While it was unusual for a conductor to "descend" to the depths of the prompter's box, Leinsdorf, happy to have something to do, agreed, and Walter expressed his appreciation by writing a "charming" dedication in Leinsdorf's score and engaging him as his assistant for next year's Maggio Musicale in Florence.[45]

In October Walter made his first recording with the Vienna Philharmonic—a splendidly elegant yet heroic reading of Beethoven's "Emperor" Concerto, with Walter Gieseking as soloist—before returning to Amsterdam for a series of concerts with that city's premier symphony orchestra. Indeed, he was to regard his work with the Concertgebouw during these years as one of the bulwarks of his musical existence. His program for October 11 included the premiere of Kurt Weill's Symphony no. 2, which the composer— another German expatriate—had begun in January of 1933 and, because of obvious interruptions, finished more than a year later in France. Weill had played through the symphony for Walter earlier in the year and was thrilled when Walter suggested performing it in Amsterdam. "It will be really wonderful if he actually does it," Weill wrote to Lotte Lenya. "Because he's now the biggest international conductor here, having had greater success in Salzburg than Toscanini!"[46] Even more excited when he actually attended a rehearsal, Weill described to Lenya how "Walter does it marvelously and everyone is really enthusiastic, especially the *entire orchestra!*"[47] But, though the work was apparently well received by the orchestra, the Amsterdam critics were somewhat unkind, implying that the symphony's harmonies and melodies were reminiscent of *Die Dreigroschenoper* (*Three-Penny Opera*) and not truly symphonic, and that it was in actuality a group of "songs" strung together (though Walter liked the work well enough to perform it again in both Vienna and New York). This same Concertgebouw program also included Prokofiev's Third Piano Concerto with the composer as soloist, as well as Brahms's Fourth Symphony, a strange intermingling of styles that one critic described as a "difficult, long but extremely interesting exercise for musicians and laymen alike."[48]

The Weill symphony figured prominently as one of the principal novelties Walter offered during this year's run of concerts in New York, but now it had taken on a new title, *Three Night Scenes: A Symphonic Fantasy*, which Walter had suggested to Weill and to which the composer had reluctantly agreed. According to Lawrence Gilman's program notes, Walter was impressed by its "nocturnal, uncanny, mysterious atmosphere," but one wonders if, after his experience in Amsterdam, Walter thought that a programmatic title would make the critics listen to the work with different expectations. If this was his plan, it failed miserably with the two most prominent New York reviewers. Olin Downes, pulling no punches, characterized the three movements as "dreary, dull and witless," and Gilman, having written positively about the work for his program notes, did an about-face and declared that it was "easily forgotten."[49] It's easy to see why this was the last purely symphonic work Weill attempted.

Walter's time in New York was somewhat shorter this season—it lasted only from December 6 until January 13—and his programming was perhaps less varied. But he did manage to include two New York premieres—Rachmaninoff's Rhapsody on a Theme of Paganini, with the composer at the piano, and Daniel Gregory Mason's *Suite after English Folksongs*—as well as Albert Roussel's Symphony no. 3 in G Minor, all of which received somewhat kinder comments than the unfortunate Weill symphony. In addition Walter continued his ongoing crusade for Mahler, offering *Das Lied von der Erde* (with Maria Olszewska and Frederick Jagel), which elicited an encomium from Lawrence Gilman and a few kind words from Olin Downes, who grudgingly grouped the final pages of the score among "the most genuinely poetical and distinguished passages in all Mahler."[50] Though Downes always admired Walter's conducting, he was not so charitable toward Walter's notes for the concert production of Gluck's *Orfeo*, which opened the season. "The conductor's annotations were without value," he carped, "badly edited, poorly phrased and lacking the slightest information about this opera."[51] Though they did indeed contain some unidiomatic awkwardnesses, Walter's notes were intended to address a problem that Downes himself mentioned: how to perform a concert version of a work that contains several ballet sequences. Instead of writing the kind of historical essay that Downes seemed to expect, Walter included a programmatic list of the numbers, summarizing the content of the arias and recitatives and describing the drama pantomimed by the dances that he and Margarete Wallmann had worked out together. This way Walter hoped to give the listener "a continued tale of the dramatic proceedings," and the notes also served to give the audience a window into his personal interpretation of a work for which he seems to have had a special affinity.

When Walter finished his concerts with the New York Philharmonic on January 13, he probably had little idea that—partly because of his own schedule, partly because of the Philharmonic's programming—he would not be returning until the 1940–41 season. Arturo Toscanini ran into Walter during his stay in New York and remarked on his "good health" and unusually cheery disposition. "He doesn't have his wife with him," Toscanini observed, "and this explains everything." But Toscanini also knew that Walter would probably not be returning to the Philharmonic for the following season. "They want to have Furtwängler split the season with me next year. There have been too many conductors this year, and not very interesting at that."[52]

Another year had passed and Walter, still barred from Germany, was becoming increasingly allied with the orchestras in two of her neighboring countries, Austria and the Netherlands. After his usual vacation in St. Moritz, Walter returned to Amsterdam in February to conduct, among other things, a concert performance of *Acis and Galatea*, then back to Vienna in March, all without passing through Germany. Of course, he had been on close terms with the Vienna Philharmonic for some years now, and a large number of the players from his early Vienna years were still members of the orchestra. Otto Strasser recalled how the atmosphere in Walter's Vienna rehearsals was loose, relaxed, almost familial, though it was always clear who was in charge.[53] The musicologist and conductor Siegmund Levarie, who as a young student in Vienna attended many of Walter's concert and opera performances, managed to slip into some of Walter's rehearsals and remembered how easy-going they were: "In his rehearsals he was kind rather than demanding." When Toscanini rehearsed, Levarie and the other conservatory students (who had made friends with the janitor in order to gain entrance to the rehearsals) had to "lie on the floor in the gallery not to be seen. But Bruno Walter was okay if he saw a few people there—he didn't kick anybody out."[54]

Walter's intimacy with this magnificent orchestral machine resulted in especially gripping performances, and we are fortunate that, by the mid-1930s, recording technology had become sophisticated enough for us to get some inkling of how intense Walter's performances with the Vienna Philharmonic could be. Their recordings of Act I and parts of Act II of *Die Walküre*, made in June 1935, are particularly riveting—the orchestra, in its every nuance, seems to be following Walter's subtlest indications, and the result is a highly expressive, supple, and unusually contrapuntal Wagner, perhaps like no other Wagnerian recording. (It didn't hurt that Walter had Melchior and Lehmann as his Siegmund and Sieglinde, along with Emanuel List as Hunding.) Throughout the spring of 1935, in fact, Walter spent a good deal of time with the Vienna Philharmonic: three concerts in March and April, a tour through England and France in April and May, and then the recording sessions in June. Many again hoped for a closer association between Walter and the opera house, and when Clemens Krauss, tainted by association with the Nazis (he had just signed a contract with the Berlin Staatsoper), left in December 1934, it seemed as if Walter might finally be secured as Vienna's opera conductor as well. But Weingartner was chosen to fill the sudden gap left by what appeared to many as Krauss's defection, though he was quick to invite Walter to bring his Salzburg *Orfeo ed Euridice* to Vienna.

Walter did not, however, spend the entire spring with the Vienna Philharmonic. In April he conducted in Budapest, Warsaw, and Prague, and in May he took part in the newly developing Maggio Musicale in Florence, concentrating mainly on Mozart, with three performances of *Die Entführung*, the Requiem, and a symphony concert in which he conducted and played the Piano Concerto no. 20 in D Minor.

Between his travels to these different countries Walter was further developing his personal philosophy that music was one of the most powerful means of coaxing nobler sentiments from humanity. It was a belief that he had held for most of his life and one that he returned to with increasing frequency in his various public statements in 1933. He had come face to face with humanity's darkest side, so it's not surprising that he felt compelled to counter it by pointing out the possibilities that existed for humankind's betterment. At some point he gave a lecture in Vienna entitled *Von den moralischen Kräften der Musik* ("On the Moral Forces of Music"), later published as a pamphlet in 1935, in which he elaborated in great detail on how he felt music's power was exercised.

In Walter's view music's great attribute was its ability to lift men and women out of the narrowness of their everyday lives and transport them to a higher plane of existence. While performing its primary mission, that of existing as pure art, music might also make the world a better place. Further, and despite his insistence that music's power was difficult to define, Walter had specific ideas about how it achieved this ennobling effect on human beings. Above all, Walter felt that dissonance in music—though it could abound freely—must ultimately resolve into consonance. (Here he betrays a possible indebtedness to Schopenhauer, who likened the resolution of dissonance into consonance to the satisfaction of the will.[55]) "The spiritual excitement created by such delays and hindrances—their emotional effect—depends precisely on the fact that dissonance strives for consonance, and unrest strives for repose, which will be withheld from it through the course of the composition and achieve fulfillment only at the conclusion."[56] There is the distinct implication that it is unnatural to deny the listener a consonant ending and, by extension, a morally uplifting experience. This was Walter's problem with truly atonal music: that it strips music of its harmonic development, and therefore the dissonances lead nowhere and have no meaning. If music has no meaning, it cannot produce its noble effect. Looked at in this light, atonal music takes on amoral characteristics, though Walter does not state this directly. Nevertheless, Walter's decision to criticize atonal composers—in print—at a time when the Nazis had also recently condemned them was perhaps injudicious.

Walter was, of course, not so naive as to believe that all one had to do to become a better person was to listen to music. But he did firmly believe that regular contact with music could, in some cases, actually improve a person's character. Further on in the essay, he tells a favorite story (he had recounted it to the London Music Club in 1933) in which an acquaintance in San Francisco who taught music to prison inmates claimed that most of the inmates he taught did not become repeat offenders when freed. Walter also placed particular importance on singing in harmony, which he found superior to "unisono" singing; he likened singing in parts to a society where different people come together for one purpose. How satisfying it was to sing in harmony with his schoolmates, he recalled, not only because of the "rich sound," but also because of the "moral satisfaction" he derived from joining with others so harmoniously.[57] (That "moral satisfaction" doubtless carried over into his collaborations with orchestras.)

By contrast, there are those who believe that, while music can be a force for good, it can just as easily be a force for evil; but Walter was very decidedly not of their number. His friend Thomas Mann, for instance, loved music but also distrusted it to a certain extent. As Katia Mann later recalled, Walter was upset after discovering in her husband's novel *Doktor Faustus* the contention that "music could signify something so sinister, so demoniacally dangerous, an out-and-out pact with the devil. He didn't want to hear of such a thing. Why music? For how can music, something as sublime as music, which suffers the little children to come unto it, endanger someone so? He wasn't prepared to acknowledge that at all."[58] Katia Mann clearly understood that, for Walter, music had to be a true gift from God and therefore could hardly be a false gift from the devil.

Inspired as he was by his belief in music's moral power, Walter was as much interested in matters on earth as the next person, and during the 1935 Salzburg Festival performances, which included the return of his *Don Giovanni* with Pinza, he was quick to perceive the growing relationship between the bass and his daughter Gretel, then the wife of Robert Neppach, whom she had married in 1934.[59] When Pinza first arrived in Salzburg that summer, Gretel greeted him somewhat distantly, showing little more interest in him than she had the previous summer. Pinza, however, having recently convinced his wife to agree to a divorce, allowed his feelings for her to blossom. "I soon knew that I could love her," he recalled, "but I said nothing, demanded nothing, and still was happy, so long as I could see her at rehearsals, at her parents' home, and have an occasional meal with her and her family in a restaurant."[60] Then one evening after a gala reception, Pinza summoned the courage to invite Gretel, along with Lotte and a Viennese music critic, for further entertainment at a night club. It proved a costly evening for Pinza, who ended up paying for the meal and two bottles of champagne; he also managed to burn his tuxedo when someone left a lighted cigarette on his chair. But these material encumbrances and accidents mattered little to Pinza, since he had at last received the impression that Gretel cared for him after all.[61]

Walter, it seems, not only knew of the relationship but approved. So he was especially upset when plans to bring Pinza to Amsterdam for concerts with the Concertgebouw did not appear to be working out, fearing that Pinza would hold him responsible. "I am afraid you have caused me a serious annoyance with Pinza," he wrote to Rudolf Mengelberg at the end of August. "Since he beamingly told my daughter that he would sing with me in

Amsterdam, I have to assume that you had made him an offer; and since he behaved much differently toward me yesterday in the last *Don Giovanni* performance, it seems to me that you let him know or suspect that the engagement had fallen through because of me."[62] Walter spent the rest of the letter stressing how important it was for him to maintain a happy working relationship with his collaborating artists. But resonating between the lines of this letter—barely legible and no doubt scribbled in haste—is the sense that, if he and Pinza somehow fell into discord, it could hurt Gretel as well. In the end Pinza did not come to Amsterdam, probably because a satisfactory financial agreement could not be reached; but whatever misunderstanding may have existed between Walter and Pinza was soon smoothed over, and Pinza recalled these years of working with Walter in Salzburg in only the happiest of lights.

During this same month, Walter was taking steps to regain some kind of regular home life. "Right now we are about to take a house in Vienna and, after years, to have a home again," Walter wrote to his brother. "I will hardly be able to spend more than three months of the year there, but gradually it will be more, and I have already gotten together my furniture, books, music, piano, etc. and, as long as I am in Vienna, my domestic life."[63] So after another trip to Amsterdam in October and a brief stint in Prague at the beginning of November conducting the Czech Philharmonic, Walter returned to Vienna to conduct six performances of *Orfeo ed Euridice*, as well as two performances of Schoenberg's *Gurre-Lieder* with the Vienna Symphony and the combined forces of the Singverein and the Bruckner Choir. But after these performances he had the luxury of returning not to a hotel but to a home, surrounded by his books and furniture, which was certainly a comforting way to round out 1935 and appeared to bode well for future years.

As 1936 began, it seemed that the pattern of his life was now firmly established: vacation in St. Moritz in January; February and part of March in Amsterdam; April, May, and June in Vienna, with little excursions throughout the first half of the year to Florence, Rome, Prague, and Paris. In May he once again cut several disks with the Vienna Philharmonic, the most notable of which was the world premiere recording of *Das Lied von der Erde* with Kerstin Thorborg and Charles Kullman, made from a live concert. As Walter's first recording of the masterpiece that he had premiered, it helped establish *Das Lied*—perhaps even more than the Ninth Symphony—as the Mahler work with which he is most closely associated. The sound quality is necessarily much inferior to that of Walter's later recordings of the song cycle, but the performance sizzles with tension, then dances with joy, and ultimately melts in poignancy. The American tenor Kullman fairly spits out the words of the opening "Trinklied," desperation ringing in his voice, and Thorborg's "Einsame im Herbst" aches with sorrowful simplicity. The rest of the songs are as finely etched, ending with Thorborg's haunting rendition of "Der Abschied." Both singers sound in excellent voice, and surrounding them is the glorious Vienna Philharmonic of the 1930s responding to Walter's supreme flexibility of tempo, offering subtly nuanced phrases and a great variety of articulation, always with a natural ease and colorful beauty of timbre.

Yet the first half of 1936 was not without one disturbing interruption to Walter's musical serenity. During one of his Viennese performances of *Tristan* in June, some Austrian Nazis threw stink bombs, sickening Anny Konetzni, who was singing Isolde. Thomas Mann, who had given a reading at the Musikverein earlier in the evening, went to the theater with the intention of catching the rest of the performance and arrived just in time for the third act and a "vile-smelling house. . . . The performance was continued," he wrote to his brother Heinrich, "ultimately with just the orchestra, for the Isolde, who had thrown up throughout the intermission, made only a lovely gesture of incapacity and did not rise from Tristan's corpse." Mann, of course, did not pull any punches, remarking that "now at least I know exactly what Nazism smells like: sweaty feet to a high power."[64] Walter deliberately chose to continue the performance, refusing to give the Nazis the satisfaction of ruining it, though naturally there were many frightened or simply nauseated people who had to leave.

As it turned out, the Nazis had also attacked other theaters that night as a thuggish demonstration of their brute force, and Walter soon received a death threat, apparently prompted by the announcement of a concert that he was to give on June 17 with Marian Anderson and the Vienna Symphony, in which the African-American contralto would sing Brahms's *Alt-Rhapsodie.* "To Nazi sympathizers," Anderson's most recent biographer has observed, "the choice of Anderson was an act of defiance of Nazi cultural policy by a Jewish musician."[65] As was his custom with all singers performing in oratorios or orchestral songs, Walter insisted that Anderson know her music by heart, which she accomplished on short notice. "Here was a departure for the Viennese," Herbert Peyser remarked in his review of the event, "and a landmark in their concert chronicles! 'What would Brahms have said if he could have known that his rhapsody would be sung by a Negress?' exclaimed one paper in amazement and (to its credit, be it said) in admiration. Well, Brahms would probably have been overjoyed could he have heard *how* she sang it—with what intuitive grasp of its poignantly human message, with what spiritual elevation, with what noble contempt of effect and outward show, with what complete subordination of herself to the ends of the composition."[66]

The next month an inner-ear infection began to plague Walter, preventing him from conducting at a Bruckner festival. By the end of the month he had rallied and was once again conducting in Salzburg. This season contained all of Walter's greatest Salzburg hits—*Don Giovanni*, *Tristan*, and *Orfeo ed Euridice*, as well as *Der Corregidor*, in which he once again won over potentially skeptical critics. Hermann Ullrich of the *Neue Freie Presse*, in particular, ended his rhapsodic review with the hope that this "beautiful work" would remain permanently in the festival program.[67]

As the Salzburg Festival came to an end, a new opportunity arose for Walter to ally himself even more closely with Austrian musical life. Erwin Kerber, a member of the Vienna Opera board and an influential person in the management of the Salzburg Festival, replaced Weingartner as director of the Staatsoper. He'd had his eye on this position for a while and managed to convince the aging conductor that it was time for him to go, a suggestion with which Weingartner complied without any protest, remaining at their disposal as a guest conductor. Prawy remarks knowingly: "It was the first time a change of Directors had been effected without animosity."[68] Kerber, whose skills lay mainly in administration, invited Walter to be his artistic director, and the gossip circulating in Vienna was that Chancellor von Schuschnigg had himself suggested to Franz and Alma Mahler Werfel that Walter be engaged. In any case, Walter eagerly accepted this "momentous offer."[69] At last he would occupy the offices that had belonged to Mahler some thirty years before, or at least he would share them with Kerber. It was a partnership that seems to have worked quite smoothly, for Kerber, as Walter recalled, was highly devoted to his conducting. Nevertheless, the responsibility of assuming artistic direction of such an illustrious institution—an opera company, with the myriad problems and complexities peculiar to that art form, which he knew all too well—nearly overwhelmed him. "A man of almost sixty, I once more took upon myself the responsibilities of a great operahouse."[70] For the next couple of years he would manage only sporadic appearances in other European countries, with the exception of Amsterdam, with which he continued to maintain close ties. Going to America was, of course, completely out of the question.

# TWELVE

# *Dies Irae*
## Vienna and Paris, 1936–1939

*They rush to their end*
*Who think themselves so strong in their existence . . .*
Wagner, *Das Rheingold*

By the time he celebrated his sixtieth birthday on September 15,
1936, Bruno Walter was firmly reestablished as a Viennese conductor, living in Vienna, conducting at the Vienna Opera and in
concerts with the Vienna Philharmonic. "Once Again in Austria"
was the heading for the last chapter of Paul Stefan's 1936 biography of Walter, the first book devoted to the conductor's life.[1] One
of Mahler's earliest biographers, Stefan had been involved with
Walter as early as 1910, when the author directed the musical activities of the Society for Art and Culture in Vienna, an organization that first made Walter's Eichendorff songs known to the public. In more recent times Stefan had devoted a short book to the
life of Arturo Toscanini, whose fame as an electrifying performer
was matched by his reputation for despising the forces of barbarism then threatening the world. What could be more natural
than that Stefan, as a tribute to Walter in his sixtieth year, should
turn his attention to the music world's other international symbol of sublime musical interpretation and the struggle against

tyranny? The biography is prefaced by contributions from Lotte Lehmann, Thomas Mann, and Stefan Zweig, and though it gives none of the rich detail provided in Walter's autobiography, it does offer the occasional informative morsel that no other source provides. As one might expect, the tone is laudatory throughout, with scarcely a word of criticism being breathed.

A similar tone pervades Walter's own biographical essay on Mahler, published in the same year by the same publisher, Herbert Reichner. The idea for the book had arisen almost immediately after Mahler's death; in fact, some elements of Walter's essay "Mahlers Weg," published in 1912, find their way into his modestly proportioned biography, which ends with an assessment of both the works and the personality behind them.[2] Though generous in his praise of his subject, Walter is not wholly uncritical. The first part of the book in particular is sprinkled with reminders of how difficult Mahler could be—there was the "violence with which he rebuffed my insufficient remarks"; he was "no educator: he was far too absorbed in himself, his work, his stormy inner life"; "his outward demeanour left much to be desired. . . . [H]e could be harsh and biting, intransigent and swift to anger."[3] The subject of the book, after all, was the man who had "a terrible side" (as Walter had once written to his parents), a man under whom Walter himself had borne his share of suffering.[4]

But most of the book shows us Walter's deep reverence for a master interpreter and a composer of genius. As a firsthand account of Mahler—and Walter makes no serious attempt to cover those areas and periods of his subject's life that were outside his personal experience—it offers many a valuable insight into the workings of a great mind. It also offers insights into Walter's own interpretive inheritance from his mentor. When reading, for example, that a "sense of something done for the first time . . . was the chief characteristic of his interpretations," we immediately recall that striving to create the first-time experience was one of Walter's constant goals as a conductor.[5] Moreover, we learn that for Walter, who freely acknowledged the invention and audacity of Mahler's creativity, the most important elements of his music were its beauty and depth: "The supreme value of Mahler's work lies not in the novelty of its being intriguing, daring, adventurous, or bizarre, but rather in the fact that this novelty was transfused into music that is beautiful, inspired, and profound."[6] It is a characteristic of Walter's interpretations of Mahler's music that they never sacrifice sublime beauty for the sake of vulgar effect.

The same year in which he paid his respects to one close friend, he had to endure the loss of another, for Ossip Gabrilowitsch passed away on September 14. Though they had long been separated geographically, Ossip and Clara had remained among Walter's closest friends, and Ossip's death, coming on the heels of Walter's recent depressing experiences, was almost more than he could bear. "An entire month has passed since our Ossip closed his eyes, and still I have not found the words to tell you how it affected me," he wrote to Clara in October. The world had lost one of the warmest-hearted people that Walter had ever known: "When I think of the best that life has given to me, I would name Ossip and you."[7] The only way to recover from the death of such a valued friend was once again to bury himself in his work.

Hardly had Walter begun his season in Vienna (which opened, not surprisingly, with *Tristan*) when it was off to Sweden and then to Amsterdam for an entire month. But by the middle of November Walter was back in Vienna and firmly entrenched in Vienna's musical life. A new production of *Don Carlo* with Alexander Kipnis, Hilde Konetzni, Franz Völker, and Elena Nikolaidi (making her debut) was the high point of December. Nikolaidi later recalled how Walter had listened to her audition and then promptly given her the score of *Don Carlo* with instructions to study it and return in a few days. "He was like a father to me," she remembered. "He was not arrogant; there was nothing pretentious."[8] Some excerpts from this production have survived in hardly bearable sound, but an intrepid listener—one who doesn't flinch at hearing Verdi sung in German—can gain some inkling of the sparkling production, its splendid cast, and the drama that Walter coaxed from Verdi's orchestral lines, lifting them out of the role of mere accompaniment to which they are too often relegated.[9] In this same month Walter also made more recordings with the Vienna Philharmonic, including Mozart's "Prague" Symphony and Beethoven's "Pastoral." While the Beethoven recording is superb, it is the "Prague" performance that really shows Walter and the Vienna Philharmonic at their best, with vigorous tempi, sighing phrases, and pure, limpid timbres similar to those of the finest period-instrument ensembles of recent times.

In February and March Walter returned again to Amsterdam, this time with a slight variation to his routine in the form of a concert production of Weber's *Euryanthe* with the Concertgebouw—the belated Amsterdam premiere. The reviewers praised the principals, who included Hans Hotter as Lysiart, but above all there was Walter, whom they regarded as the quintessential opera conductor, bringing them a new and untried work in which he was fully in his element. Some idea of the dramatic tension with which Walter seems to have infused the opera may be gleaned from his later performances of the overture, especially with the New York Philharmonic.[10]

Walter spent the rest of the spring mainly in Vienna, repeating recent productions of repertory operas such as *Don Carlo* and *Eugene Onegin* (though he managed to give concerts in Florence, Rome, and Prague). He also squeezed in a new production of Weber's *Oberon*, which he had performed at Salzburg, but which had not been performed in Vienna since 1891. The critic Josef Reitler, calling this forty-six-year gap an "archival slumber" of inordinate duration, seemed delighted with the production, Walter's conducting, and the cast, which included Helge Roswaenge and Hilde Konetzni.[11] In May there came several more recordings, mainly of Mozart, including the D Minor piano concerto with Walter as soloist. Here we finally have the opportunity to hear Walter conducting and playing a Mozart concerto, a feat that was perhaps more unusual in the first half of the twentieth century than it is today. In the best performances of classical or romantic concertos, there is certain to be a sympathetic meeting of minds between soloist and conductor, but the organic unfolding heard when the orchestra is led by the soloist is hard to match when two minds are at work. In this performance the Vienna Philharmonic follows Walter's articulation, phrasing, and rubato with breathtaking closeness—further evidence of the familiarity between Walter and the Viennese players. When he slows slightly for the second theme, the orchestra follows him exactly. And Walter's piano technique and light, pearly touch were still, in 1937, quite impressive. In the 1950s Pablo Casals once remarked that it was a pity Walter had given up his piano playing, for he judged Walter "a very great pianist."[12] Perhaps "very great" is too strong to describe Walter the pianist, but, as his recordings show, he was a sensitive player and had musical virtues that many full-time pianists could learn from.

After three performances of *Figaro* at the Maggio Musicale in Florence, Walter took the Vienna Philharmonic on tour in June, performing Mozart's Requiem in Paris at the Théâtre des Champs-Élysées. A live recording of this June 29 performance in fairly good sound has survived and, as with most live performances, there are a few strange occurrences. At the alto entrance in the "Tuba mirum," for example, which up to this point had been moving forward with a certain amount of urgency while maintaining its contemplative affect, Kerstin Thorborg can be heard slowing down, with Walter reluctantly pulling back the orchestra to match her. Elisabeth Schumann, if vulnerable to the criticism of having a small, chestless voice, sounds quite lovely in Mozart, though there are one or two shaky notes. Alexander Kipnis and the twenty-seven-year-old Anton Dermota (who was singing the part for the first time) fill out the quartet nicely, but the Vienna Staatsoper chorus wobbles from time to time. Nevertheless, the expressive phrasing and sprightly over-dotted rhythms wrought by this marvelous Mozart orchestra under Walter's guidance make the recording a compelling document in the history of pre-war classical performance practice.

Though 1937 might seem to have been a sort of "Mozartjahr" for Walter, it was his performances of Weber operas that elicited the most interest. That summer at Salzburg he conducted *Euryanthe* again, this time in a fully staged version. Articles about the production naturally made much of Weber's foreshadowing of Wagner; nevertheless, there was a certain under-lying current of skepticism in some of the reviews, to the effect that only someone of Walter's caliber, convinced as he was of the opera's worth, could make it a success. "Bruno Walter threw the entire romantic weight of his mu-sical personality into the balance in order to bring victory to this opera that he prizes so highly," commented the critic for the *Neues Wiener Journal*.[13] For his part, Walter was cautiously happy over his success, writing to Flagler that he was "not enough of an optimist to hope that from now [on] Euryan-the will become a favorite of the Opera-theaters; but perhaps this great suc-cess will induce other theaters to perform Euryanthe again and this already would give me a great joy and satisfaction."[14]

Walter's *Don Giovanni* had meanwhile turned into such a huge hit that it was performed again for the fourth summer in a row. Walter actually con-sidered the 1937 performance better than that of the previous year, remark-ing in the same letter to Flagler that "equal achievements are not obtainable so you have to make your choice to have better or worse ones; we chose to make them better and we worked hard for it." He courteously neglected to mention that the title role had been sung the previous year by Mariano Sta-bile (one of Toscanini's favorites) rather than Pinza, though we know that Walter always considered Pinza the ideal Don Giovanni. A complete record-ing of the 1937 Salzburg performance survives, and Pinza does indeed sound splendid, as do the other male singers.[15] Dino Borgioli, in particular, imbues the often weak-seeming Don Ottavio with a tender dignity. The female singers are perhaps not quite as sound vocally—Luise Helletsgruber as Donna Elvira seems to have been having a somewhat shrill evening. But there is a tautness of expression, in both the vocal lines and the orchestral ac-companiment, that lends the opera an eerie sense of inevitability. The drama set in motion in the first scene is carried through to the end—the inner scenes come off not as frivolous comic relief, as sometimes happens, but as events integral to the Don's approaching horrible fate.

Walter had barely a week to recover from the Salzburg Festival before returning to Vienna to conduct another performance of *Eugene Onegin* in early September. But the main event for the fall of 1937 was a new production of *Palestrina*. Walter had originally wanted to perform it the previous year but first had to spend some time convincing Hans Pernter, the Austrian Minister of Education, to include it in the schedule because, several years before, Pfitzner had apparently written a racist letter, declining to conduct in Salzburg. Eager to revive the opera and absolve his friend, Walter retrieved the letter from the files and, after reading it and noting its similarity to a letter sent by Sigrid Onegin, felt certain that both letters had been "dictated by the German authorities."[16] Although he eventually prevailed, Walter was still concerned that the production might give rise to polemics concerning Pfitzner, which would result in the kind of blending of art with politics that he had always taken such pains to avoid. In the event the project was shelved until the following year, and Walter, writing apologetically to Pfitzner in June 1937, had apparently decided that the composer's presence at the performance would not create any special difficulties and hoped that he would be able to be there on opening night.[17] As it turned out, Pfitzner was involved in staging and conducting a production of *Das Herz* in Frankfurt and was unable to attend. Some intriguing excerpts from the 1937 *Palestrina* have survived, revealing a brisker, more declamatory *Palestrina* with greater elasticity of tempo than is heard on more recent recordings.[18]

The other main events for what was—unknown to himself or his audience—to be his final season directing opera in Vienna were new productions of *Carmen* and Smetana's *Dalibor*. Though Walter had been conducting Bizet's popular opera since his early twenties, he had put off reviving it in Vienna because "no fascinating songstress with a fiery temperament was available for the title part."[19] But now Walter was confident that the Danish singer Elsa Brems, who had begun her career in Copenhagen singing the role, would appear sufficiently enticing. Since much depends on Carmen's acting abilility, it is naturally hard to judge from the few extant excerpts of Brems's performance whether she lived up to Walter's expectations, but in the surviving fragmentary recordings the production's overall intensity cuts through the prompter's audible barks and the obligatory surface noise.

Todor Mazaroff, another Walter discovery, comes off as an unusually compelling Don José, and the Vienna Philharmonic under Walter's guidance milks the ominous qualities of the score for all they are worth. The production's premiere, three days before Christmas, was attended by Chancellor Schuschnigg and various other prominent Viennese music-lovers, all of whom joined Walter for a celebration afterward at the Hotel Imperial. "There we all stayed until far into the night," Walter recalled in *Theme and Variations*, "*gemütlich* as only Vienna knew how to make such occasions— even in those late days."[20] And late days they proved to be—Smetana's *Dalibor* opened on February 26, little more than two weeks before the Anschluss. "This opera is a *Fidelio* with an unhappy ending," commented the critic for the *Neues Wiener Journal*, blithely unaware of the prophetic overtones these words would come to have.[21] For *Fidelio*'s message of brotherhood and freedom would soon be meaningless in Vienna.

Up to this point, however, it had been business as usual, with Walter and the Vienna Philharmonic busily turning out more recordings, including a notable rendering of Mozart's "Jupiter" Symphony. Surely the most important item, however, was the first complete recording of Mahler's Ninth, taken from a live performance at the Musikverein on January 16. In later years Walter was highly critical of this monumental effort, one of his last prewar recordings with his old friends, and was upset when RCA Victor reissued the recording in 1954 without his knowledge—he learned about it through reading the *New York Times*. In an acrid letter to George Marek he criticized the company's lack of courtesy in going ahead with the release without consulting him first. "You will have noticed the musical and technical shortcomings of this recording," he wrote. "The turbulent political happenings of March 1938 in Austria interfered drastically with my ability to concentrate on the merits of the test pressings then forwarded to me to Holland and made it very difficult for me to come to a definite approval or disapproval."[22] Marek countered by praising the recording and sent Walter a copy, suggesting that Walter might get a different impression if he listened to it again. Walter seemed somewhat mollified in his reply, though he still complained about the audible coughing, the inescapable pitfall of any live recording.[23]

Though it is understandable that Walter was distressed at not being consulted, any enthusiast of Mahler's Ninth must side with Marek on this one. The sound, aided by the Musikverein's caressingly vibrant acoustics, is remarkably good for a live recording from 1938. As for musical shortcomings,

Walter may have been thinking of the occasional flubbed note or of those tense moments in the Rondo-Burleske when the frenetic pace threatens to make the piece spin out of control. But for the rest, this earliest recorded rendition holds its own with the numerous more recent, stereo recordings and has rarely been out of the catalogue. As the first movement opens, the listener cannot help being moved by the sheer beauty of the strings' sighing figures. As it proceeds, builds, and finally unwinds, there is languidness and urgency moving as one—the effect is simply mesmerizing, and throughout the long movement (here actually under twenty-five minutes), Walter maintains this delicate balance so that one is somehow simultaneously soothed and stirred. Likewise the second movement is at once robust and questioning, with the character of each section sharply delineated, and although Walter's Tempo II is perhaps a bit more *più mosso* than *poco mosso*, the result is an exhilarating, careening waltz; the supple orchestra is more than up to the challenges posed by this dazzling tempo. The third movement is certainly *trotzig* ("brave" or "defiant") enough, and it is easy to imagine members of the audience dizzily holding on to their seats to keep from fainting in the aisles, so intense is the articulation and dramatic the gestures. There are uneasy moments near the beginning, but no real train wreck occurs, and in some ways these hints of averted disaster add to the performance's effectiveness. By the time the section marked "Mit grosser Empfindung" is reached, order has been restored, and the foreshadowing of the last movement's theme—in essence, a "turn"—is indeed played with great expression. When this theme comes to fruition in the last movement, the Viennese strings probably had no need for Walter's famous admonition to sing, for they sing freely as a matter of course, and the turn is at once expressive and ornamental. In this performance, too, the lines are so well balanced, being both independent and interconnected, that the effect is almost that of a Renaissance motet.

Mahler's Ninth had enjoyed its very first performance, of course, under Walter, and he would give one more world premiere in Vienna before taking his enforced leave of the city. One of Schoenberg's students, Egon Wellesz (who later became one of the most wide-ranging musicologists of the twentieth century), had written a suite based on a play that Walter was particularly fond of: Shakespeare's *The Tempest*. Entitled *Prosperos Beschwörungen*, the piece was introduced to the world by Walter and the Vienna Philharmonic on February 19, 1938. It offered an ingenious fusion of styles—with passages reminiscent of Schoenberg's twelve-tone works (such as the fugal section in the first movement), Stravinsky's *Le Sacre du printemps* (in the "Caliban" movement), and late Austro-German romanticism—that clearly pleased Walter, who ordinarily avoided atonality and savage roughness. According to Wellesz, Walter prepared the score with characteristic diligence: "Each time we met," he wrote, "Walter would say to me: 'Now I have learned 30 bars by heart,' the next time 'I know the first movement by heart.' When he came to the first rehearsal he hardly had to use the score."[24]

The piece was well received, and Walter included it again in his concerts with the Concertgebouw. But, as Walter himself put it, "the sands in the hourglass were running low," and the triumphs of art could hardly impede the brute menace that was approaching Austria.[25] After the fateful meeting with Hitler at Berchtesgaden on February 12, in which Schuschnigg agreed to accept the Austrian Nazi leader Arthur Seyss-Inquart into his cabinet as minister of the interior, anxiety began to spread rapidly through Vienna. Walter, soon to leave for Amsterdam, was asked by Schuschnigg himself via the theater director Ernst Lothar to sign a three-year contract with the Staatsoper. Meanwhile Walter was also asked to cable Toscanini in New York to secure him for the 1938 Salzburg Festival. He was stunned by Toscanini's refusal, sending him more cables and finally a long letter, assuring his old colleague and friend that "the chancellor defends Austria like a true Knight of the Holy Spirit," and begging him not to "leave Austria in case it goes its own independent road."[26] Toscanini, of course, had already expressed reluctance to return to Salzburg when Furtwängler had been engaged to conduct there the previous summer, and by this time the tensions between Walter and Furtwängler had grown unbearable for Walter, as he explained with undiplomatic candor to Toscanini: "Furtwängler's atmosphere is—at least for me—politically, personally, and artistically—intolerable; and particularly at Salzburg. . . . Furtwängler has one sole idea: himself, his glory, his success; he is a man of talent, of personal weight but bad-hearted, which expresses itself even in his music-making. I have now in Vienna had new proofs of how bad he is because of his 'intrigues' against me."[27] But for all Walter's pleas, Toscanini, politically the shrewder of the two conductors, remained adamant in his refusal.

Despite gloomy predictions from other colleagues, such as Bronislaw Huberman, Walter retained his faith in Chancellor Schuschnigg, even after he had made what were clearly perilous concessions to Hitler. Indeed, soon after his return from Berchtesgaden, Schuschnigg seemed to undergo a transformation; the shy, cultured man suddenly became the "lion of Vienna."[28] On February 24 he gave a stirring radio address, declaring that

Austria would not budge another inch, crying "Thus far but no further!" Walter, preparing to conduct a concert with the Czech Philharmonic, listened to the speech from his hotel room in Prague, almost regretting that he had to leave to get to the concert hall. He was convinced that Schuschnigg's speech had inflamed the Austrian people and that, had the planned plebiscite actually taken place, "Nazism in Austria would have been swept away by the wave of enthusiasm for Schuschnigg." Two days later, at the premiere of *Dalibor*, the audience rose to greet the Chancellor as he entered his box before the second act. So Walter left for the Netherlands in an optimistic mood the following day, hardly thinking that he would not return.[29]

Walter went about his business in Amsterdam as usual, performing with the Concertgebouw in a series of concerts that included, on March 17, 1938, the world premiere of Ernst Krenek's Second Piano Concerto with the composer as soloist. All the while, the political atmosphere in Vienna had been growing ever more ominous. Schuschnigg had announced that the plebiscite would take place on March 13, and through telephone conversations with Lotte back in Vienna, Walter and Elsa learned of numerous demonstrations for and against Schuschnigg. But, as Walter later recalled, they still waited trustingly for the plebiscite, holding out hope that the Austrian people would show their revulsion for Hitler in a public election. On March 11, however, Walter arrived home after a rehearsal to be informed by Elsa that Hitler had issued an ultimatum and that Schuschnigg had, after an initial show of defiance, caved in at last. Walter and Elsa spent the afternoon and evening listening to the painful farewell speech by Schuschnigg, the addresses by President Miklas and Seyss-Inquart as the new chancellor, and the news of German troops advancing on Austria, occupying one town after another. Walter felt as though he were witnessing not so much the death of Austria as her horrible disfigurement. "If you think of the most beautiful woman, whose beauty has been destroyed by smallpox or a more terrible disease and now she wanders about like a caricature of herself, resembling herself but giving horror at the same time—this is the fate of Austria and Vienna in particular," he wrote several weeks later to Harry Harkness Flagler. As the letter continues, his command of English grammar, usually impressive, nearly gives out. "I sat the night from 11th to 12th March on the Radio, I heard the incredibly terrible news I felt the growing tragedy, I listened to the change of an amiable voice in Vienna dialect to the triumphant sound of Berlin 'Jargon' and of the Vienna Valses that filled the intervals between the historic news to the Prussian Military marches, of the old Austrian hymn to the 'Horst Wessel-Lied,' the banal and profane hymn of the Third Reich."[30]

Walter and Elsa now became instant exiles from the country that had become their home; they had sent an enthusiastic telegram to Schuschnigg after his speech of February 24 and felt certain that, though they might be permitted to enter, they would never be able to leave. Walter resigned his position at the Staatsoper from a distance, and in an eerie echo of 1933 the newspapers that had so recently lionized Walter in Vienna now began to issue snide remarks instead. "Bruno Walter will not be seen wielding the baton in the awakened Vienna Staatsoper. This once 'representative' artistic messenger of Austria, who characteristically stays in Amsterdam, will move his activities to the countries in which his protector, Arturo Toscanini, also performs German music in an un-German way," the *Neues Wiener Journal* crowed, insulting him, Toscanini, and the entire Netherlands in one fell swoop.[31]

At this point, however, Walter was hardly concerned with such Nazi-induced journalistic abuse. Not only had he left most of his worldly possessions in Vienna, but, far worse, Lotte was still there and had been arrested along with a group of friends with whom she had been spending the evening, simply because, as Walter told Flagler in the same letter, "every gathering was suspect and the housekeepers denounced people just to prove sympathy with the conquerors." The news of Lotte's arrest had been announced on the radio during the intermission of one of Walter's Concertgebouw concerts, and though he managed to finish the concert, as soon as it ended, he immediately telephoned Erwin Kerber back in Vienna to see what he could discover. Then he called Gretel's husband, Robert Neppach, from whom she had not yet completely separated, and asked him to travel from Berlin (where he was living) to Vienna to work with Kerber in effecting Lotte's release. Though Kerber managed to locate the police station to which Lotte had been taken, neither he nor Neppach was able to contact her. Meanwhile Walter still had concerts to conduct in The Hague, Monte Carlo, and Nice, and he recounted how he and Elsa spent the next two weeks in a state of unrelieved anxiety: "My days and nights crawled along in a torment of waiting which would have been considered exaggerated cruelty even in Dante's infernal circles."[32] Finally, after two weeks, Lotte called her parents' hotel in Nice to tell them that she had been set free.

But there was as yet the difficult matter of getting Lotte safely out of Vienna. Walter learned that people were still able to travel, provided they could prove their trip had a professional basis, and luckily Lotte's passport still stated her profession as that of a singer. So Walter asked a concert manager in Prague to engage her for a song recital and was overwhelmed with gratitude when the "splendid fellow went so far as to have large placards announce the fictitious recital in the streets of Prague." Then, when her exit permit was delayed, the agent sent a letter threatening that "non-compliance with her obligations would have serious consequences." An agent in Zurich constructed a similar fabrication, thus opening both borders, and in the end Lotte chose the Swiss frontier in order to meet Walter and Elsa in Lugano, where they were presently staying.[33] "For two weeks Lotte has been out of the hell that Austria is now," Walter wrote to Clara Gabrilowitsch at the end of April; "we waited for her in Switzerland, at the train station in Lugano, and it was tremendously moving to embrace her after all the hardships she had lived through." As relieved as Walter was to have Lotte back safe and sound, he was now concerned for Gretel, who had to return with her husband to Berlin, where he was employed as an architect and sometime film director. "We suffer from tormented thoughts," he confessed to Clara, "knowing that she is in Germany."[34]

With all this going on, Walter attempted to regain some semblance of a normal life. He had received invitations to conduct from all over Europe, as he mentioned to both Clara and Flagler, though few from the United States—a circumstance he found somewhat puzzling. Still suffering from the strain of the last weeks and feeling even more in need of rest between engagements than usual, he accepted invitations only from France, the Netherlands, England, and Scandinavia. He and Elsa took a furnished apartment in Zurich and tried to make plans for the future, still hoping to recover a few of their possessions. Their housekeeper, who had accompanied Lotte out of Vienna, had brought some of their clothes, as did one of their maids who joined them later. A friend managed to get a portion of Walter's music across the Czech frontier, but he and Elsa still had to resign themselves to losing almost everything they'd left behind in Vienna. The fate of Walter's Cadillac turned out to be so preposterous that it bordered on black humor; it was confiscated and given to a released criminal now made *Gauleiter*. As Walter recalled ironically, "My car served the highly meritorious and qualified old party member and provided him with the comfort befitting his station."[35]

By the end of April Walter had resumed a routine that resembled his usual spring conducting schedule, directing concerts and a performance of *Fidelio* in Paris, as well as recording Schumann's Symphony no. 4 with the

London Symphony Orchestra and Haydn's Symphony no. 92 with the Paris Conservatory Orchestra. Recorded collaborations between Walter and the splendid Parisian orchestra are rare, and this sparkling Haydn performance contains perhaps crisper phrasing, with fewer "sighs," than Walter's Viennese recordings of Haydn and Mozart from this period. There is, nevertheless, a superbly polished exuberance to this Haydn symphony—the musicians seem to be following Walter's baton in every minute tempo fluctuation and inflection. After he finished in Paris, Walter was originally to have conducted the Vienna Opera in Florence in a production of *Euryanthe*, but this was clearly impossible now, and Walter intended to withdraw from the production. But the director of the festival was so desirous of having Walter conduct that he chose to change the programming and have two choral works—Beethoven's *Missa solemnis* and Brahms's *Deutsches Requiem*—performed by Italian artists instead.

Traveling to Italy, however, or indeed anywhere, was beginning to present serious problems for Walter and Elsa, since Germany had declared that Austria no longer existed and therefore their Austrian passports were invalid. Without citizenship they could neither travel nor stay in one place. To go to Florence from Paris, Walter had obtained a special permit from the Italian consulate in Paris, and years earlier he and his family had been granted the right to live in Switzerland, though they were not Swiss citizens. Since he hoped to resume his conducting activities outside Switzerland in October, Walter would somehow have to acquire new citizenship. Now a homeless musician, Walter felt, as he wrote to a friend in June, "like the bird in the poem from 'Des Knaben Wunderhorn' who pipes and trills to the end of the world."[36]

One plan he entertained was to apply for citizenship in the tiny country of Monte Carlo, known primarily for its casinos. Having lost the Salzburg Festival (though certainly there must have been many who felt that the Salzburg Festival had lost Walter), he thought perhaps he might interest the casinos' management in creating a musical and dramatic festival similar to Salzburg's and that, as a result, the government might be willing to offer him special treatment when it came to acquiring citizenship. Walter was naturally quite aware of the disparity between gambling and high culture; when describing his plan in his autobiography, he was quick to assert that "the erection of a new great operahouse on the rocks of Monaco or in the fine grounds near the Casino would have made some of the sinful riches of the gambling establishment available for a noble use."[37] Walter's plan was met with some interest but eventually foundered; he neither started a festival nor gained citizenship. As the summer dragged on, with no definite prospects for acquiring citizenship, he began to wonder how he would be able to continue his professional life.

Though the Walters' long-term plans were necessarily vague, a solution to their immediate need for a roof over their heads presented itself in Lugano, Switzerland, where Walter, Elsa, and Lotte had taken a villa with windows looking out upon Lake Lugano below and the Tessin Mountains above. The beauty of their new dwelling and the relocation of Gretel and her husband in Zurich were sources of joy, but Walter could not completely rid himself of the "wretched thought of being condemned to stay permanently on the shoal on which I seemed to have run aground."[38] In the meantime, however, a new festival had been organized in Lucerne, where Toscanini conducted a hand-picked orchestra that included members of the Busch Quartet; hearing Toscanini's rendering of the *Siegfried Idyll* in a park near Wagner's villa, Triebschen, was especially memorable for Walter. He himself conducted a highly praised concert of Weber, Schubert, and Wagner, though he and the festival's other conductors (Ansermet, Gravina, Busch, and Mengelberg) directed an orchestra composed of members from the Orchestre de la Suisse Romande and the Luzerner Kursaal-Orchester, and the favoritism shown toward Toscanini on the part of the festival's organizers did not escape the notice of at least one critic.[39]

Rescue from the fate that Walter had feared was close at hand. At the beginning of September Walter received a letter from Georges Huismans, the Directeur Général des Beaux-Arts in Paris, telling him that, having learned of his efforts to become a citizen of Monte Carlo, the French government was prepared to make him a citizen of France. Walter gratefully telegraphed his acceptance and left at once for Paris, whereupon he and Elsa were granted citizenship in a matter of weeks. "We now have regular French passports," he wrote to Rudolf Mengelberg at the end of September; "you can imagine how radiant we feel and how happy we are."[40] In return for this inestimable service, Walter was prepared to put himself at the disposal of France's musical scene as much as possible, and for a time he and Huismans even toyed with the idea of having a huge yearly music festival in Paris to be called the "Fêtes internationales à Paris," a plan which, with the Nazi occupation of France, unfortunately turned out to be little more than a pleasant fantasy on the part of Walter and Huismans.[41]

Armed with his new nationality, Walter could now begin his season in earnest. He set off first for London, where he made several recordings with the London Symphony Orchestra, including Corelli's Concerto Grosso in G Minor (the "Christmas Concerto"), one of the few recordings of Walter directing a baroque work. Though the somewhat literal interpretation of the rhythms in the opening Vivace, and the unadorned cadences throughout, might sound plodding and unimaginative today, the performance still carries a certain sense of baroque phrasing, and it is intriguing to think that Walter might himself be playing the harpsichord continuo, as he often did in Handel and Corelli concertos.

He then embarked on a tour of the Balkans and later recalled that he had agreed to this tour partly out of a desire to see Greece, especially Athens. In the end he saw more of Greece than he'd bargained for: his flight from Athens ran into some severe weather, and the plane, struck by lightning, foundered somewhere in the Peloponnesus, though Walter and the rest of the passengers were miraculously unharmed. After this little adventure, which left him in some doubt as to whether he would ever want to fly again, he returned to Paris by train, where he immersed himself in the Parisian concert scene, his activities culminating in a recital with the violinist Jacques Thibaud and two performances of the Verdi Requiem.[42]

The absolute necessity of avoiding Germany, even by air, led to further travel adventures in November. Walter returned to Amsterdam for two concerts and was then scheduled to embark on a tour of Scandinavia, to conduct concerts in Copenhagen, Stockholm, and Oslo. But since the train went through Germany and was thus out of the question and the only other obvious way to get from Amsterdam to Stockholm was to fly over Nazi Germany, Walter decided to make a detour to London and then travel on a small steamer that made regular trips from London to Gothenburg. This proved perhaps the roughest sea voyage of Walter's life, yet he still found it preferable to flying over Germany.[43] And the journey's perils were more than counterbalanced by the happy memories he retained of his concerts in Stockholm—in particular, his meetings with Prince Eugene, brother of Sweden's king, who had impressed Walter as a highly cultured man when they had previously met in Salzburg. It was at one of the prince's parties that Walter made the acquaintance of important Swedish politicians who later managed to get entry permits for Walter's brother and sister, allowing them to settle in Gothenburg.

By the time Walter returned to Lugano, it was already the middle of December, and he and Elsa were permitted some weeks' rest before they started traveling again, stopping in Paris for a few days before Walter took the Orchestre de la Société Philharmonique de Paris on a tour through Strasbourg, Lyon, and Geneva for concerts of Mozart. Then he headed for London (conducting concerts with both the BBC Symphony Orchestra and the London Philharmonic) and on to Amsterdam for a substantial number of concerts that lasted until well into February. Through the many dramatic upheavals of the last several years, the Concertgebouw had been a source of continuity in Walter's musical life. Back in the fall of 1938 Walter and Rudolf Mengelberg had made plans for Walter to conduct in the 1939–40 season, but with Nazis looming in the distance, they both must have had some presentiment that this would be Walter's last appearance in Amsterdam until after the war.

Yet even without the sense of impending doom in Europe, Walter would no doubt have been eager to renew his ties in America, which he had been forced to sever temporarily upon assuming artistic directorship of the Vienna Staatsoper. The opportunity came when the NBC Symphony Orchestra, in its second season, invited him to direct five of its Saturday night concerts in March and April. Most people, Walter included, have assumed that the orchestra, with its players selected and drilled by the formidable Artur Rodzinski, had been created expressly for Toscanini. In fact, Samuel Chotznikoff (RCA president David Sarnoff's go-between) allowed Toscanini to believe this, but NBC was all the while planning to use the orchestra for other programs as well.[44] The orchestra nevertheless had already become known as "the Toscanini orchestra" when Walter came to conduct in 1939, though the reviewers of his concerts respectfully refrained from comparisons between the two maestros and confined themselves to speaking of the merits—which they thought were plentiful—of Walter's efforts.[45]

The first concert, devoted entirely to Mozart, received perhaps the most enthusiastic reviews of Walter's NBC concerts from his old chronicler Olin Downes. Mozart's Divertimento in B-flat Major (K. 287) "could hardly have been interpreted more charmingly," while the Symphony no. 40 in G Minor was "fully in the tradition, yet so vitalized, and every phrase so instinct with comprehension and feeling, that it communicated an entirely fresh impression"; the Piano Concerto in D Minor, with Walter playing, elicited the comment that perhaps "only a conductor capable of the double task should be allowed to interpret Mozart concerti." Overall, Downes felt that Walter's debut with the NBC Symphony was one of its most "distinctive" concerts, and that the music "flashed and soared, without suspicion of the weight or cumbrousness of the mortal coil."[46] Since these concerts were radio broadcasts, many of them were privately recorded and have since been released on small labels, so we may actually compare Walter's NBC performance of the D minor piano concerto with his Viennese performance of two years earlier. The differences are striking, to say the least, particularly in the first movement, which in the earlier performance is more lyrical, alternating between agitation and reflection. The NBC performance is only slightly brisker in tempo but with a rather driving character from beginning to end—the strings use noticeably more vibrato and sometimes even sound as though they were pushing the conductor-soloist ahead. The second movement contains perhaps the closest meeting of minds between Walter and the orchestra and is not so different from the Vienna performance. And the last movement, taken at quite a clip in both performances, still has a sense of space in the Viennese account, while the NBC version borders on the frenetic. It is tempting, of course, to attribute these differences to the conducting styles of Walter and the NBC's regular fiery maestro, but we must consider the possibility that Walter himself, under the influence of what he often referred to as New York City's "allegro furioso," was mostly responsible for the performance's high-wired character. The bone-dry acoustics of Studio 8-H in Radio City, especially when compared with the warm resonance of Vienna's Musikvereinssaal, might also have been a contributing factor.

Walter's remaining four concerts were also fairly well received. The programs included Berlioz's *Symphonie fantastique*, along with the "Corsaire" Overture and excerpts from *La Damnation de Faust*; Brahms's First Symphony; and works by Weber, Wagner, and Haydn, as well as Daniel Gregory Mason's *Suite after English Folksongs*. Walter's final concert was devoted to Mahler's First Symphony. This, too, has been issued commercially and is notable for being Walter's first recorded performance of Mahler's "Titan" Symphony. While it is perhaps not as coherent, in terms of either musical expression or basic instrumental ensemble, as his two later studio recordings with the New York Philharmonic (1954) and the Columbia Symphony Orchestra (1961), it does contain many marvelously vigorous moments.

If the critics refrained from comparing Walter with the NBC's regular conductor, the musicians, for the most part staunchly loyal to Toscanini, could not help drawing comparisons, some of them invidious. William Carboni, a violist who played in both the New York Philharmonic and the NBC orchestra, recalled that Toscanini in his later years was afraid that his performances would get "draggy and heavy like Bruno Walter's."[47] Another violist, Nicolas Moldavan, described Walter's Mozart Symphony no. 40 in G

Minor as "graceful and gay," as opposed to Toscanini's version, which was "*molto drammatica*."[48] Then there is the famous story wherein Walter asked the strings to play with shorter bowings in Mozart's Fortieth, and when the musicians finally complied, Toscanini rushed furiously from the room—though the rumor that the two conductors never spoke to one another again is patently untrue.[49] Indeed, near the end of his life Toscanini reportedly told the Italian pianist Mario Delli Ponti that Walter's recording of the Fortieth (presumably that with the New York Philharmonic) was better than his own.[50] But Toscanini did not conduct Mahler, and one gets the sense that, in this work at least, the musicians were wholeheartedly committing themselves to Walter's interpretation. Instead of maintaining the sharply etched, forward-moving lines that Toscanini favored and that creep into some of Walter's performances with the NBC from time to time, the strings bend and inflect in an almost Viennese manner. Walter's countless subtle tempo changes are smoothly executed, and there is no lack of fire, particularly in the last movement.

All this time, while Americans were happily listening to the NBC playing over the radio, Hitler's troops were menacing Poland. Walter had been invited by Hans Kindler to take over one of his concerts with the National Symphony in Washington, D.C., and the headlines in the *Washington Post* on the very day that Walter was to conduct, April 12, screamed of desperate attempts by different countries to stem the tide of Nazism. Walter and Elsa and Lotte, perhaps seeing the headlines, began to fear that war would break out at any moment and that they would be separated from Gretel, still in Europe. But when they set sail for London on April 15, Europe was merely simmering, not yet boiling, and they were able to reunite with Gretel in Paris in May. Later Walter recalled this last time his whole family was together— "made radiant by all the charms of spring"—with especial wistfulness.[51]

During this time in Paris Walter made his only studio recording of Berlioz's *Symphonie fantastique*, with the Paris Conservatory Orchestra. He had programmed the work very early in his career; it was one of Mahler's favorite pieces, and Walter traced distinct similarities between Berlioz and Mahler, especially in Berlioz's "daring use of bizarre and grotesque means for the purpose of reaching the utmost keenness of expression."[52] Certainly there is no absence of expression in this 1939 recording, yet it also contains an overlay of refinement characteristic of the French orchestra and is quite different from Walter's live performances with the New York Philharmonic, at least one of which (from 1954) has been preserved. The combination of passion with restraint is particularly effective in the first movement, where it serves to highlight the general feeling of schizophrenia that persists throughout the movement. Walter's "Un Bal" movement is gentle, wistful, with a Viennese lilt, and a review of his performance with the NBC Symphony back in April criticized just this aspect of Walter's interpretation, calling his conception of "Un Bal" as a sentimental ländler "stylistically indefensible."[53] In the hands of the elegant Paris Conservatory Orchestra, however, the effect is hardly one of oversentimentality, but more a foretaste of sad times to come. The same may be said for the "Scène aux champs," an epitome of stylish exquisiteness. The last two movements are naturally more explosive, though never bordering on being out of control. The "Dies irae" theme in particular is played with an eerie sense of inevitability that sets one's hair on end—and days of wrath were inexorably approaching Walter.

It is sadly fitting that Walter's last European recording before the war should convey such sober sentiments, for all during this time he and Elsa had been expecting a catastrophe. While in Washington they had even obtained an American entry visa for Gretel so that, should war break out, she would be able to come to America with the rest of his family. But what actually happened to the Walter family in the second half of 1939 was more horrible than anything they could have imagined.

Gretel, during the last year, had been ostensibly living with her husband in Zurich, though she was still seeing Ezio Pinza whenever the opportunity arose and had been trying to prevail upon Neppach to grant her a divorce. Pinza recalled how he saw her briefly in Salzburg, and how one day she told him she had to go to Zurich to see her husband, who wanted urgently to speak with her. According to Pinza, before she boarded the train, she expressed some fear that they would not see each other again but reassured the alarmed Pinza that it was merely a "woman's whim."[54] On August 18 she and her family visited Arturo Toscanini in Kastanienbaum, near Lucerne— Toscanini recalled her beautiful smile on that occasion[55]—and then she returned to her husband. The following day Pinza received a telephone call from Toscanini's daughter, Wally, who told him that Neppach had shot Gretel as she slept, then turned the gun on himself. Pinza made the long drive from Salzburg to Zurich to find Gretel already dead and met Walter at his hotel, whereupon Walter came up to him and placed an arm around his shoulders. The funeral, he recalled, was attended only by the Walters, Toscanini and his daughter Wally, and himself. "The next day I drove the Walters to their home in Lugano, the urn with Greta's ashes in my car, the man I had grown to love like a father sitting beside me, silent with grief."[56] While the Swiss police at first announced only that a German citizen had shot his wife and then himself, Walter was informed almost immediately, receiving the shattering news while he was in his study, preparing to conduct a concert for the Lucerne Festival.[57] Completely unable to perform, he asked Toscanini to substitute for him and rushed off to Zurich, later canceling the remainder of his upcoming appearances in Lucerne.

During his many unsettling experiences of the past several years, Walter had been able to take refuge in his work, his art being his consolation. But Gretel's sudden and shocking death left him bereft of the will to carry on, even for the sake of music. "She brought light and joy into our life and now it has become dark and sad," he wrote to the Manns on August 30; "I do not know how I can make music when my soul is in such a dismal, painful condition."[58] By the middle of September Walter, feeling no better, telegrammed Rudolf Mengelberg that his nerves would not allow him to work. Then, in a letter following, he promised his old friend to try his best to resume his activities, though he still wondered whether he would be able to make music. "Here my good intentions are not sufficient, therefore the grace [of God] is needed," he wrote resignedly.[59] Indeed, he was having difficulty thinking about the future at all, as he told Alma Mahler: "I, who until now have lived only for the present and for the future, have no other thoughts or feelings than to gaze back at the past. That is where everything beautiful, noble, and charming used to be."[60]

But some thought for the future was imperative, since Walter and Elsa were beginning to have serious doubts about staying in Europe. Paris was now in constant danger of being bombed, forcing Walter to cancel any tentatively planned performances there. Though he toyed with the idea of going to London, it seemed best simply to bid Europe goodbye and head for New York, where he was to conduct concerts at the beginning of the next year. He had only dim hopes of returning to Europe in the spring. "How good that your children are still so young," he wrote to Rudolf Mengelberg, a couple of weeks before leaving for New York. "Perhaps they will become leaders and helpers in a new, better Europe." And then, knowing that this might be his last letter to Mengelberg for some time, he concluded by saying, "In this hope, I shake your hand and call to you 'auf Wiedersehen.'"[61]

On November 1 Walter, with Elsa and Lotte, boarded the *Rex* in Genoa and set sail for New York.

# THIRTEEN

# Guest Conductor on Two Coasts

## New York and Los Angeles, 1939–1947

*. . . for the miracle—*
*I mean our preservation—few in millions*
*Can speak like us; then wisely, good sir, weigh*
*Our sorrow with our comfort.*
Shakespeare, *The Tempest*

"I am thankful for the sun's warmth, which beautifies life in this part of America," Walter wrote the day after Christmas to Chaplain Helmut Fahsel, who had presided over Gretel's funeral in Lugano.[1] And indeed, living in sunny Beverly Hills, where he and Elsa and Lotte had rented a house on North Crescent Drive, was having a salubrious effect on Walter's spirits. But, even more reassuring, he was beginning to conduct again; for not long after his arrival in California, he opened the Los Angeles Philharmonic's season with five concerts—the first time he had raised his baton since Gretel's death. "Next week I shall have my first concert after the most tragic event of my life and I will do my very best to make music as I have done before. But naturally it will be very exciting for me," he wrote to Harry Harkness Flagler near the end of November.[2] His appearances with the Los Angeles Philharmonic were exciting for the audience as well, to judge by Isabel Morse

Jones's review of the fourth program, which she called "one of the outstanding concerts of its history." Throughout the next several years Jones would remain one of Walter's staunchest supporters, and, at this particular concert at least, her feelings were obviously shared by the audience. "With a spontaneity seldom seen here, the listeners rose after the rapturous performance of Beethoven's First Symphony and stood applauding the conductor in company with the orchestra. This sleepy old pueblo woke up and cheered."[3] One can't help wondering how many members of the audience knew that these concerts were, in effect, the beginning of Walter's musical rebirth, and whether such knowledge helped fuel their display of appreciation.

So, although nothing could ever fully assuage the pain Walter was to carry with him for the rest of his life, he was beginning to live with it. And being able to make music again was, in a sense, bringing him closer to Gretel's spirit. "I feel, more deeply than ever before, music as a connection to the divine," he wrote to Fahsel, "and I know that I don't deceive myself when through it I feel myself nearer to my Gretel."[4] But despite his increasing spiritual solace and his calling himself an optimist even in the face of unspeakable tragedy, there were still many earthly burdens to bear. For one thing, as he wrote in the same letter to Fahsel, even with his new, comfortable existence in America, he felt very close to the suffering of humanity back in Europe. For another, Elsa was not coping quite as well as her husband and could hardly bring herself to speak of what had taken place, even with him. In fact, in these next few years of Walter's life, as he traveled back and forth between the East and West coasts, stopping in the middle of the country in places like Kansas City to thrill audiences that had never heard him before, the dark echoes of events across the ocean would never completely leave him.

Since his high-altitude misadventure over Greece, Walter had not been fond of air travel, but he might have found it a welcome distraction from brooding on the past and the Europe that every day seemed more and more lost to him. Certainly he began a series of trips back and forth across the United States that would rival his treks between Vienna and Amsterdam in previous years. The year 1940 opened with a month-long period of rest, during which he took some time out to read Mann's *Lotte in Weimar*. Walter was deeply impressed by the work, describing it to Mann as "pure poetry, innermost beauty, beauty of the sort that could move Goethe to tears."[5] It is tempting to think that, having been so deeply moved by the novel, Walter left for New York to conduct five performances with the NBC Symphony in an especially inspired frame of mind. His rendition of Bruckner's Fourth Symphony, which dominated the opening concert, was superb in both its dramatic power and its lyricism.[6] With the NBC, Walter took somewhat brisker tempi than on his later commercial recording with the Columbia Symphony Orchestra, giving the longer movements a strong sense of forward motion but still capturing the Brucknerian spaciousness. The NBC strings sound almost Viennese in their flexibility and, particularly in the second movement, simply beautiful, in both phrasing and tone quality. Even Olin Downes, who had his reservations about what he referred to as Bruckner's "familiar structural weaknesses," concluded that "Walter did his audience a noble service in revealing the utmost of the vision and splendor of this singular music."[7] (Walter was soon to expatiate on Bruckner, comparing his singular music to Mahler's, in an essay he wrote for *Chord and Discord*, the organ of the Bruckner Society of America.[8]) The remaining concerts earned praise as well, especially Schumann's Fourth Symphony. But unknown to Walter's listeners, the critics, and perhaps even Walter himself, this was to be his last set of concerts for over ten years with what had, in effect, become Toscanini's orchestra.

Still mindful of his debt to France, Walter agreed to give a benefit recital with Lotte Lehmann for the French and American Red Cross. Before the money could even be donated, however, France fell to the Nazis, and Walter mourned the loss of France as much as he had mourned the loss of Austria and, before that, of Germany. The Anschluss, which made Austria forbidden territory, was by now two years in the past; France had since become his musical home, but he'd been granted little more than a year in which to enjoy her hospitality. Yet while France was unsuccessfully trying to ward off demons, there were "elves dancing again in Hollywood Bowl," or so Jones described Walter's rendition of Weber's *Oberon* Overture. With Mozart's Symphony no. 39 in E-flat Major, the elves became "courtiers dancing the minuet, conversing brilliantly back and forth under the direction of a kingly personality in a lyric mood" (presumably Walter himself). The contrast between the light moods that he evidently managed to evoke and the dark thoughts on France and the rest of Europe that he carried around with him could not have been greater. At one point in this first of four Hollywood Bowl concerts, however, reality did intervene; Jones described the "Funeral Music" from *Götterdämmerung* as "somber and very moving"; the "emotions this performance aroused brought tears," since the "fate of the country where this music was created came to mind and the orchestra reflected the life tragedy that is in our hearts and minds at this moment."[9]

Walter may have transported his listeners into a "musician's heaven," as Jones put it, but he himself was unable to remain in that elevated state of mind for very long. "Much of my time is absorbed by the unnumerous [i.e., innumerable] demands from musicians and other Refugees to procure them jobs or Visas or Affadavits etc.—I suffer by my inability to help," he wrote to Flagler in August.[10] And, as he told Wolfgang Stresemann in October, the "hysterical drama of the European protagonists" was having a bad effect on him, for a new book, of which he had already written a chapter, had lain untouched since the "French catastrophe." In theory he still believed in the steadfast and ever growing importance of music; but, practically speaking, he was "not in any condition to live by this realization," he admitted to his friend.[11] Back in August he had still entertained hopes of returning to Europe the following spring. "I want to go to Lugano and to the grave there," he wrote to Flagler; "my last memories are connected with our house there and the town."[12] He also wished to go to London, where he always received such "moving proofs of friendship for me personally and as musician." England now, it seemed, was Europe's last hope, and Walter likened her to St. George fighting the evil dragon; if she could only defeat this monster, "the world [would] become a place where life can be worth while again." By September, of course, Britain was surrounded by German U-boats, and the Luftwaffe was busily depositing bombs on London and other cities, so Walter's chances of returning to Europe in the near future now appeared bleak at best.

His only recourse at this point was to intensify his American activities, once again seeking refuge in his work from internal and external horrors. But he refused to regard this refuge as mere escapism. As he wrote in an article published in January 1941 for Klaus Mann's short-lived journal *Decision*, he was prompted to examine his conscience after reading a letter from Sir Adrian Boult in which the English conductor described his musical plans in great detail and made only brief mention of air raids. "I wanted to make up my mind," Walter declared, "whether now, when the battle of humanity is being fought, music should be allowed to retain the same importance as before." Not surprisingly, he decided that it could: "I began to see that music does not mean escape from world affairs; it can, in fact, play an active role in them. . . . To cultivate those things which have given meaning to our lives, and will redeem our future after the war, is the highest service to the good cause. The more decency and fair play are trampled underfoot by the enemy, the more faithfully should we observe them. The more tyrannically the other side perverts science and art, the more should we encourage a free art and a free science. The best achievements of art, as the highest manifestation of the human spirit, must ever be held up to the eyes of the world. Allies of democracy, they will deny the voice of force based on enslavement." In the end, he concluded that "the voice of music brings to those who can hear it a message of hope. It is the high duty of the musician today unfalteringly to spread its gospel of promise to all mankind."[13]

And so he began his 1940–41 season in the spirit of an evangelist, bringing his "gospel of promise" to the New World. At the end of October he conducted three concerts with the Detroit Symphony Orchestra, with which he had not appeared since 1924, when the ensemble had been the charge of his friend Ossip Gabrilowitsch. For the first two concerts he was joined by the young African-American soprano Dorothy Maynor, who had made her New York debut as recently as November 1939; she gave a sampling of a wide spectrum of styles, ranging from Mozart and Weber to Charpentier and Wagner (the "Liebestod" from *Tristan*). Walter's third concert consisted of works by Mozart, Schubert, and Strauss—and while the repertoire might now suggest overplayed symphonic war-horses, the *Detroit Free Press* noted that Schubert's "Great" C major symphony hadn't been performed there since 1933.[14]

Two weeks later Walter was back in Los Angeles conducting a series of concerts that lasted almost until Christmas. By now he and the Los Angeles Philharmonic had become quite familiar with one another. "Bruno Walter and our Philharmonic are so at one after a few rehearsals that he has but to look at them to remind them of his indications," Jones commented after the opening concert.[15] Two days later, in her Sunday column, she painted an idyllic picture of what musical life in southern California could be like with Walter as their regular music director. "Let us try to keep him here with only those absences necessary for his opera and occasional appearances elsewhere," she declared. "He draws the best from our players. He has the personal power to pull Southern California together, musically speaking."[16] Walter was deeply touched by the warmth with which he was being received on the West Coast, yet the lure of the New York musical scene, with its oldest symphony orchestra in America and grand opera house, could not be resisted. Already in October he'd signed a contract with the Metropolitan Opera for a minimum of eight performances, and at some point he had also been engaged for six weeks of New York Philharmonic concerts. As much as Walter loved California's mild climate and more moderately paced life-style, he was ready to return to New York's blustery winds and hectic existence.

First, however, Walter spent some time reacquainting himself with parts of the Midwest, becoming "untraceable" (or so he wrote in confidence to Bronislaw Huberman) in Chicago for the week around Christmas before moving over to Minneapolis for one concert with Mitropoulos's Minneapolis Symphony Orchestra, which he also had not conducted since his very first trip to America in 1923.[17] In January it was back to the New York Philharmonic, where his opening concert consisted of the unlikely coupling of Bruckner's Eighth and a Handel concerto grosso. According to Olin Downes, even in New York the Bruckner symphony "sent a number from the hall before it had finished," while he himself complained that the program could have been made "more interesting."[18]

The Bruckner symphony was repeated for the following Sunday broadcast, so the entire country could be treated (or subjected, if that was your viewpoint) to its "heavenly length." A recording has survived and, assuming that Walter's interpretation was substantially the same from one performance to the next, we may ourselves decide whom to believe. Listening to the January 26 broadcast, one can think of few conductors indeed who could successfully impose a brisker movement on this generously proportioned work, the last two movements of which do, after all, carry the marking *feierlich* ("solemnly"). What Downes called sentimental could also be heard as sensuous, especially in the beautifully phrased string lines, and instead of sounding dragged down, there is an underlying current of forward motion maintained throughout, even in the Adagio movement.[19]

After this somewhat daring beginning, Walter's remaining run of concerts settled into a fairly standard pattern of accepted masterpieces sprinkled with novelties. As he told an interviewer for the *New York Times*, he had spent the summer studying scores by American composers, and although he hadn't found many that he liked, there were a few that appealed to him.[20] One was Emerson Whithorne's symphonic poem entitled *The Dream Peddler*, which he presented on January 30. Walter also gave the New York premieres of Ernst Bloch's *Evocations* and Korngold's *Much Ado about Nothing* Suite, the latter originally composed for the Vienna Burgtheater.[21] The Korngold suite, which did not receive an especially favorable review in the *New York Times*, apparently needed a goodly amount of rehearsal—at least according to the critic B. H. Haggin, who some years later accused Walter of having callously allowed Korngold's piece to eat up time that should have been allotted to a Mozart piano concerto with the young American Webster Aitken as soloist. "If the pianist had been Schnabel the entire rehearsal would have been devoted to achieving homogeneity of phrasing and precision of execution in the joint performance of orchestra and soloist," Haggin complained, leveling the astounding charge that "the Walter of this incident was no Chevalier and Grand Seigneur, but instead a man of no artistic conscience and of ruthless inhumanity."[22] As it happened, Aitken's performance did receive a lukewarm review by Noel Straus, who praised the pianist's flawless execution but thought that there were "poetic aspects in this music which were barely hinted at in his perusal," and that his dynamics "differed at many points with those to be found in the score." At the same time, Straus praised Walter's "carefully detailed and comprehending support."[23] This being the case, one wonders whether more rehearsal would have made any difference, and Haggin—in this and other instances— seemed almost obsessively convinced that Aitken was the victim, on the one hand, of concert managers who were not interested in American pianists and, on the other, of putatively ignorant reviewers like Straus who failed to recognize the pianist's true genius.[24]

One of Walter's Sunday broadcasts included Debussy's *La Mer*, a comparative rarity in Walter's repertoire. Olin Downes remarked that Walter's performance "was far from the composer's conception" and "tended to the heavy-handed and melodramatic."[25] Though he had long admired and performed certain works of Debussy, Walter is today rarely associated with the great Impressionist composer. If his reading is more dramatic and more sharply articulated than performances by such acknowledged Debussy experts as Boulez, it must also be said that Walter's performance contains a kind of surging motion that is hardly heavy-handed and, in keeping with the three movements' descriptive titles, conjures up images of the restless sea.[26]

Walter's much-heralded Metropolitan Opera debut (his first American opera appearance) came on February 14 with a performance of *Fidelio* featuring Kirsten Flagstad, René Maison, and Alexander Kipnis in the leading roles. Even before his first performance the company hastened to honor the renowned European conductor; the previous day he had been presented with a rosewood and silver baton, and plans for a fete at the Plaza Hotel the following week were described in some detail in the *New York Times*. That Walter's debut opera dealt with such grand themes as freedom from oppression, undying love, and triumph over adversity did not escape the notice of a journalist from *Time* magazine, who was quick to contrast the opera's triumphant ending with Walter's own sad history. But Walter, ever conscious of the dichotomy between the exultant music he conducted and the recent horrors he had experienced, was by now accustomed to such questions. "Somehow this music tells us that happiness is deeper than unhappiness," he asserted to a reporter just hours before the performance.[27]

Several members of Walter's cast had, of course, sung under him across the Atlantic, but many of the orchestral musicians were encountering him for the first time, and, as violist David Berkowitz recalled, "The arrival of Bruno Walter was eagerly awaited by all of us."[28] Yet Berkowitz, and perhaps other members of the orchestra as well, found that Walter's conducting style took some getting used to. At the first rehearsal, Berkowitz admitted, he could not understand Walter's beat. "If I watched him closely, I became very confused," he owned. Apparently, as one of his colleagues explained, Walter was considered—by this orchestra at least—to be "more a musical interpreter than a technician" and that "you had to know your own part thoroughly."[29] What exactly Berkowitz's colleague meant by this is not clear; for, although many musicians have commented that Walter's beat was softer and less direct than that of a conductor like Toscanini, few of them felt he was difficult to follow. Sir Georg Solti noted that Walter "had a strange, not very clear beat, but he was proof that the beat is not an essential part of a conductor."[30] The violist David Kates, who played in the New York Philharmonic as early as 1933, remarked that Walter's "wasn't the kind of beat that Toscanini gave. Toscanini was very precise. Bruno Walter had a kind of soft downbeat—the sound would come after that." But, Kates was quick to add, "it was not disrupting."[31] The conductor and early-music pioneer Nikolaus Harnoncourt, who played the cello under Walter in the Vienna Symphony after the war, remembered "absolutely no problems. . . . It was a very clear beat." And at that time, Harnoncourt related, if a conductor's beat was not clear, the Vienna Symphony "could be so nasty."[32] The musicologist and conductor Siegmund Levarie, who studied Walter closely both in rehearsal and in concert during the 1930s, also described Walter's conducting technique as "awfully good" and thought that "it was ridiculous even to question it."[33]

Nevertheless, Walter's conducting style evidently created discomfort for some of the Metropolitan Opera Orchestra's players; at the same time, Walter appears to have had doubts about the caliber of the orchestra. Near the end of his life, when he was making plans with Columbia to record *Fidelio* (a project that was postponed indefinitely because of his ill health), Walter told John McClure confidentially that Rudolf Bing had suggested he record at the Met, but Walter did not feel the orchestra was satisfactory for recording.[34] Despite the mixed feelings evident on both sides, the recordings of Walter's broadcasts reveal that, in the end, the orchestra played perfectly well under his baton. His *Fidelio*, in particular, was a huge success; even Berkowitz referred to it as "one of the great moments in Metropolitan Opera History."[35] In what was possibly the most ebullient of his many reviews of Walter, Olin Downes nevertheless managed to interject a slighting remark about "some minor technical slips in an orchestra which is by no means equal to leading American symphonic bodies in its quality."[36] The audience, however, apparently did not find such "slips" a deterrent to enthusiasm, creating such a clamor that Walter actually took his own curtain call, a rare thing for an opera conductor. Unfortunately, no recording of the first performance has come to light, but the next performance, a Saturday broadcast, has survived, and there the orchestral playing, if rough in places, is characterized for the most part by clear phrasing, a vibrant and flexible rhythmic pulse, and highly dramatic gestures.

Walter's first season at the Metropolitan Opera also included several performances of Smetana's *Bartered Bride* (in English), as well as *Don Giovanni*, again with Pinza in the cast. The gossip concerning Pinza's relationship with Gretel had been flying thick and fast, often placing Pinza in an uncomplimentary light. Berkowitz remembered how it was rumored that Pinza had had an affair with Walter's daughter and "left her flat," and many people had mistakenly heard that Gretel had committed suicide, a story still perpetuated today.[37] Berkowitz did not go so far as to insinuate that Gretel killed herself over Pinza; nonetheless, he was surprised when Walter and Pinza's working relationship appeared to be completely amicable, recalling that Walter treated Pinza with "great courtesy and respect."[38] Although working together in the spring of 1941—so soon after the sad event—must have given rise to disturbing memories for both men, Walter never seems to have held Pinza responsible for his daughter's death. Rather, it appears to have been a shared tragedy that kept them on close terms until Pinza's own death in 1957, and afterward Walter kept up a correspondence with Pinza's wife, Dolores. In the year or so following Walter and Pinza's reunion in New York, Pinza was arraigned on suspicion of being a Fascist sympathizer, and Walter did his best to have him released, testifying in court on his behalf and afterward writing to Attorney General Francis Biddle to assure him of Pinza's innocence and integrity.[39]

After his stint with the Metropolitan Opera, Walter returned to the West Coast, which was waiting to welcome him with open arms. In May he conducted the San Francisco Symphony for one concert as part of the Berkeley Festival to celebrate the seventy-fifth anniversary of the city. In this and in his Hollywood Bowl programs during July and August, Walter stuck to standard repertoire, but his audiences didn't mind at all hearing such thrice-familiar works as Dvořák's "New World" Symphony; for, as Isabel Morse Jones commented, it was "a revelation of what happens to a familiar work when a great musician conducts it as if it were a new work."[40]

The California music critics were not, of course, always completely uncritical; yet, reading through Walter's West Coast reviews from this period, one gets the sense that they and the rest of the audience attended his concerts always expecting to be pleased, uplifted, and at times even transported. There is not that ever-present impulse to pounce on some aspect of the performance deemed inappropriate that is always lurking at the back of many New York reviews, even those by such habitual supporters as Olin Downes and Lawrence Gilman. The state also honored Walter on June 7, 1941, when the University of Southern California bestowed on him the degree of Doctor of Music, which he received in flowing academic regalia.[41] The warm support of the press and public in California, together with its mostly friendly climate, was a soothing combination, and Walter was tempted to remain there and not return to New York at all. "Our time here in California soon comes to an end," he wrote wistfully to Leo and Emma, who were still living in Sweden.[42] The Walters spent some vacation time in Monterey, which Walter described to his brother and sister as a "very beautifully located place," before returning to the East, where he made his first appearance in Montreal, conducting a concert to benefit the British War Relief and Canadian Red Cross, then proceeded to New York to take up his hectic schedule once more.

Walter's engagements with the New York Philharmonic and the Metropolitan Opera, continuing into January of the following year, this time held few surprises. The only new work Walter conducted was David Stanley Smith's *Credo*, performed in the company of Beethoven's "Eroica" and Strauss's *Don Juan*. The highlight of his Metropolitan Opera performances was a new production of Gluck's *Orfeo* in which he collaborated with Herbert Graf; it featured Kerstin Thorborg in the title role and Jarmila Novotná as Euridice, both of whom had sung the opera with Walter in his last Salzburg performances. Graf had also worked with Walter in Salzburg (on a production of *Die Entführung*); the two worked together a number of other times and remained in touch long after Walter had stopped conducting opera. When Graf left the Met in 1960, Walter helped him to obtain a position with the Zurich Opera. Like Margarete Wallmann, Graf attempted to get Walter back into opera, thinking he could persuade him to direct a production of *Così* in Zurich during his first season there, and like Wallmann he failed. Graf also tried to persuade Walter to record a concert production of *Così*, stressing what an important artistic document it would be, but Walter did not feel that particular opera would lend itself to recording; for to leave out the numerous recitatives would disturb the tonal progression, but "the endless recitatives without staging would be an intolerable burden."[43]

Their production of *Orfeo* was praised in almost every respect, though this time Walter did not have Wallmann's choreography, and Howard Taubman remarked acerbically that the ballet in the Elysian Fields "was anything but happy."[44] Though Thorborg received perhaps the most sterling reports, Novotná was also lauded for her "vibrant vocalization" and "superb mastery of the grand line in phraseology."[45] Walter himself thought highly of the Czechoslovakian soprano and would continue to work with her often in the coming years. Shortly before her death in 1994 Novotná recalled her experiences performing with Walter in the most enraptured terms: "To sing under his loving direction was the greatest joy. He seemed to love every note and tried to awaken his enthusiasm in me, in which he highly succeeded. . . . It was sublime, unforgettable. Many years have [passed], but the memory I will cherish forever."[46]

Novotná also appeared as Pamina in the new production of *Die Zauberflöte*, which opened two weeks later, the first performance of the opera at the Metropolitan Opera House in fifteen years. Herbert Graf again did the staging, and the opera was sung in English in a new translation by Ruth and Thomas Martin, the genesis of which owed a good deal to Walter's input. The translators were both musicians who had deeply admired Walter long before getting to know him personally. Ruth Martin, an American, studied violin in the 1930s at the Mozarteum in Salzburg. While abroad, she met her future husband, a Viennese conductor who, like her, had an appreciation for literature. They both witnessed memorable performances directed by Walter, and Ruth Martin made a point of attending Walter's conducting classes at the Mozarteum ("I would just sit there transfixed and not dare go near him"[47]). When the Martins settled in America, Thomas accepted a position as assistant conductor at the Chicago Opera. They decided, after a controversial performance there of Verdi's *Falstaff* sung in English, to try their hand at translating *Die Zauberflöte* into English, having found much in the standard translation "miswritten and misaccented." After some months of collaborative effort they presented the finished translation first to the St. Louis Opera and eventually to the Met, whose manager, Edward Johnson, wrote back that the company was planning to revive *Die Zauberflöte*, "because Bruno Walter wanted to do it, and that they had had seven English translations in the house, and Walter turned them all down. He didn't like any of them. He had decided a day or so before to go back to doing it in the original. And by chance ours came in, and he liked it."[48] A few weeks later, they went to New York to discuss the translation with Walter. "We used to go over there for several hours a day, and we went through every note and every word of that thing." For the most part Walter was a pleasure to work with. When asking their advice, he genuinely seemed to listen and "never pulled rank," yet he insisted on "very great literalness in the translation," and the Martins sometimes struggled in vain to give greater flexibility to their text.

In the actual performance Alexander Kipnis received the highest praise as Sarastro (a part taken by Ezio Pinza later in the season), but the remaining principals (Novotná, Rosa Bok, Charles Kullman, and John Brownlee) did not disappoint, despite the occasional continental accent. Nor did Walter's conducting disappoint, and Virgil Thomson noted with pleasure that "care for production detail, as well as for musical, had given it a general harmony and an integrity that are not easy qualities to achieve in a repertory theater," and that these qualities seemed to be appearing in the Metropolitan's productions "quite regularly this season. Somebody is taking care. I may also add, for whatever that may mean, that three of those productions were directed by Bruno Walter."[49] Walter would often feel unappreciated by the Metropolitan Opera's management, but he was certainly appreciated by Virgil Thomson, who, somewhat like Julius Korngold in Vienna and Alfred Einstein in Berlin, hinted again and again that the musical scene in New York improved tremendously when Walter was in town.

Aside from the handful of new works he conducted with the New York Philharmonic, 1941 was more a time for restoration and consolidation than for breaking fresh ground. During this year he made his first studio recordings with New York's premier orchestra—heart-stopping, intense recordings of Beethoven's Third and Fifth symphonies, as well as the "Emperor" Concerto with Rudolf Serkin, a pianist with whom Walter had worked in the past and would work again over the next two seasons and then once more in 1948.[50]

Near the end of the year Walter also saw his Mahler biography appear in a new English edition, though this, instead of being a source of satisfaction, turned into something of a nightmare. To begin with, he was never happy with James Galston's English translation, and throughout the rest of his life he would try to discourage people from turning to it—though it was in fact quite readable, and he even agreed to have Galston translate his autobiography. But he was more disturbed by the publisher's inclusion of an essay on Mahler by Ernst Krenek that, at sixty-five pages, was half as long as Walter's. Walter had apparently been told that Krenek was to write a preface, and now here was a lengthy piece of writing that, instead of introducing Walter's book, actually followed it. Even worse, Walter felt that Krenek's view of Mahler flatly contradicted his own. Certain statements of Krenek's—for example, that Mahler's Fifth, Sixth, and Seventh symphonies acted as a "catalyst in the critical stage of the musical language at that time," helping to open the door of atonality—directly conflicted with Walter's deepest beliefs.[51] For his part, Krenek heard only second-hand (from Artur Schnabel) that Walter was annoyed and wrote him a very apologetic letter, stressing that the publisher had led him to understand that Walter had been fully consulted on the matter, and that although he accepted Walter's disagreement with his view of Mahler, certainly his sincere admiration of Mahler was evident in every word of the essay. Walter replied testily that he, in Krenek's position, would have made certain that the two essays did not contradict each other, that he was upset with Krenek for agreeing to write it and upset with the publisher for putting it at the end. "I believe it is a first in publishing," Walter wrote, obviously seething with indignation, "that a publisher, without the knowledge of an author, asks another author for a foreword to the book."[52] Walter respected Krenek's compositions enough to program them from time to time; nevertheless, he had a strong aversion to the younger musician's use of jazz in *Jonny spielt auf* and disapproved of his work on Mahler's Tenth Symphony—factors that might well have made the coupling of their two essays even more distressing.

For the country of the United States as a whole, the beginning of 1942 must have seemed the opening of an entirely new and frightening—even exhilarating—chapter, for with the Japanese bombing of Pearl Harbor on December 7, 1941, America had finally entered the war. But for Walter, at least outwardly, 1942 began very much as 1941 had ended, with his time divided between the two coasts. Aside from another early January concert in Minnesota and a Metropolitan Opera performance of *Don Giovanni* in Cleveland in April, the middle of the country saw little of Walter that spring. At the end of January Walter was scheduled to conduct in Boston but was forced to cancel, owing to a regulation that no union conductor should conduct the non-union Boston Symphony. (Walter had been made an honorary member of the union after signing the Boston contract.) One of the pieces was to have been Mahler's First Symphony, and Walter was particularly disappointed at not being able to share his interpretation of the symphony with Boston audiences. But as it happened, Koussevitzky, because of his wife's recent death, had canceled three concerts with the New York Philharmonic, and Walter, still in New York, promptly agreed to take them on, conducting Mahler's Second instead of the First. Then in February it was back to California for a month-long stint of concerts, one of which included Smith's *Credo*, with a return to New York in March and April for more performances of *Don Giovanni* and *Die Zauberflöte* and four concerts with the New York Philharmonic. Again, standard repertoire was the order of the day, though his last concert included Samuel Barber's *Second Essay*. In May he returned once more to California, where he joined Lotte Lehmann in San Francisco for a lieder recital, and in July he came back for one concert at the Hollywood Bowl (with a second concert in Pasadena), where he was hailed as "Southern California's choice of orchestra conductor."[53] This was not merely journalistic hyperbole; in his sixteen concerts Walter drew the highest attendance for concerts without soloists.[54]

With this respite from the arduousness of interpreting new works or working out the details of new productions, Walter was able to concentrate on straightening out his domestic affairs. In April he rented another house on Chevy Chase Drive in Beverly Hills and, with Lotte's help, hired a chauffeur and a secretary. In September he also took an apartment in New York at 930 Fifth Avenue. More and more he felt himself attracted to the lovely weather and relaxed life-style that southern California offered; yet, as he wrote to Stresemann a few years later, he "would not be untrue to the East," where so many conducting possibilities awaited him.[55] Also, beautiful as California beaches might be, the hot California sun did not agree with Elsa, so the Walters decided to take a vacation in cooler Bar Harbor, Maine, before taking up residence in New York.[56]

As Walter prepared for the season ahead, walking through the Maine woods that were just beginning to show "the colors of autumn," he was pretty much convinced that Edward Johnson and the rest of the Metropolitan Opera administration were not very interested in having him back. The best they had offered him were repeats of his Mozart operas and a revival of

Humperdinck's *Hänsel und Gretel* to take the place of *Fidelio*, which had fallen through because of casting difficulties, and *The Bartered Bride*, which somehow didn't fit into the periods during which Walter was available. Needless to say, these suggestions did not sit well with Walter, who had unsuccessfully asked for *Tristan* and had seen his younger colleague Erich Leinsdorf conducting the bulk of the Wagner operas. "I cannot help feeling that the Management has no real interest in my activity, they have not offered me any work of interest to me," he wrote to Flagler from Maine; "they have not accepted one of my suggestions and of course I cannot accept to be treated as an old Routinier who always repeats what he has done and does not participate in the vital important artistic efforts of the Institute."[57] Walter planned to meet with Johnson the following week and—so he told Flagler— anticipated that they would go their separate ways. But evidently they came to an agreement, for Walter was engaged for several performances scattered throughout the season, including a new production of *La forza del destino*.

In the meantime he returned to conduct the New York Philharmonic, where he felt far more welcome—perhaps even too much so. At the end of 1942, as John Barbirolli's star waned, the management invited Walter to become the orchestra's new permanent director. After some agonizing, Walter decided that, for reasons of age, he must refuse. "Let me tell you," he wrote to Judson, "that my first inner reaction to your offer was a spontaneous 'yes'— the acceptance of that position seemed to me only a natural consequence of years of occasional connections with the Philharmonic in an atmosphere of ever growing understanding and friendship." But with a twenty-eight-week season and "about ninety-odd concerts," Walter didn't feel "able to cope even with half of it; but if I conduct perhaps ten of those weeks, how can I find ways and forms of responsibility for the whole season?"[58] Next year he would be celebrating his fiftieth anniversary as a conductor, and he felt himself irretrievably mired in the fatigues of old age. Little did he know that Artur Rodzinski, hired in his stead, would leave the orchestra less than four years later and that this time Walter, far from being on the brink of retirement, would feel compelled to accept the same invitation.

Assured of his role as regular guest conductor, Walter began his 1942–43 season in October with programs that once again consisted mainly of standard fare, though on October 22 he premiered John Alden Carpenter's Second Symphony. He had performed Carpenter's First Symphony with the Los Angeles Philharmonic in December 1940 and wrote to the American composer that the new work seemed to him as interesting as the First

Symphony, "and perhaps even more so," though the critics disagreed, with both Olin Downes and John Briggs thinking the Carpenter Symphony less original than his previous compositions.[59] One more somewhat novel (if not actually new) work during this run of concerts was Sibelius's Seventh Symphony. Walter performed Sibelius rarely and, despite his choice to perform this symphony, may have had mixed feelings about the Finnish composer. Somewhat later, in 1952, when Walter was awarded an honorary membership in the International Mark Twain Society, Cyril Clemens wrote to him that he might be interested to know that Sibelius, who held Walter in high esteem, was chairman of the society's music committee. Walter wrote back that he greatly appreciated the honor but made no mention of Sibelius.[60]

Having patched up his relationship with Johnson and the rest of the management at the Met, Walter began conducting there in November, with repeat performances of *Don Giovanni* and *Die Zauberflöte*. In December, however, he conducted *Figaro* for the first time in New York, with a splendid cast that included John Brownlee, Ezio Pinza, Jarmila Novotná, and Bidú Sayão, as well as a young American soprano singing her first Countess at the Met, Eleanor Steber. Herbert Graf did the staging, and, according to Howard Taubman, his direction was an improvement on that of previous productions. " 'The Marriage of Figaro' is not played for easy laughs only," he wrote. "As a result, its warmth, loveliness and enduring humanity shine through to cheer a grim world." Robert Lawrence of the *Herald Tribune*, by contrast, carped that "passages of great charm and pathos . . . alternated with pages that courted the sentimental. In sum, Mr. Walter's approach was too highly personalized."[61]

No such criticisms attended Walter's interpretation of *Forza*, which opened on January 9, 1943, and featured Zinka Milanov as Leonora, Lawrence Tibbett as Carlos, the relatively new tenor Kurt Baum as Alvaro, and Ezio Pinza in a somewhat different guise as Padre Guardino, a religious leader. Though Walter had conducted Verdi most of his life, New York audiences had yet to hear him interpret this great master, and it seems they were hardly disappointed. (Curiously enough, this seems to have been the first time Walter ever conducted *Forza*.[62]) "The opera attracted a huge audience," wrote Noel Straus, "which was roused to unusual enthusiasm by the general excellence of the interpretation."[63] The production followed an ordering of scenes devised by Franz Werfel that, among other changes, turned the first scene into a prologue and placed the overture before the second scene, where it "received a reading so remarkable for play of color and so brilliantly performed that it brought the first prolonged ovation of the evening." Baum apparently received the next ovation, and Straus was unstinting in his praise of Baum's "voice of beautiful timbre," clear quality, and warmth. Regrettably, both he and Milanov were replaced for the broadcast by Frederick Jagel and Stella Roman respectively, both of whom sang capably enough but neither of whom quite lived up to the praise lavished on their predecessors. The recorded broadcast does, however, enable us to hear Pinza's noble portrayal of the serene though consoling Abbot, as well as Walter's riveting overture—remarkable for its virtuoso runs of breathtaking flexibility, its tidal-wave crescendi, and its agonized stretching-out of the principal themes toward the conclusion.

Aside from a return trip to Minnesota at the beginning of January and a Metropolitan Opera performance of *Figaro* in Chicago in March, Walter spent the first half of 1943 in New York, alternating between the Metropolitan and the New York Philharmonic. His Philharmonic concerts began regularly enough with the usual mixture of Beethoven, Brahms, Berlioz, and Bruckner, to which was added the English composer Stanley Bate's Concertante for Piano and String Orchestra, with Bate himself performing the piano part. Then on February 6, as part of a Saturday night "Popular Concert" intended for students, Walter conducted Daniel Gregory Mason's "Lincoln" Symphony, a work he had considered performing for over two years. Having asked Mason in 1940 to send a score, Walter initially reacted to the work without enthusiasm: "It certainly *is* a strange being," he wrote to Mason in September; "the first movement seems a Finale, the fourth has a 'second movement' appearance." The opening movement was "absolutely unsymphonic, to an exceptional degree—and that from your hand, which has been so essentially symphonic." Then Walter attempted to mollify his judgment, only to end up making matters worse. He believed he understood the problem: "Lincoln and his sublime soul and great life and tragic end stood between you and your musical imagining and forming and molding. Maybe the Symphony would be the right work for a Lincoln-Celebration; but without such emphasis on its human and personal meaning, purely as a Symphony I as a musician feel embarrassed by it."[64] We can imagine Mason's shock at receiving this letter from Walter, who up to this point had been such a stalwart supporter of his compositions. On the envelope that enclosed Walter's comments, Mason jotted: "Bruno Walter's distressing letter about Lincoln Symphony."

By August 1942, however, Walter was considering the work again. This time his reservations ostensibly had more to do with his fear that there wouldn't be enough rehearsal time, though one can't help wondering whether he had really changed his mind about the work or was attempting to put Mason off gently. Given that Walter seemed worried about finding sufficient rehearsal time in the orchestra's schedule, his decision to perform the work only once and at a special student concert looks suspiciously as if he had finally agreed to conduct it not because he had become convinced of its worth but because he wished to please his old friend and thought that its programmatic nature would make it succeed with younger people.

In the midst of operas and symphonies Walter also took time out to accompany Lotte Lehmann in a concert at Town Hall in mid-March to an audience so large that the stage was filled with seats. It was New York in March rather than Salzburg in August, yet some audience members may have felt a touch of prewar nostalgia as they listened to an all-German program reminiscent of those given in happier times, as Walter himself often referred to them. During these years, Walter began more and more to restrict his accompanying activities, even declining, in 1947, to record Mozart with Desi Halban because he was afraid of offending other singers whose invitations he'd refused.[65] But he would continue to accompany Lotte Lehmann on several occasions until the end of her performing career.

The main event for the spring of 1943 was, without question, Walter's first New York performances of Bach's *Matthäus-Passion*. Having conducted the work several times in Munich with numerous cuts, Walter had long dreamed of presenting Bach's greatest oratorio in its entirety. Some twenty years after his Munich performances, he was finally granted the opportunity, though since a complete performance could run over three hours, special permission had to be obtained from the union, and the orchestra would have to be paid overtime for every fifteen minutes beyond three hours, "either for intermission or actual playing purposes."[66] There was also the little matter of translation; Walter had decided, as he related in *Of Music and Music-Making*, that the work should be performed in English, "so that the words in conjunction with the music should make an immediate emotional impression on the listeners."[67] John Finley Williamson came to the rescue, sending Walter a copy of a translation he had used by Dr. Henry S. Drinker, a lawyer by profession but an amateur choral singer and an industrious translator—in addition to the *Matthäus-Passion*, he rendered into English nearly all of Bach's vocal works, as well as those of Brahms and Mozart, along with songs by Schubert, Schumann, Wolf, and Mussorgsky.

Walter thought the translation was "excellent" but naturally wished to make a few changes, mostly having to do with his preference for keeping as much of Bach's original rhythm in the vocal lines as possible. All through the long, hot month of July, Walter and Drinker exchanged letters, hammering out various phrases and respectfully disagreeing over certain matters, such as whether it was more important to preserve Bach's sixteenth notes and occasional word painting or maintain fidelity to familiar translations of biblical passages.[68] Drinker felt strongly that with direct quotations from the Bible the King James version should be used, since it would be recognizable to the audience, even if it meant changing Bach's rhythm to a small degree. Walter, on the other hand, felt not only that Bach's rhythms should be adhered to but also that words in expressive places in the original should have their counterparts in the translation as much as possible, to the point where Drinker thought he used English words in an unusual sense and in a word order that was German, not English. For Jesus's line "denn wer das Schwert nimmt, der soll durch's Schwert umkommen," for instance, Walter wanted "For all that take the sword, shall by the sword stroke perish," an ingenious translation that allowed the operative words "sword" and "perish" to occupy roughly the same places in the recitative as *Schwert* and *umkommen*. Drinker suggested the more elegant "They that take the sword, shall perish by the sword," easier to grasp at first hearing and nearly identical to the King James reading. And Walter also felt that Bach's touches of word painting should be retained as much as possible, such as in the Evangelist's words "Und als bald krähe der Hahn," where Drinker's "immediately crew the cock" would not allow the singer to imitate the crowing of a rooster. Walter made several suggestions for this particular passage, finally writing to Drinker in mock despair that he was "very much upset that you do not like these rooster places. I worked over and thought over them literally for hours and thought I could hear him crow." Eventually, however, they arrived at a fluent translation that pleased them both, and Walter, who was often merciless with translators, could not have praised Drinker's work more highly, writing that his rendering "showed great linguistic aptitude and a real understanding of the music; it was an essential contribution to the profound impression made by this and subsequent performances of the work."[69]

There were, of course, also some questions of performance practice that Walter now finally had the time to study more fully. Already in April 1942 he had begun what he described to his brother and sister as a "musical and stylistic and historical study of the *Matthäus-Passion*."[70] Walter eventually included an entire chapter on Bach's oratorio in *Of Music and Music-Making*, where he detailed the decisions he made, and to historical-performance purists, his conclusions might seem dated or anachronistic. He did not feel, for instance, that we should employ small forces such as Bach had at his disposal at the Thomas-Kirche; "we must make allowances for the musical and emotional requirements of the work and the acoustic properties of our large concert-halls or churches."[71] With regard to orchestral size, "we may feel quite independent of Bach's Leipzig orchestra," for the same reason.[72] Whether or not to take the entire da capo in the arias, which would probably not even come into question today, also "weighed on [his] conscience," and in the end he resolved to repeat just the ritornello, attempting to "take account of the difference between our form of listening and that of Bach's time."[73] But although he felt that in performances of Bach we should "follow our hearts, and put into our performances . . . the same intensity and truthfulness of feeling that we meet on its every page," such intensity of expression should be compatible with a reverence "not only for the spirit but also for the letter of the work."[74]

Walter's three performances of the *Matthäus-Passion* were intended to close out the Philharmonic's season with a flourish, and they apparently had that effect, for the last performance drew the largest audience they had seen all season. What Olin Downes called "a noble experiment" proved such a success that the Passion was repeated for the next three years running with, as Walter requested, essentially the same soloists. "Even if there could be found one or two better ones, the tradition into which my soloists have grown by all those past performances of the Passion makes up for any improvement in a single case," he wrote to Bruno Zirato when it came time to plan his Passion for 1946, his final performance of the work.[75] (In March 1946 Zirato mentioned casually that Bach's oratorio was "an expenditure of high order for the Society"—no doubt the main reason that the performances ended.[76]) Thanks to Walter's desire to maintain an ensemble, the recorded broadcast of Part I from 1945 can give us an idea of how Walter's other performances would have sounded. To listeners accustomed to Harnoncourt, Gardiner, Leonhardt, or Herreweghe, some of Walter's tempi, particularly in the first and last choruses of Part I, as well as in the chorales, might sound ponderous. That his oboes and flutes play appoggiaturas quickly, instead of turning them into sighing figures half the length of the main notes, might also strike us as controversial, though Walter was fully aware of the debate raging even then over the duration of grace notes and had come to the decision that these little notes were not "a rhythmically exact subdivision of the melodic structure, but rather an indefinite and indefinable time-value which was to carry an element of unrest or indecision into the rhythmic plan."[77] In fact, some scholars have recently doubted that the long appoggiaturas advocated by C. P. E. Bach should be applied to J. S. Bach's music, and Gustav Leonhardt's 1990 recording of the *Matthäus-Passion* has short appoggiaturas in this duet, very similar to Walter's.

Aside from these issues, there is throughout Walter's interpretation a sensitivity of phrasing and clarity of affect from one piece to the next that distinguishes his performance from most others of its day. His soloists, particularly William Hain as the Evangelist, Mack Harrell as Jesus, the soprano Nadine Conner, and the contralto Jean Watson, have light, flexible voices and seem almost as comfortable with Bach's chromatic, expressive phrases as many recent oratorio singers, Conner perhaps less so than the others. In contrast to Walter's Munich critics, Olin Downes considered Walter's interpretation to be in a more classical vein, writing that "we have heard the score treated in a more intense and romantic spirit," and that he "expected rather more of the dramatic and climactic . . . and more emotional intensity in various expressive figures of the accompaniments, which were cooler in color and sensation than one had conceived."[78] And many of Walter's tempi, especially in the arias, seemed faster than usual to Downes, when in fact they are comparable to what has since become the stylistic norm.

Walter's interpretation of the Passion may have struck Downes as less "intense" than others he had heard, but Walter's own feelings about the story of Christ's crucifixion certainly lacked no intensity. The cellist Leonard Rose recalled how Walter's unconcealed emotion during rehearsals was often embarrassing, even distasteful, to the orchestra members, especially those with a Jewish background, at a time when Jews were being slain in Europe. "It always galled me that Bruno Walter, who was born a Jew, found it necessary to be so moved that when the text of the *St. Matthew Passion* got the roughest—for example, in the text when they sing, 'They put a crown of thorns upon his head'—Bruno Walter used to cry the hardest."[79] Rose's response was natural enough; but it is surely possible that Walter, at that moment, was inwardly drawing parallels between the humiliating crucifixion of Christ and the current plight of millions of Jews, victims of sadism and slaughter on a vast scale.

The *Matthäus-Passion* performance was one of the crowning moments of Walter's season, yet it did not completely dispel a weariness that Walter couldn't seem to shake. Already back in September of the previous year he had written to Flagler that his performance of the *Matthäus-Passion* would be the "culmination of my activity and perhaps may be my farewell."[80] By April, Walter's inner weariness was accompanied by a real physical ailment, the flu, and he feared making a trip to Philadelphia (where he was scheduled to conduct the New York Philharmonic) without the company of family or a close friend. But by this time Elsa too was suffering from what would eventually develop into more serious health problems than those of her husband and was unable to go, so Bruno Zirato wrote to the U.S. District Attorney's office to ask that Wolfgang Stresemann—presumably restricted in his movements because he was German—be granted permission to accompany Walter.[81] At the beginning of May, Walter and Elsa took a trip to Buck Hill Falls, Pennsylvania, which they doubtless hoped would prove relaxing and refreshing, though it seemed to have quite the opposite effect. "The weather is atrocious—cold and stormy, the hotel very big with lovely lounges but impersonal and bland," he wrote to Stresemann. "My wife feels very weak and each day has taken only a couple of steps outside." As for himself, as a "coda" to his flu, he now had a chronic headache for which he continued to take medication.[82]

Despite Walter's apparent difficulty in regaining his health and his worry over Elsa's continued malaise, he agreed to return to New York and conduct the Philharmonic's first two summer broadcasts. Then he and Elsa were at last able to retreat to California, where Walter had the month of June to recover before beginning a series of three Hollywood Bowl concerts in July. Evidently that was not enough, for Elsa wrote to Stresemann in July that her husband was still taking medications that didn't seem to be working, and that while her shattered nerves were calming somewhat, physical problems remained. She added, however, that they were enjoying their beautiful house and pleasant weather, so the southern California clime was apparently working at least a small bit of its magic for them.[83] But we can only speculate how Walter must have felt when, after his last concert, his "emotional goodbye" to the Bowl audience was followed by the announcement that "a sensational young singer named Frank Sinatra had been engaged as a Bowl soloist," and there was a "noticeable gasp from the audience and then shocked silence."[84] Isabel Morse Jones, for one, pulled no punches as to what she thought about the approaching clash of musical styles, headlining her article on the subject with the words, "Cash to Be Crooned Into Coffers of Bowl."[85]

But if Walter gave any thought to what Jones considered the Bowl's vanishing ideals, it was probably fleeting at best, for he would soon have to rally his forces for the start of a new concert season. So he and Elsa took a three-week vacation in the Rocky Mountains, returning to New York near the end of September. In March, Walter would be marking the fiftieth anniversary of his conducting debut, and the New York Philharmonic's management was already making plans to commemorate the event—"though I have naturally asked [the management] to refrain from a 'Festivity,'" he wrote to his brother and sister from Colorado Springs, "during a time where decisions in the course of world history must seem to put such personal matters in a vain light."[86] Nevertheless, if his health allowed it, he would at least celebrate by conducting a performance of Beethoven's Ninth Symphony, which he hoped his siblings would be able to hear when it was broadcast, along with the many other planned transmissions. "I hope I can manage it," he reflected; "fifty years of such work is a lot, and already I have the need for rest which shows itself in certain complaints of age and symptoms of fatigue." Despite his worries over his and Elsa's health, a more optimistic mood was overtaking him, perhaps because, with Italy's surrender on September 8, it looked as though the tides of war were turning in the Allies' favor. In looking back over his fifty years of music, Walter had a "feeling of sunset" and was glad that his old age coincided with the "rejuvenation of the world after the defeat of the powers of evil," almost as if he were happy to turn his baton over to the next generation of conductors if he could do it with the sense that the world was becoming a good place once more.[87] He seems to have had no idea that he had nearly twenty more years of conducting still ahead of him.

For the moment, however, Walter was looking forward to at least one more busy season, so the course of events in November must have been a source of disappointment, or at least frustration. He began his season ably enough with a very well-received concert in Montreal near the end of October. But after little more than a week of conducting in New York, Walter again fell ill with the flu and was unable to conduct the November 14 broadcast. This in itself was not a tragedy and in fact led to a tremendous break for the recently hired assistant conductor, Leonard Bernstein. Some thirty years later Bernstein recalled it as "the climax of a rather stimulating and startling week or even month, because I had just been engaged the preceding September as assistant conductor of the Philharmonic. I just turned twenty-five years old and had never conducted a professional orchestra in public before." The young Bernstein had spent the week sitting enthralled as he watched Walter work, little suspecting what was to come. "He was so kind, so gentle and so authoritative at the same time—I couldn't believe that a conductor could combine those qualities of warmth, tenderness, and absolute authority to this degree, and I was rather in love with him, an ardent admirer," he reminisced. Then on Saturday night he was informed that Walter was feeling ill and that he himself might have to conduct the next day, but Bernstein, doubting that this would come to pass, went to a song recital, then came home and spent some time looking over the scores before going to sleep in the early hours of the morning. He was awakened just a few hours later to hear that Walter couldn't leave his apartment, that Bernstein would have to go on, and that, since it was already nine in the morning, there was no time for any rehearsal.

After some pleas for help on Bernstein's part, it was arranged to have the young conductor visit Walter at his home and go over the music with him. "He was very, very gracious," Bernstein recalled; "he was sitting huddled up in a blanket, poor man, sweating and shivering and what not. And in the midst of all that misery of his, he was so kind and so helpful to me. I was there an hour, in the course of which he showed me various places where he cut off first and made a *Luftpause* and then gave an extra upbeat here, and therefore I could be helped and in front of the orchestra wouldn't be ragged. He was very helpful; I don't know what I would have done without that hour with him and he gave it to me under great duress."[88] The tremendous energy Bernstein created that night helped make his career, though William Lincer, the solo violist in *Don Quixote* (one of the evening's offerings), recalled that the fledgling conductor "certainly didn't know" Strauss's tone poem. "He jigged up and down for the whole piece and made a great spectacle," yet in the end "he did a marvelous job and was very successful."[89]

If Bernstein "didn't know" *Don Quixote*, Walter had a conception of the piece completely at odds with that of Lincer, who had recently joined the New York Philharmonic after having been principal violist with the Cleveland Orchestra. Lincer recalled that when he had initially come to a rehearsal at Walter's apartment, Walter objected to the violist's refined playing. "Mr. Lincer," he said, "you know, Sancho Panza was an idiot"—the implication being that the viola should play more roughly.

Lincer returned: "Have you read Cervantes, Maestro?" The rhetorical question affronted Walter, who had indeed read Cervantes and who long entertained fond memories of Mahler's reading aloud from *Don Quixote*.

"Yes, I have," Walter replied brusquely.

"Well, if you've read Cervantes, you know that it wasn't Sancho Panza that was an idiot; it was Don Quixote who was the idiot. Because Sancho

Panza was leading him around all the time, trying to get him out of trouble. He was a poor, sane man."

Walter refused to take the literary discussion any further: "Either we play this my way, or we don't play it at all."

Lincer later received some advice from Artur Rodzinski, who had brought the violist with him from Cleveland and was agitated to learn about the difference of opinion that had developed between Lincer and Walter: "You jackass!" he burst out. "Don't you understand? When a conductor asks you to play something a certain way, you make your head go up and down—yes, yes. Comes the performance, you play it any damned way you please. Who's going to stop you?"[90]

For the Sunday broadcast, of course, Bernstein conducted and became an overnight success. It is doubtful that Walter begrudged his young colleague his sudden fame or was particularly disappointed at missing a concert of works that, for the most part, he had conducted several times before (Rosza's Theme, Variations, and Finale was the only nonstandard piece of the evening). That he was unable to conduct *Tristan* at the Met the following week was a much a heavier blow, since it had taken him several years to convince the Met's management to give him a Wagner work at all, and now Beecham had to be engaged to replace him.

Deprived of *Tristan*, Walter at least had the opportunity of conducting Verdi's *Un ballo in maschera* at the end of December, with a cast that included Jan Peerce, Zinka Milanov, Kerstin Thorborg, and Leonard Warren. Downes commented that Walter transformed the opera from "an old-fashioned Italian piece to a lusty and full-blooded music-drama," and a recorded broadcast from later in the season with essentially the same cast certainly lends credence to Downes's opinion; the orchestra sizzles with dramatic tension from beginning to end, and the excellent singers all rise to the occasion.[91] Yet Walter's general dissatisfaction with his treatment at the hands of the Met's management would not be assuaged. Near the end of January he met with Edward Johnson over lunch to discuss his grievances. As he told Johnson, he felt he was being pegged as a Mozart conductor and insisted that he was capable of more varied things. Certainly he couldn't blame the management for the loss of *Tristan*, but he still longed to show his ability to conduct Wagner in an "interesting and exciting" manner; apparently he had been offered *Parsifal* at the last possible moment, when it was too late to reschedule his concerts with the New York Philharmonic and the Philadelphia Orchestra. "My impression is that Mr. Walter is not well and very tired," Edward Johnson noted after the meeting, adding that Walter was "re-sentful of the success and importance given to another conductor," whose identity we can only guess.[92]

Whatever Walter's conflicts with Johnson, the Met director's description of Walter as "not well and very tired" seems more than apt. Earlier in the month Walter had announced his decision to retire for a year at the close of the season and, as he put it to the press, "enjoy the privileges of a private person," by which he doubtless meant getting lots of sleep, enjoying his peaceful home in sunny California, and not having to travel back and forth between the two coasts.[93] But for now he still had a busy spring ahead of him, which was to include, in addition to his usual activities in New York, his first appearance with the Philadelphia Orchestra.

Returning to New York in March, Walter pressed on, accompanying Lotte Lehmann in *Winterreise* at Town Hall, giving the New York premiere of Barber's revised Symphony in One Movement, and conducting his first Verdi Requiem in New York, for a concert to benefit the American Red Cross. And despite Walter's best efforts, the celebration of his fiftieth anniversary as a conductor that month did somewhat resemble a festival. After his performance of Beethoven's Ninth, Walter received what the *New York Times* described as "one of the greatest ovations in the memory of old patrons of Carnegie Hall" and was then presented with several gifts: the Cambridge edition of Shakespeare from the Philharmonic's board; an album with more than a hundred letters of congratulation; an illuminated testimonial signed by numerous colleagues, including Toscanini and Beecham; and a scroll signed by the entire New York Philharmonic.[94] That very day a tribute by Thomas Mann appeared in the *New York Times Magazine* entitled "The Mission of Music," in which the author reflected on Walter's career, their similar fates at the hands of the Nazis, and, most of all, mankind's attempt to harness demoniac powers in the service of culture and the dual nature of music's power: "moral code and seduction, sobriety and drunkenness, a summons to the highest alertness and a lure to the sweetest sleep of enchantment, reason and anti-reason."[95] It may have been a mark of Mann's deep esteem for his friend that, while he privately believed that music tended perhaps more toward seduction, in this article at least he left his readers with the impression that, with the assistance of great conductors like Bruno Walter, music could instead be an ethical force.

Naturally Walter also received numerous private letters and telegrams of congratulation, perhaps the most poignant of which was a three-page memoir by Erika Mann, in which she recalled how Walter used to make up stories for her and his daughters involving a fairy godmother named "Minna Schusterbeisl." Like her brother Klaus, Erika remembered Walter as "enormously amusing." After fifty years of conducting, Walter might have felt drained and tired, but for Erika he still retained his youthful enthusiasm; going to the movies with him, she wrote, was like going to the movies with a brilliant child. And she rather doubted that he would actually get the rest he so deserved and said that even Minna Schusterbeisl could not grant him such a wish.[96] If Erika Mann had known how sadly prophetic her words would turn out to be, she might never have written them.

But meanwhile Walter finished out the season, returned to California to conduct one concert in San Francisco in July, and launched into the writing of his autobiography. Soon he was happily pestering family and friends alike with numerous queries, some factual and some more colorful, turning to his brother and sister for help in remembering their childhood. All this was probably restful compared with conducting endless concerts, and certainly compared with what was about to befall him. The Walters had gone back to Bar Harbor in June for their usual vacation when Elsa, who had never fully recovered from the blow of Gretel's death, suffered a stroke that left her hanging for months in semi-consciousness.

Walter could do nothing but bring her back to New York, see that she was cared for, and, as he wrote to Thomas Mann, hope that her suffering would come to a peaceful end. "Although this year of rest, which I had been looking forward to, has now become such a year of unrest—to put it mildly—I am content to have no professional obligations to fulfill—I could under no circumstances leave the house very often and could not concentrate on making music."[97] So he stayed at home and worked on his memoirs, which at least gave him something to think about besides the slow death of the woman who had been his companion for more than forty years. He interrupted his enforced sabbatical only twice—once in October, to conduct the New York Philharmonic in a concert for Czechoslovak Independence Day with Jarmila Novotná, and again in January, to record Samuel Barber's First Symphony.

All the while, he was receiving repeated requests from both the Philharmonic and the Metropolitan Opera boards to return, and by January he had decided that he would end his sabbatical with a Pension Fund concert at the beginning of March and then with performances of *Fidelio* (in English, with the young Regina Resnik delivering a white-hot performance as Leonore),

*Don Giovanni*, and the *Matthäus-Passion* He also found time to give Mann some musical advice for his new novel, *Doktor Faustus*. Walter in fact resumed his conducting activities at the end of February, in the country's geographic center, conducting the Kansas City Philharmonic (at the invitation of the orchestra's conductor, Efrem Kurtz) in two concerts. The local critics probably had no idea what personal tragedy Walter had left behind in New York, but they were quick to acknowledge that Walter's appearance in Kansas City was "an important item in the city's musical history," and that "the effects of his association with the orchestra will be lasting and cumulative."[98]

After eight months of suffering, Elsa at last died on March 26, just before Walter's first *Matthäus-Passion* performance that spring. "She who had fought bravely and indefatigably on behalf of one who was not born to be a fighter was now for long and painful months engaged in the last fight—a fight we all must lose," Walter reflected near the end of his autobiography. "After almost forty-four years of an all too exciting life at my side she left me and my daughter, to find in eternal life the peace she so richly deserved."[99]

Condolences came pouring in from Walter's friends and colleagues, yet as usual he found his strongest consolation in simply returning to work. Along with the resumption of his usual New York and Philadelphia activities, he made two landmark recordings. One was of Mahler's Fourth Symphony with Desi Halban (the daughter of the soprano Selma Kurz, with whom Walter had often worked in his early Vienna years), which was technically the first uncut recording of the piece, since a previous album had trimmed a few measures. The other milestone was Mendelssohn's Violin Concerto with Nathan Milstein, an incomparable performance that auspiciously ventured forth as Columbia's first twelve-inch LP.[100]

A few days before entering the studio to commit Mahler's Fourth to disk, Walter attended the world premiere of Artur Schnabel's Sonata for Violin and Piano, performed by Alexander Schneider and Bruno Eisner in Dalcrose Auditorium at New York's City Center.[101] Schnabel admired Walter's conducting enough to dash off a note to the conductor in 1943, directly after hearing the *Matthäus-Passion*: "Your accomplishment last night remains a pinnacle, a model, a blessing, and a goal. Everyone who could go must have loved you, and must remain more joyous, clear-sighted, and modest. And that is the way that the meaning of music is truly fulfilled."[102] In turn, Walter often expressed his admiration for the pianist's artistry, though he could discover no path to Schnabel's music. When Walter's old journalistic champion César Saerchinger approached Walter in 1951, asking him to sponsor a memorial committee for the purpose of organizing a concert of Schnabel's works, Walter wrote back frankly: "Let me say that I would certainly b[e] very happy to prove my lasting friendship and love for Artur Schnabel. But I could not do it by sponsoring a concert of Artur's works which have remained inaccessible to my comprehension. Much as I admired and loved Artur's personality, musicianship, and, of course, his greatness as a pianist, as a composer he has remained a stranger to me."[103] One imagines Walter squirming in his seat as he politely listened to a work composed by an old friend and colleague, an abrasively dissonant piece that could not have been to his taste. Perhaps he went not only out of a sense of loyalty to the pianist but also out of a determination to return to an active life after Elsa's death. "I have found my way back to work and music and to the completion of my book (which is near at hand)," he wrote to Flagler in May, just a few days after the recital, and also after V-E Day, "but nobody will understand better than you how hard it is to adapt myself to my present way of life."[104]

Now more than ever Walter relied on his one remaining daughter, and even after her marriage to Karl Ludwig Lindt in 1949 she remained her father's close companion, accompanying him on most of his trips to Europe after the war. In an interview some years after Walter's death, Lotte reflected that caring for her father was not a great hardship; in fact it was easy. "I don't think there can be a better relationship between father and daughter than ours was," she declared. "People sometimes asked me whether I found that this was a sacrifice that I was making, giving up very much of my own life. Well, it was no sacrifice whatsoever, mostly because he was so completely tolerant a human being. He always put himself in the place of the other person."[105] Certainly Walter and his eldest daughter had always been on close terms, and that summer they began making plans to buy a house together in Beverly Hills.

Walter was as relieved and overjoyed as anyone else that the long-awaited end to the European catastrophe had finally come. "The anti-Christ is already in hell—I feel it," he wrote to a professor of religion who had admired Walter's *Matthäus-Passion* and with whom he had struck up a correspondence.[106] But the year was not a time for unmitigated joy, for in addition to recovering from Elsa's death, Walter was also faced with the loss of Franz Werfel, who died in August. To make matters worse, by December rumors began to fly that Walter and Alma Mahler Werfel, two displaced Europeans in California, both widowed, were intending to marry. That Walter had recently purchased the house next to Alma's on North Bedford Drive did nothing to rein in such rampant gossip, and Alma described how one morning, as she lay sick in bed, she heard Hedda Hopper, the film columnist for the *Los Angeles Times*, announce the impending marriage. "I was boiling with rage at the ghouls who could think of nothing better than to marry me off while I lay heartbroken over the loss of Franz Werfel," Alma snarled. Walter, for his part, merely asked her mildly, "But would that be so terrible?"—though eventually his management sent out a press release to quash the rumor once and for all.[107]

At the same time, the translation of Walter's autobiography was not proceeding as smoothly as he could have wished, though in this Walter was partly to blame. With every chapter that James Galston translated, Walter sent him numerous suggestions, until Galston finally pleaded with him to stop sending corrections, for he had already spent a great deal of time working on the book and had to move on to other projects.[108] Walter was also not pleased when Herbert Weinstock, his editor at Knopf, called his writing style "flowery and oratorical" and suggested cutting some 30,000 words, which in Walter's estimation represented roughly a fifth of the entire book. "It may perhaps help to tell him," Walter complained indignantly to his agent, Franz Horch, "that Thomas Mann, as well as Franz Werfel, both of whom very carefully had read my book, spoke with particular satisfaction about the simplicity and seriousness of my tale."[109] In the end Walter agreed to cut the occasional sentence, mostly in passages containing references to works of German literature that Knopf deemed unfamiliar to American readers.

Perhaps with an eye toward finishing his autobiography, Walter kept his fall schedule fairly light in 1945, though he did make his first trip to Chicago, conducting several performances of *Forza* at the Civic Opera House. Zinka Milanov was to have been his Leonora but was suddenly taken ill, and Stella Roman made an overnight trip from San Francisco to take on the part, earning the appellation "heroine" of the evening. She and Walter received the greatest plaudits. "As all good operas should have, last night's 'La Forza del Destino' had both a hero and a heroine," Albert Goldberg reported, but "the hero of the occasion was not the tenor but the conductor."[110] During his stay in Chicago Walter also conducted *Figaro* with Pinza and one concert with the Chicago Symphony to benefit the orchestra's pension fund.

With the end of the war came numerous invitations for Walter to return to Europe to conduct, and some of his friends even wondered if he might come back there to live. "I don't wish to leave America anymore, except for short trips to Europe," he wrote to Leo and Emma. "I am too old to uproot myself once again."[111] Nevertheless, he was more than willing to accept as many invitations as his schedule would allow, and by the end of 1945 he had already planned a trip for the following fall that would include concerts in Stockholm, where he would be reunited with his brother and sister, and also in London, Amsterdam, Brussels, and Paris. Then he and Lotte planned to go to Lugano, to bury Elsa's ashes "where Gretel's urn rests," he told Leo and Emma, "and where we will also want to rest someday."[112]

But first he had a busy season ahead of him in New York and Philadelphia (with one concert in Montreal in October), finishing out the year with the New York Philharmonic premiere of Mahler's Ninth Symphony in December. As might be predicted, Walter received superlative reviews and Mahler somewhat mixed ones, especially from Olin Downes, who, never at the top of his critical powers when reviewing Mahler, wrote of this towering masterpiece that "there is a degree of ostentation in this music which would be funny if it were not so vulgar."[113] Other critics responded more positively to the work and appreciated the opportunity to hear it played under the direction of the conductor who had given its world premiere. (One member of the audience, Henry-Louis de La Grange, then hearing Mahler for the first time,[114] has since devoted more than four decades to researching and chronicling the composer's life.) No one, however, seemed very enthusiastic about another composer whose music Walter also championed—Hans Pfitzner. In fact, Walter's decision to program his Three Preludes from *Palestrina* in March 1946 struck many as more than questionable. Virgil Thomson reported that he had received a letter protesting the performance of Pfitzner's music on political grounds, though he remarked dryly that "this citizen has no objection to hearing any music he has not heard before, even though it were written by Hitler himself"; nevertheless, he didn't find the preludes to have much life in them.[115]

Walter himself received some anti-Pfitzner letters, one from a man who wrote that Pfitzner had supported the Nazi regime during the occupation of Poland. Upon hearing this, Walter was adamant in his refusal to believe that Pfitzner could have been anything but a victim of the Nazis: "I indeed would be horrified to think that I perform music of a composer who has identified himself in such a way as you indicate with the cause of Nazism." Pfitzner had fallen into disgrace with the Nazis, Walter wrote to his correspondent, and the terrible things reported of him seemed "incredible to me after the long years of my connection with Pfitzner."[116] His correspondent assured him that he had personally witnessed the events he described and could produce other Polish witnesses. Despite public and private condemnations of Pfitzner, Walter sent him food and went so far as to write to the United States Army's Munich Detachment to see what could be done to help his friend, who, as he learned from a fellow acquaintance, had lost all his belongings and was living in "deplorable" conditions in a sanatorium in Garmisch. "Without any doubt Pfitzner is besides Richard Strauss the most important German composer of our time," he maintained, telling the authorities that "after the long years of my personal connection with Pfitzner I felt sure that there could not be an understanding between the Nazis and a man of such value."[117]

Walter's pleas appeared to have little immediate effect, though Pfitzner wrote to him soon afterward, thanking him for performing his preludes and for the letter Walter had written on his behalf. It did his heart good, he said, that Walter still esteemed him and that they had remained faithful to each other.[118] About what he might or might not have done during the war, Pfitzner was unrepentant, writing to Walter later in the year that he thought that making all Germans accountable for Hitler's deeds, as he claimed that some Germans like Thomas Mann and Hermann Hesse were not too ashamed to do, was "as intellectually shallow and false as [it was] morally disgraceful." Showing little sensitivity to what Walter himself had endured, he wallowed in self-pity, complaining that at the end of his life he sat ignored, an "undesirable" living in a welfare home, and he claimed to be delighted that Walter, in contrast, rode "in triumph through a Europe purged of Germans," practicing his art to his "heart's content."[119] This egocentricity proved too much even for Walter, who tersely wrote back: "There is a chasm between your way of thinking and mine that I would probably only increase through a response. . . . Concerning my triumphal march, I would say to you only that my trip was undertaken for the purpose of laying my wife's ashes next to Grete's grave in Lugano, and since I was already going to Europe, I decided to conduct along the way, to accept in gratitude the most pressing and cordial invitations that had come from countries that had been kindly disposed to me and have remained so."[120] This was his last letter to Pfitzner, yet he continued to defend him until the composer's death in 1949, arguing in an unconvincing attempt to de-Nazify Pfitzner that his "unworldly idealism" and "patriotism inspired by great German culture" had caused him to be deceived by Nazi propaganda.[121] All this earned him at least one scathing letter in which the writer asked why he couldn't recall having seen a statement from Walter on behalf of Palestine or Greece or "any other decent cause"; was his schedule too demanding to allow him to defend anyone other than Nazis?[122]

As the year proceeded, Walter's thoughts turned more and more toward his upcoming trip to Europe. In April he and Lotte applied for U.S. citizenship, since in order to travel they had to obtain U.S. passports; Harry Harkness Flagler and Arthur Judson stood as Walter's witnesses. Then Walter and Lotte returned to the West Coast, where they began setting up their new house, and in September Walter conducted three concerts in San Francisco as part of a "Bruno Walter Festival." In the meantime *Theme and Variations* had finally appeared, with a German edition to be published shortly afterward by Bermann-Fischer. If Walter read Howard Taubman's mixed review in the *New York Times*, he would probably have been irked that Taubman spent the last two paragraphs discussing Walter's confessed failure to see the Nazi danger until it was nearly too late. "In Mr. Walter's case the reason for the failure was 'the tyranny of art,' not indolence," Taubman concluded. "But it wasn't a good enough excuse. One hopes the ivory-tower boys and girls are listening."[123]

While Taubman was busy casting aspersions on Walter for having left Europe at the last possible moment, Walter was in the midst of preparing to return. On September 21, just six days after his seventieth birthday, he left on the *Drottningholm* for Gothenburg, where he was at last reunited with his brother Leo and his sister Emma. Shortly afterward Walter repaired to Stockholm to conduct four concerts with the Stockholm Philharmonic Orchestra, then went on to London to conduct the London Philharmonic "after long absence," as the London *Times* reported with its wonted restraint.[124] There followed visits to Amsterdam, Brussels, Paris, and finally Zurich, where he conducted a pension fund benefit with an enlarged Tonhalle-Orchester. For the most part his programs consisted of standard repertoire, which was probably just as well, for Walter was so overwhelmed by "the wealth of impressions" that he must have found it difficult to concentrate his energies on conducting. "I've had a time of work, of private obligations, of excitement behind me such as I've hardly ever lived through in my violently shifting existence," he wrote to the Manns in the middle of December from Lugano, as his trip was nearing its end. There was so much to tell that he hardly knew where to begin, such as the striking contrast between ailing France (in spite of Paris's radiant beauty) and the "unshakable" nature of Switzerland, where he had a sense of the earlier Europe even more strongly than in Sweden. Having arrived in Lugano the day before and placed Elsa's ashes in the grave with Gretel's, Walter and Lotte were now sorting through the possessions that had remained behind in their former house, deciding what to send on to America.[125] Walter then returned to London for one more concert, flying back to New York on January 5.

Walter's months of traveling around Europe recalled his wanderings of the previous decade, and no sooner had he arrived in New York than he was off to Boston, where he had not conducted since his first trip to the United States in 1923. That Walter had recently been to the old country for the first time since the war was not lost on the Boston journalists, one of whom asked Walter how he had found Europe. "A very simple question for a complex answer," Walter replied, then went on to describe how, throughout the war, music had been of vital importance to people's daily lives. Dutch and English orchestras, he maintained, were even better than before the war. As for Central Europe, which he did not visit, it would take much "time and wisdom" for it to "come back."[126]

Instead of tiring him out, Walter's trip to Europe provided him with a fresh burst of energy. That spring, he traveled around more than he had in the previous years; in addition to conducting in New York (where his concerts featured Vaughan Williams's Fifth Symphony) and Philadelphia, he made a trip to Montreal and returned to Boston in March. He also made a number of recordings, including the world premiere release of Mahler's Fifth Symphony with the New York Philharmonic, which a few years later he said deserved a place among his "best records."[127] His letters during this time have lost the constant undercurrent of fatigue and are full of future plans. But soon he would have to curtail his wanderings once again, because he had given in to repeated requests to become the New York Philharmonic's musical adviser.

*Walter and Arturo Toscanini, on the occasion of Toscanini's European tour with the
New York Philharmonic (Leipzig, 1930).*
Courtesy of Sony Music Photo Archives.

*Ossip Gabrilowitsch and his wife, Clara (Mark Twain's daughter), both of whom
were close friends of Walter (1934).*
Courtesy of *Musical America* Archives.

*Ezio Pinza as Don Giovanni, Metropolitan Opera production (New York, early 1940s).*
Courtesy of Metropolitan Opera Archives.

*Gretel Walter, who became romantically involved with Pinza (ca. 1930).*
Courtesy of Bruno Walter Papers, Music Division, The New York Public Library
for the Performing Arts, Astor, Lenox and Tilden Foundations.

*Thomas Mann and Walter (ca. 1945).*
Courtesy of Sony Music Photo Archives.

*Walter and his wife* (left), *joined by Walter's frequent recital partner, Lotte Lehmann (ca. 1940).*
Courtesy of Sony Music Photo Archives.

*Walter in Sweden after the war, reunited with his sister Emma and brother Leo*
*(ca. 1946).*
Courtesy of Bruno Walter Papers, Music Division, The New York Public Library
for the Performing Arts, Astor, Lenox and Tilden Foundations.

*Walter conducting the New York Philharmonic (1940s).*
Courtesy of New York Philharmonic Archives.

*Walter surrounded by the members of the New York Philharmonic (1947).*
From left to right, standing: *Willi Feder, Leonard Rose, Bruno Zirato, and Walter Hendl;* seated: *Imre Pogany, Saul Goodman, Anselme Fortier, Simeon Bellison, William Lincer, Walter, Harold Gomberg, John Corigliano, William Vacchiano, John Wummer, Gordon Pulis, William Polisi, and James Chambers.*
Courtesy of New York Philharmonic Archives.

*Walter with string principals of the New York Philharmonic: John Corigliano, violin; Leonard Rose, cello; and William Lincer, viola (1947).*
Courtesy of New York Philharmonic Archives.

*Walter and Kathleen Ferrier around the time of her United States debut in 1948.*
Courtesy of *Musical America* Archives.

*Bruno Walter and Delia Reinhardt, at the time of her attempted return to the*
*concert stage (ca. 1949).*
Courtesy of Bruno Walter Papers, Music Division, The New York
Public Library for the Performing Arts, Astor, Lenox and Tilden Foundations.

*Walter and Wilhelm Furtwängler (Berlin, 1950).*
Courtesy of Bruno Walter Papers, Music Division, The New York
Public Library for the Performing Arts, Astor, Lenox and Tilden Foundations.

*Walter and Eleanor Steber (New York, ca. 1953).*
Courtesy of Yale University, Fred Plaut Collection.

*Walter at a rehearsal for* Die Zauberflöte *(New York, 1956).*
Courtesy of Metropolitan Opera Archives.

*William Warfield, Jennie Tourel, Irmgard Seefried, and Walter, listening to a*
*playback of the Mozart Requiem (New York, 1956).*
Don Hunstein, courtesy of Sony Music Photo Archives.

*Walter and his daughter Lotte, on their way to Italy (1950s).*
Courtesy of New York Philharmonic Archives.

Foreground: *Walter, Leonard Bernstein, and producer John McClure, after a recording session for* Das Lied von der Erde. *Bernstein, who listened to the session in the control booth, reportedly asked McClure: "Why does he do that?" (New York, 1960).*
Don Hunstein, courtesy of Sony Music Photo Archives.

*"You have to sing about wine, not about beer." Ernst Haefliger and Walter, during the playback session for* Das Lied. *In his last letter, dated February 16, 1962, Walter praised "the excellent Swiss tenor Ernst Haefliger."*
Don Hunstein, courtesy of Sony Music Photo Archives.

# FOURTEEN

# *Musical Adviser*
## New York, 1947–1949

*One of the main questions is how to handle persons,*
*how to handle men, how to influence these musicians . . .*
Bruno Walter to Albert Goldberg in 1958

It must have come as a shock. At the beginning of February 1947, Artur Rodzinski resigned his position as musical director of the New York Philharmonic, citing irreconcilable differences between himself and the management, especially Arthur Judson.[1] A week later the papers would announce that Walter was assuming the reins at the Philharmonic, but even before that news became public, Rodzinski, happening upon some positive words that Walter had offered about the orchestra's administration, fired off a letter to his successor. He wrote that he'd always had "tremendous respect" for Walter but considered his colleague ill informed about the "inside aspects" of the Philharmonic. Many times he had recommended Walter "as a guest conductor for at least six or eight weeks," yet his proposals were "always turned down because, in the opinion of those in power, you were not a large enough box-office attraction to warrant a longer engagement than the period you now have."[2]

If Walter was shaken by the news, his response didn't show it. Three days after the papers ran the story of Walter's becoming musical adviser, he wrote back to Rodzinski: "Let me state that in all these years the management of the Philharmonic Symphony Society offered me longer periods for guest appearances than I could accept, and in 1943 they offered me the position of their Musical Director. I do not see how these facts can be reconciled with the statements you sent me."[3] Of course, there may have been some truth to Rodzinski's charge against the Philharmonic management, yet in citing the earlier offer of the position of musical director, Walter laid down a strong hand, since it was only after he had turned down the appointment for the 1943–44 season that Rodzinski was offered the position.

It's only natural to wonder why Walter chose to take on more responsibility now, when earlier he'd said that his advanced years had prevented him from accepting the post. No doubt a number of factors came into play: he had finished his autobiography, his wife had died, and the Philharmonic desperately needed his help. It was a "moral obligation," in his words, to assist the organization in its hour of need.[4] Nevertheless, he wanted to avoid being worked beyond his strength, and experience had taught him to know his limitations. His title would be not "musical director" but only "musical adviser," and he didn't wish even that label to appear on the concert programs.[5] Furthermore, he would need adequate time to rest during the course of the season. But for all that, his work for the New York Philharmonic made plenty of demands on him, and engagements outside New York continued to keep him fully occupied.

One of the first tasks Walter tackled after being named musical adviser was to begin mapping out conductors and programs for the 1947–48 season. In this he was helped immeasurably by his friend Wolfgang Stresemann, a cultivated man from an esteemed family; his father, Gustav Stresemann, had served as Chancellor of Germany and as Foreign Minister—"the last great European political figure," as Walter characterized him in 1948.[6] Walter patently respected and admired the statesman's son. As a composer, Wolfgang Stresemann could read scores intelligently, and as an aspiring conductor, he took a personal and professional interest in newly written music. Over the course of several years Walter recommended Stresemann for a number of conducting posts. It was clear that Walter felt free to speak his mind to his younger friend, and few of Walter's correspondents could elicit such personal utterances as Stresemann drew from the usually guarded Walter. In his letters to Stresemann, Walter even went as far as to comment freely on his colleagues. For instance, on hearing thirdhand, by way of Stresemann, that

Fritz Reiner had said he'd reached the point where he bored even himself at the podium, Walter confided to his friend: "That's how he looks, and that's how it sounds."[7]

For his first season as musical adviser Walter made a conscious effort to find new American pieces. During the spring of 1947 Stresemann sifted through numerous scores in New York, sending his reports (and sometimes sheet music) to Walter in Beverly Hills. Walter also did some digging, rejecting certain composers out of hand. Works that were too dissonant stood little chance of winning him over, and the music of one contemporary composer ranked somewhat lower than construction noise, as he half-jokingly wrote to Stresemann in April 1947: "We're very happy in our new house, although a great deal of work remains to be done, and the air resounds with the noise of the workers—which, however, I prefer in any case to the compositions of Roger Sessions."[8] Music in which jazz elements played too vigorous a part was also taboo, though Walter would allow the occasional jazz-evoking harmony or syncopation. The neoclassicists and neoromantics appealed most strongly to Walter, who sought another gem from Samuel Barber. As it turned out, Barber did have something to offer. His Second Symphony had been performed in 1943 under Koussevitzky, in a version that contained electronic noises to conjure up an atmosphere of airborne maneuvers (the work was commissioned by, and dedicated to, the United States Air Force). Barber was at work on a revision of the symphony, deleting the electronic effects, and Walter hoped very much that this would supply him with a substantial American novelty. When he finally received the score, however, he was utterly repelled by it.[9] Though the revised symphony was eventually picked up by Eugene Ormandy (who performed it with the Philadelphia Orchestra in 1948), Barber himself later repudiated the piece, destroying the score and most of the parts, though recordings of the piece show the symphony to be an impressive composition, worthy of a place in Barber's canon.[10] It is a pity and a disappointment that Walter should have rejected it so vehemently.

"My novelty-headaches are being increased by a stream of unsolicited new works, not worth discussing, that wend their way into my house," Walter confessed to Stresemann in May. Growing desperate, Walter wondered whether it would be permissible to play the Barber Adagio for Strings again, though Stresemann retorted that, since the work was so well known, "performing it could scarcely be seen as promoting American music."[11] Among the other compositions that the two of them considered (mostly in reports from Stresemann to Walter) were works by Felix Borowski, Anthony Donato, Howard Hanson, Harrison Kerr, Walter Piston, Randall Thompson, David Van Vactor, and John Vewall. Some of the composers, like Thompson and Piston, had nothing new to suit the conductor's immediate needs. Nevertheless, Walter seriously considered Piston's Prelude for Organ and Strings and admired Borowski's *Requiem for a Child*, though he feared that the audience would "not regard it as substantial."[12]

Finally, in the middle of May, Stresemann exclaimed in Latinate jubilation: "Habemus Sinfoniam!" ("We have a symphony!"). He had just heard a new work by Douglas Moore—today best remembered for his opera *The Ballad of Baby Doe*—performed at Columbia University. The symphony, Stresemann wrote, though not a masterpiece, was a light, unproblematic composition with many attractions. An alternative possibility, Stresemann added, was Howard Hanson's Fourth Symphony ("Requiem"), though its third movement, the "Dies irae," struck him as weak.[13] After examining the scores, Walter voiced his doubts about both symphonies. He deemed Hanson's "Dies irae" dreadful, though that short movement (under four minutes long) is far from contemptible, and the symphony as a whole offers much that should have appealed to Walter—a distinct gravitas, skillful construction, moderate use of dissonance. As for Moore's piece, Walter allowed that it had "a certain musical quality," but the outer movements were troubling. "I can't get used to the last movement at all," Walter wrote. "And the first movement is simply too playful for me."[14] Walter's objections to both movements were certainly justified. The first movement sounds too much like a film score for a breezy American comedy, while the finale is disappointingly short—under four minutes in Walter's performance. But Stresemann, having heard it again, found the piece superior to its competitors. Since Barber, Thompson, and Piston had nothing satisfactory to offer, and "Copland, Schuman, Harris and company are not under consideration, Moore still seems the best to me," he wrote to Walter.[15] Why Copland, Schuman, and Harris were not in the running is puzzling; a few years later Stresemann himself would be programming Copland's *Appalachian Spring* for one of his concerts.[16] Meanwhile Walter had examined a new work by David Stanley Smith, *The Passing of Oedipus*, but wrote respectfully to the composer that he "could not gain a positive impression. Maybe, it is the enormous tragedy which your music tries to convey, so enormous that it defies an adequate musical expression." He suggested that Smith play the work for him in New York.[17] In any event, Moore's Symphony no. 2 was selected as the major

American novelty for Walter's first season as musical adviser to the New York Philharmonic, curiously beating out Barber's Second Symphony and Hanson's Fourth (both richer, deeper pieces). It would not, however, represent the only American piece on his programs, nor the only novelty.

One of his better choices for the coming season was a work he had conducted in 1932, his first year with the Philharmonic-Symphony Society: Daniel Gregory Mason's Symphony no. 2. This brooding work—conjuring up at times the more volatile qualities of Brahms and Elgar—had been revised since its first performances, and Walter planned to schedule it as one of his Sunday broadcasts. Mason proudly devoted two single-spaced pages in his journal to a meeting he had with Walter at the conductor's hotel on April 4, during which the two discussed the piece in great detail.[18] Walter's plan to schedule the work for a broadcast, however, was endangered by the possibility that the soloist for the evening, Vladimir Horowitz, might choose to play Brahms's Second Piano Concerto for the broadcast (as he did for the Thursday and Friday performances), in which case there would not be enough time to broadcast the symphony as well. Walter gingerly suggested substituting Mason's *Suite after English Folksongs*, a shorter and lighter work. Hearing the proposal, Mason was palpably shaken. Walter's letter threatened "a grievous disappointment" to him. "Ever since that red-letter day in my life when we went over the score of my Second Symphony at your apartment," Mason wrote, "and you promised to play it in one of your broadcasts which you convinced me were of greatest importance to knowledge of any American music, I have been convinced that you were giving me one of the supreme, and perhaps latest, opportunities of my career as a composer."[19] The suite was already well known, and the symphony had been heavily revised. Mason believed that his symphony "might be more seriously regarded now than it was fifteen years ago, even though I am now one of the older men, and out of the picture focussed on Copland, Schuman, Harris, Barber, Moore, Morton Gould, and the rest. I think people in general are more anxious to have an indigenous American music now than they were then." Walter apologized for giving his friend "a seemingly unnecessary 'shock'" and reassured him that the piece would be performed on the Sunday broadcast.[20]

In addition to fixing his own programs for the coming season, Walter oversaw and commented on the programs of his colleagues—Leopold Stokowski, Charles Munch (his old concertmaster from the Leipzig Gewandhaus Orchestra), Dimitri Mitropoulos, and the assistant conductor Walter

Hendl, who had joined the organization in 1945 and whom Walter had recommended retaining for the 1947–48 season. In most cases there was little to say about the choices his colleagues had made, though some juggling with everybody's favorite symphonic works was inevitable. But with Dimitri Mitropoulos Walter had several differences of opinion that led to outwardly polite but obviously disturbing clashes, often mediated by Bruno Zirato, associate manager of the Philharmonic in the 1946–47 season and joint manager (with Arthur Judson) the following season. Zirato, who had worked for Caruso and acted as a liaison between Toscanini and the New York Philharmonic, was also vice-president in charge of conductors at Columbia Artists Management, where he had handled Walter since the early 1930s. He and Walter were friends as well as colleagues, and Walter was a sometime dinner guest at the Zirato residence.[21] There is a refreshing frankness in the correspondence between these two professionals; Zirato, however, seems occasionally to have accepted his role as intermediary between Walter and Mitropoulos with a sigh of resignation.

The emotionally ambivalent relationship between the two conductors was akin, in some ways, to that between Furtwängler and Walter. Furtwängler, Mitropoulos, and Walter were all composer-conductors as well as pianists. The two younger conductors had admired the elder statesman, as he admired them. Yet, with such strong personalities in play, it's no wonder that friction eventually developed. During his student days in Berlin, in the early 1920s, Mitropoulos had heard Walter conduct the Berlin Philharmonic, and the experience had left a deep impression on him. His words of praise for Walter could be effusive; in 1948, on learning that he would be on the Philharmonic roster again, he oozed praise for his superior: "I almost tremble before that chance to be associated with an artist of your caliber."[22] Walter responded in kind, though with a cooler, northern choice of words: "I only can thank you and beg you to be assured that I feel very happy to have you again and for an even longer period with our orchestra. Your activity is, by its great artistic and moral meaning, a necessity in the musical life of New York."[23]

Like Walter, Mitropoulos was one of the great champions of Mahler in the first half of the twentieth century. Both conductors continued to program Mahler's symphonies in New York and other territories whose local critics had made their hostility to the composer abundantly clear over a period of decades. That being so, the men established what was at once a close bond and a potential source of conflict, since they offered markedly different interpretations of the works and had differing ideas about their presentation to the public. One symphony that Walter had avoided through the years was Mahler's Sixth. The deepest reasons for his avoidance of this powerful work—notwithstanding his statement that the symphony is "bleakly pessimistic" and "ends in hopelessness"—are ultimately shrouded in mystery, yet he claimed to be delighted that Mitropoulos was scheduling the work for the 1947–48 season.[24] Surprisingly, given the forty-odd years that had elapsed since its very first performance, this was the United States premiere of Mahler's "Tragic" Symphony. One aspect of Mitropoulos's proposed project, however, rubbed Walter the wrong way. The companion piece for the concert was to be Gershwin's Piano concerto, with Oscar Levant as soloist. The choice was not entirely frivolous. When listening to the two works in succession, one can hear a number of similarities in orchestral color and inventive boldness. But Gershwin's concerto characteristically made use of jazz idioms, and jazz-influenced classical music almost always made Walter shudder in disgust. To combine Gershwin with Mahler, a composer Walter revered as the greatest he had ever known, must have seemed tantamount to blasphemy. On June 11, 1947, he wrote a letter to Bruno Zirato on the proposed programs of his colleagues and duly noted his dissatisfaction with Mitropoulos's combination of pieces: "Interesting as I find his programs, I see one point about which I must express my *most serious* doubts. I know that Mr. Oscar Levant has been engaged to play the Gershwin Piano Concerto. But I strongly must plead against the combination of this work with Mahler's Sixth Symphony in one program. On the list of the works which Mr. Mitropoulos has chosen, I see many pieces which go far better with Gershwin than just Mahler's most tragic opus, and I would be very grateful for a 'shift.'"[25] Despite Walter's reservations, Levant did play the Gershwin Concerto on the same program as Mahler's Sixth; indeed, the Gershwin Concerto eventually edged Mahler's Sixth out of the broadcast slot, much to Mitropoulos's bitter disappointment. It was not to be the last time the two conductors would quarrel over Mahler.

Though most of Walter's contact with the media revolved around radio broadcasts and newspaper reviews, one episode with the New York Philharmonic extended his activities into the movie theater. Walter was no stranger to celluloid; he had already been shot conducting in the 1930s, but now he was in what purported to be a genuine feature film. At the beginning of May 1947 the movie *Carnegie Hall* had its New York premiere. Built on the flimsiest of plots, it tells the story of a young man, Tony Salerno, who is raised by a loving but overprotective mother. She works in the hall and wants him to become a concert pianist, with his musical education being enriched by the superb artists who grace the stage there every night. The plot conveniently allows the audience to hear performances by Walter, Stokowski, Reiner, Heifetz, Piatigorsky, Pinza, Pons, Rodzinski, Rubinstein, and other masters of the day. Tony eventually turns to jazz, much to his mother's dismay, but makes good at the end of the film by conducting and playing the piano in a piece of his own composition, which features Harry James as trumpet soloist—a fusion of jazz and classical music that must have sickened Walter. The performance takes place, inescapably, at Carnegie Hall, with Tony's proud mother seated in the same box as a congratulatory Olin Downes, who in real life would have despised the piece.

Assigned a single, far-from-challenging line in the movie ("Here you are, Tony"), Walter delivers his words with avuncular warmth as he presents his autograph to the aspiring pianist. The conductor had no delusions about his future as a potential legend of the silver screen. Lotte Lehmann, by contrast, did envision the possibility of a new career after being invited to act in the feature film *Big City*, which was released the following year. When she wrote to Walter about it in 1947, he replied with a self-deprecating sense of humor that he reserved for her and a few other intimate friends: "I certainly don't expect that you'll achieve the profound effect of my speaking scene in *Carnegie Hall*, in which the camera men, in horror, dropped their equipment."[26]

Hollywood also demanded Walter's presence in 1947, though not for film work. On July 8 he opened the twenty-sixth season of Hollywood Bowl concerts with an all-Wagner program, followed by an all-Brahms concert two days later. A third concert was a mixed bag of Dvořák, Debussy, and others. Acetates of the Wagner and Brahms concerts have circulated, one of the highlights being the Prelude and "Liebestod" of *Tristan* and the "Immolation Scene" from *Götterdämmerung*, featuring the American soprano Helen Traubel as soloist.[27] The Hollywood Bowl "Liebestod" has a special value in that it preserves a rare performance of Walter conducting this famous set piece with a first-rate vocalist. (A couple of strictly instrumental arrangements survive, as well as another sung version at the Bowl with the less satisfying Margaret Harshaw.[28]) Traubel was one of the great Wagnerian sopranos of her day, an American in the Leider and Flagstad mold, and she gave Walter a place of honor in her memoirs when listing the conductors with whom she had worked—who included Szell, Beecham, Reiner, and Busch.

"Towering among them all is Bruno Walter, a conductor who stands out in my mind not only for his clean-cut musicianship but for the fact that he begged me on a dozen occasions to learn the leading part in *Fidelio*." It was an offer the weighty Wagnerian refused for cosmetic reasons; the heroine, she noted, "wore a short coat. I admit that her boots were long, but there was that certain interval in between which, in my case, nothing could disguise."[29] At the Bowl in 1947 the combined forces of Walter and Traubel made for a performance rich in grandeur and power, despite patches of scrappy playing from the orchestra.

In an interview during the intermission of the Wagner program, Walter announced that in September he would be conducting the Vienna Philharmonic "for the first time after the tragic happenings of the last decade, at the music festival at Edinburgh, Scotland." The idea of establishing a summer music festival in Edinburgh that could compete with those in Munich, Bayreuth, and Salzburg was the brainchild of the Austrian-born Rudolf Bing, then manager of the Glyndebourne Festival and future manager of the Metropolitan Opera House, a man who had known Walter already in Vienna and Germany. According to Bing, Walter's willingness to participate in the still-conjectural festival marked the turning point in his efforts to bring it to life. "Whenever anyone asked me what all this was about, I had merely to say that Bruno Walter was coming, and no further questions were asked."[30] In 1946 Walter, Bing, and a young English contralto (or mezzo-soprano, as she was sometimes then billed), Kathleen Ferrier, met in the apartment of the publisher Hamish Hamilton to discuss preparations for the festival. Walter remembered the event clearly eight years later, by which time Ferrier had succumbed to cancer at the age of forty-one: "She came in, not shy and not bold, but in modest self-confidence, dressed in a kind of Salzburg costume, a so-called 'dirndl', looking young and lovely, pure and earnest, simple and noble, and the room seemed to become brighter from the charm of her presence."[31] With Walter at the piano, she sang some lieder and then, at the conductor's request, some passages from *Das Lied*, a work she didn't know. "She overcame their great difficulties with the ease of the born musician," he recalled, "and I recognized with delight that here was potentially one of the great singers of our time: a voice of a rare beauty, a natural production of tone, a genuine warmth of expression." *Das Lied* was in fact one of the works they performed at the first Edinburgh Festival (with Peter Pears singing the tenor part), and during piano rehearsals in London, as Walter tells the story, "We always had to interrupt the last part of the 'Farewell'—she could not continue because her emotions overwhelmed her. Tears streamed down her cheeks; with all her will-power and vigour she could not help it, and only by and by did she learn to control her feelings. But nothing could be further from her than sentimentality—in those tears spoke strength of feeling, not weakness, and a deep comprehension for another great heart."[32] The conductor was clearly taken with the lovely, svelte Ferrier, and doubtful rumors have circulated that their friendship was not simply platonic.

Another artist scheduled to sing at the inaugural season in Edinburgh was Lotte Lehmann, who told Walter over the telephone in August that she would not be able to participate because of a throat irritation. She feared that Walter would be angry with her, and although he replied that they had been friends for too long for him to be truly angry with her, he rebuked her for what he considered her selfish behavior: "Precisely because of our friendship . . . I must tell you how unfair I find the harm and disappointment you caused the people over there, without being able to justify it by a real illness. . . . This is—forgive me for my frankness—the behavior of an inconsiderate egocentricity, which allows you simply to cancel your obligations with a doctor's notice, without feeling the burden of the heavy damage done to the people in Edinburgh."[33] In an attempt to remedy the problem of Lehmann's absence, Bing suggested that Walter accompany either Elisabeth Schumann or Marian Anderson. Walter, who rarely accompanied at this point in his career (and who refused to play a Mozart piano concerto at the festival), wanted a singer with whom he had worked on many occasions. Having collaborated with Anderson only once, in Vienna, and having never accompanied her at the piano in more intimate repertoire, he favored Schumann, though he asked that his decision be kept "IN CONFIDENCE BECAUSE [I] HIGHLY APPRECIATE ANDERSON."[34]

Naturally this reunion with the Vienna Philharmonic engendered powerful feelings on both sides. Although Arnold Rosé, an exile from Austria, had died in London the previous year, another member of the Rosé Quartet, Friedrich Buxbaum, came to Edinburgh for this historic occasion. Buxbaum, Walter's old chamber music companion and former solo cellist of the Vienna Philharmonic, had also been ousted from his country in 1938. In what must have been a deeply touching moment, the orchestra asked him to resume his old place in the cello section, an offer he gladly accepted, while Walter, who didn't take the opportunity to grumble about his having been ejected from Austria, seemed to the orchestra the embodiment of reconciliation.[35] Beginning September 9 Walter and the Vienna Philharmonic performed several sold-out concerts, including in its programs Vaughan Williams's *Fantasia on a Theme of Thomas Tallis*, Beethoven's Sixth and Seventh symphonies, Schubert's "Unfinished," Mahler's *Das Lied von der Erde*, and a program of Haydn, Mozart, and Johann Strauss Jr.

Walter concertized throughout the summer in Europe and also took time out to ruminate on his personal past, returning in the latter half of September to Lugano, a place he would revisit several times more to pay his respects at the resting place of his daughter and wife. Though his concerts were rarely controversial in their choice of repertoire, Walter was surprised to find that one work, long part of the standard repertoire, had now become offensive to some listeners. The incident took place in October, when Walter was reunited with the Concertgebouw Orchestra, and the work in question was Richard Strauss's *Don Juan*—a favorite of both Mahler and Walter, and usually a surefire crowd-pleaser. Some members of the audience, however, left in protest before Walter even gave the downbeat for the piece. He later received two letters from affronted listeners, explaining that they had left because they felt Strauss's music should not be played in the Concertgebouw, since a couple of weeks before Walter's concert, Strauss's new work, the *Metamorphosen*, had been played there, a piece bearing the inscription "In memoriam," which some interpreted as an unpardonable tribute to Hitler.

Though not fond of Strauss as a man, Walter responded that, after studying the *Metamorphosen*, he could discover nothing more in it than a musical masterpiece. The words "In memoriam" surely referred to Strauss's "own glorious past," he wrote, calling attention to the allusions to *Der Rosenkavalier* and *Ein Heldenleben* and its closing musical quotation from "the funeral march of the Eroica."[36] It was therefore puzzling to him how they could conclude that the work was a memorial to Hitler. Where was their proof?

Apparently none was forthcoming, for on January 22, 1948, Walter himself gave the New York Philharmonic premiere of Strauss's *Metamorphosen*. Curiously enough, later that year Walter received a letter from Cyril Clarke asking for permission to quote a mixed judgment on Strauss, attributed to Walter, for an anthology: "I dislike Strauss as a person, and I abhor everything for which he has stood in recent years. But Strauss is a genius and some of his works are masterpieces. I cannot in all honesty boycott masterpieces because I detest their composer."[37] Walter couldn't remember having said these words and assumed that they had been translated from German. Yet he did not argue with their sentiment, giving other reasons for withholding permission: "As you ask for my permission to quote them, I regret to declare that it would be very much against my feelings to grant it, for the simple reason that Richard Strauss is today a very old man, without a home, in bad health and living in pathetic circumstances and so I feel one should not add unnecessary grief to the distress in which he finds himself."[38]

Walter returned to London for several more concerts, including a blistering account of Beethoven's Ninth with the London Philharmonic Orchestra.[39] While abroad he kept up his correspondence regarding the Philharmonic programming and again found himself in disagreement with Mitropoulos. He had read in the *New York Times* that Mitropoulos was planning to "project several titles on the front of the grand drape in Carnegie Hall" to explain the programmatic elements of Strauss's *Alpensymphonie*. After verifying that the story was accurate, Walter, then in London, wrote a long, gentle but firm letter of advice to his colleague in Minneapolis: "You know my warm sympathy with your whole personality as an artist, with your thought and practice and I have not newly to assure you of my high appreciation for your gifts and the way you use them." In this instance, however, Mitropoulos seemed to have gone astray; his plan struck Walter as "extremely unfortunate and absolutely in contrast to the very sense of concerts like ours." He continued to elaborate his point in detail, as he would have done only for someone who he thought would understand and sympathize with his reasoning:

> I am sure you will agree with my opinion that the emotional power of Music is limitless and in this field she is sovereign, whereas her descriptive capacities are—to say the least—doubtful. . . .
>
> When Strauss wrote his "Alpen-Symphonie" his purpose was, as the title proves, to write a symphony and if he could not resist the temptation "to paint" glaziers [*sic*] and cascades etc., seduced by his uncanny descriptive talent, he trespasses the noble limits of Symphonic Music and transfers methods of his dramatic works to a basically different field,—but shall we emphasize his weakness,— or worse—the weakness of Absolute Music by explaining in letters to the Public descriptive intentions, confessing their impotence to make themselves understood without such non-musical support?[40]

Ultimately, Walter left the decision up to Mitropoulos, reiterating that he found his colleague's programs "excellent" and assuring him that he would not interfere with the final choice, despite his "responsibility for the overall character of our Season."

A telegram records Mitropoulos's reponse to Walter: "NO PROJECTION WILL BE MADE WITH ALPINE SYMPHONY[;] FEEL SORRY TO BE RESPONSIBLE FOR SUCH INARTISTIC IDEAS."[41] In a letter to Zirato, Mitropoulos explained his feelings in more detail: "Thank you for sending me the letter of Mr. Bruno Walter. . . . There is no doubt that we have to please that great master. I have such an admiration and respect for him that the last thing I would want to do would be to make him unhappy. . . . I feel unhappy that my idea turned out to be inartistic and I feel mortified that I had the idea in the first place. Certainly I have my arguments and it will take a long discussion and explanation to make my apology understood or accepted."[42]

Though the issue of the titles was quickly resolved, tensions remained between the two conductors. One of the pieces Mitropoulos chose to program was Ernst Krenek's Fourth Symphony, a difficult work employing a tone row and offering a generous helping of dissonance. By this time Walter's views on such compositional techniques were well known from his own public statements and writings, and Walter apparently objected to his colleague's choice, for Mitropoulos wrote in December: "My dear and beloved master. . . . I must confess that I was a little bewildered and shocked by what you said about the Krenek Symphony." The objection was all the more painful to Mitropoulos because, as he wrote, "You have been always for me an exemplary man and artist, whom I always admired, and I tried hard to follow to the best of my abilities your wonderful principles and conceptions. This last incident of controversial ideas does not take away at all my worship of your mind."[43] Thanking him for the compliment, Walter returned that their disagreement could in no way affect Walter's "high and unalterable opinion" of Mitropoulos. "I respect the strength of your convictions and admire the virtuose [i.e., virtuosic] interpretive power which enables you to transform it into performances of such perfection."[44] A broadcast recording of the performance testifies to the passion Mitropoulos brought to Krenek's work, though it predictably elicited indifference or hostility from the press ("a very poor and labored piece of music: artificial in method, lacking in invention, ugly and tedious," to quote Downes[45]).

Whatever reservations Walter might have had about Mitropoulos, he respected his younger colleague's devotion to his art, as well as his devotion to Mahler. An even younger conductor—who would eventually be more closely associated with Mahler than any other conductor of the latter part of the twentieth century—also earned Walter's gratitude for championing the music of his old mentor. In a letter to Stresemann he wrote of his great joy that Mitropoulos was performing Mahler's Sixth and Leonard Bernstein Mahler's Second.[46] This was in fact Bernstein's debut as a performer of Mahler's works, and his orchestra was the short-lived New York City Symphony Orchestra, of which Bernstein was then music director. Although the New York press for the most part received both symphonies with as little enthusiasm as they had shown Mahler in the past, for Walter, the performances, along with other encouraging news, were "good signs and heartening counter-symptoms in view of Toscanini's friendliness to jazz!" That final snipe was probably aimed at the compositions by Gershwin that the Italian maestro was performing in the 1940s.

Throughout much of Walter's later career, especially after World War II, Walter received letters from needy musicians with whom he had once worked, most of them either German or Austrian. In August, for example, Berta Morena, one of the leading Wagnerian sopranos from his Munich years (she had also sung under Mahler), wrote to tell him of her financial burdens and health problems. Walter sympathized. "For a long time," he wrote, "I've felt that there's no situation so tragic as that of innocent Germans who now, after all they had to suffer during the Nazi era, are exposed to the same affliction and defamation as the criminals are." He later sent a "care package," which delighted her.[47] Many others approached Walter for help, and he almost always sent money to help his old friends, though he made no show of his contributions and certainly did not ask for reimbursement.[48] He also did what he could to help unemployed—or unhappily employed—musicians find work, such as Heinz Unger, Klaus Pringsheim (Thomas Mann's brother-in-law), and Maria Olszewska.

Musicians were not the only people to seek Walter's aid. In one of the more poignant episodes of 1948, the author Heinrich Eduard Jacob, who had known Walter in Berlin, Vienna, Strasbourg, and Paris, approached Walter in New York and asked him for a recommendation to help him secure a teaching position. Jacob's story is painfully familiar. After a promising career as a journalist and an author of poetry, fiction, and nonfiction, he was carted off to the concentration camps at Dachau and Buchenwald in the late 1930s, and the new regime tried to extinguish his life's work by burning his books. He eventually made his way to New York and, like so many others, had to begin his life anew. Walter agreed to help Jacob, wrote a sterling recommendation, and then, for some odd reason, wired a message to Thomas Mann, whom he believed Jacob had also approached: "Heinrich Eduard Jacob asked me for a testimony in order to get teaching position at a University and told me that you gave him such recommendation stop please wire if this is true and if your statement included recognition of his ethical qualities."[49] After learning that Mann couldn't recall having written a recommendation for Jacob, Walter himself withheld his own recommendation, much to the astonishment of Jacob, who reminded him of Mann's early support for his novels; Mann, he wrote, would never have found it necessary to ask for another person's opinion of his merits. He had tried to convey the idea that he *hoped* Mann would also write him a letter of recommendation, not that the author had already done so. Perhaps Walter had gotten the wrong idea, because Jacob had deliberately kept the interview short, knowing how busy the conductor was. Nevertheless, Jacob asserted, there was no excuse for such suspicions, since Walter knew him personally.[50] It was not Walter's finest hour.

Other claims on Walter's attention came his way in 1948. The contralto Louise Bernhardt, a rising Mahler interpreter in the late 1940s (she would be one of the soloists in Stokowski's famous performance of Mahler's Eighth with the New York Philharmonic in 1950), was singing in *Das Lied von der Erde*, and an invitation was naturally sent to Walter. The performance, however, was to be choreographed as a ballet, and Walter bristled at the very thought: "I beg you not to send me any tickets for a performance of Mahler's Lied von der Erde in the form of a ballet, an enterprise of which I most fervently disapprove."[51] When invited to the same performance by another party, he telegraphed back an even more vehement response: "THERE ARE NO LEGAL WAYS TO PROTECT SUBLIME WORKS OF ART AGAINST A PROFANATION SUCH AS PERFORMING MAHLER'S LIED VON DER ERDE AS A BALLET. BUT WHY ATTEND SUCH [AN] ACT OF BARBARISM?"[52]

The sublime work of art in question—presented as it should be—was in fact Walter's first offering in 1948 with the New York Philharmonic, where his conducting duties kept him very busy from January to April. His soloists for *Das Lied* were the contralto Kathleen Ferrier and the Swedish heldentenor Set Svanholm. Though Ferrier suffered from a cold on the first night, by the weekend she seems to have recovered, and a recently issued recording of the Sunday broadcast shows both vocalists to have been in splendid voice.[53] Even after the first performance, however, Walter expressed his enthusiasm over Ferrier's rendition of her orchestral songs. "Well," Ferrier wrote to her sister the day after her New York debut, "Bruno Walter was thrilled—I've never known him to open out so—he said I was making musical history (honest)!"[54] The performance, however, drew mixed reviews (owing partly to Ferrier's cold), but one discriminating listener found the broadcast stirring. On a drive up to Boston, Leonard Bernstein tuned in to the performance on his car radio and wrote to Walter afterward: "It was certainly one of the great musical experiences I have had. You are a very, very great master."[55] For his part, Walter found it a "real joy" to be able to "strike such a sympathetic chord" in his colleague's "heart with the performance of Mahler's work."[56]

Throughout this first season as musical adviser, Walter presented a remarkably varied set of works, including the novelties he had prepared so carefully at the beginning of the year. The week after conducting *Das Lied* he offered the New York premiere of Strauss's *Metamorphosen* coupled with Bruckner's Eighth. Two weeks later he gave the New York Philharmonic premiere of Paul Hindemith's *Symphonia serena*; the following week, the Philharmonic premiere of Douglas Moore's Second Symphony. After a brief stint with the Philadelphia Orchestra at the end of February and guest appearances in Cuba with the Patronato Pro-Musica Sinfonica of Havana at the beginning of March, he returned to conduct Daniel Gregory Mason's Second Symphony (only once, for the broadcast), and his contribution to the season ended midway through April with three performances of Beethoven's *Missa solemnis*.

Perhaps the most unexpected piece on Walter's programs for the 1947–48 season was Hindemith's *Sinfonia serena*. Although the two men had traveled in similar circles for decades, Walter had performed almost no music by Hindemith.[57] He wrote to the composer in New Haven late in January, telling him it would be "highly desirable" to go through the symphony with him before the concert; Walter didn't want to lose this rare opportunity to "receive authentic information from a composer about his work," and they scheduled a meeting in New York for February 7.[58] Judged by the yardstick of, say, Schoenberg's *Fünf Orchester-Stücke* or Krenek's Fourth Symphony (two other pieces that would be performed during Walter's years as musical adviser), Hindemith's new work was fairly accessible. Nevertheless, much in the outer movements—especially the finale—was far more abrasive than Walter's standard fare. Yet in some regards the piece shows a continuity with other modernist works that Walter performed; the trumpet fanfares at the beginning and end of the finale, in particular, are strikingly reminiscent of the conclusion to Shostakovich's First Symphony, another uncharacteristic work that Walter had once promoted. The complex counterpoint and syncopations of Hindemith's piece caused the conductor no difficulty whatsoever, to judge by the transcription disks, which show Walter not only fully in control of the score but brimming with personal insights.[59] He had already made the piece his own, and, as the reviewers noted, he conducted the challenging score from memory.

Despite the presence of a few novelties on his programs, most of Walter's selections were drawn, as usual, from the standard repertoire, and his run of New York Philharmonic concerts that season ended with Beethoven. Though Walter had written extensively about Beethoven's *Missa solemnis* and had conducted it in Vienna, Munich, Berlin, and Florence, this was the first and only occasion on which he performed it in the United States. It was also the last time he would conduct that choral masterpiece. Transcription disks of the broadcast in good sound have survived; unfortunately, recent compact-disc issues, made from grotesquely distorted sources, do a grave injustice to the sublime performances that listeners heard in Carnegie Hall midway through April 1948. The soloists were Eleanor Steber, Nan Merriman, William Hain, and Lorenzo Alvary, while the choral parts were sung by the Westminster Choir, directed by John Finley Williamson. Some rough spots aside, the reading stands as one of Walter's great triumphs, with tenderness exuding from the Kyrie, exuberant bursts of joy in the jaw-dropping Gloria, a forceful statement of convictions in the Credo, a cradle-rocking benediction in the Sanctus, and a solemn meditation on life's burdens and an imploring wish for peace in the Agnus Dei. Steber and Merriman are particularly spectacular, not so much for sweetness of tone as for the drama they instill into their parts, sounding utterly carried away by divine frenzy, but the orchestra and chorus also do their part in making this rapturously joyful noise unto the Lord. Walter's ability to communicate his tremendous vision to his large forces and his skill at changing tempo and drawing varied inflections from the singers and instrumentalists are at times breathtaking.

The burden that his position at the New York Philharmonic had placed on Walter made him hesitant to accept another season of similar demands. He had already attempted to resign his position as musical adviser when Bruno Zirato lured him back by suggesting that he conduct a Beethoven cycle with the orchestra; the idea won him over, and he agreed to resume his activity as musical adviser for another season.[60] Being in charge of the Beethoven cycle, he was under less of an obligation to seek out new American music. Nevertheless, as musical adviser, he felt it only right to include at least one new piece by an American composer in his programs. That piece, brought to his attention by Wolfgang Stresemann, was Norman Dello Joio's Variations, Chaconne and Finale, a work that Stresemann himself would later champion both in America and in Germany. When Noel Straus of the *New York Times* wrote a highly complimentary assessment of Walter's proposed programs for the 1948–49 season but erroneously stated that the conductor himself would "not provide novelties," Walter was patently disturbed and wanted to set the record straight, to stress that he was performing the New York premiere of Dello Joio's work. What would American composers and their promoters think if, during his eight weeks of conducting at the Philharmonic, he did not include "one work of American origin" on his programs?[61]

As it turns out, Dello Joio had approached Walter as early as 1946, and the two had discussed the orchestration in one of Dello Joio's other compositions.[62] In the end Walter regretfully rejected the piece, claiming that he had "no access" to the composer's "musical language." "It remains interesting to me," he wrote, "but strange like a landscape on the moon."[63] It's curious that he should have found ready access to the Variations, Chaconne and Finale, the last movement of which is patently "influenced by jazz," as the composer himself has admitted, adding, "I did play jazz for a living for quite a while."[64] According to Wolfgang Stresemann, Walter played the entire work for Dello Joio at the piano, after which the composer reportedly said, "You know, you could have become a very good jazz pianist," provoking a laugh from the jazz-hating conductor.[65] On the whole, though, Walter liked the work, calling it "very interesting and, in a certain sense, even powerful." An occasional "rawness" in the orchestration perhaps moved him to suggest revisions, as he had done with Daniel Gregory Mason.[66] Dello Joio, however, stood his ground. "There was one percussion passage," he recalled, "in which he wanted me to use a cowbell or something. He got me confused with Mahler."[67]

One other modern composer, Ralph Vaughan Williams, had written a new piece—the Sixth Symphony—that Walter wished to perform in the 1948–49 season. Again, Walter's interest in the work is somewhat surprising, especially given the jazzlike touches introduced by the saxophone in the first movement. Yet in June 1948 Walter wrote to Zirato: "Some days ago I received the score of Vaughan Williams' Sixth Symphony and began to study it at once. It is a very important work, but very difficult at the same time, and

I really do not know if I can put it on in a week when I have not the full rehearsing time at my disposal."[68] When Stokowski expressed an interest in giving the New York premiere, Walter, convinced that he himself would not have adequate rehearsal time to do the piece justice, reluctantly turned it over to his colleague.[69]

The need to build balanced programs forced Walter to allow certain works onto the Philharmonic's programs that he would almost certainly never choose to conduct himself. He gave his wholehearted approval when Mitropoulos chose to program Schoenberg's *Fünf Orchester-Stücke* (hardly a Walterian piece) and suggested calling attention to the work as the Philharmonic's "contribution to the celebration of Arnold Schoenberg's 75th birthday, either on the program itself or by a preceding note in our announcements."[70] A more delicate situation arose when a new symphony composed by the pianist Artur Schnabel was rejected, apparently by Mitropoulos. Schnabel, a longtime friend of Walter's, regarded the rejection of his symphony as a sign of the "reactionary tendencies" at the Philharmonic, and Mitropoulos gave Walter reason to believe that Schnabel was planning to discuss the decision publicly. To "avoid unpleasant publicity," Mitropoulos suggested replacing the fifty-minute symphony with a twelve-minute "Rhapsody" by Schnabel. Walter liked the solution. "This would absolutely not fall under the category of 'appeasement,'" he wrote forcefully (if not quite convincingly), adding that he thought "the performance of a short ultra-modern work belongs to the obligations of the Philharmonic Symphony Society and can be made digestible by an appropriate surrounding of familiar works."[71]

During these months Walter's thoughts turned very frequently to the woman who had once played a leading role in his emotional life, Delia Reinhardt. The war was over, and Elsa had died, so in theory there was little to keep Walter separate from Reinhardt. He tried to find a way to transplant her to America, and his friends pulled strings for her. Reinhardt, living in Switzerland, was seriously contemplating a move back to Germany because she stood to lose her meager pension if she did not return. Walter made inquiries about a possible position for her at the Carnegie Institute of Technology in Pittsburgh.[72] That he was trying to get work for Reinhardt in Pittsburgh—hardly next door to Beverly Hills—and that he was concerned about her shaky financial situation complicate the tempting view of their relationship as one hinging mainly on passion.

All the same, when Lotte Lehmann heard in April 1948 that Walter was planning to stop in Switzerland, she asked him to send her greetings to Delia, adding archly, "whom you will indeed probably see (now, now, now!!!!)."[73] We can almost see the sly wink. By March 1949 Reinhardt had moved to California and had been living there long enough to comment on the beautiful colors that the early spring had recently ushered in.[74] Professionally, however, Walter's reason for flying to Europe in the spring was to attend the reinstatement of Rodin's bust of Mahler in the Vienna Staatsoper, the bust having been removed by the Nazis. But the great opera house was in wretched shape, still in ruins after having taken a direct hit near the end of the war. Walter wistfully noticed that the window to his old office was boarded up. "There wasn't any point examining further," he reportedly said. "My old office was the same one Mahler had. It was nice to sit there."[75]

During his time in the city that continued to create such profound emotional resonance within him, Walter led the Vienna Philharmonic in two programs in mid-May, one of Bruckner's Te Deum and Beethoven's Ninth, the other of Mahler's "Resurrection" Symphony (with Maria Cebotari and Rosette Anday as soloists).[76] A broadcast recording of the Mahler program has circulated and shows the conductor vigorous and still able to draw subtleties from the orchestra.[77] For his part, Walter was pleased with the sounds he heard at the rehearsal. "The Vienna Philharmonic hasn't lost the tone introduced by Mahler. It produces the same good music as when I heard the orchestra for the first time when I was twenty-one."[78]

On his return home, an absurd situation arose, showing the confusion that now reigned in Austria, divided as it was among the Americans, British, French, and Soviets. A Soviet guard stationed at the airport in Tullin, near Vienna, detained Walter, insisting that he was a "famous mathematician" (who was no doubt trying to abscond to the West). The truth was that the guard had confused Bruno Walter with Otto Bruna, a "well-known German nuclear physicist," and the mix-up was eventually disentangled.[79] The political intrigue and ham-fisted bureaucratic fumbling could have come straight out of Graham Greene's *The Third Man*.

The strain of conducting and traveling proved debilitating to Walter, and the depressing sights he witnessed in Vienna did nothing to lift his spirits. In September he wrote to the Viennese journalist Alfred Polgar (then living in Zurich) that his condition could be called "bittersweet." He had by this time developed diabetes, and on his return home, he wrote to Polgar, the disease progressed rapidly at first, then slowed down thanks to insulin treatment. Guest engagements in Europe had to be canceled on doctor's orders.

"Nothing, incidentally, is preventing me from continuing to breathe happily in this world, even if breathing itself is less perfect than it once was. Please don't consider this emphasis on my lust for life as a compliment to the present condition of the world," he added. "Every day unfortunately brings new gloomy clouds." Yet Walter would not quite give in to despair, arguing that one could only follow the teaching of the nineteenth-century author Hieronymous Lorm (born Heinrich Landesmann), "who taught optimism without cause."[80] The optimist in Walter, however, never turned a blind eye to life's cruel strokes, and eight years later his daughter would remark that, "for relaxation," he would turn to the writings not only of the insouciant P. G. Wodehouse but also of that arch-pessimist Thomas Hardy.[81]

With his health ailing and his spirits drooping, it is little wonder that Walter decided to cut down on his responsibilities. By October he had officially announced to the New York Philharmonic that he would not be returning for another season as musical adviser. He wrote to Arthur Judson, quoting from a letter he had sent the previous year before being convinced to remain at the helm for another season: "What the Philharmonic-Symphony Society needs is not a Musical Adviser, but a real Musical Director: A conductor who, besides taking the general responsibility for the Society's contribution to the cultural life of the country, conducts a considerable part of the Philharmonic concerts himself." Such a position should be "entrusted to younger hands," he wrote, assuring the administration, however, that he would remain the Philharmonic's "faithful friend," happy to "return to a purely musical activity within the limits appropriate to [his] age."[82]

Even after canceling his European engagements for the 1948–49 season, Walter had a remarkably busy schedule. The Chicago Symphony Orchestra enjoyed a visit from him in mid-November, and he would return to Chicago every year but one (1956) until 1958. The repertoire he chose for all these concerts was entirely mainstream, with Schoenberg's *Verklärte Nacht* and Haydn's Symphony no. 96—oddly enough, a first for the orchestra— perhaps being the least familiar items among his offerings. In Chicago his broadcasts were not limited to radio transmissions but, beginning in February 1954, included the new medium of television on several occasions.[83]

Chicago demanded an ethical as well as a musical contribution to the season. A large number of musicians—including Vladimir Horowitz, Arthur Rubinstein, Fritz Busch, Jascha Heifetz, and Nathan Milstein—had drawn up a petition to protest the presence of Wilhelm Furtwängler on the Chicago Symphony Orchestra programs scheduled for the 1949–50 season.

The controversial musician had performed in Nazi Germany and had, at one time or another, entertained Nazi leaders, but he was never sympathetic to Nazism and had put himself at risk on a number of occasions to protest Nazi policies. Earlier in the year Walter had tried to help de-Nazify his friend Hans Pfitzner, which understandably struck some as a curious gesture. Now, in December, Walter was being "put under considerable pressure," as he wrote to Eric Oldberg, to join his colleagues in canceling his appearances with the Chicago Symphony Orchestra as a show of solidarity against Furtwängler. Though asserting that Furtwängler was never his friend, Walter insisted that his former rival, whose career he had once followed almost with a mentor's interest, was "only weak enough to remain in Germany and give in to the demands of the Nazis" but was himself certainly "no Nazi."[84]

Walter's position on Furtwängler seemed to have changed from what it had been in 1946, when he made it clear to Rudolf Bing that he would not attend the Edinburgh Festival if Furtwängler appeared as well.[85] Some of this change in attitude may have come from his contact with persecuted Jews who had directly profited from Furtwängler's intervention during the Nazi years. In July 1947, for example, Walter worked with the chorus master Hugo Strelitzer at the Hollywood Bowl in a performance of Brahms's *Schicksalslied*. Strelitzer's story was yet another variant on a familiar theme. Trying to eke out a living in a Berlin that made it nearly impossible for Jews to find work, he was seized by storm troopers in August 1933 and tossed into prison, where he was savagely beaten. "The only thing that was against me," he wrote, "was the fact that I was a Jew." In desperation his friends appealed to Furtwängler, who, though personally unacquainted with Strelitzer, managed to arrange his release from prison, probably saving his life in the process.[86] Exactly when Walter learned of the story is unclear, but Furtwängler's intervention in the Strelitzer affair was very much on Walter's mind in January 1949, as his statement to Bruno Zirato on the controversy surrounding Furtwängler makes clear: "The world would be condemned to a sterile condition of deadlock, if we all should perpetuate the feelings of condemnation and the attitude of collective treatment of each and everyone, who ever was connected with the Nazis. Condemnation of the real Nazi is an expression of elementary decency and of a human heart but we should try to be just and differentiate. Furtwängler never has been my friend, he is a weak person, ambitious, jealous, egocentric—but he is no Nazi, tried his best to help Jews in their need, saved one (Dr. Strelitzer) from the concentration camp and he certainly cannot be considered a moral leper."[87] But to Furtwängler himself, who seemed puzzled that so many American musicians should object to his presence in Chicago, Walter wrote that he should consider the following:

> that for years your art was used as an extremely effective means of foreign propaganda for the Regime of the Devil, that you performed valuable services for that regime through your prominent personality and great talent, that the presence and activity of an artist of your stature, even in Germany itself, helped give cultural and moral credit to vile criminals, or at least helped them considerably in acquiring it.
>
> . . . These people [Furtwängler's detractors] know nothing about your inner conflicts, problems, or depressions and little about your opposition and protests; over here, people remain skeptical about de-Nazifications. The world judges, and can only judge, by "what a person seems," not by "what a person is."[88]

Walter's response was an attempt to lay out a no-nonsense explanation for Furtwängler, whose mystification at the hostility he encountered will seem hopelessly naive to anyone who has witnessed footage of the German conductor performing (willingly or not) before Goebbels, with huge swastikas flanking the stage, then shaking the propaganda minister's hand.[89] In an effort to put Walter in the same camp as those enemies of Furtwängler who made threats against his proposed engagements in Chicago, Fred Prieberg has cited part of the letter quoted above—omitting the crucial last comments, which show that Walter did know of Furtwängler's opposition to the Nazis and was trying to judge him not by how he *seemed* but by how he *was*.[90] It took courage for Walter not to band together with others in a cause that, to the outside world, must have appeared fully justified. Yehudi Menuhin recalled that when he "interceded on behalf of Furtwängler, the one conductor who never, never said a word against Furtwängler . . . was Bruno Walter."[91]

Thanks to the Beethoven cycle, Walter's activity with the New York Philharmonic kept him busier than usual with that orchestra. His concerts commenced in December 1948 and ended at the beginning of May 1949. His first concert with the orchestra, however, had no Beethoven at all on the program; instead, it was a powerful reading of Mahler's "Resurrection," with the vocal parts sung in English. Always concerned about translation from German to English, Walter himself contributed to the English rendering of "Urlicht," though his tinkering did not result in a wholly idiomatic text. His soloists were Nadine Conner, a popular soprano at the Met and a regular soloist in Walter's performances of the *Matthäus-Passion*, and the Canadian contralto Jean Watson, whose vocal expression Walter admired for its "solemnity."[92] As transcription disks reveal, this was one of Walter's most driving accounts of the score, wholly different in mood from the more lyrical reading offered just a few months before in Vienna, and from his weightier commercial recording of the "Resurrection" with the New York Philharmonic from about a decade later. As was often the case at important performances of Mahler's works, the composer's widow, Alma, was present to enjoy the concert.

Walter's Beethoven cycle—his last outside the recording studio—began in earnest on February 24, 1949. By this time Walter was one of the grand old men of the podium, recognized as one of the greatest exponents of the Austro-German repertoire, and the reviews were predictably celebratory. Not only the nine symphonies but most of the other orchestral works were presented (excepting the concertos for solo piano): the major overtures; the Violin Concerto, with Erica Morini; and the Triple Concerto, featuring the principal cellist Leonard Rose, the concertmaster John Corigliano, and at the piano the assistant conductor Walter Hendl. A recording was made of the Triple Concerto, and Hendl recalled his eager anticipation when Walter announced the project: "I had never made a record. So, when Bruno Walter announced that he planned on conducting and recording the Triple, I was all for it, and Lenny Rose, the cellist, was worried about it, because it's one of the most difficult cello parts in the entire repertoire. (He played it beautifully, of course.) And Corigliano, the concertmaster, didn't care; he was the eternal pro. So we had quite a struggle with that before we got down to business. And then we recorded it, and Walter was extremely pleased."[93] The recording, made on March 21, three days after its last public performance, shows all three soloists in fine form, playing with grace and tender passion.

But another recording session did not fare so well. Widely regarded as the pinnacle of the symphonic repertoire, Beethoven's Ninth Symphony had thus far never been recorded by either Walter or the New York Philharmonic, though off-the-air recordings of Walter's interpretations of the

"Choral" Symphony with that ensemble exist from as early as 1944. By 1949 the new recording medium of tape had made it easier to capture the fullness of works that employed huge forces, of which the Ninth is certainly a prime example. With a superb band of soloists—Eleanor Steber, Nan Merriman, Raoul Jobin, and Mack Harrell—Walter conducted the Ninth during the Beethoven cycle in mid-April. When it came time to preserve the performance on tape, however, Steber's manager set what Walter later called "prohibitive conditions."[94] When Walter first caught wind of the potential problem, he sent a telegram to Steber, appealing to her sense of artistic "idealism": "TERRIBLY DISAPPOINTED AND REFUSE TO BELIEVE THAT FINANCIAL DEMANDS AS MADE BY YOUR MANAGER COULD HINDER EVENT OF UNIQUE IMPORTANCE LIKE RECORDING NINTH SYMPHONY. . . . AN ACT OF PRACTICAL IDEALISM FROM YOUR SIDE WOULD MAKE POSSIBLE THE DESIRABLE SOLUTION OF RECORDING WITH YOU AS SOPRANO."[95] Steber cabled Walter back the following day, telling him that, despite her own desire to participate in the recording, her manager and Columbia Records could not reach an agreement, and that she had to "leave all financial matters" in her manager's hands.[96] As a result, Walter was compelled to choose another soprano, Irma Gonzalez, at the last moment, while Nan Merriman was replaced by Walter's contralto from the Vienna Staatsoper, Elena Nikolaidi. The two male parts were sung, as in the concert, by Raoul Jobin and Mack Harrell. Although some aspects of the 1949 finale are distinctly attractive—like Mack Harrell's beautifully comforting entrance at "O Freunde" and a number of exhilarating string passages—the overall effect is anticlimactic. The recorded sound is muddy, and while Irma Gonzalez turns in a perfectly respectable performance, it has little of the ecstatic quality that Steber brought to the soprano line in concert. Walter himself felt that the final result was "disastrous," owing partly to "obstacles" presented by the hall. "The chorus was placed in such a manner as to give the male voices superiority over the female ones," he wrote to Goddard Lieberson at Columbia Records. "The placement of the microphones must have been most unfavorable to all the voices, those of the soloists as well as of the chorus, and, to shoulder my own responsibility, I was not able—perhaps I was too tired—to find out all these shortcomings by the playback at the end of our session."[97] In 1953 Walter convinced Columbia to record it again (with Frances Yeend, Martha Lipton, David Lloyd, and Mack Harrell as his quartet), offering the new version free to anyone who had bought the older set—provided that the offending disk was returned to Columbia and taken out of circulation. Yet for all Walter's concerns and anxieties, the recording as a whole, especially when heard with the later final movement, stands as an impressive monument to Walter's art.

When his second term as musical adviser drew to a close, Walter had by no means reached the end of his performing career, but he would never again have a regular position as director of a musical organization that performed before the public. Some years later he would regularly lead a recording ensemble in Los Angeles; but before beginning his work with the Columbia Symphony Orchestra, he would be kept busy answering calls from the many organizations clamoring for his presence as a guest conductor.

# FIFTEEN

# Gains and Losses

## Los Angeles, New York, Europe, 1949–1956

*Reign in my thoughts, fair hand, sweet eye, rare voice . . .*

Samuel Daniel, *Delia*

As Walter's Beethoven cycle in New York was transmitted across the country on the Sunday broadcasts, Delia Reinhardt, her eyes closed, listened to the concerts on a small radio in Hollywood, California, feeling she was present at the actual events.[1] By April 1949 she had found an apartment in Santa Monica, a city near Beverly Hills where she would reside until Walter's death. Soon after moving to California, she began to give private singing lessons for five dollars an hour—a bargain rate, though a former pupil found Reinhardt's pedagogic style less than ideal: "She could teach one to be a superb masochist. Going there was a terrifying experience, because she was the sort of teacher who would say nothing if you did something well or adequately" and offered shrivelingly "cold disapproval" if she deemed the student's performance unsatisfactory.[2]

What had happened to Reinhardt during the war? It's difficult to piece her life together, and much of the following account is based on the memories of her friends and acquaintances rather than on documented evidence. It must therefore be approached with caution. From 1924 to 1937 she was a much-admired leading soprano at the Berlin State Opera, but when Nazi politics intruded into her career, it foundered. According to her friend Irma Geering, Hermann Göring offered her a medallion, which she shunned. Another source states that she refused to give the Nazi salute and, when called to account for her actions by Göring, she simply left the room in silence.[3] Apparently as a result of her having offended Göring, she was compelled to leave the Berlin Staatsoper, and thereafter she gave only lieder recitals.[4] One eyewitness reported that at some point in 1933 she was critically ill and required medical care for three months.[5] In 1943 her house was bombed, and all her possessions destroyed; she traveled to Garmisch, where she met Irma Geering's childhood friend Hanni Christ, a sculptor from Basel. It was at this point that Reinhardt began to develop an interest in the teachings of Rudolf Steiner, though her curiosity had already been piqued during her early years in Munich. Directly after the war, she and Hanni Christ traveled to Basel, where she met the anthroposophist Wilhelm Lewerenz, who secured a pleasant apartment for Reinhardt in Dornach, a suburb of Basel and the home of the Goetheanum, the central institute for Steiner studies. This extraordinary edifice—resembling a huge, living, concrete mushroom—sits atop a hill commanding a beautiful view of the pine-filled valley below. Encompassed by "organic" architecture and natural splendor, Reinhardt spent a year delving into anthroposophy at the Goetheanum.

Many readers today will not have heard of anthroposophy, though the name of its founder, Rudolf Steiner, still has widespread currency because of the institutions around the world that follow his principles and bear his name. Part philosophy, part religion, part way of life, anthroposophy seeks knowledge and enlightenment from the spiritual world while viewing materialism as a deleterious characteristic of modern times. It draws freely on Eastern and Western thought, ancient and modern, in an attempt to synthesize a coherent system of intellectual and spiritual belief. A man of great learning, Steiner wrote a staggering number of lectures and books on the material and spiritual worlds, often offering observations of striking beauty and insight, as when he recommends the following step as preparation for "knowing higher worlds":

> The first step is to direct the soul's attention toward certain processes in the world around us. These processes are life, as it buds, grows, and flourishes; and, on the other hand, all phenomena

connected with withering, fading, and dying away. Wherever we turn our eyes, these two processes are present together. By their nature, they always evoke feelings and thoughts in us. Normally, however, we do not give ourselves sufficiently to these feelings and thoughts. We rush from one sense impression to the next. Now, however, we must consciously and intensively focus our full attention on them. Whenever we perceive a quite definite form of blossoming and flourishing, we must banish all else from our souls and, for a short time, dwell on this one impression alone.[6]

While similar ideas have been expressed before, Steiner finds the right words and images to breathe new life into advice that bears repeating, and its general trend—not to let the details and the essence of life slip through our fingers—would have appealed to Walter, who later recommended the book to others. Yet other statements in Steiner's writings (for example, that one can literally see colored auras hovering around living beings) will strike some readers as eccentric and too forcefully argued.

Delia Reinhardt was the person who kindled Walter's interest in Steiner's teachings. She and Walter seem to have corresponded during the war, and Walter had tried to arrange her passage to America as early as 1946.[7] After the war, probably during Walter's visit to Europe in the spring of 1948, the two met, and Reinhardt brought him some of Steiner's books on reincarnation and karma. He reportedly said absolutely nothing in response, but on his return to California he wrote that he would indeed be willing to learn more about anthroposophy. Assured of his open-mindedness toward Steiner's ideas, Reinhardt accepted Walter's invitation to come to California.[8] There they regularly studied a large number of books by anthroposophical authors, and Walter evidently discovered a true kindred spirit in Rudolf Steiner. The conductor's numerous letters to other anthroposophists as well as to colleagues and potential sympathizers—including Albert Schweitzer, Van Cliburn, Paul Badura-Skoda, and Jerome Hines—leave little room for doubt that Walter was genuinely swayed by Steiner's world view, which became his chief source of spiritual nourishment until his death in 1962: "Unending light poured forth from Rudolf Steiner's thoughts on the cosmos, earth, and mankind, on the physical and the spiritual world," Walter wrote in his last substantial essay. "In our epoch of dark materialism, it signified an invaluable enriching to my old age: finally a solid foundation under my feet in the certainty that everything material was the revelation of something spiritual—for in this I recognized a fundamental principle of anthroposophy."[9] These were teachings that corresponded to his longest-held beliefs; he had already written in 1905: "all phenomena of this world are merely individualizations of the spirituality that is veiled in the world."[10] He had always approached the physical as a conduit to the spiritual and metaphysical, always tried to "know higher worlds." Even anthroposophic concepts such as the auras that encircle living creatures were hardly foreign to Walter's way of thinking. In 1938, well before he had read Steiner's works, Walter wrote to Daniel Gregory Mason that it was one of "the miracles of this world, that—like the halo emanating from the head of the Saint—men and even words can be surrounded by an emanation—we may call it their atmosphere[—]and only men and words with this kind of surrounding seem to me 'worth while.'"[11]

Largely as a result of his close study of Rudolf Steiner's world view, as well as the general development of his spiritual life, Walter's own views on Christianity would alter over the years. In 1958 the Metropolitan Opera's Jerome Hines visited Walter at his house in California and was overjoyed to "know" the conductor as a "brother in Christ," as he wrote afterward. Walter responded in an unusually long letter in which he artfully tried to clarify his position without spelling out his own beliefs too clearly: "Dear friend, if you call me a brother in Christ I gratefully can accept and reciprocate it . . . but sincerity compels me to add that the course of my life and my spiritual development have led me [on] a different path to Christianity which to describe to you in words neither a letter like this nor a verbal explanation could suffice."[12] Instead of offering a brief explanation of his views, Walter recommended that Hines read his forthcoming book (*Of Music and Music-Making*) to learn more about his feelings on the subject of Christianity, obviously alluding to the anthroposophical epilogue.

Though Delia was now the central woman in Walter's life, his daughter Lotte also played a key role as he worked his way through his seventh decade, and it was apparently Lotte who prevented Walter from marrying Delia. A story circulates that Walter announced one morning that he wanted to marry Delia, and, upon hearing this, "Lotte fainted at breakfast. And therefore Walter didn't marry Delia Reinhardt."[13] Lotte herself, however, remarried in February 1949. Her husband was Karl Ludwig Lindt, a childhood friend, and, unlike her short-lived first marriage to Arthur Maria Rabenalt, this union would endure until her death in 1970.[14] Lindt was a minor movie actor, and his roles included parts in film adaptations of two novels by Thomas Mann, *Bekenntnisse des Hochstaplers Felix Krull* and *Buddenbrooks*. Lotte and her husband lived with Walter in his home in Beverly Hills—modest in comparison with the surrounding homes, though it still had the obligatory swimming pool—for the duration of the conductor's final years.

Later in 1949, balancing out the happy event of Lotte's wedding, sad tidings reached Walter. First, on May 21, 1949, Klaus Mann—one of Thomas Mann's talented brood, whose birth in 1906 nearly coincided with that of the ill-fated Gretel Walter—died from an overdose of sleeping pills in Cannes, France. As a child Klaus had played with Walter's daughters, and during the war he had defended Walter in the press and enlisted his aid in the fight against Nazism. The day after Mann's death, a man with a different set of political allegiances passed away, one of Walter's closest friends. The irascible Hans Pfitzner had fallen on hard times after the war, and the brief exchange of letters between the two musicians in 1946 shows that Walter wanted to keep the friendship intact, while Pfitzner—though welcoming the renewed communication between them—remained as difficult and egocentric as ever. Walter, despite his admiration and affection for the author of *Palestrina*, eventually chose to keep a safe distance from him. In 1948 it reached the point where Walter, when informed of the composer's destitution and asked to provide some relief, curtly and coolly responded with reports that Pfitzner was now out of the poorhouse and that his conditions had improved.[15] Yet Walter showed himself more responsive in March 1949. The ailing Pfitzner, it transpired, had expressed the wish to die in Salzburg, Mozart's birthplace, and some of his friends were trying to make his wish a reality. The Austrian government was willing to help, but no apartments were immediately available. Walter wrote several letters to try to assist his estranged friend, and Pfitzner, with aid from the Vienna Philharmonic and the Austrian authorities, indeed spent his final weeks in Salzburg, dying there, shortly after celebrating his eightieth birthday, on May 22, 1949—appropriately enough, on Wagner's birthday.[16] The news of his death struck Walter hard. On May 26 he wrote a letter of condolence to Pfitzner's widow from his second marriage, Mali, whom Walter had not met but with whom he would correspond to the last day of his life. He also sent a letter to his friend Max Brockhaus, with whom he could discuss his feelings more openly. The importance of Pfitzner's work to Walter, as well as their personal relationship, was well known to Brockhaus. "And you can equally well judge how deeply troubled I was by the difficulties in my personal relations with him," Walter added, "which had reached an intolerable level during the brief period of our postwar correspondence."[17]

The century was approaching its halfway mark, and Walter, who had sustained so many losses, was aware that his world was changing. Some of the changes, such as the increasing trend toward materialism that he perceived around him, sounded a warning bell, while others seemed part of the natural evolution of society. Addressing one change in the order of things, Olin Downes, in connection with an article he was then writing, approached Walter with a series of questions about women in orchestras—whether there was a shortage of "good men players" in the string sections, whether Walter approved of women in orchestras, whether they were as good as men, and whether (if men and women played together) sex complicated the situation. Walter, who over the decades had conducted several orchestras that included women in their ranks, cabled back a refreshingly nonsexist response: "There is no doubt that we are in danger of gradually getting short of string players in our orchestras. My experiences with women players in orchestras have nearly always been very satisfactory. They certainly are no less good musicians and instrumentalists than men. But so far I have had no experience with women players in the heavy brass sections and percussion. I [have] not found that in playing or rehearsing sex affects the work of the conductor."[18]

During the summer Walter's conducting in America included a rare collaboration with Leon Fleisher, then a twenty-year-old pupil of Artur Schnabel. On June 12, 1949, Fleisher played the solo part in Mozart's Piano Concerto no. 23 in A Major over the airwaves, supported by the Standard Symphony Orchestra under Walter. Fleisher's playing was admirably light, elegant, and probing. Impressed with his performance, Walter wrote to Schnabel afterward: "Your pupil Fleisher gave me great joy, both pianistically and musically. I found he had an unusually deep understanding of Mozart, especially in the indescribable second movement of the concerto, and the serious bearing of his nature also brought me satisfaction."[19] The promising young American would go on to make classic recordings of the five Beethoven and two Brahms piano concertos, all with the Cleveland Orchestra under George Szell, though physical problems eventually developed in his right hand, and he is best known today for his performances of the left-hand repertoire—some of the finest examples of which were composed for another acquaintance and colleague of Walter's, the one-armed Paul Wittgenstein.

Later in the summer Walter returned to Europe, and in August 1949 he made his first appearance at the Salzburg Festival since 1937; among the other participants were Wilhelm Furtwängler and Herbert von Karajan, both tainted by their activities during the Nazi years. The organizers' decision to have Walter present at the event was a wise move for political as well as aesthetic reasons, thanks to his status as an artist officially persecuted by the Nazis. In Salzburg Walter conducted *Das Lied von der Erde*, with Kathleen Ferrier and Julius Patzak. (The admirable forces of Walter, Ferrier, Patzak, and the Vienna Philharmonic would reconvene in 1952 to produce one of the most splendid readings of *Das Lied* ever recorded.) Walter also made an appearance at the Edinburgh Festival in September 1949, where he accompanied Ferrier at the piano in a now famous recital of Schubert, Brahms, and Schumann lieder.[20] The conductor rarely served as piano accompanist at this point in his career, and most of the exceptions he made were for colleagues he had worked with for many years, such as Lotte Lehmann and Elisabeth Schumann. It is a testimony to his respect (and perhaps affection) for Ferrier that he did so on this occasion. Ferrier's regular accompanist, Gerald Moore, unhappily ousted from his usual position at the keyboard, recalled Walter's idiosyncratic accompaniment with something less than affection: "Throughout the concert his habit—elementary and amateur—of playing one hand after the other in all his chording (did Kathleen know with which hand she should synchronize?) had old ladies in ecstasy, they sighed that 'It reminded them of old Vienna.'"[21] There is, of course, some truth in Moore's criticism, though the recording of the recital captures a tender rapport between soloist and accompanist that is sometimes lacking in more conventional performances. The recital was repeated in London a few weeks later, and in March 1950 the two gave another recital together at Hunter College in New York. The first commercial disk that paired Walter and Ferrier was recorded in London in October 1949, a touchingly eerie rendering of Mahler's *Kindertotenlieder* accompanied by the Vienna Philharmonic.[22]

Another singer for whom Walter was willing to make a rare appearance as piano accompanist was, as might be expected, Delia Reinhardt. A flier for the 1949–50 concert series at UCLA announced with special pride a recital by the two artists that was to take place late in November 1949. The conductor had "taken such an interest in Madame Reinhardt's re-establishment," the announcement noted, that he had "consented to appear as her accompanist in her new debut recital." It was awaited with great anticipation, and many of the venerable (and imposing) musical personages of Los Angeles came to hear, and no doubt to judge, Reinhardt. A student of hers who attended the recital said she looked and sounded "scared," and scared she must have been.[23] Her heart was fluttering so rapidly that the concert had to be canceled at the intermission. Lotte Lehmann, one of those present, wrote to Walter the following day that Delia ought to have continued with the program, except for the songs that were particularly demanding.[24] Irritated, Walter retorted that Lehmann was wrong to say that Delia should have pressed on. "With effort, one might be able to do something to counter a steadily deteriorating larynx. But when your heart is beating 120 times in a minute, your breath fails, as does your power of resistance in general." Delia's heart was weak after the horrors she had endured, Walter maintained; her throat was infected, and she was taking penicillin: anyone in her place would have had to break off the recital.[25] Not surprisingly, a recital scheduled at the Wilshire Ebell Theater a few days later vanished from the concert listings.

But the two made another attempt to give a recital at the Ojai Festival, near Los Angeles. Scheduled as the opening concert of the festival, the recital was to take place on Friday, May 26, 1950, and to include some unusual items. Along with Schumann's *Frauenliebe und -Leben* and some lieder by Richard Strauss and Brahms, they were to perform five English songs from the sixteenth and seventeenth centuries by such composers as Henry Purcell, John Dowland, Thomas Morley, and Thomas Campion.[26] The English selections were anything but standard fare for Walter, who described them, with less than historical precision, as "medieval songs," and added quite properly that they were "not only very beautiful, but have also won great popularity."[27]

Some of the strategy behind the programming was surely to allow Reinhardt to end with pieces that were beautiful but not too physically demanding, but the plan didn't help. Two hours before the concert was to begin for a capacity audience, Reinhardt announced that she had laryngitis and would not be able to perform. "So," wrote Patterson Greene in the *Los Angeles Examiner*, "for the second time this season, a last minute cancellation kept Southern Californians from hearing an artist known to most of us only through her impressive European reputation."[28] This was apparently the last time Walter and Reinhardt attempted a recital together. She soon channeled her artistic impulses into the visual arts, which she had practiced in her youth along with music.

Walter, of course, kept busy at the podium, both before and after the unsuccessful attempts at recitals with Delia, though he made few appearances with the New York Philharmonic during the 1949–50 season, no doubt enjoying his freedom from the administrative and performing duties that his official position had imposed on him over the previous two years. Midway through October 1949 he returned to Carnegie Hall for one night, conducting the "Egmont" Overture and the "Eroica," despite "acute pain in his arm," which he had been suffering all week.[29] In mid-December he again conducted the "Eroica," this time with the San Francisco Symphony Orchestra. Later, for the first two weeks in February, he conducted the New York Philharmonic in some of his favorite works, including Mozart's Piano Concerto no. 20 in D Minor (with Rudolf Firkušný as soloist), Bruckner's Ninth Symphony, and Mahler's First. All were thoroughly Walterian selections, and the programming should not have created any ripples within the Philharmonic organization. But an ugly incident developed around his choice of Mahler's First, for Mitropoulos also wanted to perform the work that season. On discovering this, Walter turned livid. "I cannot help expressing my great astonishment at Mr. Mitropoulos' intention to perform Mahler's First [S]ymphony in the same season as I am going to do it," he wrote to Bruno Zirato: "I want you to be sure that I would not have dreamed of preceding any work on Mr. Mitropoulos' program with a performance of the same one in one of my concerts during the time of my activity as musical adviser. . . . I cannot easily change my program because the 1st is the only one of the purely instrumental symphonies of Mahler's which I have not yet performed in New York, and Mr. Mitropoulos will understand my attitude with regard to Mahler and that it is important for me to play this work."[30] He added, as an afterthought, that he had also not conducted the Sixth, but he still seems to have been too enraged to think clearly. His statement that Mahler's First was "the only one of the purely instrumental symphonies of Mahler's" that he had not performed yet in New York is demonstrably untrue: he had in fact conducted the First Symphony with the New York Symphony Society in 1924 and with the New York Philharmonic in 1933 and 1942, whereas he had never conducted the purely instrumental Seventh in New York, a work he does not mention. And the First Symphony was certainly important to Mitropoulos, who had made the world premiere recording of it in 1940. The letter was accompanied by a short, unpleasant note in which Walter confided to Zirato: "I am very much disappointed in Mr. Mitropoulos' attitude and I beg you not only not to conceal my feelings toward him but to show him the enclosed letter." His oblique method of expressing anger at Mitropoulos serves as a reminder that Walter's temper was capable of flaring up, that his gentleness could give way to fierce jealousy, and also that there was, on occasion, almost palpable hostility between these two great conductors.

It was not only with the world's foremost interpreters that Walter discussed repertoire. In 1949 Wolfgang Stresemann, Walter's friend and himself an aspiring conductor, finally acquired an orchestra after years of searching for a post in a profession where the number of candidates far outweighed the number of vacant positions. The organization was a community orchestra in Toledo, Ohio—by no means a first-rate band, but a genuine symphonic ensemble nonetheless. Walter had traveled to Toledo to recommend his friend and even gave a concert there as part of his effort. Much as Walter, during his two seasons as musical adviser to the New York Philharmonic, had consulted Stresemann on his repertoire, so Stresemann in the 1950s consulted Walter. As was typical of their correspondence, Walter gave thorough answers to the questions put to him, often revealing his thoughts both on pieces he had often conducted and would conduct again ("the overture to *Fidelio* depends on the horn player") and on works outside his usual repertoire ("The *Tombeau de Couperin* is quite a difficult piece, and however simple it looks, its success is nevertheless very much contingent upon an orchestra's virtuosity").[31]

While Stresemann now had a regular post, Walter's own conducting was confined to guest appearances with various symphonic orchestras, and his days in the opera house seemed a finished chapter in his life. But the Metropolitan Opera, now under new management, was determined to recall him to the podium. In 1949 Rudolf Bing, whose company Walter had enjoyed in Edinburgh, was offered the position of general manager beginning in the 1950–51 season. When he excitedly announced this to Walter, the conductor reportedly replied: "My dear Bing, don't *touch* it."[32] Certainly when Bing wrote to Walter that he had definitely been appointed Edward Johnson's successor at the Met, Walter was more admonishing than congratulatory in his response: "Without doubt you are aware that not one, but whole hordes of dragons spitting fire and belching fumes are waiting for you. But my own experience is that optimism and courage attracts the good graces of Fortuna."[33]

Through persistence and diplomacy Bing would manage to convince Walter to return to the Met for a performance of *Fidelio* in the spring of 1951. For the present, however, it was symphonic concerts in Europe—an exhausting number of them—that drew Walter's attention and energy. From mid-August to mid-October 1950 he conducted in Lucerne, Salzburg,

Frankfurt, Stockholm, Gothenburg, Berlin, Munich, and Zurich. At the Salzburg Festival on August 23 and 24 he offered a superb traversal of Mahler's Fourth with Irmgard Seefried; with the Stockholm Philharmonic in September he treated his audience to a reading of Schubert's Ninth replete with Old World rubato; he was feted in Berlin when he conducted the Philharmonic in September in performances of Beethoven's "Egmont" Overture, Mozart's Fortieth, Strauss's *Don Juan*, and Brahms's Second. His return to Berlin, the city of his birth (he noted sadly that his birthplace had been destroyed), was clearly a bittersweet experience. His reunion with the Berlin Philharmonic, after an absence of seventeen years, brought him into contact with a substantial number of musicians—perhaps as many as twenty-five—with whom he had worked before his expulsion in 1933. Confronting those men, which might have provoked anger in another, had an almost heartening effect on Walter, who reportedly came away from the encounter saying: "Those men, and the many others with whom I have been in correspondence during the past few years, convince me that large numbers of the German people were anti-Hitler from the very beginning."[34]

Walter's return to the Berlin Philharmonic was preserved in part through the movie *Botschafter der Musik* (1954).[35] The film, a quirky history of the Berlin Philharmonic, shows in one of its first scenes Walter conducting the finale of Mozart's Fortieth. Since part of the message of the film is the regeneration of Berlin after the devastation of World War II, the opening clip purportedly shows the Philharmonie before the war, before Walter's exile. In fact, clips of the marvelous old hall (a casualty of bombing) are interspersed throughout the sequence, but the footage of Walter was surely taken from his visit of 1950, when he conducted in the Titania Palast, a large movie theater. While in Berlin, Walter gave a lecture for the students of the Municipal Conservatory—formerly his old school, the Stern Conservatory—at the students' request. He read from "Myself and Others," a section of his forthcoming book *Of Music and Music-Making*, and then held a discussion with the students, answering questions on the topic of performance practice in earlier music, especially Bach. The students themselves wrote to Walter afterward that he had brought them into contact with "a different, freer, better world," one that they had longed for during and after the war, and that they had more confidence in him than in the city fathers, their director, or any of their teachers, all of whom should have been closest to them.[36]

A little more than a week later Walter was in Munich, leading the Musikalische Akademie for its first concert of the season in a program consisting of Weber's *Euryanthe* Overture, Schubert's "Unfinished," and Mahler's First. It was an organization that had once been closely associated with Walter, and his return to war-ravaged Munich, the city where he had spent what he regarded as the most important phase of his career, awakened deep feelings. The music director of the Bayerische Staatsoper at the time was the Hungarian-born Georg Solti, who recalled that when Walter was introduced to the orchestra for the rehearsal in that familiar theater, now largely in ruins, he "was really touched. He felt nearly in tears." Indeed, he seemed so stirred that he plunged directly into the rehearsal to avoid being overcome by emotion.[37]

Such images of destruction as Walter witnessed were troubling to all who visited the hardest-hit centers of Europe, and along with the physical devastation of the immediate past there were other harsh realities—the politics of the cold war—that, on both sides of the Atlantic, inevitably created profound anxiety about the future. Wolfgang Stresemann worried about the political instability of Germany, and most intelligent thinkers knew that the atomic bomb posed a terrible threat to the entire world. Walter at this time reluctantly admitted that the atomic bomb could act as a deterrent, as he wrote to his friend on Christmas Day: "I fully share your concern over the political situation but, in an almost fatalistic way, I can scarcely feel otherwise than with Churchill, who says: If the Russians fear the atomic bomb, they won't wage a war; if they think they're prepared for it, then there will be war."[38] But his half-hearted acceptance of the atomic bomb would turn to wariness, no doubt influenced by his long-term correspondence with Albert Schweitzer, an ardent opponent of such doomsday devices. In 1959 Walter lent his name to the National Committee for a Sane Nuclear Policy.[39]

After the success of the Beethoven cycle with the New York Philharmonic, Bruno Zirato suggested that Walter present a Brahms cycle for the 1950–51 season, an idea that proved irresistible to the conductor. The Tragic Overture ushered in the cycle on January 18, 1951. In addition to the symphonies, Walter offered the Violin Concerto with Zino Francescatti, the Double Concerto with John Corigliano and Leonard Rose, the two piano concertos (with Clifford Curzon and Myra Hess as soloists), and shorter orchestral works.[40] One work absent from the program was *Ein deutsches Requiem*, which Walter wanted to include but which, because of the extra costs connected with the soloists and chorus, would have proved prohibitively expensive. The cycle concluded on February 11, with Walter having conducted the orchestra fifteen times in twenty-five days.

Then, on February 24, after an absence of more than a decade, Walter returned to conduct the NBC Symphony Orchestra in a concert that featured Joseph Szigeti in Mozart's Violin Concerto no. 3 in G Major. By this time the orchestra was associated almost exclusively with Walter's friend and rival, Arturo Toscanini, then suffering from a knee injury.[41] It was Walter's last performance with the orchestra, though he would conduct what was essentially the same ensemble, renamed the Symphony of the Air, on one sad occasion, a memorial concert for Toscanini.

A couple of weeks after the NBC concert, Walter returned to the Metropolitan Opera to conduct *Fidelio* for Bing's first season as manager; as in Walter's first *Fidelio* at the Met, Kirsten Flagstad was the Leonore. While Flagstad was one of the great Leonores of the day, her presence on the Metropolitan stage sparked controversy, for during the war she had returned to a Nazi-occupied Norway to live with her husband. Although she herself had steadfastly declined invitations to sing in Nazi-occupied countries, for some New Yorkers her decision to reside in a country under Nazi rule was unforgivable.[42] As early as December 1949 Rudolf Bing was predicting "a row" at her reappearance, even though, as he wrote to Walter, other singers on the Met roster had hardly behaved in exemplary fashion during the Nazi years but had not been ostracized. Why should Flagstad, who was a far superior artist, be prevented from singing in the house?[43] While accepting her inclusion in the cast, Walter clearly wanted to keep his distance from the inevitable "row" that Bing had predicted and asked him in confidence to announce both his own engagement and Flagstad's as utterly separate transactions.[44] Yet a few months later, having received a letter in which Flagstad was criticized on political grounds, Walter refused to condemn her and rather urged reconciliation: "I cannot see any sense in retrospective moral inexorability (if not in cases of murder, atrocities, etc.) But I most fervently believe in our moral obligation to give an example of good will, to work for reconciliation, and to fight even the remnants of hostile feelings in ourselves. Otherwise, I am afraid we just belong to the destructive forces in our time which impede progress instead of promoting peace."[45]

The controversies and rows did nothing to prevent the performances of *Fidelio* from going forward as scheduled, beginning March 6. Walter's Florestan was Set Svanholm (except for opening night, when the part was taken by Günther Treptow), and other members of the cast included Dezsö Ernster, Paul Schöffler, Jerome Hines, Nadine Conner, and Peter Klein. For this production the cast sang and spoke in German, and Walter, as usual, inserted the "Leonore" Overture no. 3 before the chorus "Heil sei dem Tag." Tapes of the broadcast show that this was again a performance of great energy and intensity, with Flagstad delivering an aptly dramatic performance. When Lotte Lehmann—another celebrated Leonore, and the polar opposite of Flagstad in temperament—heard the broadcast in Santa Barbara, she was deeply moved and wrote to Walter directly afterward: "I don't know quite what to say. You were beautiful beyond all measure today in *Fidelio*—God, how it sounded! . . . I saw you clearly standing at the podium and was consumed with envy and with burning desire to be two decades younger and to chase all the other Leonores off the stage!"[46] The powerful emotion she felt was no doubt intensified by her recent decision to withdraw from performing in public. Though inundated with rehearsals and performances, Walter wrote back to his friend and colleague of many years to tell her how touched he had been by her words. "Your letter was so thoroughly and entirely you yourself that I wonder whether the true secret of your very successful career isn't this particular directness of your nature."[47]

Before leaving the Met (for good, as he then thought), Walter gave two performances of Verdi's Requiem, the first on March 23, with Zinka Milanov, Elena Nikolaidi, Jan Peerce, and Cesare Siepi as his soloists; Milanov and Siepi also sang the "Convent Scene" from *La forza del destino*. Of course, both *Fidelio* and the Verdi Requiem were very old friends of Walter's, and familiar repertoire would pretty much monopolize his programs from now on; his days of giving premieres were nearly at an end. Nevertheless, he continued to take an interest in modern compositions, and the music of one now-forgotten composer—Harilaos Perpessa, whose "Christus" Symphony was performed by the New York Philharmonic under Mitropoulos in 1950—clearly won Walter's admiration. He heard a recording of the "Christus" Symphony and recommended it to Furtwängler and others, though Furtwängler (like others) complained that Perpessa's manuscript was difficult to decipher.[48] In July Walter sent a letter of recommendation for Perpessa to the Huntington Hartford Foundation in which he wrote: "Without any doubt, Mr. Perpessa is a composer of musical talent, dominating the technique of his work, and from the latter emanates a strong emotional power."[49] He was still writing such letters in 1956, by which time the composer had fallen on hard times. Appealing to Perpessa's compatriot Dimitri

Mitropoulos, Walter suggested that perhaps a Greek charitable institution could help out the needy composer. But Mitropoulos, whose experiences with Perpessa over the years had proved infuriating, justifiably felt he had to protect himself by not devoting any more time to a man determined to thwart all attempts to assist him.[50]

During the spring and summer Walter gave concerts in California, and then in August he and Dimitri Mitropoulos took the New York Philharmonic to Edinburgh, where the orchestra under Walter played several concerts of standard repertoire from August 22 to September 4. Martin Ormandy, brother of the conductor Eugene Ormandy and longtime cellist with the New York Philharmonic, commented that Walter wanted slower tempi in Europe and, when rehearsing the orchestra for the concerts in Edinburgh, told them: "Now, I'm going to do it a little bit different over there."[51] The principal trumpet player William Vacchiano, who joined the Philharmonic in 1935, recalled much the same concern about tempo: "I remember once Bruno Walter, when we were crossing the ocean (the first time we went to Edinburgh), called me into his room. He said: 'Remember, we have to play things a little slower in Europe than we do in America. Here, some people have to worry about making the subway, they have to get home, whereas over there they don't have to worry about time.' All the compositions were about five minutes longer there."[52] While in the capital of Scotland Walter again played piano accompaniment for Kathleen Ferrier, and he received an honorary doctorate from the University of Edinburgh. He then made his yearly pilgrimage to Lugano and later visited France, going back to the United States in late September.

Though his schedule was lighter on his return home, Walter did not simply halt his activity or his traveling. One of Walter's rare appearances in Texas took place late in November 1951, when he served as guest conductor for his former assistant Walter Hendl, now musical director of the Dallas Symphony Orchestra. At the time, the orchestra was in dire financial straits, so the board decided to invite five prominent guest conductors to drum up business: "I was being shut out of five concerts, as I saw it," Hendl recalled, "so I decided to be the soloist with each one of those conductors." As the work to be performed under Walter, he had chosen Mozart's Piano Concerto no. 9 in E-flat Major, but Walter did not consider this Mozart's best work and recommended instead the Concerto no. 27 in B-flat Major, a piece with which Hendl was less familiar. In fact, at one point in the last movement, Hendl lost track of one of his shorter solo passages:

I'm sitting there, playing with him, and we get to this spot, and I've been watching him very closely, of course, to learn more about his technique and everything, when suddenly there's a dead silence, because I forgot those four measures.

This is in the concert.

So finally (which must have been only a second or two or three), Bruno Walter looks over to me and says the equivalent in German of: "So, what are you going to do?" All he said was one word, "Nu?" And I immediately realized what was up and played the passage.[53]

Texas played host to Walter again the following month, when he conducted the Houston Symphony Orchestra, which since 1948 had been under the guidance of another conductor with a history at the New York Philharmonic, the Russian-born Efrem Kurtz, whose leadership had evidently been beneficial for the Houston ensemble. "It was indeed a pleasure to make music with this astonishingly young and enthusiastic body of musicians," Walter noted afterward, "and . . . I highly appreciate what Efrem Kurtz has achieved in the few years of his activity in Houston."[54]

Other musicians from the Old World continued to come into Walter's ambit, some seeking help or, better yet, employment. Carl Schuricht wrote from Montreux, Switzerland, midway through December 1951, to inquire whether Walter would be able to find him work as a guest conductor in New York.[55] Walter responded that he would be happy to help out, though he cautioned that if Schuricht had ever been a member of the Nazi Party, the McCarran Law would prevent him from obtaining a visa.[56] Following up on his offer, Walter wrote a letter of recommendation to Bruno Zirato, arguing that Schuricht was "a very different kind of conductor than Mr. [Hermann] Scherchen. Schuricht is absolutely no modernist, he has roots in the classics and represents in a very good way, the best German tradition."[57] Though his recommendation proved futile, Walter continued to express his admiration for Schuricht later in the decade; in 1958 he contributed an appreciation of his "friend" for a record set of the Beethoven symphonies under Schuricht.[58] It was a magnanimous gesture, since Walter himself was working on his own new Beethoven set in stereo for Columbia Records.

Relations between Columbia Records and Walter would continue till Walter's death, but the partnership was sometimes uneasy. "It is up to the Columbia Records Inc. people to improve our relations," Walter fumed at

Arthur Judson in December 1951, complaining that there had been "a certain lack of interest" on the part of Columbia in his "activities" and that his earlier grievances had been treated with "flippancy" by Goddard Lieberson—a man with whom Walter had previously enjoyed several years of happy collaboration. Walter was on the point of dissolving his relations with Columbia Records on July 26, 1952, when his current contract would expire.[59] The matter had been simmering for some time, and Judson had recently expressed his concern to Walter that, if he broke away from Columbia Records, he would necessarily put an end to his recordings with the New York Philharmonic.[60] Five of Walter's recordings were ranked as bestsellers in Columbia's classical department between 1948 and 1952, and the company must have realized how important it was to keep Walter satisfied with his working conditions.[61]

One step toward improving relations came in the form of a new producer, David Oppenheim. A performing clarinetist who had become a close friend of Leonard Bernstein and who would play under Stravinsky as well as with the Budapest String Quartet, Oppenheim worked with Walter on a large number of New York Philharmonic recordings in the first half of the 1950s. He had become director of the Masterworks division around 1952 and "made a point of supervising" the music for Walter's recording sessions and of "arranging with him what repertoire he would do and with whom he would do it."[62] The two men evidently enjoyed a satisfying work relationship. Walter, of course, had already achieved the status of a living legend, so for Oppenheim, as for many of his colleagues at Columbia, the recording sessions "were really something quite special. . . . Bruno Walter—my God! I heard about him; I never dreamed I'd ever meet him." For his part, Walter "was quite cooperative if you wanted to experiment, even with the seating of the orchestra. And I remember recording Beethoven's Second Symphony with the Philharmonic, with the winds in the front and the strings behind, and that was quite radical, I think, for a man of his age and his experience." In the studio, however, Walter sometimes lapsed into tempi that were noticeably slower than those he had taken in his live performances, so Oppenheim developed a strategy to deal with this: "I would say to him that things on recordings always sounded slower than they would in a concert hall, which I think is true. And he accepted that, and would speed the next take up, in order to compensate, so it would sound the way he wanted to do it." Certainly the New York Philharmonic recordings from the 1950s have a driving power that is often lacking from the recordings of Walter's last years, which glow with their own ripe and sensuous luster.

Early in 1952 Walter visited the East Coast and the Midwest—Chicago, Washington, D.C., Detroit, and Minneapolis—before returning to New York in March for two programs with the Philharmonic. The first offering there was Brahms's *Deutsches Requiem*, which had been absent from Walter's Brahms cycle the previous season, an omission the conductor regretted. Sung in English, this performance featured two singers who had regularly worked with Walter in sacred works: Mack Harrell and Nadine Conner. The following week offered an all-Wagner program; after conducting the familiar excerpts from *Parsifal* and *Tannhäuser*, Walter stepped down from the podium and took his seat at the piano to accompany Kirsten Flagstad in a performance of the *Wesendonk-Lieder*. Although Flagstad was apparently not fully warmed up in the songs, she stole the show in the finale to the concert, a stupendous rendition of the "Immolation Scene" from *Götterdämmerung*, which drew from the frenzied audience an ovation lasting more than twenty minutes. Among the unofficial recordings of Walter's live performances, this is one of the most ear-opening, for it affords a new insight into his approach to Wagnerian opera, so important in his career and so poorly represented in his commercial recordings. The conducting is extraordinarily flexible, dramatic, and dynamic; at a little under seventeen minutes, it moves with fleet urgency while still bearing an epic weight.[63]

As Walter's interpretations continued to be disseminated throughout the world by way of live broadcasts and studio recordings, fan mail poured in unabated, and Walter was increasingly viewed as a living heirloom from the romantic era. A particularly revealing correspondence began in April 1952 and lasted until Walter's death. The letters addressed to the conductor came from a young music student in Japan, Isao Uno. Perhaps more than any other exchange of letters between Walter and his fans, this correspondence reveals how seriously he responded to questions from total strangers who seemed sincerely interested in music. Uno, who has since become a noted conductor in Japan with many recordings to his credit (under the name Koho Uno), asked intelligent questions—often touching matters that many must have wished to explore but few dared broach—and had enough confidence in himself to persist when Walter's answers seemed incomplete or evasive. Noting that Walter was now taking brisker tempi on records made in America than he had taken in Europe, Uno asked whether the conductor was deliberately speeding up for recording sessions. Walter responded that "usually the tempo on the record differs in some way from the original, but the difference is a very small one. It may very well be that the records made in America impress you with a greater brilliancy than those of former years in Europe. The reason may be the advanced methods of recording of the present time in comparison to the older technique. I do not think that those differences of which you speak can be caused by any other reasons."[64]

Yet Uno remained unsatisfied, calling attention to Walter's different approaches to the Vienna Philharmonic ("pure, elegant, and graceful"), English orchestras ("quiet"), French ones ("light and colourful"), and American ones ("brilliant and powerful and sharp"). Moreover, the older recordings were marked by a "clear rubato . . . and a sweet brilliancy in the form of melody," while the more recent ones were "more classic." "Regardless of your letter," Uno wrote boldly, "I can't help thinking this difference is due to the transition of your artistry."[65] Walter was pleased to hear Uno's earnest questions and, instead of ignoring them, proceeded to give a more elaborate explanation of his attitude to tempo: "I myself do not know why at one time I take a tempo faster, another time slower; why my expression may change from one performance to another; and so on. I do not approach music with reason. I never understood to rationalize what I did. My only way of making music is to come as near as possible to the intentions of the composer each time I perform his works and the spontaneity which is an indispensable quality of each musical performance may very well account for differences. Your sensitivity may be perfectly reliable in feeling such differences but I am sure they cannot be very drastic as the fundamental intention and knowledge of the work could not permit it."[66]

In 1954 Uno sent a tape of two Japanese songs sung by his teacher, which Walter heard and responded to with enthusiasm: "It was with a very profound emotion that I listened to a voice and to music which spoke to me over a distance of many thousand miles and created a human message whose sincerity and kindness made [me] forget distances as well as differences of environment. Let me assure you that I highly cherish this beautiful experience." He later sent Uno a tape that he himself had recorded especially for his fan on the opposite hemisphere, in which he described his house in Beverly Hills and his daily routine.[67]

Though Walter had found a kindred spirit in Uno, there were requests that the young student made that Walter could not grant. When, for example, Uno hoped to visit America as Walter's apprentice, Walter had to disappoint him. Yet he did so in a way that encouraged the talented musician to pursue his own artistic ideals: "I hope you will understand that it is to the highest degree in your interest to develop *your own* personal potentialities—the moral and the intellectual ones, to open your thirsty soul to the innumerable resources which abound in the spiritual heritage left to mankind by the many great creative minds in the fields of art, of thought, of poetry, and so on."[68]

From the end of March to the middle of June, Walter was again in Europe, visiting Switzerland, France, Italy, Austria, and the Netherlands. Midway through April he delivered a powerful performance of Brahms's *Deutsches Requiem*—sung in Italian—with the RAI Symphony Orchestra and the Coro di Roma in Turin. The performance featured a towering Boris Christoff and an affecting Rosanna Carteri in the solo parts.[69] Before coming to Paris Walter had communicated with his old colleague Georges Sébastian, Delia Reinhardt's former husband. It's clear from Sébastian's letter to Walter that the younger conductor had lost none of his affection for the older one and that he was fully aware of Walter's relationship with Delia. Walter would be coming to Paris in April and May, and Sébastian, who had reserved a sleeping compartment on the Paris–Rome train to help his friend travel to his next engagement, wrote that he and his wife looked forward "like children" to Walter's arrival. He also regretted that he would probably not be in Paris for Walter's second visit and that his regret was all the greater because it was possible that Delia would be accompanying Walter.[70] Delia would indeed be with him for his second stay in Paris, Walter informed Sébastian, "and it would naturally be a terrible pity" if Sébastian were not in Paris at that time.[71]

In the second half of May 1952 Walter traveled to Vienna to make his first studio recording of *Das Lied von der Erde* (the 1936 release derived from a live performance), with Kathleen Ferrier and Julius Patzak as his soloists and the Vienna Philharmonic as his orchestra. Ferrier had originally been scheduled to sing in *Das Lied* with Walter in Paris early in May but was replaced at the last minute by Elsa Cavelti, perhaps because of Ferrier's declining health.[72] By this time she was already suffering from the cancer that would end her life the following year, and her moving rendition of "Der Abschied" had a pathos that was lost on no one, least of all Walter: "She stood at my side in all her beauty and vitality—and yet I remember to have felt in her singing of this farewell an ominous meaning. . . . [T]here was an overtone of finality in voice and emotion, there was a strange radiance in her eyes that made her performance—within the ideal rendering of Mahler's work—a poignant, personal message."[73] The combination of Ferrier's haunting contralto, tremulous yet secure; Patzak's nasal, almost sardonic tenor; and the Vienna Philharmonic's characteristic inflections and sweet timbres helped to make this one of Walter's most admired recordings.[74]

Before taking leave of Europe, Walter made his final guest appearances with the Concertgebouw, beginning on June 5. The program consisted of Mozart's Fortieth, Strauss's *Don Juan*, and Mahler's Fourth with Elisabeth Schwarzkopf as the soprano soloist.[75] This was apparently Schwarzkopf's first appearance with Walter, and although the conductor often praised her singing, for logistical reasons the two had to wait until Walter's farewell to Vienna in 1960 before they were to work with each other again—once more in a concert that placed Mahler's Fourth at the heart of the program.

When Walter returned to America midway through June 1952, a presidential election was in the offing. As always before an election, much talk was in the air about the two candidates—the liberal intellectual Adlai Stevenson and the war hero Dwight D. Eisenhower. Though Walter had once admired Eisenhower, his admiration had gradually turned to disappointment. Perhaps some of the reason behind Walter's change of heart had to do with Eisenhower's running mate, Richard Nixon, the future vice-president (and later president) of the United States. The outspokenly anti-Communist Nixon had already allied himself with the demagogic Joe McCarthy, whose alarmist rhetoric against alleged Communists in the United States government carried a repulsive whiff of megalomania. Walter, though no friend of the Communist Party, did not like the tactics he witnessed among the Republicans. In a lengthy letter to Eric Oldberg, an Eisenhower supporter, Walter explained his doubts and concerns:

> I still believe in him [Eisenhower] as a man of pure character, of deep earnestness of purpose and idealism, but I cannot wish to see the men coming to power with whom he is associated, whom he has endorsed, whom I cannot respect, and to whom he has made concessions which seem to me ill forebodings of happenings we might have to expect. I cannot help seeing in Adlai Stevenson the power of a great personality, the makings of a statesman and a man at home in world affairs. You certainly must know that nobody could be more opposed to the ideas of a totalitarian state than I . . . , and I am fully convinced by everything I know and have heard from Stevenson that he will be strong enough to oppose any such trends in this country.[76]

GAINS AND LOSSES

Eisenhower's easy victory over Stevenson and the brief but ominous rise of Joe McCarthy, with his ever expanding witch-hunts, could not have comforted Walter.

The political naiveté of his youth had given place to a healthy skepticism. Yet like many of his contemporaries who had witnessed the ascent and decline of politicians great and small, good and evil, he pressed on with his work, which was making music, not political campaigning; the concerts continued, on both coasts of the United States as well as in Europe. But Walter by no means accepted every offer extended to him to conduct, and among the frustrations one encounters when combing through his voluminous correspondence are the exciting projects that got away, especially those proposed late in his life, when advanced years and declining health forced him to turn them down. In November, for example, Fritz Rieger of the Munich Philharmonic invited Walter to conduct Mahler's Eighth in celebration of the orchestra's sixtieth anniversary. Walter replied that he would love to conduct the symphony in Munich—the more so because he'd heard Mahler himself conduct it there at the unforgettable world premiere—but his brief stay in Europe, if indeed he were to travel there in 1953, would not allow him adequate time to undertake such an important work.[77] The concert would almost certainly have been recorded, and we would now have a document in good sound of a major piece by Mahler that inevitably brought Walter ecstatic reviews. Another near miss was a recording of three symphonic works by Daniel Gregory Mason, a project that the composer himself had suggested ("I really do not want to have anyone but you make permanent commercial recordings of them!" Mason wrote to Walter[78]). Walter was "only too glad to comply," but the decision was up to Columbia Records. Encouraged by Walter's enthusiasm, Mason pursued the matter with Columbia, which chose, however, not to add a program of his orchestral works to its catalogue.[79]

A long-term project that Walter did finish in 1952 was his first complete recording of the Beethoven symphonies, all but one played by the New York Philharmonic (for the "Pastoral," Walter's ensemble was the Philadelphia Orchestra), with two of the symphonies—the Third and Fifth—actually recorded twice. Nevertheless, he would not be satisfied with the set until the following year, when the finale to the Ninth Symphony was re-recorded under better circumstances. While one is bombarded today with myriad Beethoven cycles on compact disc, in 1952 a complete set of the symphonies under one conductor was still a rarity. Unfortunately for Walter, recording technology had changed a great deal since he'd begun recording the symphonies with the New York Philharmonic in 1941; the old 78s had already given way to LPs, masters were taped rather than cut, and soon enough stereo would replace mono, making the set commercially obsolete. This would have its own advantages, however, since it motivated Columbia just a few years later to record the symphonies again, this time in stereo and in excellent sound.

Beginning on Christmas Day, 1952, Walter made several guest appearances with the New York Philharmonic—offering mostly his standard fare, with some selections by Bach and Corelli, as well as Vaughan Williams's *Fantasia on a Theme by Thomas Tallis,* as the least characteristic works. His stint in New York concluded on March 2, when he gave a performance of Beethoven's Ninth with Frances Yeend, Martha Lipton, David Lloyd, and Mack Harrell as soloists. The orchestra and soloists went on to record the last movement, and Walter's piano rehearsals with the vocal quartet were characteristically thorough—so thorough that Yeend, renowned for her free high notes, remembered having said, "If you don't get a take in pretty soon, I won't have anything left!"[80] The tenor, David Lloyd (who in 1951 had sung in the Ninth under Walter at the Edinburgh Festival), recalled Walter's advice to Mack Harrell when it came time to sing the notoriously difficult baritone entrance in the last movement. After the melisma on the word *freudenvollere,* the orchestra comes crashing in with a loud chord. At that point, Walter advised Harrell to "sneak a breath." That way he could sing the remaining notes "with a lot of voice left." Walter called it a *Schwindel* (a "cheat" or, to use the obvious cognate, a "swindle").[81] The story rings true, since at least one example of Walter's suggesting a *Schwindel* has been recorded for posterity. In a rehearsal of the finale of Brahms's Second Symphony, filmed in Vancouver in 1958, Walter tells the trumpets to leave out a note before their final flourish in order to have enough breath to play it effectively.

Along with concerts in Washington, D.C., Baltimore, Chicago, San Francisco, and Los Angeles, Walter also participated in a number of recording sessions in the earlier part of 1953, both with the New York Philharmonic and with an ensemble called the Columbia Symphony Orchestra. "There were any number of Columbia Symphony Orchestras," according to Loren Glickman, the regular bassoonist and also the contractor for the group in New York. "They were all pick-up orchestras. There was no such thing as the Columbia Symphony. So every time I got a call from Columbia Records, it was a new orchestra. If the conductor happened to know people, then those people were used. If he didn't, then my people were used."[82] Why did Columbia Records offer Walter an orchestra other than the Philharmonic? Economizing was surely the main goal. "It was always cheaper," Glickman pointed out, "to record with the Columbia Symphony," which was less than half the size of the Philharmonic. And when the New York Philharmonic recorded, every member—whether on the recording or not—had to be paid. Clearly for the symphonies of Mozart and Schubert, which did not require an orchestra of more than one hundred players, it was financially wise to use a separate ensemble, even if that ensemble sometimes made use of the Philharmonic's own members.

One of the notable projects that Walter and the Columbia Symphony Orchestra undertook was a Mozart recital, with Eleanor Steber as soloist. In the 1940s Walter had already conducted on two recordings of Mozart vocal recitals, one sung by Lily Pons, the other by Ezio Pinza.[83] In February 1953 Walter, Steber, and the Columbia Symphony Orchestra recorded another recital in the same genre. There were still tensions to resolve, however, between the conductor and the soloist, dating from the 1949 recording session of Beethoven's Ninth, when Steber was prevented from participating by her former manager. After shifting to Arthur Judson's management, she wrote to Walter in 1952 to explain her predicament, telling him how "grieved and sick at heart" she was about "the terrible situation that developed over the opportunity to record the Ninth Symphony" with him, and assuring him that he had been and would always be "one of the beloved inspirations and influences in [her] personal life as well as [her] musical life."[84] Walter put her at ease: "I am very happy to learn from your letter that you were not the perpetrator of the crime, but the victim, and as a fellow-victim, let me shake your hand and suggest that we unite, not only again in making music, but also in forgetting the past unpleasant incident."[85] Although the collaboration of Steber and Walter on the Mozart arias produced an affecting program, an unmistakable strain mars some passages in the upper register. Steber's vocal chords were "horribly inflamed that day," she later wrote, and her doctor had even advised her not to sing.[86]

Another Mozart recital was committed to disk in early May 1953. Splendidly sung by the bass-baritone George London in his prime, the program included five excerpts from *Le nozze di Figaro* and three concert arias. Though the orchestra is again billed as the Columbia Symphony, the musicians were this time West Coasters, including members of the Hollywood Quartet.[87] Walter was featured at the harpsichord in the recitative "Tutto è disposto" from *Figaro*, a novelty capitalized on by Columbia, which duly noted the conductor's support at the "Cembalo" on the album cover and in its promotional literature. Walter's continuo playing is discretion itself, without a trace of flamboyance, and the recording may well provide a key to his earlier approach to recitative accompaniment in eighteenth-century works.

Along with these very practical projects, Walter continued to devote time to contemplating the spiritual content and value of his art. His growing interest in anthroposophy would have strengthened any misgivings he had about the rise of materialism, and clearly that issue was among those uppermost in his mind in the 1950s. When interviewed for Elinn Hoffmann's column *Food for Thought*, Walter emphasized the spiritual importance of music and the dangers of materialism. Hoffmann sent him a typescript copy of her proposed column that quoted him as saying: "Materialism has fascinated mankind, (but) it is not the materialistic which makes life worth-while. Anything beyond the material things of life brings us to the sense of life. Music— the most sublime—is in this category. . . . Music . . . is a bridge to God." Perhaps Walter felt that he was laying out his anthroposophical cards too openly by speaking so directly of materialism; in any case, he proposed an alternative statement: "You ask me for the deeper meaning of music. Let me reply metaphorically. Imagine someone living in the midst of factories, their noises interfering with his thinking, their fumes with his breathing, their smoke with his seeing, and there is a magic power at his command to lift him to a high mountain top where he can fill his lungs with pure fresh air . . . this about describes the deeper meaning of music."[88] In a draft of the revision, he had asked the question "Do you believe that man has a soul?" The question, however, was struck from the draft. Perhaps he felt that too many readers would be made uncomfortable if he mentioned that nebulous concept, the soul. A metaphorical answer might be a more practical way of expressing the same ideas about the soul and God. In any case, only a year later, when asked to submit a brief statement for the radio program *This I Believe*, Walter expressed a "strong reluctance against a public confession of my innermost feeling and thinking."[89]

In mid-July Walter opened another season at the Hollywood Bowl. Then August and September found him once more in Europe, traveling to the Netherlands, Austria, Germany, Switzerland, and Great Britain, giving concerts in Salzburg and Edinburgh. The concerts in Edinburgh, with the Vienna Philharmonic, included a performance of Brahms's *Deutsches Requiem* in September, with Dietrich Fischer-Dieskau and Irmgard Seefried as soloists. It was the first time Walter and Fischer-Dieskau had worked with each other, and the piano rehearsal left an imprint on the twenty-eight-year-old baritone's memory: "I began to sing confidently but softly, as if I were praying. After the first syllable—'Herr!'—Bruno Walter lifted his fingers from the keys as if struck by lightning. 'No! A thousand times no! It has to sound world-weary, as if it were being sung by a high priest who seems indifferent to everything around him.'"[90]

The following day Fischer-Dieskau felt that Walter was struggling with the chorus, "mainly to elicit the expression appropriate to every measure of the work. The result in the concert itself was an unimaginably wrong intonation—almost the entire work sounding a quarter-tone lower in the chorus than in the orchestra."[91] (A recording of the Edinburgh concert belies this comment; while the chorus sounds flat on the highest notes of "Ihr habt nun Traurigkeit" and "Selig sind die Toten," for most of the Requiem the intonation could hardly be called "unimaginably wrong."[92]) For his part, Walter, who would later work with Fischer-Dieskau in Mahler's *Lieder eines fahrenden Gesellen*, commented to Mali Pfitzner in 1957 that the baritone had "enraptured" him with "the sincerity of his emotional expression and his profound musicality."[93]

For the Edinburgh concerts the Vienna Philharmonic also enjoyed the conductorship of Wilhelm Furtwängler, who, according to Fischer-Dieskau, sat through the performance of *Ein deutsches Requiem* and whispered to his wife, in a voice loud enough to be heard by Walter, that the tempi were too fast. Afterward the two great German conductors met. "The worlds of enforced exile and inner emigration, burdened by old rivalries and personal animosities, encountered each other in an electric forcefield that could not have been more explosive," Fischer-Dieskau wrote. Their conversation turned to musical interpretation, and the encounter became distinctly strained. Furtwängler, when asked how he had enjoyed the concert, "made no mention of the Requiem, responding instead to the Brahms *Haydn Variations* that had preceded the major work: 'The finale might have been somewhat more majestic!'"[94]

What was no doubt a more pleasant encounter—this of a literary nature—took place during the summer of 1953. At some point in August or September Walter visited the Goetheanum and met Albert Steffen, with whom he later engaged in a lengthy exchange of letters. Walter and Delia Reinhardt devoured Steffen's books, and it is obvious that Walter had a particularly deep admiration for the Swiss author; he seems even to have gone out of his way to write his letters to Steffen by hand instead of dictating them to his secretary—his usual procedure. The personal touch of hand-drawn characters, rather than machine-made fonts, would have been especially appreciated by a correspondent with anthroposophical beliefs.

In both Europe and, later, America Walter received numerous public tributes and personal expressions of thanks on the occasion of his seventy-seventh birthday. Hermann Obermeyer, on behalf of the Vienna Philharmonic, congratulated Walter, observing that he was "the conductor with whom we have been associated for the longest time," and that before 1938, Walter had led 128 concerts with the ensemble.[95] Rudolf Serkin sent a letter that especially touched him: "I am bound to you so much in love and gratitude that I can never tell you often enough. How often you have opened my ears and eyes to new worlds, how many splendid impressions I owe to you! And how encouraging and patient you have been with me when I've been allowed to make music with you—no, I'll never be able to give thanks enough!"[96] It was a magnanimous gesture of friendship from a musician who had already enjoyed a long and distinguished career. Columbia Records also celebrated Walter's birthday with a privately circulated LP (surely meant for air play) full of words of praise from Walter's friends and colleagues, among them Lotte Lehmann, Ezio Pinza, Eleanor Steber, George London, Lauritz Melchior, and Joseph Szigeti. It was clear that Columbia no longer wanted Walter to feel neglected.

Though he spent a substantial amount of time and effort in the recording studio in the 1950s, Walter let at least one opportunity to record a cycle of the Mahler symphonies slip away. On November 24 Heinrich Kralik invited Walter to conduct the Mahler symphonies with the Vienna Symphony. Walter responded that, while it would mean a great deal to him to leave "a kind of testament" of his Mahler interpretations, the scope and responsibilities of the project would unfortunately put too much pressure on him in his old age, and he also did not have enough time at his disposal to reside in Vienna for such an extended project; therefore, he had to decline.[97] There is no reason to doubt Walter's words, though they may not tell the whole truth. As recordings of the Vienna Symphony from the early 1950s demonstrate, it was then an ensemble by no means at the level of the Philharmonic orchestras in New York or Vienna. And if Walter had accepted, he would have had to face the Sixth and Seventh symphonies, works he had long avoided.

Though 1953 had brought its share of triumphs, it also delivered one serious blow to Walter. On October 8 Kathleen Ferrier died. The friendship that had developed between the contralto and the conductor had been brief but intense. "Despite all my efforts to see her during the last time of her life," he wrote, "I was not given the opportunity—I could only send her messages of friendship and love and receive through friends her affectionate answers. We had said good-bye to each other at the airport in Zurich. . . . I shall always see her as she stood there before me, the very image of courage and serenity, and I always shall hear her say, as she said whenever we parted, 'God bless you'. For the rest of my life I shall return these words, and think of her with the wish—God bless you, Kathleen!"[98]

It's clear that Walter's affection for Ferrier was deep, and his passionate words may well betray more than the friendship of professional colleagues. Yet Walter was likewise capable of impassioned language where his other close friends and colleagues were concerned, especially if they seemed under attack. On one occasion, for example, a self-styled "Mozart lover" wrote to Walter that Myra Hess, in her concert of Mozart's Piano Concerto no. 14 in E-flat Major (given with the New York Philharmonic in mid-January, 1954), had not played an Andantino, as Mozart had marked, but an Adagio.[99] The remark was certainly not meant as an attack on Walter, nor was it even a harsh assessment of Hess's playing, yet Walter responded to the criticism with surprising trenchancy: "I gladly answer a letter from a 'Mozart lover', even if he is entirely wrong,—morally wrong insofar as he has not humility enough to revere in a musician like Myra Hess with her life-long devotion to Mozart's music the superior insight into Mozart's musical intentions; musically wrong, as he applies the notion of andante to the quarters instead of to the eighths in the second movement of the concerto. . . .—Should you be a pianist, you could convince yourself that by applying the notion of andante to the quarters, the movement would lose its depth and variety of expression."[100] Walter was not one to let his fan mail go unanswered.

But Walter's correspondence during these years consisted of more than emphatic replies to fans. It also included appeals to his colleagues in connection with projects that he deemed particularly worthy. One area that attracted him was the developing discipline of music therapy, which overlapped with his current interest in anthroposophy and his earlier writing on the moral forces of music. In January 1954 he wrote directly to Toscanini, asking him to sign a petition that would encourage a scientific study of the powers of music: "Of course, it is, in the first line, a concern of physicians to develop a scientific method of exploiting the healing possibilities of music. But you will agree that an institution like the Ford Foundation must be informed that also the musician believes in the power of music on the human mind. And do you not believe, like me, that also educational institutions could make use of the moral influence of music on such social evils like juvenile delinquency and so on?"[101] Toscanini regretfully demurred, claiming that he had never lent his name to "any petition no matter how worthy the cause."[102] Yet Frances Paperte, founder-president of the Music Research Foundation, found Walter's arguments persuasive enough that she sought permission to use his words to Toscanini in order to promote the cause of her organization. By 1958 Walter was listed as honorary chairman of the Music Research Foundation, and while the position required little if any real effort on his part, the goals of the organization were ones he genuinely endorsed.

Engagements in Chicago and San Francisco kept Walter busy for much of February and April 1954. In May and June he traveled again through Europe, stopping first in London to share the podium with Sir John Barbirolli for a special concert on May 7, to benefit the Kathleen Ferrier Cancer Research Fund, then heading south to participate in the Maggio Musicale in Florence and to conduct the RAI Symphony Orchestra. In June he visited Dornach, Switzerland, and gave a concert in Lucerne in which the centerpiece was Bruckner's Ninth, a work that would appear more and more on his concert programs.

Walter returned to the United States early in July and spent several months in Beverly Hills. Once again he was tentatively offered the opportunity to record the complete Mahler symphonies, this time with the New York Philharmonic. In January he had committed the First Symphony to disk, and Columbia Records must have been pleased with the results, for Goddard Lieberson, then executive vice-president of the company, approached Walter in August, urging him to record Mahler's complete symphonies, an issue they had discussed "many times."[103] In this instance Walter was not prepared to reject the offer, as he had done with the Vienna Symphony's proposal, but neither was he ready to accept it: "You can imagine how much the execution of the plan to record the complete symphonic works of Mahler means to me. Of course, the reservations for my side, which you mention, are still there but on the other hand I feel deeply my obligation to keep Mahler's great work alive by all means possible. However, there are so many angles of this problem to be discussed that I do not see how to do it in a letter."[104] It is hard to know what the upshot was. Walter went on to record Mahler's Second with the New York Philharmonic, perhaps with the intention of recording the complete symphonies in succession, but a heart attack and new technology—the widespread adoption of stereo sound—brought that series, if it *was* a series, to a halt.

Another recording (this time not one of his own) engaged Walter's attention in an entirely different way. Arnold Schoenberg had died in 1951, with one of his most ambitious works unfinished and unplayed. In Hamburg on March 12, 1954, Hans Rosbaud gave the world premiere performance of the first two acts of *Moses und Aron*, Schoenberg's unfinished opera. Although Walter had publicly condemned atonality and serialism on more than one occasion and had provoked furtive insults from the readily affronted Schoenberg, the composer's widow invited Walter to hear a tape recording of the premiere of *Moses und Aron* at a gathering to take place on September 12, 1954.[105] Surprisingly, instead of finding an excuse to avoid listening to a work that he would almost certainly find rebarbative, Walter wrote that he would attend "with great joy" and even asked whether it would be possible to receive a copy of the libretto beforehand so that he could become acquainted with the text, also by Schoenberg; he hoped it would be all right to bring Delia Reinhardt along.[106] Why did he take such an interest in the event? Was his interest feigned, a sign of politeness? Did the theme of the opera pique his curiosity? Or was he genuinely eager to hear more music from the composer of *Verklärte Nacht* and *Gurre-Lieder*? He had certainly never forgotten these earlier works. In fact, *Verklärte Nacht* was one of the pieces Walter and the New York Philharmonic presented in November 1954.

Other works that Walter performed with that orchestra in November and December included the New York Philharmonic premiere of Bartók's Andante for Violin and Orchestra, Opus 5 (better known today as the first movement of his Violin Concerto no. 1), as well as the Brahms Double Concerto, with Isaac Stern and Leonard Rose, and *Ein deutsches Requiem*, with Irmgard Seefried and George London. All three works were recorded by Columbia for commercial release, but the "harsh choral and muddled orchestra sounds" on the master tape of *Ein deutsches Requiem* had not pleased Walter, who prevented its release in his lifetime.[107] As for Bartók's Andante—an unusual item for Walter, beginning as it does with a strong suggestion of atonality, though the piece ends consonantly enough on a D major chord—the sad truth is that Szigeti was by this time suffering from arthritis, and his wayward intonation was probably the reason that the recording was never issued.[108]

Although Walter found the tape of *Ein deutsches Requiem* disappointing, the performance itself proved an inspiration to many. The tenor Theodore White, then a member of the Westminster Choir, recalled the excitement of rehearsing the work under Walter. When Walter came to Westminster Choir College (in Princeton, New Jersey), classes were suspended, despite reservations on the part of the administration, who realized that none of the students would be in class, "so they just made it official: they suspended classes, because when Bruno Walter came to campus, *everybody* wanted to be there." Walter's ability to secure the attention of his singers made an immediate impact on White: "He had you spellbound from the very beginning. It was something about his persona. You sensed immediately that he was very serious about the music. Yes, this was going to be a wonderful experience, but this was not going to be a frivolous experience. . . . He knew when the choir was not giving their all. It was not just a matter of loud here and soft there; he sensed the mental commitment that the singers were giving to the music. So in the process of explaining what he would want in a particular phrase, he would always express it in a way that it wasn't a mystery. You knew exactly what he wanted." It was Walter's ability to convey the "spiritual" content of the text and music that particularly distinguished him from other choral conductors with whom White had worked.[109]

The many requiems that Walter conducted in the 1950s were well timed, for in that decade many of his old friends, acquaintances, and rivals bade farewell to this life. On November 30 Wilhelm Furtwängler died at the age of sixty-eight, putting an end to a professional rivalry that had lasted nearly four decades. Walter wrote a note of condolence to Furtwängler's widow, commenting on the grievous loss that she and the entire musical world had suffered.[110] The two conductors had achieved a kind of reconciliation after the war; a photograph of the two, taken around 1950, shows an animated Furtwängler speaking to his wary-looking older colleague.[111] Walter knew of Furtwängler's efforts to help Hugo Strelitzer, and perhaps he had since learned of others whom Furtwängler had helped.[112] When the Berlin radio station RIAS asked Walter for a tribute in Furtwängler's memory, to be aired with other such tributes on December 7, he did not decline. In his piece Walter recalled meeting Furtwängler as Pfitzner's "very promising" assistant in Strasbourg. "And I know enough of his extraordinary development," Walter continued, "to testify that the Master fulfilled in the richest measure what the apprentice foreshadowed. Without a doubt there was greatness in Wilhelm Furtwängler, a greatness which enabled him to give expression to the Great in music: and I have no doubt that his achievement, so filled with deepest devotion to music, has a significant place in musical history."[113]

Another major rival, born nearly two decades before Furtwängler, lived on, celebrating his eighty-seventh birthday on March 25, 1955. Walter sent Toscanini a warm letter of congratulation. The praise was slightly different in tone from that employed in Furtwängler's eulogy: "Your birthday gives me the welcome opportunity to express anew the deep devotion and admiration for you which since long years lives in my heart. Thinking back, I vividly visualize our first personal meeting in Milano and my ear has gratefully preserved performances of yours in Leipzig and Berlin, in Salzburg and Vienna and, of course, many unforgettable ones in New York. I want you to know that these are great memories for me and will live on as long as I live."[114] There is a far greater sense of personal engagement with the Italian maestro than with the conductor from his native land; while Furtwängler's contribution had "a significant place in musical history," Toscanini's performances left "great memories" for Walter himself to cherish.

Though Walter had not yet reached his eightieth birthday and still had half a decade's worth of productive years left to him, by 1955 his concert schedule was at last slowing down. After appearances in Chicago and San Francisco early in the year, he headed for Europe, where in May he performed with the French National Radio Orchestra and then crossed the Channel for a series of concerts with the BBC Symphony Orchestra, including a performance of the *Lieder eines fahrenden Gesellen* with Fischer-Dieskau. Although the baritone had already recorded the cycle with Furtwängler, Walter afforded him a new insight into the tempo of the songs: "When it came to my approach to the Mahler lieder, which had in part been defined by Furtwängler in Salzburg, Walter urged me to double my tempo, arguing that Mahler's intentions could be conveyed only by a kind of nervousness that betrayed no hint of assurance. And in this he was only too right." Persuaded by Walter, Fischer-Dieskau later asked Rafael Kubelik to speed up his tempo when they performed the same song cycle together.[115]

Thomas Mann became an octogenarian on June 5, 1955, and Walter was among those present in the Schauspielhaus in Zurich to celebrate his friend's birthday. Walter's contribution to the festivities was a performance of Mozart's *Eine kleine Nachtmusik* with the radio orchestra.[116] The conductor and the author had undergone many trials together since their meeting in Munich some four decades before, and now both had reached the highest rungs of their respective ladders. But Mann's eightieth birthday would be his last; he died little more than a month later, on August 12. In offering Mann's daughter some consolation and unburdening himself of his own heavy emotions, Walter wrote to Erika two days after the death of his friend: "You no doubt know how much I loved your father, and you surely know of my awareness of what his life meant to you. How should I find words for the enormity of such a loss; what could I really say to you? . . . My heart and my thoughts are with you in love and sorrow. Rarely, perhaps, has there been a father–daughter relationship more beautiful, more full of life, more fruitful than yours, and I felt myself happy for both of you when I thought of it." Walter's relationship with his daughters had been a close one, and perhaps the solace he offered had some reference to his own family life: "I should think that such a truly fruitful and harmonious relationship as that between you [two] would pour its blessings over the rest of your life, and the feeling of what you were to him and he to you must become a source of the deepest comfort to you in all the pain over your loss."[117]

Another old acquaintance—who, like Thomas Mann, had fled the Old World to find a new home in California—was trying to resurrect his reputation as a composer of lofty scores. With this end in mind, Erich Wolfgang Korngold approached Walter in the 1950s to ask for help in generating interest in his new orchestral work. Though he had been successfully writing music for Hollywood sound tracks for several years, he had not given up on "serious" music; nor had he forgotten Walter's help over the decades, having dedicated his Third String Quartet (1945) to him. Recently, Korngold's opera *Die Kathrin* had been a flop in Vienna; now in his fifties, he belatedly turned his hand to the symphony. In September 1955 Korngold visited Walter in Beverly Hills, bringing along a record of his Symphony in F-sharp Major for the conductor to hear, but Walter chose to stay outdoors on the patio, where it was cool, rather than enter the stuffy house to listen to the record. He apologized to Korngold afterward and, eager to help the composer who had shown so much promise earlier in life, offered to listen to the work at Korngold's convenience.[118]

Well constructed, brilliantly orchestrated, full of rich Korngoldian harmonies and romantic melodies, the symphony was patently a throwback to an earlier era, though its composer had done his best to give it a hard, modernist edge. Walter, impressed by the piece, wrote to his colleagues to promote the symphony, even though he felt too old to accept the challenge of conducting it himself. He later canvassed Reiner, Munch, and Mitropoulos in an attempt to get them interested in the new symphony. This was "an important work of original thematic substance, of a rare emotional power in a masterly symphonic form," he wrote to Munch in 1956. "The instrumentation is also that of a master. Here is, without any doubt, a new symphonic work with the potentialities of a genuine great success."[119] This was substantially the message he sent to the other conductors, who, unfortunately for Korngold, declined the opportunity to pursue the matter.

Walter was again conducting in Europe in October and November, visiting Milan, Rome, and Vienna. The main reason for his stop in Vienna was to conduct in the newly restored opera house, which opened on November 5 with a performance of *Fidelio* under Walter's former assistant Karl Böhm, directed by Walter's old colleague and sometime nemesis, Heinz Tietjen. To some it must have seemed ironic that Beethoven's heroic opera, condemning as it does totalitarian rule, was under the artistic direction of two men who had made no show of opposing totalitarianism in recent memory. Erich Jantsch, of the *Musical Courier*, noted that "For many, the real opening of the opera [house] occurred when Bruno Walter at a matinee conducted Bruckner's Te Deum and Beethoven's Ninth. . . . Though he does not conduct an opera during the festival, he brought back to the Vienna Opera House the high standards and the grandeur which have made it famous. Though his great performance showed up the mediocrity now prevailing, he also established firmly and categorically the *niveau* which should characterize the work of the Vienna State Opera."[120]

As one of the last living representatives of a great conducting tradition, Walter seems to have gained in stature almost daily. Columbia Records issued a two-record set of Walter conducting the New York–based Columbia Symphony Orchestra in Mozart's "Linz" Symphony; entitled *The Birth of a Performance*, it included long stretches of Walter's rehearsal with the orchestra. Though he was in principle against making his rehearsal techniques public, we can only be grateful to Columbia for preserving so many of Walter's re-creative methods. The rehearsals date from April 26 and 28, 1955, and Walter's comments are almost invariably technical rather than impressionistic. He seizes, for example, on the opening movement's introduction, in which Mozart has indicated overdotted passages by placing rests before the short notes. The orchestra seems reluctant to make the rhythms as sharp as the score demands, to the point where Walter tells the strings and woodwinds to "overdo it"; they must "be able to say *off* " at the rest before the short note ("Rah . . . Off! Da-dee . . . Off!"). His insistence on the musicians' taking a "breath" before the short note is reminiscent of attempts among early music specialists in the 1950s and 1960s to play French overtures and other similar works with stylistically appropriate overdotting (though Mozart wrote in the sharpened articulation, whereas baroque composers usually relied on understood conventions). Walter also lets us in on some of his own stylistic secrets, telling the musicians at one point to place the accent after the beat in the "Viennese" style to give one of the chords an especially dramatic presence, an effective device that untrained ears can mistake for ensemble imprecision.

On occasion Walter addressed members of the orchestra by name. Though for some players this meant immortality, for others it was cause for grievance. "I tell you what you will do, Mr. Bloom . . . ," Walter said very graciously to the first oboist, Robert Bloom, before suggesting a diminuendo on an A-flat. He later addressed Bloom again on fine points of style. When the record of the rehearsal was issued and Bloom heard himself being told how to play the phrase, he was deeply disturbed, according to Loren Glickman. Bloom "was a step above most of us orchestral players, he was like the dean of woodwinds, and he was paid more than most people for various things," Glickman noted. Bloom asked whether Glickman was aware that his name had been used during the rehearsal.

"Oh, yes, Bob," Glickman returned. "And he always says, 'Mr. Bloom, would you mind doing such and such?' . . . At one point, he says, 'Mr. Glickman, do this,' and I'm very proud that he knew my name."

"Well, I'm not very proud about it. I don't want to be known as a person who takes advice from Bruno Walter, no matter how well known he is!"[121]

It was surely not by chance that the rehearsal record was of a work by Mozart. Walter had long been associated with the great Austrian composer's music, and his interpretations—whether viewed as stylistically perfect or over-romantic—were widely admired. It will come as no surprise that in 1956, during the bicentennial of the composer's birth, performances of Mozart's music would dominate Walter's schedule.

# SIXTEEN

# Mostly Mozart

## 1956–1957

*The sun's radiant glory has vanquished the night,*
*The powers of darkness have yielded to light.*
Schikaneder and Mozart, *Die Zauberflöte*

The year 1956, two centuries after Mozart's birth, opened the sluice gates to a deluge of Mozart fetes and performances around the world. Naturally, as one of the interpreters most closely associated with Mozart, Walter was invited to take part in many of the bicentennial celebrations. But Mozart wasn't the only musician for whom 1956 had special significance; Walter himself turned eighty that year, and birthday celebrations on both sides of the Atlantic called for his presence.

Perhaps surprisingly, Walter's first concerts of the year contained no Mozart whatsoever. These took place in Chicago, where his program consisted of Schumann's *Manfred* Overture and Brahms's Third, given at the beginning of February. The next month, however, Mozart reigned. The New York Philharmonic gave a Mozart Festival in which Walter conducted several concerts, concluding with three performances of the Mozart Requiem, a piece he also recorded at that time. Walter's soloists were Irmgard Seefried, Jennie Tourel, Léopold Simoneau, and William Warfield. Preparations for the piece had begun as early as February 1955, when Walter and André Mertens of Columbia Artists Management corresponded about soloists. The bass Cesare Siepi had been discussed as a possibility, but his contract with London Records would not allow him to record for Columbia; Mertens then suggested Warfield, and Walter eagerly accepted: "I could not wish for a better soloist and one who would be more qualified for the performance of this work."[1] Two days later he wrote to Bruno Zirato: "Warfield is a great artist and has one of the most magnificent voices in the country. So, please, engage him."[2]

For his part, Warfield was delighted to sing for a conductor whom he deeply admired. Though Warfield has since achieved status as a cultural icon himself, the Requiem took place early in his career, and the experience proved an inspiration. Walter met the vocal quartet, sat at the piano, and meticulously went through the details, "polishing the work itself," Warfield recalled, "and getting us to feel the sense of the music as a quartet rather than as individual soloists just singing lines. . . . Then when it came time for the performance, it was just a matter of an indication. And in the performance we had full rein to express and to delve further into the kind of thing that we had done as a quartet."[3] Walter also made his standard request that the soloists memorize their parts—an unusual stipulation for oratorio singers: "He wanted us to be so sure of the texts and the music that it wouldn't be a matter of practicing notes." The sense of liberation Warfield felt on having dispensed with the score put him in the habit of learning oratorio parts by heart afterward.

The other surviving member of the quartet, the Canadian tenor Léopold Simoneau, also cherished his session with Walter. "He did not have to say that much because you could really sense in his accompaniment what he wanted—the phrasing he wanted, the emphasis he wanted on some phrase, on some words." Like Warfield, who emphasized Walter's ability to make the four singers a well-blended quartet, Simoneau noted that Walter knew how to make "chamber music with that beautiful composition." In the performance itself Simoneau found all the interpretive cues written clearly on Walter's face; he didn't have to act like a "traffic conductor," relying on "exaggerated gestures" to convey his ideas to the performers. "He had such a warm expression on his face, with his eyes, and his general expression, that you really knew what he wanted."[4]

For Jennie Tourel, too, singing in the Mozart Requiem under Walter proved not only intensely pleasurable but also sublime, as she wrote in a letter to Walter shortly after the performances. It had been a "transcendent musical experience," one that she would "treasure for the rest of [her] life."[5] The Requiem would be a recurring item on Walter's programs for the rest of the year. Over the summer he performed it in Milan, Salzburg, Vienna (where two of his choristers were reportedly the future conducting stars Zubin Mehta and Claudio Abbado[6]), and Los Angeles. For the performance in Milan, which took place at La Scala, Walter had negotiated the arrangements with the conductor Victor de Sabata, then artistic director of the venerable opera house. The soprano soloist of Walter's choice, Maria Stader, with whom he had collaborated on several occasions ("Bruno Walter was like a musical father to me," she later wrote[7]), was unable to sing with him because of prior commitments. De Sabata unsuccessfully tried to secure a number of attractive alternatives—Lisa Della Casa, Elisabeth Schwarzkopf, Victoria de Los Angeles—and finally suggested that Walter use either Anna Moffo or Graziella Sciutti.[8] Not familiar with either soprano, Walter left the decision in de Sabata's hands, cabling a description of the vocal qualities he desired: "NEED CLEAR SWEET FLEXIBLE VOICE WITHOUT TREMOLO," and "REQUIEM ASKS FOR VOICE LIKE MIMI BOHEME CHARMING WITHOUT TREMOLO."[9] Sciutti was eventually hired.

One other major event kept Walter busy in New York in late February and March, a performance of *Die Zauberflöte* at the Met, sung in English. What brought Walter back to that opera house, a war zone that he had vowed to avoid for the remainder of his life? There is no easy answer to that question, but retracing some of Walter's thoughts at this time might point to his motivation.

In the first half of the 1950s Walter's thoughts continually returned to the idea of leaving a "testament" that would preserve at least a portion of his art. In addition to preserving his performances on disks, Walter sought to establish a legacy by committing his thoughts to print. Although he had published his autobiography in 1946 and had written extensively on his musical career up to his departure from Europe, he had, oddly enough, only touched on the issue of musical interpretation in that work. He had scarcely finished *Theme and Variations* when he embarked in earnest on a book whose themes had preoccupied him for years, a work specifically on music and musical interpretation, which would complement his autobiography. He referred to the new book in a letter to Rudolf Mengelberg as "a kind of testament."[10] The book, published in 1957, would eventually be called *Von der Musik und vom Musizieren*. For the English title, Walter suggested *On Music and Musical Interpretation* and some variants along the same lines; Norton finally published the book in 1961 as *Of Music and Music-Making*, a translation not wholly to Walter's liking, since "music-making" did not seem lofty enough to convey the sense of high re-creativity that Walter was trying to evoke.[11]

During the years that Walter developed the ideas that appeared in this book, he identified strongly with Mozart, regarding the composer's late works as confessional. In Walter's view, for example, Mozart's last three symphonies were his "intellectual, spiritual and musical confession," representing "LIFE," "BLISS and HOPE," and "LIBERATION."[12] *Die Zauberflöte* was a similarly telling work for Walter, who wrote: "As Shakespeare, after remaining all his life the anonymous dramatist concealed behind the figures of his stage-works, at last appears before our eyes in the person of Prospero in the *Tempest*, so, I think, we at last encounter in the *Magic Flute* the human personality of Mozart himself."[13] So *Die Zauberflöte* had a special significance for the aging Bruno Walter, who was himself working on "a kind of testament." If any opera could bring him back to the theater, this could.

Bing had tried to lure Walter back to the Met several times after the conductor's official departure in 1951—always without success. But he persisted, and in May 1954 he got the first sign that Walter might bend. Walter had gathered decades' worth of fond memories connected to Mozart's operas, and when Bing offered him the opportunity to conduct either *Così fan tutte* or *Die Zauberflöte* for the two hundredth anniversary of Mozart's birth, the idea strongly appealed to Walter: "Your invitation is indeed very tempting for me because I feel I have to contribute to the best of my abilities to such an anniversary. I cannot think of 'Cosi fan tutte' because I do not feel happy in the vastness of the Metropolitan Opera with a work which needs intimacy. Very differently I feel with regard to the 'Magic Flute'. It would certainly give me great satisfaction to try again my hand on this work which is particularly near to my heart."[14] But the logistics and the headaches of putting together an opera remained. How could they find singers "fit for the numerous and problematical roles, where to find the stage-director, where the designer?" In the end, Walter wondered whether the Mozart Requiem wouldn't be a better choice. Bing, however, had clearly won the crucial battle, and it was only a matter of time before Walter would be working on another opera.

What in particular placed *Die Zauberflöte* so near to Walter's heart? His view of the work as confessional must have been a factor. Another might well have been its themes, which spoke very much to his present concerns. The climactic episode in Mozart's last opera depicts a man and a woman, joined after undergoing various trials, being initiated into a sphere of higher knowledge. The parallels between this episode and Walter's comparatively recent experience with Delia Reinhardt and anthroposophy may well have played a part in his decision. Reinhardt's very first role in Munich under Walter was Pamina, and it would have been perfectly natural for Walter to identify himself and Delia with the initiates Tamino and Pamina. By 1954 Walter was regularly exchanging ideas with the leading anthroposophists of the day, and his thoughts continually revolved around the new world picture that Steiner and his disciples offered him. In Steiner's *How to Know Higher Worlds*, a book that Walter came to know well and recommended to others, several passages bear a notable resemblance to key episodes in *Die Zauberflöte*.[15] The book maps out a path for initiation into a higher state of consciousness. Steiner writes that those who wish to be initiated must possess "courage and fearlessness," a theme stated time and again in Mozart's libretto. Shortly before Tamino and Pamina are tested, they encounter two armed men, who warn them of the trials that await them but encourage the protagonists to forge ahead. Similarly, followers of Steiner who wish to ascend to higher worlds will, in the final stages of their development, encounter two "guardians" who will explain the serious implications of continuing along the path leading to spiritual enlightenment. In Mozart's work, Tamino and Pamina must pass through fire and water to prove themselves worthy of receiving wisdom; initiates into Steiner's higher consciousness must likewise undergo trials by fire, water, and air.[16] While the parallels may have come about simply because the two works use long-established symbols to describe various stages of initiation (and of course Steiner would have been familiar with Mozart's opera), the similarities are nonetheless striking. Steiner's views on the ancient Persian religious leader Zarathustra (or Zoroaster) might also have deepened Walter's interest in *Die Zauberflöte*, whose wisest character, Sarastro, owes his name and priestly character to Zarathustra. For Steiner, who believed in reincarnation, Zarathustra was "one of the greatest Individualities who have worked in the course of human evolution."[17] Elements of Zarathustra's being, according to Steiner, entered into several important cultural and religious leaders, most notably Moses and Christ, playing a crucial role in the development of both figures.[18] So Bing's suggestion that Walter conduct *Die Zauberflöte* might well have appealed not only to Walter the Mozart-lover but also to Walter the anthroposophist. The opera's concern with love, initiation, and enlightenment coincided with the very themes that Walter found most absorbing at this time.

We know many of Walter's thoughts on Mozart's last opera thanks to his essay "The Mozart of *The Magic Flute*," written to celebrate the bicentennial of Mozart's birth.[19] In Walter's view Mozart in his final years became aware of "the growing accord of his love-filled heart with the Masonic tenets of humanity and brotherliness," and the composer projected facets of himself onto certain characters in the opera. Thus Tamino represents the lofty side of Mozart and "his ardent striving for ideal humanity," while Papageno, "the cheerful fellow, the simple son of Nature who likes to eat well and hankers after pretty girls," represents the Mozart "whose mind was bent on worldly pleasures." Sarastro, in turn, delivers pronouncements on love and forgiveness, and in his words, as Walter saw it, "the world should recognize Mozart's own spiritual testament."[20] Many will also recognize in Sarastro's sentiments a kinship with Walter's own leanings toward forgiveness and reconciliation, which he maintained during and after his own trials by fire and water.

The money for the new production of Mozart's opera came from the deep pockets of the Rockefeller family. Mrs. John D. Rockefeller III generously provided an estimated $90,000—then a hefty sum indeed.[21] Getting a cast together was the first artistic problem that Walter and Bing had to solve. Though they had discussed the possibility of using some non-Anglophone singers for the production, in the end they chose an almost all-American cast and once again used the Martins' English translation. Certainly, when the opera was finally performed, many appreciated the choice of language and casting. "The accents were homogenous, and all the performers enunciated admirably," Howard Taubman wrote. "What a delight it was to the audience to understand! What a pleasure it was to hear laughter in the Opera House in response to comic lines!"[22]

A number of the principals in the 1956 *Flute* have offered insights into Walter's thoughts on Mozart's last opera. For Sarastro, Walter had Jerome Hines, who had sung the role at the Met during the 1950–51 season and who deeply admired Walter as a conductor and as a man. He recalled years later the maestro's concern that everything be done correctly, even if doing so meant going beyond the time officially set aside for rehearsal: "We were rehearsing at the Met, and at one spot he said, 'Jerome, there is just not enough time; you must come now to my apartment, tonight or tomorrow night.' And I found myself doing private study with him in his apartment. Now there's the perfect example of the conscientious musician who really says: 'Look, I don't care how much time the corporation has allotted us, we have to do the job with great conscience and it has to be done right.'. . . I think it's the only case I've ever had of a conductor who's made me come to his home, or to his apartment, and continue the extra work that has to be done."[23] Walter accompanied Hines at the piano and carefully worked out details with all the soloists. The time and effort that he devoted to his productions, as well as his thorough knowledge of the works, also impressed Hines: "He was typical of the great conductors of that time who would personally get you to work with them, and they would just mold this thing; they put their stamp on it; they became your personal coach. . . . Nowadays, instead, the coaches prepare you, you meet the conductor for one ensemble rehearsal for three or four hours, you're with the orchestra, and *go!* Because they don't know opera as these men did. These were the giants, and I do so miss it." Despite his admiration for Walter, Hines nevertheless had reservations about some of the conductor's suggestions. When Hines first sang "Within these holy portals," he stressed the *o* sound in *holy* and *portals*. "Oh no, my dear Jerome," Walter reportedly objected; "all great vocal technique is based upon the vowel *u*." Hines tried to sing the words exactly as Walter wanted them, and he granted that this approach made his tone "much more gentle and sweet," though it made his voice sound somewhat smaller, and he missed the power that the large open vowels generated. But Walter knew what he wanted. The sweetness and gentleness were absolutely requisite for his conception of Sarastro, within whose "holy portals / Revenge remains unknown."[24]

Sarastro, the chief symbol of enlightenment and stability in the opera, is counterbalanced by the Queen of the Night, the leader of the benighted subversive contingent. Finding a suitable Queen presents special difficulties, since her part requires both dazzling agility and fierce passion; not all of Walter's Queens could satisfy these requirements as brilliantly as, say, Maria Ivogün had done in a number of Walter's early productions. The young Roberta Peters, whose ease in coloratura passages and whose crystalline tone have remained with her decades later, had sung the role at the Met in German under Kurt Adler in 1951 and had performed the second aria, "Der Hölle Rache," on national television for the *Voice of Firestone* in 1952.[25] Young, attractive, and manifestly gifted, she became Walter's Queen of the Night.

Peters characterized the Queen as "a very miserable woman, a nasty woman, and you have to portray it, not just sing the notes, but get that anger in the voice."[26] Under Walter she sang with passion and fire, and the audience burst into applause halfway through the second aria. Although she performed the Queen of the Night a great many times during her career at the Met, the experience of working on the part with Walter was memorable for her. She was still quite young at the time ("the daughter was older than the mother" in this production, she recalled) and was "in great awe" of Walter, "whose name was so revered in our work and our profession. . . . But he was absolutely wonderful, very calming, told me to relax and don't worry, everything was going to be okay. . . . He came into my dressing room and we went over the score." Both arias demand a great deal from the singer, and neither allows the soprano to warm up beforehand. Although one often remembers the second aria—with its pyrotechnical display of high Fs, arpeggios, and assorted ornaments—more vividly than the first, Walter "felt that the first aria was more difficult," and he focused his attention on it, not neglecting the slower opening section (which he wanted "very legato") in favor of the more extroverted second half.

Walter's interest in the less flashy parts of the Queen of the Night's arias also revealed itself in his comments to Laurel Hurley, who played Papagena in the 1955–56 season and in the 1956–57 season took over for Peters (then pregnant) as the Queen of the Night. Walter liked the "dark, lyric quality" in Hurley's voice and encouraged her to emphasize it when singing the Queen's arias.[27] While she enjoyed hearing Walter's praise of her vocal timbre, she respectfully submitted to him that if she made her tone too dark, the high Fs would be adversely affected. Apparently sympathizing with her dilemma, Walter said: "Why don't we cut the high F?" To this day, she feels uncertain whether Walter was joking.[28] Perhaps the most significant aspect of Walter's comment—whether uttered in jest or in earnest—is that it reveals his view of the music as a vehicle for drama rather than mere display, a characteristic of Walter's opera conducting throughout his career.

Another key role in the opera is Pamina, "to whom the thought of losing Tamino's love means death," and "who unhesitatingly goes through fire and water for him"; she represents Tamino's "feminine ideal," as Walter wrote.[29] This production's Pamina was Lucine Amara, who sang effectively but carried away far from rosy memories of the event. She remembered going to Walter's hotel to rehearse the part to Walter's piano accompaniment. When she first sang the aria, Walter objected that she was singing too loudly. She sang it again, this time more softly, but it was still too loud for Walter. (It sounded too loud to him, according to Amara, because she was singing in the confined space of his hotel room.) When they went to the theater, however, and she sang at the volume they had agreed on, Walter complained that she wasn't singing loudly enough.[30] Despite Amara's mixed feelings about the experience, the critics openly admired her Pamina, with Taubman attributing the "loveliest singing of the evening" to her.[31]

The cast boasted a number of celebrated (or soon to be celebrated) singers in the smaller roles. James McCracken, though later a star tenor at the Met, received only small roles at this point in his career. By 1961 Walter would mention McCracken, whose voice he judged "beautiful and big," as a possible Florestan for a proposed recording of *Fidelio*.[32] In *Die Zauberflöte*, however, McCracken sang one of the Two Priests; Sandra Warfield, who later married McCracken, took the part of the Third Lady, with Heidi Krall and Madelaine Chambers singing the other two. Warfield had little acquaintance with Walter at this time and at first found him almost unpleasantly self-important. "I had no idea that he was such a great, great man. But if you didn't know it before, you'd know it when he came in. . . . He took himself very seriously, you know. And I had never really seen that type of musician before." His famous conducting jacket served to reinforce his solemn image: "He was almost like a priest. He had a little bit of white shirt showing, and then the black. And that was so impressive." Walter gave her the impression of a man who treated Mozart's opera almost as a sacred work, and he was scandalized when he saw the Three Ladies' original costumes, which showed off their legs in dark navy tights. "Oh no, no. Impossible," he said immediately. The costumer, called in at once to make alterations, compromised by creating something like a chiffon "skirt, or at least some flying panels," which "covered us up enough that he thought it was decent enough for Mozart. But he couldn't bear that we were up there in these costumes . . . I mean, the Three Ladies from *The Magic Flute* with their legs out like that! He was really incensed . . . because he thought it was actually sacrilegious to do that to an opera like *The Magic Flute*."[33]

If Brian Sullivan's sometimes caustic Tamino made for a less than ideal leading male, Paul Franke made the most of his small role as the wicked, libidinous Monastatos, delivering a highly charged performance. But in some ways it was the production's Papageno, the baritone Theodor Uppman, who stole the show. The early 1950s proved a golden era for Uppman. He created Billy Budd under Britten's direction in 1951, made his Met debut as Pelléas under Pierre Monteux in 1953, and triumphed as Papageno in Walter's *Flute* in 1956. Walter had become acquainted with Uppman's singing by 1954, perhaps through the *Bell Telephone Hour* broadcasts, and must have been suitably impressed. When Bing suggested Uppman as Papageno,

Walter unhesitatingly responded: "Uppman as Papageno seems to me very good."[34]

Uppman had already performed in *Die Zauberflöte*, singing the part of the Speaker in a minor production and, during the 1951–52 season, playing Papageno at Covent Garden, with Peter Pears as Tamino. "I was not very happy with it," Uppman recalled. "It was a terrible translation. And also I didn't feel I was at that time ready to do the role justice. Didn't have much time to rehearse it."[35] His disappointment at the lack of rehearsal time in the Covent Garden production would soon be compensated by Walter's special attention to Papageno—not always treated as a "serious" role. Appearing in Walter's production was a thrilling experience for Uppman, who in his youth had admired Walter on radio broadcasts. But he felt, naturally enough, some initial anxiety about the impression he would make on the renowned conductor. "I didn't have to worry about that," he admitted. "He took me under his wing, you know, taught me really everything I have done through my whole career in that role." The teaching took several forms. Walter shared with Uppman his theory that *Die Zauberflöte* was "Mozart's last will and testament" and that Papageno represented the pleasure-loving side of Mozart's personality. As with Hines, Walter sometimes worked with Uppman away from the others. He discussed phrasing and elaborated on the text, which he cherished even in its English version. When the suggestion was made to change the translation of "Ein Mädchen oder Weibchen," for example, Walter insisted on keeping it as "A sweetheart or a maiden is Papageno's plea." "He loved those words; he thought they were just right," Uppman noted. In that aria, Walter told him, "most Papagenos forget that they have had wine to drink, and they are very sleepy. . . . You must start the first verse almost asleep." But then, Uppman added, Papageno "begins to wake up, although he's maybe still taking a drink of that wine, he still wakes up a little bit more in the second verse; and finally, by the third verse, of course, he's searching for Papagena, and he's all over the stage. . . . I don't think there are very many Papagenos who do it that way." In actual performance Uppman, like William Warfield and Léopold Simoneau, found Walter's facial expressions especially valuable and instructive. "I can't tell you how much at home I felt with him. His face was so expressive always. If I looked at him, I knew exactly what to do. And I'm sure you would hear this from anyone else who had appeared with him in the production." Walter himself had only the highest regard for Uppman as Papageno: "Believe me, our collaboration in Mozart's 'The Magic Flute' was a source of rare artistic and, at the same time, personal satisfaction to me and I shall cherish its memory. I am sure Mozart would have loved your way of interpreting—I prefer to say, of 'being'—Papageno. You brought not only your voice and your talent, but also your heart into your task and hereby could fulfill the demands of this eternal creation of Mozart."[36]

Walter took an active interest in the direction of the drama as well as in the musical side of the opera. This had been true in Munich, Berlin, and Vienna, and remained so in New York. Anne Polzer, an Austrian émigrée who was then a reporter for *Aufbau,* a German-language newspaper based in New York, attended a rehearsal of the Met *Zauberflöte* in 1957 and was struck by Walter's ability to breathe life into the action onstage when he rehearsed the Three Ladies in the opening scene. "When the rehearsal began," she wrote, "their performance was heavy, dull and lifeless, without any charm whatsoever." Yet by pointing out, "in an almost fatherly way," how they should alter their approach to the parts and suggesting new ideals to strive for, he managed to effect a dramatic transformation: "After half an hour the scene had become weightless, floating on the waves of Mozart's ravishing music."[37]

Bruno Walter came to *Die Zauberflöte* with a long-held reputation as one of the world's greatest interpreters of Mozart, and the young singers eagerly looked to him for guidance. They had been taught to interpret Mozart strictly, but Walter surprised them with what they considered a "romantic" approach. Jerome Hines found this Mozart refreshingly iconoclastic:

> We were made very much aware that one does not play around with Mozart; I mean otherwise it sounds like Rossini. You've got to do absolutely everything as written. . . . So when Bruno Walter came to do *Magic Flute,* we were all anticipating what he was going to do. I have never heard such romanticism of Mozart; he took any liberty that he felt made good sense. And I kept looking at all the coaches and saying [to myself], "Now why don't you tell him he's wrong?" And they were all there in the position of: "Salaam! Salaam!" . . .
>
> When he came to do Mozart, every coach in the place was on his knees before him. And I just got such delight out of the fact that he was doing everything they told us not to do. But he did it in consummate good musical taste, and Mozart came alive for me for the first time. It wasn't some kind of a metronomic experience; it was living Mozart, which I'm sure Mozart would have been delighted with.[38]

Despite the preponderance of Mozart on Walter's programs in 1956, other composers also demanded his attention. In March he entered the recording studio for sessions devoted to the music of Johann Strauss Jr., played by the Columbia Symphony Orchestra in New York.[39] One of the most famous waltzes, "G'schichten aus dem Wienerwald" ("Tales from the Vienna Woods"), includes a part for zither, not an instrument found in the average orchestra. Loren Glickman, the contractor, scoured the restaurants in Yorkville, then the German section of New York City, and found a talented musician who entertained the clientele by playing the zither. Glickman approached him, made sure he was a union musician, and hired him for the recording.

Everything seemed set to go. At the recording session, however, a problem arose. The introduction began, and when it came time for the zither to play, there was absolutely no coordination between his playing and Walter's conducting. Anxious, Glickman had a word with the wayward musician, advising him to follow Walter's beat.

"You've played in orchestras before?" Glickman asked hopefully.

"No." This unnerving information was followed by the equally unsettling news that he couldn't read music.

"Let's take a break, everybody," Glickman called out. He approached Walter and said, "Maestro, this man knows the music, but he doesn't know how to read music, so maybe you could tell him the tempo that you want."

Walter happily agreed. "And he got together with him and explained how he wanted it done," Glickman recounted. "After that it was perfect. The man knew how to start on the downbeat; then he never looked up again, but he played the way Walter asked him to play. And after that, it was a dream."[40]

One of the other major non-Mozartian works that Walter presented in 1956 was of a very different order from the waltzes of Strauss: Bruckner's Ninth, which Walter performed with the Vienna Symphony Orchestra. It was a special concert, commemorating the sixtieth anniversary of Bruckner's death, and took place on or around July 1 in Enns, near the composer's birthplace. When asked how much money he would want for conducting the orchestra, Walter waived his fee: "It is a pleasure to me," he wrote to an astonished Fritz Rauch of the Brucknerbund in Linz, "to be able to conduct Bruckner in the land of Bruckner."[41]

Later in the year Walter conducted a few concerts of standard repertoire with the Los Angeles Philharmonic—at the Hollywood Bowl in August and at Philharmonic Auditorium in November, where he opened the season. He was almost as much an institution at that West Coast Philharmonic as he was in New York, where his advice was still highly valued. In April 1956 he had made some frank suggestions about conductors the New York Philharmonic should consider hiring in the coming season: "It seems to me best to keep the valuable services of Dimitri Mitropoulos, even be it for a shorter period," and to include Karajan ("a *must* in view of his exceptional talent, reputation and success"), Bernstein ("a very gifted American conductor"), Cantelli ("a genuine and all-around musician" with "full command of the orchestra"), and either Previtali ("an excellent musician, conductor and a noble personality") or Giulini ("also a highly gifted conductor, and at the same time a personality of high standing").[42]

For all his closeness to the New York Philharmonic, though, he felt that the time had come for him to end his regular guest appearances with the orchestra after the 1956–57 season. He confided to Zirato (now managing director of the Philharmonic) that, for many years, "I always looked forward with joy and happy anticipation to my rehearsals and concerts with my friends of the Philharmonic Orchestra. This time, however, I feel the hour has struck for me to discontinue an activity which has meant so much to me." His eighty years had become a burden, and he preferred to leave of his own volition before being compelled to do so by age and infirmity.[43]

In the same month Walter rejected another offer that many will wish he had accepted. The composer Mario Labroca asked whether Walter would be interested in conducting a performance of Gluck's *Orfeo* for RAI Television.[44] Margareta Wallmann, who had worked with Walter on a highly successful production of *Orfeo* in Salzburg, would also be involved. It seemed like an ideal arrangement, and Walter confessed that the project piqued his interest. It was a work that Walter was famous for, and posterity would surely have cherished a television production. In the end, however, despite his great respect for Wallmann, he felt that the "special demands" of Gluck's opera could never be met "within the limited dimensions of a Television performance. Gluck's Orpheus calls for masses, for wide spaces," and he "could not compromise in such indispensable demands of so sublime a work."[45]

But other media engaged Walter's participation more readily. One project released in 1956 was an LP devoted to an interview with Walter by Arnold Michaelis. Long a Walter enthusiast, Michaelis had already interviewed the conductor in May 1955 for the New York radio station WQXR.

Goddard Lieberson, who had heard the interview, was impressed enough to offer Michaelis a job at Columbia Masterworks, where he would produce several recordings. The new interview was originally meant to furnish minute-long radio spots promoting Walter's records on Columbia as part of his eightieth-birthday celebrations. It presents Walter giving relatively unrehearsed responses to questions on his long career—his relationship with Mahler, his affection for the music of Mozart and Bruckner, his early days in Vienna, and so forth. This was an unusual format for Walter, who ordinarily avoided spontaneous interviews, preferring to read prepared responses and statements. (At one point, despite his elevated use of English, he uses the German *Brücke* instead of the English word *bridge*.) After hearing the new interview, the marketing department decided that it should be issued as an LP, which was eventually called *Bruno Walter in Conversation with Arnold Michaelis*.[46]

There were other birthday honors as well. Lotte Lehmann composed a long panegyric entitled *Bruno Walter: The Musician and the Man*, and Columbia put together a promotional record of short tributes for circulation among radio stations, similar to the collection assembled for Walter's seventy-seventh birthday and including several of the same items as well as new contributions from Leonard Bernstein, Leonard Rose, John Corigliano, William Warfield, Jennie Tourel, and Goddard Lieberson.[47] In Europe as well as America, radio programs celebrated Walter's birthday with special broadcasts. Perhaps Walter's friend Arturo Toscanini heard one of them, or one of the records issued about that time, for on September 11, 1956, he cabled a congratulatory telegram to Walter from New York: "I was moved by your beautiful performance of the symphonies and songs of Mahler . . . sung by that heavenly voice," he wrote in Italian. "I embrace you with much affection."[48] (Walter's recording of Mahler's First Symphony with the New York Philharmonic and a reissue of the *Kindertotenlieder* with Kathleen Ferrier and the Vienna Philharmonic had recently been released.)[49]

So much for the view—still widely maintained—that Toscanini hated Walter's conducting. In fact, the two remained friends until Toscanini's death, which was not far off. The Italian maestro's ninetieth birthday would have occurred on March 25, 1957, and the Symphony of the Air (the orchestra that had once been the NBC Symphony Orchestra, newly named after Toscanini's retirement) planned to celebrate the occasion with an all-star cast of conductors. The chairman of the orchestra naturally invited Walter, as well as Munch, Monteux, Ormandy, Cantelli, and Stokowski. Walter happily agreed to conduct, reserving the Prelude to *Die Meistersinger* for himself and sending his greeting to "The Orchestra that Refused to Die."[50]

But the concert didn't take place as planned. Toscanini died on January 16, 1957, and Walter now received a grim new invitation—to be a pallbearer for the funeral at St. Patrick's Cathedral in New York—an honor that his weakened constitution must have prevented him from accepting.[51] Walter prepared a short but powerful tribute to his lost friend:

> I am too deeply shocked by the passing of my dear and revered friend Arturo Toscanini to find adequate words for the statement I have been asked for. . . . Trying to touch on the secret of the unique force that emanated from Arturo Toscanini over his singers and musicians, over his audiences, over the whole musical world I believe to have found it in the rare combination of deep humility with a dictatorial willpower. Great was his humility towards the musical works and composers he interpreted and just as great the dynamic strength by which he forced his singers and musicians to perform those works according to his intentions. His ideals dominated his musical life and he dominated in their service his collaborators. In him was greatness and I am sure the memory of his glorious activities in the fields of dramatic and absolute music will live on in the hearts of all of us.[52]

The Symphony of the Air did give its concert for Toscanini, but instead of celebrating a long-lived colleague, the musicians offered a memorial tribute, led by Walter, Munch, and Monteux at Carnegie Hall on February 3, 1957. Walter's original choice of the jubilant *Meistersinger* Prelude ceded its place to the "Eroica," a more appropriate piece to commemorate the fallen titan, with its heroic first movement, its solemn "Funeral March," and its life-affirming Scherzo and Finale.[53] The performance, issued on compact disc, has much of the drive one associates with Toscanini, and one longtime admirer of Walter's, Rolland Parker, who attended the concert, later wrote to ask whether it was "possible that in matters of tempo and rhythm there was a resemblance to Toscanini's style." Characteristically, Walter not only thanked Parker for his letter but also took the trouble to answer his question regarding style: "I do not know of any change in my interpretative intentions on this occasion and I presume your impression may be explained by the fact that it was an orchestra which had played the same work under Toscanini for many years."[54] In fact, the Toscaninian element in the performance is plain for anyone to hear, and being informed that the orchestra was still perceptibly playing for the "old man" might have brought back memories of an orchestra not always willing to mold itself to Walter's wishes. When a guest conductor took over at the podium, as the violinist Felix Galimir confessed, sometimes the members of the NBC orchestra "did not even watch whatever he was doing," and it was clear that Toscanini's presence was felt by the players even when he was not physically there.[55]

With illness and death claiming his friends and his own health ailing, Walter was no doubt particularly aware of his own mortality. By January 10, 1957, he had made out his will, leaving about a quarter of his estate (or the sum of $85,000, whichever was the lesser amount) to Delia Reinhardt and the remainder to his daughter. His timing would prove providential.

The New York Philharmonic enjoyed his leadership again during February, when he performed (among other works) Bruckner's Ninth, Beethoven's Sixth, and Mahler's "Resurrection" Symphony with the contralto Maureen Forrester and the soprano Maria Stader as soloists. The young Canadian Maureen Forrester had had a successful audition in New York and recalled Walter's insistence that she come to California to go over the part with him—a proposition that Forrester, then strapped for money, heard with some uneasiness. "Now if you know the Mahler Second," she remarked, "it's not a very big piece to sing. But everybody was so excited in Montreal when they heard I was supposed to do it with Bruno Walter that I finally got enough money to go. I worked with him. He just went through it a couple of times with me and said, 'That's going to be wonderful,' and I flew back."[56] A recording session for the "Resurrection" began at that time, though the final sessions would be postponed for a year.

On March 1, 1957, Walter conducted the first performance of *Die Zauberflöte* for the 1956–57 season. For Theodor Uppman and his family the performance proved a memorable experience. After the opera, as the Uppmans drove to their home in Roslyn, New York, admiring the snow that had recently fallen and gazing up at the now limpid sky, the night continued to seem enchanted. Theodor Uppman vividly recalled the event: "We got home . . . Jean and the kids went in, and I was putting the car away, and I looked up suddenly, and there were the Northern Lights, which happen very seldom here, and it was a spectacular display, it was just flashing all over, and so I called to Jean, Margot, and Michael and said, 'You've got to see this.' We brought chairs into the back yard and sat down with the snow all around us, watching these lights. Boy, what an end to a perfect evening."[57] That night, however, marked the last operatic performance that Walter ever conducted. On March 7, 1957—twelve days before a scheduled black-tie celebration in his honor, arranged jointly by the Metropolitan Opera, the New York Philharmonic, CBS Radio, and Columbia Records—he suffered a heart attack, which forced him to withdraw completely from the demands of the stage and to restrict his musical activities to the concert hall and the recording studio.

# SEVENTEEN

# Columbia Symphony Orchestra
## Los Angeles, 1957–1962

*Something of me will remain after I have gone.*

Bruno Walter to Albert Goldberg in 1958

"The heart attack itself," Walter commented to Katia and Erika Mann, "was, judged objectively, 'mild' (though subjectively unmild); the time in the hospital, a practical lesson in patience; the return to our home, a relief."[1] He had been taken to Flower and Fifth Avenue Hospitals in Manhattan after the attack and felt greatly relieved to be back in Beverly Hills the following month. Mild or "unmild," the heart attack forced him to cancel his professional activities for the rest of the year, much to the dismay of agents who had already counted on sold-out houses through Walter's participation in their concerts. Finding comfort in a motorized chair that carried him up and down stairs, Walter relaxed and improved steadily; by July 4 he happily reported to Bruno Zirato that he was taking long walks to the ocean every afternoon.[2] Nevertheless, his condition was not good, and later in the same year he suffered another blow to his health, though it's unclear whether this was another heart attack.[3] In December Walter wrote "in confidence" to Stresemann that his health had "endured something quite serious (for the second time this year)"—"so he probably had a second heart attack," Stresemann surmised, "but it must have been milder than the other one."[4] Walter's precarious health put him in an awkward position. On the one hand, he wanted people to know that he craved and needed relaxation; on the other, he no doubt feared that his future professional activities would be jeopardized if his health were seen as dangerously frail.

If Walter was ailing through most of 1957, many of his longtime friends fared far worse. He had already lost Toscanini in January, and on May 9 Ezio Pinza died, that quintessential Don Giovanni who had shone in Walter's productions at Salzburg and the Met, the man with whom Walter's daughter Gretel had haplessly fallen in love. Emil Schipper, another singer who had worked with Walter on countless productions in Munich and Berlin, passed away on July 20. Perhaps more of a shock, however, was the death of Erich Korngold on November 29, at the age of sixty. The boy who had astonished Mahler and his contemporaries early in the century, having reached maturity, wound up writing sound tracks for Hollywood classics, never regaining the respect from the classical world that had once showered praise so bountifully upon him.

The enforced period of relaxation gave Walter more time to spend with Delia, who continued to devote her creative energy to painting. Alma Mahler Werfel sent kind words to Delia about one of her paintings, and Walter wrote to thank Alma for her praise, which had brought them both happiness.[5] As before, Walter and Reinhardt continued to read works by Steiner and his followers, and Walter maintained his correspondence with anthroposophists like Albert Steffen, Emil Bock, and Friedrich Hiebel. With the appearance of the German edition of Walter's latest book in the latter part of 1957, the conductor's allegiance to anthroposophy was made public. "There is no part of my spiritual self," he wrote in his afterword to *Of Music and Music-Making*, "to which the sublime teachings of Rudolf Steiner have not vouchsafed new light and definite advancement."[6] More and more, Walter's anthroposophical leanings would express themselves in his public and private writings. In a preface to a collection of essays to be published by the Bruckner Society in Italy, for example, Walter barely disguised his Steinerian *Weltanschauung*: "As a result of my lifelong occupation with Bruckner I am audacious enough to express the opinion that he has lived on this earth already, not in the sphere of Time but of Eternity. . . . Bruckner's music is a bridge to transcendental regions and only those longing for higher spheres will respond to the apostolic calls sounding forth from his work."[7] Reincarnation, knowledge from higher spheres—these ideas could have come directly from

Steiner (though Walter himself had long written of "higher spheres" of knowledge). Walter also ventured so far as to suggest that Mahler would have been attracted to Steiner's teachings: Mahler, he wrote to one correspondent, "was a seeker with a deeply religious disposition that most surely would have been brought gratification through contact with Rudolf Steiner, had fate brought them together."[8]

Largely in response to the epilogue concluding *Of Music and Music-Making*, the anthroposophist Emil Bock, whose works Walter had read for years, wrote a biographical essay on the conductor for the anthroposophical periodical *Christengemeinschaft*. Bock had in fact known and admired Walter as a conductor for years; in the 1920s he'd heard Gluck's *Orfeo* at the Städtische Oper in Berlin and a Bruckner concert at the Gewandhaus under Walter. Having been informed that Walter read his books, and having finally met him in 1955 when he came to conduct at the Goetheanum, Bock wrote a congratulatory letter to the conductor on his eightieth birthday. Bock was stunned when, shortly afterward, he received a long, handwritten thank-you letter from Walter, who informed the author that he and Delia had read Bock's works on the New Testament, early Christianity, and the Apostle Paul, and were now reading his book on the Apocalypse for the second time.[9] A steady correspondence ensued. When Walter read Bock's biographical essay in 1958, he was particularly pleased with a passage in which the author described Walter's Christianity as faith that had come from within, during his miserable tenure in Pressburg (six decades before), when he had been led to near-suicidal despair.[10] Though Walter had claimed, in the passage cited by Bock, that he was "never to lose" his faith in Christendom after plunging to his spiritual nadir in Pressburg, his very concept of Christ must have changed substantially if he subscribed to Steiner's view of Jesus as a historical figure who had been visited by the spirit that had once inhabited Moses and Zoroaster.

Not everyone was pleased with Walter's newfound enthusiasm for Steiner. The distinguished American publishing house Alfred A. Knopf, which published *Theme and Variations* and the revised translation of *Gustav Mahler*, would not undertake the English edition of Walter's new book so long as Walter insisted on retaining the "last chapter" (by which was surely meant the anthroposophical epilogue). Perhaps Knopf was looking for an excuse not to work with Walter again; the translation headaches involved with the Mahler biography had proved frustrating to Herbert Weinstock, Walter's editor at Knopf and himself the author of several books on musical topics. In any case, Walter refused to strike the epilogue, and the book eventually went to W. W. Norton, another prestigious publisher.[11]

Much of the negotiation for the English translation of the new book was handled by Maria Horch, Walter's literary agent and the widow of Franz Horch, who had held the same position for most of the 1940s. Walter, however, still saw to many of his business transactions, even during his convalescence. Shortly after suffering his heart attack he received a note from the financially strapped London Philharmonic, which owed him £150 and pleaded for patience. Walter cabled back that he "gladly" waived his fee and would have let the matter drop there.[12] But on April 24 another letter issued from the London Philharmonic, promising payment soon. Walter again graciously waived his fee: "I refer you to my telegram in which I told the London Philharmonic Orchestra that I did not make any claim on your check in payment of my account. It is a pleasure for me to waive any right of such kind."[13]

The London Philharmonic had been fortunate enough to enjoy a transatlantic visit from Walter before his illness had compelled him to cancel his commitments in Europe. One of the many Europeans who had hoped to present Walter in 1957 was Herbert von Karajan, who became artistic director of the Salzburg Festival that year. Though particularly saddened that Walter would not be there during his first year as director, Karajan wrote that he would try to lead the festival in the spirit that Walter had given it, a spirit that had been a continual model for Karajan since their first meeting.[14] The relationship between these two extraordinarily different musical interpreters, who belonged to opposite sides during the war, is hard to gauge. In the 1930s Karajan—whether for political or professional reasons (or both)— joined the Nazi Party, and Walter was certainly aware of Karajan's outward allegiance to the Third Reich. In 1949 he wrote to Bruno Zirato that, as far as he knew, Karajan "really [had been] a Nazi," unlike Furtwängler.[15] Yet, apparently unswayed by political motivations, Walter strongly recommended Karajan in 1956 for guest appearances with the New York Philharmonic, while knowing perfectly well that the engagement might "involve some difficulties."[16] A few months before his death, Walter characterized Karajan as "ein seltsamer Mann," an ambiguous phrase that could mean either "a peculiar man" or "a singular man."[17]

Having been forced, after his heart attack, to cancel his remaining performances for 1957, Walter conducted only a handful of concerts in 1958, the first of which took place on February 26. It was a pension fund concert with the New York Philharmonic, and the printed program reproduced in facsimile the evening's musical menu in Walter's now shaky handwriting. The works were old friends: the "Leonore" Overture no. 2, Mozart's "Linz" Symphony, Wagner's *Siegfried Idyll*, and Schubert's "Unfinished." According to Harriet Johnson, "there was no evidence" that Walter had suffered a heart attack a year before, and the audience response was predictably enthusiastic: "The entire house rose when he came on-stage to open the concert. The listeners remained to cheer him at every possible opportunity."[18]

No piece on the New York program was especially long, and Walter was careful not to overtax himself with pieces that would put him under excessive strain. In the middle of March, however, he gave two performances of Schubert's "Unfinished" and Mozart's Requiem in Chicago. In choosing the Requiem, which demands sustained concentration on the orchestra, soloists, and chorus for roughly an hour, Walter was perhaps testing himself, to see how much music he could perform without overburdening his constitution. As he remarked to Bruno Zirato in September 1957, the programs that included the Mozart Requiem would "not make demands with which [he] could not cope."[19] Nevertheless, he apparently took things gently in Chicago. "He seemed to want everything very soft in the Mozart Requiem," David Lloyd, the tenor, noted. The fine quartet of soloists on this occasion consisted of Maria Stader, Maureen Forrester, Lloyd, and Otto Edelmann, with the two female soloists making an amusing picture onstage: the diminutive Maria Stader stood beside the towering Maureen Forrester, then in an "advanced" stage of pregnancy. To make the discrepancy in their appearance less striking, Walter placed Stader on a platform.[20]

If the concerts in Chicago showed Walter testing his stamina, his choice of Bruckner's "Romantic" for performances in Los Angeles and San Francisco in April and May might well have been a further test. Unlike Mozart's Requiem, Bruckner's hour-long symphony has fewer places to pause for regrouping one's forces. It is perhaps indicative of Walter's mental preoccupations at this time that he chose, for the second half of his Los Angeles concerts on April 10 and 11, Mozart's *Masonic Funeral Music* and Strauss's *Tod und Verklärung*. Walter, as T. S. Eliot might have phrased it, was much possessed by death.

Walter's last and, in some ways, most important public engagement in 1958 was the inaugural concert of the Vancouver International Festival, given on July 19. The festival offered not only classical music but also jazz, dance, and even a performance by the renowned French mime Marcel Marceau.

Walter opened the festivities with Weber's overture to *Euryanthe*, Schubert's "Unfinished," and two works by Brahms: the *Alt-Rhapsodie* with Maureen Forrester (the alto soloist on his new recording of Mahler's "Resurrection") and the Second Symphony. The great Czech-born pianist Rudolf Firkušný was then in Vancouver and found the performance of his sometime colleague "a great inspiration." For his part, Walter was delighted to renew his acquaintance with a musician whose collaboration he had enjoyed in the past.[21]

One of the happiest results of Walter's participation in the festival is the hour-long television documentary that the Canadian Broadcasting Company made of Walter rehearsing the orchestra in the first and last movements of Brahms's Second.[22] Offering the longest video footage of Walter in action (and including a lengthy interview between Walter and Albert Goldberg, music critic for the *Los Angeles Times*), it is an invaluable record of the conductor's wizardry. According to the voice-over introduction, Walter was meeting the orchestra for the first time. The ensemble was, to quote one contemporary report, "well below top quality," though a few ringers were added to the core players.[23] In literally a matter of minutes, he transforms ragged note-reading into sensitive music-making. Animated, attentive, utterly aware of the sounds surrounding him, a constant twinkle in his eye, he gives no indication of having recently sustained a life-threatening blow to his health. Hardly glancing at the score, with every detail of the piece obviously mapped out in his mind, he adjusts balances ("Woodwinds, very *piano*; it was far too loud"), articulation ("Not too staccato . . . otherwise it gets very hard"), dynamics ("Shhh! Disappear!"), bowing ("This phrase on the frog"), and phrasing ("Always with *espressivo*, and at the end a *diminuendo*")—all this with dazzling speed and assurance. He constantly urges the players to "sing" and inflect, with a politeness verging on the courtly.

While in Vancouver, when his free time must have been at a premium, Walter was "kind enough to read through" a cello concerto by Ernst Friedlander, one of the musicians who played under him; the conductor later claimed to be "much impressed with its original musical language" and predicted that the cellist's "colleagues" would "welcome this work."[24]

The trip had a certain therapeutic value for Walter. He enjoyed the beautiful natural surroundings, and if he had earlier maintained doubts about his stamina, the concert apparently brought him renewed confidence in his powers. "The music-making there," he wrote to Wolfgang Stresemann shortly afterward, "filled me with happiness, as did the magnificent landscape of British Columbia, and I also noted with pleasure that conducting hasn't yet become excessively taxing for me."[25]

Despite his light schedule of performances before the public, Walter had been quite active musically in the earlier part of 1958, though his performances took place not on the concert stage but in the recording studio. Throughout January and for a substantial portion of February, Walter began a series of recordings with the Columbia Symphony Orchestra. The idea of putting together a recording orchestra for Walter had been proposed the previous summer, as John McClure, the young producer for many of those recordings, has described. Walter was then recuperating in Palm Springs, "taking the sun in the manner of an older European generation: with topcoat, scarf, and cloth cap against the muscular desert heat." Discovering that Walter was recovering rapidly, McClure asked him "if he were disposed to begin a large recording project using a new process called stereo." He pointed out that the new process was not only "an advance in the recording art, but also an eventual threat to already existing records."[26] Though Walter was apparently unimpressed by the "threat," he agreed to go along with the project, provided that a recording venue could be found near his home in Beverly Hills.

That desideratum was discovered in a most unlikely place: an unsightly "concrete structure built in the 1920s as a meeting place for the American Legion," which astonishingly, according to McClure, "turned out to be ideal on every point." Well, almost every point. The orchestra had to be reduced somewhat, especially in the strings, as a result of the size and resonance of the hall. The sessions, "averaging three hours each with several breaks to hear playbacks, allowed [Walter] to complete even the most turbulent movements of Mahler without suffering excessive fatigue."[27]

Those first sessions were devoted to new readings of some of the Beethoven symphonies, and a performance from those sessions became one of Walter's best-loved recordings, that of the "Pastoral." For many this became the quintessential Walter interpretation—a moderate tempo, a gentle and expansive approach to the score, sensitive shaping of the lines, sensuous orchestral playing. The Columbia Symphony Orchestra recordings were often in this mold, though there were certainly some exceptions to the rule—such as the demonic finale to Brahms's Third Symphony—and, largely because of their excellent sound, they have become the legacy by which Walter is mainly remembered. Despite their abundant virtues, however, these performances record only the last phase of Walter's long career; this is the beauty of *Winterreise* and *Parsifal* rather than *Die schöne Müllerin* and *Meistersinger*.

Though initially unimpressed by the "threat" that stereo sound posed to his monaural recordings, Walter was grateful to have one more chance to add to his legacy. Nevertheless, he was not overjoyed with the idea of re-recording all the Austro-German classics that he had committed to disks just a few years before. With evident anxiety he asked his East Coast producer, David Oppenheim, about the fate of his recordings with the New York Philharmonic: "Will our whole work over the last years, Mozart, Haydn, Strauss, etc.—will they have to be thrown into the ashcan because they are depreciated by the stereophonic method of today? Would it not be a waste of precious time and strength to remake for instance those works of Brahms (to whose Third Symphony I listened yesterday with satisfaction)? Do you not prefer to use January and February for increasing our repertoire, instead of decreasing it by depreciating our former records of Brahms and implicitly many records of the same vintage? I think in this way we would have condemned our whole former work to obsolescence. How could I, at my age, ever hope to make up for such a loss?"[28] Some have felt that Walter, in his final years, unimaginatively stuck with the same repertoire that he had recorded in the recent past, but it's worth bearing in mind that the choice of repertoire was not always his to make, and he was certainly interested in recording pieces he hadn't yet committed to disk. In 1961, with less than a year to live, Walter made a list of several projects he hoped to complete with the Columbia Symphony Orchestra, some of the more mouth-watering (and heart-breaking) of which were Mahler's Third, Bruckner's Eighth, the four Schumann symphonies, and Mendelssohn's "Scottish" Symphony. Several of these have not come down to us in any form, not even a scratchy acetate made from a poor broadcast signal. Yet Walter's plans were as realistic as they were ambitious: "Of course, we shall be lucky," he commented prophetically, "if I could finish this repertoire in my 90th year."[29]

Walter also finished a recording project with the New York Philharmonic in February, one that had been interrupted by his heart attack the previous year. He declined an invitation to conduct Mahler's Second in concert with the orchestra, maintaining that the piece would be too taxing for him to perform live: "There are very few works of the concert repertoire which demand as much strength as such a Mahler Symphony, and I think I have to renounce efforts of this kind." But studio work was another matter: "Two movements are already on record, so we have to take only the three remaining ones and I think we will do it in two sessions, which will make all the difference in the world."[30] As with the recording of the First Symphony, Walter agreed to write the liner notes, in which he urged the listener—as he had done so many years before in connection with the Third and Fourth symphonies of Mahler—to approach the purely instrumental movements as "symphonic" (rather than programmatic) music before he discussed the relations between text and music in the last two movements.

Quite apart from recording projects, Mahler continued to loom large in Walter's life. Erwin Ratz, one of the most prominent editors of Mahler's works and a key member of the Mahler Gesellschaft in Vienna, corresponded with Walter on a number of issues related to the composer. A point of contention arose over a biographical essay on Mahler in which Ratz discussed Mahler's connection with the Schoenberg circle. To Walter, Ratz seemed to be suggesting that Mahler's polyphony influenced the atonal experiments of the Second Viennese School. Always sensitive to this argument, Walter refused to endorse what Ratz had written, referring him to passages in his own writings that expressed his hostility to atonality and the twelve-tone technique, as well as his feeling that Mahler's art was in a very different category from that of the atonalists.[31] Ratz tried to appease Walter by rephrasing his comments, but Walter still bristled at the vestigial implications. In the end, Ratz struck the passage from his essay; Walter's approval, Ratz felt, was more important than his own personal ideas on the matter.[32]

Walter, of course, was far from the only conductor to present Mahler to the public in the 1950s. Heinz Unger—like Walter, one of the leading champions of Mahler in Berlin shortly before the events of 1933—was now in Canada, conducting the York Concert Society. He had recently given a performance of Mahler's Second and proudly sent Walter a newspaper review of the concert. At the "Grosse Appell" in the last movement, where the chorus sings "Auferstehen" ("Arise"), Unger thought he remembered Walter having the chorus rise from their seats, as Unger himself had recently done. Walter disabused Unger of this notion: "I am in principle against all such extra-musical aids of material effects; [but] I can imagine," he added with due sensitivity to Unger's feelings, "that your idea was very effective."[33]

One more touching link with his mentor occurred at the end of 1958. Mahler made four piano rolls in 1905 for the company M. Welte und Söhne, preserving his readings of two songs, the last movement of the Fourth Symphony, and the first movement of the Fifth. Despite some ragged playing, these are extraordinary artifacts, being the only sound documents of

Mahler's own interpretations of his works. As early as 1951 Alfred Rosé (Arnold's son and Gustav Mahler's nephew) had written to Walter about a record made from the piano rolls, the playing on which he found so "nervous," "clipped," and "conductorly" that he questioned their authenticity. Though unfamiliar with the rolls, Walter wasn't surprised to hear Rosé's comments; Mahler, after all, was not playing the piano regularly when he made the rolls, and his playing was likely to be "hard."[34] Apparently Walter did not follow up on the matter until 1958, when he noticed that Columbia had once issued the disk in question, though it was by then out of print. He wrote to Goddard Lieberson in November 1958 in the hope of convincing him to reissue the record. Lieberson explained that it included several other early performances and that the public "was rather apathetic toward these historical curiosities, and therefore they were withdrawn from our catalogue." Nevertheless, he would run off test pressings for Walter, as well as for Alma and her daughter Anna, at no charge.[35] When Walter heard the record, it must have brought back the golden days of those private recitals in Hamburg, when Mahler would play his works in progress for his young protégé. "Listening to Mahler's playing was a deeply moving experience for me," he wrote to Lieberson afterward, "which awakened great memories."[36] However hard and clipped the playing, Walter clearly enjoyed the illusion of being in Mahler's presence again.

While he occasionally turned his glance backward, the world continued to carry him forward, as the younger generation looked to him for guidance. Already in February 1958 Walter had made contact with an up-and-coming American piano virtuoso, Van Cliburn (then only twenty-three), who gained international recognition that year by winning first prize in the Tchaikovsky competition in Moscow. Walter was one of Cliburn's heroes, and the young pianist was drawn to the musical elder statesman not only for his interpretive powers but also for his philosophical interests. In fact, Cliburn took a distinct interest in anthroposophy and sought Walter's advice on whether or not to make his interests public. (Walter characteristically advised against it.) He also asked to study Brahms's Second Piano Concerto with Walter, which the conductor happily agreed to.[37] After the private lesson, Cliburn sent a check to Walter for vouchsafing some of his "precious time"; Walter, refusing any "financial relation," returned the check.[38] The following year Cliburn expressed his strong desire to record the Second Piano Concerto with Walter, but contractual restrictions—Cliburn recorded for RCA Victor, not Columbia—prevented this desirable project from being realized.[39]

In 1960, however, the two would finally collaborate on the concerto, in Walter's very last public concert.

Rare enough in 1958, Walter's public appearances were limited to three events in 1959. On March 5 and 6 he conducted the Los Angeles Philharmonic in a program consisting of the *Midsummer Night's Dream* Overture, Haydn's Symphony no. 88, and Schubert's Symphony no. 9. "Songfulness was the keynote of the conductor's interpretation," Goldberg wrote of the Schubert; "even the climaxes were treated lyrically."[40] The interpretation must have been nearly identical to the broadly paced reading Walter had just preserved with the Columbia Symphony Orchestra. He returned in November to open the Los Angeles Philharmonic's forty-first season, offering a program that featured Bruckner's Ninth, a work he recorded a few days later with the Columbia Symphony Orchestra (drawing heavily on members of the Los Angeles Philharmonic). He was apparently still in good physical form; Goldberg noted that for the opening-night concert Walter "walked on the stage with a vigor that belied his eighty-three years of life and more than sixty years of distinguished service to the art of music."[41] For the concerts and the recording, Walter presented the symphony as a three-movement work, though he was fully aware of Bruckner's drafts for a fourth movement.[42] When a fan who had enjoyed Walter's recording of the Ninth asked, in all innocence, whether any traces of a final movement existed that could perhaps be worked up into a "presentable" performing score, he unwittingly triggered a knee-jerk response:

> Indeed, *Bruckner* has not completed his 9th Symphony, but left sketches for a finale. I had the occasion to study them and they only confirmed what I had always felt, that after such an adagio, nothing could follow—similarly as is the case with Schubert's Symphony in B minor. There is a power of musical and spiritual expression which cannot allow anything to follow.
>
> I have also objected strongly to the completion and publication of Mahler's 10th Symphony. Who could dare to continue where a great master was compelled to leave incomplete one of his highest works of art?
>
> I hope I have made myself clear.[43]

As on other occasions, Walter revealed an uncongenial side of his personality when confronted with people who, in his view, felt they had the right to tamper with works of genius. But it was a genuine reverence toward musical greatness, rather than disdain for music-lovers who wanted to squeeze one or two more pieces from the legacy of their favorite composers, that elicited such prickly words from him.

The other performance of 1959, which took place earlier in the year, was Walter's farewell to the Metropolitan Opera. On March 27 and 29, Good Friday and Easter Sunday, Walter led the Met Orchestra and Chorus in Verdi's Requiem, preceded by the "Convent Scene" from *Forza*. He had given the identical program in 1951, thinking then that he was bidding the house adieu. Ironically, when he came in 1959, there was still negotiation on his possible return the following year, but this really was to be his last performance at the Met. The repertoire marked a departure from the Met's usual practice of staging *Parsifal* on Good Friday, which Rudolf Bing claimed he couldn't "bear" to see again.[44] As for the soloists, Bing suggested Zinka Milanov, who had sung the part before under Walter; Rosalind Elias, who had a bit part in Walter's *Flute* and who had since made a name for herself in Barber's *Vanessa* (Bing thought Walter might be able to help her as he had once helped Kathleen Ferrier); Carlo Bergonzi, whom Bing recommended without reservation; and either Cesare Siepi or Giorgio Tozzi, both of whom had worked with Walter on earlier occasions. There was also a distinct possibility of recording the Requiem for RCA Victor, though Walter was far from sanguine on that point: "It seems more than improbable to me that Columbia would 'lend' me to the Victor Company."[45] Eventually the soloists were chosen—Milanov, Elias, Bergonzi, and Tozzi—and in January 1959 Walter asked Bing to inform the soloists that they were expected to know their parts by heart.[46] It was a requirement common enough from Walter, especially in solemn works like the requiems of Mozart, Brahms, and Verdi. For three of the four singers, Bing replied, Walter's will would be done. Milanov, however, neither knew the part by heart nor could learn it in time for the concert, because she was away on tour and would not have sufficient time to memorize it on her return.[47]

That was perhaps an ill omen. For the Good Friday performance, Milanov was suddenly taken ill, and the soprano part went to Heidi Krall, who had sung a small role in Walter's *Flute* performances in 1956 and 1957. On Easter Sunday, Milanov sang the "Convent Scene" and took part in the Requiem through the "Dies Irae." Her voice showed noticeable strain on the high notes in the "Recordare" and the "Lacrimosa," and she collapsed near the end of the movement, to be replaced again by Krall. Through it all,

Walter kept the whole musical machine running smoothly, as a recording of the performance shows. Rolland Parker, who attended both concerts, recalled Walter's coolly professional response to Milanov's collapse: the soprano "literally fainted on stage. I was watching Bruno Walter through powerful binoculars, and he did not so much as blink an eyelash. Now, naturally he must have been a little concerned when they were dragging off his soprano in the middle of the Verdi Requiem in his ultimate performance with the Metropolitan Opera, but he had very great composure."[48]

A very different eyewitness account came from a fellow conductor, a man who had once assisted Walter during the 1930s. Erich Leinsdorf, also conducting at the Met in the 1958–59 season, attended the Good Friday performance of the Requiem. His verdict was that Walter had grown too old to be effective in a work like the Requiem, with its demanding choruses: "Age had taken physical vigor out of his arm and his beat was weak," Leinsdorf recalled in the mid-1970s. "Rarely have I perspired as much as I did during that short afternoon. Many were the moments when it was touch and go if the music would continue at all or break down in total chaos."[49] Contemporary reviews, however, reported no such problems ("Mr. Walter brought to life the fervor and the piety, the drama and lovely gentleness of Verdi's score with incomparable artistry," wrote Paul Henry Lang, while Howard Taubman noted how well the chorus and orchestra could perform "for the right maestro"); nor does the recording of the Sunday concert suggest that Walter was beyond delivering a coherent, powerful performance. His impassioned grunts and often audible comments to the soloists suggest a man fully engaged in the act of making music.[50]

Like many other bootleg recordings, the taped performance of Verdi's Requiem preserves the only interpretation of a work that Walter had performed many times throughout his career. Those interested in his development can only be grateful that enthusiasts were capturing the performances for posterity. But how did Walter himself feel about pirate recordings? Did he disapprove of them as he did the recordings of his rehearsal sessions? Apparently not at all. When Douglas Duer of the Columbia Record Club wrote that he was collecting air-checks of Walter's radio performances for the Columbia Record Club, Walter gave the project his full blessing and said he would be happy to meet Duer in New York.[51] Although Walter's attitude might seem surprising (given his hostility to reissuing the 1938 live performance of Mahler's Ninth), his eagerness to give permanence to what would otherwise be ephemeral activities corresponded to some of the most pressing concerns of his old age. He wanted to leave a legacy, and collecting off-the-air performances was just one more way of adding to that legacy.

However much he wanted to record his active repertoire, there were limits to what Walter would agree to commit to disk. When he heard early in the year that Columbia had suggested a recording of light music (Johann Strauss Jr., Suppé, and others), he promptly voiced his objections to the plan: "I am first of all an interpreter of our classical music, and I consider it my life's mission to contribute in this sense to our contemporaneous musical life as long as destiny will permit me. . . . [I]t would hurt my feelings as well as my prestige with our public if we filled the remaining sessions with light literature, be it even as charming as Strauss or Suppé. . . . Next Friday we will already do Strauss' 'Roses from the South' and it is a depressing thought for me to continue in the same vein."[52] He wrote this letter as he was finishing up one of the most penetrating and sublime recordings of his late period, that of Brahms's Fourth Symphony, the first of his stereo cycle of the Brahms symphonies.[53] There is no indication in the paperwork at Columbia that Walter ever recorded "Roses from the South" with the Columbia Symphony Orchestra, and the relationship between Columbia and Walter seems to have taken a turn for the better, since the remaining records Walter made were all of substantial material and included performances of major works by Beethoven, Bruckner, Dvořák, Mahler, Mozart, Schubert, and Wagner.

David Oppenheim had responsibilities on the East Coast apart from his work with Walter, so in August John McClure officially succeeded Oppenheim as Walter's producer. The friendly relationship between the two men is clear throughout their congenial correspondence. Although Walter felt uncomfortable about offering, at McClure's suggestion, a rehearsal session of the Beethoven symphonies with the Columbia Symphony Orchestra (it was issued anyway), he was delighted when the new set of symphonies came out. "I received the Beethoven records," he wrote to McClure in October, "and I am deeply moved by this monumental effort of Columbia, which to a great extent is your effort."[54] He also thanked his old producer Goddard Lieberson, now president of Columbia Records, not only for the set but also "for having accepted the new relation between us. It is a wonderful experience for me to have found such understanding of my situation."[55]

Although the Los Angeles–based Columbia Symphony Orchestra was the ensemble for the new Beethoven cycle, one key movement in the set—the ever problematic finale to the Ninth—was taken by the New York pickup orchestra. Once again the conclusion had to be recorded separately from the opening three movements. Walter was dissatisfied with the chorus in California, so one day the contractor Loren Glickman received a call asking for him to arrange a recording session in New York. It took place at the St. George Hotel in Brooklyn Heights. "I always thought that was a terrible, terrible thing to put upon the public," Glickman commented, "because they're buying *an* orchestra, and it turns out to be two *completely* different orchestras."[56]

Though Walter had deliberately reduced his performing schedule to almost nothing, orchestras continued to seek his services, and two offers proved too tempting to refuse. One was to conduct in the first Mahler Festival given by the New York Philharmonic during the 1959–60 season, "commemorating," as the programs stated, "the Hundredth Anniversary of Mahler's birth and the Fiftieth Anniversary of his first season as Music Director of the New York Philharmonic." Most of the conducting duties were divided between the two leading Mahlerians of their generations—Leonard Bernstein, now music director of the Philharmonic, and Dimitri Mitropoulos, a former music director of the orchestra—with Walter taking part in a single work. Though eager to participate in a celebration of his friend and mentor's work, Walter harbored doubts about spending the coldest part of the year in New York (the bulk of the festival would take place in January and February); could the Philharmonic, he asked, extend the Mahler Festival until April? There were also questions about the repertoire. Walter suggested Mahler's Fourth, since he didn't feel up to the "longer and more strenuous works."[57] In the end the festival was indeed extended to April, leaving an awkward two-month gap between the penultimate concert and the conclusion to the series, and Walter performed not the Fourth but *Das Lied von der Erde*.

The second offer that Walter accepted also involved his old mentor. The hundredth anniversary of Mahler's birth was to be celebrated in Vienna as well as in New York, not with a full-fledged cycle but with a healthy sampling of Mahler's works spread throughout the Vienna Festival Weeks in May and June 1960. No one was better suited to launch the festival than Walter, and as early as March 1959 Rudolf Gamsjäger, of the Gesellschaft der Musikfreunde in Vienna, asked the conductor if he would be able to participate. Not surprisingly, Walter wanted to perform *Das Lied*, a work he had premiered, also a work that he was scheduled to conduct with the New York Philharmonic in the same season. Unfortunately, Herbert von Karajan had already claimed Mahler's symphonic song cycle, and Gamsjäger could offer only the Fourth or Second symphonies to Walter.[58] Disappointed, Walter delicately suggested that, owing to the "atmosphere of sympathy" between himself and Karajan, it might be possible to ask him to change his program: "Perhaps you can let him know of the particularly deep personal meaning that *Das Lied von der Erde* has for me, as well as the sense of 'farewell,' which is especially apt for one of my years, and convey my wish with my warmest regards." But Gamsjäger could not offer Walter what he wanted. Already a formidable personage in the musical world, Karajan would be gaining even more power in the years to come, and Gamsjäger had no desire to get on his bad side. He urged Walter to conduct the Fourth, so loved in Vienna, and Walter somewhat grudgingly consented.[59] (As late as October, however, Walter was still inquiring whether Karajan was definitely scheduled to conduct *Das Lied*.[60]) Perhaps Karajan felt a twinge of remorse at having wrested from Walter's hands a work that the old master virtually owned, for in August Baron Heinrich Puthon of the Salzburg Festival invited Walter to conduct a program of his choice at the new Festspielhaus for the next Salzburg Festival, which, Puthon made sure to mention, was under the artistic direction of Karajan, who sent his best regards.[61] Walter appreciated the gesture but felt that adding the Salzburg engagement would overtax his system.

While Mahler's presence was still very much in the air, the ghost of one of Mahler's greatest contemporaries, Richard Strauss, also continued to haunt Walter. Strauss, who died in 1949, had not reestablished contact with Walter after World War II, and well before the war years Walter had expressed reservations about Strauss's music and his personality. Yet Strauss, as Walter was fully aware, had helped him on a number of occasions. Although Walter often performed Strauss's music throughout his career, it's unclear how far he truly admired it. Even in his autobiography there are hints that Walter's old aversion to Strauss's music had not quite disappeared. When describing a concert in which Strauss himself conducted *Tod und Verklärung* for the Berlin Philharmonic premiere, Walter, who was present, recalled feeling "perplexingly overwhelmed by it; but in spite of the intoxicating splendor of the orchestration and the dramatic force of the conception I was excited and disturbed rather than deeply moved and uplifted."[62] He didn't add that he later came to regard the work as an incomparable masterpiece, though he had performed it on countless occasions. The impression remains of a piece that had never quite taken hold of his emotions as, say, Mahler's works had done.

So it may have been with mixed feelings that Walter received a letter from Alice Strauss, the composer's daughter-in-law, who had found fourteen letters pertaining to Walter and Strauss in the Richard Strauss Archive. Walter was pleased to receive copies of the letters but regretted that he could not reciprocate by sending copies from his own collection: "All my letters from the most revered master were lost in 1938, and thereafter, of course, the connections between us were broken off."[63] Polite, but to the point: Walter had lost much during the Nazi years, when he had been driven first out of Germany, then out of Austria. No doubt he was still smarting at the thought of the events of March 1933, when Strauss agreed to take over the Berlin Philharmonic concert that the Nazis had prevented Walter from conducting.

Yet Walter was capable of offering some highly favorable words about Strauss as well. Earlier in 1959 Walter had contributed a fine eulogy to his late colleague in a pamphlet published by the Richard-Strauss-Gesellschaft: "All that I can say is that my frequent performances of his symphonic tone-poems in my early years live in my grateful memory, that I count his dramatic works among the most important events of my later activity in the theater, and that, in retrospect, I am conscious of my ever growing admiration for the expressive power and the richness of musical language as well as the mastery of formal construction in those mighty works."[64] It's hard to reconcile this assessment of Strauss with other utterances, both private and public, that Walter made about his music. And while Walter concluded his panegyric by stating that he felt "more strongly than ever the greatness of Strauss's work," that body of work never made an appearance on Walter's final recordings with the Columbia Symphony Orchestra; nor does any of it appear on the list that he submitted in 1961 of pieces that he hoped someday to record in stereo.[65]

In 1960, as in the previous year, only three occasions brought Walter onto the concert platform, but 1960 would see his very last public performance. As arranged in 1959, Walter concluded the New York Philharmonic's first Mahler Festival with four performances of *Das Lied von der Erde* (preceded by Schubert's "Unfinished") in Carnegie Hall, on April 15, 16, 21, and 24, 1960. His soloists were Maureen Forrester and the English tenor Richard Lewis. He was also making his final recording with the New York Philharmonic at this time, entering the studio on two consecutive Mondays, April 18 and 25, to tape his only stereo recording of *Das Lied*. The soloists for this project, however, were not Forrester and Lewis, who had recently recorded the work with the Chicago Symphony Orchestra under Fritz Reiner, but Mildred Miller and Ernst Haefliger.

The newspapers universally praised the concerts at Carnegie Hall, and a live recording of the performance on April 16 shows Walter to have been very much in control. As usual, he gave a passionate reading of the score and had carefully worked out the details of phrasing with the soloists, though Lewis and the orchestra fell momentarily out of synchronization at the beginning of "Der Trunkene im Frühling." Walter had been interested in using Lewis for *Das Lied* as early as 1952, when planning a performance of the work in Paris. Kathleen Ferrier had recommended Lewis then, and Walter felt that he could "fully rely on her judgment."[66] But scheduling conflicts prevented Lewis from joining Walter on that occasion, and when, eight years later, he did sing *Das Lied* with Walter, his voice showed noticeable strain in the high notes of those notoriously difficult songs.

Forrester was, of course, a known quantity to Walter, since they had worked together on Mahler's Second and Brahms's *Alt-Rhapsodie*. Having asked after the first collaboration if she was familiar with *Das Lied*, he may well have been making some mental notes for possible future performances.[67] In October 1959 he wrote to see if she could arrange a visit to his house in Beverly Hills, to "come to a full understanding" with her on *Das Lied* without the "pressure of the New York musical climate."[68] When they met, he accompanied her at the piano, as was his custom, and discussed mainly musical matters rather than approaches to the text ("Now here I take a bit of a pause, and then pick up the tempo"[69]).

While planning the concerts with one alto and tenor, Walter had to make the necessary preparations for a recording with another pair of soloists. The tenor, Ernst Haefliger, was perhaps the most renowned student of Julius Patzak, who had sung with Ferrier on Walter's recording of *Das Lied* with the Vienna Philharmonic in 1952. (Haefliger heard Patzak sing *Das Lied* under Walter at the Salzburg Festival in 1949.) Like Richard Lewis, Haefliger had been proposed for the 1952 *Das Lied*, but scheduling interfered. By 1956 he had already made a recording of *Das Lied* with the Concertgebouw under van Beinum, and Wolfgang Stresemann recommended the tenor to Walter for his 1960 recording.[70]

Preparing for the recording was difficult for the soloists, who never had a chance to rehearse with the orchestra. The week before the recording session, Haefliger met with Walter in New York, and Walter again accompanied at the piano. One entertaining comment of Walter's that Haefliger found especially memorable—the kind of aperçu that can suddenly bring a nebulous aesthetic problem into sharp focus—concerned the mood of "Das Trinklied vom Jammer der Erde," the first song in the sequence. "You have to sing about wine," Walter instructed, "not about beer."[71]

When it came time to record, Walter lightened the orchestration in places, using two horns instead of four (when the other two horns were simply doubling) to achieve a better balance between Haefliger's light voice and the large Mahlerian instrumental forces. Despite the absence of rehearsal, the opening number went so smoothly that it was done in one take. Though a lyric rather than a heroic tenor by nature, Haefliger deliberately darkened the tone of his voice in the first song to create a more "dramatic" sound. The other two tenor songs were recorded on the same day. Oddly enough, the three songs for alto (or mezzo-soprano, in this case) were not to be recorded during this session; in fact, Mildred Miller and Ernst Haefliger didn't even meet each other on this occasion, though their joint effort was soon to be available on one disk.

Mildred Miller at this time was known largely for her work at the Metropolitan Opera in such roles as Cherubino and Carmen. She was familiar to a wide audience through her appearances on television shows like the *Voice of Firestone* and the *Bell Telephone Hour*, but Walter knew nothing of this when he chose her. She had been picked from among nine recordings of different candidates, all apparently submitted anonymously to Walter. Coming from a family of German émigrés, Miller was fluent in German and had originally trained to be a lieder singer, so when she made a recording of the "Abschied" to piano accompaniment for Walter, she felt herself on firm ground. She was told when she got the recording engagement that Walter had said: "This is the one I can work with, because she is an artist." When she went to his home in Beverly Hills to work on the songs before the recording session, she was pleasantly surprised to find his methods gentler than those prevailing at the Met: "I can honestly say that no other conductor I have ever worked with got out of me such excellence—not before, not during, or after again. He did it with total respect for the human voice and for the person that he respected as an artist. And he did it with kindness. I came from the era at the Met when we artists were very browbeaten by most of the conductors."[72]

Like Haefliger, Miller entered the studio never having rehearsed the songs with the orchestra, but unlike Haefliger, she had never even sung them in concert. It must have been an intimidating situation, but, as the final recording shows, she was fully in control. Miraculously, she did the

"Abschied"—the concluding song, which lasts half an hour and demands intense concentration—in one take. Afterward, during the playback in the control booth, Walter reportedly said, "I don't think we can improve on that."[73]

Also in the control booth was John McClure, the producer, who vividly recalled a visit from another conductor during the recording of *Das Lied*. The guest was the charismatic musical director of the New York Philharmonic, Leonard Bernstein, whose fervent commitment to Mahler was already seen to rank with Walter's. Though Bernstein had learned much from Walter and claimed to have been introduced to several of the Mahler symphonies through Walter's interpretations, he had developed his own strong ideas about Mahler, many of which conflicted with Walter's. Slated to record with the Philharmonic after Walter finished his work with the orchestra, Bernstein arrived early for the session, sat next to McClure, and proceeded to criticize Walter's interpretation. "Why does he *do* that?" Bernstein asked McClure, who maintained a politic silence, despite being sorely tempted to reply, "Because it's right."[74]

Walter, pleased with Miller's performance, asked her after the session what else she wanted to record. She suggested the only Mahler song cycle she then knew well, the *Lieder eines fahrenden Gesellen*, a work he'd never recorded. Walter, however, harbored concerns that the songs might be too high for her range, so he suggested to McClure that she also work on some other Mahler songs for orchestra.[75] When she arrived at Walter's house for the piano rehearsals, she was still uncertain what they were planning to record and asked Walter what was on the agenda. "Well," he said, "you wanted to do the *Lieder eines fahrenden Gesellen*." She answered in the affirmative, to which he responded, "Well, that's it."[76] Evidently there was no problem with the songs' voice range after all. It is almost by chance, then, that we have an excellent recording of Walter doing the *Wayfarer Songs*, which Miller and the Columbia Symphony Orchestra made on June 30 and July 1, 1960.

Walter's farewell concerts of 1960 continued in Vienna, where he conducted a single performance of Schubert's "Unfinished," Mahler's Fourth, and three of Mahler's orchestral songs with the Vienna Philharmonic on May 29. For his last appearance in the lavishly gilded Musikvereinssaal, which no doubt unlocked golden memories, he had as his soloist Elisabeth Schwarzkopf, who had sung with him in Mahler's Fourth at his last performance with the Concertgebouw in 1952. Although no one could be certain that this was Walter's final concert in Vienna (there were tentative plans for him to give a performance of Bach's *Matthäus-Passion* in 1961), his presence before the Vienna Philharmonic was a major occasion, and the organization hoped to televise the concert in Austria. Unfortunately for posterity, Walter strenuously objected to the idea on aesthetic grounds. "A concert should be heard and not seen," he wrote to Egon Hilbert of the Vienna Philharmonic. The lighting equipment, cameras, and other paraphernalia would surely disturb members of the audience, Walter argued, turning them into "spectators, at the expense of the music"; moreover, as he pointed out in another letter to Hilbert, he wanted this to be not a "Celebration of Walter" but a "Celebration of Mahler."[77] Another proposed project connected with the event was a commercial recording of the concert, though contractual legalities sank that plan—and perhaps it was for the best. A recording of the entire program has circulated for some years, and the concert was not one of Walter's triumphs.[78] The orchestral playing is tentative almost throughout, and the intonation, especially in Schubert's "Unfinished," is often painfully wayward. Already in February Walter had expressed concern about not overtaxing himself during his stay in Vienna, and his age (or jet lag) was apparently catching up with him.[79]

Several months were to pass before Walter ascended the podium for the last time in public. The occasion was a pension fund concert for the Los Angeles Philharmonic, given in Shrine Auditorium on December 4, 1960. In this all-Brahms program, Van Cliburn was at last to realize his dream of performing Brahms's Second Piano Concerto under Walter. Though the young pianist was in the middle of his own tour, he arranged his recitals in such a way that he could play with his friend and sometime mentor.[80] When he spoke to Walter about the forthcoming event, Cliburn told him how much he looked forward to hearing the maestro conduct the other work on the program, Brahms's First Symphony, after the concerto. Walter, however, replied that the second half had to be reserved for Cliburn.[81] On the one hand, it set Cliburn in the place of honor, a generous gesture from such an esteemed master. On the other, it was a stratagem no doubt calculated to keep audience members in their seats till the very end of the concert. No one who found the First Symphony of Brahms plodding would be likely to leave the auditorium knowing that America's star pianist was in the wings, ready to take part in a historic collaboration. As Walter wrote in 1948, his policy was to put a "problematic work in the middle of the program" (or, in this case, at the beginning), "leaving the conclusion to the soloist, thus *compelling* the audience to stay and listen to the work in question."[82]

The combination of Cliburn and Walter proved a most successful match to Albert Goldberg. "One had the feeling that Cliburn must have studied the concerto carefully with the conductor, for their viewpoints coincided in an exceptionally unified interpretation," Goldberg noted, perhaps a little disingenuously, since he must have known that Cliburn had studied the work with Walter. "It was all first rate Brahms, and it gave Cliburn a new stature among pianists."[83]

Though Brahms and Mahler dominated the handful of concerts that Walter gave in 1960, those composers did not monopolize his attention. Bruckner remained a strong presence in Walter's later years. The conductor made his first commercial recording of Bruckner's Fourth in February with the Columbia Symphony Orchestra, not long after recording Bruckner's Ninth (for the second time, though the first recording, with the New York Philharmonic, was never officially issued); shortly afterward he wrote to Edward Neill of the Italian Bruckner Society that he felt "certain that the time for Bruckner [had] finally arrived."[84] His fondness for Bruckner prompted him to pass along one of his many prizes—the Rennerpreis of 10,000 Austrian schillings, which had been bestowed on him in 1960—to the Internationale Brucknergesellschaft.[85] When word of this typically open-handed gesture began to circulate, the Internationale Mahler-Gesellschaft evidently felt slighted. Erwin Ratz noted that Bruckner's music and reputation had not suffered during the Third Reich and that the Internationale Brucknergesellschaft currently had ample means at its disposal. For Mahler the situation was quite different. At present, much had to be done to reinstate him, and it would require hard work and encouragement. Walter, who had heard that the Brucknergesellschaft was in need of funding, was pained and surprised to hear Ratz's conflicting report and offered the Mahler Society a contribution of 8000 Austrian schillings as a sign of his "heartfelt alliance with the goals of the society."[86]

Another of the great Teutonic composers occupied Walter's thoughts in 1960. From his earliest days as a piano student, Walter had admired the contrapuntal mastery of Johann Sebastian Bach, and even in his old age he would sometimes return to the piano to play through a prelude and fugue from "The Forty-Eight." He conducted many performances of the *Matthäus-Passion* in Munich and New York, and a performance had been planned for Vienna in March 1961; but Walter, fearing the strain that such an obligation would entail, declined the invitation.[87] He was willing to lend his name, however, to the San Francisco Bach Society, allowing the organization to list him as co-chairman (a nominal office), and he wrote a brief statement:

"Bach's work is today what it was through two centuries: a pillar of our culture, and its profound beauty and greatness always prove a source of strength and happiness to the human soul."[88]

Near the end of 1960 a challenge involving another titan in musical history piqued Walter's interest. For a variety of reasons—political, economic, and contractual—Walter had never made a commercial recording of any complete opera. The closest he had come was the exhilarating but historically ill-timed *Walküre*, begun in Vienna not long before the Nazi annexation. When Columbia Records suggested that Walter record *Fidelio*, however, the operatic gap in his discography might have been filled. In October Schuyler Chapin, the new director of Masterworks at Columbia Records— a man later to become, among other things, Commissioner of the Department of Cultural Affairs in New York City—wrote to Walter that, in his meetings abroad and at home, he had heard many requests for a recording of *Fidelio* under Walter. Despite Walter's desire to cut back on his work, this idea excited him: "Believe me that the suggestion of doing a record of Beethoven's 'Fidelio' accelerates my heartbeat," he opened his response to Chapin. But there were problems. What language would be used? To his knowledge, there were no adequate English translations, so the opera would have to be performed in German. As for the dialogue, "all the single numbers of the score follow in their emotional expression the last spoken words before their beginnings. So we cannot entirely cancel the dialogue without jeopardizing a most important musical inspiration of Beethoven." Perhaps German actors could take over for the dialogue. Walter also doubted whether a "wonderful male choir" could be found in either Los Angeles or San Francisco. Nevertheless, having interjected his caveats, Walter concluded by stating that he "could not think of anything greater than doing this work."[89] For the remainder of his life, Walter intermittently corresponded with Columbia Records, especially with John McClure, about casting for the *Fidelio* recording that never was.

Some of the singers considered for Walter's *Fidelio* would appear on the famous recording under Otto Klemperer, perhaps Walter's greatest living rival in 1960. Another Mahler protégé, Klemperer had recently brought out a short book of memories about the great composer and had sent a copy to Walter, who wrote back to say how much he enjoyed reading the memoirs, particularly their meeting in Prague some fifty years before at the premiere of Mahler's Seventh.[90] Much has been made of the supposed antipathy between Klemperer and Walter, but the letters they exchanged in the last years of Walter's life suggest at least the cordiality that comes with the passage of time and with shared experiences, both triumphant and humbling. The previous year Walter had sent birthday greetings to Klemperer, who returned a warm response in which he commented that he was to conduct *Tristan* for the first time in about thirty-six years; but, he added, "we (the musicians of the old school), you know, never forget something like that."[91]

While Walter could be congenial to Klemperer (then in poor health), another conductor famous for championing Mahler inspired less complimentary words. Dead for nearly a decade, Willem Mengelberg, renowned for his breathtakingly controlled but decidedly idiosyncratic readings of the classic scores, continued to provoke controversy and commentary in 1960. One conducting student who had studied with Walter's friend Sir Adrian Boult was curious to know what Walter felt about Mengelberg's performances. Mahler had known Mengelberg personally and admired him; could Mengelberg's highly individual interpretations therefore be regarded as authentic?[92] Though normally diplomatic about the aesthetic slants of his colleagues, Walter responded with unusual frankness on this occasion: "Willem Mengelberg was a great admirer of Gustav Mahler's works, but with all his strong talent as a conductor, one could not say that he strove to satisfy the intentions of the composer. I remember having found in Amsterdam, when I conducted Mahler's First Symphony . . . the printed score full of red corrections from Mengelberg's hand—all pointing to a tendency for exaggeration." Mahler, in contrast, demanded strict fidelity to the score, and Walter claimed that his own performances were in line with what the composer desired, dominated as they were by his wish to "fulfill the intentions of the creative mind from which the work stemmed."[93]

It was fairly clear by now that Walter's career had run most of its course, and there were at least two attempts in 1960 to trace the path of his life. One was a short book by the critic Artur Holde that appeared in a series of biographies published in Berlin by Rembrandt-Verlag. A music critic for the newspaper *Aufbau*, Holde had been active as a choral conductor for Jewish organizations both in Germany before World War II and then in the United States. His modest book, running to about twenty-five pages of actual text, rarely strayed beyond the material in Walter's own memoirs, though it did offer a handsome selection of photographs following the text.[94]

Walter, "the grand old man of the podium," also became the subject of an article in *Harper's* magazine, written by Martin Mayer, who interviewed

Walter and observed him conducting the Columbia Symphony Orchestra. In preserving some of Walter's personal opinions on topics that he rarely addressed, Mayer's essay is an important contribution to our understanding of Walter's personality and tastes during his last years. Changes that the twentieth century had wrought on the sounds of orchestral instruments and the techniques used to play them, for example, did not fully please him:

> "Think what the flute has gained up top of the range," he says, "but it has lost in its beauty. Jean Paul wrote of 'the moonshine of the flute.' Who would now say, 'the moonshine of the flute'?" Approving a recording of the Schumann *Piano Concerto*, Walter sighed a little over a clarinet phrase. "That is just a *gentle* clarinet," he said. "But today they all play trumpet."[95]

As for technical precision for its own sake:

> "This idea of precision in orchestral playing is very recent. It was a necessary reaction to a certain lackadaisical way of attacking tasks, and Toscanini in forwarding it did a wonderful service. But now precision has become an ideal, which is wrong.
>
> "Music must breathe. You must get used to that, and make allowances."[96]

When Mayer submitted the article for approval in April 1960, Walter strenuously objected to the depiction of his personality and his musical aspirations. He took offense at the implication that he did not, to use Walter's words, "seem to feel seriously troubled by bits of sloppy execution." And the portrayal of his relationship with members of the orchestra also rubbed him the wrong way: "Already by calling the 'gentle friendship which shows in my relationship to my musicians' a 'technique for getting on with them', you make me appear a scheming and insincere person—which is entirely alien to my nature."[97] That objection, though understandable, isn't wholly fair; in his own memoirs he had written that, already in his Hamburg days, he'd learned to "influence the artists by psychological methods appropriate to and in conformity with [his] nature."[98] If anything, Mayer's statement is more oblique than Walter's in hinting at insincerity. In any case, having read Walter's grievances, Mayer corrected some of the factual errors in his draft but, in the end, ran the article more or less in the form that Walter had read.

From January to March 1961 Walter was busy making his final recordings with the Columbia Symphony Orchestra. The large-scale works that he preserved on tape included the First and Ninth symphonies of Mahler, Dvořák's Eighth, and Bruckner's Seventh. The recordings of the two great Mahler symphonies were landmark performances: though both were taken at slower tempi than Walter had used in his earlier recordings of the works, he still offered powerful, broad readings of the scores. According to Schuyler Chapin, who was in large part responsible for arranging these final recordings, Walter was "eager to record the First Symphony in the then new stereophonic sound."[99] An awkward problem, however, had presented itself in connection with the project, for Leonard Bernstein was also slated to record Mahler's First with Columbia, as part of his now famous cycle of the Mahler symphonies, almost all performed with the New York Philharmonic. Chapin decided to let both projects proceed, but when John McClure returned from the recording session of the symphony under Walter, he urged Chapin to listen to the performance and "be prepared." Chapin played the acetate disks that McClure had brought, and, as he tells the story, "out poured the most unbelievably beautiful performance—measured, polished, serene yet robust and filled with passion—a reading of the work by a grand old master doing final homage to his idol. After the symphony ended, I found it hard to move from my chair. I finally pulled myself together and knew I had to call Bernstein; contract or no contract, I had to ask him to cancel our plans."[100]

Asking Bernstein to cancel, or at least postpone, his plans to conduct Mahler's First must have been a difficult task. Bernstein, who did not always agree with Walter's interpretations, asked to hear what Chapin was "raving about." After listening to the recording, however, he understood: " 'Oh, my God,' he said, 'that's unbelievable! Forget about it from me. We'll do it at the end of the cycle. I couldn't bear the thought of trying to record the work now. It's *his*!'"[101]

So Bernstein's recording with the New York Philharmonic was bumped to a later date. Walter's orchestra, unlike the New York Philharmonic, was not completely familiar with Mahler's music, and Walter had to teach many of the players the Ninth Symphony—though now a staple of the symphonic repertoire—from scratch. The cellist George Neikrug confessed that the Ninth was *terra incognita* for him: "I was sight reading practically, and I had the solo part."[102] The session prompted another invaluable rehearsal record, capturing Walter's thoughts on one of the masterpieces of the symphonic repertoire, a work he premiered.[103]

John McClure, who narrated the rehearsal session, would occasionally ask Walter in private about perceived Jewish elements in Mahler's music and

Judaism in general. But whenever he brought up the topic, he was "met by total blankness. I mean, he had buried that part of him really deep."[104] It may have been a natural reaction on Walter's part to decades of musical studies that had analyzed the "Jewish elements" in Mahler's music, often to show how Mahler had "polluted" the great German musical tradition.

Along with these large symphonic works, Walter also recorded two Haydn symphonies, the overture and "Venusberg Music" from *Tannhäuser*, and several Mozart overtures (his final recordings, made on March 29 and 31). Thomas Frost, the producer for these works, recalled some of the problems encountered during these sessions. One had to do with the "Venusberg Music," which has a brief section for chorus. When the choral section arrived, Walter was astounded to find his conducting suddenly rendered ineffectual. "Walter couldn't figure out what it was," Frost remembered. "He was beating his normal time, and the choir couldn't follow him, and the orchestra and choir were playing different music." Puzzled, he asked to see the singers' sheet music and discovered, to his horror, that the chorus, from Occidental College, was using a piano–vocal score that attempted to simplify the piece rhythmically by barring the music in 3/4 rather than the 4/4 of Wagner's score. Scheduling made it imperative to finish the recording session that day, a task that seemed well-nigh impossible. But Phil Kahgan, the orchestra's contractor, made a few calls to copyists in the area who were used to the unreasonable demands and deadlines of Hollywood films, and literally within minutes the copyists were at the American Legion Hall, writing out the vocal parts in the correct meter. The day was saved.[105]

In the year of his last recordings Walter also found time to listen to the work of his colleagues, old and young. The career of George Szell, once the wunderkind pianist who had astonished Vienna concertgoers near the turn of the century, had taken a path similar to Walter's. From 1946 till his death in 1970 he held the post of musical adviser to the Cleveland Orchestra, with whom he made a large number of notable recordings, one of which was a collection of Schumann's symphonies. Szell's reading of the Fourth in particular—though far more restrained than Walter's own recorded interpretations—impressed the older conductor, who called the record "a wonderful achievement for Szell and Columbia."[106]

Another new recording deeply affected Walter: Strauss's *Elektra* under Karl Böhm, Walter's old assistant at the Munich Opera. "Let me tell you," Walter wrote Böhm, "that your masterly achievement gave me great pleasure. This record is an absolutely extraordinary high point of technical reproduction of a great masterpiece, and I congratulate you on it."[107] Böhm had recently suffered a detached retina in one eye and wrote to Walter that the other eye was also troubling him, yet he was planning to conduct *Wozzeck*. Walter, whose opinion of the Second Viennese School had hardly mellowed with age, quipped: "Well now, you're recuperating in the gentle, sunny atmosphere of *Wozzeck*, and perhaps, dear friend, for a musician addicted to work like you, that's a better way to recover than taking walks along the quiet ocean—which, however, does good to my considerably more advanced years."[108]

As late as June and July of 1961 Walter was planning to record major works in the studio—Bruckner's Eighth, Mahler's Fourth and Fifth symphonies—and the *Fidelio* project was very much alive in his correspondence with McClure till the end of 1961. Bing had even invited Walter to perform *Fidelio* at the Met and to conduct the Verdi Requiem in 1962 at the opening of Philharmonic Hall in Lincoln Center, New York's largest performing arts complex, then under construction.[109] Walter had looked so healthy when Bing had last seen him; surely he would be fit to conduct in two years' time?

But Walter knew he was losing the battle. In December he wrote to John McClure in confidence that he was subject more and more to "attacks":

> I do not feel well, and remembering my heart attack of 1957 in New York, I have to take the symptoms of my illness seriously. They are attacks of angina pectoris, a condition of strong distress which does not permit the slightest physical exertion and responds only to a use of nitroglycerin. These attacks arrive without warning and seem to be of psycho-somatic origin. But whatever be their cause, they prevent me—physically and emotionally—from conducting. I consulted an excellent heart specialist, who only could advise what I myself had already understood: That I have to postpone my recording. . . .
>
> But, you cannot imagine, dear friend, what it means to me to make such difficulties for you and for Columbia—you will have to try the cancellation or postponement of your engagements for Fidelio—so you will know how terrible I feel.[110]

Walter's apologetic confession that the attacks seemed to be psychosomatic and the sincere regret that he had burdened his colleagues—all from one with two months left to live—are typical of the man who had so often shown his sensitivity to the feelings of others.

That sensitivity made its presence felt a few days later, when Walter received a letter from a woman who had heard him conduct in Berlin in 1926. She was currently preparing a school play of *As You Like It* and wondered whether Walter could suggest some appropriate music by Mozart for incidental music. Instead of pushing the letter aside and taking a walk along the palm-lined streets of Beverly Hills, he took time to respond that he couldn't think of any better music for Shakespeare's comedy than Mozart's *Les Petits Riens*. Perhaps, as he wrote, he relived the day—nearly half a century before—when he gave the Munich premiere of Mozart's ballet music. In a postscript he told her that she could order the parts through the publisher Breitkopf und Härtel.[111]

Ill health or no, Walter continued to receive visitors at home. His date book for 1962 records numerous appointments with doctors (a Dr. Kurt and a Dr. Vincent) as well as scheduled meetings, or possible meetings, with other conductors—Schmidt-Isserstedt on January 19, "Meta" (probably Zubin Mehta, then conducting the Los Angeles Philharmonic) on January 22, and Bernstein (possibly Dr. M. A. Bernstein, who filled out his death certificate) on January 29.[112]

Walter's thoughts in his final months were much like those that had dominated his life. Others' interpretations of Mahler's music still attracted his interest, even if they did not always win his approval. A recent recording of Mahler's Ninth by Leopold Ludwig and the London Symphony Orchestra came out around March 1960, in remarkably vivid stereo sound. Records of the work were still few and far between, and this one, from a conductor who, during the Nazi years, had filled some of the same posts that Walter had previously held, must have particularly piqued his curiosity. Ludwig skillfully brought out some of the inner lines and was clearly committed to the piece, but at times he seemed eager to move the music along at places where Walter would linger over phrases. Certainly for Walter the recording proved a disappointment; it was "a thoroughly unsatisfactory recording": "a musty smell of routine pervades this performance," he wrote in disgust to Wolfgang Stresemann.[113]

Mahler's earliest symphony also prompted some personal observations from Walter, who received a letter from the Hungarian critic Mihály Meixner in late January concerning the "Blumine" movement that had originally appeared in the "Titan." Walter explained why he felt the charming piece had been dropped from the score: "I know the movement well and fully understand why Mahler didn't want to retain it. It is a gentle, purely lyrical piece, so different from the revolutionary boldness of the other movements that one might have the impression of a violation of artistic decorum."[114]

People with connections to his distant past continued to reach out to Walter. Erich Korngold's widow, Luzi, died at the end of January 1962, and Walter immediately sent a letter of condolence to her son, George Korngold. "You can imagine how nearly her departure touches me," he wrote, "and how painful it is for me to have to bid farewell to this soul—good, pure, and imbued with love. The marriage of your parents, blessed as it was by love and music, will remain as unforgettable to me as her amiable personality itself." In concluding his letter, perhaps with a thought to his own future, he offered what solace he could: "From my heart I want you to be utterly convinced that there will be a reunion with her in eternity."[115]

And of course Pfitzner was still very much alive in Walter's thoughts. Walter's last letter, addressed to Mali Pfitzner on February 16, ended on the topic of *Palestrina*, a work Walter still held dear: "From Berlin I've received the news that the excellent Swiss tenor Ernst Haefliger will be singing Palestrina in the coming new production of *Palestrina* and that he plans to come here in March to get my advice on it, which I will naturally give him with joy. Despite all the grim events of our times, I'm confident that *Palestrina* will 'endure.' The work has all the elements of imperishability."[116] Walter's own work as a conductor also had all the elements of imperishability, but he himself was only so much flesh. That evening he suffered what proved a fatal heart attack. At 5:45 on the morning of February 17, Walter was officially pronounced dead.[117]

Someone, perhaps Lotte, mysteriously jotted in his diary for February 16: "Walter +." His death certificate states that a fatal heart attack had begun its course about ten hours before the time of death, and the likelihood is that shortly before 8:00 on Thursday night Walter showed signs of serious trouble. At first he might have had some sense of what was happening, but for most of the next ten hours he would surely have been unconscious. Perhaps the person who marked February 16 as his date of death was haunted by the image of an immobile Walter, stilled on that terrible night.

On the day of Walter's death, Nadia Boulanger was in New York to conduct the Philharmonic in a performance of the Fauré Requiem. Before her performance Leonard Bernstein announced the somber news to the audience: "My dear friends, I bring you the heartbreaking news that Bruno Walter died this morning. It is almost too much to bear. Last year our beloved Mitropoulos—and now this great genius, who for forty years has been so close to us here at the Philharmonic—who has guided us so wisely, and so generously brightened and enriched our lives. Like Mitropoulos, he was one of the saints of music—a man all kindness and warmth, goodness and devotion. We can only mourn, and pay tribute."[118]

Lengthy obituaries ran in the major newspapers, and the funeral took place on Tuesday, February 20, at 4:00 p.m. in Pierce Bros. mortuary in Beverly Hills. By then, however, most of the world's attention was focused elsewhere, for John Glenn made history on that day by orbiting the earth several times in space—the first American to do so. Walter's funeral merited only a small notice in the *Los Angeles Times*. He received an anthroposophical service, conducted by Verner Hegg, a priest of the Christian Community. Over two hundred mourners—among them musicians and "representatives of the German and Austrian governments"—attended the funeral. Van Cliburn was there, accompanied by his mother. A string quartet drawn from players in the Los Angeles Philharmonic performed music by Beethoven and Haydn, two masters of the Austro-German musical tradition that Walter revered. Telegrams of condolence arrived from the German Chancellor Konrad Adenauer and from Willy Brandt, mayor of West Berlin.[119]

Walter's corpse was cremated, and his ashes were removed to the cemetery of Sant' Abbondio in Montagnola, near Lugano, Switzerland, where his remains joined those of his wife and his daughter Gretel. His daughter Lotte lived on till January 1970, dying in St. Moritz, Switzerland, shortly after the publication of an edition of her father's letters that she had worked on for several years. Within a few months of Walter's death, Delia Reinhardt had returned to Europe, moving in with her old friend Irma Geering in Dornach, near Basel, Switzerland. On August 26 Delia picked up her pen to write Alma Mahler Werfel birthday greetings and realized that this was the first time she had done so alone, without Walter. Yet, since she continued to feel very strongly "Bruno's nearness, his presence, his being-entirely-with-me," she thought it likely that Alma herself would also feel his presence when she read Delia's letter.[120]

Certainly Walter's presence continues to be felt today, even by those who have never had the pleasure of knowing him personally or hearing him conduct during his lifetime. His performances circulate continually, whether on commercial reissues of his studio recordings or on pirated releases of his broadcasts. His books still attract new readers, and his own life story has all the elements of an enduring tale. As he had wished, something of him has remained now that he is gone.

# Recommended Discographies

Several discographies devoted to Bruno Walter have appeared over the years, at least one of book length (Koho Uno's Japanese study, published in 1995 though omitted from this selection because of the language barrier). The four discographies recommended below, presented in reverse chronological order, are well researched and highly useful; those by Selvini and Chinellato, Louis, and Masini are particularly valuable in that they list both commercial and noncommercial recordings. For more recent information, the authors advise interested persons to consult the online Walter discography at www.bwdiscography.com.

Michele Selvini and Shizuko Matsui Chinellato with assistance from Michael H. Gray, in *Bruno Walter: La porta dell'eternità, 1940–1962* (Milan: Fondazione culturale della collina d'oro, 2001): 374–95.

Rémy Louis, "Bruno Walter au disque," supplement to *Diapason* no. 415 (May 1995): xiv–xviii.

"Discografia di Bruno Walter," prefaced by Umberto Masini, *Musica* 8 (June 1984): 32–39.

David A. Pickett (revised by Richard Warren Jr.), *A Bruno Walter Discography: Part One: Commercial Recordings: Issued Discs Only* (Bruno Walter Society, [1973]). (Note: Part Two was never issued.)

Robert C. Marsh, "The Heritage of Bruno Walter: A Discography," *High Fidelity* 14 (Jan. 1964): 44–48, 103–9.

# Filmography by Charles Barber

The film record of Bruno Walter in rehearsal, concert, and conversation is substantial and influential. No other documentary source reveals so clearly and compellingly his manner and charm, his baton and its eloquence, his collegiality and its demands.

The earliest known film of Walter is silent and dates from a 1929 appearance with the Los Angeles Philharmonic at the Hollywood Bowl. This event was filmed by Philip Kahgan (1892–1986), longtime principal viola with that orchestra. Walter's last film was made in 1960 at a recording session with the Columbia Symphony Orchestra and broadcast in the CBS television series *Playback*.

The single most substantial Walter document was filmed in Vancouver in 1958 by the Canadian Broadcasting Corporation, and consists of a rehearsal of the Brahms Symphony no. 2 combined with an interview filmed contemporaneously in Beverly Hills. Made near the end of a long and productive life, it conveys an extraordinary picture of serenity unyielding in its musical purposes. Several hours' work were actually filmed at these Brahms rehearsals; the outtakes were destroyed some time thereafter.

In three decades' evidence of Walter on film, one surprising fact prevails: his was a technique and an approach that changed very little over time. From first to last, the same body, eye, and gestural vocabulary is manifest. Walter's podium work seems to have matured early and thereafter to have been a sure and constant process. Walter's was a musical aesthetic felt long and deeply. The central case for that aesthetic is made in his letters, diaries, books, and conversations; it is confirmed in the visual proof of his actual work as a conductor. No better claim for his enduring musical constancy can be found than in these images.

The film and video materials described below are owned by their copyright holders, and no suggestion is made that any of them is commercially available save as noted. Most of these documents, however, are held in the Conductors on Film Collection, Archive of Recorded Sound, at Stanford University in California. Application for scholarly study of them is welcome; if permission is granted, the materials will be made available on site without charge. Because of the formidable complications of international copyright law, duplication is not possible.

Dr. Charles Barber, Founder and Curator

Conductors on Film Collection

June 2000, Stanford

### Bruno Walter Rehearsal and Performance Films

1929

Los Angeles Philharmonic, Hollywood Bowl (3:00)

Repertoire unknown, rehearsal, silent

SOURCE: Film and Television Archive, UCLA.

NOTE: The date of Walter's appearance at the Hollywood Bowl was provided by filmmaker Philip Kahgan on an insert card interpolated into the film itself.

1931

Weber, Overture to *Oberon* (8:20)

Berlin Philharmonic, Singakademie

SOURCE: Private, apparently from a series of German music films produced in this era.

1933

Gluck, *Orfeo ed Euridice* (00:17)

Salzburg Festival Orchestra, Salzburg

SOURCE: Private, appearing in the 1995 documentary "Sagt, holde Frauen . . ." produced by ORF-2 and 3-Sat.

NOTE: This fragment, in various pirate editions, has frequently (and erroneously) been described as having originated in 1944. Walter is seen working in the pit.

1947

Wagner, Prelude to *Die Meistersinger* (8:30)

New York Philharmonic, Carnegie Hall

SOURCE: *Carnegie Hall*, a Federal Films/United Artists release produced by Boris Morros and William LeBaron. It has appeared in several different versions.

NOTE: The sound track was prerecorded. The visual track was filmed later, and synchronized to audio playback. Nearly all of this film was made at Carnegie Hall in the summer of 1946.

1948
Beethoven, Symphony no. 9, fourth movement, rehearsal (1:05)
Vienna Philharmonic
SOURCE: Newsreel "Bruno Walter dirigiert," produced by Welt im Film.

1950
Mozart, Symphony no. 40, fourth movement (5:02)
Berlin Philharmonic, at Philharmonie and elsewhere
SOURCE: Private, appearing in the documentary *Botschafter der Musik.*
NOTE: Sources providing these materials have also provided three separate dates for them: Mar. 17, 1930; Sept. 25, 1950; and 1954. The longest version takes music from the end of the Menuetto into the Allegro. The film in its present form is a composite. The 1930s elements include pan shots of the old Philharmonie, destroyed by Allied bombing during the war. Long shots from the rear show the conductor working without a railing. The 1950 element shows an older Walter, with a protective railing behind him, and players working on more modern-appearing instruments. 1954 may be the year in which the composite was produced.

1955
Mahler, Symphony no. 4, conclusion of first movement (00:41)
Concertgebouw Orchestra, Amsterdam
SOURCE: Private.

1958
Brahms, Symphony no. 2, rehearsal (36:08)
Vancouver Festival Orchestra, July 1958
SOURCE: Canadian Broadcasting Corporation.
NOTE: This film is commercially available through Video Artists International (see below). It is also excerpted on the 1994 Teldec video and laser disc release, *The Art of Conducting.*

1960
Beethoven, "Leonore" Overture no. 2, conclusion (2:48)
Columbia Symphony Orchestra, studio recording session, July 1, 1960
SOURCE: Sony Music Archives.

NOTE: This footage was included in the promotional series *Playback*, introduced by Goddard Lieberson. Among the 56 minutes of outtakes in the Sony Music Archives are further rehearsal and performance sequences that present Walter head-on and primarily from below the podium; the orchestra is never seen. Also included in the footage is a playback session in which Walter and John McClure listen to and discuss the recording and the piece; Delia Reinhardt is glimpsed briefly. A silent version of the outtakes has circulated privately.

### Bruno Walter Documentaries

**1962**
"The Creative Person: Bruno Walter" (30:00)
Beethoven, "Leonore" Overture no. 2, conclusion (2:45)
Columbia Symphony Orchestra, 1960
SOURCE: Peabody Awards and Media Archives, University of Georgia.
NOTE: This is a 1962 Arnold Michaelis documentary, produced for National Educational Television. The conducting footage comes from the *Playback* episode listed above.

**1972**
"Bruno Walter: The Face of Music" (60:00)
BBC *Omnibus* television series, broadcast Feb. 13, 1972; Robert Vas, producer
SOURCE: British Broadcasting Corporation.
NOTE: This documentary includes brief excerpts from Beethoven's "Leonore" Overture no. 3, Brahms's Symphony no. 2, Mozart's Symphony no. 40, and Wagner's Prelude to *Die Meistersinger*, as well as interviews with Leonard Bernstein, Karl Böhm, Lotte Lehmann, John McClure, Georg Solti, and members of orchestras led by Walter.

**1988**
"Sound of a Century: The Concertgebouw at 100" (2:26:00)
SOURCE: Private.
NOTE: This is "Het Orkest: Geluid van een Eeuw," a Dutch documentary about the hall, orchestra, and its conductors, produced by Sieuwert Verster and others. Walter appears conducting Mahler's Symphony no. 4 and is discussed by members of the Concertgebouw Orchestra who knew him.

1996

*Bruno Walter: The Maestro, The Man* (60:00)

Brahms, Symphony no. 2, Allegro non troppo, rehearsal (22:08)

Brahms, Symphony no. 2, Allegro con spirito, rehearsal (14:00)

Vancouver Festival Orchestra, July 1958

Interview with Albert Goldberg (22:10)

SOURCE: Canadian Broadcasting Corporation, and Video Artists International release 69407.

NOTE: Interviewer Albert Goldberg (1898–1990) taught at the Chicago Musical College (1924–26), became music critic of the *Chicago Herald Examiner* (1925–36), then of the *Chicago Tribune* (1943–46). He later became music critic of the *Los Angeles Times* (1947–65), succeeding the legendary Isabel Morse Jones. This is the only known extended interview of Bruno Walter on film.

2002

"Bruno Walter" (53:00)

Television documentary by János Darvas, produced by Metropolitan in Munich

SOURCE: Metropolitan.

NOTE: This documentary exists in English and German versions, both narrated by Michele Selvini. It includes previously unreleased footage of Walter rehearsing the last movement of Mahler's Fourth Symphony with the Vienna Philharmonic and Elisabeth Schwarzkopf, shortly before the performance on May 29, 1960; a news clip of Walter disembarking from a plane with a voiceover describing his return to Vienna in May 1948; a news clip on the reopening of the Vienna Opera in November 1955 with shots of Walter, Lotte Lehmann, and others arriving for the event; and a brief German-language interview with Walter before his last perfomance in Vienna on May 29, 1960. Other clips include excerpts from the 1931 film of Weber's *Oberon* Overture with the Berlin Philharmonic, the 1955 footage of the conclusion of the first movement of Mahler's Fourth Symphony with the Concertgebouw, and Albert Goldberg's 1958 interview with Walter, as well as numerous snippets from Walter's home movies.

## Other Visual Materials

1. In 1966, in commemoration of the ninetieth anniversary of Walter's birth, the music division of Süddeutsche Rundfunk-Fernsehen in Stuttgart made a significant documentary on Walter's life and career.

2. In the mid-1950s, Bruno Walter appeared in several televised broadcasts with the Chicago Symphony Orchestra. These appearances, which included music of Mozart, Haydn, and Wagner, were produced by Chicago-based WGN-TV and broadcast on the DuMont Network. Although kinescopes (film made directly from the television image) were surely taken from these performances, and numerous efforts have been made to trace them, none appears to have survived. These broadcasts include the following musical materials:

Feb. 3, 1954
Beethoven, Triple Concerto, with soloists John Weicher, János Starker, and George Schick
Mendelssohn, Overture to *A Midsummer Night's Dream*

Jan. 5, 1955
Brahms, Double Concerto, with soloists John Weicher and János Starker
Mozart, Symphony no. 35 ("Haffner")

Jan. 12, 1955
Haydn, Symphony no. 96 ("Miracle")
Wagner, *Siegfried Idyll*
Weber, Overture to *Euryanthe*

Jan. 25, 1956
Mozart: Sinfonia concertante, with soloists John Weicher and Milton Preves
Mozart: Symphony no. 29

3. Two reels of home movies made with Bruno Walter in the 1930s, now in the New York Public Library for the Performing Arts.

# *Appendix*

## *Recent Recordings of Music Composed by Bruno Walter*

Sonata for Piano and Violin

Marco Rizzi, violin, and Alessandro Maffei, piano (Simposion 1SCL0401, recorded in 1998, issued in 2000).

Philippe Graffin, violin, and Pascal Devoyon, piano (Hyperion CDA67220, recorded in 1999, issued in 2001).

Hagai Shaham, violin, and Arnon Erez, piano (Classic Talent DOM 2910 93, recorded in 2000, issued in 2004).

In addition, a live performance dating from June 24, 2002—with Renaud Capuçon, violin, and Alexandre Gurning, piano—has been made available online as part of the Martha Argerich Project.

SONGS

*Emma Bell*, with Emma Bell, soprano, and Andrew West, piano, in a program of songs by Walter, Richard Strauss, and Joseph Marx (Linn CKD 238, recorded and issued in 2004).

Includes Walter's three "Tragödie" songs from op. 12; "Des Kindes Schlaf," "Die Lerche," and "Elfe" from Walter's Eichendorff songs; and "Waltraut's Lied I," "Waltraut's Lied II," and "Liebeslust" from op. 11 (the last three previously unrecorded).

*Gustav Mahler/Bruno Walter*, with Christian Hilz, baritone, and Katia Bouscarrut, piano, in a program of songs by Walter and Gustav Mahler (Lindberg Lyd AS 2L 18, recorded in 2003, issued in 2004).

Includes "Musikantengruss," "Der junge Ehemann," and "Der Soldat" from Walter's Eichendorff songs; "Weisst du, wie lieb ich dich hab'?" from op. 11; and "Die Linde," "Sehnsucht," and the three "Tragödie" songs from op. 12 (the last six previously unrecorded).

WALTER'S FOUR-HAND ARRANGEMENT OF MAHLER'S FIRST SYMPHONY

Zdeňka Hršel and Martin Hršel, piano (Praga Digitals PRD/DSD 250 197, recorded and issued in 2003).

# Recent Important Issues of Walter's Performances

Mozart: *Le nozze di Figaro* (Andante 3981, issued in 2002)

A three-disc set of Walter's famous Salzburg *Figaro* (1937), with superior sound to that on earlier releases.

*Vienna Philharmonic (1948–1955): Mahler, Walter* (Andante 4973, issued in 2002)

A four-disc set of live recordings by Walter and the Vienna Philharmonic performing works by Mahler: Symphony no. 2 (1948); Symphony no. 4 (with Hilde Güden, 1955); "Wo die schönen Trompeten blasen," "Ich atmet' einen linden Duft," "Wer hat dies Liedlein erdacht?" (with Hilde Güden, 1955; previously unissued); *Das Lied von der Erde* (with Julius Patzak and Kathleen Ferrier, 1952—apparently a conflation of the famous 1952 recording with Patzak and Ferrier and a live performance from the same period).

*Bruno Walter and the* NBC *Symphony* (Arbiter 133, issued in 2002)

Live performances of Walter's interpretations of Berlioz's *Symphonie fantastique* (1939; previously unissued in the West) and Ravel's *Rapsodie espagnole* (1940).

*Bruno Walter in Concert* (Arbiter 138, issued in 2003)

Live performances of Walter conducting Beethoven's First Symphony (NBC Symphony, 1939) and Mozart's Symphony no. 39 (New York Philharmonic, probably 1945; previously unissued), Beethoven's "Leonore" Overture no. 3 (New York Philharmonic, probably 1945; previously unissued), and Mozart's Violin Concerto no. 4 (New York Philharmonic, Bronilaw Huberman, 1945). The year of the New York Philharmonic selections is incorrectly given as 1946.

*Symphony Hall Centennial Celebration: From the Broadcast Archives 1943–2000* (issued in 2001)

A twelve-disc set celebrating the orchestra's history that includes a live recording of Haydn's Symphony no. 92 under Walter (1947; previously unissued in the West).

*Great Conductors of the Twentieth Century: Bruno Walter* (7243 5 75133 2 6, issued in 2002)

A two-disc set: Vienna Philharmonic recordings of Beethoven's "Pastoral" Symphony (1936); excerpt from Act II of Wagner's *Die Walküre* (with Lotte Lehmann, Ella

Flesch, Lauritz Melchoir, Alfred Jerger, and Emanuel List, 1935); the Adagietto from Mahler's Fifth Symphony (1938) and "Nun will die Sonn' so hell aufgeh'n" (with Kathleen Ferrier, 1949). New York Philharmonic recording of Brahms's Second Symphony (1953). British Symphony Orchestra recordings of the Overture to Mozart's *Le nozze di Figaro* (1932) and the Prelude to Wagner's *Die Meistersinger von Nürnberg* (1930). The Paris Conservatory Orchestra's recordings of Haydn's Symphony no. 92 (1938) and Johann Strauss's Overture to *Die Fledermaus* (1938).

### MUSIC AND ARTS

Beethoven: *Missa solemnis* (CD-1142, issued in 2004)

The New York Philharmonic with soloists Eleanor Steber, Nan Merriman, William Hain, and Lorenzo Alvary; the Westminster Choir directed by John Finley Williamson (1948). The first issue of this superb performance in decent sound.

Bruckner: Symphony no. 8 (CD-1106, issued in 2003)

A new transfer of the 1941 performance by the New York Philharmonic, with sound superior to that on previous releases.

Bruckner: Symphony no. 9 (CD-1110, issued in 2003)

A New York Philharmonic live performance of Bruckner's Symphony no. 9 (1946), coupled with Beethoven's "Leonore" Overture no. 2 from the same concert (previously unissued).

### NM CLASSICS

*Anthology of the Royal Concertgebouw Orchestra, Volume 1: 1935–1950* (NM Classics 97017, issued in 2003)

A thirteen-disc set that includes live performances of Walter conducting the overture to Wagner's *Der fliegende Holländer* (1936), Busoni's Violin Concerto in D major (with Adolf Busch, 1936), Ravel's Piano Concerto for the Left Hand (with Paul Wittgenstein, 1937), and Mahler's Symphony no. 1 (1947; previously unissued).

*Anthology of the Royal Concertgebouw Orchestra, Volume II: 1950–1960* (NM Classics 97018, issued in 2004)

A fourteen-disc set that includes live performances of Walter conducting Mozart's Symphony no. 40, Mahler's Symphony no. 4 (with Elisabeth Schwarzkopf), and Strauss's *Don Juan* (all from 1952).

### SONY CLASSICAL

Beethoven: Symphony no. 6, "Pastoral" (5087152, issued in France in 2002)

The 1946 recording with The Philadelphia Orchestra, coupled with the Columbia Symphony Orchestra recording of the "Leonore" Overture no. 2 (1960).

Brahms: Symphonies Nos. 1 and 2 (5081722, issued in France in 2002)

New York Philharmonic recordings from 1953.

Brahms: Symphonies Nos. 3 and 4 (5081732, issued in France in 2002)

New York Philharmonic recordings from 1951 (no. 4) and 1953 (no. 3).

Brahms: Symphonies 1–4 (517187 2, issued in the UK in 2004)

A two-disc set of the four symphonies performed by the New York Philharmonic in 1951 (no. 4) and 1953 (Nos. 1, 2, and 3).

*The Original Jacket Collection—Bruno Walter: Famous Mahler and Bruckner Symphonies* (SX13K 92460, issued in 2004)

A thirteen-disc set of Walter's Columbia recordings of works by Mahler, Bruckner, and Wagner, with reproductions of the original album covers.

Mahler: Symphony no. 1, "Titan" (Columbia Symphony Orchestra, 1961); Symphony no. 2, "Resurrection" (New York Philharmonic Orchestra, Maureen Forrester, Emilia Cundari, 1957 and 1958); Symphony no. 4 (New York Philharmonic, Desi Halban, 1945); Symphony no. 5 in C-sharp minor (New York Philharmonic, 1947); selections from *Lieder und Gesänge aus der Jugenzeit* (Desi Halban, soprano, and Bruno Walter, piano, 1947); *Lieder eines fahrenden Gesellen* (Columbia Symphony Orchestra, Mildred Miller, 1960); Symphony no. 9 (Columbia Symphony Orchestra, 1961); *Das Lied von der Erde* (New York Philharmonic, Mildred Miller, Ernst Haefliger, 1960).

Bruckner: Symphony no. 4, "Romantic" (Columbia Symphony Orchestra, 1960); Symphony no. 7 (Columbia Symphony Orchestra, 1961); Symphony no. 9 (Columbia Symphony Orchestra, 1959); *Te Deum* (New York Philharmonic with soloists Frances Yeend, Martha Lipton, David Lloyd, and Mack Harrel; the Westminster Choir directed by John Finley Williamson, 1953).

Wagner: Overture to *Tannhäuser* and "Venusberg Music" (Columbia Symphony Orchestra, Occidental College Concert Choir, 1961); Prelude to Act I of *Die Meistersinger von Nürnberg*, Overture to *Der fliegende Holländer*, Prelude to Act I of *Parsifal*, "Good Friday Music" from *Parsifal*, Prelude to Act I of *Lohengrin*, and *Siegfried Idyll* (Columbia Symphony Orchestra, 1959).

Also included: Bruno Walter rehearsing *Siegfried Idyll* (1959); *A Talking Portrait: Bruno Walter in Conversation with Arnold Michaelis* (1956); *A Working Portrait: Recording the Mahler Ninth Symphony* narrated by John McClure (1961).

Schubert: Symphony no. 8, "Unfinished"; Dvořák: Symphony no. 8 (5081742, issued in France in 2002)

The Philadelphia Orchestra recording of Schubert's "Unfinished" Symphony (1946) and the New York Philharmonic recording of Dvořák's Symphony no. 8 (1947).

*Bruno Walter in Amsterdam* (TAH 504, issued in 2003)

Live performances of Brahms's *Schicksalslied* (with the Amsterdam Toonkunstkoor, 1947; previously unissued) and Mahler's Symphony no. 1 (1947).

*Bruno Walter in Stockholm* (TAH 508–509, issued in 2003)

A two-disc set of live performances of Mozart's Symphony no. 40 (Vienna Philharmonic, 1952; previously unissued) and Mozart's *Eine kleine Nachtmusik* and Symphony no. 39 with Schubert's Symphony no. 9 (Stockholm Philharmonic, 1950)

*In Memoriam Kathleen Ferrier* (TAH 482, issued in 2003)

A live performance of Mahler's *Das Lied von der Erde* with Ferrier, Julius Patzak, and the Vienna Philharmonic led by Walter on May 17, 1952, just after the famous studio recording (previously unissued).

# Notes

Unattributed translations in the text, with the exception of those drawn from the sources below, are by the present authors. The rhyming couplet that serves as the epigraph to Chapter 16 is from the translation of *Die Zauberflöte* by Ruth and Thomas Martin. Italics in quoted passages reflect identical or similar treatment (such as underlining or spread characters) in the original source. In cases in which two spellings of a name are equally valid (e.g., Else/Elsa, Katja/Katia, Křenek/ Krenek), we have chosen the spelling last used by the person in question. A handful of obvious typographic and orthographic errors in correspondence have been changed, though unorthodox spellings that suggest a special pronunciation (e.g., *glaziers* for *glaciers*) have been retained.

## Abbreviations

| | |
|---|---|
| AMWC | Alma Mahler Werfel Collection, Special Collections, Van Pelt-Dietrich Library, University of Pennsylvania |
| *AZ* | *Allgemeine Zeitung* |
| BBC Walter Omnibus | An hour-long documentary on Walter produced by the BBC for its *Omnibus* series in 1972 |
| *BT* | *Berliner Tageblatt* |
| *BW Briefe* | Bruno Walter, *Briefe 1894–1962*, ed. Lotte Walter Lindt (Frankfurt: S. Fischer, 1969) |
| *BWL* | *The Bruno Walter Legacy: A Series of Commemorative Radio Programs on the 100th Anniversary of the Conductor's Birth*, a fifteen-disk set of LPs (Public Broadcasting Association, EMA-105) |
| BWP | The Bruno Walter Papers, housed in the New York Public Library for the Performing Arts, Lincoln Center, New York City. The roman numeral indicates the series in which the item appears, the arabic numeral the particular folder where the item can be found. |
| DGMP | Daniel Gregory Mason Papers, Rare Book and Manuscript Library, Columbia University |
| *GM* | Bruno Walter, *Gustav Mahler* (Vienna: Herbert Reichner, 1936); translated into English by James A. Galston (London: Kegan Paul, Trench, Trubner & Co., 1937; New York: Greystone Press, 1941); a later translation was super- |

|  | vised by Lotte Walter Lindt (1958; reprint, London: Quartet Books, 1990). Unless otherwise noted, the translation used is that supervised by Lotte Walter Lindt (1990 reprint). |
| --- | --- |
| GML | Gustav Mahler, *Selected Letters of Gustav Mahler*, trans. Eithne Wilkins, Ernst Kaiser, and Bill Hopkins, ed. Knud Martner (New York: Farrar, Straus, Giroux, 1979) |
| La Grange 1 | Henry-Louis de La Grange, *Mahler* (Garden City, N.Y.: Doubleday, 1973) |
| La Grange 2 | Henry-Louis de La Grange, *Gustav Mahler, Vienna: The Years of Challenge (1897–1904)* (Oxford: Oxford University Press, 1995) |
| La Grange 3 | Henry-Louis de La Grange, *Gustav Mahler: L'Âge d'or de Vienne (1900–1907)* (Paris: Fayard, 1983) |
| *LAT* | *Los Angeles Times* |
| LLP | Lotte Lehmann Papers, PA MSS 3, Department of Special Collections, University Libraries, University of California, Santa Barbara |
| *LNN* | *Leipziger Neueste Nachrichten* |
| *MA* | *Musical America* |
| *MC* | *Musical Courier* |
| Met Archives | Metropolitan Opera Archives, New York |
| MFCC | The Pierpont Morgan Library, Mary Flagler Cary Collection (MFC W231 F574) |
| *MK* | Bruno Walter, *Von den moralischen Kräften der Musik* (Vienna: Herbert Reichner, 1935) |
| *MM* | Bruno Walter, *Von der Musik und vom Musizieren* (Tübingen: S. Fischer, 1957); translated into English by Paul Hamburger as *Of Music and Music-Making* (New York: Norton, 1961). Unless otherwise noted, the translation of Paul Hamburger is used. |
| *MNN* | *Münchner Neueste Nachrichten* |
| *MZ* | *Münchener Zeitung* |
| *NFP* | *Neue Freie Presse* |
| *NWJ* | *Neues Wiener Journal* |
| *NYHT* | *New York Herald Tribune* |
| NYPA | New York Philharmonic Archives |
| *NYT* | *New York Times* |
| *NZM* | *Neue Zeitschrift für Musik* (*Neue* omitted in title between Aug. 1920 and Sept. 1955) |
| *TMD* | *Thomas Mann: Diaries, 1918–1939*, trans. Richard and Clara Winston (London: Robin Clark, 1984) |
| *TMGW* | Thomas Mann, *Gesammelte Werke*, 12 vols. (Frankfurt: S. Fischer, [1960–74]) |
| *TV* | Bruno Walter, *Thema und Variationen* (Stockholm: Ber- |

mann-Fischer, 1947); translated by James A. Galston as *Theme and Variations* (New York: Knopf, 1946). Unless otherwise noted, the translation of James A. Galston is used, though on rare occasions we have silently changed Galston's wording.

VZ      *Vossische Zeitung*

## Preface

1. Isaac Stern, from an interview in the BBC Walter Omnibus.
2. Hans Joachim Moser, *Musik Lexikon* (Berlin: Max Hesses Verlag, 1935), 937.
3. The first volume of Michele Selvini's beautifully produced tribute to Walter, *Bruno Walter: La porta dell'eternità* (Milan: Fondazione culturale della collina d'oro, 1999), represents the first attempt, in any language, at a full-length biography of the conductor's entire life. It appeared as we were making final adjustments to our manuscript and unfortunately could not be absorbed into our own study.

ONE

## Bruno Schlesinger

1. Many of the following facts and anecdotes come from reminiscences of Walter's mother, transcribed and typed out in a document dated Aug. 2, 1944, sent to Walter by his brother and sister (BWP II.19). According to his birth certificate, Walter's original name was simply Bruno Schlesinger, with no middle name.
2. Johanna Schlesinger's recollections (BWP II.19).
3. *TV*, 11.
4. Heinrich Ehrlich, *Wie übt man am Klavier* (Berlin, 1879).
5. Wilhelm Klatte and Ludwig Misch, *Das Sternsche Konservatorium der Musik zu Berlin* (Berlin, ca. 1926), 27.
6. *VZ*, Mar. 17, 1889; *BT*, Mar. 27, 1889.
7. *TV*, 97.
8. *National Zeitung*, Feb. 12, 1890; *VZ*, Feb. 12, 1890.
9. Johanna Schlesinger's recollections (BWP II.19).
10. *TV*, 52.
11. *TV*, 39.
12. Amy Fay, *Music-Study in Germany* (1880; reprint, New York: Dover, 1965), 119.
13. Felix Weingartner, *Über das Dirigieren* (1895; revised edition, 1905), translated by Ernest Newman as *On Conducting* in *Weingartner on Music and Conducting* (New York: Dover, 1969), 9.
14. Weingartner, *On Conducting*, 9–10.
15. Ibid., 10ff.
16. *TV*, 47.
17. *MM*, 36.
18. *TV*, 40.

19. Ibid.

20. After World War II, Wieland Wagner invited Walter to conduct Beethoven's Ninth at Bayreuth, but Walter regretfully declined, assuring Wieland of his goodwill. See Wieland Wagner to Bruno Walter (hereafter BW), Jan. 30, 1953; BW to Wieland Wagner, Feb. 9, 1953 (BWP I.633).

21. Heinrich Ehrlich, *Dreissig Jahre Künstlerleben* (Berlin, 1893), 276–77.

22. Ibid., 279.

23. BW to Sam Barlow, Mar. 21, 1946 (BWP I.467).

24. *TV*, 49.

25. Ethel Smyth, *The Memoirs of Ethel Smyth,* abridged and introduced by Ronald Crichton (Harmondsworth: Viking, 1987), 51.

26. *TV*, 41–42.

27. *TV*, 45.

28. Johanna Schlesinger's recollections (BWP II.19).

29. Paul Stefan, *Bruno Walter* (Vienna: Herbert Reichner, 1936), 23.

30. *MM*, 105–6.

31. Johanna Schlesinger's recollections (BWP II.19); *TV*, 55.

32. BW to his parents, Jan. 11, 1894 (*BW Briefe*, 9).

33. *TV*, 68.

34. Weingartner, *On Conducting*, 48.

35. *TV*, 68.

36. *TV*, 70.

37. *Kölner Tageblatt*, Mar. 21, 1894.

38. BW to his parents, Apr. 3, 1894 (*BW Briefe*, 10–11).

39. BW to his parents, Apr. 3, 1894 (*BW Briefe*, 11).

40. BW to his parents, Apr. 8, 1894 (*BW Briefe*, 11–13).

41. The antipathy between Walter and the Heydrich family carried into the next generation, for the singer's son, Reinhard, would become an infamous Nazi.

42. BW to his parents, Sept. 20, 1894 (*BW Briefe*, 13).

43. Julius Stern, *Wiener Volksblatt*, Apr. 16, 1933; Stern's anecdote is based on information he had gathered from Walter during an interview.

44. *TV*, 77 (we have slightly altered Galston's translation).

45. Arthur Foote, *Gustav Mahler: The Composer, the Conductor and the Man. Appreciations by Distinguished Contemporary Musicians* (New York: The Society of Friends of Music, 1916), 12.

46. *GM*, 18.

47. *TV*, 78.

48. Ibid.

49. *GM*, 21.

50. Alma Mahler, *Gustav Mahler: Memories and Letters*, trans. Basil Creighton, ed. Donald Mitchell, rev. ed. (New York: Viking Press, 1969), 113.

51. Ferdinand Pfohl, *Gustav Mahler: Eindrücke und Erinnerungen aus den Hamburger Jahren*, ed. Knud Martner (Hamburg: Karl Dieter Wagner, 1973), 34.

52. *TV*, 83.

53. Richard Specht, *Gustav Mahler* (Berlin: Schuster & Loeffler, 1913), 118.

54. Ibid., 119.

55. Issued on video in 1996 as *Bruno Walter: The Maestro, the Man* (VAI 69407); the rehearsal dates from July 1958.

56. Mahler to BW, July 2, 1896 (*GML*, 188–89).

57. *GM*, 33.

58. Natalie Bauer-Lechner, *Recollections of Gustav Mahler*, trans. Dika Newlin, ed. Peter Franklin (Cambridge: Cambridge University Press, 1980), 75.

59. Pfohl, *Gustav Mahler*, 49.

60. *Hamburger Nachrichten*, Sept. 10, 1895.

61. *GML*, 170.

62. See Max W. Busch and Peter Dannenberg, *Die Hamburgische Staatsoper I: 1678 bis 1945* (Zurich: M & T Verlag AG, 1988), 71–82.

63. *TV*, 89.

64. BW to his parents, Feb. 17, 1896 (*BW Briefe*, 15).

65. Ludwig Sittenfeld, *Geschichte des Breslauer Theaters von 1841 bis 1900* (Breslau: Preuss und Jünger, 1909), 309–10.

66. BW to his parents, Feb. 17, 1896 (*BW Briefe*, 15).

67. *TV*, 89.

68. BW to Leo Schlesinger, Mar. 14, 1896 (*BW Briefe*, 16).

TWO

*Kapellmeister Walter*

1. BW to his parents, Dec. 15, 1896 (*BW Briefe*, 22).

2. *TV*, 96.

3. BW to his parents, Dec. 15, 1896 (*BW Briefe*, 22).

4. *TV*, 95–96.

5. *TV*, 97.

6. *Breslauer Zeitung*, Oct. 31, 1896.

7. *TV*, 97–98.

8. *Breslauer Morgen-Zeitung*, Oct. 20, 1896.

9. *Breslauer Morgen-Zeitung*, Oct. 8, 1896.

10. *Breslauer Zeitung*, Oct. 8, 1896.

11. See Emil Bohn, *Hundert historische Concerte in Breslau. 1881–1905* (Breslau: Commissions-Verlag von Julius Hainauer, 1905).

12. In his review of *Waffenschmied*, Oct. 8, 1896.

13. *TV*, 92.

14. BW to Herbert Urban, Mar. 28, 1955 (BWP I.617).

15. BW to Emanuel Fernbach, Mar. 12, 1897 (*BW Briefe*, 25).

16. *TV*, 99.

17. *TV*, 100.

18. BW to his parents, Sept. 4, 1898 (*BW Briefe*, 26).

19. *Pressburger Zeitung*, Oct. 17, 1897.

20. *TV*, 104.
21. *TV*, 104–5.
22. *TV*, 105.
23. *Pressburger Tageblatt*, Nov. 9, 1897.
24. Interview with Regina Resnik, Feb. 18, 1997.
25. *TV*, 108.
26. *TV*, 109.
27. Undated interview with Lotte Lindt, recorded between 1962 and 1969 (*BWL*).
28. Entry for Sunday, Apr. 13, 1919 (*TMD*), 46.
29. *TV*, 110.
30. Born Else Wirthschaft, she adopted the stage name Elsa Korneck (taking her grandmother's last name), by which she was always known, though close friends continued to spell her first name *Else*.
31. Wolfgang Stresemann, . . . *und abends in die Philharmonie* (Munich: Kristall bei Langen Müller, 1981), 121.
32. The two reels of 16 mm film are part of the Rodgers and Hammerstein Sound Archive of the New York Public Library.
33. *Rigasche Rundschau*, Aug. 22, 1898.
34. *Düna Zeitung*, Aug. 29, 1898.
35. Klaus Mann, *The Turning Point* (1942; reprint, New York: Marcus Wiener Publishing, Inc., 1984), 70–71.
36. It was in his letter to Oskar Irschick that Walter gave 1899 as the date of the engagement. See Walter to Irschick, July 9, 1951 (BWP I.284).
37. BW to his parents, Sept. 4, 1898 (*BW Briefe*, 27–28).
38. *Düna Zeitung*, Aug. 22, 1898.
39. *Düna Zeitung*, Oct. 22, 1898.
40. Seen in the BBC Walter Omnibus.
41. *Rigasche Rundschau*, Aug. 22, 1898.
42. Walter also played piano accompaniment for Ferdinand Raimond's *Der Verschwender* and conducted the incidental music for a local premiere of Ernst Rosmer's *Königskinder*, whose score, by Engelbert Humperdinck, was later worked into a more substantial composition.
43. *Rigasche Rundschau*, Jan. 23, 1899.
44. Mahler to BW, Oct. 28, 1898 (*GML*, 234).
45. BW to his parents, Oct. 23, 1898 (*BW Briefe*, 29).
46. Mahler to BW, n.d. (*GML*, 235).
47. BW to his parents, Dec. 9, 1898 (*BW Briefe*, 32).
48. BW to his parents, Jan. 5, 1899 (*BW Briefe*, 33).
49. BW to Fernbach, Jan. 16, 1899 (*BW Briefe*, 34).
50. Mahler to BW, n.d. (*GML*, 239).
51. BW to his parents, Nov. 23 [1899] (*BW Briefe*, 37–38).
52. BW to his parents, Aug. 24, 1899 (*BW Briefe*, 36–37).
53. *TV*, 119.
54. BW to his parents, Feb. 8, 1900 (*BW Briefe*, 39–40).

55. The songs included in the concert (given on Apr. 30, 1900) were "Der Ring," "Die Linde," "Meine Mutter hat's gewolt," "Vorbei," "Waltrauts Lied I," and "Waltrauts Lied II."

56. *TV*, 121.

57. *VZ*, Aug. 16, 1900.

58. *Berliner Morgenpost*, Nov. 14, 1900. See also *TV*, 126–27.

59. *TV*, 88.

60. *BT*, Dec. 20, 1900; it should be added that W. B. in *VZ*, Dec. 21, 1900, gave the opera a distinctly unflattering review.

61. *TV*, 121.

THREE
## Mahler's Second-in-Command

1. *NFP*, Mar. 31, 1901.

2. Mahler to BW, [June] 1901 (*GML*, 250).

3. Mahler to BW, [June] and Aug. 1901 (*GML*, 252–53).

4. BW to Joseph Schlesinger, Aug. 15, 1901 (*BW Briefe*, 42–43).

5. Mahler to BW, [June] 1901 (*GML*, 250). Mahler himself conducted *Hoffmann* on Nov. 11, 1901; it hadn't been performed at the Hofoper since 1881 (La Grange 2, 388).

6. BW to his parents, Sept. 29, 1901 (*BW Briefe*, 44).

7. Natalie Bauer-Lechner, *Recollections of Gustav Mahler*, trans. Dika Newlin, ed. Peter Franklin (Cambridge: Cambridge University Press, 1980), 175.

8. *NFP*, Sept. 28, 1901; unsigned review.

9. Signed m. g., *NWJ*, Sept. 28, 1901.

10. K. H., *Deutsches Volksblatt*, Sept. 28, 1901.

11. BW to his parents, Sept. 29, 1901 (*BW Briefe*, 44).

12. *NFP*, Oct. 22, 1901; unsigned review.

13. Wallascheck seems surprisingly open-minded in his book *Primitive Music* (London, 1893), a survey of the music of other lands and cultures, though he offers a dubious comment concerning the music of the Jews: "the Jewish, even the synagogue, music has been modernised, notwithstanding the fact that many of the old songs have been preserved. Their sickly sweet *'lamentabile'* is still unmistakable in Mendelssohn's compositions" (62).

14. *Die Zeit*, Oct. 19, 1901.

15. Franz Mickorey (1873–1947), who later worked in Dessau, Helsinki, and Braunschweig (see La Grange 2, 292); "Herr Becher" is probably Gustav Brecher (1878–1940), a friend of Walter's mentioned as a "humble assistant conductor at the Opera" in *TV*, 163; see also La Grange 1, 625.

16. *Die Zeit*, Oct. 26, 1901.

17. Wallascheck, *Primitive Music*, 230.

18. *TV*, 157. We have been unable to locate the exact passage that Walter cites from the *Neues Wiener Tagblatt*, though abusive reviews of Walter's conducting of

*Tannhäuser* did appear in that newspaper and the *NFP* on Dec. 6, 1901 (both focusing on the overture), as well as in *Die Zeit* on Dec. 7, 1901.

19. Mahler to BW, [winter] 1901 (*GML*, 256).
20. Bauer-Lechner, *Recollections of Gustav Mahler*, 122.
21. BW to Joseph Schlesinger, Nov. 20, 1901 (*BW Briefe*, 45–46).
22. *TV*, 159.
23. BW to Ludwig Schiedermair, Dec. 6, 1901 (*BW Briefe*, 48–50).
24. Ibid. (*BW Briefe*, 51–52). Walter's interpretation, of course, owes a large debt to the text of the last movement.
25. *Die Musik* 1 (1902): 696–99.
26. *NFP*, Mar. 10, 1902.
27. BW to his parents, Dec. 30, 1901 (*BW Briefe*, 52–53).
28. BW to Hans Pfitzner, Mar. 6, 1902 (*BW Briefe*, 55–56).
29. Ibid. (*BW Briefe*, 57).
30. Pfitzner wrote to Alma on Mar. 12, 1903, asking for permission to dedicate his string quartet to her. See Susanne Keegan, *The Bride of the Wind: The Life and Times of Alma Mahler-Werfel* (New York: Viking, 1991), 115–16.
31. BW to Pfitzner, Dec. 20, 1902 (*BW Briefe*, 59–60).
32. BW to Pfitzner, Jan. 16, 1903 (*BW Briefe*, 62).
33. *NFP*, Apr. 23, May 15, and June 5, 1902; *Neues Wiener Tagblatt*, June 5, 1902.
34. *NFP*, Oct. 3, 1902.
35. *NFP*, Oct. 5 and 7, 1902.
36. *NFP*, Jan. 1, 1903. On Nov. 20, 1902, Walter had conducted a mostly vocal program (though it included Beethoven's "Egmont" Overture and Mozart's Piano Concerto no. 20 in D Minor) in the Musikvereinssaal; this was perhaps his first concert in the hall.
37. From unidentified clippings (dated Feb. 1903) in a scrapbook now at the Universität für Musik und darstellende Kunst in Vienna.
38. Interview with Mildred Miller, Oct. 21, 1996.
39. Mary Komorn-Rebhan, *Was wir von Bruno Walter lernten: Erinnerungen eines ausübenden Mitgliedes der Wiener Singakademie* (Vienna: Universal, [1913]), 4.
40. Both published by Josef Weinberger and listed in Hofmeister's *Musikalisch-literarischer Monatsbericht* (Jan. 1899), cited in Paul Banks's unpublished bibliographical study of the piano arrangements of Mahler's symphonies.
41. Walter's two collections were listed in the *Musikalisch-literarischer Monatsbericht* (Feb. and Mar. 1902), 94 and 140.
42. BW to Pfitzner, Dec. 20, 1902 (*BW Briefe*, 60).
43. BW to his parents, Feb. 2, 1907 (*BW Briefe*, 90).
44. BW to his parents, Feb. 18, 1897 (*BW Briefe*, 24).
45. The manuscript for the last three movements of Walter's Quartet is now at the Universität für Musik und darstellende Kunst in Vienna.
46. Signed "B," *Allgemeine Musikzeitung* 30 (Dec. 4, 1903): 781.
47. *NFP*, Nov. 25, 1904. The comment on "eleven thousand virgins" is an allusion to

a line in "Das himmlische Leben," the text to the last movement of Mahler's Fourth.

48. BW to Pfitzner, July 22, 1904 (*BW Briefe*, 72–73).

49. *NFP*, Dec. 2, 1903.

50. BW to Richard Strauss, Dec. 5, 1903 (*BW Briefe*, 69).

51. The manuscript for Walter's *Symphonische Phantasie*, in two movements (dated summer 1904 and Mar. 1904), is now at the Universität für Musik und darstellende Kunst in Vienna.

52. *NZM* 71 (June 15, 1904): 471.

53. From the unpublished manuscript of *Ein Leben mit Gustav Mahler*, cited in La Grange 3, 1059. Alma places this performance in 1905, but she also says that the Rosé Quartet played Walter's Quartet after this performance, which seems unlikely. Her dates must be regarded with caution.

54. *NFP*, Apr. 1, 1904.

55. BW to Pfitzner, Aug. 26, 1904 (*BW Briefe*, 74).

56. *NFP*, Nov. 9, 1904.

57. *NFP*, Nov. 13, 1904.

58. *NFP*, Dec. 28, 1904.

59. BW to Pfitzner, Sept. 25, 1904 (*BW Briefe*, 75).

60. BW to Pfitzner, Mar. 18, 1907 (*BW Briefe*, 91).

61. *NFP*, Jan. 12, 1905.

62. *TV*, 169.

63. Ibid.

64. The manuscript of the Piano Quintet is now at the Universität für Musik und darstellende Kunst in Vienna.

65. *Die Musik* 4, no. 13 (1905): 79.

66. "Über Kunstverständnis," *Österreichische Rundschau* 3 (May–July 1905): 106–10.

67. Ibid., 108–9.

68. BW to Pfitzner, [Feb. 1905] (*BW Briefe*, 79).

69. BW to Pfitzner, Apr. 15, 1905 (*BW Briefe*, 81).

70. BW to Pfitzner, Dec. 26, 1904 (*BW Briefe*, 77); *NFP*, June 7, 1905.

71. Probably either a performance of *Die Rose* on Oct. 6 or the Viennese premiere of his overture to *Käthchen von Heilbronn*, which took place on Oct. 31, 1905.

72. BW to Pfitzner, [Dec. 1905] (*BW Briefe*, 83–84).

73. See *Alma Mahler, Gustav Mahler: Memories and Letters*, trans. Basil Creighton, ed. Donald Mitchell (New York: Viking, 1969), 60.

74. BW to Pfitzner, [Dec. 1905] (*BW Briefe*, 83–84).

75. Ibid. (*BW Briefe*, 85).

76. Ibid. (*BW Briefe*, 82).

77. Marie Baumayer took Walter's place in a recital scheduled for Feb. 14, 1906, and on Mar. 8 Ferdinand Löwe stepped in for Walter, playing the piano part for the premiere of a new violin sonata by Robert Fuchs.

78. *TV*, 164–65.

79. *TV*, 167.

80. *TV*, 167.

81. *Die Musik* 5, no. 16 (1906): 214–46; Walter's piece is analyzed on 229–31.

82. Interview with Wolfgang Stresemann, Oct. 29, 1996. See also Stresemann's essay on Walter in *100 Jahre Berliner Philharmoniker: Grosse deutsche Dirigenten* (Berlin: Severin & Siedler, 1981), 133.

83. *GM*, 106–7.

84. *Die Musik* 5, no. 19 (1906): 51.

85. *NFP*, Oct. 5, 1906.

86. *Deutsche Zeitung*, Oct. 5, 1906.

87. The scrapbook at the Universität für Musik und darstellende Kunst contains no fewer than fifteen notices for the trio—a very high number, suggesting the importance of the piece to Walter. The whereabouts of Walter's Piano Trio are unknown to the authors.

88. *Die Musik* 8, no. 6 (1908–9): 374. Altmann's nationalistic tendencies, not evident in this review, emerged clearly in 1933; see Erik Levi, *Music in the Third Reich* (New York: St. Martin's Press, 1994), 183–84.

89. Gustav Mahler to Alma, Jan. 10, 1907, in *Ein Glück ohne Ruh': Die Briefe Gustav Mahlers an Alma*, ed. Henry-Louis de La Grange and Günther Weiss (Berlin: Wolf Jobst Siedler Verlag, 1995), 303.

90. BW to his parents, Feb. 2, 1907 (*BW Briefe*, 89). In an article published in the Boston *Transcript* (Mar. 31, 1923), concerning Walter's first appearance in that city, the author mentions that the Austrian conductor Wilhelm Gericke (who conducted in Boston from 1884 to 1889 and from 1898 to 1906) had reportedly "commended" Walter to Henry Higginson, the founder of the Boston Symphony Orchestra, "whereupon the 'founder and sustainer' issued edict that, were Mr. Walter ever to come to America, he should conduct at the Symphony Concerts."

91. *NFP*, Jan. 28, 1907.

92. Klemperer had played earlier recitals in Vienna during February and March. See Peter Heyworth, *Otto Klemperer: His Life and Times*, 2 vols. (Cambridge: Cambridge University Press, 1996), 1:25–26.

93. Gustav Mahler to Alma, Sept. 1, 1907 (*Ein Glück ohne Rüh'*, 334, 522). According to Mahler, Walter's symphony had been composed the previous year.

94. BW to Pfitzner, Feb. 4, 1908 (*BW Briefe*, 97–98). With Pfitzner's help, Walter himself eventually gave the German premiere in Strasbourg.

95. *NFP*, May 14, 1907.

96. *The Memoirs of Ethel Smyth*, ed. Ronald Crichton (Harmondsworth: Viking, 1987), 271.

97. BW to Pfitzner, Mar. 18, 1907 (*BW Briefe*, 91).

98. BW to his parents, May 3, 1907 (*BW Briefe*, 92–93).

99. BW to his parents, Jan. 10, 1908 (*BW Briefe*, 97).

100. Mahler to BW, [Dec. 1907] (*GML*, 305).

# FOUR

## Composer and Conductor

1. *NFP*, Jan. 3, 1908.
2. *NZM* 39 (Jan. 16, 1908): 52.
3. BW to his parents, Jan. 1, 1908 (*BW Briefe*, 97).
4. BW to Pfitzner, Feb. 4, 1908 (*BW Briefe*, 98).
5. *Deutsches Volksblatt*, Apr. 11, 1908.
6. *Die Musik* 7, no. 16 (1908): 246.
7. BW to Prof. Robert O. Weiss, Apr. 24, 1961 (BWP I.529).
8. BW to Olga Schnitzler, July 31, 1908 (*BW Briefe*, 101).
9. *TV*, 203.
10. Arthur Schnitzler, *The Road to the Open*, trans. Horace Samuel (Evanston, Ill.: Northwestern University Press, 1991), 252.
11. BW to Johanna Schlesinger, July 10, 1911 (*BW Briefe*, 124).
12. *GM*, 58.
13. Walter recalled their meeting in a letter to Klemperer dated Dec. 23, 1960 (BWP I.304).
14. *NFP*, Dec. 20, 1908.
15. *NFP*, Jan. 3, 1909.
16. Ironically, Mahler had recently introduced cuts to Wagner at the Metropolitan Opera, which elicited protests from the New York critics.
17. *NFP*, Jan. 10, 1909.
18. The parts are housed at the Universität für Musik und darstellende Kunst in Vienna.
19. BW to Pfitzner, June 17, 1908 (*BW Briefe*, 99–100). On the last page of the manuscript part for the sixth horn in F, someone has written in timings for a performance that would last fifty-two minutes: I. [Moderato 4/4], 19 minutes; II. [Adagio 4/4], $15\frac{1}{2}$ minutes; III. [Allegro con brio 3/4], $7\frac{1}{2}$ minutes; IV. [Agitato 2/2], 10 minutes.
20. BW to his parents, Mar. 12, 1909 (*BW Briefe*, 103).
21. *NFP*, Feb. 17, 1909.
22. See Elsa Bienenfeld, *NWJ*, Apr. 10, 1909; R. Batka, *Allgemeine Musikzeitung* 36 (Mar. 12, 1909): 225.
23. *Die Musik* 8, no. 12 (1909): 382.
24. *Times*, Mar. 4, 1909.
25. BW to his parents, Mar. 12, 1909 (*BW Briefe*, 103).
26. Published by Universal in 1910, it has recently been recorded by Vita and Ishmael Wallace (issued by VAI Audio, VAIA 1155).
27. Compare the first movement of Walter's sonata (p. 12, mm. 13–26), for example, with the first of Mahler's Ninth Symphony (p. 5, mm. 1–4, horns and trumpets); the motive recurs throughout Mahler's work.
28. *Die Musik* 8, no. 13 (1909): 63.

29. "Die Jungwiener Tondichter," *Die Musik* 9, no. 7 (1909–10): 1–16; the article concludes in the following issue.

30. Ibid., 8.

31. Bruno Walter, "Gustav Mahler's III. Symphonie," *Der Merker* 1 (1909): 10.

32. Ibid., 9–11.

33. *NFP*, Oct. 26, 1909.

34. *NFP*, Oct. 29, 1909.

35. BW to his parents, Dec. 5, 1909 (*BW Briefe*, 105).

36. An advertisement for the songs appeared in *NFP* on Feb. 6, 1910; "Musikantengruss" was also published separately near the end of the first issue of *Der Merker* in 1909.

37. Förstel sang Walter's songs again, on Feb. 13, at a symphony concert of the Vienna Tonkünstler Orchestra.

38. Though the dedications appear at the beginning of each set of three songs, referring specifically to "Musikantengruss" and "Die Lerche," they probably refer to the other two songs in the respective collections as well.

39. Fischer-Dieskau recorded all three songs in May 1964, with Jörg Demus at the keyboard, on an LP issued by Deutsche Grammophon (DGG 138 946); a 1975 live recording of "Der Soldat" and "Der junge Ehemann," with Wolfgang Sawallisch at the piano, was issued on CD by Orfeo (C 185 891 A) in 1989; Hägganders recording was released on LP by Bluebell of Sweden (Bell 180) in 1985. Hermann Prey recorded "Der junge Ehemann" in Dec. 1974 (Philips 6747 061 / Philips 6599 400).

40. In the 1940s, "Musikantengruss" was performed at the Czechoslovakian detainment camp Terezín. A facsimile of the program on which Walter's piece was included is given in Joza Karas, *Music in Terezín 1941–1945* (New York: Beaufort Books, 1985), [59].

41. *NFP*, Feb. 27, 1910.

42. *Times*, Feb. 22, 1910. Another performance with the same cast, not reviewed in the *Times*, took place on Feb. 24.

43. *Times*, Mar. 3, 1910. Before leaving London, Walter led one more *Tristan*, with Edyth Walker as Isolde, on Mar. 7.

44. *Times*, Dec. 23, 1912; an abbreviated translation of "Über Ethel Smyth. Ein Brief von Bruno Walter," *Der Merker* 3 (Dec. 1912): 897–98.

45. *NFP*, Apr. 22, 1910.

46. *TV*, 90, and *BW Briefe*, 19–21; BW to Hugo von Hofmannsthal, Apr. 23, 1910 (*BW Briefe*, 108).

47. *TV*, 87.

48. *AZ*, Oct. 1, 1910; *Kölnische Zeitung*, Feb. 15, 1911 (Abend Ausgabe); see also *NFP*, May 7, 1911.

49. BW to Hofmannsthal, June 12, 1910 (*BW Briefe*, 109).

50. *Der Merker* 1 (June 10, 1910): 700–1.

51. Gottfried Reinhardt, *The Genius: A Memoir of Max Reinhardt* (New York:

Knopf, 1979), 392. The memorial concert took place at Carnegie Hall on Nov. 30, 1943.

52. *TV*, 187; also Mahler to BW, Apr. 1, 1910 (*GML*, 354–55).

53. Siegfried Lipiner, *Fremden-Blatt*, Feb. 18, 1912.

54. *NFP*, Sept. 12, 1910; *TV*, 187.

55. In Paul Stefan, ed., *Gustav Mahler: Ein Bild seiner Persönlichkeit in Widmungen* (Munich: R. Piper & Co., 1910), 82–88; reprinted in *BW Briefe*, 110–16.

56. *BW Briefe*, 111.

57. *BW Briefe*, 112.

58. *GML*, 330.

59. *BW Briefe*, 113.

60. *BW Briefe*, 116.

61. The first movement of Walter's Symphony in E Major is dated Aug. 6, 1910; three movements, now at the Universität für Musik und darstellende Kunst in Vienna, are extant, and they show signs of heavy revision.

62. BW to his parents, Nov. 8, 1910 (*BW Briefe*, 117).

63. Sternberg's piece originally appeared in *Fremden-Blatt*, Mar. 25, 1916; cited and translated in Brendan Carroll, *The Last Prodigy: A Biography of Erich Wolfgang Korngold* (Portland, Ore.: Amadeus Press, 1997), 118.

64. *NFP*, Dec. 13, 1910.

65. Julius Korngold to BW, Nov. 11, 1940 (BWP I.306).

66. BW to his parents, Nov. 8, 1910 (*BW Briefe*, 116–18).

FIVE

## Premiere Performances

1. Mary Komorn-Rebhan, *Was wir von Bruno Walter lernten: Erinnerungen eines ausübenden Mitgliedes der Wiener Singakademie* (Vienna: Universal, [1913]).

2. Ibid., 7–8.

3. *La Tribuna*, Feb. 14, 1911; *NFP*, Feb. 26, 1911.

4. *MNN*, Feb. 13, 1911; *AZ*, Feb. 25, 1911.

5. *Die Musik* 10, no. 12 (1911): 377.

6. Walter remembered the year as 1909 (*TV*, 168–69), but in the parts to the symphony, on the last page of the second trumpet in B-flat, the date for the concert is given as Feb. 22, 1911.

7. Walter wrote that it gave him "joy" to conduct his symphony "with a fairly competent orchestra" in Strasbourg (*TV*, 185), suggesting that he had not been fully satisfied with the playing of the Konzertverein Orchestra at the premiere.

8. *Die Musik* 10, no. 15 (1911): 201.

9. Komorn-Rebhan, *Was wir von Bruno Walter lernten*, 13.

10. Ibid., 11.

11. Ibid., 16–18.

12. *NFP*, May 24, 1911.

13. BW to his parents, May 27, 1911 (*BW Briefe*, 122).

14. *TV*, 188.

15. BW to his parents, May 27, 1911 (*BW Briefe*, 122–23).

16. BW to Pfitzner, [May 1911] (*BW Briefe*, 120).

17. *NFP*, May 20, 1911. Walter remembered the funeral as having taken place the day after Mahler's death (*GM*, 63).

18. BW to Alma Mahler, May 21, 1911 (*BW Briefe*, 121–22).

19. BW to Justine Mahler, June 6, 1911 (The Gustav Mahler–Alfred Rosé Collection, Music Library, University of Western Ontario).

20. *Deutsches Volksblatt*, May 24, 1911.

21. *MA*, June 17, 1911.

22. *NFP*, July 3, 1911.

23. *NFP*, Sept. 24, 1911.

24. See Thomas G. Kaufman's chronology of Caruso's appearances in Michael Scott's *The Great Caruso* (New York: Knopf, 1988), 237.

25. *TV*, 175.

26. Some reviews list this performance as a "world premiere" (*Uraufführung*), others as a "first performance" (*erste Aufführung*), which usually means a local premiere.

27. *NWJ*, Nov. 10, 1911.

28. BW to his parents, Sept. 7, 1911 (*BW Briefe*, 126).

29. BW to Richard Strauss, Sept. 12, 1911 (*BW Briefe*, 127).

30. Walter and Cahier also gave a Mahler song recital in Vienna on Nov. 14.

31. *TV*, 192.

32. *AZ*, Nov. 25, 1911.

33. *MNN*, Nov. 22, 1911.

34. Cited in Peter Heyworth, *Otto Klemperer: His Life and Times*, 2 vols. (Cambridge: Cambridge University Press, 1996), 1:61.

35. *TV*, 187–88.

36. *TV*, 190–91.

37. *AZ*, Dec. 16, 1911.

38. Komorn-Rebhan, *Was wir von Bruno Walter lernten*, 21–22.

39. Acetates in good sound were made of Walter's performance of the *Missa solemnis* with the New York Philharmonic on Apr. 18, 1948; unfortunately, the only version currently available on compact disc is wretchedly distorted.

40. Komorn-Rebhan, *Was wir von Bruno Walter lernten*, 24–26.

41. *NFP*, Feb. 13, 1912.

42. *TV*, 50.

43. *NFP*, Feb. 29, 1912.

44. J. M. Corredor, *Conversations with Casals*, trans. André Mangeot (New York: E. P. Dutton, 1956), 212.

45. *Neues Wiener Tagblatt*, Mar. 15, 1912.

46. *NFP*, Mar. 16, 1912.

47. *NWJ*, Mar. 15, 1912.

48. *NFP*, Mar. 8, 1912.

49. BW to Strauss, Mar. 10, 1912 (*BW Briefe*, 133).

50. *La Tribuna*, Mar. 26, 1912.

51. Gasco's "Preludio pastorale: Presso in Clitunno" and "Scherzo orgiastico" were presented as "novelties" in Munich during the spring of 1914 under Walter; a negative review, signed A. A. N., appeared in *AZ* on Apr. 4, 1914.

52. *TV*, 182. Walter performed "Siegfried's Rhine Journey" twice at the Augusteum in Rome on Mar. 25, 1912; see *La Tribuna*, Mar. 26, 1912.

53. BW to his parents, Apr. 12, 1912 (*BW Briefe*, 134).

54. Komorn-Rebhan, *Was wir von Bruno Walter lernten*, 29.

55. Sir Adrian Boult, *My Own Trumpet* (London: Hamish Hamilton, 1973), 31.

56. *AZ*, Aug. 10, 1912.

57. *AZ*, Aug. 24, 1912. Walter may have had an aversion to the lid. Decades later, he wrote that, in a covered pit, it was impossible for the orchestral sound to achieve the brilliance it had in an open space, such as that of the Nationaltheater; see BW to Egon Hilbert, July 4, 1950 (BWP I.246).

58. *MNN*, June 10, 1912.

59. Unpublished interview with Joseph Braunstein by Rolland Parker, Sept. 18, 1993.

60. *Neues Wiener Tagblatt*, June 27, 1912; *NWJ*, June 27, 1912.

61. *NFP*, June 27, 1912; *Die Musik* 11, no. 21 (1912): 160.

62. Rudolf Louis, *MNN*, Oct. 2, 1912.

63. BW to Stresemann, Dec. 5, 1957 (BWP I.574).

64. *NFP*, Nov. 9, 1912.

65. BW to Joseph Schlesinger, [mid-July 1912] (*BW Briefe*, 134–35).

66. *TV*, 195–96. In fact, German Austria became a republic in 1918, which nullified the contract Walter had made during the imperial regime.

SIX

### *Generalmusikdirektor*

1. BW to Richard Strauss, Mar. 3, 1913 (*BW Briefe*, 144).

2. BW to Martin Mayer, Apr. 20, 1960 (BWP I.413).

3. Frederic Spotts, *Bayreuth: A History of the Wagner Festival* (New Haven: Yale University Press, 1994), 36.

4. BW to Emil Preetorius, May 5, 1959 (BWP I.501).

5. See *TV*, 202–3, and *AZ*, Jan. 18, 1913.

6. *MNN*, Jan. 7, 1913.

7. Ibid.

8. *MC*, Jan. 29, 1913.

9. *MNN*, Jan. 21, 1913.

10. *Moskovskie vedomosti*, Jan. 8 (21), 1913; also, *Die Musik* 12, no. 13 (1913): 61.

11. *TV*, 184–85.

12. Michael Kennedy, *Richard Strauss*, 2d ed. (New York: Schirmer, 1996), 52–54.

13. BW to Strauss, Sept. 29, 1912 (*BW Briefe*, 136–37).

14. Richard Strauss and Hugo von Hofmannsthal, *A Working Friendship: The Correspondence between Richard Strauss and Hugo von Hofmannsthal*, trans. Hanns Hammelmann and Ewald Osers (New York: Random House, 1961), 146.

15. *MNN*, Feb. 1, 1913.

16. BW to Strauss, Mar. 5, 1913 (*BW Briefe*, 142).

17. As a guest, Walter would return to conduct the Singakademie on many occasions through 1936, most often to perform Mahler's Eighth.

18. Review signed A. A. N., *AZ*, Mar. 15, 1913.

19. *MNN*, Feb. 25, 1913.

20. Rudolf Louis, *MNN*, Mar. 18 and 23, 1913; A. A. N., *AZ*, Mar. 29, 1913.

21. See the entry for Senius in K. J. Kutsch and Leo Riemens, *Grosses Sängerlexikon*, 3d ed., 5 vols. (Bern: K. G. Saur, 1997).

22. Walter conducted the *Matthäus-Passion* yearly from 1913 to 1920, with the exception of 1916, which seems to have passed without a performance of Bach's oratorio in Munich.

23. *MNN*, Mar. 13, 1913.

24. BW to his parents, May 20, 1913 (*BW Briefe*, 146–47).

25. *VZ*, June 22, 1913.

26. Karl Robert Blum, *Die Musik* 12, no. 20 (1913): 114–15.

27. *Die Musik* 13, no. 4 (1913): 237.

28. Rudolf Louis, *MNN*, Nov. 26, 1913; H. Sch., *AZ*, Nov. 29, 1913.

29. Reviewed in *AZ*, Dec. 27, 1913.

30. *BT*, Dec. 31, 1913.

31. *MNN*, Jan. 14, 1914. These observations may have carried some anti-Semitic overtones; in 1912 Louis had published some dubious comments on Jews in music in his book *Die deutsche Musik der Gegenwart*; see Erik Levi, *Music in the Third Reich* (New York: St. Martin's Press, 1994), 58.

32. *TV*, 285–86. Walter remembered that he had not yet turned fifty, but in fact he contracted pneumonia in the summer of 1927, shortly before his fifty-first birthday.

33. *MNN*, Jan. 14, 1914.

34. Interview with Schreker, *NFP*, Jan. 10, 1913; BW to Richard Strauss, Mar. 10, 1912 (*BW Briefe*, 133).

35. *AZ*, Mar. 7, 1914.

36. *NFP*, Jan. 10, 1913.

37. *MNN*, Mar. 2, 1914.

38. *AZ*, Mar. 7, 1914.

39. Bruno Walter, "Über Kunstverständnis," *Österreichische Rundschau* 3 (May–July 1905): 110.

40. Spotts, *Bayreuth*, 120.

41. Incidentally, Wagner's famous Festspielhaus was closed from 1915 to 1923, so during that period, the Prinzregententheater was the only venue to offer faithful stagings of works composed specifically for Bayreuth.

42. *MNN*, May 23, 1914.

43. *AZ*, May 30, 1914.

44. *MNN*, May 23, 1914.

45. *TV*, 202.

46. Alfred von Mensi, *AZ*, June 6, 1914.

47. BW to Ernst von Possart, June 26, 1914 (*BW Briefe*, 149).

48. Furtwängler expressed his gratitude for Walter's assistance in securing the Mannheim position in a letter to BW dated Jan. 1, 1949 (BWP I.208).

49. Adelheid Furtwängler to BW, Mar. 18, 1922 (BWP I.438).

50. Thomas Mann, "Musik in München," *TMGW* 11: 601 (originally published in *Der Tag*, Jan. 20 and 21, 1917).

51. Bruno Walter, "Zur Notlage der Musiker. Bierkonzerte unter berühmten Dirigenten," *Der Merker* 5 (Oct. 1914): 544.

52. Most of the concerts went unreviewed, but see *AZ*, Dec. 19, 1914, which gives a good idea of the repertoire; BW to Ossip Gabrilowitsch, June 17, 1915 (*BW Briefe*, 154).

53. *MNN*, Dec. 27, 1914.

54. *TV*, 278.

55. Ossip Gabrilowitsch to BW, Dec. 23, 1914 (BWP I.203).

56. Richard Würz, *MNN*, Dec. 30, 1914.

57. BW to his parents, Apr. 10, 1915 (*BW Briefe*, 152).

58. *MNN*, Feb. 27, 1915.

59. Max Mahler, *MNN*, Apr. 19, 1915; Walter also conducted *Elektra* in 1916, 1917, and 1919. For Strauss's complaints about Walter, see Strauss to Hofmannsthal, Aug. 17, 1915 (*Working Friendship*, 232).

60. *AZ*, Mar. 13, 1915.

61. BW to Gabrilowitsch, Aug. 21, 1915 (*BW Briefe*, 156).

SEVEN

## Delia

1. *MNN*, Aug. 31, 1915.

2. *MNN*, Sept. 7, 1915.

3. Thomas Mann, "Musik in München," *TMGW* 11:593.

4. Interview with Irma Geering, Dornach, Switzerland, Feb. 8, 1996.

5. Delia Reinhardt is referred to as Schützendorf's wife in *MNN*, Nov. 21, 1919. Schützendorf joined the Munich troupe in 1914, having previously worked in Strasbourg; he probably married Reinhardt sometime after her arrival in Munich in 1916.

6. Speech for the Korngold Memorial Concert, [Apr. 28, 1959] (BWP I.308).

7. *AZ*, Apr. 8, 1916.

8. Erich Wolfgang Korngold to BW, April 1, 1916 (BWP I.306).

9. Felix Weingartner, *Lebens Erinnerungen* (Zurich: Orellfüssli Verlag, 1929), 247–48.

10. Alexander Berrsche, *MZ*, Mar. 21, 1916.

11. BW to Ossip Gabrilowitsch, Nov. 30, 1916 (*BW Briefe*, 162–63).

12. *TMD*, June 9 and 15, 1919 (58–59).

13. Though most of the reviews Walter received in the leading papers were positive, there were evidently some dissenting voices as well. In September Wolfgang Bülau countered the negative comments leveled at Walter with his essay "Eine kleine Trutzschrift," *Signale für die musikalische Welt* (Sept. 20, 1916): 631–34.

14. Bruno Walter, "Kunst und Öffentlichkeit," *Süddeutsche Monatshefte*, Oct. 1916, 102–3.

15. Ibid., 107.

16. Thomas Mann, "Musik in München," *TMGW* 11:593–603.

17. Mann to Pfitzner, May 19, 1917, in *The Letters of Thomas Mann, 1889–1942*, trans. Richard and Clara Winston (London: Secker and Warburg, 1970), 84.

18. Mann, "Von der Tugend," in the collection *Betrachtungen eines Unpolitischen*; see *TMGW* 4:375–427, esp. 406–27.

19. BW to Sam Barlow (in English), Mar. 21, 1946 (BWP I.467).

20. *AZ*, Nov. 11, 1917.

21. Hugo Röhr had in fact given a performance of Mozart's Mass in C Minor in Munich in 1906, as Paul Ehlers noted in his review of Walter's performance (*MNN*, Nov. 6, 1917), but clearly it was very seldom performed.

22. *AZ*, Apr. 15, 1917.

23. See, in particular, the letter from BW to Max Auer of Mar. 15, 1953 (BWP I.66).

24. See Ronald Hayman, *Thomas Mann: A Biography* (New York: Scribner, 1995), 145–46, 159–60, 171, 181–82, 193, and *passim*.

25. *MNN*, Dec. 7, 1917.

26. *MNN*, Dec. 11, 1917.

27. For Trapp, see Michael Kater, *The Twisted Muse* (New York: Oxford University Press, 1997), 27–28. Ehrenberg became a member of the Nazi Party in Aug. 1932, according to Joseph Wulf, *Musik im Dritten Reich* (Hamburg: Ullstein, 1966; repr. 1983), 290 n. 1.

28. BW to Lotte Walter, June 25, 1917 (*BW Briefe*, 167).

29. BW to Lotte Walter, Oct. 2, 1917 (*BW Briefe*, 168).

30. Munich was no exception; an unusually hostile review appeared in *AZ*, Dec. 8, 1918.

31. *MNN*, Dec. 8, 1918. See also Owen Toller, *Pfitzner's* Palestrina (London: Toccata Press, 1997), 28–29.

32. BW to Wilhelm Furtwängler, Sept. 7, 1918 (*BW Briefe*, 172–73).

33. "Partiturreform," *Der Merker* 9 (July 1918): 475, 477.

34. *TMD*, 18–19.

35. Recounted in a letter from BW to Fritz Klein, May 25, 1933 (BWP I.228).

36. BW to his parents, Apr. 27, 1919 (*BW Briefe*, 176).

37. BW to his parents, June 1, 1919 (*BW Briefe*, 177).

38. *MNN*, Jan. 29, 1919.

39. *MNN*, Feb. 17, 1920.

40. *TV*, vii.

41. BW to Franz Schreker, Apr. 12, 1916 (BWP I.531).

42. BW to Schreker, Nov. 17, 1916 (*BW Briefe*, 164–65).

43. BW to Schreker, Apr. 28, 1919 (*BW Briefe*, 177).

44. *MNN*, Nov. 10, 1919.

45. *AZ*, Nov. 23, 1919.

46. *AZ*, Nov. 23, 1919.

47. *TMD*, Apr. 13, 1919 (46).

48. Reported in *MNN*, Nov. 21, 1919.

49. BW to Gabrilowitsch, Mar. 27, 1920 (*BW Briefe*, 180).

50. BW to Gabrilowitsch, May 12, 1920 (*BW Briefe*, 182).

51. Lotte Walter Lindt's note to p. 183 in *BW Briefe*, 408.

52. BW to Pfitzner, June 4, 1920 (*BW Briefe*, 182–83).

53. BW to Gretel Kraus, Apr. 8, 1950 (BWP I.311). Walter also fondly recalled, however, that Pfitzner used to play with his daughter Lotte when she was young and remarked that he had never met anyone who could play with children as well as Pfitzner; see BW to Mali Pfitzner, Jan. 27, 1961 (BWP I.480).

54. R. Hoffmann, "Musik in Wien," *Musikblätter des Anbruch* 2 (Mar. 1920): 241–42.

55. BW to Rudolf Mengelberg, June 11, 1939, in response to an invitation to conduct Mahler's Seventh with the Concertgebouw. Walter had rejected an earlier invitation to perform the Seventh with the Concertgebouw in 1934; see Rudolf Mengelberg to BW, Jan. 11, 1934, and BW to Rudolf Mengelberg, Jan. 13, 1934 (Concertgebouw Archives).

56. On Walter's desire to perform *Gurre-Lieder*, see *Arnold Schoenberg: Letters*, ed. Erwin Stein, trans. Eithne Wilkins and Ernst Kaiser (New York: St. Martin's Press, 1965), 40–42.

57. Bruno Zirato wrote to Dimitri Mitropoulos on Jan. 13, 1949, that Walter had wanted to perform *Gurre-Lieder* with the New York Philharmonic "many times, but he gave up the idea owing to the terrific cost of the production" (NYPA).

58. BW to Egon Hilbert, Oct. 4, 1960 (BWP I.248).

59. *MNN*, Apr. 22, 1920.

60. Stresemann to BW, Feb. 4, 1951 (BWP I.565). Walter performed *Gurre-Lieder* with the Vienna Symphony in 1935.

61. BW to Gabrilowitsch, July 15, 1920 (*BW Briefe*, 184).

62. *BW Briefe*, 408.

63. Entry for Oct. 31, 1920 (*TMD*, 104).

64. See, e.g., the review in *AZ*, Dec. 26, 1920.

65. Adrian Boult, "Bruno Walter," *Recorded Sound* 40 (1970): 668–69.

66. *BT*, Jan. 3, 1921.

67. From a speech of Apr. 9, 1929, cited in Brigitte Hamann, *Hitler's Vienna: A Dictator's Apprenticeship*, trans. Thomas Thornton (New York: Oxford University Press, 1999), 81. Hitler reportedly leveled the same charge in 1942; see Henry Picker, *Hitlers Tischgespräche im Führerhauptquartier 1941–1942*, 2d ed. (Stuttgart: Seewald Verlag, 1965), 302–3.

68. William Shirer, *The Rise and Fall of the Third Reich* (New York: Fawcett Crest, 1960), 81.
69. *Völkischer Beobachter*, May 15, 1921.
70. *Völkischer Beobachter*, May 22, 1921.
71. *TV*, 239.
72. *TV*, 237.
73. BW to Emanuel Fernbach, Jan. 19, 1899 (*BW Briefe*, 34).
74. *TV*, 237.
75. Recounted by Alfred Einstein in a review of *Ezio* under Robert Denzler, *BT*, Feb. 1, 1928; there the words are attributed to the singer Joseph Geis.
76. *VZ*, Nov. 8, 1916 and Jan. 22, 1919.
77. BW to Gabrilowitsch, Mar. 8, 1922 (*BW Briefe*, 189).
78. The petition in its entirety, running to about 67 pages, is in BWP I.435.
79. Dr. H. B., "Zum Fall Bruno Walter," *Völkischer Beobachter*, Mar. 25, 1922.
80. *MC*, May 25, 1922.
81. Interview with Stresemann, Oct. 29, 1996.
82. *TV*, 241.
83. Paul Bekker, "Zeitwende," *Die Musik* 15, no. 1 (1922): 3.
84. Undated interview, recorded between 1962 and 1969 (*BWL*).
85. Dr. Eckardt to Friedrich Trefz, Mar. 18, 1922 (BWP I.437) and Arthur Weisser to BW, Mar. 20, 1922 (BWP I.447).
86. See Ehlers's tribute to Hitler (1939) in Erik Levi, *Music in the Third Reich* (New York: St. Martin's Press, 1994), 236–37.
87. *TV*, 241.
88. Norbert Salter to Giulio Gatti-Casazza, Sept. 22, 1921 (Met Archives).
89. Interview with Irma Geering, Feb. 8, 1996. Walter conducted the Detroit Symphony Orchestra, Gabrilowitsch's ensemble, on his first trip to the United States, and Gabrilowitsch was responsible for arranging at least some of Walter's other American concerts.
90. Interview with Thea Dispeker, Sept. 12, 1995.
91. BWP I.443.
92. Ludwig Karl Mayer, "Bruno Walter und München," *Deutsche Tonkünstler-Zeitung* 24 (1926): 225.
93. *MZ*, Mar. 20, 1922.
94. Dr. H. B., *Völkischer Beobachter*, Oct. 7, 1922.
95. Alfred Einstein, "Bruno Walters Münchner Wirksamkeit," *Musikblätter des Anbruch* 4 (Nov. 1922): 269.
96. Adrian Boult to BW, Jan. 5, 1945 (BWP II.17). The anecdote is also related in Boult's essay "The Conductor: Foreground or Background?", reprinted in *Boult on Music* (Thetford, Norfolk: Toccata Press, 1983), 148–50.
97. George Martin, *The Damrosch Dynasty: America's First Family of Music* (Boston: Houghton Mifflin, 1983), 478–79 n. 8.
98. Walter Damrosch, *My Musical Life* (New York: Charles Scribner's Sons, 1930), 178–79.

99. BWP I.435.

100. Adolf Schiedt to BW, Oct. 4, 1922 (BWP I.441).

## New and Old Worlds

1. BW to Lotte Walter, Feb. 1, 1923 (*BW Briefe*, 195–96).

2. *NYT*, Feb. 16, 1923.

3. *Daily News*, Feb. 16, 1923.

4. *New York Evening Post*, Feb. 17, 1923.

5. *New York Herald*, Feb. 19, 1923.

6. Cited in George Martin, *The Damrosch Dynasty: America's First Family of Music* (Boston: Houghton Mifflin, 1983), 307.

7. *MA*, Feb. 24, 1923.

8. BW to Ossip Gabrilowitsch, Aug. 8, 1923 (*BW Briefe*, 203).

9. *MA*, Feb. 24, 1923.

10. BW to Lotte Walter, Feb. 21, 1923 (*BW Briefe*, 200).

11. John K. Sherman, *Music and Maestros* (Minneapolis: University of Minnesota Press, 1952), 156–57.

12. Cited in ibid., 167.

13. BW to Lotte Walter, Mar. 13, 1923 (*BW Briefe*, 201).

14. *Globe*, Mar. 31, 1923.

15. *Boston Post*, Mar. 31, 1923.

16. *Transcript*, Mar. 31, 1923.

17. Translated into German in *BW Briefe*, 201. Walter does not identify the newspaper, but he enclosed the original clipping, with his translation to be used for publicity in Vienna.

18. BW to Gabrilowitsch, Aug. 8, 1923 (*BW Briefe*, 202).

19. BW to Gabrilowitsch, Aug. 8, 1923 (*BW Briefe*, 203).

20. There is some confusion on this point even within the memoirs. Walter wrote that his family had made its "permanent home" in Vienna by the *summer* of 1923 but later claimed that he and his family chose to spend the *winter* of 1923–24 in Vienna (*TV*, 254, 267).

21. *BT*, Apr. 24, 1923.

22. *LNN*, Aug. 30, 1923.

23. *TV*, 253.

24. *De Telegraaf*, Oct. 15, 1923.

25. BW to Alma Mahler, Nov. 10, 1923 (*BW Briefe*, 203–4).

26. BW to Wolfgang Stresemann, Mar. 21, 1961 (BWP I.577).

27. BW to Alma Mahler, Mar. 14, 1961 (*BW Briefe*, 371).

28. BW to B. Krassin, Apr. 29, 1924 (*BW Briefe*, 206–7).

29. Siegfried Jacobson, *Die Musik* 17, no. 1 (1924): 71.

30. *MC*, Feb. 28, 1924; *NYT*, Mar. 10, 1924. On the Roman reception of *Verklärte Nacht*, see *TV*, 254–55.

31. *MC*, Mar. 6, 1924.

32. *MC*, Mar. 13, 1924.

33. *NYT*, Feb. 24, 1924.

34. Notice for the concert, on Mar. 25, 1924 (from the collection of Jon Samuels).

35. *Die Musik* 16, no. 11 (1924): 856.

36. BW to Franz Schreker, June 23, 1924 (*BW Briefe*, 205).

37. BW to Lotte Walter, Aug. 13, 1924 (*BW Briefe*, 209–10 and note on 411).

38. *Times*, May 7, 1924.

39. Frida Leider, *Playing My Part*, trans. Charles Osborne (New York: Meredith Press, 1966), 69.

40. *Times*, May 22, 1924.

41. Julian Herbage, Home Service typescript for Sunday, Sept. 16, 1956 (BWP I.326).

42. *TV*, 261.

43. Lotte Lehman, *Midway in My Song* (1938; reprint, Freeport, N.Y.: Books for Libraries, 1970), 155–56.

44. Listed in the *Symphony Society Bulletin* 18, no. 9 (Jan. 21, 1925).

45. *TV*, 267.

46. Paul Stefan, *Bruno Walter* (Vienna: Herbert Reichner, 1936), 57–58.

47. *TV*, 234.

48. *VZ*, Nov. 17, 1924.

49. Sergei Prokofiev to Nikolai Miaskovsky, Jan. 25, 1928; in *Selected Letters of Sergei Prokofiev*, trans. and ed. Harlow Robinson (Boston: Northeastern University Press, 1998), 270.

50. *BT*, Dec. 2, 1924.

51. *TV*, 262.

52. *Times*, Dec. 5, 1924.

53. Edward Elgar to Adela Schuster, Mar. 17, 1933; in Elgar, *Letters of a Lifetime*, ed. Jerrold Northrop Moore (Oxford: Clarendon Press, 1990), 467.

54. On the LP *Bruno Walter in Conversation with Arnold Michaelis* (Columbia Masterworks BW 80), Walter said that he'd made his first recording in Berlin in 1900. When questioned about this date by Joseph Boonin, he confidently wrote that the "prelude to Act 3 from Carmen was recorded in 1901 with the Berlin Philharmonic Orchestra"; BW to Joseph Boonin, Nov. 17, 1958 (BWP I.53).

55. *Double Sided Disc-Records-Catalogue: Polydor* (1924–25), 45.

56. Bruno Walter, "Some Thoughts about the Musical Record," *American Record Guide* 27 (1964): 374.

57. *Bruno Walter in Conversation with Arnold Michaelis.*

58. Claude G. Arnold's *The Orchestra on Record, 1896–1926* (Westport, Conn.: Greenwood Press, 1997) presents the most thorough documentation of orchestral recordings (and their dates) during the acoustic era.

59. In the series Early Recordings on 78's (Japanese Deutsche Grammophon, POCG-6067).

60. *Times*, Feb. 13, 1925.

61. Wilhelm Rode to BW, Oct. 3, 1922 (BWP I.440).

62. *Deutsche Theater-Zeitung* 42 (Apr. 8, 1938): 3; cited in Fred Prieberg, *Trial of Strength: Wilhelm Furtwängler in the Third Reich*, trans. Christopher Dolan (Boston: Northeastern University Press, 1994), 231.

63. Daniel Gregory Mason to BW, Oct. 15, 1936 (DGMP).

64. *NYT*, Mar. 16, 1925.

65. BW to Gabrilowitsch, May 14, 1925 (BWP I.212).

66. Reprinted from *The Gramophone* (July 1925) in *Herman Klein and The Gramophone*, ed. William R. Moran (Portland, Ore.: Amadeus Press, 1990), 108.

67. The history of Berlin's opera houses during the confusing period of 1923–24 is dealt with in Peter Heyworth, *Otto Klemperer: His Life and Times*, 2 vols. (Cambridge: Cambridge University Press, 1996), 1:167–95.

68. Adolf Weissmann, *Die Musik* 17, no. 10 (1925): 781.

69. BW to Thomas Mann, July 22, 1925 (*BW Briefe*, 212).

70. *NFP*, Sept. 1, 1925.

NINE

## A New Opera Company

1. *VZ*, Sept. 20, 1925.

2. In a letter to Hans Schwieger, dated May 25, 1951 (BWP I. 540), Walter recommended opening a concert that had *Das Lied* as its centerpiece with either Schubert's "Unfinished" or Mozart's Symphony no. 40; the combination of the "Unfinished" and *Das Lied* appeared again on Walter's last program with the New York Philharmonic, in 1960.

3. *TV*, 292.

4. Bruno Walter, "Kapelle und Kapellmeister," *Deutsche Tonkünstler-Zeitung* 24 (1926): 224.

5. Yehudi Menuhin, interviewed for the BBC Walter Omnibus.

6. *TV*, 266.

7. *Times*, May 31, 1926.

8. Heinz Tietjen to BW, Apr. 28, 1926 (BWP I.29).

9. Tietjen to BW, May 17, 1926 (BWP I.29).

10. Signed g. c., *Corriere della Sera*, June 24, 1926.

11. *TV*, 278.

12. Typescript, Feb. 10, 1948 (BWP I.585).

13. *BT*, Sept. 15, 1926.

14. *TV*, 272.

15. *BT*, Nov. 7, 1926.

16. *Die Musik* 19, no. 4 (1927): 285.

17. BW to Isao Uno, July 7, 1955 (BWP I.298).

18. Printed as "Dem Menschen und Musiker" in *BT*, Mar. 26, 1927, and as "Rede Bruno Walters bei der Beethovenfeier in der Philharmonie" in *Die deutsche Bühne* 19 (Apr. 1927): 85–88.

19. See Michael Kater, *The Twisted Muse* (New York: Oxford University Press, 1997), 217–18.

20. [BW] to Oberbürgermeister [Gustav Böss], Jan. 20, 1927, and Böss to BW, Feb. 5, 1927 (BWP I.30).

21. Georg Sebestyen, "Bruno Walter," *Die Musik* 17, no. 9 (1925): 677–79.

22. Anton Weiss to BW, May 9, 1927 (BWP I.620); BW to [Weiss], May 20, 1927 (Vienna Philharmonic Archives).

23. Weiss to BW, May 24, 1927 (BWP I.620).

24. BW to [Weiss], June 2, 1927 (Vienna Philharmonic Archives).

25. In the 1926–27 season Lotte Walter appeared as Fiordiligi in *Così*, Amalia in *Ballo*, Pamina in *Die Zauberflöte*, and a woman in von Schillings's *Mona Lisa*; the following season, she sang Octavian in *Der Rosenkavalier*, Adele in *Die Fledermaus*, Lisa in *Pique Dame*, Frau Fluth in *Die lustigen Weiber von Windsor*, as well as several roles in now forgotten works.

26. Rudolf Bing, *5000 Nights at the Opera* (Garden City, N.Y.: Doubleday, 1972), 38. Walter wrote that Lotte and her first husband were separated by 1933 (*TV*, 314).

27. *TV*, 278.

28. Report signed E.C., *MC*, July 7, 1927.

29. Ibid. and *MA*, July 2, 1927.

30. *San Francisco Chronicle*, July 4, 1927.

31. *LAT*, July 9, 1927.

32. *TV*, 281.

33. *TV*, 285.

34. BW to Hans Pfitzner, Aug. 29, 1927 (*BW Briefe*, 215).

35. Adolf Diesterweg, *NZM* 94 (1927): 694.

36. Bruno Walter, interviewed by Bernhard Romani, "Existenzfragen der Oper," *Die deutsche Bühne* 21 (1929): 319.

37. Interview with Albert Goldberg, aired in a documentary on Walter for the Canadian Broadcasting Company in 1958 and reissued by VAI in *Bruno Walter: The Maestro, the Man* (VAI 69407).

38. Tietjen to BW, May 11, 1927 (BWP I.31).

39. Diesterweg, *NZM* 94 (1927): 694–95.

40. Alfred Einstein, "Bruno Walters Münchner Wirksamkeit," *Musikblätter des Anbruch* 4 (1922): 268–70.

41. *BT*, Nov. 12, 1927.

42. *TV*, 153.

43. *BT*, Jan. 17, 1928.

44. *BT*, Feb. 1, 1928.

45. *TV*, 277.

46. *VZ*, Feb. 8, 1928.

47. BW to his parents, Feb. 28, 1928 (*BW Briefe*, 217).

48. *TV*, 274.

49. Brendan Carroll, *The Last Prodigy: A Biography of Erich Wolfgang Korngold* (Portland, Ore.: Amadeus Press, 1997), 211.

50. *BT*, Apr. 7, 1928.

51. See Carroll, *Last Prodigy*, 202–3.

52. *Die Musik* 20, no. 9 (1928): 687.

53. See the announcement in *BT*, Jan. 8, 1927.

54. *Le Figaro*, June 18, 1928.

55. S. Francoeur, *BT*, May 22, 1928.

56. *Le Figaro*, May 28, 1928.

57. Stravinsky, "In Re Walter," *Stereo Review* 10 (Mar. 31, 1962): [39].

58. In the BBC Walter Omnibus, Georg Solti recalled meeting Walter on a train at a time when Walter and Stravinsky were neighbors in Beverly Hills. Noticing a score that Solti was carrying, Walter asked what it was. On learning that it was *Le Sacre*, he reportedly replied: "Oh, how can you do that piece? It's terrible, a terrible piece!"

59. *Le Temps*, June 6, 1928.

60. *Le Figaro*, June 13, 1928.

61. *Le Figaro*, June 15, 1928.

62. The matrix number for the *Figaro* Overture is WAX 3844, an item first brought to our attention by James Altena, who in turn was alerted to its existence by the British dealer Raymond Glaspole.

63. *BT*, June 15, 1928.

64. See BW to Tietjen, June 4, 1928 (BWP I.32).

65. In *Wir von der Oper*, ed. Walter Firner (Munich: F. Bruckmann AG, 1932), 115–120. The book also includes commentaries on the state of opera from Fritz Busch, Wilhelm Furtwängler, Gustaf Gründgens, Maria Ivogün, Erich Kleiber, Otto Klemperer, Lotte Lehmann, Lauritz Melchior, Delia Reinhardt, and others.

66. BW to Böss, Sept. 20, 1928 (BWP I.30); an abbreviated version is given in *BW Briefe*, 217–22.

67. *LNN*, Oct. 12, 1928.

68. *BT*, Dec. 12, 1928.

69. *BT*, Jan. 2, 1929.

70. Arthur Judson to BW, Jan. 5, 1929; BW to Arthur Judson, Jan. 8, 1929 (NYPA).

71. See the first and fourth documents in BWP I.40.

72. Lotte Lehmann to BW, Mar. 26, 1929 (LLP).

73. *VZ*, Mar. 21, 1929.

74. *BT*, Mar. 20, 1929.

75. *BT*, Apr. 3, 1929.

76. Yehudi Menuhin, *Unfinished Journey* (New York: Knopf, 1977), 95.

77. *Times*, May 15, 1929.

78. *TV*, 286.

79. Bruno Walter, interviewed by Bernhard Romani, "Existenzfragen der Oper," 318.

## Gewandhauskapellmeister

1. *TV*, 288.

2. In Walter's introduction to Eberhard Creuzburg, *Die Gewandhaus-Konzerte zu Leipzig, 1781–1931* (Leipzig: Breitkopf & Härtel, 1931), 5.

3. See the letters in BWP I.323; Creuzburg, *Gewandhaus-Konzerte*, 152.

4. Johannes Forner, ed., *Die Gewandhaus-Konzerte zu Leipzig, 1781–1981*, 2d ed. (Leipzig: VEB Deutscher Verlag für Musik, 1981), 212.

5. *Die Musik* 22, no. 4 (1930): 310.

6. *TV*, 289.

7. *NZM* 97 (1930): 55.

8. *NZM* 99 (1932): 433.

9. See his announcement of Walter's appointment in *LNN*, Dec. 1, 1929.

10. *NZM* 96 (1929): 734.

11. "Über den Vortrag einiger Motive und Stellen in klassischen Werken, vornehmlich Mozart's," *NZM* 98 (1931): 666.

12. *NZM* 98 (1931): 64.

13. Take, e.g., Walter's recording of the "Prague" Symphony or Beethoven's "Pastoral," both recorded with the Vienna Philharmonic in 1936.

14. In *NZM* 90 (1923) and succeeding issues.

15. *NZM* 96 (1929): 826.

16. *NZM* 97 (1930): 55.

17. *NZM* 98 (1931): 515.

18. *BT*, Jan. 7, 1930. The same review appears in *Die Musik* 22, no. 5 (1930): 365.

19. Entry for Dec. 7, 1919 (*TMD*, 72).

20. *Bruno Walter at the Piano* (Bruno Walter Society BWS 807).

21. Quoted in Nicholas Kenyon, *The BBC Symphony Orchestra: The First Fifty Years 1930–1980* (London: BBC, 1980), 76.

22. The Strauss pieces with the Columbia Symphony Orchestra have been reissued by Sony (SMK 64467); those with the Vienna Philharmonic (a broadcast recording) were briefly available in Japan on Wing Disc (WCD 3–4).

23. From an insert in the programs for his Covent Garden performances.

24. BW to Paul Block, Mar. 8, 1930 (BWP I.185).

25. BW quoted in the *NWJ*, Mar. 27, 1930.

26. *Nachtausgabe*, Mar. 28, 1930.

27. See the correspondence between Walter and Reinhardt (BWP I.514).

28. Harold Rosenthal, *Two Centuries of Opera at Covent Garden* (London: Putnam, 1958), 467.

29. *Times*, May 7, 1930.

30. BW to Harold Rosenthal, Apr. 10, 1958 (BWP I.326).

31. It was actually Schneiderhan's secret negotiations with Furtwängler that prompted Schalk's resignation. See Marcel Prawy, *The Vienna Opera* (New York: Praeger, 1970), 131.

32. *NFP*, Dec. 23, 1928.

33. *TV*, 291–92.

34. *NZM* 98 (1931): 306. In framing his symbolic question, Junk used the familiar *du* for "you," demonstrating just how deeply and intimately he felt the Viennese cared for Walter.

35. *TV*, 293.

36. Golo Mann, *Reminiscences and Reflections: A Youth in Germany*, trans. Krishna Winston (New York: Norton, 1990), 245.

37. Ibid., 246.

38. *TV*, 293.

39. From Covent Garden insert.

40. *Times*, May 6, 1931.

41. *Times*, May 9, 1931.

42. The various behind-the-scenes maneuverings to secure Beecham, the prime mover of which appears to have been Lady Snowdon, one of the trustees of the Covent Garden Opera Syndicate, are described in detail in Francis Donaldson's *The Royal Opera House in the Twentieth Century* (London: Weidenfeld and Nicolson, 1988), 27–30. Lady Snowdon would later claim that the board of trustees had engaged Beecham without consulting her.

43. Quoted in Harold Rosenthal, *Opera at Covent Garden: A Short History* (London: Victor Gollancz Ltd., 1967), 115.

44. Roland Tenschert, *Die Musik* 24, no. 1 (1931): 46; *NWJ*, Aug. 19, 1931.

45. BW to Wolfgang Stresemann, Apr. 26, 1950 (BWP I.563).

46. BW to Margarete Wallmann, Oct. 8, 1954 (BWP I.636).

47. Creuzburg, *Gewandhaus-Konzerte*, 157. The Gewandhaus performed in Cologne, Brussels, Paris, Strasbourg, Ghent, Stuttgart, and Munich.

48. *Die Musik* 23, no. 8 (May 1931): 597.

49. See Creuzburg, *Gewandhaus-Konzerte*, 158–59.

50. *NZM* 99 (1932): 16.

51. *TV*, 294.

52. BW to Arthur Judson, May 22, 1931 (NYPA).

53. *NYT*, Jan. 15, 1932.

54. *NYT*, Feb. 5 and Jan. 22, 1932.

55. Prokofiev to Vernon Duke, June 3, 1932; in *Selected Letters of Sergei Prokofiev*, trans. and ed. Harlow Robinson (Boston: Northeastern University Press, 1998), 149.

56. BW to Daniel Gregory Mason, May 23, 1931 (DGMP).

57. *NYT*, Feb. 19, 1932.

58. *NYT*, Feb. 12, 1932.

59. Herbert F. Peyser, "Bruno Walter," *Disques* (Feb. 1932): 531–33.

60. Bruno Walter, "Konzerte und ihre Funktion," *Berliner Zeitung* (undated clipping from the second scrapbook in BWP IX, probably published in the fall of 1932).

61. Annotated comment by Mason on a letter from BW, May 23, 1931, in which Wal-

ter asked if he might keep the Shepherd score longer (DGMP); *NYHT*, Feb. 10, 1933.

62. New York *Sun*, Feb. 10, 1933; *New York Post*, Feb. 10, 1933.

63. The recording project had been discussed as early as Oct. 1932, and many letters passed between RCA Victor and the New York Philharmonic to work out the legalities involved. It is very unlikely that a recording was made, however, since the Philharmonic's Personnel Manager's Report for the week ending Feb. 26, 1933, has no notes on extra payments made to the performers for a recording (NYPA).

64. *TV*, 295.

65. *TV*, 296.

66. Forner, ed., *Gewandhaus-Konzerte*, 223.

67. *LNN*, Mar. 25, 1933.

68. See Hans-Joachim Nosselt, *Das Gewandhaus-Orchester* (Leipzig: Koehler & Amelang, 1943), 231–32.

69. Walter Vetter, "Res Severa Verum Gaudium: Die Tradition des Gewandhauses," in *Festschrift zum 175jährigen Bestehen der Gewandhauskonzerte, 1781–1956* (Leipzig; Deutscher Verlag für Musik, 1956), 34.

70. Fritz Hennenberg, *Das Leipziger Gewandhausorchester* (Leipzig: VEB Edition, 1962), 57–59.

71. Vetter, "Res Severa," 30.

72. Edith Stargardt-Wolff, *Wegbereiter grosser Musiker* (Berlin: Bote & G. Bock, 1954), 276–77.

73. *TV*, 299.

74. *TV*, 299.

75. Julius Kopsch to BW, Sept. 25, 1950 (BWP I.551).

76. BW to Kopsch, Oct. 2, 1950 (BWP I.551).

77. *Internationale Mitteilungen Richard-Strauss-Gesellschaft* 7 (May 1955): 2. See also Gerhard Splitt, *Richard Strauss 1933–1935: Ästhetik und Musikpolitik zu Beginn der nationalsozialistischen Herrschaft* (Pfaffenweiler: Centaurus Verlagsgesellschaft, 1987), 42–55. Splitt seems generally to accept the Stargardt-Wolff version.

78. BW to Stargardt-Wolff, July 5, 1955 (BWP I.544).

79. Stargardt-Wolff to BW, July 28, 1955 (BWP I.552).

80. Stargardt-Wolff to BW, Aug. 12, 1955 (BWP I.552).

81. *Völkischer Beobachter*, Mar. 19/20, 1933.

82. *Berliner Lokal-Anzeiger*, Apr. 5, 1933; quoted in Splitt, *Richard Strauss*, 46.

83. *NYT*, Apr. 9, 1933.

84. Bundesarchiv Berlin, Bestandssignatur 2236 (Bruno Walter).

85. *NZM* 100 (May 1933): 458.

86. *Deutsche Allgemeine Zeitung*, Mar. 21, 1933.

87. Quoted in *NYT*, Mar. 21, 1933.

88. Daniel Jonah Goldhagen, *Hitler's Willing Executioners* (New York: Knopf, 1996).

89. Hellmut Krug to BW, Mar. 20, 1933 (BWP I.221). The letters that Walter saved from Germans alone take up three entire folders.

90. BW to Ada Pixis, May 17, 1933 (BWP I.222). The letter to Pixis is written in a different hand, possibly Elsa's.

91. Draft of speech (BWP I.226).

92. BW to Harry Harkness Flagler, May 28, 1933 (BWP I.227).

93. BW, telegram to North American Newspaper Alliance, n. d. [after Mar. 23, 1933] (BWP I.225).

94. Quoted by Alfred Einstein, *BT*, Feb. 18, 1931.

95. BW to Kanitz, Apr. 13, 1933 (BWP I.222).

96. BW to Staatsrat Dr. Korn, Apr. 13, 1933 (BWP I.222).

97. *NZM* 100 (May 1933): 515; see Erik Levi, *Music in the Third Reich* (New York: St. Martin's Press, 1994), 10–12.

98. BW to *Deutsche Wochenschau*, May 23, 1933 (BWP I.228).

99. Gustav Bosse to BW, May 24, 1933 (BWP I.228); *NZM* 100 (June 1933): 648.

100. *Allgemeine Musikzeitung* 61 (May 4, 1934): 253.

101. Wilhelm Furtwängler, *Notebooks, 1924–54*, trans. Shaun Whiteside, rev. ed. (London: Quartet Books, 1995), 23, 41.

102. The articles are reprinted in Joseph Wulf, ed., *Musik im Dritten Reich* (Frankfurt: Ullstein, 1966), 87–89.

103. *TMD*, 128.

104. Gino Baldini to BW, Mar. 20, 1933 (BWP I.224).

105. BW to Baldini, Apr. 13, 1933 (BWP I.224).

106. BW to Harry Harkness Flagler, May 28, 1933 (BWP I.227).


ELEVEN

## Nomad Again

1. Quoted in *MC*, May 13, 1933.

2. BW to Rudolf Mengelberg, Mar. 13, 1933 (Concertgebouw Archives).

3. *Algemeen Handelsblad*, Mar. 24, 1933.

4. *TV*, 301.

5. *De Telegraaf*, Mar. 24, 1933.

6. *TV*, 301.

7. Paul Stefan, *MA*, Apr. 25, 1933.

8. *NYT*, Apr. 13, 1933.

9. *NFP*, Apr. 13, 1933.

10. Stefan, *MA*, Apr. 25, 1933.

11. *MC*, May 13, 1933.

12. *Times*, May 2, 1933.

13. Entry for Apr. 29, 1933, in Virginia Woolf, *The Diary of Virginia Woolf*, ed. Anne Olivier Bell, 5 vols. (New York: Harcourt Brace Jovanovich, 1982), 4:153.

14. BW to Harry Harkness Flagler, May 28, 1933 (BWP I.227).

15. *NFP*, Aug. 4, 1933.

16. See the account in *NYT*, Aug. 4, 1933.

17. Edith Wharton to Gaillard Lapsley, Aug. 28, 1933; in *The Letters of Edith Wharton* (New York: Charles Scribner's Sons, 1988), 56.

18. *NYT*, Aug. 20, 1933.

19. BW to Bruno Zirato, Sept. 8, 1933 (NYPA).

20. *NYT*, Sept. 28, 1933.

21. *NYHT*, Oct. 6, 1933; *NYT*, Oct. 6, 1933.

22. *NYT*, Oct. 27, 1933.

23. BW to Randall Thompson, Oct. 4, 1945 (BWP I.586).

24. *NYHT*, Nov. 27, 1933.

25. BW to Werner Bollert, Feb. 27, 1960 (BWP I.53).

26. BW to Leo Schlesinger, Nov. 29, 1933 (*BW Briefe*, 230–31).

27. *NFP*, Mar. 6, 1934.

28. Marcel Prawy, *The Vienna Opera* (New York: Praeger, 1970), 134.

29. *Neues Wiener Tagblatt*, Sept. 8, 1932.

30. *NFP*, Mar. 30, 1934.

31. *NFP*, Apr. 12, 1934.

32. Quoted in Nicholas Kenyon, *The BBC Symphony Orchestra: The First Fifty Years 1930–1980* (London: BBC, 1980), 98–99.

33. Wilhelm Backhaus to BW, May 25, 1945 (BWP I.21).

34. BW to Bruno Zirato, Dec. 30, 1948 (NYPA).

35. *TV*, 312.

36. See Gordon Brook-Shepherd, *The Austrians* (New York: Carroll & Graf, 1997), 285–94.

37. *TV*, 317.

38. Currently housed at the Rodgers and Hammerstein Sound Archive.

39. *TV*, 308.

40. *TV*, 309.

41. Ezio Pinza (with Robert Magidoff), *An Autobiography* (New York: Rinehart & Co., 1958), 151.

42. Ibid., 153.

43. Ibid., 155.

44. *NFP*, Aug. 7, 1934.

45. Erich Leinsdorf, *Cadenza* (Boston: Houghton Mifflin Company, 1976), 31–34.

46. Kurt Weill to Lotte Lenya, Sept. 16, 1934; in *Speak Low (When You Speak Love): The Letters of Kurt Weill and Lotte Lenya*, ed. and trans. Lys Symonette and Kim H. Kowalke (Berkeley: University of California Press, 1996), 143.

47. Weill to Lenya, Oct. 10, 1934 (*Speak Low*, 145).

48. *De Telegraaf*, Oct. 12, 1934.

49. *NYT*, Dec. 14, 1934; *NYHT*, Dec. 14, 1934.

50. *NYHT*, Dec. 21, 1934; *NYT*, Dec. 21, 1934.

51. *NYT*, Dec. 7, 1934.

52. Arturo Toscanini to Ada Mainardi, Jan. 19, 1935 (Arturo Toscanini's letters to

Ada Mainardi, private collection, Milan; courtesy of Harvey Sachs, who translated the letter from the original Italian).

53. Otto Strasser, *Und dafür wird man noch bezahlt: Mein Leben mit den Wiener Philharmonikern* (Vienna: Paul Neff Verlag, 1974), 54.

54. Interview with Siegmund Levarie, Mar. 24, 1996.

55. Arthur Schopenhauer, *The World as Will and Representation*, trans. E. F. J. Payne, 2 vols. (New York: Dover, 1966), 2:451.

56. *MK*, 9–10.

57. *MK*, 20.

58. Katia Mann, *Unwritten Memories*, ed. Elisabeth Plessen and Michael Mann, trans. Hunter and Hildegarde Hannum (New York: Knopf, 1975), 137.

59. Lotte Walter identifies Neppach as a film producer (*BW Briefe*, 417), while several newspapers referred to him as an architect in 1939.

60. Pinza, *Autobiography*, 156.

61. Ibid., 157–58.

62. BW to Rudolf Mengelberg, Aug. 29, 1935 (Concertgebouw Archives).

63. BW to Leo Schlesinger, Aug. 27, 1935 (*BW Briefe*, 234).

64. Thomas Mann to Heinrich Mann, July 2, 1936; in *The Letters of Thomas Mann, 1889–1942*, trans. Richard and Clara Winston (London: Secker and Warburg, 1970), 251–52.

65. Allan Keiler, *Marian Anderson: A Singer's Journey* (New York: Scribner, 2000), 172.

66. *NYT*, July 19, 1936.

67. *NFP*, Aug. 14, 1936.

68. Prawy, *Vienna Opera*, 150.

69. *TV*, 318.

70. Ibid.

TWELVE

## *Dies Irae*

1. Paul Stefan, *Bruno Walter* (Vienna: Herbert Reichner, 1936).

2. Bruno Walter, "Mahlers Weg. Ein Erinnerungsblatt," *Der Merker* 3 (Aug. 1912): 166–71.

3. *GM*, 19, 24, 125.

4. BW to his parents, Jan. 10, 1908 (*BW Briefe*, 97).

5. *GM*, 75.

6. *GM*, 111.

7. BW to Clara Gabrilowitsch, Oct. 17, 1936 (*BW Briefe*, 237).

8. Interview with Elena Nikolaidi, May 26, 1996.

9. Edition Wiener Staatsoper Live, vol. 10 (Koch Schwann, 3-1460-2).

10. Broadcast of Feb. 22, 1948, included on a New York Philharmonic/WQXR Radiothon recording (NYP 84); another performance of the overture is that with the Bavarian State Orchestra of Oct. 2, 1950, issued on AS Disc (AS 423).

11. *NFP*, May 21, 1937.
12. J. M. Corredor, *Conversations with Casals*, trans. André Mangeot (New York: E. P. Dutton, 1956), 87.
13. *NWJ*, Aug. 19, 1937.
14. BW to Harry Harkness Flagler, Sept. 4, 1937 (MFCC).
15. The performance of *Don Giovanni* from Aug. 2, 1937, has been issued by the Radio Years (RY 83.85).
16. *TV*, 318.
17. BW to Hans Pfitzner, June 9, 1937 (*BW Briefe*, 239).
18. Edition Wiener Staatsoper Live, vol. 7 (Koch Schwann, 3-1457-2).
19. *TV*, 320.
20. *TV*, 321.
21. *NWJ*, Feb. 27, 1938.
22. BW to George Marek, Sept. 28, 1954 (BWP I.407).
23. Marek to BW, Oct. 11, 1954; draft of letter from BW to Marek, Oct. 25, 1954 (BWP I.407).
24. Egon Wellesz, "Bruno Walter (1876-1962)," *Music and Letters* 43 (1962): 205.
25. *TV*, 321.
26. BW to Toscanini, Feb. 20, 1938; trans. in Harvey Sachs, "Toscanini, Hitler, and Salzburg," in *Reflections on Toscanini* (New York: Grove Weidenfeld, 1991), 130-31. The original of the letter is in The Toscanini Legacy, housed at the New York Public Library.
27. BW to Toscanini, Feb. 4, 1938; in Sachs, "Toscanini, Hitler, and Salzburg," 123-24.
28. Gordon Brook-Shepherd, *The Austrians* (New York: Carroll & Graf, 1997), 311.
29. *TV*, 322.
30. BW to Harry Harkness Flagler, Apr. 23, 1938 (MFCC).
31. *NWJ*, Mar. 15, 1938.
32. *TV*, 325.
33. Ibid.
34. BW to Clara Gabrilowitsch, Apr. 22, 1938 (*BW Briefe*, 242).
35. *TV*, 326.
36. BW to Paula Gericke, June 14, 1938 (*BW Briefe*, 245).
37. *TV*, 327.
38. *TV*, 329.
39. *Neue Zürcher Zeitung*, Aug. 31, 1938.
40. BW to Rudolf Mengelberg, Sept. 28, 1938 (Concertgebouw Archives).
41. Their correspondence and proposed lists of works and conductors are found in BWP I.186.
42. *TV*, 332-33.
43. *TV*, 334.
44. See Harvey Sachs, *Toscanini* (n.p.: Prima Publishing, 1995), 255-56, 262-63.
45. *NYT*, Mar. 26, 1939.
46. *NYT*, Mar. 12, 1939.

47. Quoted in B. H. Haggin, *The Toscanini Musicians Knew*, 2d ed. (New York: Horizon Press, 1980), reprinted in B. H. Haggin, *Arturo Toscanini: Contemporary Recollections of the Maestro*, ed. Thomas Hathaway (New York: Da Capo, 1989), 57.

48. Haggin, *The Toscanini Musicians Knew*, 77–78.

49. Story told by Josef Gingold in ibid., 254–55. A similar account is related by Frederic Waldman, also a player in the NBC orchestra, who recalled a rehearsal in which Toscanini yelled "No!" in disapproval several times as Walter rehearsed the orchestra (Waldman to Rolland Parker, Feb. 17, 1993, courtesy of Parker).

50. Quoted in Sachs, *Toscanini*, 317.

51. *TV*, 336.

52. *GM*, 84.

53. *NYHT*, Apr. 2, 1939.

54. Pinza, *Autobiography*, 159–60.

55. Arturo Toscanini to Ada Mainardi, Aug. 25, 1939 (Arturo Toscanini's letters to Ada Mainardi, private collection, Milan; courtesy of Harvey Sachs, who translated the letter from the original Italian).

56. Pinza, *Autobiography*, 160–61.

57. A small notice appeared in the *Neue Zürcher Zeitung*, Aug. 20, 1939.

58. BW to Thomas and Katia Mann, Aug. 30, 1939 (*BW Briefe*, 249–50).

59. BW to Rudolf Mengelberg, Sept. 17, 1939 (Concertgebouw Archives).

60. BW to Alma Mahler Werfel, Sept. 18, 1939 (*BW Briefe*, 250).

61. BW to Mengelberg, Oct. 17, 1939 (Concertgebouw Archives).

THIRTEEN

## Guest Conductor on Two Coasts

1. BW to Helmut Fahsel, Dec. 26, 1939 (*BW Briefe*, 253).

2. BW to Harry Harkness Flagler, Nov. 26, 1939 (MFCC).

3. *LAT*, Dec. 15, 1939.

4. BW to Fahsel, Dec. 26, 1939 (*BW Briefe*, 252).

5. BW to Thomas Mann, Jan. 16, 1940 (*BW Briefe*, 254).

6. The performance has been released on Pearl (GEMM CD 91931).

7. *NYT*, Feb. 11, 1940.

8. Bruno Walter, "Bruckner and Mahler," *Chord and Discord* 2, no. 2 (1940): 3–12.

9. *LAT*, July 27, 1940.

10. BW to Flagler, Aug. 28, 1940 (MFCC).

11. BW to Wolfgang Stresemann, Oct. 13, 1940 (*BW Briefe*, 256). The book in question was either his autobiography or an early draft of *MM*.

12. BW to Flagler, Aug. 28, 1940 (MFCC).

13. Bruno Walter, "About War and Music," *Decision* 1, no. 1 (1941): 10–11.

14. *Detroit Free Press*, Nov. 3, 1940.

15. *LAT*, Nov. 22, 1940.

16. *LAT*, Nov. 24, 1940.

17. BW to Bronislaw Huberman, Dec. 18, 1940 (BWP I.283).

18. *NYT*, Jan. 17, 1941.

19. The broadcast of Jan. 26, 1941, has been released on compact disc by AS Disc (AS 427), though better-sounding sources have survived in private collections.

20. *NYT*, Jan. 11, 1941.

21. The performance of Bloch's *Evocations* on Feb. 8, 1941, has been issued on AS Disc (AS 421).

22. *Nation*, Mar. 23, 1957; reprinted in B. H. Haggin, *35 Years of Music* (New York: Horizon Press, 1964), 194.

23. *NYT*, Feb. 2, 1941.

24. Haggin, *35 Years*, 25–26.

25. *NYT*, Jan. 20, 1941.

26. The broadcast of Jan. 19, 1941, has been released by AS Disc (AS 418).

27. *Time*, Feb. 24, 1941.

28. David Berkowitz, *Behind the Gold Curtain: Fifty Years in the Metropolitan Opera Orchestra* (Delhi, N.Y.: Birch Brook Press, 1995), 44.

29. Ibid., 44–45.

30. Sir Georg Solti (with Harvey Sachs), *Memoirs* (New York: Knopf, 1997), 114.

31. Interview with David Kates, July 24, 1997.

32. Interview with Nikolaus Harnoncourt, Nov. 22, 1996.

33. Interview with Siegmund Levarie, Mar. 24, 1996.

34. BW to John McClure, Oct. 2, 1961 (BWP I.124).

35. Berkowitz, *Behind the Gold Curtain*, 45.

36. *NYT*, Feb. 15, 1941.

37. In *The Maestro Myth* (New York: Citadel Press, 1993) Norman Lebrecht not only makes the unsubstantiated claim that Gretel killed herself, but blames Walter for her death, saying that his daughters "paid the ultimate price for his paternal shortcomings" (62).

38. Berkowitz, *Behind the Gold Curtain*, 45.

39. BW to Francis Biddle, Apr. 11, 1942 (BWP I.495).

40. *LAT*, July 19, 1941.

41. In 1950 Walter would receive an honorary Doctor of Law degree from the University of California in Los Angeles, and in 1951 another Doctor of Music degree from the University of Edinburgh.

42. BW to Leo and Emma Schlesinger, Sept. 5, 1941 (*BW Briefe*, 259).

43. BW to Herbert Graf, May 23, 1959 (BWP I.236).

44. *NYT*, Nov. 27, 1941.

45. Virgil Thomson, *NYHT*, Nov. 27, 1941.

46. Jarmila Novotná to Erik Ryding, Jan. 31, 1994.

47. Interview with Ruth Martin, May 31, 1995.

48. Ibid.

49. *NYHT*, Dec. 12, 1941.

50. Walter's early recordings of Beethoven's Fifth Symphony, the "Eroica," and the

"Emperor" with Serkin (as well as the Eighth Symphony) have been issued by the French label LYS (LYS 308–309); the "Emperor" has also appeared, in better sound, in Sony Classical's Bruno Walter Edition (SMK 64489).

51. Ernst Krenek, "Gustav Mahler," in Bruno Walter, *Gustav Mahler*, trans. James Galston (New York: Greystone Press, 1941), 206.

52. BW to Krenek, Dec. 2, 1941 (BWP I.314; also in *BW Briefe*, 262).

53. *LAT*, July 17, 1942.

54. Grace Koopal, *Miracle of Music: The History of the Hollywood Bowl* ([Los Angeles: Anderson, Ritchie and Simon], 1972), 227.

55. BW to Stresemann, Aug. 7, 1945 (BWP I.555).

56. BW to Leo and Emma Schlesinger, June 23, 1942 (*BW Briefe*, 264–65).

57. BW to Harry Harkness Flagler, Sept. 16, 1942 (MFCC).

58. BW to Arthur Judson, Dec. 11, 1942 (NYPA).

59. BW to John Alden Carpenter, July 11, 1942 (BWP I.84); *NYT* and (for Briggs) unidentified clipping, both dated Oct. 23, 1942.

60. Cyril Clemens to BW, Dec. 8, 1952, and BW to Clemens, Dec. 25, 1952 (BWP I.268).

61. *NYT*, Dec. 17, 1942; *NYHT*, Dec. 17, 1942.

62. Interview with Stresemann, Oct. 29, 1996. It is impossible to know with absolute certainty whether Walter conducted this work earlier in his career, where documentation is still spotty; but in all likelihood this was indeed his first performance of *Forza*. Stresemann commented that Walter found the overture particularly attractive.

63. *NYT*, Jan. 10, 1943.

64. BW to Daniel Gregory Mason, Sept. 26, 1940 (DGMP).

65. BW to Grete Rauch, July 7, 1947 (BWP I.106).

66. Bruno Zirato to BW, July 13, 1942 (NYPA).

67. *MM*, 170.

68. The series of letters between Walter and Drinker resides in the library of the Universität für Musik und darstellende Kunst in Vienna.

69. *MM*, 170–71.

70. BW to Leo and Emma Schlesinger, June 23, 1942 (*BW Briefe*, 264).

71. *MM*, 180.

72. *MM*, 182.

73. *MM*, 185.

74. *MM*, 174, 185.

75. BW to Zirato, July 3, 1945 (NYPA).

76. [Zirato] to BW, Mar. 20, 1946 (NYPA).

77. *MM*, 188.

78. *NYT*, Apr. 16, 1943.

79. Leonard Rose, interviewed for the BBC Walter Omnibus.

80. BW to Flagler, Sept. 16, 1942 (MFCC).

81. Zirato to Mr. Correa, U.S. District Attorney's Office, Apr. 5, 1943 (NYPA).

82. BW to Stresemann, May 4, 1943 (BWP I.555).

83. Elsa Walter to Stresemann, July 11, 1943 (BWP I.555).

84. Koopal, *Miracle of Music*, 181.

85. *LAT*, Aug. 1, 1943.

86. BW to Leo and Emma Schlesinger, Sept. 20, 1943 (*BW Briefe*, 268).

87. BW to Flagler, Sept. 27, 1943 (MFCC).

88. From Bernstein's interview with Arnold Michaelis, included in a documentary on Bruno Walter produced by Michaelis for National Educational Television.

89. Interview with William Lincer, Feb. 26, 1994. Leonard Bernstein's Philharmonic debut has been privately released on compact disc by the New York Philharmonic.

90. Interview with Lincer, Feb. 26, 1994.

91. *NYT*, Dec. 18, 1943.

92. Memo of conversation between Edward Johnson and BW, Jan. 25, 1944 (Met Archives).

93. *NYT*, Jan. 14, 1944.

94. *NYT*, Mar. 20, 1944.

95. *NYT Magazine*, Mar. 19, 1944.

96. BWP I.598.

97. BW to Thomas Mann, Oct. 1, 1944 (*BW Briefe*, 273).

98. *Kansas City Star*, Feb. 25, 1945.

99. *TV*, 343.

100. The New York Philharmonic performed on both recordings, which have been reissued by Sony Classical on SMK 64459 (Mendelssohn's Violin Concerto) and SMK 64450 (Mahler's Fourth). In 1998 Sony Classical issued a promotional CD of the Mendelssohn Violin Concerto, with the original cover reproduced in miniature, to celebrate the birth of the LP.

101. Walter's presence was noted in the *New York Post*, May 7, 1945.

102. Arthur Schnabel to BW, Apr. 16, 1943 (BWP I.528).

103. César Saerchinger to BW, Sept. 18, 1951; BW to Saerchinger, Oct. 2, 1951 (BWP I.266).

104. BW to Flagler, May 11, 1945 (MFCC).

105. Interview in *BWL*.

106. BW to Thomas Michels, May 7, 1945 (BWP I.424).

107. Alma Mahler (with E. B. Ashton), *And the Bridge Is Love* (New York: Harcourt Brace, 1958), 296; Karen Monson, *Alma Mahler: Muse to Genius* (Boston: Houghton Mifflin, 1983), 300.

108. James Galston to BW, Aug. 8, 1945 (BWP II.28).

109. BW to Franz J. Horch, Oct. 29, 1945 (BWP II.20).

110. *Chicago Tribune*, Oct. 30, 1945.

111. BW to Leo and Emma Schlesinger, July 20, 1945 (*BW Briefe*, 279).

112. BW to Leo and Emma Schlesinger, Dec. 29, 1945 (*BW Briefe*, 281).

113. *NYT*, Dec. 21, 1945.

114. Henry-Louis de La Grange to Erik Ryding, Mar. 14, 2000.

115. *NYHT*, Mar. 15, 1946.

116. BW to Tadeusz Kassern, Mar. 12, 1946 (BWP I.467).

117. BW to Munich Detachment, U.S. Army, Apr. 5, 1946 (BWP I.467).

118. Hans Pfitzner to BW, Mar. 13, 1946; in Hans Pfitzner, *Briefe* (Tutzing: Hans Schneider, 1991), 984.

119. Pfitzner to BW, Oct. 5, 1946 (Pfitzner, *Briefe*, 1021).

120. BW to Pfitzner, Nov. 4, 1946 (*BW Briefe*, 291).

121. BW to Dr. Jur. Eugen Leer, Sept. 2, 1947 (BWP I.469).

122. Sam Chapiro to BW, May 24, 1948 (BWP I.469).

123. *NYT Book Review*, Aug. 11, 1946.

124. *Times*, Oct. 21, 1946.

125. BW to Thomas and Katia Mann, Dec. 12, 1946 (*BW Briefe*, 293–94).

126. *Globe*, Jan. 15, 1947.

127. BW to Andreas Barban, July 26, 1951 (BWP I.154).

# FOURTEEN

## Musical Adviser

1. See Howard Shanet, *Philharmonic: A History of New York's Orchestra* (New York: Doubleday, 1975), 304–5.

2. Artur Rodzinski to BW, Feb. 10, 1947 (BWP I.517).

3. BW to Rodzinski, Feb. 17, 1947 (BWP I.517).

4. Unidentified newspaper clipping, Feb. 15, 1947 (Bruno Walter clipping file, New York Public Library).

5. Memorandum from Louise Fry to Miss Meyer and Miss Dennis, Oct. 2, 1947 (NYPA).

6. BW to Mrs. Charles F. Guggenheimer, Mar. 26, 1948 (BWP I.558).

7. BW to Wolfgang Stresemann, July 23, 1948 (BWP I.559).

8. BW to Stresemann, Apr. 17, 1947 (BWP I.556).

9. BW to Stresemann, May 5, 1947 (BWP I.557).

10. The most recent recording of the symphony is that of Neeme Järvi and the Detroit Symphony Orchestra (1993) for Chandos Records (CHAN 9169).

11. BW to Stresemann, May 5, 1947, and Stresemann to BW, May 9, 1947 (BWP I.557).

12. BW to Stresemann, May 5 and June 23, 1947 (BWP I.557).

13. Stresemann to BW, May 17, 1947 (BWP I.557).

14. BW to Stresemann, June 12, 1947 (BWP I.557).

15. Stresemann to BW, June 21, 1947 (BWP I.557).

16. Stresemann to BW, Oct. 27, 1951 (BWP I.566).

17. BW to David Stanley Smith, July 1, 1947 (BWP I.131).

18. Daniel Gregory Mason, Journal entry for Apr. 4, 1947 (DGMP).

19. Mason to BW, June 21, 1947 (DGMP; also BWP I.410).

20. BW to Mason, June 23, 1947 (BWP I.410).

21. Interview with Bruno Zirato Jr., Sept. 10, 1996.

22. Dimitri Mitropoulos to BW, Jan. 21, 1948 (BWP I.426).

23. BW to Mitropoulos, Feb. 2, 1948 (BWP I.426).

24. *GM*, 106–7.

25. BW to Bruno Zirato, June 11, 1947 (NYPA).

26. BW to Lotte Lehmann, Dec. 28, 1947 (BWP I.317).

27. The "Immolation Scene" is included on the CD set *Helen Traubel in Concert 1947–1951* (Eklipse EKR 56).

28. From the concert of July 14, 1953, preserved on Walter Collection 7, Historical Performers (HP 27).

29. Helen Traubel, *St. Louis Woman* (New York: Duell, Sloan and Pearce, 1959), 270–71.

30. Rudolf Bing, *5000 Nights at the Opera* (Garden City, N.Y.: Doubleday, 1972), 13, 114.

31. Bruno Walter, "Farewell," in *Kathleen Ferrier 1912–1953: A Memoir*, ed. Neville Cardus (London: Hamish Hamilton, 1954), 111.

32. Ibid., 113.

33. BW to Lotte Lehmann, Aug. 12, 1947 (BWP I.317).

34. BW to Mertens Colonert, Aug. 15, 1947 (BWP I.146).

35. The orchestra later published a pamphlet on the Edinburgh Festival, noting Walter's conciliatory attitude; see *Die Wiener Philharmoniker: ein Stück Weltgeschichte* (Vienna: Verlag der Wiener Philharmoniker, 1947), 8. According to another account, Buxbaum's return to his place in the orchestra was accompanied by a barbed comment on the sound of the orchestra as "ganz judenrein" (a pun that could mean "completely free of Jews" or "quite in tune in the Jewish manner"); see Richard Newman (with Karen Kirtley), *Alma Rosé: Vienna to Auschwitz* (Portland, Ore.: Amadeus, 2000), 322.

36. BW to L. C. Mazirel, Oct. 19, 1947 (BWP I.550; also in *BW Briefe*, 299).

37. Cited in a letter from Cyril Clarke to BW, June 30, 1948 (BWP I.550). In a letter to Julius Kopsch dated Oct. 2, 1950, Walter recorded his continuing resentment that Strauss had taken over his Berlin Philharmonic concert in 1933: "But naturally," he added, "my admiration for the great musician, as well as my promotion of his works, has remained unaffected by this incident" (BWP I.551).

38. BW to Clarke, July 26, 1948 (BWP I.550).

39. The broadcast of Nov. 13, 1947, has been reissued on Music and Arts (CD 733).

40. BW to Mitropoulos, Oct. 28, 1947 (BWP I.426).

41. Mitropoulos to BW, Oct. 28, 1947 (BWP I.426).

42. Quoted in a letter from Zirato to BW, Oct. 31, 1947 (BWP I.486).

43. Mitropoulos to BW, Dec. 18, 1947 (BWP I.426).

44. BW to Mitropoulos, Dec. 22, 1947 (BWP I.426).

45. *NYT*, Nov. 28, 1947.

46. BW to Stresemann, Nov. 4, 1947 (BWP I.558).

47. BW to Berta Morena, Oct. 14, 1947; Morena to BW, Feb. 19, 1951 (BWP I.428).

48. Norman Lebrecht, in *The Maestro Myth* (New York: Citadel Press, 1993), claims that after the Anschluss Walter responded to Arnold Rosé's need for financial assistance by pleading poverty and offering only "a few hundred dollars" (a con-

siderable sum at that time). "The following year," Lebrecht writes, "basking in the Californian sunshine, he demanded the return of his 'loan'" (62). The incident, if it happened as Lebrecht represents it, would have been highly uncharacteristic. It is perhaps significant that Rosé's son, Alfred, wrote to BW affectionately as "Dear Uncle Bruno" on June 2, 1951 (BWP I.517).

49. BW to Thomas Mann, Mar. 26, 1948 (BWP I.291).

50. H. E. Jacob to BW, Apr. 8, 1948 (BWP I.291).

51. BW to Godfrey Turner, Apr. 12, 1948 (BWP I.354).

52. BW to Alma Clayburgh, undated telegram (BWP I.354).

53. The broadcast of Jan. 18, 1948, is included in *New York Philharmonic: The Mahler Broadcasts, 1948–82* (New York Philharmonic Special Editions NYP 9801/12).

54. Cited in Winifred Ferrier, *The Life of Kathleen Ferrier* (London: Hamish Hamilton, 1955), 89.

55. Leonard Bernstein to BW, Jan. 22, 1948 (BWP I.46).

56. BW to Bernstein, Feb. 2, 1948 (Leonard Bernstein Collection, Library of Congress).

57. Walter conducted the overture to Hindemith's *Neues vom Tage* with the Gewandhaus Orchestra on Dec. 17, 1931.

58. BW to Paul Hindemith, Jan. 26, 1948 (Paul-Hindemith-Institut, Frankfurt am Main). We are indebted to Luitgard Anna Schader of the Paul-Hindemith-Institut for calling this letter to our attention, as well as the date and place of the meeting marked in Hindemith's pocket calendar and a notation by Gertrud Hindemith that the meeting was to take place on Saturday, Feb. 7, at 11:30 a.m.

59. The performance has been issued by AS Disc (AS 421).

60. BW to Zirato, Apr. 18, 1949 (NYPA).

61. *NYT*, Sept. 19, 1948; BW to Zirato, Sept. 24, 1948 (NYPA).

62. See the correspondence in BWP I.127.

63. BW to Norman Dello Joio, July 28, 1946 (BWP I.127).

64. Interview with Dello Joio, Nov. 10, 1994.

65. Interview with Stresemann, Oct. 29, 1996.

66. BW to Stresemann, July 23, 1948 (BWP I.559).

67. Interview with Dello Joio, Nov. 10, 1994.

68. BW to Zirato, June 22, 1948 (NYPA).

69. BW to Zirato, June 29, 1948 (NYPA).

70. BW to Zirato, May 31, 1948 (NYPA).

71. BW to Zirato, May 25, 1948 (NYPA).

72. BW to Lotte Lehmann, Aug. 10, 1948 (BWP I.317).

73. Lehmann to BW, Apr. 16, 1948 (LLP).

74. Delia Reinhardt to Alma Mahler Werfel, Mar. 21, 1949 (AMWC).

75. *NYHT*, May 8, 1948.

76. A brief promotional film clip of Walter rehearsing the last movement of Beethoven's Ninth with the Vienna Philharmonic has circulated and been reissued on video by Parnassus Records (PCV 2).

77. The performance has circulated on Nuova Era (2314/15) as well as other labels.

78. *NYHT*, May 8, 1948.

79. *NYT*, May 25, 1948.

80. BW to Alfred Polgar, Sept. 10, 1948 (BWP I.497; abbreviated version in *BW Briefe*, 304–5).

81. Quoted in Albert Goldberg, "Bruno Walter: Poet of Conductors," *NYT Magazine* (Sept. 9, 1956), 36.

82. BW to Arthur Judson, Oct. 4, 1948 (NYPA).

83. Sadly, kinescopes of Walter's programs seem not to exist, though some have survived for other Chicago Symphony Orchestra broadcasts of the same vintage.

84. BW to Eric Oldberg, Dec. 31, 1948 (BWP I.457).

85. BW to Rudolf Bing, Mar. 26, 1946 (BWP I.145). On the two drafts of this letter see Sam Shirakawa, *The Devil's Music Master* (New York: Oxford University Press, 1992), 306.

86. See Strelitzer's contribution to *Furtwängler Recalled*, ed. Daniel Gillis (Tuckahoe, N.Y.: John De Graff, Inc., 1965), 97–99.

87. BW to Zirato, Jan. 31, 1949 (NYPA).

88. BW to Wilhelm Furtwängler, Jan. 13, 1949 (BWP I.208; also in *BW Briefe*, 308–10), cited and translated in Shirakawa, *Devil's Music Master*, 364. We have altered the translation in places.

89. The footage of Furtwängler conducting the finale of Beethoven's Ninth before Goebbels is available on the videotape *Great Conductors of the Third Reich*, issued by the Bel Canto Society (BCS 0052), which also shows Furtwängler conducting the Prelude to *Die Meistersinger* at the AEG factory, the background of which is decorated with images of large swastikas enclosed in gears.

90. Fred Prieberg, *Trial of Strength: Wilhelm Furtwängler in the Third Reich*, trans. Christopher Dolan (Boston: Northeastern University Press, 1994), 5.

91. Interview with Yehudi Menuhin, May 1, 1996. See also Menuhin, *Unfinished Journey* (New York: Knopf, 1977), 95.

92. BW to Zirato, Feb. 24, 1948 (NYPA).

93. Interview with Walter Hendl, Sept. 24, 1995.

94. BW to Zirato, Feb. 26, 1952 (NYPA).

95. BW to Eleanor Steber, Apr. 6, 1949 (NYPA).

96. Steber to BW, Apr. 7, 1949 (NYPA).

97. BW to Goddard Lieberson, Oct. 27, 1949 (Sony Music Archives).

FIFTEEN

## Gains and Losses

1. Delia Reinhardt to Alma Mahler Werfel, Mar. 21, 1949 (AMWC).

2. Interview with a former student of Delia Reinhardt's, Nov. 19, 1995.

3. Frieda Margarete Reuschle, in an obituary tribute to Delia Reinhardt (an unidentified item among the papers on Reinhardt at the Goetheanum).

4. Interview with Irma Geering, Feb. 8, 1996. Unless otherwise noted, the follow-

ing biographical comments come from either this interview or the obituary by Reuschle cited above.

5. Otto Rennefeld to BW, June 30, 1948 (BWP I.3).
6. Rudolf Steiner, *Wie erlangt man Erkenntnisse der höheren Welt* (Berlin, 1909), trans. by Christopher Bamford as *How to Know Higher Worlds* (Hudson, N.Y.: Anthroposophic Press, 1994), 39–40.
7. See Gerard Van Loon to BW, Apr. 26 and July 10, 1946 (BWP I.467 and 468).
8. Interview with Irma Geering, Feb. 8, 1996.
9. Bruno Walter, "Mein Weg zur Anthroposophie," *Das Goetheanum* 52 (Dec. 24, 1961): 418.
10. Bruno Walter, "Über Kunstverständnis," *Österreichische Rundschau* 3 (May–July 1905): 107.
11. BW to Daniel Gregory Mason, May 1, 1938 (DGMP).
12. BW to Jerome Hines, Nov. 12, 1958 (courtesy of Jerome Hines).
13. Interview with Henry-Louis de La Grange, Feb. 13, 1998. De La Grange heard the story from Walter's longtime secretary Susie Danziger.
14. See Lotte's own note on her marriage in *BW Briefe*, 430.
15. Claire Norden to BW, undated; BW to Norden, Nov. 29, 1948 (BWP I.470).
16. See Max Brockhaus's typescript "Hans Pfitzner's letzte Tage" (BWP I.471).
17. BW to Brockhaus, May 26, 1949 (*BW Briefe*, 313).
18. BW to Olin Downes, June 29, 1949 (BWP I.143).
19. BW to Artur Schnabel, June 26, 1949 (BWP I.528). Fleisher's performance is preserved on Bruno Walter Rarities 12 (AS 412).
20. Issued as vol. 9 of London's Kathleen Ferrier Jubilee series (London 433 476–2).
21. Gerald Moore, *Collected Memoirs* (Harmondsworth: Penguin, 1986), 238.
22. The Ferrier–Walter *Kindertotenlieder* has been reissued in EMI's series Great Performances of the Century (EMI 66963–2).
23. Interview with a former student of Delia Reinhardt's, Nov. 19, 1995.
24. Lotte Lehmann to BW, Nov. 30, 1949 (LLP).
25. BW to Lehmann, Dec. 12, 1949 (LLP).
26. BW to John Bauer, Apr. 28, 1950 (BWP I.455).
27. BW to John Bauer, Apr. 12, 1950 (BWP I.454).
28. *Los Angeles Examiner*, May 29, 1950.
29. Unsigned memo, Oct. 15, 1949 (NYPA).
30. BW to Bruno Zirato, May 21, 1949 (NYPA).
31. BW to Wolfgang Stresemann, Mar. 21, 1950 (BWP I.563).
32. Rudolf Bing, *5000 Nights at the Opera* (Garden City, N.Y.: Doubleday, 1972), 14.
33. Bing to BW, May 27, 1949; BW to Bing, June 1, 1949 (BWP I.50).
34. Undated typescript (probably from 1951) of an interview with Walter, apparently submitted for Walter's approval by Elizabeth Sloper (BWP IV.2). Walter in fact objected to several ideas attributed to him in the interview, but the passages cited were not among those he rejected and are in keeping with ideas he expressed elsewhere.

35. The performance of Mahler's Fourth from Aug. 24, 1950, one of Walter's finest readings of the score to be preserved, was issued on CD by MCA Classics (MCAD-42337). The Stockholm performance of Schubert's Symphony no. 9 in C Major has appeared on AS Disc (AS 306). Hunt Productions issued a recording of most of the Berlin Philharmonic Program of Sept. 24, 1950 (HUNTCD 738), while the footage from the Mozart symphony has been issued on video in *Botschafter der Musik* (PCV 1) by Parnassus Records.

36. Der Studentenrat des Städtischen Konservatoriums to BW, Oct. 23, 1950 (BWP I.25).

37. Georg Solti (BBC Walter Omnibus).

38. BW to Stresemann, Dec. 25, 1950 (BWP I.564).

39. Donald Keys to BW, Dec. 1, 1959; BW to Keys, Dec. 8, 1959 (BWP I.274).

40. The performance of the Brahms Double Concerto with Corigliano and Rose has been issued by Nuova Era (2226), while the broadcast of the Second Piano Concerto with Hess has appeared on AS Disc, Bruno Walter Rarities 15 (AS 415). The Brahms First Piano Concerto has circulated privately.

41. *NYT*, Feb. 25, 1951.

42. See Robert Tuggle, "Clouds of War," *Opera News* 60, no. 1 (July 1995): 10–17, esp. 15–16.

43. Bing to BW, Dec. 14, 1949 (Met Archives).

44. BW to Bing, Dec. 30, 1949 (Met Archives).

45. BW to Clayburgh, June 17, 1950 (BWP I.184).

46. Lehmann to BW, "Saturday, after the broadcast" [Mar. 10, 1951] (LLP).

47. BW to Lehmann, Mar. 17, 1951 (*BW Briefe*, 323–24).

48. Wilhelm Furtwängler to BW, Apr. 14, 1951 (BWP I.208).

49. BW to Michael Gaszynski, July 6, 1951 (BWP I.460).

50. BW to Dimitri Mitropoulos, Mar. 2, 1956; Mitropoulos to BW, Mar. 7, 1956 (BWP I.426). See also William Trotter, *Priest of Music: The Life of Dimitri Mitropoulos* (Portland, Ore.: Amadeus Press, 1995), 309–10.

51. Interview with Martin Ormandy, Feb. 19, 1994.

52. Interview with William Vacchiano, Dec. 21, 1996.

53. Interview with Walter Hendl, Sept. 24, 1995.

54. BW to Zirato, Dec. 13, 1951 (NYPA).

55. Carl Schuricht to BW, Dec. 15, 1951 (BWP I.533).

56. BW to Schuricht, Dec. 28, 1951 (BWP I.533).

57. BW to Zirato, Jan. 25, 1952 (BWP I.533).

58. BW to René Nicoly, Sept. 9, 1958 (BWP I.533).

59. BW to Arthur Judson, Dec. 7, 1951 (NYPA).

60. Judson to BW, Nov. 23, 1951 (BWP I.490).

61. Undated internal memo, ca. 1957 (Sony Music Archives).

62. Interview with David Oppenheim, Jan. 17, 1995.

63. An excellent transfer of the "Immolation Scene" from Mar. 23, 1952, was issued in 1997 on New York Philharmonic Special Editions (NYP 9707). The *Wesendonk-Lieder* are available on Music and Arts (CD-838).

64. BW to Isao Uno, June 29, 1953 (BWP I.297).

65. Uno to BW, Sept. 15, 1953 (BWP I.297).

66. BW to Uno, Oct. 23, 1953 (BWP I.297).

67. BW to Uno, July 12, 1954 (BWP I. 298).

68. Uno to BW, June 25, 1955; BW to Uno, July 7, 1955 (BWP I.298). Koho Uno has since published books and articles in Japanese on Walter.

69. The performance of Apr. 16, 1952, was issued by Cetra in 1994 (CDAR 2029).

70. Georges Sébastian to BW, Feb. 23, 1952 (BWP I.201).

71. BW to Sébastian, Feb. 26, 1952 (BWP I.201).

72. *Le Figaro*, May 6, 1952.

73. Bruno Walter, "Farewell," in *Kathleen Ferrier, 1912–1953: A Memoir*, ed. Neville Cardus (London: Hamish Hamilton, 1954), 109.

74. The recording is currently available on Decca Records (Decca 414 194–2).

75. The performance of Mahler's Fourth has been issued as part of the six-disk set *Fifty Years Holland Festival: A Dutch Miracle* (Globe 6900).

76. BW to Eric Oldberg, Oct. 24, 1952 (BWP I.457).

77. Fritz Rieger to BW, Nov. 11, 1952; BW to Rieger, Dec. 6, 1952 (BWP I.433).

78. Mason to BW, Nov. 18, 1952 (DGMP; also BWP I.410).

79. BW to Mason, Dec. 13, 1952 (BWP I.410). See also Mason to Goddard Lieberson, Dec. 18, 1952; to BW, Dec. 2, 1952; to David Oppenheim, Jan. 8, 1953 (all in DGMP).

80. Interview with Frances Yeend and James Benner, May 26, 1996.

81. Interview with David Lloyd, Oct. 16, 1996.

82. Interview with Loren Glickman, Feb. 17, 1994.

83. The Mozart recitals by Lily Pons (1942) and Ezio Pinza (1946–47) have been reissued, along with Mozart recitals by Steber (1953) and George London (1953) and the Mozart Requiem (1956), by Sony Classical in its Legendary Interpretations series (SM3K 47211).

84. Eleanor Steber to BW, [fall–winter, 1952] (BWP I.544).

85. BW to Steber, Dec. 22, 1952 (BWP I.544).

86. Steber to BW, Apr. 14, 1953 (BWP I.544).

87. Interview with George Neikrug, Mar. 24, 1996.

88. BW to [Elinn] Hoffman, July 9, 1953 (BWP IV.2).

89. BW to Raymond Swing, Dec. 18, 1954 (BWP I.580).

90. Dietrich Fischer-Dieskau, *Reverberations*, trans. Ruth Hein (New York: Fromm International Publishing Corporation, 1989), 159.

91. Ibid., 160.

92. Issued in Japan on King Records "Seven Seas" (K30Y 310).

93. BW to Mali Pfitzner, Nov. 14, 1957 (BWP I.476).

94. Fischer-Dieskau, *Reverberations*, 160.

95. Hermann Obermeyer to BW, Sept. 3, 1953 (BWP I.622).

96. Rudolf Serkin to BW, [Sept. 1953] (BWP I.542).

97. Heinrich Kralik to BW, Nov. 24, 1952; BW to Kralik, Dec. 6, 1952 (BWP I.310).

98. Bruno Walter, "Farewell," 114.

99. A. F. Schmidt to BW, Jan. 15, 1954 (BWP I.527). The performance has been issued by AS Disc (AS 401).
100. BW to Schmidt, Jan. 19, 1954 (BWP I.527).
101. BW to Arturo Toscanini, Jan. 27, 1954 (BWP I.590).
102. Toscanini to BW, Feb. 2, 1954 (BWP I.590).
103. Lieberson to BW, Aug. 10, 1954 (BWP I.108).
104. BW to Lieberson, Aug. 12, 1954 (BWP I.108).
105. Invitation from Mrs. Arnold Schoenberg (BWP I.530).
106. BW to Mrs. Arnold Schoenberg, Sept. 7, 1954 (BWP I.530).
107. BW to Oppenheim, Dec. 20, 1955 (BWP I.111). Sony has issued compact-disc recordings of the Brahms Double Concerto with Stern and Rose (a studio performance) in vol. 1 of The Isaac Stern Collection (SM3K 45952) and *Ein deutsches Requiem* in Bruno Walter: The Edition (SMK 64469).
108. At least one live recording of the Bartók Andante (as well as the rest of the concert of Dec. 23, 1954) is preserved in the Sony Archives.
109. Interview with Theodore White, Mar. 24, 1995.
110. Draft, probably for a telegram, from BW to Frau Professor Wilhelm [i.e., Elisabeth] Furtwängler, n.d. (BWP I.209).
111. The photograph, dated 1950, is marked as having been taken in Berlin, though it may date from the 1949 Salzburg Festival (BWP XI, box 2).
112. For an overview of those whom Furtwängler helped during the war, see Sam Shirakawa, *The Devil's Music Master* (New York: Oxford University Press, 1992), 261–64; Shirakawa addresses the issue in detail through much of his book.
113. Walter's tribute is taken from the English translation that appeared in *Furtwängler Recalled*, ed. Daniel Gillis (Tuckahoe, N.Y.: John de Graff, Inc., 1965), 43.
114. BW to Toscanini, Mar. 21, 1955 (BWP I.591).
115. Fischer-Dieskau, *Reverberations*, 161, 189.
116. Program for Thomas Mann's eightieth birthday (BWP I.403).
117. BW to Erika Mann, Aug. 14, 1955 (*BW Briefe*, 338–39).
118. BW to Erich Wolfgang Korngold, Sept. 12, 1955 (BWP I.307).
119. BW to Charles Munch, May 26, 1956 (BWP I.307).
120. *MC*, Dec. 1, 1955.
121. Interview with Loren Glickman, Feb. 17, 1994.

SIXTEEN

*Mostly Mozart*

1. André Mertens to BW, Feb. 17, 1955; BW to Mertens, Feb. 19, 1955 (BWP I.492).
2. BW to Bruno Zirato, Feb. 21, 1955 (NYPA).
3. Interview with William Warfield, Apr. 24, 1996.
4. Interview with Léopold Simoneau and Pierrette Alarie, Sept. 18, 1995.
5. Jennie Tourel to BW, Mar. 17, 1955 (BWP I.595).
6. Martin Bookspan and Ross Yockey, *Zubin* (New York: Harper and Row, 1978), 37.

7. Maria Stader to Erik Ryding and Rebecca Pechefsky, Feb. 2, 1996.

8. Victor de Sabata to BW, May 15, 1956 (BWP I.287).

9. BW to Victor de Sabata, two drafts for telegrams [May 1956] (BWP I.287).

10. BW to Rudolf Mengelberg, Feb. 13, 1959 (BWP I.414).

11. BW to Eric P. Swenson, Apr. 24, 1958 (BWP II.52).

12. From an unpublished typescript essay, written for the Mozart bicentennial year (BWP I.429).

13. *MM*, 195, 199.

14. BW to Rudolf Bing, May 27, 1954 (BWP I.418).

15. Rudolf Steiner, *Wie erlangt man Erkenntnisse der höheren Welt?* (Berlin, 1909), trans. by Christopher Bamford as *How to Know Higher Worlds* (Hudson, N.Y.: Anthroposophic Press, 1994); further references are to Bamford's translation. In "Mein Weg zur Anthroposophie," BW mentions the book as one of the first works by Steiner that he read (419); he also recommended the book in a letter to Count R. Bethusy-Huc, Apr. 21, 1961 (BWP I.14).

16. Steiner, *How to Know Higher Worlds*, 65, 184–206. In a letter of May 1956 to Albert Schweitzer on his article about *Die Zauberflöte*, Walter said he was convinced that "it was the trial by fire and water—that is, the mystical process of initiation—that drew Mozart's soul, which strove for purity, to Schikaneder's libretto" (*BW Briefe*, 343).

17. Rudolf Steiner, *Das Lukas-Evangelium*, trans. by D. S. Osmond with the assistance of Owen Barfield as *The Gospel of St. Luke* (Hudson, N.Y.: Anthroposophic Press, 1964), 85.

18. Ibid., 32–33, 90–92, 100–2.

19. Originally published as a pamphlet in German entitled *Vom Mozart der Zauberflöte* (Frankfurt: S. Fischer, 1955); then as an article in the *Saturday Review* (Jan. 28, 1956), trans. Ruth and Thomas P. Martin; finally incorporated into *MM* as chap. 6.

20. *MM*, 195, 197–99.

21. Irving Kolodin, *The Metropolitan Opera 1883–1966: A Candid History* (New York: Knopf, 1966), 563.

22. *NYT*, Feb. 24, 1956. The broadcast of Mar. 3, 1956, has circulated on AS Disc (AS 425/26).

23. Interview with Jerome Hines, Nov. 7, 1994. Further quotations are from this interview.

24. A visual record of Hines singing this aria, which he performed on television during the run at the Met (May 7, 1956), is preserved on *The Voice of Firestone: Jerome Hines in Opera and Song* (VAI 69129).

25. Preserved on *The Voice of Firestone: Roberta Peters in Opera and Song*, vol. 1 (VAI 69115).

26. Interview with Roberta Peters, Apr. 7, 1994. Further quotations from Peters are from this interview.

27. Interview with Laurel Hurley, June 22, 1994.

28. Josephine Antoine does in fact omit the high F in her performance of the first

aria in the broadcast of Dec. 26, 1942, singing (perhaps at Walter's suggestion) B-flat, C, D rather than Mozart's B-flat, D, F. The performance has been issued on compact disc by Walhall (WHL2).

29. *MM*, 197.
30. Interview with Lucine Amara, Nov. 1, 1994.
31. *NYT*, Feb. 24, 1956.
32. BW to John McClure, Aug. 12, 1961 (BWP I.123).
33. Interview with Sandra Warfield, May 29, 1995. Further quotations are from this interview.
34. BW to Bing, Oct. 1, 1954 (BWP I.419).
35. Interview with Theodor and Jean Uppman, Feb. 3, 1994; subsequent quotations are from this interview.
36. BW to Theodor Uppman, Apr. 10, 1957 (courtesy of Theodor Uppman).
37. Anne Polzer, unpublished memoir (courtesy of Rolland Parker).
38. Interview with Hines.
39. The Strauss waltzes have been reissued on CD by Sony Classical (SMK 64467).
40. Interview with Loren Glickman, Feb. 17, 1994.
41. BW to Fritz Rauch, Feb. 4, 1956 (BWP I.69).
42. BW to Zirato, Apr. 10, 1956 (NYPA).
43. BW to Zirato, Oct. 1, 1956 (NYPA).
44. Mario Labroca to BW, Oct. 22, 1956 (BWP I.288).
45. BW to Labroca, Oct. 29, 1956 (BWP I.288).
46. Interview with Arnold Michaelis, Feb. 23, 1994. (The LP had the catalogue number BW 80.)
47. The typescript of Lehmann's essay is entitled *Bruno Walter, Musiker und Mensch*, probably delivered on Sept. 15, 1956 (BWP I.316). The Masterworks recording of tributes (not for sale) had the identification numbers LP 39039 and 39040.
48. Toscanini to BW, Sept. 11, 1956 (BWP I.591).
49. Mahler's First Symphony was released by Columbia in Jan. 1955 (ML 4958; reissued on compact disc by Sony Classical as MHK 63328); and the *Kindertotenlieder* with Ferrier, though recorded in 1949, was reissued by Columbia on LP in Apr. 1955 (ML 4980; reissued on compact disc by EMI Classics as 7243-5-66963-2-7).
50. David Walter to BW, Nov. 14 and 21, 1956; BW to David Walter, Dec. 18, 1956 (BWP I.592).
51. Constance Hope to BW, Jan. 17, 1957 (BWP I.592). Walter's response is not among the Bruno Walter Papers.
52. BW's statement on the death of Arturo Toscanini (BWP I.592).
53. Walter's performance of the "Eroica" with the Symphony of the Air has been preserved on Music and Arts (CD-1010).
54. Rolland Parker to BW, Sept. 15, 1959; BW to Parker, Oct. 8, 1959 (courtesy of Parker; both letters are now in the Carnegie Hall Archives).
55. Interview with Felix Galimir, Oct. 19, 1996.

56. Interview with Maureen Forrester, Dec. 11, 1994.
57. Interview with Theodor Uppman.

SEVENTEEN

## Columbia Symphony Orchestra

1. BW to Katia and Erika Mann, Apr. 30, 1957 (*BW Briefe*, 349).
2. BW to Alma Mahler Werfel, May 13, 1957 (BWP I.344); BW to [Bruno Zirato], July 4, 1957 (NYPA).
3. See BW to Emil Bock, Nov. 15, 1957 (BWP I.6).
4. BW to Wolfgang Stresemann, Dec. 5, 1957 (BWP I.574), in a passage omitted from the version in *BW Briefe* (355–56); interview with Stresemann, Oct. 29, 1996.
5. BW to Alma Mahler Werfel, July 5, 1957 (BWP I.344).
6. *MM*, 212.
7. Bruno Walter, "About Anton Bruckner" [1961] (BWP I.77). We have not been able to locate the Italian publication in which Walter's essay was to have appeared. Walter also expressed interest in reincarnation, without saying openly that he believed in it, in a letter to Anna Gertrud Huber, Feb. 10, 1961 (BWP I.283).
8. BW to Ferdinand Rauter, Feb. 21, 1961 (BWP I.379).
9. Emil Bock, "Bruno Walter: Bekenntnis zum Geist aus reifster Lebensleistung," *Christengemeinschaft* 30, no. 2 (1958): 46–51, esp. 46–47. See also *TV*, 102–7.
10. Bock, "Bruno Walter," 50; BW to Bock, June 6, 1958 (BWP I.7); *TV*, 105.
11. See Maria Horch to BW, Oct. 3, 1957 (BWP I.280).
12. Eric Bravington to BW, Mar. 11, 1957, with BW's typed draft of a response (BWP I.332).
13. BW to [Bravington], May 16, 1957 (BWP I.332).
14. Herbert von Karajan to BW, May 3, 1957 (BWP I.631).
15. BW to Bruno Zirato, Jan. 20, 1949 (BWP I.208).
16. BW to Zirato, Apr. 10, 1956 (NYPA).
17. See Wolfgang Stresemann, *Herbert von Karajan: "Ein seltsamer Mann . . . "* (Frankfurt: Ullstein, 1991), 7.
18. *New York Post*, Feb. 27, 1958.
19. BW to Zirato, Sept. 6, 1957 (NYPA).
20. Interview with David Lloyd, Oct. 16, 1996.
21. Rudolf Firkušný to BW, Aug. 22, 1959; BW to Firkušný, Aug. 27, 1959 (BWP I.178).
22. Released on video as *Bruno Walter: The Maestro, the Man* (VAI 69407).
23. Irving Kolodin, *Saturday Review*, Aug. 2, 1958.
24. Ernst Friedlander to BW, Sept. 2, 1959; BW to Friedlander, Aug. 10, 1959 (BWP I.128).
25. BW to Stresemann, July 28, 1958 (BWP I.575; also in *BW Briefe*, 359).
26. John McClure, "An Education and a Joy," *High Fidelity* 14 (Jan. 1964): 41.
27. Ibid., 42.
28. BW to David Oppenheim, Aug. 28, 1958 (BWP I.115).

29. BW to McClure, Apr. 28, 1961 (BWP I.121). Other planned recordings included Mendelssohn's "Hebrides" Overture and incidental music to *A Midsummer Night's Dream*; the "Funeral Music" and "Siegfried's Rhine Journey" from Wagner's *Götterdämmerung*, as well as the overture to *Rienzi*; Schumann's *Manfred* Overture; the overtures to Weber's *Freischütz, Euryanthe, Oberon*, and *Abu Hassan*; Berlioz's "Carnaval romain" Overture, *Benvenuto Cellini* Overture, and selections from *La Damnation de Faust*; Mahler's Fourth and Fifth symphonies; Haydn's symphonies nos. 92 and 86; and Beethoven's "Leonore" overtures nos. 1 and 3, as well as the "Egmont" and "Creatures of Prometheus" overtures.

30. BW to Zirato, Sept. 6, 1957 (NYPA).

31. BW to Erwin Ratz, Mar. 28, 1958 (BWP I.390).

32. Ratz to BW, Apr. 24, 1958 (BWP I.390).

33. BW to Heinz Unger, Feb. 28, 1958 (BWP I.614).

34. Alfred Rosé to BW (June 2, 1951), and BW to Rosé, June 5, 1951 (BWP I.518).

35. BW to Goddard Lieberson, Nov. 24, 1958; Lieberson to BW, Dec. 3, 1958 (BWP I.367).

36. BW to Lieberson, Dec. 29, 1958 (BWP I.116). The Mahler piano rolls have recently been issued on Golden Legacy (GLRS 101).

37. BW to Zirato, Dec. 2, 1958 (I.98).

38. Van Cliburn to BW, Dec. 21, 1958; BW to Cliburn, Dec. 26, 1958 (BWP I.98).

39. Van Cliburn to BW, Nov. 9, 1959 (BWP I.99).

40. *LAT*, Mar. 7, 1959.

41. *LAT*, Nov. 13, 1959.

42. Sony Classical has reissued the Columbia Symphony Orchestra recordings of Schubert's Ninth (SMK 64478) and Bruckner's Ninth (SMK 64483). Columbia had taped a live performance of Bruckner's Ninth with the New York Philharmonic under Walter in December 1953, but the recording was never released commercially.

43. BW to Joseph M. Ganster, Dec. 14, 1960 (BWP I.75).

44. Rudolf Bing to BW, May 6, 1958 (Met Archives).

45. Bing to BW, May 7, 1958; BW to Bing, May 12, 1958 (Met Archives).

46. BW to Bing, Jan. 17, 1959 (Met Archives).

47. Bing to BW, Feb. 3, 1959 (Met Archives).

48. Interview with Rolland Parker, Oct. 5, 1996. The Verdi Requiem broadcast of Mar. 29, 1959, has been issued by AS Disc (AS 408).

49. Erich Leinsdorf, *Cadenza: A Musical Career* (Boston: Houghton Mifflin, 1976), 7.

50. *NYHT*, Mar. 28, 1959; *NYT*, Mar. 28, 1959.

51. Douglas Duer to BW, Dec. 30, 1958; BW to Duer, Jan. 6, 1959 (BWP I.116).

52. BW to Oppenheim, Feb. 18, 1959 (BWP I.116).

53. The remaining three symphonies were recorded by the end of January 1960; all are available on Sony Classical's Bruno Walter Edition, SMK 64470 (Symphony no. 1), SMK 64471 (nos. 2 and 3), and SMK 64472 (no. 4).

54. BW to McClure, Oct. 27, 1959 (BWP I.117).

55. BW to Lieberson, Nov. 3, 1959 (BWP I.117).

56. Interview with Loren Glickman, Feb. 17, 1996.

57. BW to Zirato, Jan. 10, 1959 (BWP I.494).

58. Rudolf Gamsjäger to BW, Mar. 19 and June 2, 1959 (BWP I.232).

59. BW to Gamsjäger, June 9, 1959; Gamsjäger to BW, June 30, 1959; BW to Gamsjäger, July 13, 1959 (BWP I.232).

60. BW to Gamsjäger, Oct. 6, 1959 (BWP I.232).

61. Heinrich Puthon to BW, Aug. 31, 1959; BW to Puthon, Sept. 8, 1959 (BWP I.525).

62. *TV*, 50.

63. BW to Alice Strauss, Dec. 13, 1959 (BWP I.549).

64. *Internationale Mitteilungen Richard-Strauss-Gesellschaft* 22 (Aug. 1959) (BWP I.550).

65. BW to McClure, Apr. 28, 1961 (BWP I.121).

66. BW to Nicolas Nabokov, Feb. 9, 1952 (BWP I.200).

67. Interview with Maureen Forrester, Dec. 11, 1994.

68. BW to Forrester, Oct. 10, 1959 (BWP I.185).

69. Interview with Forrester, Dec. 11, 1994.

70. Interview with Ernst Haefliger, May 25, 1995.

71. Ibid.

72. Interview with Mildred Miller, Oct. 21, 1996.

73. Ibid.

74. Interview with McClure, Oct. 20, 1996.

75. BW to McClure, May 13, 1960 (BWP I.118).

76. Interview with Miller, Oct. 21, 1996.

77. BW to Egon Hilbert, Mar. 3, 1960 (BWP I.234) and Mar. 17, 1960 (*BW Briefe*, 365).

78. *Bruno Walter: Farewell Concert in Vienna*, Music and Arts CD 705.

79. BW to Stresemann, Feb. 3, 1960 (BWP I.577).

80. *LAT*, Dec. 3, 1960.

81. Personal communication with Van Cliburn, Nov. 14, 1994.

82. BW to Zirato, June 9, 1948 (NYPA).

83. *LAT*, Dec. 5, 1960.

84. BW to Edward Neill, Feb. 27, 1960 (BWP I.75).

85. Leopold Hager to BW, June 3, 1960 (BWP I.75).

86. Ratz to BW, Aug. 5, 1960; BW to Ratz, Aug. 9, 1960 (BWP I.392).

87. BW to Stresemann, Sept. 26, 1960 (BWP I.577).

88. Paul FitzGerald to BW, July 24, 1960; BW to FitzGerald, July 28, 1960 (BWP I.274).

89. BW to Schuyler Chapin, Oct. 27, 1960 (BWP I.119).

90. BW to Otto Klemperer, Dec. 23, 1960 (BWP I.304).

91. Klemperer to BW, May 18, 1959 (BWP I.304).

92. J. C. Knappe to BW, Feb. 29, 1960 (BWP I.373).

93. BW to Knappe, Mar. 10, 1960 (BWP I.373).

94. Artur Holde, *Bruno Walter* (Berlin: Rembrandt-Verlag, 1960). In 1956 the organist and critic Bernard Gavoty published his pamphlet *Bruno Walter*, based on *Theme and Variations*, which included many photographs taken by Roger Hauert of Walter in his later years (Geneva: René Kister, 1956); originally written in French, it appeared also in German, Italian, and English translations.

95. Martin Mayer, "Bruno Walter: The Working Musician of Beverly Hills," *Harper's Magazine*, Feb. 1961, 75.

96. Ibid., 76.

97. BW to Mayer, Apr. 20, 1960 (BWP I.413).

98. *TV*, 83.

99. Schuyler Chapin, *Leonard Bernstein: Notes from a Friend* (New York: Walker, 1992), 35.

100. Ibid., 35–36.

101. Ibid., 36.

102. Interview with George Neikrug, Mar. 24, 1996.

103. The Ninth Symphony, along with the rehearsal segment, has been issued on compact disc by Sony Classical (SM2K 64452).

104. Interview with McClure, Oct. 20, 1996.

105. Interview with Thomas Frost, Jan. 11, 1995. Frost also recounts this story, with some other details, in "Bruno Walter's Last Recording Session," *HiFi/Stereo Review*, Dec. 1963, 50–54.

106. BW to McClure, June 9, 1961 (BWP I.122).

107. BW to Karl Böhm, July 25, 1961 (BWP I.52).

108. Böhm to BW, Feb. 26, 1961; BW to Böhm, Mar. 3, 1961 (BWP I.52).

109. BW to McClure, Oct. 2, 1961 (BWP I.124); Bing to BW, Oct. 5, 1961 (BWP I.422).

110. BW to McClure, Dec. 16, 1961 (BWP I.125).

111. Irmgard Müller to BW, Dec. 29, 1961; BW to Müller, Jan. 6, 1962 (BWP I.430).

112. Leonard Bernstein Collection, box 57, folder 24 (Library of Congress); Zubin Mehta had written a thank-you note to Walter on Nov. 24, 1961, for his kind words about Mehta's performance of Mahler's First Symphony (BWP I.414).

113. BW to Stresemann, Jan. 12, 1962 (BWP I.578).

114. BW to Mihály Meixner, Jan. 26, 1962 (*BW Briefe*, 381).

115. BW to George Korngold, Jan. 28, 1962 (copy courtesy of Gregor Benko).

116. BW to Mali Pfitzner, Feb. 16, 1962 (BWP I.481).

117. The time of death given on the Certificate of Death.

118. Leonard Bernstein's address, Feb. 17, 1962 (NYPA).

119. *LAT*, Feb. 21, 1962.

120. Delia Reinhardt to Alma [Mahler Werfel], Aug. 26, 1962 (AMWC).

# Index